*The Oxford Book of the Sea*

# The Oxford Book of
# The Sea

EDITED BY
JONATHAN RABAN

Oxford   New York
OXFORD UNIVERSITY PRESS
1992

Oxford University Press, Walton Street, Oxford OX2 6DP
Oxford New York Toronto
Delhi Bombay Calcutta Madras Karachi
Petaling Jaya Singapore Hong Kong Tokyo
Nairobi Dar es Salaam Cape Town
Melbourne Auckland
and associated companies in
Berlin Ibadan

Oxford is a trade mark of Oxford University Press

© Oxford University Press, 1992

British Library Cataloguing in Publication Data
Data available

Library of Congress Cataloging in Publication Data
The Oxford book of the sea / edited by Jonathan Raban.
p. cm.
1. English literature. 2. American literature. 3. Ocean—Literary collections.
I. Raban. Jonathan.
PR1111.O24097 1992 820'.8'032162—dc20 91–25929
ISBN 0–19–214197–X

Typeset by Hope Services (Abingdon) Ltd.
Printed in Great Britain by
The Bath Press, Avon

*For Jean Lenihan*

# Acknowledgements

FOR the last two years I have been badgering friends and acquaintances for their favourite marine passages in literature. Miles Clark generously sent me his own private anthology of sea writing, and I have incorporated many of his suggestions. Jane Steinberg came up with a sheaf of contemporary poems about the sea, several of which appear here. I am grateful to T. J. Binyon, Professor Nicholas Brooke, Margaret Drabble, Claire Kirkman, Commander Kenneth Lilly, Professor Dean McManus, Christopher MacLehose, Belle Randall, Lorna Sage, and Linda Taylor for their suggestions and advice.

The Lavender Hill branch of Battersea Public Library, hard-pressed by local government cuts, was extremely helpful in the early stages, and proved to have a goldmine Victorian collection in its basement. Later, I had the good luck to be able to use the superbly stocked and expertly staffed Seattle Public Library—a model institution which puts to shame the parsimony with which British public libraries have been treated recently (though it is now—in 1991—in the throes of a very British story about cuts in the civic budget). The Allen Library of the University of Washington allowed me access to a rare edition of William Falconer's *The Shipwreck*, and Dr William R. Jones of Southampton University, the lone expert on Falconer's work, declared that text to be a faulty one and supplied a definitive version.

# Contents

# Note on the Selection

WHEN I started to assemble material for this collection, I meant to take my title literally and compile a book of the *sea*—not a book of voyages, naval battles, shipboard life, fishing, or any of the other activities that take place in, or on, or at the edge of, the sea. That is a rather sloppy distinction, but a useful one. It at least enabled me to reject a lot of passages that I was tempted to include. For the record, I tried to build the collection around a handful of pieces which seemed to me to define its heart: Poe's 'A Descent into the Maelström', Gerard Manley Hopkins's journal-entries on breaking waves, Conrad's description of the Indian Ocean at the beginning of *The Nigger of the 'Narcissus'*, Hilaire Belloc on the Portland Race in *The Cruise of the Nona*, Henry Beston on waves in *The Outermost House*, Rachel Carson on the colour of the sea in *The Sea About Us*, and Charles Tomlinson's anatomy of a great wave in 'The Atlantic'. In all of these, the focus is squarely on the water itself, and I looked for passages that would supplement and deepen these first-hand studies of the sea.

I have restricted the selection to writing in English. The French sea, the German sea, the Japanese sea are importantly different places— and the meanings of the sea in English alone are so rich and various that I felt it would unnecessarily complicate matters to introduce, say, Baudelaire, or Rilke, to the anthology. I have, though, included a taste of George Chapman's *Homer's Odysseys*, on the grounds that 'Chapman's Homer' is at least as much Chapman's as it is Homer's, and that it has long been regarded as a work of 'English' literature.

My general emphasis, with some exceptions, has been on the sea in literature rather than on the 'literature of the sea'. Generic sea stories, sea shanties, and associated nauticalia are well represented in other collections (as, for instance, in Captain John Coote's *The Faber Book of the Sea*, published in the US as *The Norton Book of the Sea*).

These ground-rules were intended to make things manageable, but the sea is an unmanageably great subject. My selection plots an arbitrary course across an ocean of writing, on which the solo editor carries his own limited horizon with him as he goes. I am uncomfortably aware of the great quantity of writing that I have not even glimpsed from my position here in the wheelhouse, just a few feet above sea-level.

J.R.

*Seattle*
*August 1991*

# INTRODUCTION

'I want to know what it says. The sea, Floy, what is it that it keeps on saying?'

Charles Dickens, *Dombey and Son*

IT is no surprise that one of the earliest works in the literature of English is a powerful poem about the sea. People generally write about the things that give them most difficulty in their lives, and maritime peoples are chronically oppressed and fascinated by the sea. 'The Seafarer' was copied, possibly from an oral source, perhaps from a written one, into the Exeter Book, a miscellany of Anglo-Saxon writing, which dates from about the year 904 and which was given by the eleventh-century Bishop Leofric to Exeter Cathedral, where it is still kept.

The dramatic impact of the poem, its metaphoric richness, are beyond question. The ancient mariner, telling of the loneliness, danger, and discomfort of his life afloat, is so here-and-now that he speaks straight through the superficial oddities of Anglo-Saxon vocabulary and grammar. But his precise meaning and tone are bafflingly hard to gauge. Every modern translator has given the poem a different twist. Where they disagree most is over the question of whether the seafarer has, in Richard Hamer's phrase, 'a love of the sea'.

Hamer (in *A Choice of Anglo-Saxon Verse*) thinks he has. This is the way he renders a crucial six lines (33–8) of the poem:

> And yet the heart's desires
> Incite me now that I myself should go
> On towering seas, among the salt waves' play;
> And constantly the heartfelt wishes urge
> The spirit to venture, that I should go forth
> To see the lands of strangers far away.

We are only a step away here from Masefield's 'Sea Fever', and the jaded urbanite's ache to get away from it all to the lonely sea and the sky.

Hamer's seafarer sounds disconcertingly like a modern yachtsman, in stormgear and yellow wellingtons, heading for an early-season crossing of the Channel from Ramsgate to Calais.

Michael Alexander (in *The Earliest English Poems*) strikes a much tougher and less illusioned note:

> Now come thoughts
> knocking my heart, of the high waves,
> clashing salt-crests, I am to cross again.
> Mind-lust maddens, moves as I breathe
> soul to set out, seek out the way
> to a far folk-land flood-beyond.

The thoughts that 'come' are both involuntary and fearful. 'I am to cross again' suggests that it is merely the mariner's fate, not his desire, to return to the sea, and 'Mind-lust maddens' hardly conveys the kind of emotion usually associated with the romantic pleasures and adventures of boating. Alexander's seafarer takes to the water unwillingly, as a necessity. He needs to reach 'a far folk-land', and a hazardous sea-crossing is his only way of getting there. For islanders like the British, this was one of the grim facts of life until the age of the charter flight. All foreign countries are known in English as 'overseas', and for good reason. Wanting to go to Paris was not at all the same thing as wanting to go to sea, but the journey to Paris inevitably entailed a long voyage that was more often endured than enjoyed.

Ezra Pound's 'The Seafarer' is more a modern replica of the Anglo-Saxon poem than a translation of it. Here is his version of the same six lines:

> Nathless there knocketh now
> The heart's thought that I on high streams
> The salt-wavy tumult traverse alone.
> Moaneth alway my mind's lust
> That I fare forth, that I afar hence
> Seek out a foreign fastness.

Like Alexander, Pound puts the weight of his seafarer's feelings on his ambition to go abroad, rather than his desire to go to sea. Yet in the solitude and danger of the 'high streams' and the 'salt-wavy tumult', this seafarer is a Romantic hero in a very recognizable mould. Outcast from society, with gannets and gulls for company, he stands aloof from other men on his wilderness of water. Pound, the heir to Byron, Shelley, Coleridge, Dana, Melville, and Conrad, has created a character who is on kissing-cousin terms with the Ancient Mariner and Captain Ahab. Even in the cold depths of misery, his tone is heroically defiant. The sea on which Pound sets him afloat is a post-nineteenth-century sea; an epic backdrop of wild Nature, against which the lonely individual spirit strives.

It is probably impossible for a modern reader ever to live in 'The Seafarer' on the terms in which it was originally written. We have sailed on too many literary seas to avoid infecting the Anglo-Saxon sea with meanings of which it was almost certainly innocent. The poem says that the sea is a nasty, bitter, dangerous, and lonely place, but we—translators all—know better. *Our* sea is the realm of the sublime, the theatre of heroic action, beautiful, treacherous, and all the rest. So the poem gets continually rewritten in the light of our own assumptions about the meaning of a life at sea.

What happens to the poem in that process happens on a far grander scale to the sea itself. The sea is one of the most 'universal' symbols in literature; it is certainly the most protean. It changes in response to shifts of sensibility as dramatically as it does to shifts of wind and the phases of the moon. The sea in eighteenth-century literature is one place, the sea in nineteenth-century literature quite another; as the American sea is importantly different from the British sea. Conrad's title for his collection of maritime essays, *The Mirror of the Sea*, puts it nicely: the writer who goes to sea finds himself confronting a disturbed reflection of his own age, personality, and preoccupations. The sea in literature is not a verifiable object, to be described, with varying degrees of success and shades of emphasis, by writers of different periods; it is, rather, the supremely liquid and volatile element, shaping itself newly for every writer and every generation.

The literature of the English Renaissance is crammed with ships, voyages, quadrants, compasses, and nautical slang. The surprising thing is that there is so little sea in it. Reading Hakluyt's *Voyages*, for instance, one is continually immersed in the business of seagoing, yet the glimpses one gets of the water itself are few and far between. In part, this reflects Hakluyt's personal taste as he edited the accounts of his correspondents. He was interested in the sea as the road to colonial conquest, and he was looking for descriptions of what lay at the end of the road rather than for assessments of the character and composition of the road surface. His successor, Samuel Purchas, author of *Hakluytus Posthumus: Or Purchas His Pilgrimes* (1626), was much more hospitable to the idea of the sea as a worthy subject in its own right. In a splendid catalogue of the manifold properties of the sea, Purchas wrote that the sea 'presents the eye with diversified Colours and Motions . . . multiplicity of Natures for Contemplation . . . manifold affections in it selfe, to affect and stupifie the subtilest Philosopher . . . '

Yet only rarely do either Hakluyt's or Purchas's captains write directly about the sea. Their concerns are overwhelmingly practical. A storm is a storm, to be survived, not described. The sea interests them for its depth, for the quality of its bottom as a holding-ground, for the strength and direction of its tidal streams; and these features are routinely logged, without elaboration. The main exceptions to this brusque approach occur when the sea is itself an object of colonial exploration, as in the voyages in search of the north-east and north-west passages and in the surveys of the fishing grounds on the Grand Banks of Newfoundland.

Hakluyt's most accomplished literary contributor was Sir Walter Raleigh, whose poems are studded with marine images and whose vision of paradise resembles nothing so much as a diver's-eye-view of a tropical coral reef:

> . . . the holy paths we'll travel,
> Strewed with rubies thick as gravel,
> Ceilings of diamonds, sapphire floors,
> High walls of coral and pearl bowers . . .

Even Raleigh writes regrettably tersely about the sea in the log of his voyage to Guiana. Twenty-two degrees of latitude, including the Bay of Biscay and the onset of the north-east trade winds, disappear in his first sentence:

On Thursday, the sixth of February, in the year 1595, we departed *England*, and the Sunday following had sight of the north cape of *Spain*, the wind for the most part continuing prosperous; we passed in sight of the *Burlings*, and the Rock, and fell with *Fuertaventura* the 17. of the same month . . .

It is not until he is within sight of Guiana that Raleigh's narrative speed slows down and he relaxes into prose description. On the landscape of his discovery, on sailing up its estuaries and inland rivers, he is wonderful at creating pictures in words for his patron, Queen Elizabeth; on the sea, he is surprisingly uninformative.

Raleigh sets a pattern which repeats itself over two hundred years, down to the voyages of Captains Cook and Vancouver. The professionals of the sea take its hazards and its beauties for granted. For them, the land is always full of interest, but the sea is merely a space to be traversed. The ship is another matter. A ship is—legally and socially—a detached fragment of the country whose flag it sails under, and its affairs merit description. But the water on which it floats is a *waste*, and sometimes a *rude waste*. For generations of highly literate captains, the sea held nothing in itself that was seriously worth describing. It was the occasional passengers—especially those passengers who knew the *Odyssey*, either in the original Greek or, after 1616, in Chapman's superb English version—who saw the sea as a fit subject in its own right. Raleigh's close friend, Edmund Spenser, who voyaged back and forth between England and his estate in Ireland, wrote far more vividly of the sea than did Raleigh himself.

There is nothing by Shakespeare in this anthology, which may seem odd at first blush. For the sea is an immensely important source of image and metaphor in his work. Twenty-six of the references to the word 'sea' in the *Oxford Dictionary of Quotations* are to Shakespeare. Several scenes from his plays are set at sea, as in *The Tempest* and *Pericles*. There are such famous marine passages as Clarence's dream in *Richard III*:

> As we paced along
> Upon the giddy footing of the hatches,
> Methought that Gloucester stumbled, and in falling
> Struck me, that thought to stay him, overboard,
> Into the tumbling billows of the main.
> Lord, Lord! Methought what pain it was to drown!
> What dreadful noise of waters in mine ears!
> What ugly sights of death within mine eyes!
> Methought I saw a thousand fearful wrecks,
> Ten thousand men that fishes gnawed upon,
> Wedges of gold, great anchors, heaps of pearl,
> Inestimable stones, unvalued jewels,
> All scattered in the bottom of the sea.
> Some lay in dead men's skulls, and in those holes
> Where eyes did once inhabit there were crept,
> As 'twere in scorn of eyes, reflecting gems,
> Which wooed the slimy bottom of the deep
> And mocked the dead bones that lay scattered by.

Even here the sea—*as* sea—is not quite in the foreground. Entirely appropriately, it is a sea one might conceive in a bad dream, fuelled by hearsay and late-night reading. In part at least, it is furnished from stock. The grotto of pearls and precious stones is queerly kin to Raleigh's underwater heaven, and it anticipates Ariel's song in *The Tempest*:

> Full fathom five thy father lies,
>     Of his bones are coral made,
> Those are pearls that were his eyes.

Shakespeare's sea—the silver sea; the triumphant sea; the hungry sea; the sea of glory; the boundless sea; the multitudinous seas incarnadined by Macbeth's bloody hands—has a quality of brilliant irrealism. It is not known whether Shakespeare ever went to sea, or even whether he set eyes on it. Some critics, including G. B. Harrison, have championed the notion that Shakespeare's allusions to the sea are so vivid and powerful, his nautical expertise (as in the sail-handling involved in the first scene of *The Tempest*) so flawless, that he must have had extensive first-hand experience of the sea, probably on a long foreign voyage. Perhaps he did; but to insist on the point is seriously to undervalue Shakespeare's capacity to imagine the world and make it palpable.

What is certain is that he wrote from the heart of a maritime culture, in a nation whose chief theatre of war, commerce, adventure, and colonial expansion was the sea. He lived in a city of ships and seamen, on the banks of a great tidal estuary. He was in a position to meet and talk to the great navigators of the day, like Raleigh and Drake. He had read the published voyages. *The Tempest* owes a good deal to the reports of the captains and travellers (including Strachey's *A True Reportory of the Wreck and Redemption of Sir Thomas Gates upon and from the Islands of the Bermudas*, Parry's *New and Large Discourse of the Travels of Sir Anthony Shirley, Knight*, and others).

The idea of the sea radiates through Shakespeare's plays, as it radiated through the culture of his age. Yet nowhere in his work is the sea confronted head on. It exists, rather, as a magical realm, a reservoir of glittering tropes and figures, like a mirror-image of the triumphant and boundless imagination itself.

To live in sixteenth-century English was to live in the language of seamanship and the sea. It is in Shakespeare's most casual allusions, rather than in his extended marine passages, that this comes out most clearly. As when, for instance, Guildenstern reports to the King on Hamlet's strange behaviour:

Nor do we find him forward to be nounded,
But, with a crafty madness, keeps aloof
When we would bring him on to some confession
Of his true state.

Elias Canetti (in *Crowds and Power*) has written of how every
Englishman is prone to see himself as the captain of a ship at sea, and
Hamlet here is seen to be managing himself like a ship threatened
with grounding on a lee shore. *Aloof* (that most English of postures)
is *a-luff*. Faced with Rosencranz and Guildenstern's impertinent
enquiries, Hamlet has luffed up into the wind to gain sea-room away
from them. Modern English is littered with dead nautical metaphors
like *aloof*, which were alive and well when Shakespeare was writing.
To have things *above board* ... to be *taken aback* ... to see something
out *to the bitter end* (the last extremity of the anchor-chain, where it
is attached to the bitt, and a sure sign of desperate circumstances)—the
most landlubberly speaker of colloquial English is prone to talk
unconsciously in terms that come out of the sea. In Shakespeare's
English the terms have a precise, allusive meaning. Even if he never
saw the sea, he was in a sense its creature because he spoke its
language.

Between 1685 and 1703, the loquacious and resourceful gentlewoman,
Celia Fiennes, rode side-saddle across the length and breadth of
England. Her journeys kept on bringing her to the sea's edge. Yet she
saw nothing of the sea. At Scarborough, she counted the number of
'sayle' on the far horizon; at Dover, she saw the coast of France; at
Land's End, she stood on the cliff and peered into the distance,
looking for the Isles of Scilly. What intervened between her and these
signs of distant civilization was a colourless blank—a vacancy on
which she wasted no words at all.

Fiennes's blindness to the ocean was a common English affliction.
There was some social snobbery in it. Sailors (except in times of war)
were vagrant ruffians. They lived in the lowest and most malodorous
quarters of town. The element from which they derived their horrid
living was a vast, uncivil desert of waters, from which a person of
sensibility could expect to derive little or no education and pleasure.
To someone like Celia Fiennes, with her taste for titles and grand
houses, the sea was beneath her notice, one suspects, because it was
irredeemably lower class.

In 1700, Fiennes stood on the brink of a great upheaval of ideas about the sea. She was just ten years older than Joseph Addison, the disciple of John Locke and forerunner of Edmund Burke. Addison's essay on the sea in the *Spectator* of 1712 is a major landmark in sea writing. He identifies the sea as the archetype of the Sublime in nature:

of all objects that I have ever seen, there is none which affects my imagination so much as the sea or ocean. I cannot see the heaving of this prodigious bulk of waters, even in a calm, without a very pleasing astonishment; but when it is worked up in a tempest, so that the Horizon on every side is nothing but foaming billows and floating mountains, it is impossible to describe the agreeable horrour that rises from such a prospect. A troubled ocean, to a man who sails upon it, is, I think, the biggest object that he can see in motion, and consequently gives his imagination one of the highest kinds of pleasure that can arise from greatness.

Addison's eighteenth-century sublime sea is the immediate ancestor of the modern romantic sea. Suddenly, the water itself is in focus and in the foreground of the picture. Where in Charles Cotton's poem, 'The Tempest', a vividly rendered storm at sea had been created as an emblem of the turbulent and ungovernable emotions of the human heart, in Addison the sea is a sufficient subject in its own right. The sensation of 'agreeable horrour' provoked by the sight of great waves is one that will reverberate through the writing of the next three centuries.

Burke's epic treatise, 'On the Sublime and Beautiful' (1757), created for the ocean a philosophical space in the very centre of things. His primary definition of the Sublime tacitly invokes the power of ocean:

Whatever is fitted in any sort to excite the ideas of pain and danger, that is to say, whatever is in any sort terrible, or is conversant about terrible objects, or operates in a manner analogous to terror, is a source of the *sublime*; that is, it is productive of the strongest emotion which the mind is capable of feeling. I say the strongest emotion, because I am satisfied the ideas of pain are much more powerful than those which enter on the part of pleasure.

The sea makes its first direct appearance under the section-heading, 'Terror'.

A level plain of a vast extent on land, is certainly no mean idea; the prospect of such a plain may be as extensive as a prospect of the ocean: but can it ever fill the mind with anything so great as the ocean itself? This is owing to several causes; but it is owing to none more than this, that the ocean is an object of no small terror. Indeed, terror is in all cases whatsoever, either more openly or latently, the ruling principle of the sublime.

Under 4. VII, 'Exercise Necessary for the Finer Organs', Burke describes the joint operation of physical pain and mental terror: 'they are capable of producing delight; not pleasure, but a sort of delightful horror, a sort of tranquillity tinged with terror'. My own sailing companion tells me that this is the best description she has yet read of the feelings induced by being in a small boat at sea.

Burke's theory of the sublime was enormously influential on both painting and writing in the eighteenth century. It effectively legitimized the sea as a great subject for art, and gave rise to scores of fictional and painted tempests. It also provided a vital connecting link between neo-classical theory and the later, Romantic poems and paintings of the sea by Byron, Shelley, Coleridge, and J. M. W. Turner.

The most extended of the sublime tempests is William Falconer's *The Shipwreck* (1762), which went through scores of editions and enjoyed a vast popular reputation as the greatest marine poem in language until well into the nineteenth century. Falconer (1732–70) was a professional seaman who gained the patronage of the Duke of York for his literary work, and his three-canto epic, in laboured rhymed couplets, tries to marry the theories of Addison and Burke to actual shiphandling in an actual storm. It bristles with technical nauticalia at the same time as it wallows fashionably in delightful horror. Falconer went on to compile the first sea-dictionary, *An Universal Dictionary of the Marine* (1769), which is a fine and detailed portrait of the sea as it was encountered by the eighteenth-century sailor. He met a sailor's end. On 27 December 1769, the warship *Aurora*, in which he was travelling as a passenger, left Cape Town harbour and was never heard of again.

Between Addison's essay and Burke's treatise, another important shift of taste was taking place. By the early 1730s, Scarborough, with its chalybeate spring, had become the first of the English seaside resorts. Just as the sea was being recognized as sublime, so it was beginning to be seen as healthful. Dr Wittie of Hull (Scarborough's commercial near-neighbour) promoted the idea of drinking seawater as a cure for gout and worms. This practice occasioned a splendidly unpleasant poem by John Winstanley, 'To the Revd. Mr—— on his Drinking Sea-Water' (1751), which is, I believe, the first of what have

since become an avalanche of diatribes on the pollution of the North
Sea:

> Methinks, dear Tom, I see thee stand demure
> Close by old Ocean's side, with arms erect,
> Gulping the brine; and, with gigantic quaff,
> Pledge the proud whale, and from ten thousand springs
> Dilute the hyp, concomitant unkind!
>   For thee th'Euphrates from her spicy banks,
> Conveys her healing stream; for thee the Caspian
> Filters his balsam; while the fragrant Nile
> Tinges with balmy dew the greeting seas,
> Conscious of thee; whose tow'ring pyramids
> Would pride to lodge thy consecrated urn.
>   For thee the sage Batavian, from his stern,
> With face distorted and convulsive grin,
> Disgorges eastern gums, in bowels pent,
> And streaks the surge with salutary hue.
>   For thee the Thames, impregnated with steam
> Mercurial, wafts her complicated dose
> From reeking vaults, full copiously supplied
> By bums venereal, ruefully discharged
> By Ward's mysterious drop or magic pill.

The 'Batavian' is a Dutchman.

Sea-bathing, as a general tonic, turned in the first years of the
eighteenth century from an eccentric fad into a social rage. What
began at Scarborough soon spread round the English coast in a long
draggle of boarding houses and bathing machines. In Smollett's *The
Expedition of Humphry Clinker* (1771), one can see the sublime sea
merging with the therapeutic sea in a letter from Scarborough written
by Jerry Melford to his friend Sir Watkin Phillips:

Scarborough, though a paltry town, is romantic from its situation along a
cliff that overhangs the sea . . . You and I have often plunged together into the
Isis; but the sea is a much more noble bath, for health as well as pleasure. You
cannot conceive what a flow of spirits it gives, and how it braces every sinew
of the human frame . . .

By the time the Prince of Wales (later Prince Regent) came to
Brighton in 1783 and began to furnish it with pleasure domes, the
seaside holiday was a British institution, and it drastically altered the
way in which the sea was conventionally viewed. Fishermen, their
boats and hovels, turned picturesque—fit subjects for new versions

of pastoral. Watching waves break, like poking into rockpools, became a genteel occupation. What had been a vacancy only a few years earlier was transformed into a noble prospect. The sea now commanded description, in increasingly obsessive detail.

This was also the century of middle class travel for pleasure; of ferry boats and packets in which suffering passengers paid the price for their new freedom to go abroad. Where the voyagers of the sixteenth and seventeenth centuries were usually too familiar with the sea to be much excited by its motions and variety, the eighteenth-century travellers were transfixed by its awful novelty. Almost every major writer of the period, including Fielding, Smollett, Johnson, Boswell, left a record of being made sick, bewildered, and (more rarely) exhilarated by their brief excursions on the sea. Their descriptions—especially of the English Channel on a rough night, with the wind and tide at odds—are notably free of philosophical notions of the sublime.

The gothic novels of Ann Radcliffe are in thrall to Burke's aesthetic theory. Their aim—made plain on almost every page—is to stimulate sensations of delicious terror, and the sea forms an inevitable component of their machinery. The tempest and shipwreck in *The Mysteries of Udolpho* (1794) offers a fine example of sea writing in the style of the classical-sublime.

Radcliffe takes a despotic line with the contingent details of her story. The eastern horizon, where the storm brews up, is turned into the western horizon when she requires the sun to set there. Consulting a map of the Val de L'Aude and Golfe de Lion, where the episode takes place, only confuses things further. Radcliffe conjures a conveniently mixed-sex monastery which is ruined when seen from the outside, with its 'shattered towers', but turns out to be in full working order when the party of visitors enters it.

Her disregard for documentary realism is an essential part of her method. She constructs a highly artificial reality with pools of real water and sporadic outbursts of real weather. The overall effect of the piece is of a large landscape painting framed in heavy ornamental gilt. Within the frame, the landscape is—artfully landscaped, in the craggy-vista manner of Claude Lorrain, with trim turf and cleverly pruned foliage. This landscape manages somehow to contain the sea, which is, nevertheless, seen as an 'immense expanse' with a 'vast horizon', and which produces an 'emotion of sublimest rapture'. The sublime, according to Burke, was characterized by magnificence, greatness, and obscurity; the beautiful by littleness, proportion, and delicacy. Radcliffe's sea, at once vast and terrifying, and diminished by the park-like landscape which frames and contains it, gets the best of both worlds. It is sublime, and it is as pretty as a picture.

Indeed, it *is* a picture:

Blanche withdrew to a window, the lower panes of which, being without painting, allowed her to observe the progress of the storm over the Mediterranean, whose dark waves, that had so lately slept, now came boldly swelling, in long succession, to the shore, where they burst in white foam, and threw up a high spray over the rocks. A red sulphureous tint overspread the long line of clouds, that hung above the western horizon, beneath whose dark skirts the sun looking out, illumined the distant shores of Languedoc, as well as the tufted summits of the nearer woods, and shed a partial gleam on the western waves. The rest of the scene was in deep gloom, except where a sunbeam, darting between the clouds, glanced on the white wings of the seafowl, that circled high among them, or touched the swelling sail of a vessel, which was seen labouring in the storm. Blanche, for some time, anxiously watched the progress of the bark, as it threw the waves in foam around it, and, as the lightnings flashed, looked to the opening heavens, with many a sigh for the fate of the poor mariners.

This is a description—not of the sea, but of an eighteenth-century marine painting, complete with brushwork ('A red sulphureous tint overspread . . . '); it is art at one conscious remove from reality. It is vital to the effect of the piece that the sea is viewed through a painted casement window: the coloured designs on the upper panes of the window turn the 'scene' observed through the lower panes into an animated pictorial representation of nature—another coloured picture.

Yet Radcliffe's weather—for all her meddling with compass points and meteorology—is vivid; her sea, although one is made to perceive it through a coat of thick and somewhat cracked varnish, is a sea in which real people might drown. Her tempest is a very modest one by the standards of Shakespeare's or Charles Cotton's tempests; it is no more than a summer thunderstorm. But it has enough watery immediacy and power to overwhelm a small vessel, improvidently sailed (a competent captain of that particular bark would have reefed his sail and headed south for the open sea, instead of running before the wind for a harbourless shore).

Radcliffe was eight years older than Coleridge, twenty-four years older than Byron, but she belonged to another age. Her Gothic sea

and their Romantic sea are divided by a great upheaval in the history
of ideas, even though they remain connected by the tenuous umbilical
of the Sublime.

When he wrote *The Ancient Mariner* (1798), Coleridge had never
been to sea. (Shortly after finishing the poem, he had his first taste
of seagoing when he sailed on the Hamburg packet from Yarmouth;
he was 'exceedingly' disappointed by the experience.) Growing
up in Ottery St Mary, Devon, he was just six miles from the coast.
He was an addict of Hakluyt, Purchas, and the more recent
voyages. The combination of the seaside at Lyme Bay and a pile of
salty books was sufficient for him to recreate, with thrilling dramatic
force, the mariner's voyage south to the Antarctic pack-ice, north
through the storm-latitudes and the trades and into the equatorial
doldrums.

The poem is a triumph of what Coleridge himself labelled the
'esemplastic power' of the imagination. His invented, phantasmagoric
sea is more vividly real than Radcliffe's Mediterranean, which she
drew from the life. And one is tempted to read his 'painted ship upon
a painted ocean' as a kind of fortuitous footnote to Radcliffe. Where
art was for her a necessary frame for life (like the 'Claude Glass' with
which great landowners used to view their estates, as if they were
pictures); for Coleridge, art is here used as a teasing image of
lifelessness. The limp sails of the becalmed ship and the inert water on
which it floats are dead in the way that conventional marine painting
is dead—because it lacks an imagination to quicken it with life. Here
Coleridge's theology nicely coincides with his aesthetics: the ship is
dead because it has lost God and the divine imagination which
breathes life into the world. Living in a godless world, as the Ancient
Mariner finds himself doing, is like falling into the hands of a
mechanical draughtsman and colourist.

In the most important sense, Coleridge's imaginary sea *is* first-
hand. It comes to us in the language and character of the mariner
himself—that archetypal solitary outsider. The primacy of the self,
and its essential nakedness in the world of nature and experience, is
the cornerstone of Romantic theory. So Coleridge posts his mariner
to sea as a representative self, going abroad on its own, dealing with
the world hands-on, without benefit of filtering and distancing
conventions. The mariner's sea, alive with all its fearful meaning, is
his alone. It is a private reality, to which the reader is admitted as a
privileged intimate. Sailing into nightmare with the ancient mariner,

one is brought breathtakingly close to the water and the great moral secret which the water is there to reveal.

It is Byron, though, who has taken most of the credit for inventing the nineteenth-century sea, in *Childe Harold's Pilgrimage* (1812–16).

> There is a pleasure in the pathless woods,
> There is a rapture on the lonely shore,
> There is society where none intrudes,
> By the deep Sea, and music in its roar . . .

The outcast Byronic hero, apostrophizing the ocean as his darling, patting the 'mane' of its white breakers, glorying in its fickle moods, and craving for death in its capacious bosom, was the man, not just of the hour, but of the century. When Byron went to the beach, he mingled with the Universe. Stripping off, he laid himself on the breast of Ocean, to be 'borne, like thy bubbles, onward'. Much as Regency Brighton came to dictate the social habits of the age in respect of the sea, so Byron came to dictate its mental ones.

Byron's brand of Romantic sea, in which every swimmer—let alone every Corinthian sailor—could wallow in the boundless, endless, and sublime and still be home in time for tea and muffins, took hold on the popular imagination with a tenacity that has survived even into the late twentieth century. The ground for it had been prepared long before, in the eighteenth century, and when Byron began to write about the sea in his inimitably extravagant terms, it found an immediate mass audience.

The ink was not yet dry on *Childe Harold's Pilgrimage* before Jane Austen presented the new Romantic sea as a banal cliché. In *Sanditon* (1817), Byron, Shelley, and Scott show up, in the mouth of a young baronet on the make:

He began, in a tone of great taste and feeling, to talk of the sea and the sea shore—and ran with energy through all the usual phrases employed in praise of their sublimity, and descriptive of the *undescribable* emotions they excite in the mind of sensibility. The terrific grandeur of the ocean in a storm, its glassy surface in a calm, its gulls and its samphire, and the deep fathoms of its abysses, its quick vicissitudes, its direful deceptions, its mariners tempting it in sunshine and overwhelmed by the sudden tempest, all were eagerly and fluently touched; rather commonplace perhaps—but doing very well from the lips of a handsome Sir Edward . . .

It is a very funny passage, and full of wounding accuracy. One only wishes that every writer who treated the sea, from the early nineteenth century to the present day, had kept it pinned above his or her desk as an acerbic warning.

There were good geographical and demographic reasons why an English audience should have been so eager to embrace Byron's vision of the sea. Romanticism sanctified nature, solitude, wilderness at a time when in England (if not yet in Ireland, Wales, and Scotland), solitude and nature were both in increasingly short supply, and there was no real wilderness at all. Germany had its forests, the United States its open frontier; England's only untamed wilderness, where man might still feel small and alone in the vastness of Creation, was the sea. As England developed the biggest cities and the most mechanized industries in the world, so its access to the sea—that alternative universe—became more and more precious. For the sea was the realm of man as solitary creature, the hero struggling with elemental forces, and to go to sea was to escape from the city and the machine, and from the regulated and repetitive patterns of life in a complex industrial society. As Byron himself put it:

> Roll on, thou deep and dark blue Ocean —roll!
> Ten thousand fleets sweep over thee in vain;
> Man marks the earth with ruin—his control
> Stops with the shore;—upon the watery plain
> The wrecks are all thy deed, nor doth remain
> A shadow of man's ravage . . .

Uncontrolled, unravaged, unbuilt-over, the sea was the last refuge of the free spirit raised in the land of dark Satanic mills and the great wen of metropolitan London.

It was this sea that Turner painted—a sea of pure, unpent nature at its wildest and most magnificent. He gave pictorial representation to the mysterious and hallucinogenic sea of Coleridge (as in 'Sunrise with Sea-Monsters') and to the gale-swept, mighty sea of Byron. He also encouraged a happy myth about himself. While working on a preliminary sketch for his painting of the boat approaching Yarmouth harbour in a storm, he had been, so he said, roped to the mast of a fishing smack. Drenched to the skin, half-drowned, rolling through an arc of eighty degrees, the artist remained at his post, drawing the enormous waves under a sky of blown spume. The story (which has been generally doubted) has the essential rightness of fiction. It portrays the artist as a heroically manly figure whose devotion, both to the artistic endeavour and to nature, is touched with religious self-sacrifice. Turner, making himself a hostage of the wind and sea, becomes the solitary outcast hero of Romantic iconography—he becomes the Ancient Mariner and Childe Harold.

Turner's fragmentary sea poem, 'Foam's Frail Power', has all the obscurity prescribed by Burke in his recipe for the Sublime ('A clear idea is another name for a little idea'). It is impressively confused and uncertain. It also carries the argument about painted oceans an interesting stage further. The poem is phrased in a grammar and vocabulary derived from conventional eighteenth-century verse. It reveals a sea composed entirely of paint—streaks of white, saffron, and ultramarine, laid thickly on the canvas, which itself turns into the canvas of sails on a real sea.

> . . . blanched spots of canvas creep
> Upon the dark medium as village spires

So the boats show at once as triangles of bare white canvas, their outlines perhaps cut into the surrounding paint with a palette-knife, and as looking like 'village spires'—those triumphs of high artifice in a rural landscape. There is no resolving the contradiction: the poem remains a fascinatingly suggestive muddle, in which one glimpses Turner's genius wrestling with an unfamiliar medium, as he tries to put—in gummed-up words—what he does so freely, and with such bold assurance, in paint.

Literature is usually supposed to make nothing happen, but, in the case of Romantic writing about the sea, it has had a distinct and curious influence on the labour market. One would not have thought that a career in the navy, the merchant fleet, or the fishing industry, with all its dangers and privations, its hugger-mugger, boarding school atmosphere, would have been likely to attract the kind of sensitive and bookish young man who sees his eventual future in literary work. Yet the post-Byronic world is liberally spotted with careers that began afloat, with hemp and tar, and continued smoothly into the study, with ink and galley proofs.

Byron and his contemporaries made the sea into a proper habitat for aspiring authors. Captain Marryat . . . Fenimore Cooper . . . Richard Henry Dana . . . Herman Melville . . . Joseph Conrad . . .

John Masefield—along with many more minor and specialized writers like Frank Bullen and Albert Richard Wetjen, as well as more recent ones like Malcolm Lowry, Nicholas Monsarrat, or the young Anglo-American novelist, Paul Watkins—the literary seamen are so thick on the ground that they constitute a class in themselves.

To turn one's back on the overcivilized urban world by running away to sea in search of transcendent verities was a romantic (with a small r) gesture, performed so often that it became something dangerously close to an established social ritual. In the dreamscape in which such actions are plotted, the sea-life was natural, pure, free of the constraints of the factory and the city. Yet in reality, the sea itself was beginning to be invaded by industrial machinery.

In nineteenth- and early twentieth-century literature—in Conrad, in Masefield—the sea still belongs to sail. The ship moves in nature, propelled by the natural force of the wind. When steam engines, turbines, and diesels show up, they are there for special purposes, as intruders on a world over which the sailing ship rightfully reigns. When Masefield longs to go down to the sea again, it is not to gain passage in his dirty British coaster with a salt-caked smoke stack, but in a tall ship where the wind's song is audible over the white sail's shaking. When Conrad puts Captain MacWhirr at the wheel of the steamship, *Nan-Shan*, in *Typhoon*, the ship is like a great physical extension of the captain's dim and mechanical personality. The name 'MacWhirr' suggests the stupid revolution of a flywheel in an engine, and when ship and man drive blindly through the typhoon (as no ship should, and as no sailing ship could), they are affronting the nature of the sea. MacWhirr represents the unimaginative, industrial world that Conrad detested, and it is an anomaly that he should be at sea at all.

The truth is that MacWhirr and his ships' engines had long been in the ascendant in the actual nineteenth-century sea. Melville, for instance, was a professional seaman from 1839 to 1844; while he was gaining the experience that would enable him to write the supreme prose epic of the age of sail, Brunel's steam paddle-wheeler, the *Great Western*, went into regular transatlantic service in 1838, and his screw-driven *Great Britain* was launched in 1843. *The Nigger of the 'Narcissus'* was published in the same year (1892) that saw the invention of the diesel engine. By the time that Masefield published his *Salt-Water Ballads* in 1902, the turbine had been in general use for nearly five years.

Sea writing in the nineteenth century was aggressively reactionary and backward looking. Even Kipling, who loved and celebrated the machine age, set his sea novel, *Captains Courageous*, aboard sailing schooners on the Grand Banks. For the sea was hallowed as the province of Nature—it was *the* elemental reality, and the engine room, with its smells of Manchester and Birmingham and Sheffield, had no place in it.

Romanticism had begun as a radical movement. It equated libertarianism with democracy. Coleridge with his projected Pantisocratic community in New England—Wordsworth in France, endorsing the Revolution—Byron in Greece—the Romantic forefathers were democrats and freedom-fighters. It is ironic that their immediate heirs should have found in the Romantic programme a validation for their new and angry kind of conservatism. The political colour of late Romantic writing about the sea is a very deep blue.

In December 1885, Conrad (still then K. N. Korzeniowski) wrote to a fellow Polish exile in England, Spiridion Kliszczewski, about the disappointing results of the recent British general election, in which the Liberals, led by Gladstone, had won 86 more seats than the Conservatives:

Where's the man to stop the rush of social-democratic ideas? The opportunity and the day have come and are gone! Believe me: gone for ever! For the sun is set and the last barrier removed. England was the only barrier to the pressure of infernal doctrines born in continental back-slums. Now, there is nothing! The destiny of this nation and of all nations is to be accomplished in darkness amid much weeping and gnashing of teeth, to pass through robbery, equality, anarchy and misery under the iron rule of a militarism despotism! Such is the lesson of common sense logic.

Socialism must end in Caesarism.

. . . I live mostly in the past and the future. The present has, you understand, but few charms for me. I look with the serenity of despair and the indifference of contempt upon the passing events. Disestablishment, Land Reform, Universal Brotherhood are but like milestones on the road to ruin . . .

Thus the second mate of the sailing ship, *Tilkhurst*, then in Calcutta waiting for its cargo.

One cannot separate Conrad's writing about the sea from his far-right political beliefs: they are two sides of the same coin. The land was polluted beyond repair—by socialism and 'radical reform'.

'Every disreputable ragamuffin in Europe feels that the day of universal brotherhood, despoliation and disorder is coming apace, and nurses day-dreams of well-plenished pockets amongst the ruin of all that is respectable, venerable, and holy.' For Conrad, the sea was the last untainted, venerable, and holy place left on the earth's surface, and that conviction fires his most brilliant writing, and gives his vision of the sea its incandescent quality.

He was happy on board ship, as he was never quite happy on shore. A tight ship, sailing under the Red Ensign in the 1880s, was something like a small monarchy, with an aristocratic class wielding unquestioned power over a loyal mass of inferior citizens. It was not in the least blemished by democracy. So Conrad, moving, as it were, from a marquisate to a dukedom, with his eye on the crown (briefly worn) of captaincy, managed to live, at sea, in a social order that had been largely banished, or heavily diluted, or overthrown by revolution on the land.

He pined for the sea when he was away from it. Condemned to a post on the River Congo, aboard a steamboat, and to having to take orders from a manager who was 'a common ivory dealer . . . a shop-keeper', Conrad fretted that 'Everything here is repellent to me.'

I feel homesick for the sea, the desire to look again on the level expanse of salt water which has so often lulled me, which has smiled at me so frequently under the sparkling sunshine of a lovely day, which many times too has hurled the threat of death in my face with a swirl of white foam whipped by the wind under the dark December sky . . . (translated from the French)

After he had given up the profession of the sea for a life of writing, Conrad kept on going back to the ocean as a yachtsman. He crewed for his friend, G. F. W. Hope (the 'Director of Companies' in Heart of Darkness), aboard his boats, Nellie and Ildegonde, and always the sea was a source of idyllic renewal. The roughest and coldest excursions provoked Conrad to rapture:

We have spent entire days without trysails, in the fog and the high seas of the Atlantic. The little 'Ildegonde' (which is a cutter of 23 tons burden) danced on the steep swells like a cockleshell. For two magnificent weeks I have been tossed about in the open sea, with the sad song of the wind in the rigging rising over the accompaniment of the immense and monotonous voice of enormous waves, breaking continually in an infinity of grey sky and green water, and foam of brilliant whiteness. (translated from the French)

The sea for Conrad was a primal theatre. It babied and punished him—smiling, lulling, threatening him with death—like a combination of indulgent mother and terrifying father.

The great achievement of his fiction was to give the sea—each sea—a local habitation and a name. The opening chapter of *Heart of Darkness*, with its luminous prose-painting of the sea reach of the Thames estuary, is a superb case in point: it gives to water a character and geography as particular as that of Gloucestershire or Massachusetts. It is a place where people live; not a vacancy, or a symbol, or apostrophized Ocean, or even *the* ocean—but a named and measured stretch of sea with its own distinct face. So the western Pacific in *Typhoon* and the Indian Ocean in *The Nigger of the 'Narcissus'* are as different in their characters as MacWhirr and James Wait. The range of sea-portraits in Conrad's fiction is almost as great as the range of his own seagoing.

One never loses the sense that, in this obsessive limning of water, Conrad is building a counterworld; a mirror-world of shimmering lucidity, unblighted by the horrors of nineteenth-century industrial democratic life. His love for the one is sustained by his hatred of the other, and it is poignantly sharpened by Conrad's knowledge that he is writing about a dying age in the life of the sea. These are the last days. When the *Narcissus* leaves Bombay harbour, it has to be hauled out of port by a steam tug which 'resembled an enormous and aquatic black beetle'. The tug leaves on the surface of the sea 'a round black patch of soot . . . an unclean mark of the creature's rest'. In Conrad's work, the patch of soot has an organic life of its own: it is growing; and soon, perhaps very soon, it will have polluted every one of his various and beautiful seas.

For the English writer (and I include Conrad, whose adopted Englishness made him a more fiery patriot than most native-born Englishmen—as one can see in the opening to *Heart of Darkness*), the sea was swollen with historical significance. The sea shaped and defined the nation. It was the terrain on which the Englishman's major wars had been fought, his road to the markets of the world, his route to Empire. It was his wilderness and the chief testing-ground of his young manhood. It was impossible for him (or her) to write about the sea without summoning some or all of these clangorous echoes. He could barely look out over the end of a pier without thinking of Drake, Hawkins, Raleigh, Nelson. 'Britannia rules the waves . . . ',

wrote Thomas Campbell, comfortably ensconced in a house over-
looking a placid reach of the upper Thames at the time of writing; and
Emerson, crossing the Atlantic in 1832, noted with amused scepticism
that the English were inclined to regard the seas of the world as their
exclusive colonial possession.

It was not so for the American writer. American history began in
sea voyages. As William Bradford wrote in *Of Plymouth Plantation*
(1630):

Having found a good haven and being brought safely in sight of land, they
fell upon their knees and blessed the God of Heaven who had brought them
over the vast and furious ocean, and delivered them from all the perils and
miseries of it, again to set their feet upon the firm and stable earth, their
proper element.

That firm and stable earth was the proper element of American
history—a record, in very large part, of the great drive to explore and
settle the interior of the continent. The sea was the beginning of
English journeys; it was the end of American ones. When the Lewis
and Clark expedition at last reached the Columbia River estuary in
November 1805, Clark wrote in his journal: 'Great joy in camp we
are in *View* of the *Ocian*, this great Pacific Octean which we been So
long anxious to See . . . ' This first glimpse of the sea (a deluded one, as
it turned out) was so welcome precisely because the sea did not have
to be travelled. Nor did either Lewis or Clark spare any words on a
description of its appearance; they were merely thankful that it was
there.

The American wilderness lay inside the country. The sea stories of
Fenimore Cooper, like *The Pilot* (1823), whose detailed descriptions
of the water and ship-handling far surpassed those of its British
model, *The Pirate* (1821) by Sir Walter Scott, were only a rehearsal
for Cooper's later tales of life 'in the woods', on the Frontier. Natty
Bumppo, the wise man of the woods, was the man, not Long Tom the
coxwain, who, in a phrase that foreshadows Bumppo's claim to be
the true child of nature, says: 'These waves, to me, are what the land is
to you; I was born on them, and I have always meant that they should
be my grave'. Substitute *woods* for *waves*, and you have Natty to
the life.

Only in the enormous geography of nineteenth-century America
could the sea itself turn into a metaphor for the even more belittling

vastness of the land—as it does in William Cullen Bryant's 'The
Prairies' (1834):

> The Prairies. I behold them for the first,
> And my heart swells, while the dilated sight
> Takes in the encircling vastness. Lo! they stretch
> In airy undulations, far away,
> As if the ocean, in his gentlest swell,
> Stood still, with all his rounded billows fixed,
> And motionless forever.—Motionless?—
> No—they are all unchained again. The clouds
> Sweep over with their shadows, and, beneath,
> The surface rolls and fluctuates to the eye;
> Dark hollows seem to glide along and chase
> The sunny ridges. Breezes of the South!
> . . . —have ye fanned
> A nobler or a lovelier scene than this?

This pulls the whole tradition of English sea writing inside out, with
the ocean being used as a familiar, domestic object to convey the
sublimity of a stretch of farmland.

This did not mean that American writers were generally less
interested in the sea. Far from it: between 1800 and the present day,
the sea figures in American literature as often, and as importantly, as
it does in British. But the American writer brings to it a quite
different geographical perspective, as he brings to it a quite different
national history.

In 1726, at the time of his 'tedious and dangerous' return voyage from
Southampton to Philadelphia, Benjamin Franklin would undoubtedly
have thought of himself as a loyal Englishman; but there is something
very un-English about Franklin's log. Intellectually, Franklin was
closer to being a French Enlightenment *philosophe* than he was to
being an English Augustan—a kindred spirit to contemporaries like
Buffon and Rousseau. Franklin's sea is an engrossing naturalist's
aquarium, as he investigates the life of the shark, the colour of the
flying fish and the generation of crabs in gulfweed:

Observing the weed more narrowly, I spied a very small crab crawling
among it, about as big as the head of a ten-penny nail, and of a yellowish
colour, like the weed itself. This gave me some reason to think that he was a
native of the branch, that he had not long since been in the same condition
with the rest of those little embrios that appeared in the shells, this being the

method of their generation; and that consequently all the rest of this odd kind of fruit might be crabs in due time. To strengthen my conjecture, I have resolved to keep the weed in salt water, renewing it every day till we come on shore, by this experiment to see whether any more crabs will be produced or not in this manner . . .

His theory was happily confirmed the next morning, with the appearance of a new crab, though the weed had withered and the 'embrios' were dead.

Franklin produced a speculative chart of the course of the Gulf Stream, and pressed it on captains of mail-ships in an attempt to shorten transatlantic journey times. His sea, cram-full of wonders, curiosities, and lessons, is already recognizably 'American' in its composition. It is an absorbing natural phenomenon not an over-bearing national symbol.

Liberated from the weight of sea-history that the British carried on their shoulders, American writers were able to adopt a tone towards the sea that was characteristically lighter and spryer. Of course the American sea is the realm of danger and death: as many ships go down in it, and sailors drown, as in its British counterpart. But it is nearly always seen through a more transparent, less darkly coloured, glass. One thinks of Marryat versus Dana. The British naval sea of *Mr Midshipman Easy* (1836) is an education into discipline, duty and tradition, where *Two Years Before the Mast* (1840), also the story of an induction into manhood and the exemplary society of the ship, is an education in the marvels of the natural world—though Dana is far more realistic than Marryat about the bodily discomforts of life at sea. Dana can spend a paragraph on the difficulty of drying out socks and trousers, and on the leakiness of composition boot-soles, in a way that must have struck many of his British readers as deplorably unmanly. Equally, while rounding the Horn—the great ritual passage for sorting out the men from the boys—Dana lets his attention wander to the entrancing prettiness of small icebergs:

No pencil has ever yet given anything like the true effect of an iceberg. In a picture they are huge, uncouth masses, stuck in the sea, while their chief beauty and grandeur—their slow, stately motion, the whirling of the snow about their summits, and the fearful groaning and cracking of their parts—the picture cannot give. This is the large iceberg; while the small and distant islands, floating on the smooth sea, in the light of a clear day, look like little floating fairy isles of sapphire.

It is hard to imagine Marryat ever allowing the sea off the Horn to be 'smooth'; and harder still to imagine one of his young heroes thinking in terms of 'little floating fairy isles of sapphire'.

The note struck by Dana is sounded again and again in American writing: by Thoreau, beachcombing around Cape Cod; Melville, dissertating on cetology in *Moby Dick*; Stephen Crane, taking a considered, oceanographer's view of wave formation, even in the catastrophic circumstances described in 'The Open Boat'; Samuel Eliot Morison and E. B. White, both using their sailboats as floating observation platforms, from which to study the working of the tides, marine bird life, and much else; Henry Beston, anatomizing waves in *The Outermost House*; Rachel Carson, exploring marine physics, chemistry, and biology in *The Sea Around Us*. In the United States, as not in Britain, writing about the sea has been contiguous with 'nature writing', as if the sea offered not so much a counterworld as a liquid extension of the green fields and forests within the land itself. The classic British opposition between wild sea and tame land, between *nature* and *culture*, has simply not applied to the American experience. The great transfixing stories of cannibalism in Britain (of man gone savage through too much contact with unconfined nature), like the fate of the crew of the *Mignonette*, all took place at sea. In the United States, their locations were inland—in the Rocky Mountains, with Alfred Packer, who ate five of the six Democrats in Hinsdale County, Colorado, or the Donner Party. When Joshua Slocum left Boston in 1895 to sail alone around the world in *Spray*, the sea did not offer the only path available to him of solitary adventure, as it did to the British. Slocum could have packed his bags and taken the train to Oregon or New Mexico. It is an important difference.

In 'The Open Boat', Stephen Crane wrote: 'In a ten-foot dinghy one can get an idea of the resources of the sea in the line of waves that is not probable to the average experience which is never at sea in a dinghy'. The small-boat sailor, dealing on intimate terms with each breaking crest, studying its wrinkled skin, its planes and contours, in close-up, and doing so in earnest, for dear life, has a—sometimes distressingly—conjugal relationship with the sea. This close to the water, he or she is like Gulliver in Brobdignag; and the main contribution of the yachtsmen to marine literature has been a kind of Brobdignagian description of the sea's magnified pores, exuding beads of sweat in which a human-sized creature might drown.

It is not surprising that so many of the Romantic poets were passionate amateur sailors. Wordsworth, probably wisely, confined his meditative boating to the Lakes. Byron kept a substantial yacht with a paid crew, the *Bolivar*, on the Mediterranean. Shelley had a schooner (though, at 24 feet long, it was hardly bigger than a dinghy), which he moored outside his beach-house in Lerici. For some time before he became a boat-owner, Shelley had been apostrophizing the sea as a fit grave for a poet. In 'Alastor', he wrote:

> The boat fled on
> With unrelaxing speed. 'Vision and Love!'
> The poet cried aloud, 'I have beheld
> The path of thy departure. Sleep and death
> Shall not divide us long!'

Nor did they. Eight weeks after taking delivery of the *Don Juan* from its builder, Shelley, with a friend and an English teenage boy whom he had hired as a deckhand, drowned in the Gulf of Spezia.

On 8 July 1822, they sailed from Livorno, homeward bound for Lerici. In the early evening, a squall came up from the south-west. An Italian fisherman, who passed the *Don Juan* as he ran for shelter, said that he had remonstrated with Shelley, who refused to reef or take down the sails of his vastly overcanvassed boat, despite the gale-force wind and rapidly rising sea. The *Don Juan* was swamped ten miles west of Viareggio. This foolhardy piece of seamanship ensured Shelley's apotheosis as a romantic hero. For his luckless companions, Edward Williams and Charles Vivian, there was no such compensation.

The small, private sailing vessel (of anything from 20 to 40 feet) was a natural vehicle for Englishmen who nursed Byronic, Shelleyan, or Turnerian dreams of battling alone against the elements, and it produced its own body of minor literature. By the time that Slocum came to write *Sailing Alone Around the World* in the United States at the end of the century, the small-boat voyage was a well-established genre in Britain, with a set of rigid formal conventions. Books like *The Voyage Alone in the Yawl 'Rob Roy'* by John MacGregor (1867), R. T. McMullen's *Down Channel* (1869) and E. E. Middleton's *The Cruise of the Kate* (1870) were Victorian bestsellers, and they inspired dozens of imitators.

The typical sailing-alone book opens with a portrait of the author on the streets of a large English city, or riding to work on a suburban commuter train, beset by the ills of modern urban civilization. The second chapter is devoted to a minute description of the planning and building—or the finding in a boatyard—of a suitable dream craft in which to make an escape, complete with half-hull drawings and rigging diagrams. The provisioning of the galley is fully inventorized, down to such items as 'pepper (coarse, or it is blown away)'. Thereafter, the book describes courses sailed, storms weathered, sunsets observed, tide-races caught in, fog lost in, harbourmasters and fishermen encountered, seasickness conquered and tranquillity achieved on—usually—the domestic seas around the British Isles, with the Thames Estuary and the English Channel as its most common location.

Most of these books were not so much records of voyages as instructional manuals in anecdotal form. They aimed at fleshing out the daydreams of readers who planned, sometime, to take their own long vacation from the crowds and timetables of nineteenth-century England, and they represented the sea as the last refuge of natural, self-reliant man.

MacGregor, McMullen, and Middleton all went to sea to teach the land a lesson, and the *Rob Roy*, the *Perseus*, and the *Kate* were miniature ships of state—models of order that (or so their captains insinuated) England would do well to observe and copy. MacGregor called for 'strong Tory government' and an evangelical revival, and distributed bibles, tracts, and cheap editions of *Pilgrim's Progress* around the coasts of England and France. His ship was a floating advertisement for muscular Christianity. McMullen abominated Roman Catholics, trades unions ('Idlers' unions'), and untidiness, in society at large, as aboard his boat: 'In language too mild to express my real sentiments, I dislike a sloven; a slovenly reef, a slovenly furl and a dirty mast look disgraceful on a yacht of any pretensions.' E. E. Middleton, the oddest and most humanly interesting of the three, loaded the *Kate* with a cargo of pamphlets promoting his theory that the world was saucer-shaped, his cures for gout and rheumatism and his verse translation of Virgil's *Aeneid*.

For these early yachtsmen, the sea was that biblical wilderness in which the true prophet must temporarily dwell, and they embraced it as a place of hardship and voluntary suffering. Images of romantic sublimity mingle in their writing with the idea that the sea is a kind of alembic, created by God as an instrument for testing the resolution of the British character. As he weathered a storm off Beachy Head in the 21-foot *Rob Roy*, John MacGregor revelled (or so he later claimed) in the 'splendours for the eye, and deep long thrills of the sublime, that stirred deep the whole inner being with feelings vivid and strong and loosed the most secret folds of consciousness with thoughts I had never felt before, and perhaps shall never know again'. A mile or so off a tame holiday beach, MacGregor found a nature that exceeded in his account, Mont Blanc, Etna, Vesuvius, and Niagara in 'grandeur'. Who else in Sussex sees Psalm 18 come to life before his eyes, but the lone yachtsman, at once so near and yet so far from home?

Implicit in each of these books is the notion that the author's capacity to fend for himself at sea, to survive the tumult of the storm, is a guarantee of his claims to be taken seriously ashore. MacGregor used his voyages to raise money for his charities, the Ragged Schools, the Shoeblack Brigade, and the Canoe Club—all devoted to the moral rescue of boys from the industrial working class. The subtext of McMullen's *Down Channel* is an acrimonious sermon on laziness and backsliding in Victorian society. Middleton's *Cruise of the Kate* is a long plea for recognition by a man whose literary efforts, geographical theories, and medical discoveries have been cruelly scorned by the shoreside establishment.

In Britain, the sea and the land interpenetrate. The small-boat voyagers were rarely out of sight of the society they were trying to call to order, and they used the sea to prove something to the land— to the larger craft of Great Britain herself, that unwieldy ship, wallowing on a dangerous course through the second industrial revolution.

The contrast between these British yachtsmen and the American, Joshua Slocum, is sharp in the extreme. Slocum had clearly read Conrad, and was familiar with the growing literature of small-boat sailing. In *Sailing Alone Around the World*, he struck a firm dissenting note. On page 1: 'The wonderful sea charmed me from the first.' On the last page of the book: 'The *Spray* . . . did not . . . sail to powwow about the dangers of the seas. The sea has been much maligned.' Slocum's sea is a remarkably benign and, on the whole, comfortable terrain. He presents his voyage, not as a battle of man against nature, nor as the renunciation of civilization in favour of wilderness, but as the humdrum life of a born-and-bred sea creature.

His training as a professional seaman led Slocum to a modest taciturnity in his descriptions of the sea. He never exaggerated the size of a wave (as the English yachtsmen habitually did) or dwelt indulgently on the personal danger of his voyage. Difficult passages, of several days' duration, are often dismissed in a sentence—and *Sailing Alone Around the World* devotes many more pages to Slocum's engagements ashore than it does to the long months he spent afloat. Yet his reading and his temperament inclined Slocum to a keen appreciation of the physical beauty of water under the influence of wind and tide, and, at regular intervals throughout the book, his customarily gruff manner suddenly breaks, to make way for a paragraph-long prose-poem. Even here, though, on the lyrical pinnacles of the book, Slocum seems curiously detached from the seascapes he describes.

It is a necessary conceit in the writing of *Sailing Alone* (and a much quibbled-over feature of the voyage itself ) that the *Spray* was capable of sailing itself for long periods, with the helm of the boat lashed and its captain otherwise engaged. On passage from Thursday Island to the Keeling Cocos Islands, for instance, Slocum claimed that he covered 2,700 miles in 23 days, spending only three hours of that time on the tiller. No one since has managed to replicate that feat, and I suspect it of being, in part at least, an ingenious literary device.

By crediting his boat with extraordinary powers of self-sufficiency, Slocum is able to efface himself from the scene. It is the *Spray* that makes the voyage, while her master stands back, observing the interaction of boat and sea with a kind of serene alienation. As a narrative strategy, this works a great deal better than the many attempts to lash the helms of the boats that have followed in the *Spray's* wake. It gives Slocum's kindly sea an appearance of credible objectivity, and it is a sturdily anti-Romantic way of writing about the water.

Any oceanographer, I think, would recognize Slocum's sea as his own. 'One could not be lonely in a sea like this,' wrote Slocum of the South Atlantic, observing the tumbling whitecaps, the porpoises, and the flying-fish ('Shooting out of the waves like arrows, and with outstretched wings, they sailed on the wind in graceful curves; then falling till again they touched the crest of the waves to wet their delicate wings and renew the flight'). For Slocum, the sea was simply the area of nature he knew best, and there are times in *Sailing Alone Around the World* when, far out at sea, he manages to sound endearingly like Gilbert White pottering in his Selborne garden.

Oceanography—a bundle of different sciences with a common marine application—has produced some of the most original writing about the sea in the twentieth century, as it has produced some of the most lucid and accessible prose in any scientific discipline. It began with buckets lowered over the sides of becalmed ships and with experiments of the sort conducted by Benjamin Franklin on his transatlantic passage, and it developed into long voyages of research and exploration, like Darwin's *Voyage of the Beagle* (1839). For a long time, well into this century, oceanography was inseparable from narratives of voyages and the names of the ships that made them: the *Challenger*, the *Arcturus*, the *Atlantis*. Inevitably, it was half science, half adventure, and even the most sober physicists' accounts of their time at sea are strongly influenced by their reading of writers like Dana, Melville, and Conrad.

In two fields especially—the circulation of ocean currents and the process of wave formation—oceanographers have focused on the same features of the sea that have most engaged the attention of the poets, novelists, and voyage-writers. An oceanographer's view of a wave is strikingly different from that of the non-scientist. Where the novelist and the navigator tend to be preoccupied with large, life-threatening waves, the overwhelming interest of the oceanographers has been with the capillary wave—the scallop-shaped wrinkle on the smooth surface of the water. Where the lay writers have taken the existence of waves for granted, oceanographers have addressed the question of why the wind should impart waves to the sea, and not some other kind of motion. That question turns out to be unexpectedly complex, and did not find a satisfactory answer until as late as the 1960s.

Oceanographers of the generation born before 1920—like Sir George Deacon, Willard Bascom, and Henry Stommel—have, in effect, taken the sea of the nineteenth-century novelists and poets and subjected it to a fastidious quantitative analysis, while retaining a Romantic sense of wonder at the sea's power and mystery. Bascom, particularly, writes of the sea with such frank passion that his *Waves and Beaches* has the eccentric and engaging character of a monograph by a swaggering adventurer.

For the first half of the twentieth century, oceanography continued to be written by people who were at least as happy roughing it aboard ship, or glorying in a storm on a Pacific beach, as they were in a university laboratory. A taste for seagoing was an essential qualification for the job. Yet as they amassed more and more first-hand data about the sea, so they were led increasingly into the language of mathematics to express their findings—and led away from the research vessel and the exploratory voyage, into the computer-room.

It is infuriating for the non-mathematical reader to discover that, just as oceanography began to formulate radical new perceptions of the sea, so it became a closed book. I had hoped, for instance, to include something here from Henry Stommel's *The Gulf Stream*. Stommel is not a 'mathematical' oceanographer in the sense that his students and juniors are; but beyond the first, historical background chapter, his book is not comprehensible to an audience unable to follow the logic of algebraic equations. I cannot follow that logic, and it is not the job of an editor to select passages that he cannot himself understand.

For the innumerate (and we are many), the best that one can hope to do is to taste the exhaust fumes of modern oceanography in the pages of popularizing magazines like *Scientific American*. Willard Bascom (in *The Crest of the Wave*) has already looked forward to a time when the latest generation of oceanographic Ph.D.s will have no need to set eyes upon the ocean. So the gap between the lay reader, and the lay writer, and the professionals of the sea widens.

That is literature's loss. For writing about the sea in the twentieth century needed some fresh understanding, some shift of knowledge or sensibility, to liberate it from the nineteenth-century masterpieces to which it is in thrall.

There is a great deal of modern writing which is set at sea. The period immediately after the Second World War saw a spate of novels by writers who had served in the British and US navies. Gore Vidal's first novel, *Williwaw*, published when he was 19, is a sea story, by Hemingway out of Conrad. Nicholas Monsarrat's *The Cruel Sea*, set on a corvette on escort duty in the North Atlantic, is much the richest and most complicated of its author's books. William Golding's *Pincher Martin* is at once an elegant theological fable and a brilliantly horrible account of a seaman's drowning after his ship has been torpedoed.

In these novels the sea is, above all else, *cruel*; its coldness and turbulence reflect the universal derangement of a world at war. Yet, side-by-side with the war novels, came a series of books in which the sea figures as a realm of escape and renewal. Written by ex-servicemen who were unable to settle to peacetime life, they chronicled the purchase of rotting Brixham trawlers and derelict yachts, their loving

restoration and their eventual sailing-away from welfare-state England
to seas untainted by Attleeite socialism. Thus Brigadier Miles Smeeton's
*Once is Enough*, Peter Pye's *Red Mains'l*, George Millar's *Isabel and
the Sea* and *A White Boat from England*, and Ann Davidson's grim
story of a dream of freedom that ended, a few days out, in the
drowning of her husband in Portland Race, *Last Voyage*. In style, in
politics, in their vision of the sea, the post-war voyage-writers hark
directly back to their Victorian antecedents. One could stitch together
sentences from Pye and Smeeton, McMullen and MacGregor, without a visible seam.

The sea continues to provide a natural backdrop for works of
contemporary fiction. In 1989, the US National Book Award went to
*Spartina* by John Casey—a novel about a Rhode Island fisherman, in
which much of the action takes place at sea. In 1990, the same prize
went to *Middle Passage* by Charles Johnson, which is set almost
entirely at sea, aboard a slave ship on the Atlantic. There is a lot of life
still left in the literary sea.

Yet both *Spartina* and *Middle Passage* are understandably uneasy
in their handling of the sea. Casey and Johnson are sophisticated
writers: their work shows them to be aware of being latecomers, of
writing in the lengthening shadows of Melville and Conrad. Their
ships and men are new, but the water on which they are set afloat is
nineteenth-century water. It has been written before.

Two-thirds of the way through *Spartina*, the boat which provides
the novel with its title and her builder, Dick Pierce, are tested in a
hurricane. The scene is one of the basic archetypes of fiction at sea, of
which the finest example is Conrad's *Typhoon*. In this anthology
alone (and I have tried to prefer calms to storms when presented with
a choice), there are twenty-something tempests, ranging from the
Atlantic hurricane in Edward Hay's account of Sir Humphrey
Gilbert's voyage to Newfoundland, to the hurricane in Richard
Hughes's *In Hazard*. In each one a boat or ship—that emblem of
human labour and aspiration—is either tested to breaking-point or
entirely destroyed. These are hard acts to follow.

John Casey builds up his set-piece storm with cautious minimalism.
The rhetoric of grand marine description is exhausted: waves have
towered too high, too often—as they have blotted out the sky,
broken like rolls of thunder, collapsed in snowy avalanches, et cetera,
et cetera. As one answer to economic inflation is to tighten up on the
money supply, so Casey deals with this linguistic inflation by putting

harsh controls on the supply of figurative language. Here is how he manages an early stage in the hurricane:

What faint light there was began to darken. Dick could still see the dark of the sea against the lighter blur of sky, but now he lost his short glimpses across the trough to the defined planes of the wave face, facets of chipped flint. He still had a sense of the enormous distance between waves. Each trough a small valley. And he had an even more puzzled sense of whether it was *Spartina* who moved toward the wave or the wave which came toward her, until she lifted up and went blind in the blown spray across her windshield.

It was full dark when he sensed that the seas were growing confused. From the direction of the spattering across the windshield he figured the wind had pulled around to the southwest. Maybe west. The main roll of the sea was still from the south, but he could feel *Spartina* responding to bulges and shoves of wind on her starboard bow.

This is crisp and particular writing. Yet one can feel Casey tiptoeing nervously in the large footprints left by the novelists of the past who have been this way before. On the whole, he is committed to the avoidance of metaphor—and when a metaphor does crop up, it is part of the worn common coinage of sea writing, like the 'defined planes of the wave face, facets of chipped flint'. It is remarkable how often the sight of an advancing wave has brought thoughts of flint-knapping to mind. So, too, a wave-trough is seen as a 'valley', though Casey slightly enlivens that dull image by modifying it to a 'small valley'. One is grateful for small things here, like the 'bulges and shoves of wind'—minor, marginal variations on a standard theme.

It is *allusive*, in the sense that it invites one to fill the gaps left in Casey's descriptive writing with one's memories of other, more richly palpable literary hurricanes. It allows the reader to recall, for instance, the corresponding two paragraphs from *Typhoon*:

Sprawling over the table with arrested pen, he glanced out of the door, and in that frame of his vision he saw all the stars flying upwards between the teakwood jambs on a black sky. The whole lot took flight together and disappeared, leaving only a blackness flecked with white flashes, for the sea was as black as the sky and speckled with foam afar. The stars that had flown to the roll came back on the return swing of the ship, rushing downwards in their glittering multitude, not of fiery points, but enlarged to tiny discs brilliant with a clear wet sheen.

Jukes watched the flying big stars for a moment, and then wrote: '8 P.M. Swell increasing. Ship laboring and taking water on her decks. Battened down the coolies for the night. Barometer still falling.' He paused, and

thought to himself, 'Perhaps nothing whatever'll come of it.' And then he
resolutely closed his entries: 'Every appearance of a typhoon coming on.'

The better stocked one's head is with such memories, the more
powerful and ominous Casey's sea becomes. Dick Pierce, sharing his
lonely wheelhouse with ghostly captains like Ahab and MacWhirr,
gathers weight from their presence.

*Spartina* is a fine novel, and Casey deals gracefully with the
problem of creating a seascape that has been created many times
before. At a lower and less self-aware level of literary performance,
much modern marine writing seems merely light-fingered. There
have been wholesale purloinings of Conrad's subtle palette of violets,
greys, and olive-greens. Melville's white whale has been variously
recast as a shark, a marlin, a German U-Boat. A depressing quantity
of prose writing about the sea in the late twentieth century has been
content to recycle the language and iconography of its nineteenth-
century predecessors.

It is a problem confined to prose. The sea in twentieth-century
poetry is a far livelier and more original place. The chief difficulty
under which the novelists and voyage-writers have laboured is the
exhaustion of descriptive metaphor. The thesaurus has been ransacked,
the reservoir emptied. In recent poetry, though, the sea itself is the
metaphor. 'The Sea is History', writes Derek Walcott, and, unconsciously rhyming with him, Mary Oliver comes back:

> The sea
> isn't a place
> but a fact, and
> a mystery

Description is not the point. The sea exists to be listened to and
decoded, an ocean of meanings and associations. Where the seas of
their prose-writing contemporaries have tended to coalesce into a
single, Conradian body of water, the individual seas of Bishop,
Lowell, Larkin, Tomlinson, and the rest are each private, posted
against trespassers.

Larkin's band of urban holidaymakers, 'Coming to water clumsily
undressed', attend the sea as one might attend church, to awaken
some answering sense of profundity in themselves—and 'To the Sea'
reads like a companion-poem to Larkin's earlier 'Churchgoing':

> A serious house on serious earth it is,
> In whose blent air all our compulsions meet,

> Are recognised, and robed as destinies.
> And that much never can be obsolete,
> Since someone will forever be surprising
> A hunger in himself to be more serious,
> And gravitating with it to this ground,
> Which, he once heard, was proper to grow wise in,
> If only that so many dead lie round.

The summer tourists enact, *en masse*, the same ritual performed by the churchgoer in solitude:

> Everything crowds under the low horizon:
> Steep beach, blue water, towels, red bathing caps,
> The small hushed waves' repeated fresh collapse
> Up the warm yellow sand, and further off
> A white steamer stuck in the afternoon—
>
> Still going on, all of it, still going on!
> To lie, eat, sleep in hearing of the surf
> (Ears to transistors, that sound tame enough
> Under the sky), or gently up and down
> Lead the uncertain children, frilled in white
> And grasping at enormous air, or wheel
> The rigid old along for them to feel
> A final summer . . .

In a secular world, it is this sacral quality of the sea that survives most vividly in the poetry of our own time. The sea lies on the far margin of society, and it is—as nothing else is—serious and deep. The last line of Derek Walcott's epic narrative poem, *Omeros*, has Achilles (a West Indian fisherman who, in Walcott's poem as in Homer's *Iliad*, is the prototype of busy, mortal man) walking away from the end of the story:

> When he left the beach the sea was still going on.

## ANON.

## from 'The Seafarer'

Mæg ic be mē sylfum     sōðgied wrecan,
sīþas secgan,     hū ic geswincdagum
carfoðhwīle     oft þrōwade,
bitre brēostccare     gebiden hæbbe,
gecunnad in cēole     cearselda fela,
atol ȳþa gewealc.     Þær mec oft bigeat
nearo nihtwaco     æt nacan stefnan,
þonne hē be clifum cnossað.     Calde geþrungen
wæron fēt mīne,     forste gebunden,
caldum clommum,     þær þā ceare seofedun
hāte ymb heortan;     hungor innan slāt
merewērges mōd.     Þæt se mon ne wāt,
þe him on foldan     fægrost limpeð,
hū ic earmcearig     īscealdne sǣ
winter wunade     wræccan lastum,
winemǣgum bidroren,     *   *   *
bihongen hrīmgicelum;     hægl scūrum flēag
Þær ic ne gehȳrde     būtan hlimman sǣ,
īscaldne wǣg.     Hwīlum ylfete song
dyde ic mē tō gomene,     ganetes hlēoþor
and huilpan swēg     fore hleahtor wera,
mǣw singende     fore medodrince.
Stormas þær stānclifu bēotan,     þær him stearn oncwæð
īsigfeþera;     ful oft þæt earn bigeal
ūrigfeþra.     Nǣnig hlēomǣga
fēasceaftig ferð     frēfran meahte.
For þon him gelȳfeð lȳt     sē þe āh līfes wyn
gebiden in burgum,     bealosīþa hwōn,
wlonc and wīngāl,     hū ic wērig oft
in brimlāde     bīdan sceolde.
Nāp nihtscua,     norþan snīwde,
hrīm hrūsan bond,     hægl fēol on eorþan,

corna caldast.    For þon cnyssað nū
heortan geþōhtas,        þæt ic hēan strēamas,
sealtȳþa gelāc      sylf cunnige;
monað mōdes lust        mǣla gehwylce
ferð tō fēran,      þæt ic feor heonan
elþēodigra        eard gesēce;
for þon nis þæs mōdwlonc        mon ofer eorþan,
ne his gifena þæs gōd,      ne in geoguþe tō þæs hwæt,
ne in his dǣdum tō þæs dēor,      ne him his dryhten tō þæs hold,
þæt hē ā his sǣfōre      sorge næbbe,
tō hwon hine Dryhten        gedōn wille.
Ne biþ him tō hearpan hyge,        ne tō hringþege,
ne tō wīfe wyn,      ne tō worulde hyht,
ne ymbe ōwiht elles,        nefne ymb ȳða gewealc;
ac ā hafað longunge        sē þe on lagu fundað.
Bearwas blōstmum nimað,        byrig fægriað,
wongas wlitig[i]að,        woruld ōnetteð;
ealle þā gemoniað        mōdes fūsne,
sefan tō sīþe,        þām þe swā þenceð
on flōdwegas      feor gewītan.
Swylce gēac monað        geōmran reorde,
singeð sumeres weard,        sorge bēodeð
bittre in brēosthord.        Þæt se beorn ne wāt,
sēftēadig secg,      hwæt þā sume drēogað,
þe þā wræclāstas        wīdost lecgað.
For þon nū mīn hyge hweorfeð        ofer hreþerlocan;
mīn mōdsefa      mid mereflōde
ofer hwæles ēþel        hweorfeð wīde,
eorþan scēatas,        cymeð eft tō mē
gifre and grǣdig;        gielleð ānfloga,
hweteð on hwælweg        hreþer unwearnum
ofer holma gelagu.

c.900

## Translation of 'The Seafarer'
## by Kevin Crossley-Holland

I can sing a true song about myself,
tell of my travels, how in days of tribulation
I often endured a time of hardship,
how I have harboured bitter sorrow in my heart
and often learned that ships are homes of sadness.
Wild were the waves when I often took my turn,
the arduous night-watch, standing at the prow
while the boat tossed near the rocks. My feet
were afflicted by cold, fettered in frost,
frozen chains; there I sighed out the sorrows
seething round my heart; a hunger within tore
at the mind of the sea-weary man. He who lives
most prosperously on land does not understand
how I, careworn and cut off from my kinsmen,
have as an exile endured a winter
on the icy sea . . .
hung round with icicles; hail showers flew.
I heard nothing there but the sea booming—
the ice-cold wave, at times the song of the swan.
The cry of the gannet was all my gladness,
the call of the curlew, not the laughter of men,
the mewing gull, not the sweetness of mead.
There, storms beat the rocky cliffs; the icy-feathered
tern answered them; and often the eagle,
dewy-winged, screeched overhead. No protector
could console the cheerless heart.
Wherefore he who is used to the comforts of life
and, proud and flushed with wine, suffers
little hardship living in the city,
will scarcely believe how I, weary,
have had to make the ocean paths my home.
The night-shadow grew long, it snowed from the north,
frost fettered the earth; hail fell on the ground,
coldest of grain. But now my blood
is stirred that I should make trial

of the mountainous streams, the tossing salt waves;
my heart's longings always urge me
to undertake a journey, to visit the country
of a foreign people far across the sea.
On earth there is no man so self-assured,
so generous with his gifts or so bold in his youth,
so daring in his deeds or with such a gracious lord,
that he harbours no fears about his seafaring
as to what the Lord will ordain for him.
He thinks not of the harp nor of receiving rings,
nor of rapture in a woman nor of worldly joy,
nor of anything but the rolling of the waves;
the seafarer will always feel longings.
The groves burst with blossom, towns become fair,
meadows grow green, the world revives;
all these things urge the heart of the eager man
to set out on a journey, he who means
to travel far over the ocean paths.
And the cuckoo, too, harbinger of summer,
sings in a mournful voice, boding bitter sorrow
to the heart. The prosperous man knows not
what some men endure who tread
the paths of exile to the end of the world.

Wherefore my heart leaps within me,
my mind roams with the waves
over the whale's domain, it wanders far and wide
across the face of the earth, returns again to me
eager and unsatisfied; the solitary bird screams,
irresistible, urges the heart to the whale's way
over the stretch of the seas.

# EDMUND SPENSER

c.1552–1599

# from *The Faerie Queene*

## Cant. XII

2

Two dayes now in that sea he sayled has,
  Ne ever land beheld, ne living wight,
  Ne ought save perill, still as he did pas:
  Tho when appeared the third *Morrow* bright,
  Upon the waves to spred her trembling light,
  An hideous roaring farre away they heard,
  That all their senses filled with affright,
  And streight they saw the raging surges reard
Up to the skyes, that them of drowning made affeard.

3

Said then the Boteman, Palmer stere aright,
  And keepe an even course; for yonder way
  We needes must passe (God do us well acquight,)
  That is the *Gulfe of Greedinesse*, they say,
  That deepe engorgeth all this worldes pray:
  Which having swallowd up excessively,
  He soone in vomit up againe doth lay,
  And belcheth forth his superfluity,
That all the seas for feare do seeme away to fly.

4

On th'other side an hideous Rocke is pight,
  Of mightie *Magnes* stone, whose craggie clift
  Depending from on high, dreadfull to sight,
  Over the waves his rugged armes doth lift,
  And threatneth downe to throw his ragged rift

On who so commeth nigh; yet nigh it drawes
All passengers, that none from it can shift:
For whiles they fly that Gulfes devouring jawes,
They on this rock are rent, and sunck in helplesse wawes.


5

Forward they passe, and strongly he them rowes,
  Until they nigh unto that Gulfe arrive,
  Where streame more violent and greedy growes:
Then he with all his puissance doth strive
To strike his oares, and mightily doth drive
The hollow vessell through the threatfull wave,
  Which gaping wide, to swallow them alive,
  In th'huge abysse of his engulfing grave,
Doth rore at them in vaine, and with great terror rave.


6

They passing by, that griesly mouth did see,
  Sucking the seas into his entralles deepe,
  That seem'd more horrible then hell to bee,
Or that darke dreadfull hole of *Tartare* steepe,
Through which the damned ghosts doen often creepe
Backe to the world, bad livers to torment:
  But nought that falles into this direfull deepe,
  Ne that approcheth nigh the wide descent,
May backe returne, but is condemned to be drent.


7

On th'other side, they saw that perilous Rocke,
  Threatning it selfe on them to ruinate,
  On whose sharpe clifts the ribs of vessels broke,
And shivered ships, which had bene wrecked late,
Yet stuck, with carkasses exanimate
Of such, as having all their substance spent
  In wanton joyes, and lustes intemperate,
  Did afterwards make shipwracke violent,
Both of their life, and fame for ever fowly blent.

8

For thy, this hight *The Rocke of* vile *Reproch*,
A daungerous and detestable place,
To which nor fish nor fowle did once approch,
But yelling Meawes, with Scagulles hoarse and bace,
And Cormoyrants, with birds of ravenous race,
Which still sate waiting on that wastfull clift,
For spoyle of wretches, whose unhappie cace,
After lost credite and consumed thrift,
At last them driven hath to this despairefull drift.


9

The Palmer seeing them in safetie past,
Thus said; Behold th'ensamples in our sights,
Of lustfull luxurie and thriftlesse wast:
What now is left of miserable wights,
Which spent their looser daies in lewd delights,
But shame and sad reproch, here to be red,
By these rent reliques, speaking their ill plights?
Let all that live, hereby be counselled,
To shunne *Rocke of Reproch*, and it as death to dred.


10

So forth they rowed, and that *Ferryman*
With his stiffe oares did brush the sea so strong,
That the hoare waters from his frigot ran,
And the light bubbles daunced all along,
Whiles the salt brine out of the billowes sprong.
At last farre off they many Islands spy,
On every side floting the floods emong:
Then said the knight, Loe I the land descry,
Therefore old Syre thy course do thereunto apply.


11

That may not be, said then the *Ferryman*
Least we unweeting hap to be fordonne:
For those same Islands, seeming now and than,
Are not firme lande, nor any certein wonne,
But straggling plots, which to and fro do ronne

In the wide waters: therefore are they hight
The *wandring Islands*. Therefore doe them shonne;
For they have oft drawne many a wandring wight
Into most deadly daunger and distressed plight.


12

Yet well they seeme to him, that farre doth vew,
  Both faire and fruitfull, and the ground dispred
With grassie greene of delectable hew,
  And the tall trees with leaves apparelled,
  Are deckt with blossomes dyde in white and red,
That mote the passengers thereto allure;
  But whosoever once hath fastened
  His foot thereon, may never it recure,
But wandreth ever more uncertein and unsure.


13

As th'Isle of *Delos* whylome men report
  Amid th'*Aegean* sea long time did stray,
Ne made for shipping any certaine port,
  Till that *Latona* traveiling that way,
  Flying from *Iunoes* wrath and hard assay,
Of her faire twins was there delivered,
  Which afterwards did rule the night and day;
  Thenceforth it firmely was established,
And for *Apolloes* honor highly herried.


14

They to him hearken, as beseemeth meete,
  And passe on forward: so their way does ly,
That one of those same Islands, which doe fleet
  In the wide sea, they needes must passen by,
  Which seemd so sweet and pleasant to the eye,
That it would tempt a man to touchen there:
  Upon the banck they sitting did espy
  A daintie damzell, dressing of her heare,
By whom a litle skippet floting did appeare.

15

She them espying, loud to them can call,
  Bidding them nigher draw unto the shore;
  For she had cause to busie them withall;
  And therewith loudly laught: But nathemore
  Would they once turne, but kept on as afore:
  Which when she saw, she left her lockes undight,
  And running to her boat withouten ore
  From the departing land it launched light,
And after them did drive with all her power and might.

16

Whom overtaking, she in merry sort
  Them gan to bord, and purpose diversly,
  Now faining dalliance and wanton sport,
  Now throwing forth lewd words immodestly;
  Till that the Palmer gan full bitterly
  Her to rebuke, for being loose and light
  Which not abiding, but more scornefully
  Scoffing at him, that did her justly wite,
She turnd her bote about, and from them rowed quite.

17

That was the wanton *Phaedria*, which late
  Did ferry him over the *Idle lake*:
  Whom nought regarding, they kept on their gate,
  And all her vaine allurements did forsake,
  When them the wary Boateman thus bespake;
  Here now behoveth us well to avyse,
  And of our safetie good heede to take;
  For here before a perlous passage lyes,
Where many Mermayds haunt, making false melodies.

18

But by the way, there is a great Quicksand,
  And a whirlepoole of hidden jeopardy,
  Therefore, Sir Palmer, keepe an even hand;
  For twixt them both the narrow way doth ly.
  Scarse had he said, when hard at hand they spy

That quicksand nigh with water covered;
But by the checked wave they did descry
It plaine, and by the sea discoloured:
It called was the quicksand of *Unthriftyhed.*


### 19

They passing by, a goodly Ship did see,
  Laden from far with precious merchandize,
  And bravely furnished, as ship might bee,
  Which through great disaventure, or mesprize,
  Her selfe had runne into that hazardize;
  Whose mariners and merchants with much toyle,
  Labour'd in vaine, to have recur'd their prize,
  And the rich wares to save from pitteous spoyle,
But neither toyle nor travell might her backe recoyle.


### 20

On th'other side they see that perilous Poole,
  That called was the *Whirlepoole of decay,*
  In which full many had with haplesse doole
  Beene suncke, of whom no memorie did stay:
  Whose circled waters rapt with whirling sway,
  Like to a restlesse wheele, still running round,
  Did covet, as they passed by that way,
  To draw their boate within the utmost bound
Of his wide *Labyrinth*, and then to have them dround.


### 21

But th'heedfull Boateman strongly forth did stretch
  His brawnie armes, and all his body straine,
  That th'utmost sandy breach they shortly fetch,
  Whiles the dred daunger does behind remaine.
  Suddeine they see from midst of all the Maine,
  The surging waters like a mountaine rise,
  And the great sea puft up with proud disdaine,
  To swell above the measure of his guise,
As threatning to devoure all, that his powre despise.

22

The waves come rolling, and the billowes rore
 Outragiously, as they enraged were,
 Or wrathfull *Neptune* did them drive before
 His whirling charet, for exceeding feare:
 For not one puffe of wind there did appeare,
 That all the three thereat woxe much afrayd,
 Unweeting, what such horrour straunge did reare.
 Eftsoones they saw an hideous hoast arrayd,
Of huge Sea monsters, such as living sence dismayd.


23

Most ugly shapes, and horrible aspects,
 Such as Dame Nature selfe mote feare to see,
 Or shame, that ever should so fowle defects
 From her most cunning hand escaped bee;
 All dreadfull pourtraicts of deformitee:
 Spring-headed *Hydraes*, and sea-shouldring Whales,
 Great whirlpooles, which all fishes make to flee,
 Bright Scolopendraes, arm'd with silver scales,
Mighty *Monoceros*, with immeasured tayles.


24

The dreadfull Fish, that hath deserv'd the name
 Of Death, and like him lookes in dreadfull hew,
 The griesly Wasserman, that makes his game
 The flying ships with swiftnesse to pursew,
 The horrible Sea-satyre, that doth shew
 His fearefull face in time of greatest storme,
 Huge *Ziffius*, whom Mariners eschew
 No lesse, then rocks (as travellers informe)
And greedy *Rosmarines* with visages deforme.


25

All these, and thousand thousands many more,
 And more deformed Monsters thousand fold,
 With dreadfull noise, and hollow rombling rore,
 Came rushing in the fomy waves enrold,
 Which seem'd to fly for feare, them to behold:

Ne wonder, if these did the knight appall;
For all that here on earth we dreadfull hold,
Be but as bugs to fearen babes withall,
Compared to the creatures in the seas entrall.

1589

# RICHARD HAKLUYT

## 1552–1616

# Edward Hay's account of Sir Humphrey Gilbert's voyage to Newfoundland

Wednesday toward night the wind came South, and wee bare with the land all that night, Westnorthwest, contrary to the mind of master Cox: neverthelesse wee followed the Admirall, deprived of power to prevent a mischiefe, which by no contradiction could be brought to hold other course, alleaging they could not make the ship to worke better, nor to lie otherwaies.

The evening was faire and pleasant, yet not without token of storme to ensue, and most part of this Wednesday night, like the Swanne that singeth before her death, they in the Admiral, or Delight, continued in sounding of Trumpets, with Drummes, and Fifes: also winding the Cornets, Haughtboyes: and in the end of their jolitie, left with the battell and ringing of dolefull knels.

Towards the evening also we caught in the Golden Hinde a very mighty Porpose, with a harping iron, having first striken divers of them, and brought away part of their flesh, sticking upon the iron, but could recover onely that one. These also passing through the Ocean, in heardes, did portend storme. I omit to recite frivolous reportes by them in the Frigat, of strange voyces, the same night, which scarred some from the helme.

Thursday the 29 of August, the wind rose, and blew vehemently at South and by East, bringing withal raine, and thicke mist, so that we could not see a cable length before us. And betimes in the morning we were altogether runne and folded in amongst flats and sands, amongst which we found shoale and deepe in every three or foure shippes length, after wee began to sound: but first-we were upon them unawares, untill master Cox looking out, discerned (in his judgement) white cliffes, crying (land) withall, though we could not afterward descrie any land, it being very likely the breaking of the sea white, which seemed to be white cliffes, through the haze and thicke weather.

Immediatly tokens were given unto the Delight, to cast about to seaward, which, being the greater ship, and of burden 120 tunnes, was yet formost upon the breach, keeping so ill watch, that they knew not the danger, before they felt the same, too late to recover it: for presently the Admirall strooke a ground, and had soone after her sterne and hinder partes beaten in pieces: whereupon the rest (that is to say, the Frigat in which was the Generall and the Golden Hinde) cast about Eastsoutheast, bearing to the South, even for our lives into the windes eye, because that way caried us to the seaward. Making out from this danger, wee sounded one while seven fathome, then five fathome, then foure fathome and lesse, againe deeper, immediatly foure fathome, then but three fathome, the sea going mightily and high. At last we recovered (God be thanked) in some despaire, to sea roome enough.

In this distresse, wee had vigilant eye unto the Admirall, whom wee sawe cast away, without power to give the men succour, neither could we espie any of the men that leaped overboord to save themselves, either in the same Pinnesse or Cocke, or upon rafters, and such like meanes, presenting themselves to men in those extremities: for we desired to save the men by every possible meanes. But all in vaine, sith God had determined their ruine: yet all that day, and part of the next, we beat up and downe as neere unto the wracke as was possible for us, looking out, if by good hap we might espie any of them.

This was a heavy and grievous event, to lose at one blow our chiefe shippe fraighted with great provision, gathered together with much travell, care, long time, and difficultie. But more was the losse of our men, which perished to the number almost of a hundreth soules. Amongst whom was drowned a learned man, an Hungarian, borne in the citie of Buda, called thereof Budaeus, who of pietie and zeale to good attempts, adventured in this action, minding to record in the Latine tongue, the gests and things worthy of remembrance, happening in this discoverie, to the honour of our nation, the same being adorned with the eloquent stile of this Orator, and rare Poet of our time.

Here also perished our Saxon Refiner and Discoverer of inestimable riches, as it was left amongst some of us in undoubted hope.

No lesse heavy was the losse of the Captaine Maurice Browne, a vertuous, honest, and discreete Gentleman, overseene onely in liberty given late before to men, that ought to have bene restrained, who shewed himselfe a man resolved, and never unprepared for death, as by his last act of this tragedie appeared, by report of them that escaped this wracke miraculously, as shall bee hereafter declared. For when all hope was past of recovering the ship, and that men began to give over, and to save themselves, the Captaine was advised before to shift also for his life, by the Pinnesse at the sterne of the ship: but refusing that counsell, he would not give example with the first to leave the shippe, but used all meanes to exhort his people not to despaire, nor so to leave off their labour, choosing rather to die, then to incurre infamie, by forsaking his charge, which then might be thought to have perished through his default, shewing an ill president unto his men, by leaving the ship first himselfe. With this mind hee mounted upon the highest decke, where hee attended imminent death, and unavoidable: how long, I leave it to God, who withdraweth not his comfort from his servants at such times.

In the meane season, certaine, to the number of foureteene persons, leaped into a small Pinnesse (the bignes of a Thames barge, which was made in the New found land) cut off the rope wherewith it was towed, and committed themselves to Gods mercy, amiddest the storme, and rage of sea and windes, destitute of foode, not so much as a droppe of fresh water. The boate seeming overcharged in foule weather with company, Edward Headly a valiant souldier, and well reputed of his companie, preferring the greater to the lesser, thought better that some of them perished then all, made this motion to cast lots, and them to bee throwen overboord upon whom the lots fell, thereby to lighten the boate, which otherwayes seemed impossible to live, offred himself with the first, content to take his adventure gladly: which nevertheles Richard Clarke, that was Master of the Admirall, and one of this number, refused, advising to abide Gods pleasure, who was able to save all, as well as a few.

The boate was caried before the wind, continuing six dayes and nights in the Ocean, and arrived at last with the men (alive, but weake) upon the New found land, saving that the foresayd Headly (who had bene late sicke) and another called of us Brasile, of his travell into those Countreys, died by the way, famished, and lesse able to holde out, then those of better health. For such was these poore mens extremitie, in cold and wet, to have no better sustenance then their owne urine, for sixe dayes together.

Thus whom God delivered from drowning, hee appointed to bee famished, who doth give limits to mans times, and ordaineth the manner and circumstance of dying: whom againe he will preserve, neither Sea, nor famine can confound. For those that arrived upon the Newe found land, were brought into France by certaine French men, then being upon that coast.

After this heavie chance, wee continued in beating the sea up and downe, expecting when the weather would cleere up, that we might yet beare in with the land, which we judged not farre off, either the continent or some Island. For we many times, and in sundry places found ground at 50, 45, 40 fathomes, and lesse. The ground comming upon our lead, being sometimes oazie sand, and otherwhile a broad shell, with a little sand about it.

Our people lost courage dayly after this ill successe, the weather continuing thicke and blustering, with increase of cold, Winter drawing on, which tooke from them all hope of amendement, setling an assurance of worse weather to growe upon us every day. The Leeside of us lay full of flats and dangers inevitable, if the wind blew hard at South. Some againe doubted we were ingulfed in the Bay of S. Laurence, the coast full of dangers, and unto us unknowen. But above all, provision waxed scant, and hope of supply was gone, with losse of our Admirall.

Those in the Frigat were already pinched with spare allowance, and want of clothes chiefly: Whereupon they besought the Generall to returne for England, before they all perished. And to them of the Golden Hinde, they made signes of their distresse, pointing to their mouthes, and to their clothes thinne and ragged: then immediately they also of the Golden Hinde, grew to be of the same opinion and desire to returne home.

The former reasons having also moved the Generall to have compassion of his poore men, in whom he saw no want of good will, but of meanes fit to performe the action they came for, resolved upon retire: and calling the Captaine and Master of the Hinde, he yeelded them many reasons, inforcing this unexpected returne, withall protesting himselfe, greatly satisfied with that hee had seene, and knew already.

Reiterating these words, Be content, we have seene enough, and take no care of expence past: I will set you foorth royally the next Spring, if God send us safe home. Therefore I pray you let us no longer strive here, where we fight against the elements.

Omitting circumstance, how unwillingly the Captaine & Master of the Hinde condescended to this motion, his owne company can testifie: yet comforted with the Generals promises of a speedie returne at Spring, and induced by other apparant reasons, proving an impossibilitie, to accomplish the action at that time, it was concluded on all hands to retire.

So upon Saturday in the afternoone the 31 of August, we changed our course, and returned backe for England, at which very instant, even in winding about, there passed along betweene us and towards the land which we now forsooke a very lion to our seeming, in shape, hair and colour, not swimming after the maner of a beast by mooving of his feete, but rather sliding upon the water with his whole body (excepting the legs) in sight, neither yet diving under, and againe rising above the water, as the maner is, of Whales, Dolphins, Tunise, Porposes, and all other fish: but confidently shewing himselfe above water without hiding: Notwithstanding, we presented our selves in open view and gesture to amase him, as all creatures will be commonly at a sudden gaze and sight of men. Thus he passed along turning his head to and fro, yawning and gaping wide, with ugly demonstration of long teeth, and glaring eyes, and to bidde us a farewell (comming right against the Hinde) he sent forth a horrible voyce, roaring or bellowing as doeth a lion, which spectacle wee all beheld so farre as we were able to discerne the same, as men prone to wonder at every strange thing, as this doubtlesse was, to see a lion in the Ocean sea, or fish in shape of a lion. What opinion others had thereof, and chiefly the Generall himselfe, I forbeare to deliver: But he tooke it for Bonum Omen, rejoycing that he was to warre against such an enemie, if it were the devill.

The wind was large for England at our returne, but very high, and the sea rough, insomuch as the Frigat wherein the Generall went was almost swalowed up.

Munday in the afternoone we passed in the sight of Cape Race, having made as much way in little more then two dayes and nights backe againe, as before wee had done in eight dayes from Cape Race, unto the place where our ship perished. Which hindrance thitherward, and speed back againe, is to be imputed unto the swift current, as well as to the winds, which we had more large in our returne.

This Munday the Generall came aboord the Hind to have the Surgeon of the Hind to dresse his foote, which he hurt by treading upon a naile: At what time we comforted ech other with hope of hard successe to be all past, and of the good to come. So agreeing to cary out lights alwayes by night, that we might keepe together, he departed into his Frigat, being by no meanes to be intreated to tarie in the Hind, which had bene more for his security  Immediatly after followed a sharpe storme, which we overpassed for that time. Praysed be God.

The weather faire, the Generall came aboord the Hind againe, to make merrie together with the Captaine, Master, and company, which was the last meeting, and continued there from morning untill night. During which time there passed sundry discourses, touching affaires past, and to come, lamenting greatly the losse of his great ship, more of the men, but most of all of his bookes and notes, and what els I know not, for which hee was out of measure grieved, the same doubtles being some matter of more importance then his bookes, which I could not draw from him: yet by circumstance I gathered, the same to be the Ore which Daniel the Saxon had brought unto him in the New found land. Whatsoever it was, the remembrance touched him so deepe, as not able to containe himselfe, he beat his boy in great rage, even at the same time, so long after the miscarying of the great ship, because upon a faire day, when wee were becalmed upon the coast of the New found land, neere unto Cape Race, he sent his boy aboord the Admirall, to fetch certaine things: amongst which, this being chiefe, was yet forgotten and left behind. After which time he could never conveniently send againe aboord the great ship, much lesse hee doubted her ruine so neere at hand.

Herein my opinion was better confirmed diversly, and by sundry conjectures, which maketh me have the greater hope of this rich Mine. For where as the Generall had never before good conceit of these North parts of the world: now his mind was wholly fixed upon the New found land. And as before he refused not to grant assigne-ments liberally to them that required the same into these North parts, now he became contrarily affected, refusing to make any so large grants, especially of S. Johns, which certaine English merchants made suite for, offering to imploy their money and travell upon the same:

yet neither by their owne suite, nor of others of his owne company, whom he seemed willing to pleasure, it could be obtained.

Also laying downe his determination in the Spring following, for disposing of his voyage then to be reattempted: he assigned the Captaine & Master of the Golden Hind, unto the South discovery, and reserved unto himselfe the North, affirming that this voyage had wonne his heart from the South, and that he was now become a Northerne man altogether.

Last, being demanded what means he had at his arrivall in England, to compasse the charges of so great preparation as he intended to make the next Spring: having determined upon two fleetes, one for the South, another for the North: Leave that to mee (hee replied) I will aske a pennie of no man. I will bring good tidings unto her Majesty, who wil be so gracious, to lend me 10000 pounds, willing us therefore to be of good cheere: for he did thanke God (he sayd) with al his heart, for that he had seene, the same being enough for us all, and that we needed not to seeke any further. And these last words he would often repeate, with demonstration of great fervencie of mind, being himselfe very confident, and setled in beliefe of inestimable good by this voyage: which the greater number of his followers nevertheles mistrusted altogether, not being made partakers of those secrets, which the Generall kept unto himselfe. Yet all of them that are living, may be witnesses of his words and protestations, which sparingly I have delivered.

Leaving the issue of this good hope unto God, who knoweth the trueth only, & can at his good pleasure bring the same to light: I will hasten to the end of this tragedie, which must be knit up in the person of our Generall. And as it was Gods ordinance upon him, even so the vehement perswasion and intreatie of his friends could nothing availe, to divert him from a wilfull resolution of going through in his Frigat, which was overcharged upon their deckes, with fights, nettings, and small artillerie, too cumbersome for so small a boate, that was to passe through the Ocean sea at that season of the yere, when by course we might expect much storme of foule weather, whereof indeed we had enough.

But when he was intreated by the Captaine, Master, and other his well willers of the Hinde, not to venture in the Frigat, this was his answere: I will not forsake my little company going homeward, with whom I have passed so many stormes and perils. And in very trueth, hee was urged to be so over hard, by hard reports given of him, that he was afraid of the sea, albeit this was rather rashnes, then advised resolution, to preferre the wind of a vaine report to the weight of his owne life.

Seeing he would not bend to reason, he had provision out of the Hinde, such as was wanting aboord his Frigat. And so we committed him to Gods protection, & set him aboord his Pinnesse, we being more then 300 leagues onward of our way home.

By that time we had brought the Islands of Azores South of us, yet wee then keeping much to the North, until we had got into the height and elevation of England: we met with very foule weather, and terrible seas, breaking short and high Pyramid wise. The reason whereof seemed to proceede either of hilly grounds high and low within the sea (as we see hilles and dales upon the land) upon which the seas doe mount and fall: or else the cause proceedeth of diversitie of winds, shifting often in sundry points: al which having power to move the great Ocean, which againe is not presently setled, so many seas do encounter together, as there had bene diversitie of windes. Howsoever it commeth to passe, men which all their life time had occupied the Sea, never saw more outragious Seas. We had also upon our maine yard, an apparition of a little fire by night, which seamen doe call Castor and Pollux. But we had onely one, which they take an evill signe of more tempest: the same is usuall in stormes.

Munday the ninth of September, in the afternoone, the Frigat was neere cast away, oppressed by waves, yet at that time recovered: and giving foorth signes of joy, the Generall sitting abaft with a booke in his hand, cried out unto us in the Hind (so oft as we did approch within hearing) We are as neere to heaven by sea as by land. Reiterating the same speech, well beseeming a souldier, resolute in Jesus Christ, as I can testifie he was.

The same Monday night, about twelve of the clocke, or not long after, the Frigat being ahead of us in the Golden Hinde, suddenly her lights were out, whereof as it were in a moment, we lost the sight, and withall our watch cryed, the Generall was cast away, which was too true. For in that moment, the Frigat was devoured and swallowed up of the Sea. Yet still we looked out all that night, and ever after, untill wee arrived upon the coast of England: Omitting no small saile at sea, unto which we gave not the tokens betweene us, agreed upon, to have perfect knowledge of each other, if we should at any time be separated.

In great torment of weather, and perill of drowning, it pleased God to send safe home the Golden Hinde, which arrived in Falmouth, the 22 day of September, being Sonday, not without as great danger escaped in a flaw, comming from the Southeast, with such thicke mist, that we could not discerne land, to put in right with the Haven.

From Falmouth we went to Dartmouth, & lay there at anker before the Range, while the captaine went aland, to enquire if there had bene any newes of the Frigat, which sayling well, might happily have bene before us. Also to certifie Sir John Gilbert, brother unto the Generall of our hard successe, whom the Captaine desired (while his men were yet aboord him, and were witnesses of all occurrents in that voyage), it might please him to take the examination of every person particularly, in discharge of his and their faithfull endevour. Sir John Gilbert refused so to doe, holding himselfe satisfied with report made by the Captaine: and not altogether dispairing of his brothers safetie, offered friendship and curtesie to the Captaine and his company, requiring to have his Barke brought into the harbour: in furtherance whereof, a boate was sent to helpe to tow her in.

Neverthelesse, when the Captaine returned aboord his ship, he found his men bent to depart, every man to his home: and then the winde serving to proceede higher upon the coast they demanded money to carie them home, some to London, others to Harwich, and elsewhere (if the barke should be carried into Dartmouth, and they discharged, so farre from home) or else to take benefite of the wind, then serving to draw neerer home, which should be a lesse charge unto the Captaine, and great ease unto the men, having els farre to goe.

Reason accompanied with necessitie perswaded the Captaine, who sent his lawfull excuse and cause of his sudden departure unto sir John Gilbert, by the boate of Dartmouth, and from thence the Golden Hind departed, and tooke harbour at Waimouth. Al the men tired with the tediousnes of so unprofitable a voyage to their seeming: in which their long expence of time, much toyle and labour, hard diet and continuall hazard of life was unrecompensed: their Captaine neverthelesse by his great charges, impaired greatly thereby, yet comforted in the goodnes of God, and his undoubted providence following him in all that voyage, as it doth alwaies those at other times, whosoever have confidence in him alone. Yet have we more neere feeling and perseverance of his powerfull hand and protection, when God doth bring us together with others into one same peril, in which he leaveth them, and delivereth us, making us thereby the beholders, but not partakers of their ruine.

Even so, amongst very many difficulties, discontentments, mutinies, conspiracies, sicknesses, mortalitie, spoylings, and wracks by sea, which were afflictions, more then in so small a Fleete, or so short a time may be supposed, albeit true in every particularitie, as partly by the former relation may be collected, and some I suppressed with silence for their sakes living, it pleased God to support this company (of which onely one man died of a maladie inveterate, and long infested): the rest kept together in reasonable contentment and concord, beginning, continuing, and ending the voyage, which none els did accomplish, either not pleased with the action, or impatient of wants, or prevented by death.

1598–1600

# THE ENGLISH BIBLE

## (1611)

## from Psalm 107

They that go down to the sea in ships, that do business in great
    waters;
These see the works of the Lord, and his wonders in the deep.
For he commandeth, and raiseth the stormy wind, which lifteth up
    the waves thereof.
They mount up to the heaven, they go down again to the depths: their
    soul is melted because of trouble.
They reel to and fro, and stagger like a drunken man, and are at their
    wit's end.
Then they cry unto the Lord in their trouble, and he bringeth them
    out of their distresses.
He maketh the storm a calm, so that the waves thereof are still.
Then are they glad because they be quiet; so he bringeth them unto
    their desired haven.

Verses 23–30

# GEORGE CHAPMAN
## 1559–1634

## from *Homer's Odysseys*

In meantime flew our ships, and straight we fetch'd
The Sirens' isle; a spleenless wind so stretch'd
Her wings to waft us, and so urged our keel.
But having reach'd this isle, we could not feel
The least gasp of it, it was stricken dead,
And all the sea in prostrate slumber spread:
The Sirens' devil charm'd all. Up then flew
My friends to work, strook sail, together drew,
And under hatches stow'd them, sat, and plied
Their polish'd oars, and did in curls divide
The white-head waters. My part then came on:
A mighty waxen cake I set upon,
Chopp'd it in fragments with my sword, and wrought
With strong hand every piece, till all were soft.
The great power of the sun, in such a beam
As then flew burning from his diadem,
To liquefaction help'd us. Orderly
I stopp'd their ears; and they as fair did ply
My feet and hands with cords, and to the mast
With other halsers made me soundly fast.
    Then took they seat, and forth our passage strook,
The foamy sea beneath their labour shook.
    Row'd on, in reach of an erected voice,
The Sirens soon took note, without our noise;
Tuned those sweet accents that made charms so strong,
And these learn'd numbers made the Sirens' song:
    'Come here, thou worthy of a world of praise,
That dost so high the Grecian glory raise;
Ulysses! stay thy ship, and that song hear
That none pass'd ever but it bent his ear,
But left him ravish'd, and instructed more
By us, than any ever heard before.

For we know all things whatsoever were
In wide Troy labour'd; whatsoever there
The Grecians and the Trojans both sustain'd
By those high issues that the Gods ordain'd.
And whatsoever all the earth can show
T' inform a knowledge of desert, we know.'
    This they gave accent in the sweetest strain
That ever open'd an enamour'd vein.
When my constrain'd heart needs would have mine ear
Yet more delighted, force way forth, and hear.
To which end I commanded with all sign
Stern looks could make (for not a joint of mine
Had power to stir) my friends to rise, and give
My limbs free way. They freely strived to drive
Their ship still on. When, far from will to loose,
Eurylochus and Perimedes rose
To wrap me surer, and oppress'd me more
With many a halser than had use before.
When, rowing on without the reach of sound,
My friends unstopp'd their ears, and me unbound,
And that isle quite we quitted. But again
Fresh fears employ'd us. I beheld a main
Of mighty billows, and a smoke ascend,
A horrid murmur hearing. Every friend
Astonish'd sat; from every hand his oar
Fell quite forsaken, with the dismal roar
Where all things there made echoes: stone-still stood
Our ship itself, because the ghastly flood
Took all men's motions from her in their own.
I through the ship went, labouring up and down
My friends' recover'd spirits. One by one
I gave good words, and said: That well were known
These ills to them before; I told them all;
And that these could not prove more capital
Than those the Cyclop block'd us up in; yet
My virtue, wit, and heaven-help'd course's set
Their freedoms open. I could not believe
But they remember'd it, and wish'd them give
My equal care and means now equal trust.
The strength they had for stirring up they must

Rouse and extend, to try if Jove had laid
His powers in theirs up, and would add his aid
To scape even that death. In particular then,
I told our pilot, that past other men
He most must bear firm spirits, since he sway'd
The continent that all our spirits convey'd,
In his whole guide of her. He saw there boil
The fiery whirlpools that to all our spoil
Inclosed a rock, without which he must steer,
Or all our ruins stood concluded there.
    All heard me and obey'd, and little knew
That, shunning that rock, six of them should rue
The wrack another hid. For I conceal'd
The heavy wounds, that never would be heal'd,
To be by Scylla open'd; for their fear
Would then have robb'd all of all care to steer,
Or stir an oar, and made them hide beneath;
When they and all had died an idle death.
But then even I forgot to shun the harm
Circe forewarn'd; who will'd I should not arm,
Nor shew myself to Scylla, lest in vain
I ventured life. Yet could not I contain,
But arm'd at all parts, and two lances took,
Up to the foredeck went, and thence did look
That rocky Scylla would have first appear'd
And taken my life with the friends I fear'd.
    From thence yet no place could afford her sight,
Though through the dark rock mine eye threw her light,
And ransack'd all ways. I then took a strait
That gave myself, and some few more, receipt
'Twixt Scylla and Charybdis; whence we saw
How horridly Charybdis' throat did draw
The brackish sea up, which when all abroad
She spit again out, never caldron sod
With so much fervour, fed with all the store
That could enrage it; all the rock did roar
With troubled waters; round about the tops
Of all the steep crags flew the foamy drops.
But when her draught the sea and earth dissunder'd,
The troubled bottoms turn'd up, and she thunder'd,

Far under shore the swart sands naked lay.
Whose whole stern sight the startled blood did fray
From all our faces. And while we on her
Our eyes bestow'd thus to our ruin's fear,
Six friends had Scylla snatch'd out of our keel,
In whom most loss did force and virtue feel.
When looking to my ship, and lending eye
To see my friends' estates, their heels turn'd high,
And hands cast up, I might discern, and hear
Their calls to me for help, when now they were
To try me in their last extremities.
And as an angler medicine for surprise
Of little fish sits pouring from the rocks,
From out the crook'd horn of a fold-bred ox,
And then with his long angle hoists them high
Up to the air, then sleightly hurls them by,
When helpless sprawling on the land they lie;
So easely Scylla to her rock had rapt
My woful friends, and so unhelp'd, entrapt
Struggling they lay beneath her violent rape;
Who in their tortures, desperate of escape,
Shriek'd as she tore, and up their hands to me
Still threw for sweet life. I did never see,
In all my sufferance ransacking the seas,
A spectacle so full of miseries.

And when the seventh day Jove reduced the wind
That all the month raged, and so in did bind
Our ship and us, was turn'd and calm'd, and we
Launch'd, put up masts, sails hoisted, and to sea.
   The island left so far that land nowhere
But only sea and sky had power t'appear,
Jove fix'd a cloud above our ship, so black
That all the sea it darken'd. Yet from wrack
She ran a good free time, till from the West
Came Zephyr ruffling forth, and put his breast
Out in a singing tempest, so most vast
It burst the gables that made sure our mast:
Our masts came tumbling down; our cattle down
Rush'd to the pump, and by our pilot's crown

The main-mast pass'd his fall, pash'd all his skull,
And all this wrack but one flaw made at full.
Off from the stern the sternsman diving fell,
And from his sinews flew his soul to hell.
Together all this time Jove's thunder chid,
And through and through the ship his lightning glid,
Till it embraced her round; her bulk was fill'd
With nasty sulphur, and her men were kill'd,
Tumbled to sea, like sea-mews swum about,
And there the date of their return was out.
  I toss'd from side to side still, till all broke
Her ribs were with the storm, and she did choke
With let-in surges; for the mast torn down
Tore her up piecemeal, and for me to drown
Left little undissolved. But to the mast
There was a leather thong left, which I cast
About it and the keel, and so sat tost
With baneful weather, till the West had lost
His stormy tyranny. And then arose
The South, that bred me more abhorred woes;
For back again his blasts expell'd me quite
On ravenous Charybdis. All that night
I totter'd up and down, till Light and I
At Scylla's rock encounter'd, and the nigh
Dreadful Charybdis. As I drave on these,
I saw Charybdis supping up the seas,
And had gone up together, if the tree
That bore the wild figs had not rescued me;
To which I leapt, and left my keel, and high
Clambering upon it did as close imply
My breast about it as a reremouse could;
Yet might my feet on no stub fasten hold
To ease my hands: the roots were crept so low
Beneath the earth, and so aloft did grow
The far-spread arms that (though good height I gat)
I could not reach them. To the main bole flat
I therefore still must cling; till up again
She belch'd my mast, and after that amain
My keel came tumbling. So at length it chanced
To me, as to a judge that long advanced

To judge a sort of hot young fellows' jars,
At length time frees him from their civil wars,
When glad he riseth and to dinner goes;
So time, at length, released with joys my woes,
And from Charybdis' mouth appear'd my keel.
To which, my hand now loosed and now my heel,
I altogether with a huge noise dropp'd;
Just in her midst fell, where the mast was propp'd;
And there row'd off with owers of my hands.
God and man's Father would not from her sands
Let Scylla see me; for I then had died
That bitter death that my poor friends supplied.
  Nine days at sea I hover'd: the tenth night
In th'isle Ogygia, where, about the bright
And right renown'd Calypso, I was cast
By power of Deity; where I lived embraced
With love and feasts.

                                        1616


# SAMUEL PURCHAS

## c.1575–1626

# from *Purchas His Pilgrimes*

As God hath combined the Sea and Land into one Globe, so their joynt
combination and mutuall assistance is necessary to Secular happinesse
and glory. The Sea covereth one halfe of this Patrimony of Man,
whereof God set him in possession when he said, replenish the earth
and subdue it, and have dominion over the fish of the Sea, and over
the fowle of the Aire, and over every living thing that mooveth upon
the Earth. And when the Sea had, as it were, rebelled against
rebellious Man, so that all in whose nostrils was the breath of life, and
all that was in the dry Land died, yet then did it all that time indure
the yoke of Man, in that first of ships the Arke of Noah; and soone
after the Goad also, when God renewed the former Covenant, and

imposed the feare and dread of Man upon everie beast of the Earth, and upon every foule of the Aire, upon all that mooveth upon the Earth, and upon all the fishes of the Sea.

Thus should Man at once lose halfe his Inheritance, if the Art of Navigation did not inable him to manage this untamed Beast, and with the Bridle of the Winds, and Saddle of his Shipping to make him serviceable. Now for the services of the Sea, they are innumerable; it is the great Purveyor of the Worlds Commodities to our use, Conveyor of the Excesse of Rivers, Uniter by Traffique of al Nations; it presents the eye with diversified Colours and Motions, and is as it were with rich Brooches, adorned with various Ilands; it is an open field for Merchandize in Peace, a pitched field for the most dreadfull fights of Warre; yeelds diversitie of Fish and Fowle for diet, Materials for Wealth, Medicine for Health, Simples for Medicines, Pearles and other Jewels for Ornament, Amber and Ambergrise for delight, the wonders of the Lord in the Deepe for instruction, variety of Creatures for use, multiplicity of Natures for Contemplation, diversity of accidents for admiration, compendiousnesse to the way, to full bodies healthfull evacuation, to the thirsty earth fertile moysture, to distant friends pleasant meeting, to weary persons delightfull refreshing; to studious and religious minds a Map of Knowledge, Mystery of Temperance, Exercise of Continence, Schoole of Prayer, Meditation, Devotion, and Sobrietie: refuge to the distressed, Portage to the Merchant, passage to the Traveller, Customes to the Prince, Springs, Lakes, Rivers, to the Earth; it hath on it Tempests and Calmes to chastise the Sinnes, to exercise the faith of Sea-men; manifold affections in it selfe, to affect and stupifie the subtilest Philosopher; sustaineth moveable Fortresses for the Souldier, mayntayneth (as in our Iland) a Wall of defence and waterie Garrison to guard the State; entertaines the Sunne with vapours, the Moone with obsequiousnesse, the Starres also with a naturall Looking-glasse, the Skie with Clouds, the Aire with temperatenesse, the Soyle with supplenesse, the Rivers with Tydes, the Hils with moysture, the Valleyes with fertilitie; contayneth most diversified matter for Meteors, most multiforme shapes, most various, numerous kindes, most immense, difformed, deformed, unformed Monsters; Once (for why should I longer detayne you?) the Sea yeelds Action to the bodie, Meditation to the Minde, the World to the World, all parts thereof to each part, by this Art of Arts, Navigation.

*

*Henry Hudson's narrative*

This day and night wee had cleere weather, and we were here come into a blacke blue Sea.

The ninth, cleere weather, the wind came at South-east and by East: from the last day till this day noone, wee had a good way North-east, in latitude of 75 degrees 29 minutes: then wee entred into Ice, being the first we saw in this Voyage: our hope was to goe through it, we stood into it, and held our course betweene North-east, and East North-east, loosing for one, and bearing roome for another, till foure in the after-noone: at which time we were so farre in, and the Ice so thicke and firme ahead, being in it foure or five leagues, that wee had endangered us somewhat too farre; wee returned as wee went in, and with a few rubbes of our ship against the Ice; by eight a clocke this Eevening wee got free of it. Wee made our way till next day at noone, South-west and by South, 18 leagues: in the middest of this way wee had no ground at 180 fathoms. The tenth, in the morning hasey weather; but at noone it cleered up, and then we cast about, and stood away North and by East, the wind being at East South-east, two watches, five leagues: then we had the wind at East, we cast about, and stood South South-east, and made a South way, sixe leagues. The eleventh, in the morning a hard storme at East, and East and by South we strooke a hull.

The twelfth, in the morning fog, and all day after cleere weather, the wind at South South-west, we steered East and by North: at noone being in the latitude 75 degrees 30 minutes. From noone till foure a clocke, five leagues East and by North; then we saw Ice ahead of us, and under our Lee trending from the North-west to the North and East of us: We had sounding 100 fathom, greenish Oze. Here we saw divers pieces of drift wood by us driving, and streame Leeches lying South South-west, and North North-east. We many times saw the like since we saw the North Cape. The thirteenth, cleere weather, the wind at East, we made a South way 6 leagues, two watches: then we cast about, and made a North way one watch 3 leagues ½: At twelve at night, much wind with fog, we strooke ahull and layed our ships head to the Southward. The fourteenth, in the fore-noone fog, and our shroudes were frozen: the after-noone was cleer Sun-shine, and so was all the night.

The fifteenth, all day and night cleere sun-shine; the wind at East, the latitude at noone 75 degrees 7 minutes. We held Westward by our account 13 leagues. In the after-noone the Sea was asswaged; and the wind being at East we set sayle, and stood South and by East, and South South-east as we could. This morning, one of our companie looking over boord saw a Mermaid, and calling up some of the companie to see her, one more came up, and by that time shee was come close to the ships side, looking earnestly on the men: a little after, a Sea came and overturned her: from the Navill upward, her backe and breasts were like a womans (as they say that saw her) her body as big as one of us; her skin very white; and long haire hanging downe behind, of colour blacke: in her going downe they saw her tayle, which was like the tayle of a Porposse, and speckled like a Macrell. Their names that saw her, were Thomas Hilles and Robert Rayner.

The sixteenth, cleere weather, the wind being at East. From the last day till this day noone, we made our way South and by East 9 leagues; and from noon to eight a clocke in the Eevening, 6 leagues: then we cast about and stood to the Northwards.

The seventeenth, cleere weather, the wind at South-east and by East: from the last day till this day noone, our way was North-east and by East, at noone being in the latitude of 74 degrees 40 minutes. At after-noone we sounded, and had ground at 86 fathom, greene Oze, and our water whitish greene: Here we saw Whales, Porpoises, and the Sea full of Fowles.

※

A Ruter, or briefe direction for readie sayling into the East-India, digested into a plaine method by Master John Davis of Lime-house, upon experience of his five Voyages thither, and home againe.

Nauticall Observation of places betwixt the Lizard and Saint Augustine in the Ile of Saint Laurence.

First, the Lizard hath in latitude fiftie degrees ten minutes. The Cape Finisterre in Galicia hath in latitude forty three degrees twentie minutes, and longitude from the Meridian of the Lizard, two degrees thirtie six minutes West. The Iland of Lancerota hath in latitude twentie eight degrees, forty minutes, and longitude from the Lizard five degrees twentie foure minutes West. The variation of the Compasse six degrees six minutes from North to East. And when you are in the latitude of thirtie three degrees thirtie minutes, and chance to have five degrees twentie minutes of variation, you may assure

your selfe to be North North-east from the said Iland, and your
course is South South-west to goe with it.

The Grand Canaria hath in latitude twenty seven degrees fortie
minutes, and longitude from the Lizard six degrees thirtie minutes
West. The variation is six degrees from North to East. Likewise in
the latitude thirty degrees thirty minutes: when you have five degrees
and fiftie minutes variation, you have the said Iland South and by
West from you.

The Iland of Saint Marie, being the Eastermost of the Azores, hath
in latitude thirtie seven degrees; and longitude from the Lizard
fourteene degrees West. The variation of the Compasse one degree
fortie minutes from North to East. But when you are in the latitude
of thirtie degrees thirtie minutes comming home-ward, and finde five
degrees variation, and would see the Ilands in your course, goe
North-east for Saint Marie: but it is better to goe more Northerly,
and so you shall bee sure to see some of them: for the variation is
much upon that rate in the North-east course, till you come in with
the Ilands.

The latitude of Sal, which is one of the Ilands of Cape Verde, is ten
degrees thirtie minutes, and longitude from the Lizard twelve degrees
twelve minutes. The variation three degrees, thirtie minutes from
North to East.

Bonavista is from Sal sixe leagues. The mid-way betweene the
Meridian of Cape Verde and these Ilands in the latitude of nine
degrees, you have two degrees fifteene minutes of variation to the
East-ward: and the neerer you are to the Maine land, the lesse
variation. But when you come in five degrees of latitude, if the
Ternados doe not meete with you before, there you shall beginne to
have them, which are winds blowing everywhere.

But if you will passe the Equinoctiall, use what diligence you may,
in plying to get from these unhealthfull and troublesome windes: but
keepe your selfe so, that you may bee but South and by East, or South
South-east from Maio, because it may bee in your minde, that your
much going to the East-ward will bee a helpe when you stand over
with the generall wind. But you may there spend much time, and get
little advantage. Now assoone as you have the wind at South South-
east, and are in two or three degrees off the line, stand away with it.
For if you may passe the Line in ten degrees of longitude from the
Lizard, your variation will be sixe degrees ten minutes from North to
East, and you shall feele neither the East South-east streame to hurt

you, nor the North-west and by West streame, that setteth over to the West-Indies.

But if the wind doe hinder you much, feare not to passe the Line in fourteene degrees of longitude from the Lizard, your variation will bee in that place six degrees fortie five minutes. And beeing past, make your way to the South-ward as speedily as you may: but if the wind be at East North-east or East, as many times it will bee, doe not goe to the East-ward of the South-east and by East, although in your minde it were the best course: for if you doe, you shall find the wind at South-east and South South-east, and it will bring you downe to your South course againe, although you have spent so much time as in your South course would have carried you without the Tropicke into the variable winds way, which is in twentie sixe or twentie eight degrees.

For it is great oddes, when a man may saile thirtie six leagues in foure and twentie houres, and will sayle but foure and twentie close upon a wind. For when you have brought your selfe into the variable winds way, it cannot be long before you have a slent to get up to the Cape of Good Hope, where you shall note, that your variation will increase in running South from the Line. For when you come in twentie degrees to the South-ward, you shall have fifteene degrees of variation, and more to the West-ward fourteene. Whereby if you note it well, you shall perceive, that in these parts, betweene the Tropickes I meane, it keepeth no method in Easting or Westing, as it doth without them: as you may see at the Ile De Fernando de Loronha, the latitude whereof is foure degrees South, and longitude from the Lizard nineteene degrees twentie minutes West. The variation is there eight degrees ten minutes, from North to East: if you come there to ride, the Roade is upon the North-east side, but it is ill ground in some place. The depth, nine, eight and seven fathomes water, sandie grounds, with a stone or Rocke heere and there.

This land riseth like Paules steeple, and that land like the steeple will bee when you are in the Roade South South-west from you. There is much broken ground and Ilands by the Ile it selfe. Heere is good refreshing and good water, but dangerous landing for the Sea to sinke your Boats and drowne your men.

The Portugals of Fernamburo have some few Slaves heere that make Cotton and keepe their Cattell. They have Guiney Wheate there growing.

The Iland of Santa Helena hath in South latitude sixteen degrees, &

longitude from the Lizard foure degrees thirtie minutes East: and from the Cape of Good Hope twentie three degrees thirtie minutes West. The variation is seven degrees thirtie minutes from North to East. This Iland is one of the best for the bignesse thereof for the refreshing of men, that I know in the Sea: it standeth so healthy, and hath so good a Roade for Shippes, as a man can desire. The Roade is open to the North-west side: right before the Chappell you may ride in twelve, tenne, nine, eight, or seven fathomes water, good ground and no danger, but what you see a long the shoare.

The Iland is little, but very high land, a man may see it eighteene leagues off. Upon it are all things fitting for a mans comfort, comming with it in distresse. If you will see this Iland, you have the wind alway at South-east or thereabouts. Therefore keepe your selfe in the latitude of sixteene degrees tenne minutes, or fifteene degrees, and runne West upon that height, and you cannot misse it: whether it bee day or night you need not feare, but this you may assure your selfe, that in your course from the Cape of Good Hope, there is nothing that will wrong you. I meane no streame nor Current. For I have seene that my selfe three times comming from the Cape the South-east wind will take you in thirtie degrees, and sometimes before, and will carrie you to the North-ward of the Equinoctiall Line.

Saldanha, which is the Bay where we doe commonly anchor out-ward bound, hath in latitude thirtie foure degrees twentie five minutes, and longitude from the Lizard twentie eight degrees East. The variation thirtie minutes from North to East. For the knowing of the land hereabout Saldanha, it is all high land. But commonly when you come from the West-ward it is foggie and darke upon it, so that you shall see the breach of the shoare, before you can come to make it, or know it. If you see the land when you are in the Offing rise like a Table, and other round hils by it, one like a Sugar-loafe; bring this Table East by South, and then stirre so see, till you come close under the land, for this course will bring you in with the point of the Souther land going into the Roade. Now when you see the point it selfe, which is low land, you shall see the Ile of Penguin: but keepe your selfe neerer the point then to Penguin Iland, because there are sunken Rockes all toward the Iland: keepe your Lead going, for toward the point you shall have ground at fifteene fathomes, and then you may bee bold to goe by it in ten fathomes water. Then the Roade is South-east by East from this point in six fathomes, or five if you

list. The Table will bee South South-west the middle of it, and the
Sugar-loafe South-west halfe Westerly. The worst winds for that
Roade are from the North-west to the North-east. Heere is good
watering and fresh victuals, when the people come downe with it.

There is fresh-fish in the River to bee had at sometime of the tyde
with a seine: it doth high sometimes five foote water, and sometimes
sixe, sometimes more, and sometimes lesse.

Betweene the Coast of Brasil and this Roade the Compasse hath
twentie degrees variation, and more or lesse as you are to the Northward or South. For the more you are to the South-ward, the more
you have, and to the North-ward the lesse. But in thirtie three
degrees thirty minutes, you have the highest variation twenty one
degrees from North to East, & longitude from the Lizard seven deg.
thirtie minutes, or from the Cape of Good Hope, thirtie five deg.
thirtie minutes West: Now when you come in eleven degrees no
minutes of variation, you may assure your selfe, if your variation bee
good, you are three hundred and thirtie leagues short: and it will
keepe a good method in decreasing after the rate of thirtie or eight and
twentie leagues to a degree: for when you are in two degrees of
variation, you shall be eight and fortie or fiftie leagues short: and
when you have fortie minutes, and cannot see the land, you are but
ten leagues off.

Now if you can see the Land close by the waters side, before you
can see the other high land, the fogge hanging upon the shoare, and
are in thirtie foure degrees of latitude, you may see white sandie
wayes close by the waters side, your course is to the point, if they
beare East South-east from you, and beeing neere the shoare is
North-east. For these white sandie wayes are almost three leagues
short of that point going into the Roade, and fast by the point to the
South-west from the said point going for the Roade, the two points
doe lye North-east and South-west. And then the land toward the
Cape lyeth South-east and by East, and South South-east. So likewise
the land lyeth to the North-ward off the Bay North North-west, and
South South-west.

Penguin Iland and this Point lye North and by West, and South
and by East.

To the Northward of this Iland is an Iland called Connie Iland, and
it lyeth in latitude thirtie three degrees twentie seven minutes, and
North North-west from Penguine Ile. This Connie Ile hath bad
ground about it: but you may goe betweene the Maine and that Iland.

If you will anchor, this Ile upon the Wester-side hath a dangerous ledge of Rockes lying off it to the Seaward. The Maine all along the shoare is bold, but what you may see.

Chapmans Chance hath in latitude thirtie foure degrees tenne minutues, and is an Harbour, which lyeth within the South-west point under a little Hill like Charing Crosse, close hanging by the Sea-side of the South South-west side of the land like a Table, standing in the very bottome of the Bay.

This is a very good Harbour for the ships: for the maine land of the Cape will be shut in upon the Westerside of the land: and there is good ground, and a good depth to ride in, as ten, nine, eight, seven, sixe, or five fathomes.

This Harbor is not past ten miles over land to Soldanha from it: and a man may come away with that wind that you cannot come forth withall from Soldanha. Wherefore when any shall have beene there with a ship, they shall better know it. Wee went not in with our ship, because we were all fit to goe about, before wee did know it to bee a Harbor. For wee did suspect it by chance standing in with a scant wind, and being toward night our Captaine Master Edmund Marlow sent one of the Masters Mates in the Pinnasse to see whether it were a Harbor or not, having little wind, and by that time hee came in with it, the Sunne was downe, so that he could not see and take that notice he would for quick returning to the ship.

Cape Falso hath in latitude thirty foure degrees thirty minutes, and is distant from the Cape of Good Hope, nine leagues East South-cast.

Betweene these two Capes there is a deepe Bay, and before it there is a Rocke even with the water; but it lyeth neere the Cape of Good Hope. In this Bay is the great River called Rio Dolce, that runneth farre up in the Land. There is good refreshing, as the Hollanders report, for they have beene there with their ships.

Heere at Cape Falso is no variation that I can find by observing South from it. The Land lyeth to the Cape das Aguilhas East South-east from the Cape of Good Hope, and is distant sixe and twentic leagues: no danger is to be seene, but a bould shoare along the coast. And so it is bould sixtie leagues to the Eastward: for so farre I have sailed to the East-ward of Cape Das Aguilhas the land lyeth East Northerly for one hundred leagues.

The very Cape Das Aguilhas hath in latitude thirtie foure degrees, fiftie minutes South, and is very low land. But there is high land to the East-ward of the last named Cape. You may have ground with your

Lead in seven or eight leagues off the land, for one hundred leagues East, at seventie, sixtie, sixtie five, fiftie five, fiftie, fortie fathomes, sandie blacke ground upon your Leade, which will helpe you much in comming home if you cannot observe the variation nor latitude. The variation of Cape Das Aguilhas is no degrees thirtie minutes from North to West. And at the Cape of Good Hope the Compasse is varied from North to East five and twentie minutes. Assoone as you are to the West-ward of Cape Das Aguilhas, you shall have Ozie and deepe water; whereby you may see that this will helpe you well in darke weather to know how the lands are from you, and how to hale in with the Cape of Good Hope.

When you saile into the East-India from the Cape of Good Hope, you must bee very carefull in your course: for till you come up to have seven or eight degrees of variation, you shall find it sometimes very uncertaine, shouts of streames that will set a man sometimes one way, sometimes another as I have often found it to bee so, and have had none other meanes to helpe my selfe, but by the variation which is very sure, if you bee carefull in observing. But after you passe eight degrees of variation, you shall not need to feare the streames, if you bee bound to the East-ward, for the streames or tydes doe set betweene the variation aforesaid, and the Cape Das Aguilhas.

Now if you find betweene the Cape and this variation of seven or eight degrees that you doe not alter it to your ship running East; for this is your fittest course, if you bee bound for Bantam, or within for any place of the Ile of Saint Laurence, till you come up to the variation aforesaid, as you may chance at five or sixe degrees, assure your selfe you are wrong with it. For the variation will increase by the rate of nine and twentie or thirtie leagues, to the Ile of Saint Laurence. I meane these leagues in Easting from the Meridians, and not the course you saile by, for if you saile North-east and by East, and you shall have thirtie sixe leagues for one degree and halfe Easting, or longitude, which will alter one degree of variation.

And the more North-ward your course is, the lesse variation you have, as you shall plainly understand: for in five and twentie of latitude in sight of Saint Laurence, you have sixteene degrees no minutes. And running North by the land to the River of Saint Augustine, you shall have but fifteene degrees in the latitude of twentie three degrees and thirtie minutes, which is plaine that it is lesse to the North-ward, then to the South-ward. So likewise up to the East-ward in the latitude of eleven degrees no minutes, the

highest variation is twentie three degrees forty minutes. And in the
latitude of thirtie three degrees no minutes, the highest variation is
twentie seven degrees ten minutes, as I have seene and observed my
selfe, and in my judgement in ten leagues Easting and Westing of the
same Meridian, as hereafter shall more plainely appeare in their due
places.

1625

# JOHN DONNE
## 1572–1631

### 'The Storme'

Thou which art I ('tis nothing to be soe)
Thou which art still thy selfe, by these shalt know
Part of our passage; And, a hand, or eye
By *Hilliard* drawne, is worth an history,
By a worse painter made; and (without pride)
When by thy judgment they are dignifi'd,
My lines are such: 'Tis the preheminence
Of friendship onely to 'impute excellence.
England to whom we'owe, what we be, and have,
Sad that her sonnes did seeke a forraine grave
(For, Fates, or Fortunes drifts none can soothsay,
Honour and misery have one face and way.)
From out her pregnant intrailes sigh'd a winde
Which at th'ayres middle marble roome did finde
Such strong resistance,that it selfe it threw
Downeward againe; and so when it did view
How in the port, our fleet deare time did leese,
Withering like prisoners,which lye but for fees,
Mildly it kist our sailes, and, fresh and sweet,
As to a stomack sterv'd, whose insides meete,
Meate comes, it came; and swole our sailes, when wee
So joyd, as *Sara*'her swelling joy'd to see.

But 'twas but so kinde, as our countrimen,
Which bring friends one dayes way, and leave them then.
Then like two mighty Kings, which dwelling farre
Asunder, meet against a third to warre,
The South and West winds joyn'd, and, as they blew,
Waves like a rowling trench before them threw.
Sooner than you read this line, did the gale,
Like shot, not fear'd till felt, our sailes assaile;
And what at first was call'd a gust, the same
Hath now a stormes, anon a tempests name.
*Jonas*, I pitty thee, and curse those men,
Who when the storm rag'd most, did wake thee then;
Sleepe is paines easiest salve, and doth fulfill
All offices of death, except to kill.
But when I wakt, I saw, that I saw not;
Ay, and the Sunne, which should teach mee'had forgot
East, West, Day, Night, and I could onely say,
If the world had lasted, now it had been day.
Thousands our noyses were, yet wee'mongst all
Could none by his right name, but thunder call:
Lightning was all our light, and it rain'd more
Than if the Sunne had drunke the sea before.
Some coffin'd in their cabbins lye, 'equally
Griev'd that they are not dead, and yet must dye;
And as sin-burd'ned soules from graves will creepe,
At the last day, some forth their cabbins peepe:
And tremblingly'aske what newes, and doe heare so,
Like jealous husbands, what they would not know.
Some sitting on the hatches, would seeme there,
With hideous gazing to feare away feare.
Then note they the ships sicknesses, the Mast
Shak'd with this ague, and the Hold and Wast
With a salt dropsie clog'd, and all our tacklings
Snapping, like too-high-stretched treble strings.
And from our totterd sailes, ragges drop downe so,
As from one hang'd in chaines, a yeare agoe.
Even our Ordinance plac'd for our defence,
Strive to breake loose, and scape away from thence.
Pumping hath tir'd our men, and what's the gaine?
Seas into seas throwne, we suck in againe;

Hearing hath deaf'd our saylers; and if they
Knew how to heare, there's none knowes what to say,
Compar'd to these stormes, death is but a qualme,
Hell somewhat lightsome, and the'Bermuda calme.
Darknesse, lights elder brother, his birth-right
Claims o'er this world, and to heaven hath chas'd light.
All things are one, and that one none can be,
Since all formes, uniforme deformity
Doth cover, so that wee, except God say
Another *Fiat*, shall have no more day.
So violent, yet long these furies bee,
'That though thine absence sterve me,'I wish not thee.

1633

# 'The Calme'

Our storme is past, and that storms tyrannous rage,
A stupid calme, but nothing it, doth swage.
The fable is inverted, and farre more
A blocke afflicts, now, than a storke before.
Stormes chafe, and soon weare out themselves, or us;
In calmes, Heaven laughs to see us languish thus.
As steady'as I can wish, that my thoughts were,
Smooth as thy mistresse glasse, or what shines there,
The sea is now. And, as the Iles which wee
Seeke, when wee can move, our ships rooted bee.
As water did in stormes, now pitch runs out:
As lead, when a fir'd Church becomes one spout.
And all our beauty, and our trimme, decayes,
Like courts removing, or like ended playes.
The fighting place now seamens ragges supply;
And all the tackling is a frippery.
No use of lanthornes; and in one place lay
Feathers and dust, to day and yesterday.
Earths hollownesses, which the worlds lungs are,
Have no more winde than the upper valt of aire.
We can nor lost friends, nor sought foes recover,
But meteorlike, save that wee move not, hover.

Onely the Calenture together drawes
Deare friends, which meet dead in great fishes jawes:
And on the hatches as on Altars lyes
Each one, his owne Priest, and owne Sacrifice.
Who live, that miracle do multiply
Where walkers in hot Ovens, doe not dye.
If in despite of these, wee swimme, that hath
No more refreshing, than our brimstone Bath,
But from the sea, into the ship we turne,
Like parboyl'd wretches, on the coales to burne.
Like *Bajazet* encag'd, the shepheards scoffe,
Or like slacke sinew'd *Sampson*, his haire off,
Languish our ships. Now, as a Miriade
Of Ants, durst th'Emperours lov'd snake invade,
The crawling Gallies, Sea-gaols, finny chips,
Might brave our Pinnaces, now bed-ridde ships.
Whether a rotten state, and hope of gaine,
Or to disuse mee from the queasie paine
Of being belov'd, and loving, or the thirst
Of honour, or faire death, out pusht mee first,
I lose my end: for here as well as I
A desperate may live, and a coward die.
Stagge, dogge, and all which from, or towards flies,
Is paid with life, or pray, or doing dyes.
Fate grudges us all, and doth subtly lay
A scourge, 'gainst which wee all forget to pray,
He that at sea prayes for more winde, as well
Under the poles may begge cold, heat in hell.
What are wee then? How little more alas
Is man now, than before he was? he was
Nothing; for us, wee are for nothing fit;
Chance, or our selves still disproportion it.
Wee have no power, no will, no sense; I lye,
I should not then thus feele this miserie.

                                              1633

# JOHN MILTON
## 1608–1674

## from 'Lycidas'

But now my oat proceeds,
And listens to the herald of the sea
That came in Neptune's plea,
He asked the waves, and asked the felon winds,
What hard mishap hath doomed this gentle swain?
And questioned every gust of rugged wings
That blows from off each beaked promontory;
They knew not of his story,
And sage Hippotades their answer brings,
That not a blast was from his dungeon strayed,
The air was calm, and on the level brine,
Sleek Panope with all her sisters played.
It was that fatal and perfidious bark
Built in the eclipse, and rigged with curses dark,
That sunk so low that sacred head of thine.

1638

---

## *Book of Common Prayer*
### 1662

### *Prayers to be used in Storms at Sea*

O most powerful and glorious Lord God, at whose command the
winds blow, and lift up the waves of the sea, and who stillest the rage
thereof; We thy creatures, but miserable sinners, do in this our great
distress cry unto thee for help; Save, Lord, or else we perish. We
confess, when we have been safe and seen all things quiet about us, we
have forgot thee our God, and refused to hearken to the still voice of

thy word, and to obey thy commandments: But now we see how terrible thou art in all thy works of wonder; the great God to be feared above all: and therefore we adore thy divine Majesty, acknowledging thy power, and imploring thy goodness. Help, Lord, and save us for thy mercies sake in Jesus Christ thy Son our Lord.

*Amen.*

## Or this

O most glorious and gracious Lord God, who dwellest in heaven, but beholdest all things below; Look down, we beseech thee, and hear us, calling out of the depth of misery, and out of the jaws of this death, which is ready now to swallow us up: Save, Lord, or else we perish. The living, the living shall praise thee. O send thy word of command to rebuke the raging winds, and the roaring sea, that we being delivered from this distress, may live to serve thee, and to glorify thy name all the days of our life. Hear, Lord, and save us, for the infinite merits of our blessed Saviour thy Son, our Lord Jesus Christ.    *Amen.*

# JOHN DRYDEN

## 1631–1700

# from *Annus Mirabilis*

### CLV

Digression concerning shipping and navigation.

By viewing Nature, Nature's handmaid Art
    Makes mighty things from small beginnings grow:
Thus fishes first to shipping did impart
    Their tail the rudder, and their head the prow.

### CLVI

Some log, perhaps, upon the waters swam,
    An useless drift, which, rudely cut within,
And hollow'd, first a floating trough became,
    And cross some riv'let passage did begin

### CLVII

In shipping such as this, the Irish *kern*,
  And untaught Indian, on the stream did glide:
Ere sharp-keel'd boats to stem the flood did learn,
  Or fin-like oars did spread from either side.

### CLVIII

Add but a sail, and Saturn so appear'd,
  When from lost empire he to exile went,
And with the golden age to Tiber steer'd,
  Where coin and first commerce he did invent.

### CLIX

Rude as their ships was navigation then;
  No useful compass or meridian known;
Coasting, they kept the land within their ken,
  And knew no North but when the Polestar shone.

### CLX

Of all who since have us'd the open sea,
  Than the bold English none more fame have won;
*(s) Extra anni*
*solisque vias.*   (s) Beyond the year, and out of heav'n's high way,
*—Virg.*   They make discoveries where they see no sun.

### CLXI

But what so long in vain, and yet unknown,
  By poor mankind's benighted wit is sought,
Shall in this age to Britain first be shown,
  And hence be to admiring nations taught.

### CLXII

The ebbs of tides and their mysterious flow,
  We, as arts' elements, shall understand,
And as by line upon the ocean go,
  Whose paths shall be familiar as the land.

### CLXIII

(t) By a more
exact measure
of longitude.
(t) Instructed ships shall sail to quick commerce,
    By which remotest regions are allied;
Which makes one city of the universe;
    Where some may gain, and all may be supplied.

### CLXIV

Then, we upon our globe's last verge shall go,
    And view the ocean leaning on the sky:
From thence our rolling neighbors we shall know,
    And on the lunar world securely pry.

### CLXV

Apostrophe
to the Royal
Society.
This I foretell from your auspicious care,
    Who great in search of God and Nature grow;
Who best your wise Creator's praise declare,
    Since best to praise his works is best to know.

1667

---

# MARGARET CAVENDISH, DUCHESS OF NEWCASTLE

## c.1624–1674

## 'The Sea-goddess'

My cabinets are oyster-shells,
In which I keep my orient pearls;
To open them I use the tide,
As keys to locks, which opens wide
The oyster shells, then out I take
Those orient pearls and crowns do make;
And modest coral I do wear,
Which blushes when it touches air.

On silver waves I sit and sing,
And then the fish lie listening:
Then sitting on a rocky stone
I comb my hair with fishes' bone;
The whilst Apollo with his beams
Doth dry my hair from watery streams.
His light doth glaze the water's face,
Make the large sea my looking-glass:
So when I swim on waters high,
I see myself as I glide by:
But when the sun begins to burn,
I back into my waters turn,
And dive unto the bottom low:
Then on my head the waters flow
In curlëd waves and circles round,
And thus with waters am I crowned.

1668

# CHARLES COTTON

## 1630–1687

# 'The Tempest'

Standing upon the margent of the Main,
    Whilst the high boiling Tide came tumbling in,
I felt my fluctuating thoughts maintain
    As great an Ocean, and as rude, within;
        As full of Waves, of Depths, and broken Grounds,
        As that which daily laves her chalky bounds.

Soon could my sad Imagination find
    A Parallel to this half World of Floud,
An Ocean by my walls of Earth confin'd,
    And Rivers in the Chanels of my Bloud:

Discovering man, unhappy man, to be
Of this great Frame Heaven's Epitome.

There pregnant *Argosies* with full Sails ride,
   To shoot the Gulphs of Sorrow and Despair,
Of which the Love no Pilot has to guide,
   But to her Sea-born Mother steers by Pray'r,
When, oh! the Hope her Anchor lost, undone,
Rolls at the mercy of the Regent Moon.

'Tis my ador'd *Diana*, then must be
   The Guid'ress to this beaten Bark of mine,
'Tis she must calm and smooth this troubled Sea,
   And waft my hope over the vaulting Brine:
Call home thy venture *Dian* then at last,
And be as merciful as thou art chaste.

                                                    1689

# JOSEPH ADDISON
## 1672–1719

# from *The Spectator*

*SIR*,
Upon reading your *Essay*, concerning the pleasures of the imagination, I find among the three sources of those pleasures which you
have discovered, that *Greatness* is one. This has suggested to me the
reason why, of all objects that I have ever seen, there is none which
affects my imagination so much as the sea or ocean. I cannot see the
heavings of this prodigious bulk of waters, even in a calm, without a
very pleasing astonishment; but when it is worked up in a tempest, so
that the Horizon on every side is nothing but foaming billows and
floating mountains, it is impossible to describe the agreeable horrour
that rises from such a prospect. A troubled ocean, to a man who sails

upon it, is, I think, the biggest object that he can see in motion, and consequently gives his imagination one of the highest kinds of pleasure that can arise from greatness. I must confess, it is impossible for me to survey this world of fluid matter, without thinking on the hand that first poured it out, and made a proper channel for its reception. Such an object naturally raises in my thoughts the idea of an almighty Being, and convinces me of his existence as much as a metaphysical demonstration. The imagination prompts the understanding, and by the greatness of the sensible object, produces in it the idea of a Being who is neither circumscribed by time nor space.

As I have made several voyages upon the sea, I have often been tossed in storms, and on that occasion have frequently reflected on the descriptions of them in antient Poets. I remember *Longinus* highly recommends one in *Homer*, because the Poet has not amused himself with little fancies upon the occasion, as Authors of an inferior genius, whom he mentions, had done, but because he has gathered together those circumstances which are the most apt to terrify the imagination, and which really happen in the raging of a tempest. It is for the same reason, that I prefer the following description of a ship in a storm, which the Psalmist has made, before any other I have ever met with. *They that go down to the sea in ships, that do business in great waters: these men see the works of the Lord, and his wonders in the deep. For he commandeth and raiseth the stormy wind, which lifteth up the waters thereof. They mount up to Heaven, they go down again to the depths, their Soul is melted because of trouble. They reel to and fro, and stagger like a drunken man, and are at their wits-end. Then they cry unto the Lord in their trouble, and he bringeth them out of their distresses. He maketh the storm a calm, so that the waves thereof are still. Then they are glad because they be quiet, so he bringeth them unto their desired haven.*

By the way, how much more comfortable, as well as rational, is this system of the Psalmist, than the pagan scheme in *Virgil*, and other Poets, where one Deity is represented as raising a storm, and another as laying it? Were we only to consider the Sublime in this piece of poetry, what can be nobler than the idea it gives us of the supreme Being thus raising a tumult among the elements, and recovering them out of their confusion, thus troubling and becalming nature?

Great Painters do not only give us Landskips of gardens, groves, and meadows, but very often employ their pencils upon sea-pieces: I could wish you would follow their example. If this small sketch may

deserve a place among your works, I shall accompany it with a divine
Ode, made by a Gentleman upon the conclusion of his travels.

I.

How are thy servants blest, O Lord!
　How sure is their defence!
Eternal wisdom is their guide,
　Their help Omnipotence.

II.

In foreign realms, and lands remote,
　Supported by thy care,
Thro' burning climes I pass'd unhurt,
　And breath'd in tainted air.

III.

Thy mercy sweetned ev'ry soil,
　Made ev'ry region please;
The hoary *Alpine* hills it warm'd,
　And smooth'd the *Tyrrhene* seas.

IV.

Think, O my Soul, devoutly think,
　How with affrighted eyes
Thou saw'st the wide extended deep
　In all its horrors rise!

V.

Confusion dwelt in ev'ry face,
　And fear in ev'ry heart;
When waves on waves, and gulphs in gulphs,
　O'ercame the pilot's art.

VI.

Yet then from all my griefs, O Lord,
　Thy mercy set me free,
Whilst in the confidence of pray'r
　My soul took hold on thee.

## VII.

For tho' in dreadful whirles we hung
  High on the broken wave,
I knew thou wert not slow to hear,
  Nor impotent to save.

## VIII.

The storm was laid, the winds retir'd,
  Obedient to thy will;
The sea that roar'd at thy command,
  At thy command was still.

## IX.

In midst of dangers, fears and death,
  Thy goodness I'll adore,
And praise thee for thy mercies past;
  And humbly hope for more.

## X.

My life, if thou preserv'st my life,
  Thy sacrifice shall be;
And death, if death must be my doom,
  Shall join my soul to thee.

1712

# DANIEL DEFOE

## c.1660–1731

# from *Robinson Crusoe*

On the first of September 1651 I went on board a ship bound for London; never any young adventurer's misfortunes, I believe, began sooner, or continued longer, than mine. The ship was no sooner gotten out of the Humber, but the wind began to blow and the waves to rise in a most frightful manner; and as I had never been at sea before, I was most inexpressibly sick in body and terrify'd in my mind. I began now seriously to reflect upon what I had done, and how justly I was overtaken by the judgment of Heaven for my wicked leaving my father's house, and abandoning my duty; all the good counsel of my parents, my father's tears and my mother's entreaties, came now fresh into my mind; and my conscience, which was not yet come to the pitch of hardness to which it has been since, reproach'd me with the contempt of advice, and the breach of my duty to God and my father.

All this while the storm encreas'd, and the sea, which I had never been upon before, went very high, tho' nothing like what I have seen many times since; no, nor like what I saw a few days after: but it was enough to affect me then, who was but a young sailor, and had never known any thing of the matter. I expected every wave would have swallowed us up, and that every time the ship fell down, as I thought, in the trough or hollow of the sea, we should never rise more; and in this agony of mind I made many vows and resolutions, that if it would please God here to spare my life this one voyage, if ever I got once my foot upon dry land again, I would go directly home to my father, and never set it into a ship again while I liv'd; that I would take his advice, and never run my self into such miseries as these any more. Now I saw plainly the goodness of his observations about the middle station of life, how easy, how comfortably he had liv'd all his days, and never had been expos'd to tempests at sea or troubles on shore;

and I resolv'd that I would, like a true repenting prodigal, go home to
my father.

These wise and sober thoughts continued all the while the storm
continued, and indeed some time after; but the next day the wind was
abated and the sea calmer, and I began to be a little inur'd to it.
However, I was very grave for all that day, being also a little sea-sick
still; but towards night the weather clear'd up, the wind was quite
over, and a charming fine evening follow'd; the sun went down
perfectly clear and rose so the next morning; and having little or no
wind and a smooth sea, the sun shining upon it, the sight was, as I
thought, the most delightful that ever I saw.

I had slept well in the night, and was now no more sea-sick but very
chearful, looking with wonder upon the sea that was so rough and
terrible the day before, and could be so calm and so pleasant in so little
time after. And now, least my good resolutions should continue, my
companion, who had indeed entic'd me away, comes to me. 'Well,
Bob,' says he, clapping me on the shoulder, 'how do you do after it? I
warrant you were frighted, wa'n't you, last night, when it blew but a
cap full of wind?' 'A cap full d'you call it?' said I, ''twas a terrible
storm.' 'A storm, you fool, you,' replies he, 'do you call that a storm?
Why, it was nothing at all; give us but a good ship and sea room, and
we think nothing of such a squall of wind as that; but you're but a fresh
water sailor, Bob; come, let us make a bowl of punch and we'll forget
all that; d'ye see what charming weather 'tis now?' To make short
this sad part of my story, we went the old way of all sailors, the punch
was made, and I was made drunk with it, and in that one night's
wickedness I drowned all my repentance, all my reflections upon my
past conduct, and all my resolutions for my future. In a word, as the
sea was returned to its smoothness of surface and settled calmness by
the abatement of that storm, so the hurry of my thoughts being over,
my fears and apprehensions of being swallow'd up by the sea being
forgotten, and the current of my former desires return'd, I entirely
forgot the vows and promises that I made in my distress. I found
indeed some intervals of reflection, and the serious thoughts did, as it
were, endeavour to return again sometimes, but I shook them off,
and rouz'd my self from them as it were from a distemper, and
applying my self to drink and company, soon mastered the return of
those fits, for so I call'd them, and I had in five or six days got as
compleat a victory over conscience as any young fellow that resolv'd
not to be troubled with it could desire. But I was to have another trial

for it still; and Providence, as in such cases generally it does, resolv'd to leave me entirely without excuse. For if I would not take this for a deliverance, the next was to be such a one as the worst and most harden'd wretch among us would confess both the danger and the mercy.

The sixth day of our being at sea we came into Yarmouth roads; the wind having been contrary and the weather calm, we had made but little way since the storm. Here we were obliged to come to an anchor, and here we lay, the wind continuing contrary, viz. at south-west, for seven or eight days, during which time a great many ships from Newcastle came into the same roads, as the common harbour where the ships might wait for a wind for the river.

We had not, however, rid here so long, but should have tided it up the river, but that the wind blew too fresh, and, after we had lain four or five days, blew very hard. However, the roads being reckoned as good as a harbour, the anchor good, and our ground-tackle very strong, our men were unconcerned, and not in the least apprehensive of danger, but spent the time in rest and mirth, after the manner of the sea; but the eighth day in the morning, the wind increased, and we had all hands at work to strike our top-masts and make every thing snug and close, that the ship might ride as easy as possible. By noon the sea went very high indeed, and our ship rid forecastle in, shipp'd several seas, and we thought once or twice our anchor had come home; upon which our master order'd out the sheet anchor; to that we rode with two anchors a-head, and the cables vered out to the better end.

By this time it blew a terrible storm indeed, and now I began to see terror and amazement in the faces even of the seamen themselves. The master, tho' vigilant to the business of preserving the ship, yet as he went in and out of his cabbin by me, I could hear him softly to himself say several times, 'Lord, be merciful to us, we shall be all lost, we shall be all undone'; and the like. During these first hurries I was stupid, lying still in my cabbin, which was in the steerage, and cannot describe my temper. I could ill re-assume the first penitence, which I had so apparently trampled upon and harden'd my self against: I thought the bitterness of death had been past, and that this would be nothing too, like the first. But when the master himself came by me, as I said just now, and said we should be all lost, I was dreadfully frighted. I got up out of my cabbin, and look'd out; but such a dismal sight I never saw: the sea went mountains high, and broke upon us

every three or four minutes; when I could look about, I could see
nothing but distress round us. Two ships that rid near us we found
had cut their masts by the board, being deep loaden; and our men
cry'd out that a ship which rid about a mile a-head of us was
foundered. Two more ships, being driven from their anchors, were
run out of the roads to sea at all adventures, and that with not a mast
standing. The light ships fared the best, as not so much labouring in
the sea; but two or three of them drove, and came close by us,
running away with only their sprit-sail out before the wind.

Towards evening the mate and boat-swain begg'd the master of
our ship to let them cut away the foremast, which he was very
unwilling to: but the boat-swain protesting to him that if he did not,
the ship would founder, he consented; and when they had cut away
the foremast, the main-mast stood so loose, and shook the ship so
much, they were obliged to cut her away also, and make a clear deck.

Any one may judge what a condition I must be in at all this, who
was but a young sailor, and who had been in such a fright before at
but a little. But if I can express at this distance the thoughts I had
about me at that time, I was in tenfold more horror of mind upon
account of my former convictions, and the having returned from
them to the resolutions I had wickedly taken at first, than I was at
death it self; and these, added to the terror of the storm, put me into
such a condition, that I can by no words describe it. But the worst
was not come yet; the storm continued with such fury, that the
seamen themselves acknowledged they had never known a worse.
We had a good ship, but she was deep loaden, and wallowed in the
sea, that the seamen every now and then cried out she would founder.
It was my advantage in one respect, that I did not know what they
meant by 'founder' till I enquir'd. However, the storm was so
violent, that I saw what is not often seen, the master, the boat-swain,
and some others more sensible than the rest, at their prayers, and
expecting every moment when the ship would go to the bottom. In
the middle of the night, and under all the rest of our distresses, one of
the men that had been down on purpose to see, cried out we had
sprung a leak; another said there was four foot water in the hold.
Then all hands were called to the pump. At that very word my heart,
as I thought, died within me, and I fell backwards upon the side of my
bed where I sat, into the cabbin. However, the men roused me, and
told me that I that was able to do nothing before, was as well able to
pump as another; at which I stirr'd up and went to the pump, and

work'd very heartily. While this was doing, the master, seeing some
light colliers, who not able to ride out the storm, were oblig'd to slip
and run away to sea and would come near us, ordered to fire a gun as a
signal of distress. I, who knew nothing what that meant, was so
surprised that I thought the ship had broke, or some dreadful thing
had happen'd. In a word, I was so surprised that I fell down in a
swoon. As this was a time when every body had his own life to think
of, no body minded me, or what was become of me; but another man
stept up to the pump, and thrusting me aside with his foot, let me lye,
thinking I had been dead; and it was a great while before I came to my
self.

   We work'd on, but the water encreasing in the hold, it was
apparent that the ship would founder, and tho' the storm began to
abate a little, yet as it was not possible she could swim till we might
run into a port, so the master continued firing guns for help; and a
light ship who had rid it out just a head of us ventured a boat out to
help us. It was with the utmost hazard the boat came near us, but it
was impossible for us to get on board, or for the boat to lie near the
ship side, till at last, the men rowing very heartily and venturing their
lives to save ours, our men cast them a rope over the stern with a buoy
to it, and then vered it out a great length, which they after great labour
and hazard took hold of, and we hawl'd them close under our stern
and got all into their boat. It was to no purpose for them or us after we
were in the boat to think of reaching to their own ship, so all agreed to
let her drive and only to pull her in towards shore as much as we
could, and our master promised them that if the boat was stav'd upon
shore he would make it good to their master; so partly rowing and
partly driving, our boat went away to the norward sloaping towards
the shore almost as far as Winterton Ness.

   We were not much more than a quarter of an hour out of our
ship but we saw her sink, and then I understood for the first time
what was meant by a ship foundering in the sea; I must acknowledge I
had hardly eyes to look up when the seamen told me she was sinking;
for from that moment they rather put me into the boat than that I
might be said to go in, my heart was as it were dead within me, partly
with fright, partly with horror of mind and the thoughts of what was
yet before me.

   While we were in this condition, the men yet labouring at the oar to
bring the boat near the shore, we could see, when, our boat mounting
the waves, we were able to see the shore, a great many people running

along the shore to assist us when we should come near, but we made but slow way towards the shore, nor were we able to reach the shore, till being past the light-house at Winterton, the shore falls off to the westward towards Cromer, and so the land broke off a little the violence of the wind. Here we got in, and, tho' not without much difficulty, got all safe on shore, and walk'd afterwards on foot to Yarmouth, where, as unfortunate men, we were used with great humanity as well by the magistrates of the town, who assign'd us good quarters, as by particular merchants and owners of ships, and had money given us sufficient to carry us either to London or back to Hull, as we thought fit.

1719

# from *A Tour through the Whole Island of Great Britain*

From Yarmouth I resolved to pursue my first design, (viz.) to view the sea-side on this coast, which is particularly famous for being one of the most dangerous and most fatal to the sailors in all England, I may say in all Britain; and the more so, because of the great number of ships which are continually going and coming this way, in their passage between London and all the northern coasts of Great-Britain. From Winterton Ness, which is the utmost northerly point of land in the county of Norfolk, and about four miles beyond Yarmouth, the shore falls off for near sixty miles to the west, as far as Lynn and Boston, till the shore of Lincolnshire tends north again for about sixty miles more, as far as the Humber, whence the coast of Yorkshire, or Holderness, which is the East Riding, shoots out again into the sea, to the Spurn, and to Flambro' Head, as far east almost as the shore of Norfolk had given back at Winterton, making a very deep gulf or bay, between those two points of Winterton and the Spurn Head; so that the ships going north, are obliged to stretch away to sea from Winterton Ness, and leaving the sight of land in that deep bay which I have mentioned, that reaches to Lynn, and the shore of Lincolnshire, they go, I say, N. or still NNW to meet the shore of Holderness, which I said runs out into the sea again at the Spurn; this they leave also and the first land they make, or desire to make, is called as above, Flambro' Head; so that Winterton Ness and Flambro' Head, are the two extremes of this course, there is, as I said, the Spurn Head indeed between; but as it lies too far in towards the Humber, they keep out to the north to avoid coming near it.

In like manner the ships which come from the north, leave the shore at Flambro' Head, and stretch away SSE for Yarmouth Roads; and the first land they make is Winterton Ness (as above). Now, the danger of the place is this: if the ships coming from the north are taken with a hard gale of wind from the SE or from any point between NE and SE so that they cannot, as the seamen call it, weather Winterton Ness, they are thereby kept in within that deep bay; and if the wind blows hard, are often in danger of running on shore upon the rocks about Cromer, on the north coast of Norfolk, or stranding upon the flat shore between Cromer and Wells. All the relief they have, is good ground tackle to ride it out, which is very hard to do there, the sea coming very high upon them, or if they cannot ride it out then, to run into the bottom of the great bay I mentioned, to Lynn or Boston, which is a very difficult and desperate push: so that sometimes in this distress whole fleets have been lost here all together.

The like is the danger to ships going northward, if after passing by Winterton they are taken short with a north-east wind, and cannot put back into the Roads, which very often happens, then they are driven upon the same coast, and embayed just at the latter. The dangers of this place being thus considered, 'tis no wonder, that upon the shore beyond Yarmouth, there are no less than four light-houses kept flaming every night, besides the lights at Castor, north of the town, and at Goulston S, all which are to direct the sailors to keep a good offing, in case of bad weather, and to prevent their running into Cromer Bay, which the seamen call the Devil's Throat.

As I went by land from Yarmouth northward, along the shore towards Cromer aforesaid, and was not then fully master of the reason of these things, I was surprised to see, in all the way from Winterton, that the farmers, and country people had scarce a barn, or a shed, or a stable; nay, not the pales of their yards, and gardens, not a hogsty, not a necessary-house, but what was built of old planks, beams, wales and timbers, &c. the wrecks of ships, and ruins of mariners' and merchants' fortunes.

About the year 1692 (I think it was that year) there was a melancholy example of what I have said of this place; a fleet of 200 sail of light colliers (so they call the ships bound northward empty to fetch coals

from Newcastle to London) went out of Yarmouth Roads with a fair
wind, to pursue their voyage, and were taken short with a storm of
wind at NE, after they were past Winterton Ness, a few leagues;
some of them, whose masters were a little more wary than the rest, or
perhaps, who made a better judgement of things, or who were not so
far out as the rest, tacked, and put back in time, and got safe into the
roads; but the rest pushing on, in hopes to keep out to sea, and
weather it, were by the violence of the storm driven back, when they
were too far embayed to weather Winterton Ness, as above; and so
were forced to run west, every one shifting for themselves, as well as
they could. Some run away for Lyn Deeps but few of them, (the night
being so dark) could find their way in there; some but very few rid it
out, at a distance; the rest being above 140 sail were all driven on
shore, and dashed to pieces, and very few of the people on board were
saved. At the very same unhappy juncture, a fleet of loaden ships
were coming from the north, and being just crossing the same bay,
were forcibly driven into it, not able to weather the Ness, and so were
involved in the same ruin as the light fleet was; also some coasting
vessels loaden with corn from Lyn, and Wells, and bound for
Holland, were with the same unhappy luck just come out, to begin
their voyage, and some of them lay at anchor; these also met with the
same misfortune, so that in the whole, above 200 sail of ships, and
above a thousand people perished in the disaster of that one miserable
night, very few escaping.

1724–6

# BENJAMIN FRANKLIN
## 1706–1790

## from *Journal of a Voyage*

Wednesday, August 3

This morning we were hurried on board, having scarce time to dine, weighed anchor, and stood away for Yarmouth again, though the wind is still westerly; but meeting with a hoy when we were near half way there that had some goods on board for us to take in, we tacked about for Cowes, and came to anchor there a third time, about four in the afternoon.

Thursday, August 4

Stayed on board till about five in the afternoon, and then went on shore and stopped all night.

Friday, August 5

Called up this morning and hurried aboard, the wind being North-West. About noon we weighed and left Cowes a third time, and sailing by Yarmouth we came into the channel through the Needles; which passage is guarded by Hurst Castle, standing on a spit of land which runs out from the main land of England within a mile of the Isle of Wight. Towards night the wind veered to the Westward, which put us under apprehensions of being forced into port again: but presently after it fell a flat calm, and then we had a small breeze that was fair for half an hour, when it was succeeded by a calm again.

Saturday, August 6

This morning we had a fair breeze for some hours, and then a calm that lasted all day. In the afternoon I leaped overboard and swam round the ship to wash myself. Saw several Porpoises this day. About eight o'clock we came to an anchor in forty fathom water against the tide of flood, somewhere below Portland, and weighed again about eleven, having a small breeze.

Sunday, August 7

Gentle breezes all this day. Spoke with a ship, the *Ruby*, bound for London from Nevis, off the Start of Plymouth. This afternoon spoke

with Captain Homans in a ship bound for Boston, who came out of
the River when we did, and had been beating about in the Channel all
the time we lay at Cowes in the Wight.

Monday, August 8

Fine weather, but no wind worth mentioning, all this day; in the
afternoon saw the Lizard.

Tuesday, August 9

Took our leave of the land this morning. Calms the fore part of the
day. In the afternoon a small gale, fair. Saw a grampus.

Wednesday, August 10

Wind NW. Course SW about four knots. By observation in
latitude 48°50′. Nothing remarkable happened.

Thursday, August 11

Nothing remarkable. Fresh gale all day.

Calms and fair breezes alternately.

| | |
|---|---|
| Friday, August 12 | |
| Saturday, —— 13 | |
| Sunday, —— 14 | |

No contrary winds, but calms and
fair breezes alternately.

| | |
|---|---|
| Monday, —— 15 | |
| Tuesday, —— 16 | |
| Wednesday, — 17 | |

Thursday, August 18

Four dolphins followed the ship for some hours: we struck at them
with the fizgig, [harpoon], but took none.

Friday, August 19

This day we have had a pleasant breeze at East. In the morning we
spied a sail upon our larboard bow, about two leagues distance.
About noon she put out English colours, and we answered with our
ensign, and in the afternoon we spoke with her. She was a ship of
New York, Walter Kippen Master, bound from Rochelle in France to
Boston with salt. Our captain and Mr D. went on board and stayed
till evening, it being fine weather. Yesterday complaints being made
that a Mr G——n one of the passengers had with a fraudulent design
marked the cards, a Court of Justice was called immediately, and he
was brought to his trial in form. A Dutchman who could speak no
English deposed by his interpreter, that when our mess was on shore

at Cowes, the prisoner at the bar marked all the court cards on the back with a pen.

I have sometimes observed that we are apt to fancy the person that cannot speak intelligibly to us, proportionably stupid in understanding, and when we speak two or three words of English to a foreigner, it is louder than ordinary, as if we thought him deaf, and that he had lost the use of his ears as well as his tongue. Something like this I imagine might be the case of Mr G——n; he fancied the Dutchman could not see what he was about because he could not understand English, and therefore boldly did it before his face.

The evidence was plain and positive, the prisoner could not deny the fact, but replied in his defence, that the cards he marked were not those we commonly played with, but an imperfect pack, which he afterwards gave to the cabin-boy. The Attorney-General observed to the court that it was not likely he should take the pains to mark the cards without some ill design, or some further intention than just to give them to the boy when he had done, who understood nothing at all of cards. But another evidence being called, deposed that he saw the prisoner in the main top one day when he thought himself unobserved, marking a pack of cards on the backs, some with the print of a dirty thumb, others with the top of his finger, &c. Now there being but two packs on board, and the prisoner having just confessed the marking of one, the court perceived the case was plain. In fine the jury brought him in guilty, and he was condemned to be carried up to the round top, and made fast there in view of all the ship's company during the space of three hours, that being the place where the act was committed, and to pay a fine of two bottles of brandy. But the prisoner resisting authority, and refusing to submit to punishment, one of the sailors stepped up aloft and let down a rope to us, which we with much struggling made fast about his middle and hoisted him up into the air, sprawling, by main force. We let him hang, cursing and swearing, for near a quarter of an hour; but at length he crying out murder! and looking black in the face, the rope being overtort about his middle, we thought proper to let him down again; and our mess have excommunicated him till he pays his fine, refusing either to play, eat, drink, or converse with him.

Saturday, August 20

We shortened sail all last night and all this day, to keep company with the other ship. About noon Captain Kippen and one of his passengers came on board and dined with us; they stayed till evening. When they were gone we made sail and left them.

Sunday, August 21

This morning we lost sight of the Yorker, having a brisk gale of wind at East. Towards night a poor little bird came on board us, being almost tired to death, and suffered itself to be taken by the hand. We reckon ourselves near two hundred leagues from land, so that no doubt a little rest was very acceptable to the unfortunate wanderer, who 'tis like was blown off the coast in thick weather, and could not find its way back again. We receive it hospitably and tender it victuals and drink; but he refuses both, and I suppose will not live long. There was one came on board some days ago in the same circumstances with this, which I think the cat destroyed.

Monday, August 22

This morning I saw several flying-fish, but they were small. A favourable wind all day.

Fair winds, nothing remarkable. $\begin{cases} \text{Tuesday, August 23} \\ \text{Wednesday, ——— 24} \end{cases}$

Thursday, August 25

Our excommunicated ship-mate thinking proper to comply with the sentence the court passed upon him, and expressing himself willing to pay the fine, we have this morning received him into unity again. Man is a sociable being, and it is for aught I know one of the worst of punishments to be excluded from society. I have read abundance of fine things on the subject of solitude, and I know 'tis a common boast in the mouths of those that affect to be thought wise, *that they are never less alone than when alone*. I acknowledge solitude an agreeable refreshment to a busy mind; but were these thinking people obliged to be always alone, I am apt to think they would quickly find their very being insupportable to them. I have heard of a gentleman who underwent seven years close confinement, in the Bastile at Paris. He was a man of sense, he was a thinking man; but being deprived of all conversation, to what purpose should he think? for he was denied even the instruments of expressing his thoughts in writing. There is no burden so grievous to man as time that he knows not how to dispose of. He was forced at last to have recourse to this invention: he daily scattered pieces of paper about the floor of his little room, and then employed himself in picking them up and sticking them in rows and figures on the arm of his elbow-chair; and he used to tell his friends, after his release, that he verily believed if he had not taken this method he should have lost his senses. One of the philosophers, I think it was Plato, used to say, that he had rather be the veriest stupid block in nature, than the possessor of all knowledge without some intelligent being to communicate it to.

What I have said may in a measure account for some particulars in my present way of living here on board. Our company is in general very unsuitably mixed, to keep up the pleasure and spirit of conversation: and if there are one or two pair of us that can sometimes entertain one another for half an hour agreeably, yet perhaps we are seldom in the humour for it together. I rise in the morning and read for an hour or two perhaps, and then reading grows tiresome. Want of exercise occasions want of appetite, so that eating and drinking affords but little pleasure. I tire myself with playing at draughts, then I go to cards; nay there is no play so trifling or childish, but we fly to it for entertainment. A contrary wind, I know not how, puts us all out of good humour; we grow sullen, silent and reserved, and fret at each other upon every little occasion. 'Tis a common opinion among the ladies, that if a man is ill-natured he infallibly discovers it when he is in liquor. But I, who have known many instances to the contrary, will teach them a more effectual method to discover the natural temper and disposition of their humble servants. Let the ladies make one long sea voyage with them, and if they have the least spark of ill nature in them and conceal it to the end of the voyage, I will forfeit all my pretensions to their favour. The wind continues fair.

Friday, August 26

The wind and weather fair till night came on; and then the wind came about, and we had hard squalls with rain and lightning till morning.

Saturday, August 27

Cleared up this morning, and the wind settled westerly. Two dolphins followed us this afternoon: we hooked one and struck the other with the fizgig; but they both escaped us, and we saw them no more.

Sunday, August 28

The wind still continues westerly, and blows hard. We are under a reefed mainsail and foresail.

Monday, August 29

Wind still hard West. Two dolphins followed us this day; we struck at them, but they both escaped.

Tuesday, August 30

Contrary wind still. This evening the moon being near full, as she rose after eight o'clock, there appeared a rainbow in a western cloud to windward of us. The first time I ever saw a rainbow in the night caused by the moon.

Wednesday, August 31

Wind still West, nothing remarkable.

Thursday, September 1

Bad weather, and contrary winds.

Friday, September 2

This morning the wind changed, a little fair. We caught a couple of dolphins, and fried them for dinner. They tasted tolerably well. These fish make a glorious appearance in the water: their bodies are of a bright green, mixed with a silver colour, and their tails of a shining golden yellow; but all this vanishes presently after they are taken out of their element, and they change all over to a light grey. I observed that cutting off pieces of a just-caught living dolphin for baits, those pieces did not lose their lustre and fine colours when the dolphin died, but retained them perfectly. Every one takes notice of that vulgar error of the painters, who always represent this fish monstrously crooked and deformed, when it is in reality as beautiful and well shaped a fish as any that swims. I cannot think what should be the original of this chimera of theirs (since there is not a creature in nature that in the least resembles their dolphin) unless it proceeded at first from a false imitation of a fish in the posture of leaping, which they have since improved into a crooked monster with a head and eyes like a bull, a hog's snout, and a tail like a blown tulip. But the sailors give me another reason, though a whimsical one, viz. that as this most beautiful fish is only to be caught at sea, and that very far to the Southward, they say the painters wilfully deform it in their representations, lest pregnant women should long for what it is impossible to procure for them.

Wind still westerly; nothing remarkable.

{ Saturday, September 3
{ Sunday, —— 4
{ Monday, —— 5

Tuesday, September 6

This afternoon the wind continuing still in the same quarter, increased till it blew a storm, and raised the sea to a greater height than I had ever seen it before.

Wednesday, September 7

The wind is somewhat abated, but the sea is very high still. A dolphin kept us company all this afternoon: we struck at him several times, but could not take him.

Thursday, September 8

This day nothing remarkable has happened. Contrary wind.

Friday, September 9

This afternoon we took four large dolphins, three with a hook and line, and the fourth we struck with a fizgig. The bait was a candle with two feathers stuck in it, one on each side, in imitation of a flying-fish, which are the common prey of the dolphins. They appeared extremely eager and hungry, and snapped up the hook as soon as ever it touched the water. When we came to open them, we found in the belly of one, a small dolphin half digested. Certainly they were half famished, or are naturally very savage to devour those of their own species.

Saturday, September 10

This day we dined upon the dolphins we caught yesterday, three of them sufficing the whole ship, being twenty-one persons.

Sunday, September 11

We have had a hard gale of wind all this day, accompanied with showers of rain. 'Tis uncomfortable being upon deck; and though we have been all together all day below, yet the long continuance of these contrary winds has made us so dull, that scarce three words have passed between us.

Nothing remarkable;      { Monday, September 12
wind contrary.      { Tuesday,   ——— 13

Wednesday, September 14

This afternoon about two o'clock, it being fair weather and almost calm, as we sat playing Draughts upon deck, we were surprised with a sudden and unusual darkness of the sun, which as we could perceive was only covered with a small thin cloud: when that was passed by, we discovered that that glorious luminary laboured under a very great eclipse. At least ten parts out of twelve of him were hid from our eyes, and we were apprehensive he would have been totally darkened.

Thursday, September 15

For a week past we have fed ourselves with the hopes that the change of the moon (which was yesterday) would bring us a fair wind; but to our great mortification and disappointment, the wind seems now settled in the westward, and shews as little signs of an alteration as it did a fortnight ago.

Friday, September 16

Calm all this day. This morning we saw a *Tropic bird*, which flew round our vessel several times. It is a white fowl with short wings; but one feather appears in his tail, and he does not fly very fast. We reckon ourselves about half our voyage; latitude 38 and odd minutes. These birds are said never to be seen further North than the latitude of 40.

Saturday, September 17

All the forenoon the calm continued, the rest of the day some light breezes easterly; and we are in great hopes the wind will settle in that quarter.

Sunday, September 18

We have had the finest weather imaginable all this day, accompanied with what is still more agreeable, a fair wind. Every one puts on a clean shirt and a cheerful countenance, and we begin to be very good company. Heaven grant that this favourable gale may continue! for we have had so much of turning to windward, that the word *helm-a-lee* is become almost as disagreeable to our ears as the sentence of a judge to a convicted malefactor.

Monday, September 19

The weather looks a little uncertain, and we begin to fear the loss of our fair wind. We see Tropic birds every day, sometimes five or six together; they are about as big as pigeons.

Tuesday, September 20

The wind is now westerly again, to our great mortification; and we are come to an allowance of bread, two biscuits and a half a day.

Wednesday, September 21

This morning our Steward was brought to the geers and whipped, for making an extravagant use of flour in the puddings, and for several other misdemeanors. It has been perfectly calm all this day, and very hot. I was determined to wash myself in the sea to-day, and should have done so had not the appearance of a shark, that mortal enemy to swimmers, deterred me: he seemed to be about five feet long, moves round the ship at some distance in a slow majestic manner, attended by near a dozen of those they call pilot-fish, of different sizes; the largest of them is not so big as a small mackerel, and the smallest not bigger than my little finger. Two of these diminutive pilots keep just before his nose, and he seems to govern himself in his motions by their direction; while the rest surround him on every side indifferently. A shark is never seen without a retinue of these, who are his purveyors, discovering and distinguishing his prey for him; while he in return gratefully protects them from the ravenous hungry dolphin. They are commonly counted a very greedy fish; yet this refuses to meddle with the bait we have thrown out for him. 'Tis likely he has lately made a full meal.

Thursday, September 22

A fresh gale at West all this day. The shark has left us.

Friday, September 23

This morning we spied a sail to windward of us about two leagues. We shewed our jack upon the ensign-staff, and shortened sail for them till about noon, when she came up with us. She was a snow from Dublin, bound to New York, having upwards of fifty servants on board, of both sexes; they all appeared upon deck, and seemed very much pleased at the sight of us. There is really something strangely cheering to the spirits in the meeting of a ship at sea, containing a society of creatures of the same species and in the same circumstances with ourselves, after we had been long separated and excommunicated as it were from the rest of mankind. My heart fluttered in my breast with joy when I saw so many human countenances, and I could scarce refrain from that kind of laughter which proceeds from some degree of inward pleasure. When we have been for a considerable time tossing on the vast waters, far from the sight of any land or ships, or any mortal creature but ourselves (except a few fish and sea birds) the whole world, for aught we know, may be under a second deluge, and we (like Noah and his company in the Ark) the only surviving remnant of the human race. The two Captains have mutually promised to keep each other company; but this I look upon to be only matter of course, for if ships are unequal in their sailing they seldom stay for one another, especially strangers. This afternoon the wind that has been so long contrary to us, came about to the eastward (and looks as if it would hold), to our no small satisfaction. I find our mess-mates in a better humour, and more pleased with their present condition than they have been since we came out; which I take to proceed from the contemplation of the miserable circumstances of the passengers on board our neighbour, and making the comparison. We reckon ourselves in a kind of paradise, when we consider how they live, confined and stifled up with such a lousy stinking rabble in this sultry latitude.

Saturday, September 24

Last night we had a very high wind, and very thick weather; in which we lost our consort. This morning we spied a sail a-head of us, which we took to be her; but presently after we spied another, and then we plainly perceived that neither of them could be the snow, for one of them stemmed with us, and the other bore down directly upon us, having the weather gage of us. As the latter drew near we were a little surprised, not knowing what to make of her; for by the course she steered she did not seem designed for any port, but looked as if she intended to clap us aboard immediately. I could perceive concern in every face on board; but she presently eased us of our apprehensions by bearing away a-stern of us. When we hoisted our jack she answered with French colours, and presently took them down again; and we soon lost sight of her. The other ran by us in less than half an hour, and answered our jack with an English ensign; she stood to the eastward, but the wind was too high to speak with either of them. About nine o'clock we spied our consort, who had got a great way a-head of us. She, it seems, had made sail in the night, while we lay-by with our main yard down during the hard gale. She very civilly shortened sail for us, and this afternoon we came up with her; and now we are running along very amicably together side by side, having a most glorious fair wind.

> On either side the parted billows flow,
> While the black ocean foams and roars below.

Sunday, September 25

Last night we shot a-head of our consort pretty far. About midnight having lost sight of each other, we shortened sail for them:

but this morning they were got as far a-head of us as we could see, having run by us in the dark unperceived. We made sail and came up with them about noon; and if we chance to be a-head of them again in the night, we are to show them a light, that we may not lose company by any such accident for the future. The wind still continues fair, and we have made a greater run these last four-and-twenty hours than we have done since we came out. All our discourse now is of Philadelphia, and we begin to fancy ourselves on shore already. Yet a small change of weather, attended by a westerly wind, is sufficient to blast all our blooming hopes, and quite spoil our present good humour.

### Monday, September 26

The wind continued fair all night. In the twelve o'clock watch our consort, who was about a league a-head of us, showed us a light, and we answered with another. About six o'clock this morning we had a sudden hurry of wind at all points of the compass, accompanied with the most violent shower of rain I ever saw, insomuch that the sea looked like a *cream dish*. It surprised us with all our sails up, and was so various, uncertain, and contrary, that the mizen topsail was full, while the head sails were all aback; and before the men could run from one end of the ship to the other, 'twas about again. But this did not last long ere the wind settled to the North-East again, to our great satisfaction. Our consort fell astern of us in the storm, but made sail and came up with us again after it was over. We hailed one another on the morrow, congratulating upon the continuance of the fair wind, and both ran on very lovingly together.

### Tuesday, September 27

The fair wind continues still. I have laid a bowl of punch that we are in Philadelphia next Saturday sen'night, for we reckon ourselves not above 150 leagues from land. The snow keeps us company still.

### Wednesday, September 28

We had very variable winds and weather last night, accompanied with abundance of rain; and now the wind is come about westerly again, but we must bear it with patience. This afternoon we took up several branches of gulf weed (with which the sea is spread all over from the Western Isles to the coast of America); but one of these branches had something peculiar in it. In common with the rest it had a leaf about three quarters of an inch long, indented like a saw, and a small yellow berry filled with nothing but wind; besides which it bore a fruit of the animal kind, very surprising to see. It was a small shell-fish like a heart, the stalk by which it proceeded from the branch being partly of a gristly kind. Upon this one branch of the weed there were near forty of these vegetable animals; the smallest of them near the end contained a substance somewhat like an oyster, but the larger were visibly animated, opening their shells every moment, and thrusting out a set of unformed claws, not unlike those of a crab; but the inner part was still a kind of soft jelly. Observing the weed more narrowly, I spied a very small crab crawling among it, about as big as the head of a ten-penny nail, and of a yellowish colour, like the weed itself. This gave me some reason to think that he was a native of the branch, that he had not long since been in the same condition with the rest of those little embrios that appeared in the shells, this being the method of their generation; and that consequently all the rest of this odd kind of fruit might be crabs in due time. To strengthen my conjecture, I have resolved to keep the weed in salt water, renewing it every day till we come on shore, by this experiment to see whether any more crabs will be produced or not in this manner. I remember that the last calm we had, we took notice of a large crab upon the surface of the sea, swimming from one branch of weed to another, which he seemed to prey upon; and I likewise recollect that at Boston, in New England, I have often seen small crabs with a shell like a snail's upon their backs, crawling about in the salt water; and likewise at Portsmouth in England. It is likely nature has provided this hard shell to secure them till their own proper shell has acquired a sufficient hardness, which once perfected, they quit their old habitation and venture abroad safe in their own strength. The various changes that silk-worms, butterflies, and several other insects go through, make such alterations and metamorphoses not improbable. This day the captain of the snow with one of his passengers came on board us; but the wind beginning to blow, they did not stay dinner, but returned to their own vessel.

Thursday, September 29

Upon shifting the water in which I had put the weed yesterday, I found another crab, much smaller than the former, who seemed to have newly left his habitation. But the weed begins to wither, and the rest of the embrios are dead. This new comer fully convinces me, that at least this sort of crabs are generated in this manner. The snow's Captain dined on board us this day. Little or no wind.

Friday, September 30

I sat up last night to observe an eclipse of the moon, which the calendar calculated for London informed us would happen at five o'clock in the morning, September 30. It began with us about eleven last night, and continued till near two this morning, darkening her body about six digits, or one half; the middle of it being about half an hour after twelve, by which we may discover that we are in a meridian of about four hours and a half from London, or 67½ degrees of longitude, and consequently have not much above one hundred leagues to run. This is the second eclipse we have had within these fifteen days. We lost our consort in the night, but saw him again this morning near two leagues to windward. This afternoon we spoke with him again. We have had abundance of dolphins about us these three or four days; but we have not taken any more than one, they being shy of the bait. I took in some more gulf-weed to-day with the boat-hook, with shells upon it like that before mentioned, and three living perfect crabs, each less than the nail of my little finger. One of them had something particularly observable, to wit, a thin piece of the white shell which I before noticed as their covering while they remained in the condition of embrios, sticking close to his natural shell upon his back. This sufficiently confirms me in my opinion of the manner of their generation. I have put this remarkable crab with a piece of the gulf-weed, shells, &c. into a glass phial filled with salt water (for want of spirits of wine) in hopes to preserve the curiosity till I come on shore. The wind is South-West.

Saturday, October 1

Last night our consort, who goes incomparably better upon a wind than our vessel, got so far to windward and a-head of us, that this morning we could see nothing of him, and 'tis like shall see him no more. These South-Wests are hot damp winds, and bring abundance of rain and dirty weather with them.

Sunday, October 2

Last night we prepared our line with a design to sound this morning at four o'clock; but the wind coming about again to the North West, we let it alone. I cannot help fancying the water is changed a little, as is usual when a ship comes within soundings, but 'tis probable I am mistaken; for there is but one besides myself of my opinion, and we are very apt to believe what we wish to be true.

**Monday, October 3**

The water is now very visibly changed to the eyes of all except the Captain and Mate, and they will by no means allow it; I suppose because they did not see it first. Abundance of dolphins are about us, but they are very shy, and keep at a distance. Wind North West.

**Tuesday, October 4**

Last night we struck a dolphin, and this morning we found a flying-fish dead under the windlass. He is about the bigness of a small mackarel, a sharp head, a small mouth, and a tail forked somewhat like a dolphin, but the lowest branch much larger and longer than the other, and tinged with yellow. His back and sides of a darkish blue, his belly white, and his skin very thick. His wings are of a finny substance, about a span long, reaching, when close to his body, from an inch below his gills to an inch above his tail. When they fly it is straight forward, for (they cannot readily turn) a yard or two above the water, and perhaps fifty yards is the farthest before they dip into the water again, for they cannot support themselves in the air any longer than while their wings continue wet. These flying-fish are the common prey of the dolphin, who is their mortal enemy. When he pursues them they rise and fly, and he keeps close under them till they drop, and then snaps them up immediately. They generally fly in flocks, four or five, or perhaps a dozen together, and a dolphin is seldom caught without one or more in his belly. We put this flying-fish upon the hook, in hopes of catching one, but in a few minutes they got it off without hooking themselves; and they will not meddle with any other bait.

**Tuesday Night**

Since eleven o'clock we have struck three fine dolphins, which are a great refreshment to us. This afternoon we have seen abundance of grampuses, which are seldom far from land; but towards evening we had a more evident token, to wit, a little tired bird, something like a lark, came on board us, who certainly is an American, and 'tis likely was ashore this day. It is now calm. We hope for a fair wind next.

**Wednesday, October 5**

This morning we saw a heron, who had lodged aboard last night. 'Tis a long-legged, long-necked bird, having as they say but one gut. They live upon fish, and will swallow a living eel thrice sometimes before it will remain in their body. The wind is West again. The ship's crew was brought to a short allowance of water.

#### Thursday, October 6

This morning abundance of grass, rock-weed, &c. passed by us; evident tokens that land is not far off. We hooked a dolphin this morning that made us a good breakfast. A sail passed by us about twelve o'clock, and nobody saw her till she was too far astern to be spoken with. 'Tis very near calm: we saw another sail a-head this afternoon; but night coming on, we could not speak with her, though we very much desired it: she stood to the Northward, and it is possible might have informed us how far we are from land. Our artists on board are much at a loss. We hoisted our jack to her, but she took no notice of it.

#### Friday, October 7

Last night, about nine o'clock, sprung up a fine gale at North East, which run us in our course at the rate of seven miles an hour all night. We were in hopes of seeing land this morning, but cannot. The water, which we thought was changed, is now as blue as the sky; so that unless at that time we were running over some unknown shoal our eyes strangely deceived us. All the reckonings have been out these several days; though the captain says 'tis his opinion we are yet an hundred leagues from land: for my part I know not what to think of it, we have run all this day at a great rate; and now night is come on we have no soundings. Sure the American continent is not all sunk under water since we left it.

#### Saturday, October 8

The fair wind continues still; we ran all night in our course, sounding every four hours, but can find no ground yet, nor is the water changed by all this day's run. This afternoon we saw an *Irish Lord*, and a bird which flying looked like a yellow duck. These they say are not seen far from the coast. Other signs of land have we none. Abundance of large porpoises ran by us this afternoon, and we were followed by a shoal of small ones, leaping out of the water, as they approached. Towards evening we spied a sail a-head and spoke with her just before dark. She was bound from New York for Jamaica, and left Sandy Hook yesterday about noon, from which they reckon themselves forty-five leagues distant. By this we compute that we are not above thirty leagues from our capes, and hope to see land to-morrow.

Sunday, October 9

We have had the wind fair all the morning: at twelve o'clock we sounded, perceiving the water visibly changed, and struck ground at twenty-five fathoms, to our universal joy. After dinner one of our mess went up aloft to look out, and presently pronounced the long-wished for sound, *Land! Land!* In less than an hour we could descry it from the deck, appearing like tufts of trees. I could not discern it so soon as the rest; my eyes were dimmed with the suffusion of two small drops of joy. By three o'clock we were run in within two leagues of the land, and spied a small sail standing along shore. We would gladly have spoken with her, for our captain was unacquainted with the coast, and knew not what land it was that we saw. We made all the sail we could to speak with her. We made a signal of distress; but all would not do, the ill-natured dog would not come near us. Then we stood off again till morning, not caring to venture too near.

Monday, October 10

This morning we stood in again for land; and we, that had been here before, all agreed that it was Cape Henlopen; about noon we were come very near, and to our great joy saw the pilot-boat come off to us, which was exceeding welcome. He brought on board about a peck of apples with him; they seemed the most delicious I ever tasted in my life: the salt provisions we had been used to, gave them a relish. We had an extraordinary fair wind all the afternoon and ran above an hundred miles up the Delaware before ten at night. The country appears very pleasant to the eye, being covered with woods, except here and there a house and plantation. We cast anchor when the tide turned, about two miles below Newcastle, and there lay till the morning tide.

Tuesday, October 11

This morning we weighed anchor with a gentle breeze, and passed by Newcastle, whence they hailed us and bade us welcome. 'Tis extreme fine weather. The sun enlivens our stiff limbs with his glorious rays of warmth and brightness. The sky looks gay, with here and there a silver cloud. The fresh breezes from the woods refresh us, the immediate prospect of liberty after so long and irksome confine-ment ravishes us. In short all things conspire to make this the most joyful day I ever knew. As we passed by Chester some of the company went on shore, impatient once more to tread on *terra firma*, and designing for Philadelphia by land. Four of us remained on board, not caring for the fatigue of travel when we knew the voyage had much weakened us. About eight at night, the wind failing us, we cast anchor at Redbank, six miles from Philadelphia, and thought we must be obliged to lie on board that night: but some young Philadelphians happening to be out upon their pleasure in a boat, they came on board, and offered to take us up with them: we accepted of their kind proposal, and about ten o'clock landed at Philadelphia, heartily congratulating each other upon our having happily completed so tedious and dangerous a voyage. Thank God!

1726

# JAMES THOMSON
## 1700–1748

## from *The Seasons*

> The cormorant on high
> Wheels from the deep, and screams along the land.
> Loud shrieks the soaring hern; and with wild wing
> The circling sea-fowl cleave the flaky clouds.
> Ocean, unequal pressed, with broken tide
> And blind commotion heaves; while from the shore,
> Eat into caverns by the restless wave,
> And forest-rustling mountain comes a voice
> That, solemn-sounding, bids the world prepare.
> Then issues forth the storm with sudden burst,
> And hurls the whole precipitated air
> Down in a torrent. On the passive main
> Descends the ethereal force, and with strong gust
> Turns from its bottom the discoloured deep.
> Through the black night that sits immense around,
> Lashed into foam, the fierce-conflicting brine
> Seems o'er a thousand raging waves to burn.
> Meantime the mountain-billows, to the clouds

In dreadful tumult swelled, surge above surge,
Burst into chaos with tremendous roar,
And anchored navies from their stations drive
Wild as the winds, across the howling waste
Of mighty waters: now the inflated wave
Straining they scale, and now impetuous shoot
Into the secret chambers of the deep,
The wintry Baltic thundering o'er their head.
Emerging thence again, before the breath
Of full-exerted heaven they wing their course,
And dart on distant coasts—if some sharp rock
Or shoal insidious break not their career,
And in loose fragments fling them floating round.

1726–30

# GEORGE ANSON
## 1697–1762

# from *A Voyage Around the World*†

We had scarcely reached the southern extremity of the Streights of *Le Maire*, when our flattering hopes were instantly lost in the apprehensions of immediate destruction: For before the sternmost ships of the squadron were clear of the Streights, the serenity of the sky was suddenly changed, and gave us all the presages of an impending

† George (later Admiral Lord) Anson's *A Voyage Around the World* (1748) is worth inclusion in its own right, although its authorship is doubtful (it was probably ghosted for Anson either by Richard Walter, the chaplain aboard Anson's ship, the *Centurion*, or by the scientific pamphleteer, Benjamin Robins). Its interest is the more poignant because it supplied the story, reproduced here, which was to form the basis of William Cowper's 'The Castaway' (see below).
  One term used in the last paragraph of this extract, and germane to Cowper's poem, needs annotation. Where Anson (or Walter, or Robins) writes of 'putting the helm a weather and manning the fore-shrouds', he describes a horrible piece of heavy-weather seamanship. When the wind was too high to carry any sail, men were made to climb up

storm; and immediately that wind shifted to the southward, and blew in such violent squalls, that we were obliged to hand our top-sails, and reef our main-sail: The tide too, which had hitherto favoured us, now turned against us, and drove us to the eastward with prodigious rapidity, so that we were in great anxiety for the *Wager* and the *Anna Pink*, the two sternmost vessels, fearing they would be dashed to pieces against the shore of *Staten-land*; nor were our apprehensions without foundation, for it was with the utmost difficulty they escaped. And now the whole squadron, instead of pursuing their intended course to the SW, were driven to the eastward by the united force of the storm, and of the currents; so that next day in the morning we found ourselves near seven leagues to the eastward of *Staten-land*, which then bore from us NW. The violence of the current, which had set us with so much precipitation to the eastward, together with the force and constancy of the westerly winds, soon taught us to consider the doubling of Cape *Horn* as an enterprize, that might prove too mighty for our efforts, though some amongst us had lately treated the difficulties which former voyagers were said to have met with in this undertaking, as little better than chimerical, and had supposed them to arise rather from timidity and unskilfulness, than from the real embarrassments of the winds and seas; but we were now severely convinced, that these censures were rash and ill-grounded. For the distresses with which we struggled, during the three succeeding months, will not easily be paralleled in the relation of any former naval expedition. This will, I doubt not, be readily allowed by those who shall carefully peruse the ensuing narration.

From the storm which came on before we had well got clear of Streights *Le Maire*, we had a continual succession of such tempestuous weather, as surprized the oldest and most experienced Mariners on board, and obliged them to confess, that what they had hitherto called storms were inconsiderable gales, compared with the violence of these winds, which raised such short, and at the same time such mountainous waves, as greatly surpassed in danger all seas known in any other part of the globe: And it was not without great reason, that this unusual appearance filled us with continual terror; for had any one of these waves broke fairly over us, it must, in all probability, have sent us to the bottom. Nor did we escape with terror only; for

into the shrouds, so that the combined wind resistance of their bodies did the work of a storm-jib and gave the ship some minimal steerageway. It was the misfortune of Cowper's castaway to suffer this fate of being used as human canvas.

the ship rolling incessantly gunwale to, gave us such quick and violent motions, that the men were in perpetual danger of being dashed to pieces against the decks, or sides of the ship. And though we were extremely careful to secure ourselves from these shocks, by grasping some fixed body, yet many of our people were forced from their hold, some of whom were killed, and others greatly injured; in particular, one of our best seamen was canted over-board and drowned, another dislocated his neck, a third was thrown into the main-hold and broke his thigh, and one of our Boatswain's Mates broke his collar-bone twice; not to mention many other accidents of the same kind. These tempests, so dreadful in themselves, though unattended by any other unfavourable circumstance, were yet rendered more mischievous to us by their inequality, and the deceitful intervals which they at sometimes afforded; for though we were oftentimes obliged to lie to for days together under a reefed mizen, and were sometimes reduced to lie at the mercy of the waves under our bare poles, yet now and then we ventured to make sail with our courses double reefed; and the weather proving more tolerable, would perhaps encourage us to set our top-sails; after which the wind, without any previous notice, would return upon us with redoubled force, and would in an instant tear our sails from the yards. And that no circumstance might be wanting which could aggrandize our distress, these blasts generally brought with them a great quantity of snow and sleet, which cased our rigging, and froze our sails, thereby rendring them and our cordage brittle, and apt to snap upon the slightest strain, adding great difficulty and labour to the working of the ship, benumbing the limbs of our people, and making them incapable of exerting themselves with their usual activity, and even disabling many of them, by mortifying their toes and fingers. It were indeed endless to enumerate the various disasters of different kinds which befel us; and I shall only mention the most material, which will sufficiently evince the calamitous condition of the whole squadron, during the course of this navigation.

It was on the 7th of March, as hath been already observed, that we passed Streights *Le Maire*, and were immediately afterwards driven to the eastward by a violent storm, and the force of the current which set that way. For the four or five succeeding days we had hard gales of wind from the same quarter, with a most prodigious swell; so that though we stood, during all that time, towards the SW, yet we had no reason to imagine, we had made any way to the westward. In this interval we had frequent squalls of rain and snow, and shipped great quantities of water; after which, for three or four days, though the seas ran mountains high, yet the weather was rather more moderate: But, on the 18th, we had again strong gales of wind with extreme cold, and at midnight the main top-sail split, and one of the straps of the main dead eyes broke. From hence, to the 23d, the weather was more favourable, though often intermixed with rain and sleet, and some hard gales; but as the waves did not subside, the ship, by labouring in this lofty sea, was now grown so loose in her upper works, that she let in the water at every seam, so that every part within board was constantly exposed to the sea-water, and scarcely any of the Officers ever lay in dry beds. Indeed it was very rare, that two nights ever passed without many of them being driven from their beds, by the deluge of water that came upon them.

On the 23d, we had a most violent storm of wind, hail, and rain, with a very great sea; and though we handed the main top-sail before the height of the squall, yet we found the yard sprung; and soon after the foot-rope of the main-sail breaking, the main-sail itself split instantly to rags, and, in spite of our endeavours to save it, much the greater part of it was blown over-board. On this, the Commodore made the signal for the squadron to bring to; and the storm at length flattening to a calm, we had an opportunity of getting down our main top-sail yard to put the Carpenters at work upon it, and of repairing our rigging; after which, having bent a new mainsail, we got under sail again with a moderate breeze; but in less than twenty-four hours we were attacked by another storm still more furious than the former; for it proved a perfect hurricane, and reduced us to the necessity of lying to under our bare poles. As our ship kept the wind better than any of the rest, we were obliged, in the afternoon, to wear ship, in order to join the squadron to the leeward, which otherwise we should have been in danger of losing in the night: And as we dared not venture any sail abroad, we were obliged to make use of an expedient, which answered our purpose; this was putting the helm a weather, and manning the fore-shrouds. But though this method proved successful for the end intended, yet in the execution of it, one of our ablest seaman was canted over-board; and notwithstanding the prodigious agitation of the waves, we perceived that he swam very strong, and it was with the utmost concern that we found ourselves incapable of assisting him; and we were the more grieved at his unhappy fate, since we lost sight of him struggling with the waves,

and conceived from the manner in which he swam, that he might
continue sensible for a considerable time longer, of the horror
attending his irretrievable situation.

1748

# HENRY FIELDING

## 1707–1754

# from *A Voyage to Lisbon*

*Monday* [29 July]. At noon the captain took an observation, by
which it appeared that Ushant bore some leagues northward of us,
and that we were just entering the Bay of Biscay. We had advanced a
very few miles in this bay before we were entirely becalmed: we
furled our sails, as being of no use to us while we lay in this most
disagreeable situation, more detested by the sailors than the most
violent tempest: we were alarmed with the loss of a fine piece of salt
beef, which had been hung in the sea to freshen it; this being, it seems,
the strange property of salt water. The thief was immediately suspected,
and presently afterwards taken by the sailors. He was, indeed, no
other than a huge shark, who, not knowing when he was well off,
swallowed another piece of beef, together with a great iron crook on
which it was hung, and by which he was dragged into the ship.

I should scarce have mentioned the catching this shark, though so
exactly conformable to the rules and practice of voyage-writing, had
it not been for a strange circumstance that attended it. This was the
recovery of the stolen beef out of the shark's maw, where it lay
unchewed and undigested, and whence, being conveyed into the pot,
the flesh, and the thief that had stolen it, joined together in furnishing
variety to the ship's crew.

During this calm we likewise found the mast of a large vessel,
which the captain thought had lain at least three years in the sea. It
was stuck all over with a little shellfish or reptile, called a barnacle,
and which probably are the prey of the rock-fish, as our captain calls

it, asserting that it is the finest fish in the world; for which we are obliged to confide entirely to his taste; for, though he struck the fish with a kind of harping-iron, and wounded him, I am convinced, to death, yet he could not possess himself of his body; but the poor wretch escaped to linger out a few hours with probably great torments.

In the evening our wind returned, and so briskly, that we ran upwards of twenty leagues before the next day's [Tuesday's] observation, which brought us to lat. 47° 42'. The captain promised us a very speedy passage through the bay; but he deceived us, or the wind deceived him, for it so slackened at sunset, that it scarce carried us a mile in an hour during the whole succeeding night.

*Wednesday*. A gale struck up a little after sun-rising, which carried us between three and four knots or miles an hour. We were this day at noon about the middle of the Bay of Biscay, when the wind once more deserted us, and we were so entirely becalmed, that we did not advance a mile in many hours. My fresh-water reader will perhaps conceive no unpleasant idea from this calm: but it affected us much more than a storm could have done; for, as the irascible passions of men are apt to swell with indignation long after the injury which first raised them is over, so fared it with the sea. It rose mountains high, and lifted our poor ship up and down, backwards and forwards, with so violent an emotion, that there was scarce a man in the ship better able to stand than myself. Every utensil in our cabin rolled up and down, as we should have rolled ourselves, had not our chairs been fast lashed to the floor. In this situation, with our tables likewise fastened by ropes, the captain and myself took our meal with some difficulty, and swallowed a little of our broth, for we spilt much the greater part. The remainder of our dinner being an old, lean, tame duck roasted, I regretted but little the loss of, my teeth not being good enough to have chewed it.

Our women, who began to creep out of their holes in the morning, retired again within the cabin to their beds, and were no more heard of this day, in which my whole comfort was to find by the captain's relation that the swelling was sometimes much worse; he did, indeed, take this occasion to be more communicative than ever, and informed me of such misadventures that had befallen him within forty-six years at sea as might frighten a very bold spirit from undertaking even the shortest voyage. Were these, indeed, but universally known, our matrons of quality would possibly be deterred from venturing their tender offspring at sea; by which means our navy would lose the honour of many a young commodore, who at twenty-two is better versed in maritime affairs than real seamen are made by experience at sixty.

And this may, perhaps, appear the more extraordinary, as the education of both seems to be pretty much the same; neither of them having had their courage tried by Virgil's description of a storm, in which, inspired as he was, I doubt whether our captain doth not exceed him.

In the evening the wind, which continued in the NW, again freshened, and that so briskly that Cape Finisterre appeared by this day's observation to bear a few miles to the southward. We now indeed sailed, or rather flew, near ten knots an hour; and the captain, in the redundancy of his good-humour, declared he would go to church at Lisbon on Sunday next, for that he was sure of a wind; and, indeed, we all firmly believed him. But the event again contradicted him; for we were again visited by a calm in the evening.

But here, though our voyage was retarded, we were entertained with a scene, which as no one can behold without going to sea, so no one can form an idea of anything equal to it on shore. We were seated on the deck, women and all, in the serenest evening that can be imagined. Not a single cloud presented itself to our view, and the sun himself was the only object which engrossed our whole attention. He did indeed set with a majesty which is incapable of description, with which, while the horizon was yet blazing with glory, our eyes were called off to the opposite part to survey the moon, which was then at full, and which in rising presented us with the second object that this world hath offered to our vision. Compared to these the pageantry of theatres, or splendour of courts, are sights almost below the regard of children.

We did not return from the deck till late in the evening; the weather being inexpressibly pleasant, and so warm that even my old distemper perceived the alteration of the climate. There was indeed a swell, but nothing comparable to what we had felt before, and it affected us on the deck much less than in the cabin.

*Friday* [2 Aug.]. The calm continued till sun-rising, when the wind likewise arose, but unluckily for us it came from a wrong quarter; it was SSE, which is that very wind which Juno would have solicited of Aeolus, had Aeneas been in our latitude bound for Lisbon.

The captain now put on his most melancholy aspect, and resumed his former opinion that he was bewitched. He declared with great solemnity that this was worse and worse, for that a wind directly in his teeth was worse than no wind at all. Had we pursued the course which the wind persuaded us to take we had gone directly for Newfoundland, if we had not fallen in with Ireland in our way. Two ways remained to avoid this; one was to put into a port of Galicia; the other, to beat to the westward with as little sail as possible: and this was our captain's election.

As for us, poor passengers, any port would have been welcome to us; especially as not only our fresh provisions, except a great number of old ducks and fowls, but even our bread was come to an end, and nothing but sea-biscuit remained, which I could not chew. So that now for the first time in my life I saw what it was to want a bit of bread.

The wind, however, was not so unkind as we had apprehended; but, having declined with the sun, it changed at the approach of the moon, and became again favourable to us, though so gentle that the next day's observation carried us very little to the southward of Cape Finisterre. This evening at six the wind, which had been very quiet all day, rose very high, and continuing in our favour drove us seven knots an hour.

This day we saw a sail, the only one, as I heard of, we had seen in our whole passage through the bay. I mention this on account of what appeared to me somewhat extraordinary. Though she was at such a distance that I could only perceive she was a ship, the sailors discovered that she was a snow, bound to a port in Galicia.

*Sunday* [4 Aug.]. After prayers, which our good captain read on the deck with an audible voice, and with but one mistake, of a lion for Elias, in the second lesson for this day, we found ourselves far advanced in 42°, and the captain declared we should sup off Porte. We had not much wind this day; but, as this was directly in our favour, we made it up with sail, of which we crowded all we had. We went only at the rate of four miles an hour, but with so uneasy a motion, continually rolling from side to side, that I suffered more than I had done in our whole voyage; my bowels being almost twisted out of my belly. However, the day was very serene and bright, and the captain, who was in high spirits, affirmed he had never passed a pleasanter at sea.

1755

# ANON

## 'Ode on a Storm'

With gallant pomp, and beauteous pride
   The floating pile in harbour rode,
Proud of her freight, the swelling tide
Reluctant left the vessel's side,
   And rais'd it as she flow'd.

The waves with Eastern breezes curl'd,
   Had silver'd half the liquid plain;
The anchors weigh'd, the sails unfurl'd,
Serenely mov'd the wooden world,
   And stretch'd along the main

The scaly natives of the deep,
   Press to admire the vast machine,
In sporting gambols round it leap,
Or swimming low, due distance keep,
   In homage to their queen

Thus, as life glides in gentle gale
   Pretended friendship waits on pow'r,
But early quits the borrow'd veil
When adverse Fortune shifts the sail,
   And hastens to devour.

In vain we fly approaching ill,
   Danger can multiply its form;
Expos'd we fly like Jonas still,
And heaven, when 'tis heaven's will,
   O'ertakes us in a storm.

The distant surges foamy white
   Foretel the furious blast;

Dreadful, tho' distant was the sight,
Confed'rate winds and waves unite,
    And menace ev'ry mast.

Winds whistling thro' the shrouds, proclaim
    A fatal harvest on the deck,
Quick in pursuit as active flame,
Too soon the rolling ruin came,
    And ratify'd the wreck.

Thus, Adam smil'd with new-born grace,
    Life's flame inspir'd by heav'nly breath;
Thus the same breath sweeps off his race,
Disorders Nature's beauteous face,
    And spreads disease and death.

Stripp'd of her pride, the vessel rolls,
    And as by sympathy she knew
The secret anguish of our souls,
With inward deeper groans condoles
    The danger of her crew.

Now what avails it to be brave,
    On liquid precipices hung?
Suspended on a breaking wave,
Beneath us yawn'd a sea-green grave,
    And silenc'd ev'ry tongue.

The faithless flood forsook her keel,
    And downward launch'd the lab'ring hull,
Stun'd she forgot awhile to reel
And feel almost, or seem'd to feel
    A momentary lull.

Thus in the jaws of death we lay,
    Nor light, nor comfort found us there,
Lost in the gulph and floods of spray
No sun to chear us, nor a ray
    Of hope, but all despair.

The nearer shore, the more despair,
  While certain ruin waits on land;
Should we pursue our wishes there,
Soon we recant the fatal pray'r,
  And strive to shun the strand.

At length, the Being whose behest
  Reduc'd this Chaos into form,
His goodness and his pow'r express'd,
He spoke—and, as a God, suppress'd
  Our troubles, and the storm.

                                    1758

# WILLIAM FALCONER

## 1732–1770

## from *The Shipwreck*

'All hands unmoor!' proclaims a boisterous cry:
'All hands unmoor,' the cavern'd rocks reply!
Rous'd from repose, aloft the sailors swarm,
And with their levers soon the windlass arm.
The order given, up-springing with a bound,
They lodge the bars, and wheel their engine round:
At every turn the clanging pauls resound.
Uptorn reluctant from its oozy cave,
The ponderous anchor rises o'er the wave.
Along their slippery masts the yards ascend,
And high in air, the canvas wings extend:
Redoubling cords the lofty canvas guide,
And thro' inextricable mazes glide.
The lunar rays with long reflection gleam,
To light the vessel o'er the silver stream:

Along the glassy plane serene she glides,
While azure radiance trembles on her sides.
From east to north the transient breezes play;
And in th'Egyptian quarter soon decay.
A calm ensues; they dread th'adjacent shore;
The boats with rowers arm'd are sent before:
With cordage fasten'd to the lofty prow,
Aloof to sea the stately ship they tow.

When from the left approaching, they descry
A liquid column towering shoot on high.
The foaming base an angry whirlwind sweeps,
Where curling billows rouse the fearful deeps.
Still round and round the fluid vortex flies,
Scattering dun night and horror thro' the skies,
The swift volution and th'enormous train
Let sages vers'd in nature's lore explain!
The horrid apparition still draws nigh,
And white with foam the whirling surges fly!—
The guns were prim'd; the vessel northward veers
Till her black battery on the column bears.
The nitre fir'd; and while the dreadful sound,
Convulsive, shook the slumbering air around,
The watry volume, trembling to the sky,
Burst down a dreadful deluge from on high!
Th'affrighted surge, recoiling as it fell,
Rolling in hills disclos'd th'abyss of hell.
But soon, this transient undulation o'er,
The sea subsides; the whirlwinds rage no more.

For, while with boundless inundation o'er
The sea-beat ship th'involving waters roar,
Displaced beneath by her capacious womb,
They rage, their ancient station to resume;
By secret ambushes, their force to prove,
Thro' many a winding channel first they rove;
Till, gathering fury, like the fever'd blood,
Thro' her dark veins they roll a rapid flood.
While unrelenting thus the leaks they found,
The pumps with ever-clanking strokes resound.

Around each leaping valve, by toil subdu'd,
The tough bull-hide must ever be renew'd.

'Starboard again!' the watchful pilot cries;
'Starboard,' th'obedient timoneer replies.
Then to the left the ruling helm returns;
The wheel revolves; the ringing axle burns!
The ship no longer, foundering by the lee,
Bears on her side th'invasions of the sea:
All lonely o'er the desart waste she flies,
Scourged on by surges, storm and bursting skies.
As when the masters of the lance assail,
In Hyperborean seas, the slumbering whale;
Soon as the javelins pierce his scaly hide,
With anguish stung, he cleaves the downward tide.
In vain he flies, no friendly respite found;
His life-blood gushes thro' th'inflaming wound.

    The wounded bark, thus smarting with her pain,
Scuds from pursuing waves along the main;
While, dash'd apart by her dividing prow,
Like burning adamant the waters glow.
Her joints forget their firm elastic tone;
Her long keel trembles, and her timbers groan.
Upheaved behind her, in tremendous height,
The billows frown, with fearful radiance bright!
Now shivering, o'er the topmost wave she rides,
While, deep beneath th'enormous gulf divides.
Now, launching headlong down the horrid vale,
She hears no more the roaring of the gale;
Till up the dreadful height again she flies,
Trembling beneath the current of the skies.

High o'er the poop th'audacious seas aspire,
Uprolled in hills of fluctuating fire.
As some fell conqueror, frantic with success,
Sheds o'er the nations ruin and distress;
So, while the watry wilderness he roams,
Incens'd to sevenfold rage the tempest foams;

And o'er the trembling pines, above, below,
Shrill thro' the cordage howls, with notes of woe.
Now thunders, wafted from the burning zone,
Growl from afar, a deaf and hollow groan!
The ship's high battlements, to either side
For ever rocking, drink the briny tide:
Her joints unhing'd, in palsied langours play,
As ice dissolves beneath the noon-tide ray.
The skies asunder torn, a deluge pour;
Th'impetuous hail descends in whirling shower.
High on the masts, with pale and livid rays,
Amid the gloom portentous meteors blaze.
Th'aetherial dome, in mournful pomp array'd,
Now lurks behind impenetrable shade,
Now, flashing round intolerable light,
Redoubles all the terrors of the night.

And now, lash'd on by destiny severe,
With horror fraught, the dreadful scene drew near!
The ship hangs hovering on the verge of death,
Hell yawns, rocks rise, and breakers roar beneath!—
In vain alas! the sacred shades of yore
Would arm the mind with philosophic lore;
In vain they'd teach us, at the latest breath,
To smile serene amid the pangs of death.
Even Zeno's self, and Epictetus old,
This fell abyss had shudder'd to behold.
Had Socrates, for godlike virtue fam'd,
And wisest of the sons of men proclaim'd,
Beheld this scene of frenzy and distress,
His soul had trembled to its last recess!—
O yet confirm my heart, ye powers above,
This last tremendous shock of fate to prove.
The tottering frame of reason yet sustain!
Nor let this total ruin whirl my brain!

In vain the cords and axes were prepar'd,
For now th'audacious seas insult the yard;
High o'er the ship they throw a horrid shade,
And o'er her burst, in terrible cascade.

Uplifted on the surge, to heaven she flies,
Her shatter'd top half-buried in the skies,
Then headlong plunging thunders on the ground,
Earth groans! air trembles! and the deeps resound!
Her giant-bulk the dread concussion feels,
And quivering with the wound, in torment reels:
So reels, convuls'd with agonising throes,
The bleeding bull beneath the murd'rer's blows—
Again she plunges! hark! a second shock
Tears her strong bottom on the marble rock!
Down on the vale of death, with dismal cries,
The fated victims shuddering roll their eyes,
In wild despair; while yet another stroke,
With deep convulsion, rends the solid oak.
Till like the mine, in whose infernal cell,
The lurking demons of destruction dwell,
At length asunder torn her frame divides;
And crashing spreads in ruin o'er the tides.

1762

# from *An Universal Dictionary of the Marine*

CURRENT, in navigation, *courans*, (*currens*, Lat.) a certain progressive movement of the water of the sea, by which all bodies floating therein are compelled to alter their course, or velocity, or both, and submit to the laws imposed on them by the current.

In the sea currents are either natural and general, as arising from the diurnal rotation of the earth about it's axis; or accidental and particular, caused by the waters being driven against promontories, or into gulfs and streights; where, wanting room to spread, they are driven back, and thus disturb the ordinary flux of the sea.

'Currents are various, and directed towards different parts of the ocean, of which some are constant, and others periodical. The most extraordinary current of the sea is that by which part of the Atlantic or African ocean moves about Guinea from Cape Verd towards the curvature or bay of Africa, which they call Fernando Poo, viz. from west to east, contrary to the general motion. And such is the force of this current, that when ships approach too near the shore, it carries them violently towards that bay, and deceives the mariners in their reckoning.

'There is a great variety of shifting currents, which do not last, but return at certain periods; and these do, most of them, depend upon, and follow the anniversary winds or monsoons, which by blowing in one place may cause a current in another.' *Varenius.*

In the streights of Gibraltar the currents almost constantly drive to the eastward, and carry ships into the Mediterranean: they are also found to drive the same way into St George's-channel.

The setting or progressive motion of the current, may be either quite down to the bottom, or to a certain determinate depth.

As the knowledge of the direction and velocity of currents is a very material article in navigation, it is highly necessary to discover both, in order to ascertain the ship's situation and course with as much accuracy as possible. The most successful method which has been hitherto attempted by mariners for this purpose, is as follows. A common iron pot, which may contain four or five gallons, is suspended by a small rope fastened to it's ears or handles, so as to hang directly upright, as when placed upon the fire. This rope, which may be from 70 to 100 fathoms in length, being prepared for the experiment, is coiled in the boat, which is hoisted out of the ship at a proper opportunity, when there is little or no wind to ruffle the surface of the sea. The pot being then thrown overboard into the water, and immediately sinking, the line is slackened till about seventy or eighty fathoms run out, after which the line is fastened to the boat's stem, by which she is accordingly restrained, and rides as at anchor. The velocity of the current is then easily tried by the *log* and half-minute glass, the usual method of discovering the rate of a ship's sailing at sea. The course of the stream is next obtained by means of the compass provided for this operation.

Having thus found the seting and drift of the current, it remains to apply this experiment to the purposes of navigation. If the ship sails along the direction of the current, then the motion of the ship is increased by as much as is the drift or velocity of the current.

If a current sets directly against the ship's course, then her motion is retarded in proportion to the strength of the current. Hence it is plain, 1. If the velocity of the current be less than that of the ship, then the ship will advance so much as is the difference of these velocities. 2. If the velocity of the current be more than that of the ship, then will the ship fall as much *astern* as is the difference of these velocities. 3. If

the velocity of the current be equal to that of the ship, then will the
ship stand still, the one velocity destroying the other.

If the current thwarts the course of a ship, it not only diminishes or
increases her velocity, but gives her a new direction, compounded of
the course she steers, and the setting of the current, as appears by the
following

### LEMMA.

If a body at A be impelled by two
forces at the same time, the one in
the direction AB, carrying it from
A to B in a certain space of time,
and the other in the direction AD,
pushing it from A to D in the same
time; complete the parallelogram ABCD, and draw the diagonal AC:
then the body at A, (which let us suppose a ship agitated by the wind
and current; AB being the line along which she advances as impressed
by the wind, and AD the line upon which she is driven by the current)
will move along the diagonal AC, and will be in the point C, at the
end of the time in which it would have moved along AD or AB, as
impelled by either of those forces (the wind or current) separately.

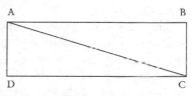

WATER-SPOUT, an extraordinary and dangerous meteor, consisting
of a large mass of water, collected into a sort of column by the force of
a whirlwind, and moved with rapidity along the surface of the sea.

A variety of authors have written on the cause and effects of these
meteors, with different degrees of accuracy and probability. As it
would be superfluous to enter minutely into their various conjectures,
which are frequently grounded on erroneous principles, we shall
content ourselves with selecting a few of the latest remarks; and
which are apparently supported by philosophical reasoning.

Dr Franklin, in his physical and meteorological observations,
supposes a water-spout and a whirlwind to proceed from the same
cause, their only difference being, that the latter passes over the land,
and the former over the water. This opinion is coroborated by *M. de
la Pryme*, in the *Philosophical Transactions*; where he describes two
spouts observed at different times in Yorkshire, whose appearances
in the air were exactly like those of the spouts at sea; and their effects
the same as those of real whirlwinds.

Whirlwinds have generally a progressive as well as a circular motion; so had what is called the spout at *Topsham*, described in the *Transactions*; and this also by it's effects appears to have been a real whirlwind. Water-spouts have also a progressive motion, which is more or less rapid; being in some violent, and in others barely perceptible.

Whirlwinds generally rise after calms and great heats: the same is observed of water-spouts, which are therefore most frequent in the warm latitudes.

The wind blows every way from a large surrounding space to a whirlwind. Three vessels, employed in the whale-fishery, happening to be *becalmed*, lay in sight of each other, at about a league distance, and in the form of a triangle. After some time a water-spout appeared near the middle of the triangle; when a brisk gale arose, and every vessel made sail. It then appeared to them all by the *triming* of their sails, and the course of each vessel, that the spout was to leeward of every one of them; and this observation was further confirmed by the comparing of accounts, when the different observers afterwards confered about the subject. Hence whirlwinds and water-spouts agree in this particular likewise.

But if the same meteor, which appears a water-spout at sea, should, in it's progressive motion, encounter and pass over land, and there produce all the phaenomena and effects of a whirlwind, it would afford a stronger conviction that a whirlwind and a water-spout are the same thing. An ingenious correspondent of Dr Franklin gives one instance of this that fell within his own observation.[1]

---

[1] I had often seen water-spouts at a distance, and heard many strange stories of them, but never knew any thing satisfactory of their nature or cause, until that which I saw at Antigua; which convinced me that a water-spout is a whirlwind, which becomes visible in all its dimensions by the water it carries up with it.

There appeared, not far from the mouth of the harbour of St John's, two or three water-spouts, one of which took it's course up the harbour. It's progressive motion was slow and unequal, not in a strait line, but as it were by jerks or starts. When just by the wharf, I stood about 100 yards from it. There appeared in the water a circle of about twenty yards diameter, which to me had a dreadful though pleasing appearance. The water in this circle was violently agitated, being whisked about, and carried up into the air with great rapidity and noise, and reflected a lustre, as if the sun shined bright on that spot, which was more conspicuous, as there appeared a dark circle around it. When it made the shore, it carried up with the same violence shingles, staves, large pieces of the roofs of houses, &c. and one small wooden house it lifted entirely from the foundation on which it stood, and carried it to the distance of fourteen feet, where it settled without breaking or overseting; and, what is remarkable, though the whirlwind moved from west to east, the house moved from east to west. Two or three

A fluid moving from all points horizontally towards a center must, at that center, either mount or descend. If a hole be opened in the middle of the bottom of a tub filled with water, the water will flow from all sides to the center, and there descend in a whirl. But air flowing on or near the surface of land or water, from all sides towards a center, must at that center ascend; because the land or water will hinder it's descent.

If these concentring currents of air be in the upper region, they may indeed descend in the spout or whirlwind; but then, when the united current reached the earth or water, it would spread, and probably blow every way from the center. There may be whirlwinds of both kinds; but from the effects commonly observed, Dr Franklin suspects the rising one to be most frequent: when the upper air descends, it is perhaps in a greater body extending wider, as in thunder-gusts, and without much whirling; and when air descends in a spout or whirlwind, he conceives that it would rather press the roof of a house *inwards*, or force *in* the tiles, shingles, or thatch, and force a boat down into the water, or a piece of timber into the earth, than snatch them upwards, and carry them away.

The whirlwinds and spouts are not always, though most frequently, in the day-time. The terrible whirlwind which damaged a great part of *Rome*, June 11, 1749, happened in the night; and was supposed to have been previously a water-spout, it being asserted as an undoubted fact, that it gathered in the neighbouring sea, because it could be traced from Ostia to Rome.

This whirlwind is said to have appeared as a very black, long, and lofty cloud, discoverable, notwithstanding the darkness of the night, by it's continually lightning, or emiting flashes on all sides, pushing along with a surprising swiftness, and within three or four feet of the ground. It's general effects on houses were, striping off the roofs, blowing away chimneys, breaking doors and windows, *forcing up the floors, and unpaving the rooms* (some of these effects seem to agree well with the supposed vacuum in the center of the whirlwind) and the very rafters of the houses were broke and dispersed, and even hurled against houses at a considerable distance, &c.

negroes and a white woman were killed by the fall of the timber, which it carried up into the air, and dropt again. After passing through the town, I believe it was soon dissipated; for, except tearing a large limb from a tree, and part of the cover of a sugar-work near the town, I do not remember any further damage done by it. I conclude, wishing you success in your enquiry, and am, &c.                    W.M.

The Doctor, in proceeding to explain his conceptions, begs to be allowed two or three positions, as a foundation for his hypothesis. 1. That the lower region of air is often more heated, and so more rarified, than the upper; and by consequence specifically lighter. The coldness of the upper region is manifested by the hail, which sometimes falls from it in warm weather. 2. That heated air may be very moist, and yet the moisture so equally diffused and rarefied as not to be visible till colder air mixes with it, at which time it condenses and becomes visible. Thus our breath, although invisible in summer, becomes visible in winter.

These circumstances being granted, he presupposes a tract of land or sea, of about sixty miles in extent, unsheltered by clouds and unrefreshed by the wind, during a summer's day, or perhaps for several days without intermission, till it becomes violently heated, together with the lower region of the air in contact with it, so that the latter becomes specifically lighter than the superincumbent higher region of the atmosphere, wherein the clouds are usually floated: he supposes also that the air surrounding this tract has not been so much heated during those days, and therefore remains heavier. The consequence of this, he conceives, should be, that the heated lighter air should ascend, and the heavier descend; and as this rising cannot operate throughout the whole tract at once, because that would leave too extensive a vacuum, the rising will begin precisely in that colum which happens to be lightest, or most rarified; and the warm air will flow horizontally from all parts to this column, where the several currents meeting, and joining to rise, a whirl is naturally formed, in the same manner as a whirl is formed in a tub of water, by the descending fluid receding from all sides of the tub towards the hole in the center.

And as the several currents arrive at this central rising column, with a considerable degree of horizontal motion, they cannot suddenly change it to a vertical motion; therefore, as they gradually, in approaching the whirl, decline from right to curve or circular lines, so, having joined the whirl, they ascend by a spiral motion; in the same manner as the water descends spirally through the hole in the tub before mentioned.

Lastly, as the lower air nearest the surface is more rarified by the heat of the sun, it is more impressed by the current of the surrounding cold and heavy air which is to assume it's place, and consequently it's motion towards the whirl is swiftest, and so the force of the lower part of the whirl strongest, and the centrifugal force of it's particles greatest. Hence the vacuum which encloses the axis of the whirl should be greatest near the earth or sea, and diminish gradually as it approaches the region of the clouds, till it ends in a point.

This circle is of various diameters, sometimes very large.

If the vacuum passes over water, the water may rise in a body or column therein to the height of about thirty-two feet. This whirl of air may be as invisible as the air itself, though reaching in reality from the water to the region of cool air, in which our low summer thunder-clouds commonly float; but it will soon become visible at it's extremities. The agitation of the water under the whirling of the circle, and the swelling and rising of the water in the commencement of the vacuum, renders it visible below. It is perceived above by the warm air being brought up to the cooler region, where it's moisture begins to be condensed by the cold into thick vapour; and is then first discovered at the highest part; which being now cooled condenses what rises behind it, and this latter acts in the same manner on the succeeding body; where, by the contact of the vapours, the cold operates faster in a right line downwards, than the vapours themselves can climb in a spiral line upwards; they climb, however, and as by continual addition they grow denser, and by consequence increase their centrifugal force, and being risen above the concentrating currents that compose the whirl, they fly off, and form a cloud.

It seems easy to conceive, how, by this successive condensation from above, the spout appears to drop or descend from the cloud, although the materials of which it is composed are all the while ascending. The condensation of the moisture contained in so great a quantity of warm air as may be supposed to rise in a short time in this prodigiously rapid whirl, is perhaps sufficient to form a great extent of cloud: and the friction of the whirling air on the sides of the column may detach great quantities of it's water, disperse them into drops, and carry them up in the spiral whirl mixed with the air. The heavier drops may indeed fly off, and fall into a shower about the spout; but much of it will be broken into vapour, and yet remain visible.

As the whirl weakens, the tube may apparently separate in the middle; the column of water subsiding, the superior condensed part drawing up to the cloud. The tube or whirl of air may nevertheless remain entire, the middle only becoming invisible, as not containing any visible matter.

Dr Stuart, in the *Philosophical Transactions*, says, 'It was observable of all the spouts he saw, but more perceptible of a large one, that towards the end it began to appear like a hollow canal, only black in the borders, but white in the middle; and though it was at first altogether black and opaque, yet the sea-water could very soon after be perceived to fly up along the middle of this canal like smoke in a chimney.'

When Dr Stuart's Spouts were full charged, that is, when the whirling pipe of air was filled with quantities of drops and vapour torn off from the column, the whole was rendered so dark that it could not be seen through, nor the spiral ascending motion discovered; but when the quantity ascending lessened, the pipe became more transparent, and the ascending motion visible. The spiral motion of the vapours, whose lines intersect each other on the nearest and furthest side of this transparent part, appeared therefore to Stuart like smoke ascending in a chimney; for the quantity being still too great in the line of sight through the sides of the tube, the motion could not be discovered there, and so they represented the solid sides of the chimney.

Dr Franklin concludes by supposing a whirlwind or spout to be stationary, when the concuring winds are equal; but if unequal, the whirl acquires a progressive motion in the direction of the strongest pressure. When the wind that communicates this progression becomes stronger above than below, or below than above, the spout will be bent or inclined. Hence the horizontal process and obliquity of water-spouts are derived.


WAVE, a volume of water elevated by the action of the wind upon it's surface, into a state of fluctuation.

Mr Boyle has proved, by a variety of experiments, that the utmost force of the wind never penetrates deeper than six feet into the water; and it should seem a natural consequence of this, that the water put in motion by it can only be elevated to the same height of six feet from the level of the surface in a calm. This six feet of elevation being then added to the six of excavation, in the part whence that water was raised, should give twelve feet for the greatest elevation of a wave, when the height of it is not increased by whirlwinds, or the interruption of rocks or shoals, which always gives an additional elevation to the natural swell of the waves.

We are not to suppose, from this calculation, that no wave of the sea can rise more than six feet above it's natural level in open and deep water; for some immensely higher than these are formed in violent tempests, in the great seas. These, however, are not to be accounted waves in their natural state; but they are single waves composed of many others: for in these wide plains of water, when one wave is raised by the wind, and would elevate itself up to the exact height of six feet, and no more, the motion of the water is so great, and the succession of the waves so quick, that during the time wherein this rises, it receives into it several other waves, each of which would have been of the same height with itself. These accordingly run into the first wave, one after another as it rises: by this means it's rise is continued much longer than it would naturally have been, and it becomes accumulated to an enormous size. A number of these complicated waves arising together, and being continued in a long succession by the duration of the storm, make the waves so dangerous to shipping, which the sailors, in their phrase, call *mountains high*.

1769

---

# TOBIAS SMOLLET

## 1721–1771

# from *Travels through France and Italy*†

Dover is commonly termed a den of thieves; and I am afraid it is not altogether without reason, it has acquired this appellation. The people are said to live by piracy in time of war; and by smuggling and fleecing strangers in time of peace: but I will do them the justice to say, they make no distinction between foreigners and natives. Without

---

† Smollet's *Travels through France and Italy* is now best remembered as the object of a famous satire, Sterne's *A Sentimental Journey*. Sterne ridiculed Smollett as 'Smelfungus', the ultimately disgruntled traveller: 'The learned SMELFUNGUS travelled from Boulogne to Paris—from Paris to Rome—and so on—but he set out with the spleen and jaundice, and every object he pass'd by was discoloured or

all doubt a man cannot be much worse lodged and worse treated in
any part of Europe; nor will he in any other place meet with more
flagrant instances of fraud, imposition, and brutality. One would
imagine they had formed a general conspiracy against all those who
either go to, or return from the continent. About five years ago, in my
passage from Flushing to Dover, the master of the packet-boat
brought to all of a sudden off the South Foreland, although the wind
was as favourable as it could blow. He was immediately boarded by a
custom-house boat, the officer of which appeared to be his friend. He
then gave the passengers to understand, that as it was low water, the
ship could not go into the harbour; but that the boat would carry
them ashore with their baggage.

The custom-house officer demanded a guinea for this service, and
the bargain was made. Before we quitted the ship, we were obliged to
gratify the cabin-boy for his attendance, and to give drink-money to
the sailors. The boat was run aground on the open beach; but we
could not get ashore without the assistance of three or four fellows,
who insisted upon being paid for their trouble. Every parcel and
bundle, as it was landed, was snatched up by a separate porter: one
ran away with a hat-box, another with a wig-box, a third with a
couple of shirts tied up in a handkerchief, and two were employed in
carrying a small portmanteau that did not weigh forty pounds. All
our things were hurried to the custom-house to be searched, and the
searcher was paid for disordering our cloaths: from thence they were
removed to the inn, where the porters demanded half a crown each
for their labour. It was in vain to expostulate; they surrounded the
house like a pack of hungry hounds, and raised such a clamour, that
we were fain to comply. After we had undergone all this imposition,
we were visited by the master of the packet, who, having taken our
fares, and wished us joy of our happy arrival in England, expressed
his hope that we would remember the poor master, whose wages
were very small, and who chiefly depended upon the generosity of
the passengers. I own I was shocked at his meanness, and could not
help telling him so. I told him, I could not conceive what title he had

distorted—He wrote an account of them, but 'twas nothing but the account of his
miserable feelings.' The first thing that Smollet found to detest on his journey was the
'invidious strait' of the English Channel. His description of his passage, and its
attendant hazards and miseries, is particularly interesting for its portrayal of seafarers
as a gang of thievish ruffians. This view, later sentimentally overlaid by images of Jolly
Jack Tar and Ye Mariners of England, had a wide currency. Except in times of war,
seamen were generally regarded as a desperate underclass.

to any such gratification: he had sixteen passengers, who paid a guinea each, on the supposition that every person should have a bed; but there were no more than eight beds in the cabin, and each of these was occupied before I came on board; so that if we had been detained at sea a whole week by contrary winds and bad weather, one half of the passengers must have slept upon the boards, howsoever their health might have suffered from this want of accommodation. Notwithstanding this check, he was so very abject and importunate, that we gave him a crown a piece, and he retired.

The first thing I did when I arrived at Dover this last time, was to send for the master of a packet-boat, and agree with him to carry us to Boulogne at once, by which means I saved the expence of travelling by land from Calais to this last place, a journey of four-and-twenty miles. The hire of a vessel from Dover to Boulogne is precisely the same as from Dover to Calais, five guineas, but this skipper demanded eight, and, as I did not know the fare, I agreed to give him six. We embarked between six and seven in the evening, and found ourselves in a most wretched hovel, on board what is called a Folkstone cutter. The cabin was so small that a dog could hardly turn in it, and the beds put me in mind of the holes described in some catacombs, in which the bodies of the dead were deposited, being thrust in with the feet foremost; there was no getting into them but end-ways, and indeed they seemed so dirty, that nothing but extreme necessity could have obliged me to use them. We sat up all night in a most uncomfortable situation, tossed about by the sea, cold, and cramped and weary, and languishing for want of sleep. At three in the morning the master came down, and told us we were just off the harbour of Boulogne; but the wind blowing off shore, he could not possibly enter, and therefore advised us to go ashore in the boat. I went upon deck to view the coast, when he pointed to the place where he said Boulogne stood, declaring at the same time we were within a short mile of the harbour's mouth. The morning was cold and raw, and I knew myself extremely subject to catch cold; nevertheless we were all so impatient to be ashore, that I resolved to take his advice. The boat was already hoisted out, and we went on board of it, after I had paid the captain and gratified his crew. We had scarce parted from the ship, when we perceived a boat coming towards us from the shore; and the master gave us to understand, it was coming to carry us into the harbour. When I objected to the trouble of shifting from one boat to another in the open sea, which (by the bye) was a little rough; he said it was a privilege which the watermen of Boulogne had, to carry all passengers ashore, and that this privilege he durst not venture to infringe. This was no time nor place to remonstrate. The French boat came alongside half filled with water, and we were handed from the one to the other. We were then obliged to lie upon our oars, till the captain's boat went on board and returned from the ship with a packet of letters. We were afterwards rowed a long league, in a rough sea, against wind and tide, before we reached the harbour, where we landed; benumbed with cold, and the women excessively sick: from our landing-place we were obliged to walk very near a mile to the inn where we purposed to lodge, attended by six or seven men and women, bare-legged, carrying our baggage. This boat cost me a guinea, besides paying exorbitantly the people who carried our things; so that the inhabitants of Dover and of Boulogne seem to be of the same kidney, and indeed they understand one another perfectly well. It was our honest captain who made the signal for the shore-boat before I went upon deck; by which means he not only gratified his friends, the watermen of Boulogne, but also saved about fifteen shillings portage, which he must have paid had he gone into the harbour; and thus he found himself at liberty to return to Dover, which he reached in four hours. I mention these circumstances as a warning to other passengers. When a man hires a packet-boat from Dover to Calais or Boulogne, let him remember that the stated price is five guineas; and let him insist upon being carried into the harbour in the ship, without paying the least regard to the representations of the master, who is generally a little dirty knave. When he tells you it is low water, or the wind is in your teeth, you may say you will stay on board till it is high water, or till the wind comes favourable. If he sees you are resolute, he will find means to bring his ship into the harbour, or at least to convince you, without a possibility of your being deceived, that it is not in his power.

1766

# from *The Expedition of Humphry Clinker*

From Harrigate, we came hither, by the way of York, and here we shall tarry some days, as my uncle and Tabitha are both resolved to make use of the waters. Scarborough, though a paltry town, is romantic from its situation along a cliff that overhangs the sea. The harbour is formed by a small elbow of land that runs out as a natural mole, directly opposite to the town; and on that side is the castle, which stands very high, of considerable extent, and, before the invention of gun-powder, was counted impregnable. At the other end of Scarborough are two public rooms for the use of the company, who resort to this place in the summer, to drink the waters and bathe in the sea; and the diversions are pretty much on the same footing here as at Bath. The Spa is a little way beyond the town, on this side, under a cliff, within a few paces of the sea, and thither the drinkers go every morning in dishabille; but the descent is by a great number of steps, which invalids find very inconvenient. Betwixt the well and the harbour, the bathing machines are ranged along the beach, with all their proper utensils and attendants. You have never seen one of these machines. Image to yourself a small, snug, wooden chamber, fixed upon a wheel-carriage, having a door at each end, and on each side a little window above, a bench below. The bather, ascending into this apartment by wooden steps, shuts himself in, and begins to undress, while the attendant yokes a horse to the end next the sea, and draws the carriage forwards, till the surface of the water is on a level with the floor of the dressing-room, then he moves and fixes the horse to the other end. The person within being stripped, opens the door to the sea-ward, where he finds the guide ready, and plunges headlong into the water. After having bathed, he re-ascends into the apartment, by the steps which had been shifted for that purpose, and puts on his clothes at his leisure, while the carriage is drawn back again upon the dry land; so that he has nothing further to do, but to open the door, and come down as he went up. Should he be so weak or ill as to require a servant to put off and on his clothes, there is room enough in the apartment for half a dozen people. The guides who attend the ladies in the water, are of their own sex, and they and the female bathers have a dress of flannel for the sea; nay, they are provided with other conveniences for the support of decorum. A certain number of the machines are fitted with tilts, that project from the sea-ward ends of them, so as to screen the bathers from the view of all persons whatsoever. The beach is admirably adapted for this practice, the descent being gently gradual, and the sand soft as velvet; but then the machines can be used only at a certain time of the tide, which varies every day; so that sometimes the bathers are obliged to rise very early in the morning. For my part, I love swimming as an exercise, and can enjoy it at all times of the tide, without the formality of an apparatus. You and I have often plunged together into the Isis; but the sea is a much more noble bath, for health as well as pleasure. You cannot conceive what a flow of spirits it gives, and how it braces every sinew of the human frame. Were I to enumerate half the diseases which are every day cured by sea-bathing, you might justly say you had received a treatise, instead of a letter, from

your affectionate friend and servant,<br>J. Melford.

1771

———

# JAMES BOSWELL

## 1740–1795

## from *Journal of a Tour to the Hebrides*

### *Sunday, 3d October.*

Joseph reported that the wind was still against us. Dr Johnson said, 'A wind, or not a wind? that is the question'; for he can amuse himself at times with a little play of words, or rather of sentences. I remember when he turned his cup at Aberbrothick, where we drank tea, he muttered, *Claudite iam rivos, pueri.* I must again and again apologize to fastidious readers, for recording such minute particulars. They prove the scrupulous fidelity of my Journal. Dr Johnson said it was a very exact picture of a portion of his life.

While we were chatting in the indolent stile of men who were to stay here all this day at least, we were suddenly roused by being told that the wind was fair, that a little fleet of herring-busses was passing by for Mull, and that Mr Simpson's vessel was about to sail. Hugh M'Donald, the skipper, came to us, and was impatient that we should get ready, which we soon did. Dr Johnson, with composure and solemnity, repeated the observation of Epictetus, that, 'as man has the voyage of death before him,—whatever may be his employment, he should be ready at the master's call; and an old man should never be far from the shore, lest he should not be able to get himself ready.' He rode, and I and the other gentlemen walked, about an English mile to the shore, where the vessel lay. Dr Johnson said, he should never forget Sky, and returned thanks for all civilities. We were carried to the vessel in a small boat which she had, and we set sail very briskly about one o'clock. I was much pleased with the motion for many hours. Dr Johnson grew sick, and retired under cover, as it rained a good deal. I kept above, that I might have fresh air, and finding myself not affected by the motion of the vessel, I exulted in being a stout seaman, while Dr Johnson was quite in a state of annihilation. But I was soon humbled; for after imagining that I could go with ease to America or the East-Indies, I became very sick, but kept above board, though it rained hard.

As we had been detained so long in Sky by bad weather, we gave up the scheme that Col had planned for us of visiting several islands, and contented ourselves with the prospect of seeing Mull, and Icolmkill and Inchkenneth, which lie near to it.

Mr Simpson was sanguine in his hopes for a while, the wind being fair for us. He said, he would land us at Icolmkill that night. But when the wind failed, it was resolved we should make for the sound of Mull, and land in the harbour of Tobermorie. We kept near the five herring vessels for some time; but afterwards four of them got before us, and one little wherry fell behind us. When we got in full view of the point of Ardnamurchan, the wind changed, and was directly against our getting into the sound. We were then obliged to tack, and get forward in that tedious manner. As we advanced, the storm grew greater, and the sea very rough. Col then began to talk of making for Egg, or Canna, or his own island. Our skipper said, he would get us into the Sound. Having struggled for this a good while in vain, he said, he would push forward till we were near the land of Mull, where we might cast anchor, and lie till the morning; for although, before this, there had been a good moon, and I had pretty distinctly seen not only the land of Mull, but up the Sound, and the country of Morven as at one end of it, the night was now grown very dark. Our crew consisted of one M'Donald, our skipper, and two sailors, one of whom had but one eye; Mr Simpson himself, Col, and Hugh M'Donald his servant, all helped. Simpson said, he would willingly go for Col, if young Col or his servant would undertake to pilot us to a harbour; but, as the island is low land, it was dangerous to run upon it in the dark. Col and his servant appeared a little dubious. The scheme of running for Canna seemed then to be embraced; but Canna was ten leagues off, all out of our way; and they were afraid to attempt the harbour of Egg. All these different plans were successively in agitation. The old skipper still tried to make for the land of Mull; but then it was considered that there was no place there where we could anchor in safety. Much time was lost in striving against the storm. At last it became so rough, and threatened to be so much worse, that Col and his servant took more courage, and said they would undertake to hit one of the harbours in Col.—'Then let us run for it in God's name,' said the skipper; and instantly we turned towards it. The little wherry which had fallen behind us, had hard work. The master begged that, if we made for Col, we should put out a light to him. Accordingly one of the sailors waved a glowing peat for some time. The various difficulties that were started, gave me a good deal of apprehension, from which I was relieved, when I found we were to run for a harbour before the wind. But my relief was but of short duration; for I soon heard that our sails were very bad, and were in danger of being torn in pieces, in which case we should be driven upon the rocky shore of Col. It was very dark, and there was a heavy and incessant rain. The sparks of the burning peat flew so much about, that I dreaded the vessel might take fire. Then, as Col was a sportsman, and had powder on board, I figured that we might be blown up. Simpson and he appeared a little frightened, which made me more so; and the perpetual talking, or rather shouting, which was carried on in Erse, alarmed me still more. A man is always suspicious of what is saying in an unknown tongue; and, if fear be his passion at the time, he grows more afraid. Our vessel often lay so much on one side, that I trembled lest she should be overset; and indeed they told me afterwards, that they had run her sometimes to within an inch of the water, so anxious were they to make what haste they could before the night should be worse. I now saw what I never saw before, a prodigious sea, with immense billows coming upon a vessel, so as that it seemed hardly possible to escape. There was something grandly horrible in the sight. I am glad I have seen it once. Amidst all these terrifying circumstances, I endeavoured to compose my mind. It was not easy to do it; for all the stories that I had heard of the dangerous sailing among the Hebrides, which is proverbial, came full upon my recollection. When I thought of those who were dearest to me, and would suffer severely, should I be lost, I upbraided myself, as not having a sufficient cause for putting myself in such danger. Piety afforded me comfort; yet I was disturbed by the objections that have been made against a particular providence, and by the arguments of those who maintain that it is in vain to hope that the petitions of an individual, or even of congregations, can have any influence with the Deity; objections which have been often made, and which Dr Hawkesworth has lately revived, in his Preface to the Voyages to the South Seas; but Dr Ogden's excellent doctrine on the efficacy of intercession prevailed.

It was half an hour after eleven before we set ourselves in the course for Col. As I saw them all busy doing something, I asked Col, with much earnestness, what I could do. He, with a happy readiness, put into my hand a rope, which was fixed to the top of one of the masts, and told me to hold it till he bade me pull. If I had considered the matter, I might have seen that this could not be of the least service; but his object was to keep me out of the way of those who were busy working the vessel, and at the same time to divert my fear, by employing me, and making me think that I was of use. Thus did I stand firm to my post, while the wind and rain beat upon me, always expecting a call to pull my rope.

The man with one eye steered; old M'Donald, and Col and his servant, lay upon the fore-castle, looking sharp out for the harbour. It was necessary to carry much *cloth*, as they termed it, that is to say, much sail, in order to keep the vessel off the shore of Col. This made violent plunging in a rough sea. At last they spied the harbour of Lochiern, and Col cried, 'Thank God, we are safe!' We ran up till we were opposite to it, and soon afterwards we got into it, and cast anchor.

Dr Johnson had all this time been quiet and unconcerned. He had lain down on one of the beds, and having got free from sickness, was satisfied. The truth is, he knew nothing of the danger we were in: but, fearless and unconcerned, might have said, in the words which he has chosen for the motto to his *Rambler*,

> *Quo me cunque rapit tempestas, deforor hospes.*[1]

Once, during the doubtful consultations, he asked whither we were going; and upon being told that it was not certain whether to Mull or Col, he cried, 'Col for my money!'—I now went down, with Col and Mr Simpson, to visit him. He was lying in philosophick tranquillity, with a greyhound of Col's at his back, keeping him warm. Col is quite the *Juvenis qui gaudet canibus.* He had, when we left Talisker, two greyhounds, two terriers, a pointer, and a large Newfoundland water-dog. He lost one of his terriers by the road, but had still five dogs with him. I was very ill, and very desirous to get to shore. When I was told that we could not land that night, as the storm had now increased, I looked so miserably, as Col afterwards informed me, that what Shakspeare has made the Frenchman say of the English soldiers, when scantily dieted, '*Piteous they will look, like drowned mice!*' might, I believe, have been well applied to me.

1785

## ANN RADCLIFFE
### 1764–1823

# from *The Mysteries of Udolpho*

The cheerfulness, with which Blanche rejoined the party, vanished, on her reaching the margin of the sea; she gazed with apprehension upon the immense expanse of waters, which, at a distance, she had beheld only with delight and astonishment, and it was by a strong effort, that she so far overcame her fears as to follow her father into the boat.

[1] For as the tempest drives, I shape my way. FRANCIS.

As she silently surveyed the vast horizon, bending round the distant verge of the ocean, an emotion of sublimest rapture struggled to overcome a sense of personal danger. A light breeze played on the water, and on the silk awning of the boat, and waved the foliage of the receding woods, that crowned the cliffs, for many miles, and which the Count surveyed with the pride of conscious property, as well as with the eye of taste . . .

A dead calm had succeeded the light breeze, that wafted them hither, and the men took to their oars. Around, the waters were spread into one vast expanse of polished mirror, reflecting the grey cliffs and feathery woods, that over-hung its surface, the glow of the western horizon and the dark clouds, that came slowly from the east. Blanche loved to see the dipping oars imprint the water, and to watch the spreading circles they left, which gave a tremulous motion to the reflected landscape, without destroying the harmony of its features . . .

The Count, looking up, now perceived, that the twilight of evening was anticipated by an approaching storm. In the east a tempest was collecting; a heavy gloom came on, opposing and contrasting the glowing splendour of the setting sun. The clamorous sea-fowl skimmed in fleet circles upon the surface of the sea, dipping their light pinions in the wave, as they fled away in search of shelter. The boatmen pulled hard at their oars; but the thunder, that now muttered at a distance, and the heavy drops, that began to dimple the water, made the Count determine to put back to the monastery for shelter, and the course of the boat was immediately changed. As the clouds approached the west, their lurid darkness changed to a deep ruddy glow, which, by reflection, seemed to fire the tops of the woods and the shattered towers of the monastery.

The appearance of the heavens alarmed the Countess and Mademoiselle Bearn, whose expressions of apprehension distressed the Count, and perplexed his men; while Blanche continued silent, now agitated with fear, and now with admiration, as she viewed the grandeur of the clouds, and their effect on the scenery, and listened to the long, long peals of thunder, that rolled through the air.

The boat having reached the lawn before the monastery, the Count sent a servant to announce his arrival, and to entreat shelter of the Superior, who, soon after, appeared at the great gate, attended by several monks, while the servant returned with a message, expressive at once of hospitality and pride, but of pride disguised in submission. The party immediately disembarked, and, having hastily crossed the lawn—for the shower was now heavy—were received at the gate by the Superior, who, as they entered, stretched forth his hands and gave his blessing; and they passed into the great hall, where the lady abbess waited, attended by several nuns, clothed, like herself, in black, and veiled in white. The veil of the abbess was, however thrown half back, and discovered a countenance, whose chaste dignity was sweetened by the smile of welcome, with which she addressed the Countess, whom she led, with Blanche and Mademoiselle Bearn, into the convent parlour, while the Count and Henri were conducted by the Superior to the refectory.

The Countess, fatigued and discontented, received the politeness of the abbess with careless haughtiness, and had followed her with indolent steps, to the parlour, over which the painted casements and wainscot of larch-wood threw, at all times, a melancholy shade, and where the gloom of evening now loured almost to darkness.

While the lady abbess ordered refreshment, and conversed with the Countess, Blanche withdrew to a window, the lower panes of which, being without painting, allowed her to observe the progress of the storm over the Mediterranean, whose dark waves, that had so lately slept, now came boldly swelling, in long succession, to the shore, where they burst in white foam, and threw up a high spray over the rocks. A red sulphureous tint overspread the long line of clouds, that hung above the western horizon, beneath whose dark skirts the sun looking out, illumined the distant shores of Languedoc, as well as the tufted summits of the nearer woods, and shed a partial gleam on the western waves. The rest of the scene was in deep gloom, except where a sun-beam, darting between the clouds, glanced on the white wings of the sea-fowl, that circled high among them, or touched the swelling sail of a vessel, which was seen labouring in the storm. Blanche, for some time, anxiously watched the progress of the bark, as it threw the waves in foam around it, and, as the lightnings flashed, looked to the opening heavens, with many a sigh for the fate of the poor mariners.

The sun, at length, set, and the heavy clouds, which had long impended, dropped over the splendour of his course; the vessel, however, was yet dimly seen, and Blanche continued to observe it, till the quick succession of flashes, lighting up the gloom of the whole horizon, warned her to retire from the window, and she joined the Abbess, who, having exhausted all her topics of conversation with the Countess, had now leisure to notice her.

But their discourse was interrupted by tremendous peals of thunder; and the bell of the monastery soon after ringing out, summoned the inhabitants to prayer. As Blanche passed the windows, she gave another look to the ocean, where, by the momentary flash, that illumined the vast body of the waters, she distinguished the vessel she had observed before, amidst a sea of foam, breaking the billows, the mast now bowing to the waves, and then rising high in air.

She sighed fervently as she gazed, and then followed the Lady Abbess and the Countess to the chapel. Meanwhile, some of the Count's servants, having gone by land to the chateau for carriages, returned soon after vespers had concluded, when, the storm being somewhat abated, the Count and his family returned home. Blanche was surprised to discover how much the windings of the shore had deceived her, concerning the distance of the chateau from the monastery, whose vesper bell she had heard, on the preceding evening, from the windows of the west saloon, and whose towers she would also have seen from thence, had not twilight veiled them.

On their arrival at the chateau, the Countess, affecting more fatigue, than she really felt, withdrew to her apartment, and the Count, with his daughter and Henri, went to the supper-room, where they had not been long, when they heard, in a pause of the gust, a firing of guns, which the Count understanding to be signals of distress from some vessel in the storm, went to a window, that opened towards the Mediterranean, to observe further; but the sea was now involved in utter darkness, and the loud howlings of the tempest had again overcome every other sound. Blanche, remembering the bark, which she had before seen, now joined her father, with trembling anxiety. In a few moments, the report of guns was again borne along the wind, and as suddenly wafted away; a tremendous burst of thunder followed, and, in the flash that had preceded it, and which seemed to quiver over the whole surface of the waters, a vessel was discovered, tossing amidst the white foam of the waves at some distance from the shore. Impenetrable darkness again involved the scene, but soon a second flash shewed the bark, with one sail unfurled, driving towards the coast. Blanche hung upon her father's arm, with looks full of the agony of united terror and pity, which were unnecessary to awaken the heart of the Count, who gazed upon the sea with a piteous expression, and, perceiving, that no boat could live in the storm, forbore to send one; but he gave orders to his people to carry torches out upon the cliffs, hoping they might prove a kind of beacon to the vessel, or, at least, warn the crew of the rocks they were approaching. While Henri went out to direct on what part of the cliffs the lights should appear, Blanche remained with her father, at the window, catching, every now and then, as the lightning flashed, a glimpse of the vessel; and she soon saw, with reviving hope, the torches flaming on the blackness of night, and, as they waved over the cliffs, casting a red gleam on the gasping billows. When the firing of guns was repeated, the torches were tossed high in the air, as if answering the signal, and the firing was then redoubled; but, though the wind bore the sound away, she fancied, as the lightnings glanced, that the vessel was much nearer the shore.

The Count's servants were now seen, running to and fro, on the rocks; some venturing almost to the point of the crags, and bending over, held out their torches fastened to long poles; while others, whose steps could be traced only by the course of the lights, descended the steep and dangerous path that wound to the margin of the sea, and, with loud halloos, hailed the mariners, whose shrill whistle, and then feeble voices, were heard, at intervals, mingling with the storm. Sudden shouts from the people on the rocks increased the anxiety of Blanche to an almost intolerable degree: but her suspense, concerning the fate of the mariners was soon over, when Henri, running breathless into the room, told that the vessel was anchored in the bay below, but in so shattered a condition, that it was feared she would part before the crew could disembark. The Count immediately gave orders for his own boats to assist in bringing them to shore, and that such of these unfortunate strangers as could not be accommodated in the adjacent hamlet should be entertained at the chateau. Among the latter, were Emily St. Aubert, Monsieur Du Pont, Ludovico and Annette, who, having embarked at Leghorn and reached Marseilles, were from thence crossing the Gulf of Lyons, when this storm overtook them. They were received by the Count with his usual benignity, who, though Emily wished to have proceeded immediately to the monastery of St Claire, would not allow her to leave the chateau, that night; and, indeed, the terror and fatigue she had suffered would scarcely have permitted her to go farther.

1795

# SAMUEL TAYLOR COLERIDGE

## 1772–1834

# The Rime of the Ancient Mariner

### ARGUMENT

How a Ship having passed the Line was driven by storms to the cold Country towards the South Pole; and how from thence she made her course to the tropical Latitude of the Great Pacific Ocean; and of the strange things that befell; and in what manner the Ancyent Marinere came back to his own Countr.

### PART I

An ancient
Mariner
meeteth three
Gallants bidden
to a wedding-
feast, and
detaineth one.

It is an ancient Mariner,
And he stoppeth one of three.
'By thy long grey beard and glittering eye,
Now wherefore stopp'st thou me?

The Bridegroom's doors are opened wide,
And I am next of kin;
The guests are met, the feast is set:
May'st hear the merry din.'

The Wedding-
Guest is spell-
bound by the
eye of the old
sea-faring man,
and constrained
to hear his tale.

He holds him with his skinny hand,
'There was a ship,' quoth he.
'Hold off! unhand me, grey-beard loon!'
Eftsoons his hand dropt he.

He holds him with his glittering eye—
The Wedding-Guest stood still,
And listens like a three years' child:
The Mariner hath his will.

The Wedding-Guest sat on a stone:
He cannot choose but hear;
And thus spake on that ancient man,
The bright-eyed Mariner.

The Mariner tells how the ship sailed southward with a good wind and fair weather, till it reached the line.

'The ship was cheered, the harbour cleared,
Merrily did we drop
Below the kirk, below the hill,
Below the lighthouse top.

The Sun came up upon the left,
Out of the sea came he!
And he shone bright, and on the right
Went down into the sea.

Higher and higher every day,
Till over the mast at noon—
The Wedding-Guest here beat his breast,
For he heard the loud bassoon.

The Wedding-Guest heareth the bridal music; but the Mariner continueth his tale.

The bride hath paced into the hall,
Red as a rose is she;
Nodding their heads before her goes
The merry minstrelsy.

The Wedding-Guest he beat his breast,
Yet he cannot choose but hear;
And thus spake on that ancient man,
The bright-eyed Mariner.

The ship driven by a storm toward the south pole.

'And now the STORM-BLAST came, and he
Was tyrannous and strong:
He struck with his o'ertaking wings,
And chased us south along.

With sloping masts and dipping prow,
As who pursued with yell and blow
Still treads the shadow of his foe,
And forward bends his head,
The ship drove fast, loud roared the blast,
And southward aye we fled.

And now there came both mist and snow,
And it grew wondrous cold:
And ice, mast-high, came floating by,
As green as emerald.

The land of ice, and of fearful sounds where no living thing was to be seen.

And through the drifts the snowy clifts
Did send a dismal sheen:
Nor shapes of men nor beasts we ken—
The ice was all between.

The ice was here, the ice was there,
The ice was all around:
It cracked and growled, and roared and howled,
Like noises in a swound!

Till a great sea-bird, called the Albatross, came through the snow-fog, and was received with great joy and hospitality.

At length did cross an Albatross,
Thorough the fog it came;
As if it had been a Christian soul,
We hailed it in God's name.

It ate the food it ne'er had eat,
And round and round it flew.
The ice did split with a thunder-fit;
The helmsman steered us through!

And lo! the Albatross proveth a bird of good omen, and followeth the ship as it returned northward through fog and floating ice.

And a good south wind sprung up behind;
The Albatross did follow,
And every day, for food or play,
Came to the mariners' hollo!

In mist or cloud, on mast or shroud,
It perched for vespers nine;
Whiles all the night, through fog-smoke white,
Glimmered the white Moon-shine.'

The ancient Mariner inhospitably killeth the pious bird of good omen.

'God save thee, ancient Mariner!
From the fiends, that plague thee thus!—
Why look'st thou so?'—With my crossbow
I shot the ALBATROSS.

### PART II

The Sun now rose upon the right:
Out of the sea came he,
Still hid in mist, and on the left
Went down into the sea.

And the good south wind still blew behind,
But no sweet bird did follow,
Nor any day for food or play
Came to the mariners' hollo!

His shipmates
cry out against
the ancient
Mariner, for
killing the bird
of good luck.

And I had done a hellish thing,
And it would work 'em woe:
For all averred, I had killed the bird
That made the breeze to blow.
Ah wretch! said they, the bird to slay,
That made the breeze to blow!

But when the
fog cleared off,
they justify the
same, and thus
make
themselves
accomplices in
the crime.

Nor dim nor red, like God's own head,
The glorious Sun uprist:
Then all averred, I had killed the bird
That brought the fog and mist.
'Twas right, said they, such birds to slay,
That bring the fog and mist.

The fair breeze
continues; the
ship enters the
Pacific Ocean,
and sails
northward,
even till it
reaches the Line.
The ship hath
been suddenly
becalmed.

The fair breeze blew, the white foam flew,
The furrow followed free;
We were the first that ever burst
Into that silent sea.

Down dropt the breeze, the sails dropt down,
'Twas sad as sad could be;
And we did speak only to break
The silence of the sea!

All in a hot and copper sky,
The bloody Sun, at noon,
Right up above the mast did stand,
No bigger than the Moon.

Day after day, day after day,
We stuck, nor breath, nor motion;
As idle as a painted ship
Upon a painted ocean.

And the
Albatross
begins to be
avenged.

Water, water, every where,
And all the boards did shrink;
Water, water, every where,
Nor any drop to drink.

The very deep did rot: O Christ!
That ever this should be!
Yea, slimy things did crawl with legs
Upon the slimy sea.

About, about, in reel and rout
The death-fires danced at night;
The water, like a witch's oils,
Burnt green, and blue and white.

A Spirit had
followed them;
one of the
invisible
inhabitants of
this planet,

And some in dreams assuréd were
Of the Spirit that plagued us so;
Nine fathom deep he had followed us
From the land of mist and snow.

neither departed souls nor angels; concerning whom the learned Jew, Josephus, and the Platonic
Constantinopolitan, Michael Psellus, may be consulted. They are very numerous, and there is no
climate or element without one or more.

And every tongue, through utter drought,
Was withered at the root;
We could not speak, no more than if
We had been choked with soot.

The shipmates,
in their sore
distress, would
fain throw the
whole guilt on
the ancient

Ah! well a-day! what evil looks
Had I from old and young!
Instead of the cross, the Albatross
About my neck was hung.

Mariner; in sign whereof they hang the dead sea-bird round his neck.

## PART III

There passed a weary time. Each throat
Was parched, and glazed each eye.
A weary time! a weary time!

The ancient
Mariner
beholdeth a sign
in the element
afar off.

How glazed each weary eye,
When looking westward, I beheld
A something in the sky.

At first it seemed a little speck,
And then it seemed a mist;
It moved and moved, and took at last
A certain shape, I wist.


A speck, a mist, a shape, I wist!
And still it neared and neared:
As if it dodged a water-sprite,
It plunged and tacked and veered.

At its nearer
approach, it
seemeth him to
be a ship; and at
a dear ransom
he freeth his
speech from the
bonds of thirst.

With throats unslaked, with black lips baked,
We could nor laugh nor wail;
Through utter drought all dumb we stood!
I bit my arm, I sucked the blood,
And cried, A sail! a sail!


With throats unslaked, with black lips baked,
Agape they heard me call:

A flash of joy;

Gramercy! they for joy did grin,
And all at once their breath drew in,
As they were drinking all.

And horror
follows. For can
it be a ship that
comes onward
without wind or
tide?

See! see! (I cried) she tacks no more!
Hither to work us weal;
Without a breeze, without a tide,
She steadies with upright keel!


The western wave was all a-flame.
The day was well nigh done!
Almost upon the western wave
Rested the broad bright Sun;
When that strange shape drove suddenly
Betwixt us and the Sun.

It seemeth him
but the skeleton
of a ship.

And straight the Sun was flecked with bars,
(Heaven's Mother send us grace!)
As if through a dungeon-grate he peered
With broad and burning face.

Alas! (thought I, and my heart beat loud)
How fast she nears and nears!
Are those *her* sails that glance in the Sun,
Like restless gossameres?

*And its ribs are seen as bars on the face of the setting Sun. The Spectre-Woman and her Death-mate, and no other on board the skeleton ship.*

Are those *her* ribs through which the Sun
Did peer, as through a grate?
And is that Woman all her crew?
Is that a DEATH? and are there two?
Is DEATH that woman's mate?

*Like vessel, like crew!*

*Her* lips were red, *her* looks were free,
Her locks were yellow as gold:
Her skin was as white as leprosy,
The Night-mare LIFE-IN-DEATH was she,
Who thicks man's blood with cold.

*Death and Life-in-Death have diced for the ship's crew, and she (the latter) winneth the ancient Mariner.*

The naked hulk alongside came,
And the twain were casting dice;
'The game is done! I've won! I've won!'
Quoth she, and whistles thrice.

*No twilight within the courts of the Sun.*

The Sun's rim dips; the stars rush out:
At one stride comes the dark;
With far-heard whisper, o'er the sea,
Off shot the spectre-bark.

*At the rising of the Moon,*

We listened and looked sideways up!
Fear at my heart, as at a cup,
My life-blood seemed to sip!
The stars were dim, and thick the night,
The steersman's face by his lamp gleamed white;
From the sails the dew did drip—

Till clomb above the eastern bar
The hornéd Moon, with one bright star
Within the nether tip.

One after
another,

One after one, by the star-dogged Moon,
Too quick for groan or sigh,
Each turned his face with a ghastly pang,
And cursed me with his eye.

His shipmates
drop down
dead.

Four times fifty living men,
(And I heard nor sigh nor groan)
With heavy thump, a lifeless lump,
They dropped down one by one.

But Life-in-
Death begins
her work on the
ancient
Mariner.

The souls did from their bodies fly,—
They fled to bliss or woe!
And every soul, it passed me by,
Like the whizz of my cross-bow!

PART IV

The Wedding-
Guest feareth
that a Spirit is
talking to him;

'I fear thee, ancient Mariner!
I fear thy skinny hand!
And thou art long, and lank, and brown,
As is the ribbed sea-sand.

But the ancient
Mariner
assureth him of
his bodily life,
and proceedeth
to relate his
horrible
penance.

I fear thee and thy glittering eye,
And thy skinny hand, so brown.'—
Fear not, fear not, thou Wedding-Guest!
This body dropt not down.

Alone, alone, all, all alone,
Alone on a wide wide sea!
And never a saint took pity on
My soul in agony.

He despiseth
the creatures of
the calm,

The many men, so beautiful!
And they all dead did lie:
And a thousand thousand slimy things
Lived on; and so did I.

And envieth
that *they* should
live, and so
many lie dead.

I looked upon the rotting sea,
And drew my eyes away;
I looked upon the rotting deck,
And there the dead men lay.

I looked to heaven, and tried to pray;
But or ever a prayer had gusht,
A wicked whisper came, and made
My heart as dry as dust.

I closed my lids, and kept them close,
And the balls like pulses beat;
For the sky and the sea, and the sea and the sky
Lay like a load on my weary eye,
And the dead were at my feet.

*But the curse*
*liveth for him in*
*the eye of the*
*dead men.*

The cold sweat melted from their limbs,
Nor rot nor reek did they:
The look with which they looked on me
Had never passed away.

An orphan's curse would drag to hell
A spirit from on high;
But oh! more horrible than that
Is the curse in a dead man's eye!
Seven days, seven nights, I saw that curse,
And yet I could not die.

*In his loneliness*
*and fixedness he*
*yearneth*
*towards the*
*journeying*
*Moon, and the*
*stars that still*
*sojourn, yet still*
*move onward;*
*and every where*
*the blue sky*
*belongs to*
*them, and is*
*their appointed*
*rest, and their*
*native country*

The moving Moon went up the sky,
And no where did abide:
Softly she was going up,
And a star or two beside—

Her beams bemocked the sultry main,
Like April hoar-frost spread;
But where the ship's huge shadow lay,
The charmèd water burnt alway
A still and awful red.

*and their own natural homes, which they enter unannounced, as lords that are certainly expected*
*and yet there is a silent joy at their arrival.*

*By the light of*
*the Moon he*
*beholdeth*
*God's creatures*
*of the great*
*calm.*

Beyond the shadow of the ship,
I watched the water-snakes:
They moved in tracks of shining white,
And when they reared, the elfish light
Fell off in hoary flakes.

Within the shadow of the ship
I watched their rich attire:
Blue, glossy green, and velvet black,
They coiled and swam; and every track
Was a flash of golden fire.

Their beauty
and their
happiness.

O happy living things! no tongue
Their beauty might declare:
A spring of love gushed from my heart,
And I blessed them unaware:

He blesseth
them in his
heart.

Sure my kind saint took pity on me,
And I blessed them unaware.

The spell begins
to break.

The self-same moment I could pray;
And from my neck so free
The Albatross fell off, and sank
Like lead into the sea.

PART V

Oh sleep! it is a gentle thing,
Beloved from pole to pole!
To Mary Queen the praise be given!
She sent the gentle sleep from Heaven,
That slid into my soul.

By grace of the
holy Mother,
the ancient
Mariner is
refreshed with
rain.

The silly buckets on the deck,
That had so long remained,
I dreamt that they were filled with dew;
And when I awoke, it rained.

My lips were wet, my throat was cold,
My garments all were dank;
Sure I had drunken in my dreams,
And still my body drank.

I moved, and could not feel my limbs:
I was so light—almost
I thought that I had died in sleep,
And was a blessèd ghost.

He heareth
sounds and
seeth strange
sights and
commotions in
the sky and the
element.
And soon I heard a roaring wind:
It did not come anear;
But with its sound it shook the sails,
That were so thin and sere.

The upper air burst into life!
And a hundred fire-flags sheen,
To and fro they were hurried about!
And to and fro, and in and out,
The wan stars danced between.

And the coming wind did roar more loud,
And the sails did sigh like sedge;
And the rain poured down from one black cloud;
The Moon was at its edge.

The thick black cloud was cleft, and still
The Moon was at its side:
Like waters shot from some high crag,
The lightning fell with never a jag,
A river steep and wide.

The bodies of
the ship's crew
are inspired and
the ship moves
on;
The loud wind never reached the ship,
Yet now the ship moved on!
Beneath the lightning and the Moon
The dead men gave a groan.

They groaned, they stirred, they all uprose,
Nor spake, nor moved their eyes;
It had been strange, even in a dream,
To have seen those dead men rise.

The helmsman steered, the ship moved on;
Yet never a breeze up-blew;
The mariners all 'gan work the ropes,
Where they were wont to do;
They raised their limbs like lifeless tools—
We were a ghastly crew.

The body of my brother's son
Stood by me, knee to knee:
The body and I pulled at one rope,
But he said nought to me.

'I fear thee, ancient Mariner!'
Be calm, thou Wedding-Guest!
'Twas not those souls that fled in pain,
Which to their corses came again,
But a troop of spirits blest:

For when it dawned—they dropped their arms,
And clustered round the mast;
Sweet sounds rose slowly through their mouths,
And from their bodies passed.

Around, around, flew each sweet sound,
Then darted to the Sun;
Slowly the sounds came back again,
Now mixed, now one by one.

Sometimes a-dropping from the sky
I heard the sky-lark sing;
Sometimes all little birds that are,
How they seemed to fill the sea and air
With their sweet jargoning!

And now 'twas like all instruments,
Now like a lonely flute;
And now it is an angel's song,
That makes the heavens be mute.

It ceased; yet still the sails made on
A pleasant noise till noon,
A noise like of a hidden brook
In the leafy month of June,
That to the sleeping woods all night
Singeth a quiet tune.

> But not by the souls of the men, nor by daemons of earth or middle air, but by a blessed troop of angelic spirits, sent down by the invocation of the guardian saint.

The lonesome Spirit from the south-pole carries on the ship as far as the Line, in obedience to the angelic troop, but still requireth vengeance.

Till noon we quietly sailed on,
Yet never a breeze did breathe:
Slowly and smoothly went the ship,
Moved onward from beneath.

Under the keel nine fathom deep,
From the land of mist and snow,
The spirit slid: and it was he
That made the ship to go.
The sails at noon left off their tune,
And the ship stood still also.

The Sun, right up above the mast,
Had fixed her to the ocean:
But in a minute she 'gan stir,
With a short uneasy motion—
Backwards and forwards half her length
With a short uneasy motion.

The Polar Spirit's fellow-daemons, the invisible inhabitants of the element, take part in his wrong; and two of them relate, one to the other, that penance long and heavy for the ancient Mariner hath been accorded to the Polar Spirit, who returneth southward.

Then like a pawing horse let go,
She made a sudden bound:
It flung the blood into my head,
And I fell down in a swound.

How long in that same fit I lay,
I have not to declare;
But ere my living life returned,
I heard and in my soul discerned
Two voices in the air.

'Is it he?' quoth one, 'Is this the man?
By him who died on cross,
With his cruel bow he laid full low
The harmless Albatross.

The spirit who bideth by himself
In the land of mist and snow,
He loved the bird that loved the man
Who shot him with his bow.'

The other was a softer voice,
As soft as honey-dew:
Quoth he, 'The man hath penance done,
And penance more will do.'


PART VI

*First Voice*

'But tell me, tell me! speak again,
Thy soft response renewing—
What makes that ship drive on so fast?
What is the ocean doing?'


*Second Voice*

'Still as a slave before his lord,
The ocean hath no blast;
His great bright eye most silently
Up to the Moon is cast—


If he may know which way to go;
For she guides him smooth or grim.
See, brother, see! how graciously
She looketh down on him.'


*First Voice*

The Mariner
hath been cast       'But why drives on that ship so fast,
into a trance;        Without or wave or wind?'
for the angelic
power causeth
the vessel to         *Second Voice*
drive
northward           'The air is cut away before,
faster than          And closes from behind.
human life
could endure.

Fly, brother, fly! more high, more high!
Or we shall be belated:
For slow and slow that ship will go,
When the Mariner's trance is abated.'

I woke, and we were sailing on
As in a gentle weather:
'Twas night, calm night, the moon was high;
The dead men stood together.

All stood together on the deck,
For a charnel-dungeon fitter:
All fixed on me their stony eyes,
That in the Moon did glitter.

The pang, the curse, with which they died,
Had never passed away:
I could not draw my eyes from theirs,
Nor turn them up to pray.

And now this spell was snapt: once more
I viewed the ocean green,
And looked far forth, yet little saw
Of what had else been seen—

Like one, that on a lonesome road
Doth walk in fear and dread,
And having once turned round walks on,
And turns no more his head;
Because he knows, a frightful fiend
Doth close behind him tread.

But soon there breathed a wind on me,
Nor sound nor motion made:
Its path was not upon the sea,
In ripple or in shade.

It raised my hair, it fanned my cheek
Like a meadow-gale of spring—
It mingled strangely with my fears,
Yet it felt like a welcoming.

Swiftly, swiftly flew the ship,
Yet she sailed softly too:
Sweetly, sweetly blew the breeze—
On me alone it blew.

The supernatural motion is retarded; the Mariner awakes, and his penance begins anew.

The curse is finally expiated.

*And the ancient Mariner beholdeth his native country.*

Oh! dream of joy! is this indeed
The light-house top I see?
Is this the hill? is this the kirk?
Is this mine own countree?

We drifted o'er the harbour-bar,
And I with sobs did pray—
O let me be awake, my God!
Or let me sleep alway.

The harbour-bay was clear as glass,
So smoothly it was strewn!
And on the bay the moonlight lay,
And the shadow of the Moon.

The rock shone bright, the kirk no less,
That stands above the rock:
The moonlight steeped in silentness
The steady weathercock.

And the bay was white with silent light,
Till rising from the same,
Full many shapes, that shadows were,
In crimson colours came.

*The angelic spirits leave the dead bodies, And appear in their own forms of light.*

A little distance from the prow
Those crimson shadows were:
I turned my eyes upon the deck—
Oh, Christ! what I saw there!

Each corse lay flat, lifeless and flat,
And, by the holy rood!
A man all light, a seraph-man,
On every corse there stood.

This seraph-band, each waved his hand:
It was a heavenly sight!
They stood as signals to the land,
Each one a lovely light;

This seraph-band, each waved his hand,
No voice did they impart—
No voice; but oh! the silence sank
Like music on my heart.

But soon I heard the dash of oars,
I heard the Pilot's cheer;
My head was turned perforce away
And I saw a boat appear.

The Pilot and the Pilot's boy,
I heard them coming fast:
Dear Lord in Heaven! it was a joy
The dead men could not blast.

I saw a third—I heard his voice:
It is the Hermit good!
He singeth loud his godly hymns
That he makes in the wood.
He'll shrieve my soul, he'll wash away
The Albatross's blood.

## PART VII

*The Hermit of the Wood,*

This Hermit good lives in that wood
Which slopes down to the sea.
How loudly his sweet voice he rears!
He loves to talk with marineres
That come from a far countree.

He kneels at morn, and noon, and eve—
He hath a cushion plump:
It is the moss that wholly hides
The rotted old oak-stump.

The skiff-boat neared: I heard them talk,
'Why, this is strange, I trow!
Where are those lights so many and fair,
That signal made but now?'

Approacheth
the ship with
wonder.

'Strange, by my faith!' the Hermit said—
'And they answered not our cheer!
The planks looked warped! and see those sails,
How thin they are and sere!
I never saw aught like to them,
Unless perchance it were

Brown skeletons of leaves that lag
My forest-brook along;
When the ivy-tod is heavy with snow,
And the owlet whoops to the wolf below,
That eats the she-wolf's young.'

'Dear Lord! it hath a fiendish look—
(The Pilot made reply)
I am a-feared'—'Push on, push on!'
Said the Hermit cheerily.

The boat came closer to the ship,
But I nor spake nor stirred;
The boat came close beneath the ship,
And straight a sound was heard.

The ship
suddenly
sinketh.

Under the water it rumbled on,
Still louder and more dread:
It reached the ship, it split the bay;
The ship went down like lead.

The ancient
Mariner is saved
in the Pilot's
boat.

Stunned by that loud and dreadful sound,
Which sky and ocean smote,
Like one that hath been seven days drowned
My body lay afloat;
But swift as dreams, myself I found
Within the Pilot's boat.

Upon the whirl, where sank the ship,
The boat spun round and round;
And all was still, save that the hill
Was telling of the sound.

I moved my lips—the Pilot shrieked
And fell down in a fit;
The holy Hermit raised his eyes,
And prayed where he did sit.

I took the oars: the Pilot's boy,
Who now doth crazy go,
Laughed loud and long, and all the while
His eyes went to and fro.
'Ha! ha!' quoth he, 'full plain I see,
The Devil knows how to row.'

And now, all in my own countree,
I stood on the firm land!
The Hermit stepped forth from the boat,
And scarcely he could stand.

The ancient Mariner earnestly entreated the Hermit to shrieve him; and the penance of life falls on him.

'O shrieve me, shrieve me, holy man!'
The Hermit crossed his brow.
'Say quick,' quoth he, 'I bid thee say
What manner of man art thou?'

Forthwith this frame of mine was wrenched
With a woful agony,
Which forced me to begin my tale;
And then it left me free.

And ever and anon throughout his future life an agony constraineth him to travel from land to land;

Since then, at an uncertain hour,
That agony returns:
And till my ghastly tale is told,
This heart within me burns.

I pass, like night, from land to land;
I have strange power of speech;
That moment that his face I see,
I know the man that must hear me:
To him my tale I teach.

What loud uproar bursts from that door!
The wedding-guests are there:

But in the garden-bower the bride
And bride-maids singing are:
And hark the little vesper bell,
Which biddeth me to prayer!

O Wedding-Guest! this soul hath been
Alone on a wide wide sea:
So lonely 'twas, that God himself
Scarce seeméd there to be.

O sweeter than the marriage-feast,
'Tis sweeter far to me,
To walk together to the kirk
With a goodly company!—

To walk together to the kirk,
And all together pray,
While each to his great Father bends,
Old men, and babes, and loving friends
And youths and maidens gay!

And to teach,
by his own
example, love
and reverence to
all things that
God made and
loveth.

Farewell, farewell! but this I tell
To thee, thou Wedding-Guest!
He prayeth well, who loveth well
Both man and bird and beast.

He prayeth best, who loveth best
All things both great and small;
For the dear God who loveth us,
He made and loveth all.

The Mariner, whose eye is bright,
Whose beard with age is hoar,
Is gone: and now the Wedding-Guest
Turned from the bridegroom's door.

He went like one that hath been stunned,
And is of sense forlorn:
A sadder and a wiser man,
He rose the morrow morn.

1798

# from *Biographia Literaria*

[In the North Sea, sailing from Yarmouth to Hamburg on the packet
. . . ]†

At four o'clock I observed a wild duck swimming on the waves, a
single solitary wild duck. It is not easy to conceive, how interesting a
thing it looked in that round objectless desert of waters. I had
associated such a feeling of immensity with the ocean, that I felt
exceedingly disappointed, when I was out of sight of all land, at the
narrowness and nearness, as it were, of the circle of the horizon. So
little are images capable of satisfying the obscure feelings connected
with words.

1817

---

# WILLIAM COWPER

1731–1800

# 'The Castaway'

Obscurest night involved the sky,
　The Atlantic billows roared,
When such a destined wretch as I,
　Washed headlong from on board,
Of friends, of hope, of all bereft,
His floating home for ever left.

---

† This was in 1798—shortly after Coleridge had completed *The Rime of the Ancient
Mariner.*

No braver chief could Albion boast
    Than he with whom he went,
Nor ever ship left Albion's coast,
    With warmer wishes sent.
He loved them both, but both in vain,
Nor him beheld, nor her again.

Not long beneath the whelming brine,
    Expert to swim, he lay;
Nor soon he felt his strength decline,
    Or courage die away;
But waged with death a lasting strife,
Supported by despair of life.

He shouted: nor his friends had failed
    To check the vessel's course,
But so the furious blast prevailed,
    That, pitiless perforce,
They left their outcast mate behind,
And scudded still before the wind.

Some succour yet they could afford;
    And, such as storms allow,
The cask, the coop, the floated cord,
    Delayed not to bestow.
But he (they knew) nor ship, nor shore,
Whate'er they gave, should visit more.

Nor, cruel as it seemed, could he
    Their haste himself condemn,
Aware that flight, in such a sea,
    Alone could rescue them;
Yet bitter felt it still to die
Deserted, and his friends so nigh.

He long survives, who lives an hour
    In ocean, self-upheld;
And so long he, with unspent power,
    His destiny repelled;
And ever, as the minutes flew,
Entreated help, or cried—Adieu!

At length, his transient respite past,
  His comrades, who before
Had heard his voice in every blast,
  Could catch the sound no more.
For then, by toil subdued, he drank
The stifling wave, and then he sank.

No poet wept him: but the page
  Of narrative sincere,
That tells his name, his worth, his age,
  Is wet with Anson's tear.
And tears by bards or heroes shed
Alike immortalize the dead.

I therefore purpose not, or dream,
  Descanting on his fate,
To give the melancholy theme
  A more enduring date:
But misery still delights to trace
Its semblance in another's case.

No voice divine the storm allayed,
  No light propitious shone;
When, snatched from all effectual aid,
  We perished, each alone:
But I beneath a rougher sea,
And whelmed in deeper gulfs than he.

                    1803

# J. M. W. TURNER

## 1779–1851

## 'Foam's Frail Power'

    the gay occident of saffron hue
In tenderest medium of distance blue
While the deep ocean heaves (in) a smooth trance
Calm foamless far distance
The beauties and the wonder of the deep
While the blanchd spots of canvas creep
Upon the dark medium as village spires
Point as in foam where Hope aspires
The blanchd sand within the reach of tide
Glimers in lucid interval the washing pride
With little murmurs breaks along the shore
In t(r)eacherous smoothness scarcely whited o'r
With foam(s) frail power undulating

1811

# PERCY BYSSHE SHELLEY
## 1792–1822

## from 'Lines Written among the Euganean Hills'

Many a green isle needs must be
In the deep wide sea of misery,
Or the mariner, worn and wan,
Never thus could voyage on
Day and night, and night and day,
Drifting on his dreary way,
With the solid darkness black
Closing round his vessel's track;
Whilst above the sunless sky,
Big with clouds, hangs heavily,
And behind the tempest fleet
Hurries on with lightning feet,
Riving sail, and cord, and plank,
Till the ship has almost drank
Death from the o'er-brimming deep;
And sinks down, down, like that sleep
When the dreamer seems to be
Weltering through eternity;
And the dim low line before
Of a dark and distant shore
Still recedes, as ever still
Longing with divided will,
But no power to seek or shun,
He is ever drifted on
O'er the unreposing wave
To the haven of the grave.

1818

# from letter to Thomas Love Peacock

We set off an hour after sunrise one radiant morning in a little boat;
there was not a cloud in the sky, nor a wave upon the sea, which was
so translucent that you could see the hollow caverns clothed with the
glaucous sea-moss, and the leaves and branches of those delicate
weeds that pave the unequal bottom of the water. As noon approached,
the heat, and especially the light, became intense. We passed Posilipo,
and came first to the eastern point of the bay of Puzzoli, which is
within the great bay of Naples, and which again incloses that of Baiae.
Here are lofty rocks and craggy islets, with arches and portals of
precipice standing in the sea, and enormous caverns, which echoed
faintly with the murmur of the languid tide. This is called La Scuola di
Virgilio. We then went directly across to the promontory of Misenum,
leaving the precipitous island of Nisida on the right. Here we were
conducted to see the Mare Morto, and the Elysian Fields; the spot on
which Virgil places the scenery of the Sixth Aeneid. Though extremely
beautiful, as a lake, and woody hills, and this divine sky must make it,
I confess my disappointment. The guide showed us an antique
cemetery, where the niches used for placing the cinerary urns of the
dead yet remain. We then coasted the bay of Baiae to the left, in which
we saw many picturesque and interesting ruins; but I have to remark
that we never disembarked but we were disappointed—while from
the boat the effect of the scenery was inexpressibly delightful. The
colours of the water and the air breathe over all things here the
radiance of their own beauty. After passing the bay of Baiae, and
observing the ruins of its antique grandeur standing like rocks in the
transparent sea under our boat, we landed to visit lake Avernus. We
passed through the cavern of the Sibyl (not Virgil's Sibyl) which
pierces one of the hills which circumscribe the lake, and came to a
calm and lovely basin of water, surrounded by dark woody hills, and
profoundly solitary. Some vast ruins of the temple of Pluto stand on a
lawny hill on one side of it, and are reflected in its windless mirror. It
is far more beautiful than the Elysian Fields—but there are all the
materials for beauty in the latter, and the Avernus was once a chasm
of deadly and pestilential vapours. About half a mile from Avernus, a
high hill, called Monte Novo, was thrown up by volcanic fire.

---

P. B. SHELLEY 171

Passing onward we came to Pozzoli, the ancient Dicaearchea, where there are the columns remaining of a temple to Serapis, and the wreck of an enormous amphitheatre, changed, like the Coliseum, into a natural hill of the overteeming vegetation. Here also is the Solfatara, of which there is a poetical description in the Civil War of Petronius, beginning—'Est locus,' and in which the verses of the poet are infinitely finer than what he describes, for it is not a very curious place. After seeing these things we returned by moonlight to Naples in our boat. What colours there were in the sky, what radiance in the evening star, and how the moon was encompassed by a light unknown to our regions!

22 December 1818

## from *Alastor*

Startled by his own thoughts, he looked around.
There was no fair fiend near him, not a sight
Or sound of awe but in his own deep mind.
A little shallop floating near the shore
Caught the impatient wandering of his gaze.
It had been long abandoned, for its sides
Gaped wide with many a rift, and its frail joints
Swayed with the undulations of the tide.
A restless impulse urged him to embark
And meet lone Death on the drear ocean's waste;
For well he knew that mighty Shadow loves
The slimy caverns of the populous deep.

The day was fair and sunny: sea and sky
Drank its inspiring radiance, and the wind
Swept strongly from the shore, blackening the waves.
Following his eager soul, the wanderer
Leaped in the boat, he spread his cloak aloft
On the bare mast, and took his lonely seat,
And felt the boat speed o'er the tranquil sea
Like a torn cloud before the hurricane.

As one that in a silver vision floats
Obedient to the sweep of odorous winds
Upon resplendent clouds, so rapidly
Along the dark and ruffled waters fled
The straining boat.—A whirlwind swept it on,
With fierce gusts and precipitating force,
Through the wide ridges of the chafed sea.
The waves arose. Higher and higher still
Their fierce necks writhed beneath the tempest's scourge
Like serpents struggling in a vulture's grasp.
Calm and rejoicing in the fearful war
Of wave ruining on wave, and blast on blast
Descending, and black flood on whirlpool driven
With dark obliterating course, he sate:
As if their genii were the ministers
Appointed to conduct him to the light
Of those beloved eyes, the Poet sate
Holding the steady helm. Evening came on,
The beams of sunset hung their rainbow hues
High 'mid the shifting domes of sheeted spray
That canopied his path o'er the waste deep;
Twilight, ascending slowly from the east,
Entwin'd in duskier wreaths her braided locks
O'er the fair front and radiant eyes of day;
Night followed, clad with stars. On every side
More horribly the multitudinous streams
Of ocean's mountainous waste to mutual war
Rushed in dark tumult thundering, as to mock
The calm and spangled sky. The little boat
Still fled before the storm; still fled, like foam
Down the steep cataract of a wintry river;
Now pausing on the edge of the riven wave;
Now leaving far behind the bursting mass
That fell, convulsing ocean. Safely fled—
As if that frail and wasted human form
Had been an elemental god.

                    At midnight
The moon arose: and lo! the etherial cliffs
Of Caucasus, whose icy summits shone

Among the stars like sunlight, and around
Whose cavern'd base the whirlpools and the waves
Bursting and eddying irresistibly
Rage and resound for ever.—Who shall save?—
The boat fled on,—the boiling torrent drove,—
The crags closed round with black and jagged arms,
The shattered mountain overhung the sea,
And faster still, beyond all human speed,
Suspended on the sweep of the smooth wave,
The little boat was driven. A cavern there
Yawned, and amid its slant and winding depths
Ingulfed the rushing sea. The boat fled on
With unrelaxing speed. 'Vision and Love!'
The Poet cried aloud, 'I have beheld
The path of thy departure. Sleep and death
Shall not divide us long!'

1816

# from letter to Captain Daniel Roberts

Dear Sir,

The *Don Juan* arrived safe on the evening of Sunday after a long and stormy passage and I have been waiting the clearing up of the weather and the return of the man to write to you. She is a most beautiful boat and so far surpasses both mine and Williams's expectations that it was with some difficulty that we could persuade ourselves that you had not sent us the *Bolivar* by mistake. I do not know how I can express, much less repay, my obligation to you for having sacrificed so much of your time and attention as must have been requisite to produce anything so complete. We were out this morning and for a short time on Sunday evening though the weather was very squally. Yesterday it blew a gale from the South West and she required more reefs than we found in her sails. Today we went from Lerici to Spezzia and back again on a wind in a little more than an hour and a half. I hope, however, soon to see you here, and although I cannot boast very capital accommodation, that you will put up with such quarters as we can afford which after all will be better than the Inn.

Tell Trelawny I write to him by the post; he will arrange with you in what manner I am to remit the rest of the expenses of the boat; I think he told me he wished me to procure him Tuscan crowns to that amount.

Believe me, Dear Sir,
Your very obliged and faithful
P. B. Shelley.

13 May 1822

## from letter to John Gisborne

I have a boat here. It cost me £80 and reduced me to some difficulty in point of money. However, it is swift and beautiful, and appears quite a vessel. Williams is captain, and, we drive along this delightful bay in the evening wind under the summer moon until earth appears another world. Jane brings her guitar, and if the past and future could be obliterated, the present would content me so well that I could say with Faust to the passing moment 'Remain thou, thou art so beautiful.'

18 June 1822

# JANE AUSTEN
## 1775–1817

## from *Sanditon*

He began, in a tone of great taste and feeling, to talk of the sea and the sea shore—and ran with energy through all the usual phrases employed in praise of their sublimity, and descriptive of the *undescribable* emotions they excite in the mind of sensibility. The terrific grandeur of the ocean in a storm, its glassy surface in a calm, its gulls and its samphire, and the deep fathoms of its abysses, its quick vicissitudes, its direful deceptions, its mariners tempting it in sunshine and overwhelmed by the sudden tempest, all were eagerly and fluently touched; rather commonplace perhaps—but doing very well from the lips of a handsome Sir Edward, and she could not but think him a man of feeling—till he begun to stagger her with the number of his quotations, and the bewilderment of some of his sentences.

'Do you remember,' said he, 'Scott's beautiful lines on the sea? Oh! what a description they convey! They are never out of my thoughts when I walk here. That man who can read them unmoved must have the nerves of an assassin! Heaven defend me from meeting such a man un-armed.'

'What description do you mean?' said Charlotte. 'I remember none at this moment, of the sea, in either of Scott's poems.'

'Do you not indeed? Nor can I exactly recall the beginning at this moment—But—you cannot have forgotten his description of Woman—

Oh! Woman in our hours of ease—

1817

---

GEORGE GORDON, LORD BYRON
1788–1824

# verse letter to Francis Hodgson

I

Huzza! Hodgson, we are going,
   Our embargo's off at last
Favourable Breezes blowing
   Bend the canvass oer the mast,
From aloft the signal's streaming
   Hark! the farewell gun is fired,
Women screeching, Tars blaspheming,
   Tells us that our time's expired

Here's a rascal
Come to task all
Prying from the custom house,
Trunks unpacking
Cases cracking
Not a corner for a mouse
Scapes unsearched amid the racket
Ere we sail on board the Packet.


2

Now our boatmen quit their mooring
     And all hands must ply the oar;
Baggage from the quay is lowering,
     We're impatient—push from shore—
'Have a care! that Case holds liquor
     'Stop the boat—I'm sick—oh Lord!
'Sick Maam! damme, you'll be sicker
     Ere you've been an hour on board
          Thus are screaming
          Men & women
     Gemmen, Ladies, servants, Jacks,
          Here entangling
          All are wrangling
     Stuck together close as wax,
Such the genial noise & racket
Ere we reach the Lisbon Packet.


3

Now we've reached her, lo! the Captain
     *Gallant* Kidd commands the crew
Passengers *now* their berths are clapt in
     Some to grumble, some to spew,
Heyday! call you that a Cabin?
     Why tis hardly three feet square
Not enough to stow Queen Mab in,
     Who the deuce can harbour there?
          Who Sir? plenty
          Nobles twenty

Did at once my vessel fill
  Did they—Jesus!
    How you squeeze us
  Would to God, they did so still,
Then I'd scape the heat & racket
Of the good ship, Lisbon Packet.

———

Note + Erratum—
  For 'gallant' read 'gallows.'


4

Fletcher, Murray, Bob, where are you?
  Stretched along the deck like logs
Bear a hand—you jolly tar you!
  Here's a rope's end for the dogs,
Hobhouse muttering fearful curses
  As the hatchway down he rolls
Now his breakfast, now his verses
  Vomits forth & damns our souls,
    Here's a stanza
    On Braganza
  Help!—a couplet— no, a cup
    Of warm water,
      What's the matter?
  Zounds! my liver's coming up,
I shall not survive the racket
Of this brutal Lisbon Packet.


5

Now at length we're off for Turkey,
  Lord knows when we shall come back,
Breezes foul, & tempests murkey,
  May unship us in a crack,
But since life at most a jest is
  As Philosophers allow
Still to laugh by far the best is,
  Then laugh on—as I do now,

Laugh at all things
Great & small things,
Sick or well, at sea or shore,
While we're quaffing
Let's have laughing
Who the Devil cares for more?
Save good wine, & who would lack it?
Even on board the Lisbon Packet.

30 June 1809

## letter to his mother

Two days ago I was nearly lost in a Turkish ship of war owing to the ignorance of the captain & crew though the storm was not violent. Fletcher yelled after his wife, the Greeks called on all the Saints, the Mussulmen on Alla, the Captain burst into tears & ran below deck telling us to call on God, the sails were split, the mainyard shivered, the wind blowing fresh, the night setting in, & all our chance was to make Corfu which is in possession of the French, or (as Fletcher *pathetically* termed it) 'a *watery* grave'. I did what I could to console Fletcher but finding him incorrigible wrapped myself up in my Albanian capote (an immense cloak) & lay down on deck to wait the worst, I have learnt to philosophize on my travels, & if I had not, complaint was useless. Luckily the wind abated & only drove us on the coast of Suli on the main land where we landed & proceeded by the help of the natives to Prevesa again; but I shall not trust Turkish Sailors in future.

12 November 1809

## from *Childe Harold's Pilgrimage*, Canto IV

### CLXXVIII

There is a pleasure in the pathless woods,
There is a rapture on the lonely shore,
There is society where none intrudes,
By the deep Sea, and music in its roar:
I love not man the less, but Nature more,

From these our interviews, in which I steal
From all I may be, or have been before,
To mingle with the Universe, and feel
What I can ne'er express, yet cannot all conceal.

## CLXXIX

Roll on, thou deep and dark blue Ocean—roll!
Ten thousand fleets sweep over thee in vain;
Man marks the earth with ruin—his control
Stops with the shore;—upon the watery plain
The wrecks are all thy deed, nor doth remain
A shadow of man's ravage, save his own,
When for a moment, like a drop of rain,
He sinks into thy depths with bubbling groan,
Without a grave, unknell'd, uncoffin'd and unknown.

## CLXXXIII

Thou glorious mirror, where the Almighty's form
Glasses itself in tempests; in all time,
Calm, or convulsed—in breeze, or gale, or storm,
Icing the pole, or in the torrid clime
Dark heaving; boundless, endless, and sublime—
The image of Eternity—the throne
Of the Invisible; even from out thy slime
The monsters of the deep are made; each zone
Obeys thee; thou goest forth, dread, fathomless, alone.

## CLXXXIV

And I have loved thee, Ocean! and my joy
Of youthful sports was on thy breast to be
Borne like thy bubbles, onward: from a boy
I wanton'd with thy breakers—they to me
Were a delight; and if the freshening sea
Made them a terror—'twas a pleasing fear,
For I was as it were a child of thee,
And trusted to thy billows far and near,
And laid my hand upon thy mane—as I do here.

1818

# from *Don Juan*, Canto II

### 24

The ship, called the most holy *Trinidada*,
  Was steering duly for the port Leghorn,
For there the Spanish family Moncada
  Were settled long ere Juan's sire was born.
They were relations, and for them he had a
  Letter of introduction, which the morn
Of his departure had been sent him by
His Spanish friends for those in Italy.

### 25

His suite consisted of three servants and
  A tutor, the licentiate Pedrillo,
Who several languages did understand,
  But now lay sick and speechless on his pillow,
And rocking in his hammock, longed for land,
  His headache being increased by every billow.
And the waves oozing through the porthole made
His berth a little damp, and him afraid.

### 26

'Twas not without some reason, for the wind
  Increased at night until it blew a gale;
And though 'twas not much to a naval mind,
  Some landsmen would have looked a little pale,
For sailors are in fact a different kind.
  At sunset they began to take in sail,
For the sky showed it would come on to blow
And carry away perhaps a mast or so.

### 27

At one o'clock the wind with sudden shift
  Threw the ship right into the trough of the sea,

Which struck her aft and made an awkward rift,
    Started the sternpost, also shattered the
Whole of her stern-frame, and ere she could lift
    Herself from out her present jeopardy
The rudder tore away. 'Twas time to sound
The pumps, and there were four feet water found.


28

One gang of people instantly was put
    Upon the pumps and the remainder set
To get up part of the cargo and what not,
    But they could not come at the leak as yet.
At last they did get at it really, but
    Still their salvation was an even bet.
The water rushed through in a way quite puzzling,
While they thrust sheets, shirts, jackets, bales of muslin


29

Into the opening, but all such ingredients
    Would have been vain, and they must have gone down,
Despite of all their efforts and expedients,
    But for the pumps. I'm glad to make them known
To all the brother tars who may have need hence,
    For fifty tons of water were upthrown
By them per hour, and they had all been undone
But for the maker, Mr Mann, of London.


30

As day advanced the weather seemed to abate,
    And then the leak they reckoned to reduce
And keep the ship afloat, though three feet yet
    Kept two hand and one chain pump still in use.
The wind blew fresh again; as it grew late
    A squall came on, and while some guns broke loose,
A gust, which all descriptive power transcends,
Laid with one blast the ship on her beam ends.

### 31

There she lay, motionless, and seemed upset.
　　The water left the hold and washed the decks
And made a scene men do not soon forget,
　　For they remember battles, fires, and wrecks,
Or any other thing that brings regret
　　Or breaks their hopes or hearts or heads or necks.
Thus drownings are much talked of by the divers
And swimmers who may chance to be survivors.


### 32

Immediately the masts were cut away,
　　Both main and mizen. First the mizen went,
The mainmast followed, but the ship still lay
　　Like a mere log and baffled our intent.
Foremast and bowsprit were cut down, and they
　　Eased her at last (although we never meant
To part with all till every hope was blighted),
And then with violence the old ship righted.


### 33

It may be easily supposed, while this
　　Was going on, some people were unquiet,
That passengers would find it much amiss
　　To lose their lives as well as spoil their diet,
That even the able seaman, deeming his
　　Days nearly o'er, might be disposed to riot,
As upon such occasions tars will ask
For grog and sometimes drink rum from the cask.


### 34

There's nought no doubt so much the spirit calms
　　As rum and true religion; thus it was,
Some plundered, some drank spirits, some sung psalms
　　The high wind made the treble, and as bass
The hoarse harsh waves kept time. Fright cured the qualms
　　Of all the luckless landsmen's seasick maws.

Strange sounds of wailing, blasphemy, devotion
Clamoured in chorus to the roaring ocean.

1819 24

―――

## JOHN KEATS
### 1795–1821

## 'The Sea'

It keeps eternal whisperings around
   Desolate shores, and with its mighty swell
   Gluts twice ten thousand caverns, till the spell
Of Hecate leaves them their old shadowy sound.
Often 'tis in such gentle temper found,
   That scarcely will the very smallest shell
   Be moved for days from whence it sometime fell,
When last the winds of heaven were unbound.
Oh ye! who have your eye-balls vex'd and tired,
   Feast them upon the wideness of the Sea;
Oh ye! whose ears are dinn'd with uproar rude,
   Or fed too much with cloying melody—
Sit ye near some old cavern's mouth, and brood
Until ye start, as if the sea-nymphs quired!

1820?

―――

# CHARLES LAMB

## 1775–1834

# from 'The Old Margate Hoy'

Will it be thought a digression (it may spare some unwelcome comparisons) if I endeavour to account for the *dissatisfaction* which I have heard so many persons confess to have felt (as I did myself feel in part on this occasion), *at the sight of the sea for the first time*? I think the reason usually given—referring to the incapacity of actual objects for satisfying our preconceptions of them—scarcely goes deep enough into the question. Let the same person see a lion, an elephant, a mountain for the first time in his life, and he shall perhaps feel himself a little mortified. The things do not fill up that space which the idea of them seemed to take up in his mind. But they have still a correspond-ency to his first notion, and in time grow up to it, so as to produce a very similar impression: enlarging themselves (if I may say so) upon familiarity. But the sea remains a disappointment. It is not, that in *the latter* we had expected to behold (absurdly, I grant, but, I am afraid, by the law of imagination, unavoidably) not a definite object, as those wild beasts, or that mountain compassable by the eye, but *all the sea at once*, THE COMMENSURATE ANTAGONIST OF THE EARTH? I do not say we tell ourselves so much, but the craving of the mind is to be satisfied with nothing less. I will suppose the case of a young person of fifteen (as I then was) knowing nothing of the sea, but from description. He comes to it for the first time—all that he has been reading of it all his life, and *that* the most enthusiastic part of life—all he has gathered from narratives of wandering seamen—what he has gained from true voyages, and what he cherishes as credulously from romance and poetry—crowding their images, and exacting strange tributes from expectation. He thinks of the great deep, and of those who go down unto it; of its thousand isles, and of the vast continents it washes; of its receiving the mighty Plata, or Orellana, into its bosom, without disturbance, or sense of augmentation; of Biscay swells, and the mariner

> For many a day, and many a dreadful night,
> Incessant labouring round the stormy Cape;

of fatal rocks, and the 'still-vexed Bermoothes'; of great whirlpools, and the water-spout; of sunken ships, and sumless treasures swallowed up in the unrestoring depths; of fishes and quaint monsters, to which all that is terrible on earth—

> Be but as buggs to frighten babes withal,
> Compared with the creatures in the sea's entral;

of naked savages, and Juan Fernandez; of pearls, and shells; of coral beds, and of enchanted isles; of mermaids' grots—

I do not assert that in sober earnest he expects to be shown all these wonders at once, but he is under the tyranny of a mighty faculty, which haunts him with confused hints and shadows of all these; and when the actual object opens first upon him, seen (in tame weather, too, most likely) from our unromantic coasts—a speck, a slip of sea-water, as it shows to him—what can it prove but a very unsatisfying and even diminutive entertainment? Or if he has come to it from the mouth of a river, was it much more than the river widening? and, even out of sight of land, what had he but a flat watery horizon about him, nothing comparable to the vast o'er-curtaining sky, his familiar object, seen daily without dread or amazement? Who, in similar circumstances, has not been tempted to exclaim with Charoba, in the poem of Gebir,

> Is this the mighty ocean? is this all?

I love town, or country; but this detestable Cinque Port is neither. I hate these scrubbed shoots, thrusting out their starved foliage from between the horrid fissures of dusty innutritious rocks; which the amateur calls 'verdure to the edge of the sea'. I require woods, and they show me stunted coppices. I cry out for the water-brooks, and pant for fresh streams, and inland murmurs. I cannot stand all day on the naked beach, watching the capricious hues of the sea, shifting like the colours of a dying mullet. I am tired of looking out at the windows of this island-prison. I would fain retire into the interior of my cage. While I gaze upon the sea, I want to be on it, over it, across it. It binds me in with chains, as of iron. My thoughts are abroad. I should not so feel in Staffordshire. There is no home for me here. There is no sense of home at Hastings. It is a place of fugitive resort, an heterogeneous assemblage of sea-mews and stock-brokers, Amphitrites of the town, and misses that coquet with the Ocean. If it were what it was in its primitive shape, and what it ought to have remained, a fair, honest fishing-town, and no more, it were something—with a few straggling fishermen's huts scattered about, artless as its cliffs, and with their materials filched from them, it were something. I could abide to dwell with Mesheck; to assort with fisher-swains, and smugglers. There are, or I dream there are, many of this latter occupation here. Their faces become the place. I like a smuggler. He is the only honest thief. He robs nothing but the revenue—an abstraction I never greatly cared about. I could go out with them in their mackerel boats, or about their less ostensible business, with some satisfaction. I can even tolerate those poor victims to monotony, who from day to day pace along the beach, in endless progress and recurrence, to watch their illicit countrymen—townsfolk or brethren, perchance—whistling to the sheathing and unsheathing of their cutlasses (their only solace), who, under the mild name of preventive service, keep up a legitimated civil warfare in the deplorable absence of a foreign one, to show their detestation of run hollands, and zeal for Old England. But it is the visitants from town, that come here to *say* that they have been here, with no more relish of the sea than a pond-perch or a dace might be supposed to have, that are my aversion. I feel like a foolish dace in these regions, and have as little toleration for myself here as for them. What can they want here? If they had a true relish of the ocean, why have they brought all this land luggage with them? or why pitch their civilized tents in the desert? What mean these scanty book-rooms—marine libraries as they entitle them—if the sea were, as they would have us believe, a book 'to read strange matter in'? What are their foolish concert-rooms, if they come, as they would fain be thought to do, to listen to the music of the waves? All is false and hollow pretension. They come because it is the fashion, and to spoil the nature of the place. They are, mostly, as I have said, stock-brokers; but I have watched the better sort of them—now and then, an honest citizen (of the old stamp), in the simplicity of his heart, shall bring down his wife and daughters to taste the sea breezes. I always know the date of their arrival. It is easy to see it in their countenance. A day or two they go wandering on the shingles, picking up cockle-shells, and thinking them great things; but, in a poor week, imagination slackens: they begin to discover that cockles produce no pearls, and then—O then!—if I could interpret for the pretty creatures (I know they have not the courage to confess it themselves), how gladly would they exchange their seaside rambles for a Sunday walk on the green sward of their accustomed Twickenham meadows!

I would ask one of these sea-charmed emigrants, who think they truly love the sea, with its wild usages, what would their feelings be if some of the unsophisticated aborigines of this place, encouraged by their courteous questionings here, should venture, on the faith of such assured sympathy between them, to return the visit, and come up to see—London. I must imagine them with their fishing-tackle on their back, as we carry our town necessaries. What a sensation would it cause in Lothbury! What vehement laughter would it not excite among

> The daughters of Cheapside, and wives of Lombard-street!

I am sure that no town-bred or inland-born subjects can feel their true and natural nourishment at these sea-places. Nature, where she does not mean us for mariners and vagabonds, bids us stay at home. The salt foam seems to nourish a spleen. I am not half so good-natured as by the milder waters of my natural river. I would exchange these sea-gulls for swans, and scud a swallow for ever about the banks of Thamesis.

1823

# JAMES FENIMORE COOPER

## 1789–1851

# from *The Pilot*

The Ariel continued to struggle against the winds and ocean for several hours longer before the day broke on the tempestuous scene, and the anxious mariners were enabled to form a more accurate estimate of their real danger. As the violence of the gale increased, the canvas of the schooner had been gradually reduced, until she was unable to show more than was absolutely necessary to prevent her driving helplessly on the land. Barnstable watched the appearance of the weather, as the light slowly opened upon them, with an intense anxiety, which denoted that the presentiments of the cockswain were no longer deemed idle. On looking to windward, he beheld the green masses of water that were rolling in toward the land, with a violence that seemed irresistible, crowned with ridges of foam; and there were moments when the air appeared filled with sparkling gems, as the rays of the rising sun fell upon the spray that was swept from wave to wave. Toward the land the view was still more appalling. The cliffs, but a short half league under the lee of the schooner, were, at all times, nearly hid from the eye by the pyramids of water, which the furious element, so suddenly restrained in its violence, cast high into the air, as if seeking to overlap the boundaries that Nature had fixed to its dominion. The whole coast, from the distant headland at the south to the well-known shoals that stretched far beyond their course in the opposite direction, displayed a broad belt of foam, into which it would have been certain destruction for the proudest ship that ever swam to enter. Still the Ariel floated on the billows, lightly and in safety, though yielding to the impulses of the waters, and, at times, appearing to be engulfed in the yawning chasms, which, apparently, opened beneath her to receive the little fabric. The low rumor of acknowledged danger had found its way through the schooner, and the seamen, after fastening their hopeless looks on the small spot of canvas that they were still able to show to the tempest, would turn to view the dreary line of coast that seemed to offer so gloomy an alternative. Even Dillon, to whom the report of their danger had found its way, crept from his place of concealment in the cabin, and moved about the decks, unheeded, devouring, with greedy ears, such opinions as fell from the lips of the sullen mariners.

At this moment of appalling apprehension, the cockswain exhibited the calmest resignation. He knew all had been done that lay in the power of man to urge their little vessel from the land, and it was now too evident to his experienced eyes that it had been done in vain; but, considering himself as a sort of fixture in the schooner, he was quite prepared to abide her fate, be it for better or for worse. The settled look of gloom that gathered around the frank brow of Barnstable was in no degree connected with any considerations of himself; but proceeded from that sort of parental responsibility from which the sea-commander is never exempt. The discipline of the crew, however, still continued perfect and unyielding. There had, it is true, been a slight movement made by one or two of the older seamen, which indicated an intention to drown the apprehensions of death in inebriety; but Barnstable had called for his pistols, in a tone that checked the procedure instantly, and, although the fatal weapons were, untouched by him, left to lie exposed on the capstan, where they had been placed by his servant, not another symptom of insubordination appeared among the devoted crew. There was even what, to a landsman, might seem an appalling affectation of attention to the most trifling duties of the vessel; and the men who, it should seem, ought to be devoting the brief moments of their existence to the mighty business of the hour, were constantly called to attend to the most trivial details of their profession. Ropes were coiled, and the slightest damages occasioned by the waves, which, at short intervals, swept across the low decks of the Ariel, were repaired, with the same precision and order as if she yet lay embayed in the haven from which she had just been driven. In this manner the arm of authority was kept extended over the silent crew, not with the vain desire to preserve a lingering though useless exercise of power, but with a view to maintain that unity of action that now could alone afford them even a ray of hope.

'She can make no head against this sea, under that rag of canvas,' said Barnstable, gloomily, addressing the cockswain, who, with folded arms, and an air of cool resignation, was balancing his body on the verge of the quarter-deck, while the schooner was plunging madly into waves that nearly buried her in their bosom; 'the poor little thing trembles like a frightened child, as she meets the water.'

Tom sighed heavily, and shook his head, before he answered:

'If we could have kept the head of the mainmast an hour longer, we might have got an offing, and fetched to windward of the shoals; but as it is, sir, mortal man can't drive a craft to windward—she sets bodily in to land, and will be in the breakers in less than an hour, unless God wills that the wind shall cease to blow.'

'We have no hope left us but to anchor; our ground tackle may yet bring her up.'

Tom turned to his commander, and replied, solemnly, and with that assurance of manner that long experience only can give a man in moments of great danger:

'If our sheet-cable was bent to our heaviest anchor, this sea would bring it home, though nothing but her launch was riding by it. A north-easter in the German Ocean must and will blow itself out; nor shall we get the crown of the gale until the sun falls over the land. Then indeed it may lull; for the winds do often seem to reverence the glory of the heavens too much to blow their might in its very face!'

'We must do our duty to ourselves and the country,' returned Barnstable. 'Go, get the two bowers spliced, and have a kedge bent to a hawser; we'll back our two anchors together, and veer to the better end of two hundred and forty fathoms; it may yet bring her up. See all clear there for anchoring, and cutting away the mast! We'll leave the wind nothing but a naked hull to whistle over.'

'Ay, if there was nothing but the wind, we might yet live to see the sun sink behind them hills,' said the cockswain, 'but what hemp can stand the strain of a craft that is buried, half the time, to her foremast in the water?'

The order was, however, executed by the crew, with a sort of desperate submission to the will of their commander; and, when the preparations were completed, the anchors and kedge were dropped to the bottom, and the instant that the Ariel tended to the wind, the axe was applied to the little that was left of her long, raking masts. The crash of the falling spars, as they came, in succession, across the decks of the vessel, appeared to produce no sensation amid that scene of complicated danger; but the seamen proceeded in silence to their hopeless duty of clearing the wrecks. Every eye followed the floating timbers, as the waves swept them away from the vessel, with a sort of feverish curiosity to witness the effect produced by their collision with those rocks that lay so fearfully near them; but long before the spars entered the wide border of foam, they were hid from view by the furious element in which they floated. It was now felt by the whole crew of the Ariel that their last means of safety had been adopted; and, at each desperate and headlong plunge the vessel took, into the bosom of the seas that rolled upon her forecastle, the anxious seamen thought that they could perceive the yielding of the iron that yet clung to the bottom, or could hear the violent surge of the parting strands of the cable, that still held them to their anchors. While the minds of the sailors were agitated with the faint hopes that had been excited by the movements of their schooner, Dillon had been permitted to wander about the deck unnoticed; his rolling eyes, hard breathing, and clinched hands, excited no observation among the men, whose thoughts were yet dwelling on the means of safety. But now, when with a sort of frenzied desperation he would follow the retiring waters along the decks, and venture his person nigh the group that had collected around and on the gun of the cockswain, glances of fierce or of sullen vengeance were cast at him, that conveyed threats of a nature that he was too much agitated to understand.

'If ye are tired of this world, though your time, like my own, is probably but short in it,' said Tom to him, as he passed the cockswain in one of his turns, 'you can go forward among the men; but if we have need of the moments to foot up the reck'ning of your doings among men, afore ye're brought to face your Maker, and hear the logbook of Heaven, I would advise you to keep as nigh as possible to Captain Barnstable or myself.'

'Will you promise to save me if the vessel is wrecked?' exclaimed Dillon, catching at the first sounds of friendly interest that had reached his ears since he had been recaptured. 'Oh! if you will, I can secure your future ease, yes, wealth, for the remainder of your days!'

'Your promises have been too ill kept afore this, for the peace of your soul,' returned the cockswain, without bitterness, though sternly; 'but it is not in me to strike even a whale that is already spouting blood.'

The intercessions of Dillon were interrupted by a dreadful cry, that arose among the men forward, and which sounded with increased horror, amid the roarings of the tempest. The schooner rose on the breast of a wave at the same instant, and, falling off with her broadside to the sea, she drove in towards the cliffs, like a bubble on the rapids of a cataract.

'Our ground-tackle has parted,' said Tom, with his resigned patience of manner undisturbed; 'she shall die as easy as man can make her!' While he yet spoke, he seized the tiller, and gave to the vessel such a direction as would be most likely to cause her to strike the rocks with her bows foremost.

There was for one moment an expression of exquisite anguish betrayed in the dark countenance of Barnstable; but at the next it passed away, and he spoke cheerfully to his men:

'Be steady, my lads, be calm: there is yet a hope of life for you— our light draught will let us run in close to the cliffs, and it is still falling water—see your boats clear, and be steady.'

The crew of the whale-boat, aroused by this speech from a sort of stupor, sprang into their light vessel, which was quickly lowered into the sea, and kept riding on the foam, free from the sides of the schooner, by the powerful exertions of the men. The cry for the cockswain was earnest and repeated, but Tom shook his head, without replying, still grasping the tiller, and keeping his eyes steadily bent on the chaos of waters into which they were driving. The launch, the largest boat of the two, was cut loose from the 'gripes', and the bustle and exertions of the moment rendered the crew insensible to the horror of the scene that surrounded them. But the loud, hoarse call of the cockswain, to 'look out—secure yourselves!' suspended even their efforts, and at that instant the Ariel settled, on a wave that melted from under her, heavily on the rocks. The shock was so violent as to throw all who disregarded the warning cry from their feet, and the universal quiver that pervaded the vessel was like the last shudder of animated nature. For a time long enough to breathe, the least experienced among the men supposed the danger to be past; but a wave of great height followed the one that had deserted them, and raising the vessel again, threw her roughly still farther on the bed of rocks, and at the same time its crest broke over her quarter, sweeping the length of her decks with a fury that was almost resistless. The shuddering seamen beheld their loosened boat driven from their grasp, and dashed against the base of the cliffs, where no fragment of her wreck could be traced at the receding of the waters. But the passing billow had thrown the vessel into a position which in some measure, protected her decks from the violence of those that succeeded it.

'Go, my boys, go,' said Barnstable, as the moment of dreadful uncertainty passed; 'you have still the whale-boat, and she, at least, will take you nigh the shore. Go into her, my boys. God bless you, God bless you all! You have been faithful and honest fellows, and I believe He will not desert you; go, my friends, while there is a lull.'

The seamen threw themselves, in a mass, into the light vessel, which nearly sank under the unusual burden; but when they looked around them, Barnstable and Merry, Dillon and the cockswain, were yet to be seen on the decks of the Ariel. The former was pacing, in deep and perhaps bitter melancholy, the wet planks of the schooner, while the boy hung, unheeded on his arm, uttering disregarded petitions to his commander to desert the wreck. Dillon approached the side where the boat lay, again and again, but the threatening countenances of the seamen as often drove him back in despair. Tom had seated himself on the heel of the bowsprit, where he continued, in an attitude of quiet resignation, returning no other answers to the loud and repeated calls of his shipmates, than by waving his hand toward the shore.

'Now hear me,' said the boy, urging his request to tears; 'if not for my sake or for your own sake, Mr Barnstable, or for the hope of God's mercy, go into the boat, for the love of my cousin Katherine.'

The young lieutenant paused in his troubled walk, and for a moment he cast a glance of hesitation at the cliffs; but at the next instant his eyes fell on the ruin of his vessel, and he answered:

'Never, boy, never; if my hour has come, I will not shrink from my fate.'

'Listen to the men, dear sir; the boat will be swamped, alongside the wreck, and their cry is, that without you they will not let her go.'

Barnstable motioned to the boat, to bid the boy enter it, and turned away in silence.

'Well,' said Merry, with firmness, 'if it be right that a lieutenant shall stay by the wreck, it must also be right for a midshipman! Shove off; neither Mr Barnstable nor myself will quit the vessel.'

'Boy, your life has been entrusted to my keeping, and at my hands will it be required,' said the commander, lifting the struggling youth and tossing him into the arms of the seamen. 'Away with ye, and God be with you; there is more weight in you now than can go safe to land.'

Still the seamen hesitated, for they perceived the cockswain moving, with a steady tread, along the deck, and they hoped he had relented and would yet persuade the lieutenant to join his crew. But Tom, imitating the example of his commander, seized the latter suddenly in his powerful grasp, and threw him over the bulwarks with an irresistible force. At the same moment he cast the fast of the boat from the pin that held it, and, lifting his broad hands high into the air, his voice was heard in the tempest:

'God's will be done with me!' he cried. 'I saw the first timber of the Ariel laid, and shall live just long enough to see it torn out of her bottom; after which I wish to live no longer.'

But his shipmates were swept far beyond the sound of his voice before half these words were uttered. All command of the boat was rendered impossible by the numbers it contained, as well as the raging of the surf; and, as it rose on the white crest of a wave, Tom saw his beloved little craft for the last time. It fell into a trough of the sea, and in a few moments more its fragments were ground into splinters on the adjacent rocks. The cockswain still remained where he had cast off the rope, and beheld the numerous heads and arms that appeared rising, at short intervals, on the waves; some making powerful and well-directed efforts to gain the sands, that were becoming visible as the tide fell, and others wildly tossed in the frantic movements of helpless despair. The honest old seaman gave a

cry of joy, as he saw Barnstable issue from the surf, bearing the form
of Merry in safety to the sands, where one by one several seamen
soon appeared also, dripping and exhausted. Many others of the crew
were carried, in a similar manner, to places of safety; though, as Tom
returned to his seat on the bowsprit, he could not conceal from his
reluctant eyes the lifeless forms that were, in other spots, driven
against the rocks with a fury that soon left them but few of the
outward vestiges of humanity.

Dillon and the cockswain were now the sole occupants of their
dreadful station. The former stood in a kind of stupid despair, a
witness of the scene we have related; but, as his curdled blood began
again to flow more warmly through his heart, he crept close to the
side of Tom, with that sort of selfish feeling that makes even hopeless
misery more tolerable, when endured in participation with another.

'When the tide falls,' he said, in a voice that betrayed the agony of
fear, though his words expressed the renewal of hope, 'we shall be
able to walk to land.'

'There was One, and only One, to whose feet the waters were the
same as a dry deck,' returned the cockswain; 'and none but such as
have His power will ever be able to walk from these rocks to the
sands.' The old seaman paused, and turning his eyes, which exhibited
a mingled expression of disgust and compassion, on his companion,
he added, with reverence: 'Had you thought more of Him in fair
weather, your case would be less to be pitied in this tempest.'

'Do you still think there is much danger?' asked Dillon.

'To them that have reason to fear death. Listen; do you hear that
hollow noise beneath ye?'

''Tis the wind driving by the vessel!'

''Tis the poor thing herself,' said the affected cockswain, 'giving
her last groans. The water is breaking up her decks, and, in a few
minutes more, the handsomest model that ever cut a wave will be like
the chips that fell from her timbers in framing!'

'Why, then, did you remain here?' cried Dillon, wildly.

'To die in my coffin, if it should be the will of God,' returned Tom.
'These waves, to me, are what the land is to you; I was born on them,
and I have always meant that they should be my grave.'

1823

# CHARLES DARWIN
## 1809–1882

# from *The Voyage of the* Beagle

While sailing a little south of the Plata on one very dark night, the sea presented a wonderful and most beautiful spectacle. There was a fresh breeze, and every part of the surface, which during the day is seen as foam, now glowed with a pale light. The vessel drove before her bows two billows of liquid phosphorus, and in her wake she was followed by a milky train. As far as the eye reached, the crest of every wave was bright, and the sky above the horizon, from the reflected glare of these livid flames, was not so utterly obscure as over the vault of the heavens.

As we proceed further southward the sea is seldom phosphorescent; and off Cape Horn I do not recollect more than once having seen it so, and then it was far from being brilliant. This circumstance probably has a close connexion with the scarcity of organic beings in that part of the ocean. After the elaborate paper by Ehrenberg, on the phosphorescence of the sea, it is almost superfluous on my part to make any observations on the subject. I may however add, that the same torn and irregular particles of gelatinous matter, described by Ehrenberg, seem in the southern as well as in the northern hemisphere, to be the common cause of this phenomenon. The particles were so minute as easily to pass through fine gauze; yet many were distinctly visible by the naked eye. The water when placed in a tumbler and agitated, gave out sparks, but a small portion in a watch-glass scarcely ever was luminous. Ehrenberg states that these particles all retain a certain degree of irritability. My observations, some of which were made directly after taking up the water, gave a different result. I may also mention, that having used the net during one night, I allowed it to become partially dry, and having occasion twelve hours afterwards to employ it again, I found the whole surface sparkled as brightly as when first taken out of the water. It does not appear probable in this case, that the particles could have remained so long alive. On one occasion having kept a jelly-fish of the genus Dianaea till it was dead, the water in which it was placed became luminous. When the waves scintillate with bright green sparks, I believe it is generally owing to minute crustacea. But there can be no doubt that very many other pelagic animals, when alive, are phosphorescent.

On two occasions I have observed the sea luminous at considerable depths beneath the surface. Near the mouth of the Plata some circular and oval patches, from two to four yards in diameter, and with defined outlines, shone with a steady but pale light; while the surrounding water only gave out a few sparks. The appearance resembled the reflection of the moon, or some luminous body; for the edges were sinuous from the undulations of the surface. The ship, which drew thirteen feet of water, passed over, without disturbing these patches. Therefore we must suppose that some animals were congregated together at a greater depth than the bottom of the vessel.

Near Fernando Noronha the sea gave out light in flashes. The appearance was very similar to that which might be expected from a large fish moving rapidly through a luminous fluid. To this cause the sailors attributed it; at the time, however, I entertained some doubts, on account of the frequency and rapidity of the flashes. I have already remarked that the phenomenon is very much more common in warm than in cold countries; and I have sometimes imagined that a disturbed electrical condition of the atmosphere was most favourable to its production. Certainly I think the sea is most luminous after a few days of more calm weather than ordinary, during which time it has swarmed with various animals. Observing that the water charged with gelatinous particles is in an impure state, and that the luminous appearance in all common cases is produced by the agitation of the fluid in contact with the atmosphere, I am inclined to consider that the phosphorescence is the result of the decomposition of the organic particles, by which process (one is tempted to call it a kind of respiration) the ocean becomes purified.

What are the boasted glories of the illimitable ocean? A tedious waste, a desert of water, as the Arabian calls it. No doubt there are some delightful scenes. A moonlight night, with the clear heavens and the dark glittering sea, and the white sails filled by the soft air of a gently blowing trade-wind; a dead calm, with the heaving surface polished like a mirror, and all still except the occasional flapping of the canvas. It is well once to behold a squall with its rising arch and coming fury, or the heavy gale of wind and mountainous waves. I confess, however, my imagination had painted something more grand, more terrific in the full-grown storm. It is an incomparably finer spectacle when beheld on shore, where the waving trees, the wild flight of the birds, the dark shadows and bright lights, the rushing of the torrents, all proclaim the strife of the unloosed elements. At sea the albatross and little petrel fly as if the storm were their proper sphere, the water rises and sinks as if fulfilling its usual task, the ship alone and its inhabitants seem the objects of wrath. On a forlorn and weather-beaten coast, the scene is indeed different, but the feelings partake more of horror than of wild delight.

1839

---

# ADMIRAL SIR FRANCIS BEAUFORT

## 1774–1857

### The Beaufort Scale†                        c.1830

(see pp. 198–9)

† Admiral Beaufort constructed his scale for relating wind forces to sea states as early as 1805, but it was not until around 1830 that the Admiralty adopted it as a standard tool for use in the British Navy. "Beaufort Scales" come in a variety of dates, shapes and sizes, and I have preferred this recent Canadian example on the grounds that it combines the maximum of information with reasonable fidelity to the phrasing of the original.

# BEAUFORT WIND SCALE

| Beaufort number or force | Wind speed | | | | World Meteorological Organization (1964) | Estimating wind speed |
| | knots | mph | metres per second | km per hour | | Effects observed far from land |
|---|---|---|---|---|---|---|
| 0 | under 1 | under 1 | 0.0–0.2 | under 1 | Calm | Sea like mirror. |
| 1 | 1–3 | 1–3 | 0.3–1.5 | 1–5 | Light air | Ripples with appearance of scales; no foam crests. |
| 2 | 4–6 | 4–7 | 1.6–3.3 | 6–11 | Light breeze | Small wavelets; crests of glassy appearance, not breaking. |
| 3 | 7–10 | 8–12 | 3.4–5.4 | 12–19 | Gentle breeze | Large wavelets; crests begin to break; scattered whitecaps. |
| 4 | 11–16 | 13–18 | 5.5–7.9 | 20–28 | Moderate breeze | Small waves, becoming longer; numerous whitecaps. |
| 5 | 17–21 | 19–24 | 8.0–10.7 | 29–38 | Fresh breeze | Moderate waves, taking longer form; many whitecaps; some spray. |
| 6 | 22–27 | 25–31 | 10.8–13.8 | 39–49 | Strong breeze | Larger waves forming; whitecaps everywhere; more spray. |
| 7 | 28–33 | 32–38 | 13.9–17.1 | 50–61 | Near gale | Sea heaps up; white foam from breaking waves begins to be blown in streaks. |
| 8 | 34–40 | 39–46 | 17.2–20.7 | 62–74 | Gale | Moderately high waves of greater length; edges of crests begin to break into spindrift; foam is blown in well-marked streaks. |
| 9 | 41–47 | 47–54 | 20.8–24.4 | 75–88 | Strong gale | High waves; sea begins to roll; dense streaks of foam; spray may reduce visibility. |
| 10 | 48–55 | 55–63 | 24.5–28.4 | 89–102 | Storm | Very high waves with overhanging crests; sea takes white appearance as foam is blown in very dense streaks; rolling is heavy and visibility reduced. |
| 11 | 56–63 | 64–72 | 28.5–32.6 | 103–117 | Violent storm | Exceptionally high waves; sea covered with white foam patches; visibility still more reduced. |
| 12 | 64 and over | 73 and over | 32.7 and over | 118 and over | Hurricane | Air filled with foam; sea completely white with driving spray; visibility greatly reduced. |

| Effects observed near coast | Effects observed on land | Sea State | |
|---|---|---|---|
| | | Term and height of waves, in metres | Code |
| Calm. | Calm; smoke rises vertically. | Calm, glassy, 0 | 0 |
| ...shing smack just has steerage way. | Smoke drift indicates wind direction; vanes do not move. | | |
| ...'ind fills the sails of smacks which then travel at about 1–2 miles per hour. | Wind felt on face; leaves rustle; vanes begin to move. | Calm, rippled, 0–0.1 | 1 |
| ...macks begin to careen and travel about 3–4 miles per hour. | Leaves, small twigs in constant motion; light flags extended. | Smooth, wavelets, 0.1–0.5 | 2 |
| ...ood working breeze, smacks carry all canvas with good list. | Dust, leaves, and loose paper raised up; small branches move. | Slight, 0.5–1.25 | 3 |
| ...macks shorten sail. | Small trees in leaf begin to sway. | Moderate, 1.25–2.5 | 4 |
| ...macks have doubled reef in mainsail; care required when fishing. | Larger branches of trees in motion; whistling heard in wires. | Rough, 2.5–4 | 5 |
| ...macks remain in harbour and those at sea lie-to. | Whole trees in motion; resistance felt in walking against wind. | | |
| ...ll smacks make for harbour, if near. | Twigs and small branches broken off trees; progress generally impeded. | Very rough, 4–6 | 6 |
| | Slight structural damage occurs; slate blown from roofs. | | |
| | Seldom experienced on land; trees broken or uprooted; considerable structural damage occurs. | High, 6–9 | 7 |
| | | Very high, 9–14 | 8 |
| | Very rarely experienced on land; usually accompanied by widespread damage. | Phenomenal, over 14 | 9 |

# RICHARD HENRY DANA, JR.

## 1815–1882

# from *Two Years Before the Mast*

In our first attempt to double the Cape, when we came up to the latitude of it, we were nearly seventeen hundred miles to the westward, but, in running for the straits of Magellan, we stood so far to the eastward, that we made our second attempt at a distance of not more than four or five hundred miles; and we had great hopes, by this means, to run clear of the ice; thinking that the easterly gales, which had prevailed for a long time, would have driven it to the westward. With the wind about two points free, the yards braced in a little, and two close-reefed top-sails and a reefed fore-sail on the ship, we made great way toward the southward; and, almost every watch, when we came on deck, the air seemed to grow colder, and the sea to run higher. Still, we saw no ice, and had great hopes of going clear of it altogether, when, one afternoon, about three o'clock, while we were taking a *siesta* during our watch below, 'All hands!' was called in a loud and fearful voice. 'Tumble up here, men!—tumble up!—don't stop for your clothes—before we're upon it!' We sprang out of our berths and hurried upon deck. The loud, sharp voice of the captain was heard giving orders, as though for life or death, and we ran aft to the braces, not waiting to look ahead, for not a moment was to be lost. The helm was hard up, the after yards shaking, and the ship in the act of wearing. Slowly, with the stiff ropes and iced rigging, we swung the yards round, everything coming hard and with a creaking and rending sound, like pulling up a plank which has been frozen into the ice. The ship wore round fairly, the yards were steadied, and we stood off on the other tack, leaving behind us, directly under our larboard quarter, a large ice island, peering out of the mist, and reaching high above our tops, while astern; and on either side of the island, large tracts of field-ice were dimly seen, heaving and rolling in the sea. We were now safe, and standing to the northward; but, in a few minutes more, had it not been for the sharp look-out of the watch, we should have been fairly upon the ice, and left our ship's old bones adrift in the Southern ocean. After standing to the northward a few hours, we wore ship, and, the wind having hauled, we stood to the southward and eastward. All night long, a bright lookout was kept from every part of the deck; and whenever ice was seen on the one bow or the other, the helm was shifted and the yards braced, and by quick working of the ship she was kept clear. The accustomed cry of 'Ice ahead!'—'Ice on the lee bow!'—'Another island!' in the same tones, and with the same orders following them, seemed to bring us directly back to our old position of the week before. During our watch on deck, which was from twelve to four, the wind came out ahead, with a pelting storm of hail and sleet, and we lay hove-to, under a close-reefed main top-sail, the whole watch. During the next watch it fell calm, with a drenching rain, until daybreak, when the wind came out to the westward, and the weather cleared up, and showed us the whole ocean, in the course which we should have steered, had it not been for the head wind and calm, completely blocked up with ice. Here then our progress was stopped, and we wore ship, and once more stood to the northward and eastward; not for the straits of Magellan, but to make another attempt to double the Cape, still farther to the eastward; for the captain was determined to get round if perseverance could do it, and the third time, he said, never failed.

With a fair wind we soon ran clear of the field-ice, and by noon had only the stray islands floating far and near upon the ocean. The sun was out bright, the sea of a deep blue, fringed with the white foam of the waves which ran high before a strong south-wester; our solitary ship tore on through the water as though glad to be out of her confinement; and the ice islands lay scattered upon the ocean here and there, of various sizes and shapes, reflecting the bright rays of the sun, and drifting slowly northward before the gale. It was a contrast to much that we had lately seen, and a spectacle not only of beauty, but of life; for it required but little fancy to imagine these islands to be animate masses which had broken loose from the 'thrilling regions of thick-ribbed ice', and were working their way, by wind and current, some alone, and some in fleets, to milder climes. No pencil has ever yet given anything like the true effect of an iceberg. In a picture, they are huge, uncouth masses, stuck in the sea, while their chief beauty and grandeur—their slow, stately motion, the whirling of the snow about their summits, and the fearful groaning and cracking of their parts—the picture cannot give. This is the large iceberg; while the small and distant islands, floating on the smooth sea, in the light of a clear day, look like little floating fairy isles of sapphire.

From a north-east course we gradually hauled to the eastward, and after sailing about two hundred miles, which brought us as near to the western coast of Terra del Fuego as was safe, and having lost sight of the ice altogether, for the third time we put the ship's head to the southward, to try the passage of the Cape. The weather continued clear and cold, with a strong gale from the westward, and we were fast getting up with the latitude of the Cape, with a prospect of soon being round. One fine afternoon, a man who had gone into the fore-top to shift the rolling tackles, sung out, at the top of his voice, and with evident glee, 'Sail ho!' Neither land nor sail had we seen since leaving San Diego; and any one who has traversed the length of a whole ocean alone, can imagine what an excitement such an announcement produced on board. 'Sail ho!' shouted the cook, jumping out of his galley; 'Sail ho!' shouted a man, throwing back the slide of the scuttle, to the watch below, who were soon out of their berths and on deck; and 'Sail ho!' shouted the captain down the companion-way to the passenger in the cabin. Beside the pleasure of seeing a ship and human beings in so desolate a place, it was important for us to speak a vessel, to learn whether there was ice to the eastward, and to ascertain the longitude; for we had no chronometer, and had been drifting about so long that we had nearly lost our reckoning, and opportunities for lunar observations are not frequent or sure in such a place as Cape Horn. For these various reasons, the excitement in our little community was running high, and conjectures were made, and everything thought of for which the captain would hail, when the man aloft sung out—'Another sail, large on the weather bow!' This was a little odd, but so much the better, and did not shake our faith in their being sails. At length the man in the top hailed, and said he believed it was land, after all. 'Land in your eye!' said the mate, who was looking through the telescope; 'they are ice islands, if I can see a hole through a ladder'; and a few moments showed the mate to be right; and all our expectations fled; and instead of what we most wished to see, we had what we most dreaded, and what we hoped we had seen the last of. We soon, however, left these astern, having passed within about two miles of them; and at sundown the horizon was clear in all directions.

Having a fine wind, we were soon up with and passed the latitude of the Cape, and having stood far enough to the southward to give it a wide berth, we began to stand to the eastward, with a good prospect of being round and steering to the northward on the other side, in a very few days. But ill luck seemed to have lighted upon us. Not four hours had we been standing on in this course, before it fell dead calm; and in half an hour it clouded up; a few straggling blasts, with spits of snow and sleet, came from the eastward; and in an hour more, we lay hove-to under a close-reefed main top-sail; drifting bodily off to leeward before the fiercest storm that we had yet felt, blowing dead ahead, from the eastward. It seemed as though the genius of the place had been roused at finding that we had nearly slipped through his fingers, and had come down upon us with tenfold fury. The sailors said that every blast, as it shook the shrouds, and whistled through the rigging, said to the old ship, 'No, you don't!'—'No, you don't!'

For eight days we lay drifting about in this manner. Sometimes—generally towards noon—it fell calm; once or twice a round copper ball showed itself for a few moments in the place where the sun ought to have been; and a puff or two came from the westward, giving some hope that a fair wind had come at last. During the first two days, we made sail for these puffs, shaking the reefs out of the top-sails and boarding the tacks of the courses, but finding that it only made work for us when the gale set in again, it was soon given up, and we lay-to under our close-reefs. We had less snow and hail than when we were farther to the westward, but we had an abundance of what is worse to a sailor in cold weather—drenching rain. Snow is blinding, and very bad when coming upon a coast, but, for genuine discomfort, give me rain with freezing weather. A snow-storm is exciting, and it does not wet through the clothes (which is important to a sailor); but a constant rain there is no escaping from. It wets to the skin, and makes all protection vain. We had long ago run through all our dry clothes, and as sailors have no other way of drying them than by the sun, we had nothing to do but to put on those which were the least wet. At the end of each watch, when we came below, we took off our clothes and wrung them out; two taking hold of a pair of trowsers,—one at each end,—and jackets in the same way. Stockings, mittens, and all, were wrung out also, and then hung up to drain and chafe dry against the bulkheads. Then, feeling of all our clothes, we picked out those which were the least wet, and put them on, so as to be ready for a call, and turned-in, covered ourselves up with blankets, and slept until three knocks on the scuttle and the dismal sound of 'All starbowlines ahoy! Eight bells, there below! Do you hear the news?' drawled out from on deck, and the sulky answer of 'Aye, aye!' from below, sent us up again.

On deck, all was as dark as a pocket, and either a dead calm, with the rain pouring steadily down, or, more generally, a violent gale dead ahead, with rain pelting horizontally, and occasional variations of hail and sleet; decks afloat with water swashing from side to side, and constantly wet feet; for boots would not be wrung out like drawers, and no composition could stand the constant soaking. In fact, wet and cold feet are inevitable in such weather, and are not the least of those little items which go to make up the grand total of the discomforts of a winter passage round the Cape. Few words were spoken between the watches as they shifted, the wheel was relieved, the mate took his place on the quarter deck, the look-outs in the bows; and each man had his narrow space to walk fore and aft in, or, rather, to swing himself forward and back in, from one belaying pin to another, for the decks were too slippery with ice and water to allow of much walking. To make a walk, which is absolutely necessary to pass away the time, one of us hit upon the expedient of sanding the deck; and afterwards, whenever the rain was not so violent as to wash it off, the weather-side of the quarter-deck, and a part of the waist and forecastle were sprinkled with the sand which we had on board for holystoning; and thus we made a good promenade, where we walked fore and aft, two and two, hour after hour, in our long, dull, and comfortless watches. The bells seemed to be an hour or two apart, instead of half an hour, and an age to elapse before the welcome sound of eight bells. The sole object was to make the time pass on. Any change was sought for, which would break the monotony of the time; and even the two hours' trick at the wheel, which came round to each of us, in turn, once in every other watch, was looked upon as a relief. Even the never-failing resource of long yarns, which eke out many a watch, seemed to have failed us now; for we had been so long together that we had heard each other's stories told over and over again, till we had them by heart; each one knew the whole history of each of the others, and we were fairly and literally talked out. Singing and joking, we were in no humour for, and, in fact, any sound of mirth or laughter would have struck strangely upon our ears, and would not have been tolerated, any more than whistling, or a wind instrument. The last resort, that of speculating upon the future, seemed now to fail us, for our discouraging situation, and the danger we were really in (as we expected every day to find ourselves drifted back among the ice) 'clapped a stopper' upon all that. From saying—'*when* we get home'—we began insensibly to alter it to—'*if* we get home'—and at last the subject was dropped by a tacit consent.

*Thursday, September 15th.* This morning the temperature and peculiar appearance of the water, the quantities of gulf-weed floating about, and a bank of clouds lying directly before us, showed that we were on the border of the Gulf Stream. This remarkable current, running north-east, nearly across the ocean, is almost constantly shrouded in clouds, and is the region of storms and heavy seas. Vessels often run from a clear sky and light wind, with all sail, at once into a heavy sea and cloudy sky, with double-reefed top-sails. A sailor told me that on a passage from Gibraltar to Boston, his vessel neared the Gulf Stream with a light breeze, clear sky, and studding-sails out, alow and aloft; while, before it, was a long line of heavy, black clouds, lying like a bank upon the water, and a vessel coming out of it, under double-reefed top-sails, and with royal yards sent down. As they drew near, they began to take in sail after sail, until they were reduced to the same conditon; and, after twelve or fourteen hours of rolling and pitching in a heavy sea, before a smart gale, they ran out of the bank on the other side, and were in fine weather again, and under their royals and sky-sails. As we drew into it, the sky became cloudy, the sea high, and everything had the appearance of the going off, or the coming on, of a storm. It was blowing no more than a stiff breeze; yet the wind, being north-east, which is directly against the course of the current, made an ugly, chopping sea, which heaved and pitched the vessel about, so that we were obliged to send down the royal yards, and to take in our light sails. At noon, the thermometer, which had been repeatedly lowered into the water, showed the temperature to be seventy; which was considerably above that of the air,—as is always the case in the centre of the Stream. A lad who had been at work at the royal mast-head, came down upon deck, and took a turn round the long-boat; and looking very pale, said he was so sick that he could stay aloft no longer, but was ashamed to acknowledge it to the officer. He went up again, but soon gave out and came down, and leaned over the rail, 'as sick as a lady passenger'. He had been to sea several years, and had, he said, never been sick before. He was made so by the irregular, pitching motion of the vessel, increased by the height to which he had been above the hull, which is like the fulcrum of the lever. An old sailor, who was at work on the top-gallant yard, said he felt disagreeably all the time, and was glad, when his job was done, to get down into the top, or upon deck. Another hand was sent to the royal mast-head, who staid nearly an hour, but gave up. The work must be done, and the mate sent me. I did very well for some time, but began at length to feel very unpleasantly, though I had never been sick since the first two days from Boston, and had been in all sorts of weather and situations. Still, I kept my place, and did not come down, until I had got through my work, which was more than two hours. The ship certainly never acted so badly before. She was pitched and jerked about in all manner of ways; the sails seeming to have no steadying power over her. The tapering points of the masts made various curves and angles against the sky overhead, and some-times, in one sweep of an instant, described an arc of more than forty-five degrees, bringing up with a sudden jerk which made it necessary to hold on with both hands, and then sweeping off, in another long, irregular curve. I was not positively sick, and came down with a look of indifference, yet was not unwilling to get upon the comparative terra firma of the deck. A few hours more carried us through, and when we saw the sun go down, upon our larboard beam, in the direction of the continent of North America, we had left the bank of dark, stormy clouds astern, in the twilight.

There is a witchery in the sea, its songs and stories, and in the mere sight of a ship, and the sailor's dress, especially to a young mind, which has done more to man navies, and fill merchantmen, than all the pressgangs of Europe. I have known a young man with such a passion for the sea, that the very creaking of a block stirred up his imagination so that he could hardly keep his feet on dry ground; and many are the boys, in every seaport, who are drawn away, as by an almost irresistible attraction, from their work and schools, and hang about the decks and yards of vessels, with a fondness which, it is plain, will have its way. No sooner, however, has the young sailor begun his new life in earnest, than all this fine drapery falls off, and he learns that it is but work and hardship, after all. This is the true light in which a sailor's life is to be viewed; and if in our books, and anniversary speeches, we would leave out much that is said about 'blue water', 'blue jackets', 'open hearts', 'seeing God's hand on the deep', and so forth, and take this up like any other practical subject, I am quite sure we should do full as much for those we wish to benefit.

1840

# CHARLES DICKENS
## 1812–1870

# from *American Notes*

We all dined together that day; and a rather formidable party we were: no fewer than eighty-six strong. The vessel being pretty deep in the water, with all her coals on board and so many passengers, and the weather being calm and quiet, there was but little motion; so that before the dinner was half over, even those passengers who were most distrustful of themselves plucked up amazingly; and those who in the morning had returned to the universal question, 'Are you a good sailor?' a very decided negative, now either parried the inquiry with the evasive reply, 'Oh! I suppose I'm no worse than anybody else;' or, reckless of all moral obligations, answered boldly 'Yes': and with some irritation too, as though they would add, 'I should like to know what you see in *me*, sir, particularly, to justify suspicion!'

Notwithstanding this high tone of courage and confidence, I could not but observe that very few remained long over their wine; and that everybody had an unusual love of the open air; and that the favourite and most coveted seats were invariably those nearest to the door. The tea-table, too, was by no means as well attended as the dinner-table; and there was less whist-playing than might have been expected. Still, with the exception of one lady, who had retired with some precipitation at dinner-time, immediately after being assisted to the finest cut of a very yellow boiled leg of mutton with very green capers, there were no invalids as yet; and walking, and smoking, and drinking of brandy-and-water (but always in the open air), went on with unabated spirit, until eleven o'clock or thereabouts, when 'turning in'—no sailor of seven hours' experience talks of going to bed—became the order of the night. The perpetual tramp of boot-heels on the decks gave place to a heavy silence, and the whole human freight was stowed away below, excepting a very few stragglers, like myself, who were probably, like me, afraid to go there.

To one unaccustomed to such scenes, this is a very striking time on shipboard. Afterwards, and when its novelty had long worn off, it never ceased to have a peculiar interest and charm for me. The gloom through which the great black mass holds its direct and certain course; the rushing water, plainly heard, but dimly seen; the broad, white, glistening track, that follows in the vessel's wake; the men on the look-out forward, who would be scarcely visible against the dark sky, but for their blotting out some score of glistening stars; the helmsman at the wheel, with the illuminated card before him, shining, a speck of light amidst the darkness, like something sentient and of Divine intelligence; the melancholy sighing of the wind through block, and rope, and chain; the gleaming forth of light from every crevice, nook, and tiny piece of glass about the decks, as though the ship were filled with fire in hiding, ready to burst through any outlet, wild with its resistless power of death and ruin. At first, too, and even when the hour, and all the objects it exalts, have come to be familiar, it is difficult, alone and thoughtful, to hold them to their proper shapes and forms. They change with the wandering fancy; assume the semblance of things left far away; put on the well-remembered aspect of favourite places dearly loved; and even people them with shadows. Streets, houses, rooms; figures so like their usual occupants, that they have startled me by their reality, which far exceeded, as it seemed to me, all power of mine to conjure up the absent; have, many and many a time, at such an hour, grown suddenly out of objects with whose real look, and use, and purpose, I was as well acquainted as with my own two hands.

My own two hands, and feet likewise, being very cold, however, on this particular occasion, I crept below at midnight. It was not exactly comfortable below. It was decidedly close; and it was impossible to be unconscious of the presence of that extraordinary compound of strange smells, which is to be found nowhere but on board ship, and which is such a subtle perfume that it seems to enter at every pore of the skin, and whisper of the hold. Two passengers' wives (one of them my own) lay already in silent agonies on the sofa; and one lady's maid (*my* lady's) was a mere bundle on the floor, execrating her destiny, and pounding her curl-papers among the stray boxes. Everything sloped the wrong way: which in itself was an aggravation scarcely to be borne. I had left the door open, a moment before, in the bosom of a gentle declivity, and, when I turned to shut it, it was on the summit of a lofty eminence. Now every plank and timber creaked, as if the ship were made of wicker-work; and now crackled, like an enormous fire of the driest possible twigs. There was nothing for it but bed; so I went to bed.

It was pretty much the same for the next two days, with a tolerably fair wind and dry weather. I read in bed (but to this hour I don't know what) a good deal; and reeled on deck a little; drank cold brandy-and-water with an unspeakable disgust, and ate hard biscuit perseveringly: not ill, but going to be.

It is the third morning. I am awakened out of my sleep by a dismal shriek from my wife, who demands to know whether there's any danger. I rouse myself, and look out of bed. The water-jug is plunging and leaping like a lively dolphin; all the smaller articles are afloat, except my shoes, which are stranded on a carpet-bag, high and dry, like a couple of coal-barges. Suddenly I see them spring into the air, and behold the looking-glass, which is nailed to the wall, sticking fast upon the ceiling. At the same time the door entirely disappears, and a new one is opened in the floor. Then I begin to comprehend that the state-room is standing on its head.

Before it is possible to make any arrangement at all compatible with this novel state of things, the ship rights. Before one can say 'Thank Heaven!' she wrongs again. Before one can cry she is wrong, she seems to have started forward, and to be a creature actually running of its own accord, with broken knees and failing legs, through every variety of hole and pitfall, and stumbling constantly. Before one can so much as wonder, she takes a high leap into the air. Before she has well done that, she takes a deep dive into the water. Before she has gained the surface, she throws a summerset. The instant she is on her legs, she rushes backward. And so she goes on staggering, heaving, wrestling, leaping, diving, jumping, pitching, throbbing, rolling, and rocking: and going through all these movements, sometime by turns, and sometimes all together: until one feels disposed to roar for mercy.

A steward passes. 'Steward!' 'Sir?' 'What is the matter? what do you call this?' 'Rather a heavy sea on, sir, and a head-wind.'

A head-wind! Imagine a human face upon the vessel's prow, with fifteen thousand Samsons in one bent upon driving her back, and hitting her exactly between the eyes whenever she attempts to advance an inch. Imagine the ship herself, with every pulse and artery of her huge body swoln and bursting under this mal-treatment, sworn to go on or die. Imagine the wind howling, the sea roaring, the rain beating: all in furious array against her. Picture the sky both dark and wild, and the clouds, in fearful sympathy with the waves, making another ocean in the air. Add to all this, the clattering on deck and down below; the tread of hurried feet; the loud hoarse shouts of seamen; the gurgling in and out of water through the scuppers; with, every now and then, the striking of a heavy sea upon the planks above, with the deep, dead, heavy sound of thunder heard within a vault; and there is the head-wind of that January morning.

I say nothing of what may be called the domestic noises of the ship: such as the breaking of glass and crockery, the tumbling down of stewards, the gambols, overhead, of loose casks and truant dozens of bottled porter, and the very remarkable and far from exhilarating sounds raised in their various state-rooms by the seventy passengers who were too ill to get up to breakfast. I say nothing of them: for although I lay listening to this concert for three or four days, I don't think I heard it for more than a quarter of a minute, at the expiration of which term, I lay down again, excessively sea-sick.

Not sea-sick, be it understood, in the ordinary acceptation of the term: I wish I had been: but in a form which I have never seen or heard described, though I have no doubt it is very common. I lay there, all the day long, quite coolly and contentedly; with no sense of weariness, with no desire to get up, or get better, or take the air; with no curiosity, or care, or regret, of any sort or degree, saving that I think I can remember, in this universal indifference, having a kind of lazy joy—of fiendish delight, if anything so lethargic can be dignified with the title—in the fact of my wife being too ill to talk to me. If I may be allowed to illustrate my state of mind by such an example, I should say that I was exactly in the condition of the elder Mr Willet, after the incursion of the rioters into his bar at Chigwell. Nothing would have surprised me. If, in the momentary illumination of any ray of intelligence that may have come upon me in the way of thoughts of Home, a goblin postman, with a scarlet coat and bell, had come into that little kennel before me, broad awake in broad day, and, apologising for being damp through walking in the sea, had handed me a letter directed to myself, in familiar characters, I am certain I should not have felt one atom of astonishment: I should have been perfectly satisfied. If Neptune himself had walked in, with a toasted shark on his trident, I should have looked upon the event as one of the very commonest everyday occurrences.

Once—once—I found myself on deck. I don't know how I got

there, or what possessed me to go there, but there I was; and
completely dressed too, with a huge pea-coat on, and a pair of boots
such as no weak man in his senses could ever have got into. I found
myself standing, when a gleam of consciousness came upon me,
holding on to something. I don't know what. I think it was the
boatswain: or it may have been the pump: or possibly the cow. I can't
say how long I had been there; whether a day or a minute. I recollect
trying to think about something (about anything in the whole wide
world, I was not particular) without the smallest effect. I could not
even make out which was the sea, and which the sky, for the horizon
seemed drunk, and was flying wildly about, in all directions. Even in
that incapable state, however, I recognised the lazy gentleman standing
before me: nautically clad in a suit of shaggy blue, with an oilskin hat.
But I was too imbecile, although I knew it to be he, to separate him
from his dress; and tried to call him, I remember, *Pilot*. After another
interval of total unconsciousness, I found he had gone, and recognised
another figure in its place. It seemed to wave and fluctuate before me
as though I saw it reflected in an unsteady looking-glass; but I knew it
for the captain; and such was the cheerful influence of his face, that I
tried to smile: yes, even then I tried to smile. I saw by his gestures that
he addressed me; but it was a long time before I could make out that
he remonstrated against my standing up to my knees in water—as I
was; of course I don't know why. I tried to thank him, but couldn't. I
could only point to my boots—or wherever I supposed my boots to
be—and say in a plaintive voice, 'Cork soles': at the same time
endeavouring, I am told, to sit down in the pool. Finding that I was
quite insensible, and for the time a maniac, he humanely conducted
me below.

There I remained until I got better: suffering, whenever I was
recommended to eat anything, an amount of anguish only second to
that which is said to be endured by the apparently drowned, in the
process of restoration to life. One gentleman on board had a letter of
introduction to me from a mutual friend in London. He sent it below
with his card, on the morning of the head-wind; and I was long
troubled with the idea that he might be up, and well, and a hundred
times a day expecting me to call upon him in the saloon. I imagined
him one of those cast-iron images—I will not call them men—who
ask, with red faces, and lusty voices, what sea-sickness means,
and whether it really is as bad as it is represented to be. This was
very torturing indeed; and I don't think I ever felt such perfect

gratification and gratitude of heart, as I did when I heard from the ship's doctor that he had been obliged to put a large mustard poultice on this very gentleman's stomach. I date my recovery from the receipt of that intelligence.

It was materially assisted though, I have no doubt, by a heavy gale of wind, which came slowly up at sunset, when we were about ten days out, and raged with gradually increasing fury until morning, saving that it lulled for an hour a little before midnight. There was something in the unnatural repose of that hour, and in the after gathering of the storm, so inconceivably awful and tremendous, that its bursting into full violence was almost a relief.

The labouring of the ship in the troubled sea on this night I shall never forget. 'Will it ever be worse than this?' was a question I had often heard asked, when everything was sliding and bumping about, and when it certainly did seem difficult to comprehend the possibility of anything afloat being more disturbed, without toppling over and going down. But what the agitation of a steam-vessel is, on a bad winter's night in the wild Atlantic, it is impossible for the most vivid imagination to conceive. To say that she is flung down on her side in the waves, with her masts dipping into them, and that, springing up again, she rolls over on the other side, until a heavy sea strikes her with the noise of a hundred great guns, and hurls her back—that she stops, and staggers, and shivers, as though stunned, and then, with a violent throbbing at her heart, darts onward like a monster goaded into madness, to be beaten down, and battered, and crushed, and leaped on by the angry sea—that thunder, lightning, hail, and rain, and wind, are all in fierce contention for the mastery—that every plank has its groan, every nail its shriek, and every drop of water in the great ocean its howling voice—is nothing. To say that all is grand, and all appalling and horrible in the last degree, is nothing. Words cannot express it. Thoughts cannot convey it. Only a dream can call it up again, in all its fury, rage, and passion.

And yet, in the very midst of these terrors, I was placed in a situation so exquisitely ridiculous, that even then I had as strong a sense of its absurdity as I have now, and could no more help laughing than I can at any other comical incident, happening under circumstances the most favourable to its enjoyment. About midnight we shipped a sea, which forced its way through the skylights, burst open the doors above, and came raging and roaring down into the ladies' cabin, to the unspeakable consternation of my wife and a little Scotch lady—who,

by the way, had previously sent a message to the captain by the
stewardess, requesting him, with her compliments, to have a steel
conductor immediately attached to the top of every mast, and to the
chimney, in order that the ship might not be struck by lightning.
They, and the handmaid before mentioned, being in such ecstasies of
fear that I scarcely knew what to do with them, I naturally bethought
myself of some restorative or comfortable cordial; and nothing better
occurring to me, at the moment, than hot brandy-and-water, I
procured a tumbler-full without delay. It being impossible to stand
or sit without holding on, they were all heaped together in one corner
of a long sofa—a fixture extending entirely across the cabin— where
they clung to each other in momentary expectation of being drowned.
When I approached this place with my specific, and was about to
administer it, with many consolatory expressions, to the nearest
sufferer, what was my dismay to see them all roll slowly down to the
other end! And when I staggered to that end, and held out the glass
once more, how immensely baffled were my good intentions by the
ship giving another lurch, and their all rolling back again! I suppose I
dodged them up and down this sofa, for at least a quarter of an hour,
without reaching them once; and by the time I did catch them, the
brandy-and-water was diminished, by constant spilling, to a tea-
spoonful. To complete the group, it is necessary to recognise in this
disconcerted dodger, a very pale individual, who had shaved his
beard and brushed his hair, last, at Liverpool: and whose only articles
of dress (linen not included) were a pair of dreadnought trousers; a
blue jacket, formerly admired upon the Thames at Richmond; no
stockings; and one slipper.

1842


# from *David Copperfield*


As we struggled on, nearer and nearer to the sea, from which this
mighty wind was blowing dead on shore, its force became more and
more terrific. Long before we saw the sea, its spray was on our lips,
and showered salt rain upon us. The water was out, over miles and
miles of the flat country adjacent to Yarmouth; and every sheet and
puddle lashed its banks, and had its stress of little breakers setting
heavily towards us. When we came within sight of the sea, the waves

on the horizon, caught at intervals above the rolling abyss, were like glimpses of another shore with towers and buildings. When at last we got into the town, the people came out to their doors, all aslant, and with streaming hair, making a wonder of the mail that had come through such a night.

I put up at the old inn, and went down to look at the sea; staggering along the street, which was strewn with sand and seaweed, and with flying blotches of sea-foam; afraid of falling slates and tiles; and holding by people I met, at angry corners. Coming near the beach, I saw, not only the boatmen, but half the people of the town, lurking behind buildings; some, now and then braving the fury of the storm to look away to sea, and blown sheer out of their course in trying to get zigzag back.

Joining these groups, I found bewailing women whose husbands were away in herring or oyster boats, which there was too much reason to think might have foundered before they could run in anywhere for safety. Grizzled old sailors were among the people, shaking their heads, as they looked from water to sky, and muttering to one another; ship-owners, excited and uneasy; children, huddling together, and peering into older faces; even stout mariners, disturbed and anxious, levelling their glasses at the sea from behind places of shelter, as if they were surveying an enemy.

The tremendous sea itself, when I could find sufficient pause to look at it, in the agitation of the blinding wind, the flying stones and sand, and the awful noise, confounded me. As the high watery walls came rolling in, and, at their highest, tumbled into surf, they looked as if the least would engulf the town. As the receding wave swept back with a hoarse roar, it seemed to scoop out deep caves in the beach, as if its purpose were to undermine the earth. When some white-headed billows thundered on, and dashed themselves to pieces before they reached the land, every fragment of the late whole seemed possesed by the full might of its wrath, rushing to be gathered to the composition of another monster. Undulating hills were changed to valleys, undulating valleys (with a solitary storm-bird sometimes skimming through them) were lifted up to hills; masses of water shivered and shook the beach with a booming sound; every shape tumultuously rolled on, as soon as made, to change its shape and place, and beat another shape and place away; the ideal shore on the horizon, with its towers and buildings, rose and fell; the clouds fell fast and thick; I seemed to see a rending and upheaving of all nature. . . .

There was a dark gloom in my solitary chamber, when I at length
returned to it; but I was tired now, and, getting into bed again, fell—
off a tower and down a precipice—into the depths of sleep. I have an
impression that for a long time, though I dreamed of being elsewhere
and in a variety of scenes, it was always blowing in my dream. At
length, I lost that feeble hold upon reality, and was engaged with two
dear friends, but who they were I don't know, at the siege of some
town in a roar of cannonading.

The thunder of the cannon was so loud and incessant, that I could
not hear something I much desired to hear, until I made a great
exertion and awoke. It was broad day—eight or nine o'clock; the
storm raging, in lieu of the batteries; and someone knocking and
calling at my door.

'What is the matter?' I cried.

'A wreck! Close by!'

I sprung out of bed, and asked, what wreck?

'A schooner, from Spain or Portugal, laden with fruit and wine.
Make haste, sir, if you want to see her! It's thought, down on the
beach, she'll go to pieces every moment.'

The excited voice went clamouring along the staircase; and I wrapped
myself in my clothes as quickly as I could, and ran into the street.

Numbers of people were there before me, all running in one
direction, to the beach. I ran the same way, outstripping a good
many, and soon came facing the wild sea.

The wind might by this time have lulled a little, though not more
sensibly than if the cannonading I had dreamed of, had been diminished
by the silencing of half-a dozen guns out of hundreds. But, the sea,
having upon it the additional agitation of the whole night, was
infinitely more terrific than when I had seen it last. Every appearance
it had then presented, bore the expression of being *swelled*; and the
height to which the breakers rose, and, looking over one another, bore
one another down, and rolled in, in interminable hosts, was most
appalling.

In the difficulty of hearing anything but wind and waves, and in the
crowd, and the unspeakable confusion, and my first breathless efforts
to stand against the weather, I was so confused that I looked out to
sea for the wreck, and saw nothing but the foaming heads of the great
waves. A half-dressed boatman, standing next me, pointed with his
bare arm (a tattoo'd arrow on it, pointing in the same direction) to the
left. Then, O great Heaven, I saw it, close in upon us!

One mast was broken short off, six or eight feet from the deck, and lay over the side, entangled in a maze of sail and rigging; and all that ruin, as the ship rolled and beat—which she did without a moment's pause, and with a violence quite inconceivable—beat the side as if it would stave it in. Some efforts were even then being made, to cut this portion of the wreck away; for, as the ship, which was broadside on, turned towards us in her rolling, I plainly descried her people at work with axes, especially one active figure with long curling hair, conspicuous among the rest. But, a great cry, which was audible even above the wind and water, rose from the shore at this moment; the sea, sweeping over the rolling wreck, made a clean breach, and carried men, spars, casks, planks, bulwarks, heaps of such toys, into the boiling surge.

The second mast was yet standing, with the rags of a rent sail, and a wild confusion of broken cordage flapping to and fro. The ship had struck once, the same boatman hoarsely said in my ear, and then lifted in and struck again. I understood him to add that she was parting amidships, and I could readily suppose so, for the rolling and beating were too tremendous for any human work to suffer long. As he spoke, there was another great cry of pity from the beach; four men arose with the wreck out of the deep, clinging to the rigging of the remaining mast; uppermost, the active figure with the curling hair.

There was a bell on board; and as the ship rolled and dashed, like a desperate creature driven mad, now showing us the whole sweep of her deck, as she turned on her beam-ends towards the shore, now nothing but her keel, as she sprung wildly over and turned towards the sea, the bell rang; and its sound, the knell of those unhappy men, was borne towards us on the wind. Again we lost her, and again she rose. Two men were gone. The agony on the shore increased. Men groaned, and clasped their hands; women shrieked, and turned away their faces. Some ran wildly up and down along the beach, crying for help where no help could be. I found myself one of these, frantically imploring a knot of sailors whom I knew, not to let those two lost creatures perish before our eyes.

They were making out to me, in an agitated way—I don't know how, for the little I could hear I was scarcely composed enough to understand—that the lifeboat had been bravely manned an hour ago, and could do nothing; and that as no man would be so desperate as to attempt to wade off with a rope, and establish a communication with the shore, there was nothing left to try; when I noticed that some new sensation moved the people on the beach, and saw them part, and Ham come breaking through them to the front.

I ran to him—as well as I know, to repeat my appeal for help. But, distracted though I was, by a sight so new to me and terrible, the determination in his face, and his look out to sea—exactly the same look as I remembered in connexion with the morning after Emily's flight—awoke me to a knowledge of his danger. I held him back with both arms; and implored the men with whom I had been speaking, not to listen to him, not to do murder, not to let him stir from that sand!

Another cry arose on shore; and looking to the wreck, we saw the cruel sail, with blow on blow, beat off the lower of the two men, and fly up in triumph round the active figure left alone upon the mast.

Against such a sight, and against such determination as that of the calmly desperate man who was already accustomed to lead half the people present, I might as hopefully have entreated the wind. 'Mas'r Davy,' he said, cheerily grasping me by both hands, 'if my time is come, 'tis come. If 'tan't, I'll bide it. Lord above bless you, and bless all! Mates, make me ready! I'm a-going off!'

I was swept away, but not unkindly, to some distance, where the people around me made me stay; urging, as I confusedly perceived, that he was bent on going, with help or without, and that I should endanger the precautions for his safety by troubling those with whom they rested. I don't know what I answered, or what they rejoined; but, I saw hurry on the beach, and men running with ropes from a capstan that was there, and penetrating into a circle of figures that hid him from me. Then, I saw him standing alone, in a seaman's frock and trousers: a rope in his hand, or slung to his wrist: another round his body: and several of the best men holding, at a little distance, to the latter, which he laid out himself, slack upon the shore, at his feet.

The wreck, even to my unpractised eye, was breaking up. I saw that she was parting in the middle, and that the life of the solitary man upon the mast hung by a thread. Still, he clung to it. He had a singular red cap on—not like a sailor's cap, but of a finer colour; and as the few yielding planks between him and destruction rolled and bulged, and his anticipative death-knell rung, he was seen by all of us to wave it. I saw him do it now, and though I was going distracted, when his action brought an old remembrance to my mind of a once dear friend.

Ham watched the sea, standing alone, with the silence of suspended breath behind him, and the storm before, until there was a great retiring wave, when, with a backward glance at those who held the rope which was made fast round his body, he dashed in after it, and in a moment was buffeting with the water; rising with the hills, falling with the valleys, lost beneath the foam; then drawn again to land. They hauled in hastily.

He was hurt. I saw blood on his face, from where I stood; but he took no thought of that. He seemed hurriedly to give them some directions for leaving him more free—or so I judged from the motion of his arm—and was gone as before.

And now he made for the wreck, rising with the hills, falling with the valleys, lost beneath the rugged foam, borne in towards the shore, borne on towards the ship, striving hard and valiantly. The distance was nothing, but the power of the sea and wind made the strife deadly. At length he neared the wreck. He was so near, that with one more of his vigorous strokes he would be clinging to it, when a high, green, vast hill-side of water, moving on shoreward, from beyond the ship, he seemed to leap up into it with a mighty bound, and the ship was gone!

Some eddying fragments I saw in the sea, as if a mere cask had been broken, in running to the spot where they were hauling in. Consternation was in every face. They drew him to my very feet—insensible—dead. He was carried to the nearest house; and, no one preventing me now, I remained near him, busy, while every means of restoration were tried; but he had been beaten to death by the great wave, and his generous heart was stilled for ever.

As I sat beside the bed, when hope was abandoned and all was done, a fisherman, who had known me when Emily and I were children, and ever since, whispered my name at the door.

'Sir,' said he, with tears starting to his weather-beaten face, which, with his trembling lips, was ashy pale, 'will you come over yonder?'

The old remembrance that had been recalled to me, was in his look. I asked him, terror-stricken, leaning on the arm he held out to support me:

'Has a body come ashore?'

He said, 'Yes.'

'Do I know it?' I asked then.

He answered nothing.

But, he led me to the shore. And on that part of it where she and I had looked for shells, two children—on that part of it where some lighter fragments of the old boat, blown down last night, had been scattered by the wind—among the ruins of the home he had wronged—I saw him lying with his head upon his arm, as I had often seen him lie at school.

1850

# FRANCES CALDERÓN DE LA BARCA
## 1804–1882[†]

## from *Life in Mexico*

Packet ship 'Norma',
Oct. 27th, 1839.

This morning, at ten o'clock, we stepped on board the steamboat Hercules, destined to convey us to our packet with its musical name. The day was foggy and gloomy, as if refusing to be comforted, even by an occasional smile from the sun. All prognosticated that the Norma would not sail to-day, but 'where there's a will', etc. Several of our friends accompanied us to the wharf; the Russian Minister, the Minister of Buenos Ayres, Mr ——, who tried hard to look sentimental, and even brought tears into his eyes by some curious process; Judge ——, Mr ——, and others, from whom we were truly sorry to part.

The Norma was anchored in one of the most beautiful points of the bay, and the steamboat towed us five miles, until we had passed the Narrows. The wind was contrary, but the day began to clear up, and the sun to scatter the watery clouds.

Still there is nothing so sad as a retreating view. It is as if time were visibly in motion; and as here we had to part from ——, we could

[†] Frances Calderón de la Barca was born Frances Inglis in Edinburgh. When her father died in debt in Normandy, she and her mother emigrated to the United States, where they eventually settled in Washington. Here she met Don Angel Calderón de la Barca. Shortly after their marriage in 1838, Don Angel was posted to Mexico as the first Spanish Envoy to the new republic.

only distinguish, as through a misty veil, the beauties of the bay; the shores covered to the water's edge with trees rich in their autumnal colouring; the white houses on Staten Island—the whole gradually growing fainter, till, like a dream, they faded away.

The pilot has left us, breaking our last link with the land. We still see the mountains of Neversink, and the lighthouse of Sandy Hook. The sun is setting, and in a few minutes we must take our leave, probably for years, of places long familiar to us.

Our fellow-passengers do not appear very remarkable. There is Madame A——, returning from being prima donna in Mexico, in a packet called after the opera in which she was there a favourite, with her husband Señor V—— and her child. There is M. B—— with moustaches like a bird's nest; a pretty widow in deep affliction, at least in deep mourning; a maiden lady going out as a governess, and every variety of Spaniard and Havanero. So now we are alone, C——n and I, and my French femme-de-chambre, with her air of Dowager Duchess, and moreover sea-sick.

28th.—When I said I liked a sea life, I did not mean to be understood as liking a merchant ship, with an airless cabin, and with every variety of disagreeable odour. As a French woman on board, with the air of an afflicted porpoise, and with more truth than elegance, expresses it: 'Tout devient puant, même l'eau-de-cologne.'

The wind is still contrary, and the Norma, beating up and down, makes but little way. We have gone seventy-four miles, and of these advanced but forty. Every one being sick to-day, the deck is nearly deserted. The most interesting object I have discovered on board is a pretty little deaf and dumb girl, very lively and with an intelligent face, who has been teaching me to speak on my fingers. The infant heir of the house of —— has shown his good taste by passing the day in squalling. M. B——, pale, dirty, and much resembling a brigand out of employ, has traversed the deck with uneasy footsteps and a cigar appearing from out his moustaches, like a light in a tangled forest, or a jack-o-lantern in a marshy thicket. A fat Spaniard has been discoursing upon the glories of olla podrida. *Au reste*, we are slowly pursuing our way, and at this rate might reach Cuba in three months.

And the stars are shining, quiet and silvery. All without is soft and beautiful, and no doubt the Norma herself looks all in unison with the scene, balancing herself like a lazy swan, white and graciously. So it is without, and within, there is miserable sea-sickness, bilge-water, and all the unavoidable disagreeables of a small packet.

31st.—Three days have passed without anything worthy of notice having occurred, except that we already feel the difference of temperature. The passengers are still enduring sea-sickness in all its phases.

This morning opened with an angry dispute between two of the gentlemen, on the subject of Cuban lotteries, and they ended by applying to each other epithets which, however much they might be deserved, were certainly rather strong; but by dinner time, they were amicably engaged in concocting together an enormous tureen of *gaspachos*, a sort of salad, composed of bread, oil, vinegar, sliced onion and garlic—and the fattest one declares that in warm weather, a dish of *gaspachos*, with plenty of garlic in it, makes him feel as fresh as a rose. He must indeed be a perfect bouquet.

The opening of morning is dramatic in our narrow cabin. About twenty voices in Spanish, German, Italian, and broken English, strike up by degrees. From a neighbouring state room, *Nid d'oiseau* puts forth his head. 'Stooar! a toomlar! here is no vater!' 'Comin, sir, comin.' '*Caramba*! Stooard!' 'Comin, sir, comin!' 'Stuart? vasser und toel!' 'Here, sir.' 'Amigo! how is the wind?' (This is the waking up of el Señor Ministro, putting his head half suffocated out of his berth.) 'Oh steward! steward!' 'Yes, miss,' 'come here, and look at *this*!' 'I'll fix it, miss,'—etc.

1st November.—A fair wind after a stifling night, and strong hopes of seeing the Bahama Banks on Sunday. Most people are now gradually ascending from the lower regions, and dragging themselves on deck with pale and dejected countenances. Madam A—— has such a sweet-toned voice in speaking, especially in her accents of her *bella Italia*, that it is refreshing to listen to her. I have passed all day in reading, after a desultory fashion, 'Les Enfants d'Edouard', by Casimir Delavigne, Washington Irving, D'Israeli's 'Curiosities of Literature', etc.; and it is rather singular that while there is a very tolerable supply of English and French books here, I see but one or two odd volumes in Spanish, although these packets are constantly filled with people of that nation, going and coming. Is it that they do not care for reading, or that less attention is paid to them than to the French or American passengers? One would think Cervantes, Lope de Vega, Calderon, or Moratin, better worth buying than many commonplace novels which I find here.

3rd.—Yesterday the wind blew soft as on a summer morning. A

land-bird flew into the ship. To-day the wind has veered round, but the weather continues charming. The sea is covered with multitudes of small flying-fish. An infantile water-spout appeared, and died in its birth. Mr ——, the consul, has been giving me an account of the agreeable society in the Sandwich Islands! A magnificent sunset, the sight of which compensates for all the inconveniences of the voyage. The sky was covered with black clouds lined with silver, and surrounded by every variety of colour; deep blue, fleecy, rose, violet, and orange. The heavens are now thickly studded with stars, numbers shooting across the blue expanse like messengers of light, glancing and disappearing as if extinguished.

It is well to read the History of Columbus at sea, but especially in these waters, where he wandered in suspense, high-wrought expectation, and firm faith; and to watch the signs which the noble mariner observed in these latitudes; the soft serenity of the breezes, the clear blue of the heavens, the brilliancy and number of the stars, the sea-weeds of the gulf, which always drift in the direction of the wind, the little land-birds that come like harbingers of good tidings, the frequency of the shooting stars, and the multitude of flying-fish.

As the shades of evening close around, and the tropical sky glitters with the light of innumerable stars, imagination transports us back to that century which stands out in bold relief amidst other ages rolling by comparatively undistinguished, and we see as in a vision the Discoverer of a World, standing on the deck of his caravel, as it bounded over the unknown and mysterious waste of waters, his vigilant eyes fixed on the west, like a Persian intently watching the rising of his god; though his star was to arise from whence the day-god sets. We see him bending his gaze on the first dark line that separated the watery sea from the blue of the heavens, striving to penetrate the gloom of night, yet waiting with patient faith until the dawn of day should bring the long-wished for shores in sight.

6th.—For three days, three very long and uncomfortable days, the wind, with surprising constancy, has continued to blow dead ahead. In ancient days, what altars might have smoked to Aeolus! Now, except in the increased puffing of consolatory cigar-smoke, no propitiatory offerings are made to unseen powers. There are indeed many mourning signs amongst the passengers. Every one has tied up his head in an angry-looking silken bandana, drawn over his nose with a dogged air. Beards are unshaven, a black stubble covering the lemon-coloured countenance, which occasionally bears a look of sulky defiance, as if its owner were, like Juliet, 'past hope, past cure, past help'.

7th.—This morning the monotony of fine weather was relieved by a hearty squall, accompanied by torrents of rain, much thunder, and forked lightning. The ship reeled to and fro like a drunken man, and the passengers, as usual in such cases, performed various involuntary evolutions, cutting right angles, sliding, spinning round, and rolling over, as if Oberon's magic horn were playing an occasional blast amidst the roaring winds; whilst the stewards alone, like Horace's good man, walked serene amidst the wreck of crockery and the fall of plates. Driven from our stronghold on deck, indiscriminately crammed in below like figs in a drum; 'weltering', as Carlyle has it, 'like an Egyptian pitcher of tamed vipers', the cabin windows all shut in, we tried to take it coolly, in spite of the suffocating heat.

There is a child on board who is certainly possessed, not by a witty malicious demon, a *diable boiteux*, but by a teasing, stupid, wicked imp, which inspires him with the desire of tormenting everything human that comes within his reach. Should he escape being thrown overboard, it will show a wonderful degree of forbearance on the part of the passengers.

8th.—The weather is perfect, but the wind inexorable; and the passengers, with their heads tied up, look more gloomy than ever. Some sit dejected in corners, and some quarrel with their neighbours, thus finding a safety-valve by which their wrath may escape.

9th.—There is no change in the wind, yet the gentlemen have all brightened up, taken off their handkerchiefs and shaved, as if ashamed of their six days' impatience, and making up their minds to a sea-life. This morning we saw land; a long, low ridge of hills on the island of Eleuthera, where they make salt, and where there are many negroes. Neither salt nor negroes visible to the naked eye; nothing but the gray outline of the hills, melting into the sea and sky; and having tacked about all day, we found ourselves in the evening precisely opposite to this same island. There are Job's comforters on board, who assure us that they have been thirty-six days between New York and la 'joya más preciosa de la corona de España'.[1]

For my part, I feel no impatience, having rather a dislike to changing my position when tolerable, and the air is so fresh and laden with balm, that it seems to blow over some paradise of sweets, some

---

[1] The most precious jewel in the Spanish crown, the name given to Cuba.

land of fragrant spices. The sea also is a mirror, and I have read Marryat's 'Pirate' for the first time.

Thus then we stand at eight o'clock, p.m.; wind ahead, and little of it, performing a zigzag march between Eleuthera and Abaco. On deck, the pretty widow lies in an easy chair, surrounded by her countrymen, who discourse about sugar, molasses, chocolate, and other local topics, together with the relative merits of Cuba as compared with the rest of the known world. Madame A—— is studying her part of Elizabetta in the opera of Roberto Devereux, which she is to bring out in Havana, but the creaking of the Norma is sadly at variance with harmony. A pale German youth, in dressing-gown and slippers, is studying Schiller. An ingenious youngster is carefully conning a well-thumbed note, which looks like a milliner's girl's last billet-doux. The little *possédé* is burning brown paper within an inch of the curtains of a state-room, while the steward is dragging it from him. Others are gradually dropping into their berths, like ripe nuts from a tree. Thus are we all pursuing our vocations.

9th.—Wind dead ahead! I console myself with Cinq-Mars and Jacob Faithful. But the weather is lovely. A young moon in her first quarter, like a queen in her minority, glitters like a crescent on the brow of night.

Towards evening the long wished for lighthouse of Abaco (built by the English) showed her charitable and revolving radiance. But our ship, Penelope-like, undoes by night what she has performed by day, and her course is backward and crabbish. A delicious smell of violets is blowing from the land.

10th.—A fair wind. The good tidings communicated by the A——, *toute rayonnante de joie*. A fair wind and a bright blue sea, cool and refreshing breezes, the waves sparkling, and the ship going gallantly over the waters. So far, our voyage may have been tedious, but the most determined landsman must allow that the weather has been charming.

Sunday at sea; and though no bells are tolling, and no hymns are chanted, the blue sky above and the blue ocean beneath us, form one vast temple, where, since the foundations of the earth and sea were laid, *Day unto day uttereth speech, and night unto night showeth knowledge.*

This morning we neared the Berry Islands, unproductive and rocky, as the geography books would say. One of these islands belongs to a coloured man, who bought it for fifty dollars—a cheaply purchased sovereignty. He, his wife and children, with their *negro slaves!* live there, and cultivate vegetables to sell at New York, or to the different ships that pass that way. Had the wind been favourable, they would probably have sent us out a boat with fresh vegetables, fish, and fruit, which would have been very acceptable. We saw, not far from the shore, the wreck of a two-masted vessel; sad sight to those who pass over the same waters to see

A brave vessel,
Who had, no doubt, some noble creatures in her,
Dashed all to pieces!

Who had, at least, some of God's creatures in her. Anything but that! I am like Gonzalo, and 'would fain die a dry death'.

We are now on the Bahama Banks, the water very clear and blue, with a creamy froth, looking as if it flowed over pearls and turquoises. An English schooner man-of-war (a *boy*-of-war in size) made all sail towards us, doubtless hoping we were a slaver; but, on putting us to the test of his spy-glass, the captain, we presume, perceived that the general tinge of countenance was lemon rather than negro, and so abandoned his pursuit.

This evening on the Banks. It would be difficult to imagine a more placid and lovely scene. Everything perfectly calm, all sail set, and the heavens becoming gradually sprinkled with silver stars. The sky blue, and without a cloud, except where the sun has just set, the last crimson point sinking in the calm sea and leaving a long retinue of rainbow-coloured clouds, deep crimson tinged with bright silver, and melting away into gray, pale vapour.

On goes the vessel, stately and swanlike; the water of the same turquoise blue, covered with a light pearly froth, and so clear that we see the large sponges at the bottom. Every minute they heave the lead. 'By the mark three.' 'By the mark three, less a quarter.' 'By the mark twain and a half' (fifteen feet, the vessel drawing thirteen), two feet between us and the bottom. The sailor sings it out like the first line of a hymn in a short metre, doled out by the parish clerk. I wish Madame A—— were singing it instead of he, 'By the mark three, less a quarter.' To this tune, the only sound breaking the stillness of the night, I dropped to sleep. The captain passed the night anxiously, now looking out for lights on the Banks, now at the helm, or himself sounding the lead:

For some must watch whilst others sleep;
Thus wags the world away.

11th.—Beautiful morning, and fair wind. About eight we left the Banks. Just then we observed, that the sailor who sounded, having sung out five, then six, then in a few minutes seven, suddenly found no bottom, as if we had fallen off all at once from the brink of the Bank into an abyss.

A fellow-captain, and passenger of our captain's, told me this morning, that he spoke the ship which carried out Governor and Mrs McLean to Cape-Coast Castle—the unfortunate L. E. L. It does not seem to me at all astonishing that the remedies which she took in England without injury, should have proved fatal to her in that wretched climate.

We have been accompanied all the morning by a fine large ship, going full sail, the Orleans, Captain Sears, bound for New Orleans. . . . A long semicircular line of black rocks in sight; some of a round form, one of which is called the Death's Head; another of the shape of a turtle, and some two or three miles long. At the extremity of one of these the English are building a lighthouse.

12th.—We are opposite the Pan of Matanzas, about sixty miles from Havana. Impatience becomes general, but the breeze rocks up and down, and we gain little. This day, like all last days on board, has been remarkably tedious, though the country gradually becomes more interesting. There is a universal brushing-up amongst the passengers; some shaving, some with their heads plunged into tubs of cold water. So may have appeared Noah's ark, when the dove did not return, and the passengers prepared for *terra firma*, after a forty days' voyage. Our Mount Ararat was the Morro Castle, which, dark and frowning, presented itself to our eyes, at six o'clock, p.m.

Nothing can be more striking than the first appearance of this fortress, starting up from the solid rock, with its towers and battlements, while here, to remind us of our latitude, we see a few feathery cocoas growing amidst the herbage that covers the banks near the castle. By its side, covering a considerable extent of ground, is the fortress called the *Cabaña*, painted rose-colour, with the angles of its bastions white.

But there is too much to look at now. I must finish my letter in Havana.

1843

# EDGAR ALLAN POE

## 1809–1849

# 'A Descent into the Maelström'

*The ways of God in Nature, as in Providence, are not as our ways; nor are the models that we frame any way commensurate to the vastness, profundity, and unsearchableness of His works, which have a depth in them greater than the well of Democritus.*

Joseph Glanville

We had now reached the summit of the loftiest crag. For some minutes the old man seemed too much exhausted to speak.

'Not long ago,' said he at length, 'and I could have guided you on this route as well as the youngest of my sons; but, about three years past, there happened to me an event such as never happened before to mortal man—or at least such as no man ever survived to tell of—and the six hours of deadly terror which I then endured have broken me up body and soul. You suppose me a *very* old man—but I am not. It took less than a single day to change these hairs from a jetty black to white, to weaken my limbs, and unstring my nerves, so that I tremble at the least exertion, and am frightened at a shadow. Do you know I can scarcely look over this little cliff without getting giddy?'

The 'little cliff', upon whose edge he had so carelessly thrown himself down to rest that the weightier portion of his body hung over it, while he was only kept from falling by the tenure of his elbow on its extreme and slippery edge—this 'little cliff' arose, a sheer unob-structed precipice of black shining rock, some fifteen or sixteen hundred feet from the world of crags beneath us. Nothing would have tempted me to be within half a dozen yards of its brink. In truth so deeply was I excited by the perilous position of my companion, that I fell at full length upon the ground, clung to the shrubs around me, and dared not even glance upward at the sky—while I struggled in vain to divest myself of the idea that the very foundations of the mountain were in danger from the fury of the winds. It was long before I could reason myself into sufficient courage to sit up and look out into the distance.

'You must get over these fancies,' said the guide, 'for I have
brought you here that you might have the best possible view of the
scene of that event I mentioned—and to tell you the whole story with
the spot just under your eye.'

'We are now,' he continued, in that particularizing manner which
distinguished him—'we are now close upon the Norwegian coast—
in the sixty-eighth degree of latitude—in the great province of
Nordland—and in the dreary district of Lofoden. The mountain
upon whose top we sit is Helseggen, the Cloudy. Now raise yourself
up a little higher—hold on to the grass if you feel giddy—so—and
look out, beyond the belt of vapor beneath us, into the sea.'

I looked dizzily, and beheld a wide expanse of ocean, whose waters
wore so inky a hue as to bring at once to my mind the Nubian
geographer's account of the *Mare Tenebrarum*. A panorama more
deplorably desolate no human imagination can conceive. To the right
and left, as far as the eye could reach, there lay outstretched, like
ramparts of the world, lines of horridly black and beetling cliff,
whose character of gloom was but the more forcibly illustrated by the
surf which reared high up against it its white and ghastly crest,
howling and shrieking for ever. Just opposite the promontory upon
whose apex we were placed, and at a distance of some five or six miles
out at sea, there was visible a small, bleak-looking island; or, more
properly, its position was discernible through the wilderness of
surge in which it was enveloped. About two miles nearer the land,
arose another of smaller size, hideously craggy and barren, and
encompassed at various intervals by a cluster of dark rocks.

The appearance of the ocean, in the space between the more distant
island and the shore, had something very unusual about it. Although,
at the time, so strong a gale was blowing landward that a brig in the
remote offing lay to under a double-reefed try-sail, and constantly
plunged her whole hull out of sight, still there was here nothing like a
regular swell, but only a short, quick, angry cross dashing of water in
every direction—as well in the teeth of the wind as otherwise. Of
foam there was little except in the immediate vicinity of the rocks.

'The island in the distance,' resumed the old man, 'is called by the
Norwegians Vurrgh. The one midway is Moskoe. That a mile to the
northward is Ambaaren. Yonder are Iflesen, Hoeyholm, Keildholm,
Suarven, and Buckholm. Further off—between Moskoe and Vurrgh—
are Otterholm, Flimen, Sandflesen, and Skarholm. These are the true
names of the places—but why it has been thought necessary to name

them at all, is more than either you or I can understand. Do you hear any thing? Do you see any change in the water?'

We had now been about ten minutes upon the top of Helseggen, to which we had ascended from the interior of Lofoden, so that we had caught no glimpse of the sea until it had burst upon us from the summit. As the old man spoke, I became aware of a loud and gradually increasing sound, like the moaning of a vast herd of buffaloes upon an American prairie; and at the same moment I perceived that what seamen term the *chopping* character of the ocean beneath us, was rapidly changing into a current which set to the eastward. Even while I gazed, this current acquired a monstrous velocity. Each moment added to its speed—to its headlong impetuosity. In five minutes the whole sea, as far as Vurrgh, was lashed into ungovernable fury; but it was between Moskoe and the coast that the main uproar held its sway. Here the vast bed of the waters, seamed and scarred into a thousand conflicting channels, burst suddenly into phrensied convulsion—heaving, boiling, hissing—gyrating in gigantic and innumerable vortices, and all whirling and plunging on to the eastward with a rapidity which water never elsewhere assumes, except in precipitous descents.

In a few minutes more, there came over the scene another radical alteration. The general surface grew somewhat more smooth, and the whirlpools, one by one, disappeared, while prodigious streaks of foam became apparent where none had been seen before. These streaks, at length, spreading out to a great distance, and entering into combination, took unto themselves the gyratory motion of the subsided vortices, and seemed to form the germ of another more vast. Suddenly—very suddenly—this assumed a distinct and definite existence, in a circle of more than half a mile in diameter. The edge of the whirl was represented by a broad belt of gleaming spray; but no particle of this slipped into the mouth of the terrific funnel, whose interior, as far as the eye could fathom it, was a smooth, shining, and jet-black wall of water, inclined to the horizon at an angle of some forty-five degrees, speeding dizzily round and round with a swaying and sweltering motion, and sending forth to the winds an appalling voice, half shriek, half roar, such as not even the mighty cataract of Niagara ever lifts up in its agony to Heaven.

The mountain trembled to its very base, and the rock rocked. I threw myself upon my face, and clung to the scant herbage in an excess of nervous agitation.

'This,' said I at length, to the old man—'this *can* be nothing else than the great whirlpool of the Maelström.'

'So it is sometimes termed,' said he. 'We Norwegians call it the Moskoe-ström, from the island of Moskoe in the midway.'

The ordinary account of this vortex had by no means prepared me for what I saw. That of Jonas Ramus, which is perhaps the most circumstantial of any, cannot impart the faintest conception either of the magnificence, or of the horror of the scene—or of the wild bewildering sense of *the novel* which confounds the beholder. I am not sure from what point of view the writer in question surveyed it, nor at what time; but it could neither have been from the summit of Helseggen, nor during a storm. There are some passages of his description, nevertheless, which may be quoted for their details, although their effect is exceedingly feeble in conveying an impression of the spectacle.

'Between Lofoden and Moskoe,' he says, 'the depth of the water is between thirty-six and forty fathoms; but on the other side, towards Ver (Vurrgh) this depth decreases so as not to afford a convenient passage for a vessel, without the risk of splitting on the rocks, which happens even in the calmest weather. When it is in flood, the stream runs up the country between Lofoden and Moskoe with a boisterous rapidity; but the roar of its impetuous ebb to the sea is scarce equalled by the loudest and most dreadful cataracts; the noise being heard several leagues off, and the vortices or pits are of such an extent and depth, that if a ship comes within its attraction, it is inevitably absorbed and carried down to the bottom, and there beat to pieces against the rocks; and when the water relaxes, the fragments thereof are thrown up again. But these intervals of tranquillity are only at the turn of the ebb and flood, and in calm weather, and last but a quarter of an hour, its violence gradually returning. When the stream is most boisterous, and its fury heightened by a storm, it is dangerous to come within a Norway mile of it. Boats, yachts, and ships have been carried away by not guarding against it before they were within its reach. It likewise happens frequently, that whales come too near the stream, and are overpowered by its violence; and then it is impossible to describe their howlings and bellowings in their fruitless struggles to disengage themselves. A bear once, attempting to swim from Lofoden to Moskoe, was caught by the stream and borne down, while he roared terribly, so as to be heard on shore. Large stocks of firs and pine trees, after being absorbed by the current, rise again broken and torn to such a degree as if bristle grew upon them. This plainly shows the bottom to consist of craggy rocks, among which they are whirled to and fro. This stream is regulated by the flux and reflux of the sea—it being constantly high and low water every six hours. In the year 1645, early in the morning of Sexagesima Sunday, it raged with such a noise and impetuosity that the very stones of the houses on the coast fell to the ground.'

In regard to the depth of the water, I could not see how this could have been ascertained at all in the immediate vicinity of the vortex. The 'forty fathoms' must have reference only to portions of the channel close upon the shore either of Moskoe or Lofoden. The depth in the centre of the Moskoe-ström must be unmeasurably greater; and no better proof of this fact is necessary than can be obtained from even the sidelong glance into the abyss of the whirl which may be had from the highest crag of Helseggen. Looking down from this pinnacle upon the howling Phlegethon below, I could not help smiling at the simplicity with which the honest Jonas Ramus records, as a matter difficult of belief, the anecdotes of the whales and the bears, for it appeared to me, in fact, a self-evident thing, that the largest ships of the line in existence, coming within the influence of that deadly attraction, could resist it as little as a feather the hurricane, and must disappear bodily and at once.

The attempts to account for the phenomenon—some of which, I remember, seemed to me sufficiently plausible in perusal—now wore a very different and unsatisfactory aspect. The idea generally received is that this, as well as three smaller vortices among the Feroe islands, 'have no other cause than the collision of waves rising and falling, at flux and reflux, against a ridge of rocks and shelves, which confines the water so that it precipitates itself like a cataract; and thus the higher the flood rises, the deeper must the fall be, and the natural result of all is a whirlpool or vortex, the prodigious suction of which is sufficiently known by lesser experiments.'—These are the words of the Encyclopaedia Britannica. Kircher and others imagine that in the centre of the channel of the maelström is an abyss penetrating the globe, and issuing in some very remote part—the Gulf of Bothnia being somewhat decidedly named in one instance. This opinion, idle in itself, was the one to which, as I gazed, my imagination most readily assented; and, mentioning it to the guide, I was rather surprised to hear him say that, although it was the view almost universally entertained of the subject by the Norwegians, it nevertheless was not his own. As to the former notion he confessed his inability to comprehend it; and here I agreed with him—for, however conclusive on paper, it becomes altogether unintelligible, and even absurd, amid the thunder of the abyss.

'You have had a good look at the whirl now,' said the old man, 'and if you will creep round this crag, so as to get in its lee, and deaden the roar of the water, I will tell you a story that will convince you I ought to know something of the Moskoe-ström.'

I placed myself as desired, and he proceeded.

'Myself and my two brothers once owned a schooner-rigged smack of about seventy tons burthen, with which we were in the habit of fishing among the islands beyond Moskoe, nearly to Vurrgh. In all violent eddies at sea there is good fishing, at proper opportunities, if one has only the courage to attempt it; but among the whole of the Lofoden coastmen, we three were the only ones who made a regular business of going out to the islands, as I tell you. The usual grounds are a great way lower down to the southward. There fish can be got at all hours, without much risk, and therefore these places are preferred. The choice spots over here among the rocks, however, not only yield the finest variety, but in far greater abundance; so that we often got in a single day, what the more timid of the craft could not scrape together in a week. In fact, we made it a matter of desperate speculation—the risk of life standing instead of labor, and courage answering for capital.

'We kept the smack in a cove about five miles higher up the coast than this; and it was our practice, in fine weather, to take advantage of the fifteen minutes' slack to push across the main channel of the Moskoe-ström, far above the pool, and then drop down upon anchorage somewhere near Otterholm, or Sandflesen, where the eddies are not so violent as elsewhere. Here we used to remain until nearly time for slack-water again, when we weighed and made for home. We never set out upon this expedition without a steady side wind for going and coming—one that we felt sure would not fail us before our return—and we seldom made a miscalculation upon this point. Twice, during six years, we were forced to stay all night at anchor on account of a dead calm, which is a rare thing indeed just about here; and once we had to remain on the grounds nearly a week, starving to death, owing to a gale which blew up shortly after our arrival, and made the channel too boisterous to be thought of. Upon this occasion we should have been driven out to sea in spite of everything (for the whirlpools threw us round and round so violently, that, at length, we fouled our anchor and dragged it) if it had not been that we drifted into one of the innumerable cross currents—here to day and gone to-morrow—which drove us under the lee of Flimen, where, by good luck, we brought up.

'I could not tell you the twentieth part of the difficulties we encountered "on the ground"—it is a bad spot to be in, even in good weather—but we make shift always to run the gauntlet of the Moskoe-ström itself without accident; although at times my heart has been in my mouth when we happened to be a minute or so behind or before the slack. The wind sometimes was not as strong as we thought it at starting, and then we made rather less way than we could wish, while the current rendered the smack unmanageable. My eldest brother had a son eighteen years old, and I had two stout boys of my own. These would have been of great assistance at such times, in using the sweeps, as well as afterward in fishing—but, somehow, although we ran the risk ourselves, we had not the heart to let the young ones get into the danger—for, after all said and done, it *was* a horrible danger, and that is the truth.

'It is now within a few days of three years since what I am going to tell you occurred. It was on the tenth of July, 18—, a day which the people of this part of the world will never forget—for it was one in which blew the most terrible hurricane that ever came out of the heavens. And yet all the morning, and indeed until late in the afternoon, there was a gentle and steady breeze from the south-west, while the sun shone brightly, so that the oldest seaman among us could not have foreseen what was to follow.

'The three of us—my two brothers and myself—had crossed over to the islands about two o'clock p.m., and soon nearly loaded the smack with fine fish, which, we all remarked, were more plenty that day than we had ever known them. It was just seven, *by my watch*, when we weighed and started for home, so as to make the worst of the Ström at slack water, which we knew would be at eight.

'We set out with a fresh wind on our starboard quarter, and for some time spanked along at a great rate, never dreaming of danger, for indeed we saw not the slightest reason to apprehend it. All at once we were taken aback by a breeze from over Helseggen. This was most unusual—something that had never happened to us before—and I began to feel a little uneasy, without exactly knowing why. We put the boat on the wind, but could make no headway at all for the eddies, and I was upon the point of proposing to return to the anchorage, when, looking astern, we saw the whole horizon covered with a singular copper-colored cloud that rose with the most amazing velocity.

'In the meantime the breeze that had headed us off fell away and we were dead becalmed, drifting about in every direction. This state of things, however, did not last long enough to give us time to think about it. In less than a minute the storm was upon us—in less than two the sky was entirely overcast—and what with this and the driving spray, it became suddenly so dark that we could not see each other in the smack.

'Such a hurricane as then blew it is folly to attempt describing. The oldest seaman in Norway never experienced any thing like it. We had let our sails go by the run before it cleverly took us; but, at the first puff, both our masts went by the board as if they had been sawed off—the mainmast taking with it my youngest brother, who had lashed himself to it for safety.

'Our boat was the lightest feather of a thing that ever sat upon water. It had a complete flush deck, with only a small hatch near the bow, and this hatch it had always been our custom to batten down when about to cross the Ström, by way of precaution against the chopping seas. But for this circumstance we should have foundered at once—for we lay entirely buried for some moments. How my elder brother escaped destruction I cannot say, for I never had an opportunity of ascertaining. For my part, as soon as I had let the foresail run, I threw myself flat on deck, with my feet against the narrow gunwale of the bow, and with my hands grasping a ring-bolt near the foot of the foremast. It was mere instinct that prompted me to do this— which was undoubtedly the very best thing I could have done—for I was too much flurried to think.

'For some moments we were completely deluged, as I say, and all this time I held my breath, and clung to the bolt. When I could stand it no longer I raised myself upon my knees, still keeping hold with my hands, and thus got my head clear. Presently our little boat gave herself a shake, just as a dog does in coming out of the water, and thus rid herself, in some measure, of the seas. I was now trying to get the better of the stupor that had come over me, and to collect my senses so as to see what was to be done, when I felt somebody grasp my arm. It was my elder brother, and my heart leaped for joy, for I had made sure that he was overboard—but the next moment all this joy was turned into horror—for he put his mouth close to my ear, and screamed out the word *"Moskoe-ström!"*

'No one ever will know what my feelings were at that moment. I shook from head to foot as if I had had the most violent fit of the ague. I knew what he meant by that one word well enough—I knew what he wished to make me understand. With the wind that now drove us on, we were bound for the whirl of the Ström, and nothing could save us!

'You perceive that in crossing the Ström *channel*, we always went a long way up above the whirl, even in the calmest weather, and then had to wait and watch carefully for the slack—but now we were driving right upon the pool itself, and in such a hurricane as this! "To be sure," I thought, "we shall get there just about the slack—there is some little hope in that"—but in the next moment I cursed myself for being so great a fool as to dream of hope at all. I knew very well that we were doomed, had we been ten times a ninety-gun ship.

'By this time the first fury of the tempest had spent itself, or perhaps we did not feel it so much, as we scudded before it, but at all events the seas, which at first had been kept down by the wind, and lay flat and frothing, now got up into absolute mountains. A singular change, too, had come over the heavens. Around in every direction it was still as black as pitch, but nearly overhead there burst out, all at once, a circular rift of clear sky—as clear as I ever saw—and of a deep bright blue—and through it there blazed forth the full moon with a lustre that I never before knew her to wear. She lit up every thing about us with the greatest distinctness—but, oh God, what a scene it was to light up!

'I now made one or two attempts to speak to my brother—but in some manner which I could not understand, the din had so increased that I could not make him hear a single word, although I screamed at the top of my voice in his ear. Presently he shook his head, looking as pale as death, and held up one of his fingers, as if to say "listen!"

'At first I could not make out what he meant—but soon a hideous thought flashed upon me. I dragged my watch from its fob. It was not going. I glanced at its face by the moonlight, and then burst into tears as I flung it far away into the ocean. *It had run down at seven o'clock! We were behind the time of the slack, and the whirl of the Ström was in full fury!*

'When a boat is well built, properly trimmed, and not deep laden, the waves in a strong gale, when she is going large, seem always to slip from beneath her—which appears strange to a landsman—and this is what is called *riding*, in sea phrase.

'Well, so far we had ridden the swells very cleverly; but presently a gigantic sea happened to take us right under the counter, and bore us with it as it rose—up—up—as if into the sky. I would not have believed that any wave could rise so high. And then down we came with a sweep, a slide, and a plunge that made me feel sick and dizzy, as if I was falling from some lofty mountain-top in a dream. But while we were up I had thrown a quick glance around—and that one glance was all sufficient. I saw our exact position in an instant. The Moskoe-ström whirlpool was about a quarter of a mile dead ahead—but no more like the every-day Moskoe-ström than the whirl, as you now see it, is like a mill-race. If I had not known where we were, and what we had to expect, I should not have recognised the place at all. As it was, I involuntarily closed my eyes in horror. The lids clenched themselves together as if in a spasm.

'It could not have been more than two minutes afterwards until we suddenly felt the waves subside, and were enveloped in foam. The boat made a sharp half turn to larboard, and then shot off in its new direction like a thunderbolt. At the same moment the roaring noise of the water was completely drowned in a kind of shrill shriek—such a sound as you might imagine given out by the water-pipes of many thousand steam-vessels letting off their steam all together. We were now in the belt of surf that always surrounds the whirl; and I thought, of course, that another moment would plunge us into the abyss—down which we could only see indistinctly on account of the amazing velocity with which we were borne along. The boat did not seem to sink into the water at all, but to skim like an air-bubble upon the surface of the surge. Her starboard side was next the whirl, and on the larboard arose the world of ocean we had left. It stood like a huge writhing wall between us and the horizon.

'It may appear strange, but now, when we were in the very jaws of the gulf, I felt more composed than when we were only approaching it. Having made up my mind to hope no more, I got rid of a great deal of that terror which unmanned me at first. I supposed it was despair that strung my nerves.

'It may look like boasting—but what I tell you is truth—I began to reflect how magnificent a thing it was to die in such a manner, and how foolish it was in me to think of so paltry a consideration as my own individual life, in view of so wonderful a manifestation of God's power. I do believe that I blushed with shame when this idea crossed my mind. After a little while I became possessed with the keenest curiosity about the whirl itself. I positively felt a *wish* to explore its depths, even at the sacrifice I was going to make; and my principal grief was that I should never be able to tell my old companions on shore about the mysteries I should see. These, no doubt, were singular fancies to occupy a man's mind in such extremity—and I have often thought since, that the revolutions of the boat around the pool might have rendered me a little light-headed.

'There was another circumstance which tended to restore my self-possession; and this was the cessation of the wind, which could not reach us in our present situation—for, as you saw for yourself, the belt of the surf is considerably lower than the general bed of the ocean, and this latter now towered above us, a high, black, mountainous ridge. If you have never been at sea in a heavy gale, you can form no idea of the confusion of mind occasioned by the wind and spray together. They blind, deafen, and strangle you, and take away all power of action or reflection. But we were now, in a great measure, rid of these annoyances—just as death-condemned felons in prison are allowed petty indulgences, forbidden them while their doom is yet uncertain.

'How often we made the circuit of the belt it is impossible to say. We careered round and round for perhaps an hour, flying rather than floating, getting gradually more and more into the middle of the surge, and then nearer and nearer to its horrible inner edge. All this time I had never let go of the ring-bolt. My brother was at the stern, holding on to a large empty water-cask which had been securely lashed under the coop of the counter, and was the only thing on deck that had not been swept overboard when the gale first took us. As we approached the brink of the pit he let go his hold upon this, and made for the ring, from which, in the agony of his terror, he endeavored to force my hands, as it was not large enough to afford us both a secure grasp. I never felt deeper grief than when I saw him attempt this act—although I knew he was a madman when he did it—a raving maniac through sheer fright. I did not care, however, to contest the point with him. I knew it could make no difference whether either of us held on at all; so I let him have the bolt, and went astern to the cask. This there was no great difficulty in doing; for the smack flew round steadily enough, and upon an even keel—only swaying to and fro with the immense sweeps and swelters of the whirl. Scarcely had I secured myself in my new position, when we gave a wild lurch to starboard, and rushed headlong into the abyss. I muttered a hurried prayer to God, and thought all was over.

'As I felt the sickening sweep of the descent, I had instinctively tightened my hold upon the barrel, and closed my eyes. For some seconds I dared not open them—while I expected instant destruction, and wondered that I was not already in my death-struggles with the water. But moment after moment elapsed. I still lived. The sense of falling had ceased; and the motion of the vessel seemed much as it had been before while in the belt of foam, with the exception that she now lay more along. I took courage and looked once again upon the scene.

'Never shall I forget the sensation of awe, horror, and admiration with which I gazed about me. The boat appeared to be hanging, as if by magic, midway down, upon the interior surface of a funnel vast in circumference, prodigious in depth, and whose perfectly smooth sides might have been mistaken for ebony, but for the bewildering rapidity with which they spun around, and for the gleaming and ghastly radiance they shot forth, as the rays of the full moon, from that circular rift among the clounds which I have already described, streamed in a flood of golden glory along the black walls, and far away down into the inmost recesses of the abyss.

'At first I was too much confused to observe any thing accurately. The general burst of terrific grandeur was all that I beheld. When I recovered myself a little, however, my gaze fell instinctively downward. In this direction I was able to obtain an unobstructed view, from the manner in which the smack hung on the inclined surface of the pool. She was quite upon an even keel—that is to say, her deck lay in a plane parallel with that of the water—but this latter sloped at an angle of more than forty-five degrees, so that we seemed to be lying upon our beam-ends. I could not help observing, nevertheless, that I had scarcely more difficulty in maintaining my hold and footing in this situation, than if we had been upon a dead level; and this, I suppose, was owing to the speed at which we revolved.

'The rays of the moon seemed to search the very bottom of the profound gulf; but still I could make out nothing distinctly, on account of a thick mist in which every thing there was enveloped, and over which there hung a magnificent rainbow, like that narrow and tottering bridge which Musselmen say is the only pathway between Time and Eternity. This mist, or spray, was no doubt occasioned by the clashing of the great walls of the funnel, as they all met together at

the bottom—but the yell that went up to the Heavens from out of
that mist I dare not attempt to describe.

'Our first slide into the abyss itself, from the belt of foam above,
had carried us to a great distance down the slope; but our farther
descent was by no means proportionate. Round and round we
swept—not with any uniform movement—but in dizzying swings
and jerks, that sent us sometimes only a few hundred feet—sometimes
nearly the complete circuit of the whirl. Our progress downward, at
each revolution, was slow, but very perceptible.

'Looking about me upon the wide waste of liquid ebony on which
we were thus borne, I perceived that our boat was not the only object
in the embrace of the whirl. Both above and below us were visible
fragments of vessels, large masses of building timber and trunks of
trees, with many smaller articles, such as pieces of house furniture,
broken boxes, barrels and staves. I have already described the unnatural
curiosity which had taken the place of my original terrors. It appeared to
grow upon me as I drew nearer and nearer to my dreadful doom.
Now I began to watch, with a strange interest, the numerous things
that floated in our company. I *must* have been delirious—for I even
sought *amusement* in speculating upon the relative velocities of their
several descents toward the foam below. "This fir tree," I found
myself at one time saying, "will certainly be the next thing that takes
the awful plunge and disappears,"—and then I was disappointed to
find that the wreck of a Dutch merchant ship overtook it and went
down before. At length, after making several guesses of this nature,
and being deceived in all—this fact—the fact of my invariable
miscalculation, set me upon a train of reflection that made my limbs
again tremble, and my heart beat heavily once more.

'It was not a new terror that thus affected me, but the dawn of a
more exciting *hope*. This hope arose partly from memory, and partly
from present observation. I called to mind the great variety of
buoyant matter that strewed the coast of Lofoden, having been
absorbed and then thrown forth by the Moskoe-ström. By far the
greater number of the articles were shattered in the most extraordinary
way—so chafed and roughened as to have the appearance of being
stuck full of splinters—but then I distinctly recollected that there
were *some* of them which were not disfigured at all. Now I could not
account for this difference except by supposing that the roughened
fragments were the only ones which had been *completely absorbed*—
that the others had entered the whirl at so late a period of the tide, or,

from some reason, had descended so slowly after entering, that they did not reach the bottom before the turn of the flood came, or of the ebb, as the case might be. I conceived it possible, in either instance, that they might thus be whirled up again to the level of the ocean, without undergoing the fate of those which had been drawn in more early or absorbed more rapidly. I made, also, three important observations. The first was, that as a general rule, the larger the bodies were, the more rapid their descent; the second, that, between two masses of equal extent, the one spherical, and the other *of any other shape*, the superiority in speed of descent was with the sphere; the third, that, between two masses of equal size, the one cylindrical, and the other of any other shape, the cylinder was absorbed the more slowly. Since my escape, I have had several conversations on this subject with an old school-master of the district; and it was from him that I learned the use of the words "cylinder" and "sphere". He explained to me—although I have forgotten the explanation—how what I observed was, in fact, the natural consequence of the forms of the floating fragments—and showed me how it happened that a cylinder, swimming in a vortex, offered more resistance to its suction, and was drawn in with greater difficulty than an equally bulky body, of any form whatever.[1]

'There was one startling circumstance which went a great way in enforcing these observations, and rendering me anxious to turn them to account, and this was that, at every revolution, we passed something like a barrel, or else the broken yard or the mast of a vessel, while many of these things, which had been on our level when I first opened my eyes upon the wonders of the whirlpool, were now high up above us, and seemed to have moved but little from their original station.

'I no longer hesitated what to do. I resolved to lash myself securely to the water-cask upon which I now held, to cut it loose from the counter, and to throw myself with it into the water. I attracted my brother's attention by signs, pointing to the floating barrels that came near us, and did every thing in my power to make him understand what I was about to do. I thought at length that he comprehended my design—but, whether this was the case or not, he shook his head despairingly, and refused to move from his station by the ring-bolt. It was impossible to force him; the emergency admitted of no delay; and so, with a bitter struggle, I resigned him to his fate, fastened myself to the cask by means of the lashings which secured it to the

---

[1] See Archimedes, *De Incidentibus in Fluido*, lib. 2

counter, and precipitated myself with it into the sea, without another moment's hesitation.

'The result was precisely what I had hoped it might be. As it is myself who now tell you this tale—as you see that I *did* escape—and as you are already in possession of the mode in which this escape was effected, and must therefore anticipate all that I have farther to say—I will bring my story quickly to conclusion. It might have been an hour, or thereabout, after my quitting the smack, when, having descended to a vast distance beneath me, it made three or four wild gyrations in rapid succession, and, bearing my loved brother with it, plunged headlong, at once and forever, into the chaos of foam below. The barrel to which I was attached sunk very little farther than half the distance between the bottom of the gulf and the spot at which I leaped overboard, before a great change took place in the character of the whirlpool. The slope of the sides of the vast funnel became momently less and less steep. The gyrations of the whirl grew, gradually, less and less violent. By degrees, the froth and the rainbow disappeared, and the bottom of the gulf seemed slowly to uprise. The sky was clear, the winds had gone down, and the full moon was setting radiantly in the west, when I found myself on the surface of the ocean, in full view of the shores of Lofoden, and above the spot where the pool of the Moskoe-ström *had been*. It was the hour of the slack—but the sea still heaved in mountainous waves from the effects of the hurricane. I was borne violently into the channel of the Ström, and in a few minutes, was hurried down the coast into the "grounds" of the fishermen. A boat picked me up—exhausted from fatigue—and (now that the danger was removed) speechless from the memory of its horror. Those who drew me on board were my old mates and daily companions—but they knew me no more than they would have known a traveller from the spirit-land. My hair, which had been raven black the day before, was as white as you see it now. They say too that the whole expression of my countenance had changed. I told them my story—they did not believe it. I now tell it to *you*—and I can scarcely expect you to put more faith in it than did the merry fishermen of Lofoden.'

1845

# HERMAN MELVILLE
## 1819–1891

# from *Journal*

### Saturday Oct 13

Rose early this morning, opened my bulls eye window, & looked out
to the East. The sun was just rising, the horizon was red; a familiar
sight to me, reminding me of old times. Before breakfast went up to
the mast-head, by way of gymnastics. About 10 o'clock a.m. the
wind rose, the rain fell, & the deck looked dismally enough. By
dinner time, it blew half a gale, & the passengers mostly retired to
their rooms, sea sick. After dinner, the rain ceased, yet it still blew
stiffly, & we were slowly forging along under close-reefed topsails—
mainsail furled. I was walking the deck, when I perceived one of the
steerage passengers looking over the side; I looked too, & saw a man
in the water, his head completely lifted above the water—about
twelve feet from the ship, right abreast the gangway. For an instant, I
thought I was dreaming; for no one seemed to see what I did. Next
moment, I shouted 'Man overboard!' & turned to go aft. The Captain
ran forward, greatly confused. I dropped overboard the tackle-fall of
the quarter-boat, & swung it towards the man, who was now
drifting close to the ship. He did not get hold of it, & I got over the
side, within a foot or two of the sea, & again swung the rope towards
him. He now got hold of it. By this time, a crowd of people—sailors
& others—were clustering about the bulwarks; but none seemed
very anxious to save him. They warned *me* however, not to fall
overboard. After holding on to the rope, about a quarter of a minute
the man let go of it, & drifted astern under the mizzen chains. Four or
five of the seamen jumped over into the chains & swung him more
ropes. But his conduct was unaccountable; he could have saved
himself, had he been so minded. I was struck by the expression of his
face in the water. It was merry. At last he drifted off under the ship's
counter, & all hands cried 'He's gone!' Running to the taffrail, we
saw him again, floating off—saw a few bubbles, & never saw him
again. No boat was lowered, no sail was shortened, hardly any noise
was made. The man drowned like a bullock. It afterwards turned out,

that he was crazy, & had jumped overboard. He had declared he
would do so several times; & just before he *did* jump, he had tried to
get possession of his child, in order to jump into the sea, with the
child in his arms. His wife was miserably sick in her berth. The
Captain said that this was the fourth or fifth instance he had known of
people jumping overboard. He told a story of a man who did so, with
his wife on deck at the time. As they were trying to save him, the wife
said it was no use; & when he was drowned, she said 'there were
plenty more men to be had.' Amiable creature!—By night, it blew a
terrific gale, & we hove to. Miserable time! nearly every one sick,
& the ship rolling & pitching in an amazing manner. About midnight,
I rose & went on deck. It was blowing horribly—pitch dark, &
raining. The Captain was in the cuddy & directed my attention 'to
those fellows' as he called them—meaning several 'Corposant balls'
on the yard arms & mast heads. They were the first I had ever seen,
& resembled large, dim stars in the sky.

1849

# from *Moby Dick*

## I. THE SPIRIT-SPOUT

Days, weeks passed, and under easy sail, the ivory Pequod had
slowly swept across four several cruising-grounds; that off the
Azores; off the Cape de Verdes; on the Plate (so called), being off the
mouth of the Rio de la Plata; and the Carrol Ground, an unstaked,
watery locality, southerly from St Helena.

It was while gliding through these latter waters that one serene and
moonlight night, when all the waves rolled by like scrolls of silver;
and, by their soft, suffusing seethings, made what seemed a silvery
silence, not a solitude: on such a silent night a silvery jet was seen far
in advance of the white bubbles at the bow. Lit up by the moon, it
looked celestial; seemed some plumed and glittering god uprising
from the sea. Fedallah first descried this jet. For of these moonlight

nights, it was his wont to mount to the main-mast head, and stand a look-out there, with the same precision as if it had been day. And yet, though herds of whales were seen by night, not one whaleman in a hundred would venture a lowering for them. You may think with what emotions, then, the seamen beheld this old Oriental perched aloft at such unusual hours; his turban and the moon, companions in one sky. But when, after spending his uniform interval there for several successive nights without uttering a single sound; when, after all this silence, his unearthly voice was heard announcing that silvery, moon-lit jet, every reclining mariner started to his feet as if some winged spirit had lighted in the rigging, and hailed the mortal crew. 'There she blows!' Had the trump of judgment blown, they could not have quivered more; yet still they felt no terror; rather pleasure. For though it was a most unwonted hour, yet so impressive was the cry, and so deliriously exciting, that almost every soul on board instinctively desired a lowering.

Walking the deck with quick, side-lunging strides, Ahab commanded the t'gallant sails and royals to be set, and every stunsail spread. The best man in the ship must take the helm. Then, with every mast-head manned, the piled-up craft rolled down before the wind. The strange, upheaving, lifting tendency of the taffrail breeze filling the hollows of so many sails, made the buoyant, hovering deck to feel like air beneath the feet; while still she rushed along, as if two antagonistic influences were struggling in her—one to mount direct to heaven, the other to drive yawingly to some horizontal goal. And had you watched Ahab's face that night, you would have thought that in him also two different things were warring. While his one live leg made lively echoes along the deck, every stroke of his dead limb sounded like a coffin-tap. On life and death this old man walked. But though the ship so swiftly sped, and though from every eye, like arrows, the eager glances shot, yet the silvery jet was no more seen that night. Every sailor swore he saw it once, but not a second time.

This midnight-spout had almost grown a forgotten thing, when, some days after, lo! at the same silent hour, it was again announced: again it was descried by all; but upon making sail to overtake it, once more it disappeared as if it had never been. And so it served us night after night, till no one heeded it but to wonder at it. Mysteriously jetted into the clear moonlight, or starlight, as the case might be; disappearing again for one whole day, or two days, or three; and somehow seeming at every distinct repetition to be advancing still further and further in our van, this solitary jet seemed for ever alluring us on.

Nor with the immemorial superstition of their race, and in accordance with the preternaturalness, as it seemed, which in many things invested the Pequod, were there wanting some of the seamen who swore that whenever and wherever descried; at however remote times, or in however far apart latitudes and longitudes, that unnearable spout was cast by one self-same whale; and that whale, Moby Dick. For a time, there reigned, too, a sense of peculiar dread at this flitting apparation, as if it were treacherously beckoning us on and on, in order that the monster might turn round upon us, and rend us at last in the remotest and most savage seas.

These temporary apprehensions, so vague but so awful, derived a wondrous potency from the contrasting serenity of the weather, in which, beneath all its blue blandness, some thought there lurked a devilish charm, as for days and days we voyaged along, through seas so wearily, lonesomely mild, that all space, in repugnance to our vengeful errand, seemed vacating itself of life before our urn-like prow.

But, at last, when turning to the eastward, the Cape winds began howling around us, and we rose and fell upon the long, troubled seas that are there; when the ivory-tusked Pequod sharply bowed to the blast, and gored the dark waves in her madness, till, like showers of silver chips, the foam-flakes flew over her bulwarks; then all this desolate vacuity of life went away, but gave place to sights more dismal than before.

Close to our bows, strange forms in the water darted hither and thither before us; while thick in our rear flew the inscrutable sea-ravens. And every morning, perched on our stays, rows of these birds were seen; and spite of our hootings, for a long time obstinately clung to the hemp, as though they deemed our ship some drifting, uninhabited craft; a thing appointed to desolation, and therefore fit roosting-place for their homeless selves. And heaved and heaved, still unrestingly heaved the black sea, as if its vast tides were a conscience; and the great mundane soul were in anguish and remorse for the long sin and suffering it had bred.

## 2. THE PACIFIC

When gliding by the Bashee isles we emerged at last upon the great South Sea; were it not for other things, I could have greeted my dear

Pacific with uncounted thanks, for now the long supplication of my youth was answered; that serene ocean rolled eastwards from me a thousand leagues of blue.

There is, one knows not what sweet mystery about this sea, whose gently awful stirrings seem to speak of some hidden soul beneath; like those fabled undulations of the Ephesian sod over the buried Evangelist St John. And meet it is, that over these sea-pastures, wide-rolling watery prairies and Potters' Fields of all four continents, the waves should rise and fall, and ebb and flow unceasingly; for here, millions of mixed shades and shadows, drowned dreams, somnambulisms, reveries; all that we call lives and souls, lie dreaming, dreaming, still; tossing like slumberers in their beds; the ever-rolling waves but made so by their restlessness.

To any meditative Magian rover, this serene Pacific, once beheld, must ever after be the sea of his adoption. It rolls the midmost waters of the world, the Indian ocean and Atlantic being but its arms. The same waves wash the moles of the new-built Californian towns, but yesterday planted by the recentest race of men, and lave the faded but still gorgeous skirts of Asiatic lands, older than Abraham; while all between float milky-ways of coral isles, and low-lying, endless, unknown Archipelagoes, and impenetrable Japans. Thus this mysterious, divine Pacific zones the world's whole bulk about; makes all coasts one bay to it; seems the tide-beating heart of earth. Lifted by those eternal swells, you needs must own the seductive god, bowing your head to Pan.

But few thoughts of Pan stirred Ahab's brain, as standing like an iron statue at his accustomed place beside the mizen rigging, with one nostril he unthinkingly snuffed the sugary musk from the Bashee isles (in whose sweet woods mild lovers must be walking), and with the other consciously inhaled the salt breath of the new found sea; that sea in which the hated White Whale must even then be swimming. Launched at length upon these almost final waters, and gliding towards the Japanese cruising-ground, the old man's purpose intensified itself. His firm lips met like the lips of a vice; the Delta of his forehead's veins swelled like overladen brooks; in his very sleep, his ringing cry ran through the vaulted hull, 'Stern all! the White Whale spouts thick blood!'

### 3. THE CHASE—FIRST DAY

That night, in the mid-watch, when the old man—as his wont at intervals—stepped forth from the scuttle in which he leaned, and went to his pivot-hole, he suddenly thrust out his face fiercely, snuffing up the sea air as a sagacious ship's dog will, in drawing nigh to some barbarous isle. He declared that a whale must be near. Soon that peculiar odor, sometimes to a great distance given forth by the living sperm whale, was palpable to all the watch; nor was any mariner surprised when, after inspecting the compass, and then the dog-vane, and then ascertaining the precise bearing of the odor as nearly as possible, Ahab rapidly ordered the ship's course to be slightly altered, and the sail to be shortened.

The acute policy dictating these movements was sufficiently vindicated at daybreak, by the sight of a long sleek on the sea directly and lengthwise ahead, smooth as oil, and resembling in the pleated watery wrinkles bordering it, the polished metallic-like marks of some swift tide-rip, at the mouth of a deep, rapid stream.

'Man the mast-heads! Call all hands!'

Thundering with the butts of three clubbed handspikes on the forecastle deck, Daggoo roused the sleepers with such judgment claps that they seemed to exhale from the scuttle, so instantaneously did they appear with their clothes in their hands.

'What d'ye see?' cried Ahab, flattening his face to the sky.

'Nothing, nothing, sir!' was the sound hailing down in reply.

'T'gallant sails!—stunsails! alow and aloft, and on both sides!'

All sail being set, he now cast loose the life-line, reserved for swaying him to the main royal-mast head; and in a few moments they were hoisting him thither, when, while but two thirds of the way aloft, and while peering ahead through the horizontal vacancy between the main-top-sail and top-gallant-sail, he raised a gull-like cry in the air, 'There she blows!—there she blows! A hump like a snow-hill! It is Moby Dick!'

Fired by the cry which seemed simultaneously taken up by the three look-outs, the men on deck rushed to the rigging to behold the famous whale they had so long been pursuing. Ahab had now gained his final perch, some feet above the other look-outs, Tashtego standing just beneath him on the cap of the top-gallant mast, so that the Indian's head was almost on a level with Ahab's heel. From this height the whale was now seen some mile or so ahead, at every roll of the sea revealing his high sparkling hump, and regularly jetting his silent spout into the air. To the credulous mariners it seemed the same silent spout they had so long beheld in the moonlit Atlantic and Indian Oceans.

'And did none of ye see it before?' cried Ahab, hailing the perched men all around him.

'I saw him almost that same instant, sir, that Captain Ahab did, and I cried out,' said Tashtego.

'Not the same instant; not the same—no, the doubloon is mine, Fate reserved the doubloon for me. *I* only; none of ye could have raised the White Whale first. There she blows! there she blows!— there she blows! There again!—there again! he cried, in long-drawn, lingering, methodic tones, attuned to the gradual prolongings of the whale's visible jets. 'He's going to sound! In stunsails! Down top-gallant-sails; Stand by three boats. Mr Starbuck, remember, stay on board, and keep the ship. Helm there! Luff, luff a point! So; steady, man, steady! There go flukes! No, no; only black water! All ready the boats there? Stand by, stand by! Lower me, Mr Starbuck; lower, lower,—quick, quicker!' and he slid through the air to the deck.

'He is heading straight to leeward, sir,' cried Stubb, 'right away from us; cannot have seen the ship yet.'

'Be dumb, man! Stand by the braces! Hard down the helm!—brace up! Shiver her!—shiver her! So; well that! Boats, boats!'

Soon all the boats but Starbuck's were dropped; all the boat-sails set—all the paddles plying; with rippling swiftness, shooting to leeward; and Ahab heading the onset. A pale, death-glimmer lit up Fedallah's sunken eyes; a hideous motion gnawed his mouth.

Like noiseless nautilus shells, their light prows sped through the sea; but only slowly they neared the foe. As they neared him, the ocean grew still more smooth; seemed drawing a carpet over its waves; seemed a noon-meadow, so serenely it spread. At length the breathless hunter came so nigh his seemingly unsuspecting prey, that his entire dazzling hump was distinctly visible, sliding along the sea as if an isolated thing, and continually set in a revolving ring of finest, fleecy, greenish foam. He saw the vast, involved wrinkles of the slightly projecting head beyond. Before it, far out on the soft Turkish-rugged waters, went the glistening white shadow from his broad, milky forehead, a musical rippling playfully accompanying the shade; and behind, the blue waters interchangeably flowed over into the moving valley of his steady wake; and on either hand bright bubbles arose and danced by his side. But these were broken again by the light toes of hundreds of gay fowl softly feathering the sea, alternate with their fitful flight; and like to some flagstaff rising from the painted hull of an argosy, the tall but shattered pole of a recent

lance projected from the white whale's back; and at intervals one of
the cloud of soft-toed fowels hovering, and to and fro skimming like a
canopy over the fish, silently perched and rocked on this pole, the
long tail feathers streaming like pennons.

A gentle joyousness—a mighty mildness of repose in swiftness,
invested the gliding whale. Not the white bull Jupiter swimming
away with ravished Europa clinging to his graceful horns; his lovely,
leering eyes sideways intent upon the maid; with smooth bewitching
fleetness, rippling straight for the nuptial bower in Crete; not Jove,
not that great majesty Supreme! did surpass the glorified White
Whale as he so divinely swam.

On each soft side—coincident with the parted swell, that but once
leaving him, then flowed so wide away—on each bright side, the
whale shed off enticings. No wonder there had been some among the
hunters who namelessly transported and allured by all serenity, had
ventured to assail it; but had fatally found that quietude but the
vesture of tornadoes. Yet calm, enticing calm, oh, whale! thou glidest
on, to all who for the first time eye thee, no matter how many in that
same way thou may'st have bejuggled and destroyed before.

And thus, through the serene tranquillities of the tropical sea,
among waves whose hand-clappings were suspended by exceeding
rapture, Moby Dick moved on, still withholding from sight the full
terrors of his submerged trunk, entirely hiding the wrenched hideous-
ness of his jaw. But soon the fore part of him slowly rose from the
water; for an instant his whole marbleized body formed a high arch,
like Virginia's Natural Bridge, and warningly waving his bannered
flukes in the air, the grand god revealed himself, sounded, and went
out of sight. Hoveringly halting, and dipping on the wing, the white
sea-fowls longingly lingered over the agitated pool that he left.

With oars apeak, and paddles down, the sheets of their sails adrift,
the three boats now stilly floated, awaiting Moby Dick's reappearance.

'An hour,' said Ahab, standing rooted in his boat's stern; and he
gazed beyond the whale's place, towards the dim blue spaces and
wide wooing vacancies to leeward. It was only an instant; for again
his eyes seemed whirling round in his head as he swept the watery
circle. The breeze now freshened; the sea began to swell.

'The birds!—the birds!' cried Tashtego.

In long Indian file, as when herons take wing, the white birds were
now all flying towards Ahab's boat; and when within a few yards
began fluttering over the water there, wheeling round and round,

with joyous, expectant cries. Their vision was keener than man's; Ahab could discover no sign in the sea. But suddenly as he peered down and down into its depths, he profoundly saw a white living spot no bigger than a white weasel, with wonderful celerity uprising, and magnifying as it rose, till it turned, and then there were plainly revealed two long crooked rows of white, glistening teeth, floating up from the undiscoverable bottom. It was Moby Dick's open mouth and scrolled jaw; his vast, shadowed bulk still half blending with the blue of the sea. The glittering mouth yawned beneath the boat like an open-doored marble tomb; and giving one sidelong sweep with his steering oar, Ahab whirled the craft aside from this tremendous apparition. Then, calling upon Fedallah to change places with him, went forward to the bows, and seizing Perth's harpoon, commanded his crew to grasp their oars and stand by to stern.

Now, by reason of this timely spinning round the boat upon its axis, its bow, by anticipation, was made to face the whale's head while yet under water. But as if perceiving this strategem, Moby Dick, with that malicious intelligence ascribed to him, sidelingly transplanted himself, as it were, in an instant, shooting his pleated head lengthwise beneath the boat.

Through and through; through every plank and each rib, it thrilled for an instant, the whale obliquely lying on his back, in the manner of a biting shark, slowly and feelingly taking its bows full within his mouth, so that the long, narrow, scrolled lower jaw curled high up into the open air, and one of the teeth caught in a row-lock. The bluish pearl-white of the inside of the jaw was within six inches of Ahab's head, and reached higher than that. In this attitude the White Whale now shook the slight cedar as a mildly cruel cat her mouse. With unastonished eyes Fedallah gazed, and crossed his arms; but the tiger-yellow crew were tumbling over each other's heads to gain the uttermost stern.

And now, while both elastic gunwales were springing in and out, as the whale dallied with the doomed craft in this devilish way; and from his body being submerged beneath the boat, he could not be darted at from the bows, for the bows were almost inside of him, as it were; and while the other boats involuntarily paused, as before a quick crisis impossible to withstand, then it was that monomaniac Ahab, furious with this tantalizing vicinity of his foe, which placed him all alive and helpless in the very jaws he hated; frenzied with all this, he seized the long bone with his naked hands, and wildly strove to wrench it from its gripe. As now he thus vainly strove, the jaw slipped from him; the frail gunwales bent in, collapsed, and snapped, as both jaws, like an enormous shears, sliding further aft bit the craft completely in twain, and locked themselves fast again in the sea, midway between the two floating wrecks. These floated aside, the broken ends drooping, the crew at the stern-wreck clinging to the gunwales, and striving to hold fast to the oars to lash them across.

At that preluding moment, ere the boat was yet snapped, Ahab, the first to perceive the whale's intent, by the crafty upraising of his head, a movement that loosed his hold for the time; at that moment his hand had made one final effort to push the boat out of the bite. But only slipping further into the whale's mouth, and tilting over sideways as it slipped, the boat had shaken off his hold on the jaw; spilled him out of it, as he leaned to the push; and so he fell flat-faced upon the sea.

Ripplingly withdrawing from his prey, Moby Dick now lay at a little distance, vertically thrusting his oblong white head up and down in the billows; and at the same time slowly revolving his whole spindled body; so that when his vast wrinkled forehead rose—some twenty or more feet out of the water—the now rising swells, with all their confluent waves, dazzlingly broke against it, vindictively tossing their shivered spray still higher into the air. So, in a gale, the but half-baffled Channel billows only recoil from the base of the Eddystone, triumphantly to overleap its summit with their scud. . . .

1851

## 'Far Off-Shore'

Look, the raft, a signal flying,
   Thin—a shred;
None upon the lashed spars lying,
   Quick or dead.

Cries the sea-fowl, hovering over,
   'Crew, the crew?'
And the billow, reckless rover,
   Sweeps anew!

1888

# CHARLOTTE BRONTË
## 1816–1855

# from *Villette*

'Shall you be sea-sick?'

'Shall you?'

'Oh, immensely! as soon as ever we get in sight of the sea: I begin, indeed, to feel it already. I shall go below; and won't I order about that fat odious stewardess! Heureusement je sais faire aller mon monde.' Down she went.

It was not long before the other passengers followed her: throughout the afternoon I remained on deck alone. When I recall the tranquil, and even happy mood in which I passed those hours, and remember, at the same time, the position in which I was placed: its hazardous—some would have said its hopeless—character; I feel that, as—

> Stone walls do not a prison make,
> Nor iron bars—a cage,

so peril, loneliness, an uncertain future, are not oppressive evils, so long as the frame is healthy and the faculties are employed; so long, especially, as Liberty lends us her wings, and Hope guides us by her star.

I was not sick till long after we passed Margate, and deep was the pleasure I drank in with the sea breeze; divine the delight I drew from the heaving Channel waves, from the seabirds on their ridges, from the white sails on their dark distance, from the quiet yet beclouded sky, overhanging all. In my reverie, methought I saw the continent of Europe, like a wide dreamland, far away. Sunshine lay on it, making the long coast one line of gold; tiniest tracery of clustered town and snow-gleaming tower, of woods deep massed, of heights serrated, of smooth pasturage and veiny stream, embossed the metal-bright prospect. For background, spread a sky, solemn and dark blue, and—grand with imperial promise, soft with tints of enchantment—strode from north to south a God-bent bow, an arch of hope.

Cancel the whole of that, if you please, reader—or rather let it stand, and draw thence a moral—an alliterative, text-hand copy—

Day-dreams are delusions of the demon.

Becoming excessively sick, I faltered down into the cabin.

Miss Fanshawe's berth chanced to be next to mine; and, I am sorry to say, she tormented me with an unsparing selfishness during the whole time of our mutual distress. Nothing could exceed her impatience and fretfulness. The Watsons, who were very sick too, and on whom the stewardess attended with shameless partiality, were stoics compared with her. Many a time since have I noticed, in persons of Ginevra Fanshawe's light, careless temperament, and fair, fragile style of beauty, an entire incapacity to endure: they seem to sour in adversity, like small beer in thunder. The man who takes such a woman for his wife, ought to be prepared to guarantee her an existence all sunshine. Indignant at last with her teasing peevishness, I curtly requested her 'to hold her tongue'. The rebuff did her good, and it was observable that she liked me no worse for it.

As dark night drew on, the sea roughened: larger waves swayed strong against the vessel's side. It was strange to reflect that blackness and water were round us, and to feel the ship ploughing straight on her pathless way, despite noise, billow, and rising gale. Articles of furniture began to fall about, and it became needful to lash them to their places; the passengers grew sicker than ever; Miss Fanshawe declared, with groans, that she must die.

'Not just yet, honey,' said the stewardess. 'We're just in port.' Accordingly, in another quarter of an hour, a calm fell upon us all; and about midnight the voyage ended.

1853

# WALT WHITMAN
## 1819–1892

## from *Song of Myself*

You sea! I resign myself to you also—I guess what you mean,
I behold from the beach your crooked inviting fingers,
I believe you refuse to go back without feeling of me,
We must have a turn together, I undress, hurry me out of sight of the
    land,
Cushion me soft, rock me in billowy drowse,
Dash me with amorous wet, I can repay you.

Sea of stretch'd ground-swells,
Sea breathing broad and convulsive breaths,
Sea of the brine of life and of unshovell'd yet always-ready graves,
Howler and scooper of storms, capricious and dainty sea,
I am integral with you, I too am of one phase and of all phases.

1855

## 'In Cabin'd Ships at Sea'

In cabin'd ships at sea,
The boundless blue on every side expanding,
With whistling winds and music of the waves, the large imperious
    waves,
Or some lone bark buoy'd on the dense marine,
Where joyous full of faith, spreading white sails,
She cleaves the ether mid the sparkle and the foam of day, or under
    many a star at night,
By sailors young and old haply will I, a reminiscence of the land, be
    read,
In full rapport at last.

*Here are our thoughts, voyagers' thoughts,*
*Here not the land, firm land, alone appears,* may then by them be said,
*The sky o'erarches here, we feel the undulating deck beneath our feet,*
*We feel the long pulsation, ebb and flow of endless motion,*
*The tones of unseen mystery, the vague and vast suggestions of the*
     *briny world, the liquid-flowing syllables,*
*The perfume, the faint creaking of the cordage, the melancholy*
     *rhythm,*
*The boundless vista and the horizon far and dim are all here,*
*And this is ocean's poem.*

Then falter not O book, fulfil your destiny,
You not a reminiscence of the land alone,
You too as a lone bark cleaving the ether, purpos'd I know not
     whither, yet ever full of faith,
Consort to every ship that sails, sail you!
Bear forth to them folded my love (dear mariners, for you I fold it
     here in every leaf);
Speed on my book! spread your white sails my little bark athwart the
     imperious waves,
Chant on, sail on, bear o'er the boundless blue from me to every sea,
This song for mariners and all their ships.

                                                   1856–60

# 'Patroling Barnegat'

Wild, wild the storm, and the sea high running,
Steady the roar of the gale, with incessant undertone muttering,
Shouts of demoniac laughter fitfully piercing and pealing.
Waves, air, midnight, their savagest trinity lashing,
Out in the shadows there milk-white combs careering,
On beachy slush and sand spirts of snow fierce slanting,
Where through the murk the easterly death-wind breasting,
Through cutting swirl and spray watchful and firm advancing
(That in the distance! is that a wreck? is the red signal flaring?),
Slush and sand of the beach tireless till daylight wending.

Steadily, slowly, through hoarse roar never remitting,
Along the midnight edge by those milk-white combs careering,
A group of dim, weird forms, struggling, the night confronting,
That savage trinity warily watching.

1856–60

## 'After the Sea-Ship'

After the sea-ship, after the whistling winds,
After the white-gray sails taut to their spars and ropes,
Below, a myriad myriad waves hastening, lifting up their necks,
Tending in ceaseless flow toward the track of the ship,
Waves of the ocean bubbling and gurgling, blithely prying,
Waves, undulating waves, liquid, uneven, emulous waves,
Toward that whirling current, laughing and buoyant, with curves,
Where the great vessel sailing and tacking displaced the surface,
Larger and smaller waves in the spread of the ocean yearnfully
    flowing,
The wake of the sea-ship after she passes, flashing and frolicsome
    under the sun,
A motley procession with many a fleck of foam and many fragments,
Following the stately and rapid ship, in the wake following.

1856–60

## EMILY DICKINSON
### 1830–1886

## 'Exultation is the going'

Exultation is the going
Of an inland soul to sea,
Past the houses—past the headlands—
Into deep Eternity—

Bred as we, among the mountains,
Can the sailor understand
The divine intoxication
Of the first league out from land?

1890

---

# ANTHONY TROLLOPE
## 1815–1882

## from *The West Indies and the Spanish Main*

I am beginning to write this book on board the brig ——, trading
between Kingston, in Jamaica, and Cien Fuegos, on the southern
coast of Cuba. At the present moment there is not a puff of wind,
neither land breeze nor sea breeze; the sails are flapping idly against
the masts; there is not motion enough to give us the command of the
rudder; the tropical sun is shining through upon my head into the
miserable hole which they have deluded me into thinking was a cabin.
The marine people—the captain and his satellites—are bound to
provide me; and all that they have provided is yams, salt pork,
biscuit, and bad coffee. I should be starved but for the small ham—
would that it had been a large one—which I thoughtfully purchased
in Kingston; and had not a kind medical friend, as he grasped me by
the hand at Port Royal, stuffed a box of sardines into my pocket. He
suggested two boxes. Would that I had taken them!

It is now the 25th January, 1859, and if I do not reach Cien Fuegos
by the 28th, all this misery will have been in vain. I might as well in
such case have gone to St Thomas, and spared myself these experiences
of the merchant navy. Let it be understood by all men that in these
latitudes the respectable, comfortable, well-to-do route from every
place to every other place is via the little Danish island of St Thomas.
From Demerara to the Isthmus of Panama, you go by St Thomas.
From Panama to Jamaica and Honduras, you go by St Thomas. From
Honduras and Jamaica to Cuba and Mexico, you go by St Thomas.

From Cuba to the Bahamas, you go by St Thomas—or did when this was written. The Royal Mail Steam Packet Company dispense all their branches from that favoured spot.

But I was ambitious of a quicker transit and a less beaten path, and here I am lying under the lee of the land, in a dirty, hot, motionless tub, expiating my folly. We shall never make Cien Fuegos by the 28th, and then it will be eight days more before I can reach the Havana. May God forgive me all my evil thoughts!

Motionless, I said: I wish she were. Progressless should have been my word. She rolls about in a nauseous manner, disturbing the two sardines which I have economically eaten, till I begin to fear that my friend's generosity will become altogether futile. To which result greatly tends the stench left behind it by the cargo of salt fish with which the brig was freighted when she left St John, New Brunswick, for these ports. 'We brought but a very small quantity,' the skipper says. If so, that very small quantity was stowed above and below the very bunk which has been given up to me as a sleeping-place. Ugh!

'We are very poor,' said the blue-nosed skipper when he got me on board. 'Well; poverty is no disgrace,' said I, as one does when cheering a poor man. 'We are very poor indeed; I cannot even offer you a cigar.' My cigar-case was immediately out of my pocket. After all, cigars are but as coals going to Newcastle when one intends to be in Cuba in four days.

'We are very poor indeed, sir,' said the blue-nosed skipper again when I brought out my solitary bottle of brandy—for I must acknowledge to a bottle of brandy as well as to the small ham. 'We have not a drop of spirits of any kind on board.' Then I altered my mind, and began to feel that poverty was a disgrace. What business had this man to lure me into his stinking boat, telling me that he would take me to Cien Fuegos, and feed me on the way, when he had not a mouthful to eat, or a drop to drink, and could not raise a puff of wind to fill his sails? 'Sir,' said I, 'brandy is dangerous in these latitudes, unless it be taken medicinally; as for myself, I take no other kind of physic.' I think that poverty on shipboard is a disgrace, and should not be encouraged. Should I ever be on shore again, my views may become more charitable.

Oh, for the good ship 'Atrato', which I used to abuse with such objurgations because the steward did not come at my very first call; because the claret was only half iced; because we were forced to close our little whist at 11 p.m., the serjeant-at-arms at that hour inexorably extinguishing all the lights! How rancorous were our tongues! 'This comes of monopoly,' said a stern and eloquent neighbour at the dinner-table, holding up to sight a somewhat withered apple. 'And dis,' said a grinning Frenchman from Martinique with a curse, exhibiting a rotten walnut—'dis, dis! They give me dis for my moneys—for my thirty-five pounds!' And glancing round with angry eye, he dropped the walnut on to his plate.

Apples! and walnuts!! What would I give for the 'Atrato' now; for my berth, then thought so small; for its awning; for a bottle of its soda water; for one cut from one of all its legs of mutton; for two hours of its steam movement! And yet it is only now that I am learning to forgive that withered apple and that ill-iced claret. . . .

Oh; we are getting into the trade-winds, are we? Let Aeolus be thanked at last. I should be glad to get into a monsoon or a simoom at the present moment, if there be monsoons and simooms in these parts. Yes; it comes rippling down upon us with a sweet, cool, airy breeze; the sails flap rather more loudly, as though they had some life in them, and then fill themselves with a grateful motion. Our three or four sailors rise from the deck where they have been snoring, and begin to stretch themselves. 'You may put her about,' says the skipper, for be it known that for some hours past her head has been lying back towards Port Royal. 'We shall make fine track now, sir,' he says, turning to me, 'And be at Cien Fuegos on the 28th?' I demanded. 'Perhaps, sir; perhaps. We've lost twenty-four hours, sir, doing nothing, you know.'

Oh, wretched man that I am! the conveyance from Cien Fuegos to the Havana is but once a week.

The sails are still flopping against the yard. It is now noon on the 29th of January, and neither captain, mate, crew, nor the one solitary passenger have the least idea when the good brig —— will reach the port of Cien Fuegos; not even whether she will reach it at all. Since that time we have had wind enough in all conscience—lovely breezes as the mate called them. But we have oversailed our mark; and by how much no man on board this vessel can tell. Neither the captain nor the mate were ever in Cien Fuegos before; and I begin to doubt whether they ever will be there. No one knows where we are. An old stove has, it seems, been stowed away right under the compass, giving a false bias to the needle, so that our only guide guides us wrong. There is not a telescope on board. I very much doubt the skipper's power of taking an observation, though he certainly goes through the form of holding a machine like a brazen spider up to his eye about midday. My brandy and cigars are done; and altogether we are none of us jolly.

Flap, flap, flap! roll, roll, roll! The time passes in this way very tediously. And then there has come upon us all a feeling not expressed, though seen in the face of all, of utter want of confidence in our master. There is none of the excitement of danger, for the land is within a mile of us; none of the exhaustion of work, for there is nothing to do. Of pork and biscuits and water there is, I believe, plenty. There is nothing tragic to be made out of it. But comic misery wears one quite as deeply as that of a sterner sort.

It is hardly credible that men should be sent about a job for which they are so little capable, and as to which want of experience must be so expensive! Here we are, beating up the coast of Cuba against the prevailing wind, knowing nothing of the points which should guide us, and looking out for a harbour without a sea-glass to assist our eyes. When we reach port, be it Cien Fuegos or any other, the first thing we must do will be to ask the name of it! It is incredible to myself that I should have found my way into such circumstances.

1859

## ALFRED, LORD TENNYSON
### 1809–1892

## 'The Voyage'

We left behind the painted buoy
    That tosses at the harbour-mouth;
And madly danced our hearts with joy,
    As fast we fleeted to the South:
How fresh was every sight and sound
    On open main or winding shore!
We knew the merry world was round,
    And we might sail for evermore.

Warm broke the breeze against the brow,
   Dry sang the tackle, sang the sail:
The Lady's-head upon the prow
   Caught the shrill salt, and sheer'd the gale.
The broad seas swell'd to meet the keel,
   And swept behind; so quick the run,
We felt the good ship shake and reel,
   We seem'd to sail into the Sun!

How oft we saw the Sun retire,
   And burn the threshold of the night,
Fall from his Ocean-lane of fire,
   And sleep beneath his pillar'd light!
How oft the purple-skirted robe
   Of twilight slowly downward drawn,
As thro' the slumber of the globe
   Again we dash'd into the dawn!

New stars all night above the brim
   Of waters lighten'd into view;
They climb'd as quickly, for the rim
   Changed every moment as we flew.
Far ran the naked moon across
   The houseless ocean's heaving field,
Or flying shone, the silver boss
   Of her own halo's dusky shield;

The peaky islet shifted shapes,
   High towns on hills were dimly seen,
We past long lines of Northern capes
   And dewy Northern meadows green.
We came to warmer waves, and deep
   Across the boundless east we drove,
Where those long swells of breaker sweep
   The nutmeg rocks and isles of clove.

By peaks that flamed, or, all in shade,
   Gloom'd the low coast and quivering brine
With ashy rains, that spreading made
   Fantastic plume or sable pine;

By sands and steaming flats, and floods
  Of mighty mouth, we scudded fast,
And hills and scarlet-mingled woods
  Glow'd for a moment as we past.

O hundred shores of happy climes,
  How swiftly stream'd ye by the bark!
At times the whole sea burn'd, at times
  With wakes of fire we tore the dark;
At times a carven craft would shoot
  From havens hid in fairy bowers,
With naked limbs and flowers and fruit,
  But we nor paused for fruit nor flowers.

For one fair Vision ever fled
  Down the waste waters day and night,
And still we follow'd where she led,
  In hope to gain upon her flight.
Her face was evermore unseen,
  And fixt upon the far sea-line;
But each man murmur'd, 'O my Queen,
  I follow till I make thee mine.'

And now we lost her, now she gleam'd
  Like Fancy made of golden air,
Now nearer to the prow she seem'd
  Like Virtue firm, like Knowledge fair,
Now high on waves that idly burst
  Like Heavenly Hope she crown'd the sea,
And now, the bloodless point reversed,
  She bore the blade of Liberty.

And only one among us—him
  We pleased not—he was seldom pleased:
He saw not far: his eyes were dim:
  But ours he swore were all diseased.
'A ship of fools,' he shriek'd in spite,
  'A ship of fools,' he sneer'd and wept.
And overboard one stormy night
  He cast his body, and on we swept.

And never sail of ours was furl'd,
  Nor anchor dropt at eve or morn;
We lov'd the glories of the world,
  But laws of nature were our scorn.
For blasts would rise and rave and cease,
  But whence were those that drove the sail
Across the whirlwind's heart of peace,
  And to and thro' the counter gale?


Again to colder climes we came,
  For still we follow'd where she led:
Now mate is blind and captain lame,
  And half the crew are sick or dead,
But, blind or lame or sick or sound,
  We follow that which flies before.
We know the merry world is round,
  And we may sail for evermore.

                                      1864


# 'The Sailor Boy'


He rose at dawn and, fired with hope,
  Shot o'er the seething harbour-bar,
And reach'd the ship and caught the rope,
  And whistled to the morning star.


And while he whistled long and loud
  He heard a fierce mermaiden cry,
'O boy, tho' thou art young and proud,
  I see the place where thou wilt lie.


'The sands and yeasty surges mix
  In caves about the dreary bay,
And on thy ribs the limpet sticks,
  And in thy heart the scrawl shall play.'

'Fool,' he answer'd, 'death is sure
   To those that stay and those that roam,
But I will nevermore endure
   To sit with empty hands at home.

'My mother clings about my neck,
   My sisters crying, "Stay for shame";
My father raves of death and wreck,
   They are all to blame, they are all to blame.

'God help me! save I take my part
   Of danger on the roaring sea,
A devil rises in my heart,
   Far worse than any death to me.'

1861

## 'Crossing the Bar'

Sunset and evening star,
   And one clear call for me!
And may there be no moaning of the bar,
   When I put out to sea,

But such a tide as moving seems asleep,
   Too full for sound and foam,
When that which drew from out the boundless deep
   Turns again home.

Twilight and evening bell,
   And after that the dark!
And may there be no sadness of farewell,
   When I embark;

For tho' from out our bourne of Time and Place
   The flood may bear me far,
I hope to see my Pilot face to face
   When I have crost the bar.

1889

# PROFESSOR ANSTED

# from 'The Representation of Water'

The mobility of water is at the bottom of all the properties which render the element artistic. It is the life which ensures such incessant power to express ideas; it is the perpetual change which gives the highest of all interest. 'To paint water in all its perfection is as impossible as to paint the soul.' This remark of Mr Ruskin's, as striking as it is accurately true, is only one of the innumerable passing hints by which that suggestive writer has enriched the literature of Art.

The variety of colour of water is not less remarkable than its infinite mobility. Water has its own tint; it reflects and transmits a true shade. But the colour actually seen depends on the transparency of the water, on the nature of the light that it is exposed to, on the nature of the bottom if of any moderate depth, on the angle at which the light falls, and on the objects around, whose colour is also reflected. Look, for example, at a spit of flat sand, just covered by a few inches of water on an advancing tide: at first, and close to the observer, the sand will be seen through the water; but at a little distance, shallow as the water really is, it will look to grow deeper and deeper, because the reflected rays from its surface are more and more in excess of any transmitted rays, in proportion as the distance of the water from the eye increases. This is easily verified if we watch the tide. As a larger extent of the sand becomes covered, so does the position of the deeper water seem to advance. Just in the same way the reflection from a pond or shallow pool of fresh water, whether clear or muddy, differs according to the distance. What seems, and is, muddy when quite near, loses that appearance altogether a little farther off. Under these circumstances, the colour is modified by the distance in reality, and the depth in appearance.

That water has a colour of its own is almost certain, but it is also the case that it very easily assumes, or appears to assume, different tints. Entering the British Channel from the Atlantic, every sailor knows, and passengers soon learn to know, the diminished depth from the altered colour. A nearer approach to land is yet more marked; and yet the comparatively shallow water thus first observed is several hundred feet deep, and the actual quantity of transmitted colour cannot much differ. The effect is, perhaps, derived from other causes than the absolute tint of the water, as we know that in open sea marine currents will have a somewhat similar effect.

Of the physical properties that help to lead the artist in the right direction in the delineation of water, that power of acting upon almost all substances in nature which especially characterises it, is, perhaps, the most important; it is certainly the most remarkable. Water acts directly on all rocks, partly by dissolving and helping to decompose them, and partly by eating away and bodily removing all such broken portions as come under its influence. In this sense, and in this manner, the whole surface of the earth—every rock, every cliff, every plain and valley—certainly owes its peculiarities of form, and all that in itself is characteristic, to water action. Almost every rock has been deposited from water, has been washed and worn by the waves, has been eaten into by marine currents and rivers, has been bored through by water trickling down from the surface into the interior, or up from the interior to the surface. Thus, water being connected with all natural appearances, and with most changes, the study of it is really the most important of all studies, and to understand the nature of its action is desirable for every artist.

Proceeding now to special phenomena, let us first consider that vast reservoir covering three-fifths of the surface of our globe, presenting, from time to time, all conceivable differences of condition,—now raging and furious, presently calm and peaceful; its bosom gently heaving with the rising or falling tide, or lashed into foam by the tempest and the whirlwind.

The colour of water in the open ocean we have already alluded to, and it is not less varied than it is beautiful. In fine weather, of the deepest and most exquisite clear blue, it is so sensitive as to thicken and become muddy with approaching change. During a great storm, it is sometimes of one uniform dead whiteness of foam, and soon black and colourless, having lost all the tints so characteristic of it at other times. Immediately after a storm, the air and water appear worked into a strange and fitful state—fearful to watch, but hardly to be expressed either by the pencil or pen. But, not only does the colour vary with these extremes of weather. From day to day, and even from hour to hour, as he is carried into other latitudes, and departs more and more from his starting-place, the traveller sees new phases of

beauty; sea-weed drifts past him of unfamiliar forms, and this alters
the tone of the water in which it floats. A fringe of snow-white
breakers marks a dangerous coral reef, or a low mist on the surface a
treacherous shoal. Each change in depth, or in the current he is
crossing, is indicated by a fresh tint; and whether he is able to look
down scores of fathoms to white rocks and shells below, or his eye
seeks in vain for repose in the unfathomable blue deep on whose
bosom he is gently rocked, there is always enough to satisfy the most
restless and curious student, and always abundant interest in contemplating the reflections of the ever-changing sky.

But the phenomena of waves are, perhaps, more striking, and are
quite as difficult to represent. They also involve variety without end.
From the gentlest ripple to the most violent disturbance the gradations
are infinite; and the waves vary, not only with their magnitude, but
with the depth of the water in which they are formed. Every wave
surface, besides having its own height and width as a wave, is also
covered with small ripples, so that perfectly smooth surfaces of water
are rare and exceptional appearances. The waves on a rocky shore
often exhibit a metallic greenness, and a rich depth of colour, that is
illustrated, but not exaggerated, in Hook's admirable and well-
known pictures. In them the pure water-character is retained, in spite
of the apparent hardness of the tone, and they afford studies of a high
order, teaching some most difficult and little known truths.

1863

# HENRY DAVID THOREAU
## 1817–1862

# from *Cape Cod*

The next summer I saw a sloop from Chatham dragging for anchors
and chains just off this shore. She had her boats out at the work while
she shuffled about on various tacks, and, when anything was found,
drew up to hoist it on board. It is a singular employment, at which
men are regularly hired and paid for their industry, to hunt to-day in

pleasant weather for anchors which have been lost—the sunken faith and hope of mariners, to which they trusted in vain; now, perchance, it is the rusty one of some old pirate's ship or Norman fisherman, whose cable parted here two hundred years ago; and now the best bower anchor of a Canton or a California ship, which has gone about her business. If the roadsteads of the spiritual ocean could be thus dragged, what rusty flukes of hope deceived and parted chain-cables of faith might again be windlassed aboard! enough to sink the finder's craft, or stock new navies to the end of time. The bottom of the sea is strewn with anchors, some deeper and some shallower, and alternately covered and uncovered by the sand, perchance with a small length of iron cable still attached—to which where is the other end? So many unconcluded tales to be continued another time. So, if we had diving-bells adapted to the spiritual deeps, we should see anchors with their cables attached, as thick as eels in vinegar, all wriggling vainly toward their holding-ground. But that is not treasure for us which another man has lost; rather it is for us to seek what no other man has found or can find—not be Chatham men, dragging for anchors.

The annals of this voracious beach! Who could write them, unless it were a shipwrecked sailor? How many who have seen it have seen it only in the midst of danger and distress, the last strip of earth which their mortal eyes beheld. Think of the amount of suffering which a single strand has witnessed. The ancients would have represented it as a sea-monster with open jaws, more terrible than Scylla and Charybdis. An inhabitant of Truro told me that about a fortnight after the *St John* was wrecked at Cohasset he found two bodies on the shore at the Clay Pounds. They were those of a man, and a corpulent woman. The man had thick boots on, though his head was off, but 'it was alongside'. It took the finder some weeks to get over the sight. Perhaps they were man and wife, and whom God had joined the ocean currents had not put asunder. Yet by what slight accidents at first may they have been associated in their drifting. Some of the bodies of those passengers were picked up far out at sea, boxed up and sunk; some brought ashore and buried. There are more consequences to a shipwreck than the underwriters notice. The Gulf Stream may return some to their native shores, or drop them in some out-of-the-way cave of Ocean, where time and the elements will write new riddles with their bones.

The sea-shore is a sort of neutral ground, a most advantageous point from which to contemplate this world. It is even a trivial place. The

waves forever rolling to the land are too far-travelled and untamable
to be familiar. Creeping along the endless beach amid the sun-squall
and the foam, it occurs to us that we, too, are the product of sea-
slime.

It is a wild, rank place, and there is no flattery in it. Strewn with
crabs, horse-shoes, and razor-clams, and whatever the sea casts up—
a vast *morgue*, where famished dogs may range in packs, and crows
come daily to glean the pittance which the tide leaves them. The
carcasses of men and beasts together lie stately up upon its shelf,
rotting and bleaching in the sun and waves, and each tide turns them
in their beds, and tucks fresh sand under them. There is naked
Nature, inhumanly sincere, wasting no thought on man, nibbling at
the cliffy shore where gulls wheel amid the spray.

We saw this forenoon what, at a distance, looked like a bleached
log with a branch still left on it. It proved to be one of the principal
bones of a whale, whose carcass, having been stripped of blubber at
sea and cut adrift, had been washed up some months before. It
chanced that this was the most conclusive evidence which we met
with to prove, what the Copenhagen antiquaries assert, that these
shores were the *Furdustrandas* which Thorhall, the companion of
Thorfinn during his expedition to Vinland in 1007, sailed past in
disgust. It appears that after they had left the Cape and explored the
country about Straum-Fiordr (Buzzards' Bay!), Thorhall, who was
disappointed at not getting any wine to drink there, determined to
sail north again in search of Vinland. Though the antiquaries have
given us the original Icelandic, I prefer to quote their translation,
since theirs is the only Latin which I know to have been aimed at
Cape Cod.

> Cum parati erant, sublato
> velo, cecinit Thorhallus:
> Eò redeamus, ubi conterranei
> sunt nostri! faciamus aliter,
> expansi arenosi peritum,
> lata navis explorare curricula:
> dum procellam incitantes gladii
> morae impatientes, qui terram
> collaudant, Furdustrandas
> inhabitant et coquunt balaenas.

In other words: 'When they were ready and their sail hoisted,
Thorhall sang: Let us return thither where our fellow-countrymen

are. Let us make a bird[1] skilful to fly through the heaven of sand,[2] to explore the broad track of ships; while warriors who impel to the tempest of swords,[3] who praise the land, inhabit Wonder-Strands, *and cook whales.*' And so he sailed north past Cape Cod, as the antiquaries say, 'and was shipwrecked on to Ireland'.

Though once there were more whales cast up here, I think that it was never more wild than now. We do not associate the idea of antiquity with the ocean, nor wonder how it looked a thousand years ago, as we do of the land, for it was equally wild and unfathomable always. The Indians have left no traces on its surface, but it is the same to the civilized man and the savage. The aspect of the shore only has changed. The ocean is a wilderness reaching round the globe, wilder than a Bengal jungle, and fuller of monsters, washing the very wharves of our cities and the gardens of our sea-side residences. Serpents, bears, hyenas, tigers, rapidly vanish as civilization advances, but the most populous and civilized city cannot scare a shark far from its wharves. It is no further advanced than Singapore, with its tigers, in this respect. The Boston papers had never told me that there were seals in the harbor. I had always associated these with the Esquimaux and other outlandish people. Yet from the parlor windows all along the coast you may see families of them sporting on the flats. They were as strange to me as the merman would be. Ladies who never walk in the woods, sail over the sea. To go to sea! Why, it is to have the experience of Noah—to realize the deluge. Every vessel is an ark.

1864

[1] i.e. a vessel.
[2] The sea, which is arched over its sandy bottom like a heaven.
[3] Battle.

# RALPH WALDO EMERSON
## 1803–1882

# from *English Traits*

I find the sea-life an acquired taste, like that for tomatoes and olives. The confinement, cold, motion, noise, and odour are not to be dispensed with. The floor of your room is sloped at an angle of twenty or thirty degrees, and I waked every morning with the belief that some one was tipping up my berth. Nobody likes to be treated ignominiously, upset, shoved against the side of the house, rolled over, suffocated with bilge, mephitis, and stewing oil. We get used to these annoyances at last, but the dread of the sea remains longer. The sea is masculine, the type of active strength. Look, what egg-shells are drifting all over it, each one, like ours, filled with men in ecstasies of terror, alternating with cockney conceit, as the sea is rough or smooth. Is this sad-coloured circle an eternal cemetery? In our graveyards we scoop a pit, but this aggressive water opens mile-wide pits and chasms, and makes a mouthful of a fleet. To the geologist, the sea is the only firmament; the land is in perpetual flux and change, now blown up like a tumour, now sunk in a chasm, and the registered observations of a few hundred years find it in a perpetual tilt, rising and falling. The sea keeps its old level; and 'tis no wonder that the history of our race is so recent, if the roar of the ocean is silencing our traditions. A rising of the sea, such as has been observed, say an inch in a century, from east to west on the land, will bury all the towns, monuments, bones, and knowledge of mankind, steadily and insensibly. If it is capable of these great and secular mischiefs, it is quite as ready at private and local damage; and of this no landsman seems so fearful as the seaman. Such discomfort and such danger as the narratives of the captain and mate disclose are bad enough as the costly fee we pay for entrance to Europe; but the wonder is always new that any sane man can be a sailor. And here, on the second day of our voyage, stepped out a little boy in his shirt-sleeves, who had hid himself, whilst the ship was in port, in the bread-closet, having no money, and wishing to go to England. The sailors have dressed him in Guernsey frock, with a knife in his belt, and he is climbing nimbly about after them, 'likes the work first-rate, and, if the captain will take him, means now to come back again in the ship'. The mate avers that this is the history of all sailors; nine out of ten are runaway boys; and adds, that all of them are sick of the sea, but stay in it out of pride. Jack has a life of risks, incessant abuse, and the worst pay. It is a little better with the mate, and not very much better with the captain. A hundred dollars a month is reckoned high pay. If sailors were contented, if they had not resolved again and again not to go to sea any more, I should respect them.

Of course, the inconveniences and terrors of the sea are not of any account to those whose minds are pre-occupied. The water-laws, arctic frost, the mountain, the mine, only shatter Cockneyism; every noble activity makes room for itself. A great mind is a good sailor, as a great heart is. And the sea is not slow in disclosing inestimable secrets to a good naturalist.

'Tis a good rule in every journey to provide some piece of liberal study to rescue the hours which bad weather, bad company, and taverns, steal from the best economist. Classics which at home are drowsily read have a strange charm in a country inn, or in the transom of a merchant brig. I remember that some of the happiest and most valuable hours I have owed to books, passed, many years ago, on shipboard. The worst impediment I have found at sea is the want of light in the cabin.

We found on board the usual cabin library; Basil Hall, Dumas, Dickens, Bulwer, Balzac, and Sand, were our sea-gods. Among the passengers, there was some variety of talent and profession; we exchanged our experiences, and all learned something. The busiest talk with leisure and convenience at sea, and sometimes a memorable fact turns up, which you have long had a vacant niche for, and seize with the joy of a collector. But, under the best conditions, a voyage is one of the severest tests to try a man. A college examination is nothing to it. Sea-days are long—these lack-lustre, joyless days which whistled over us; but they were few—only fifteen, as the captain counted, sixteen according to me. Reckoned from the time when we left soundings, our speed was such that the captain drew the line of his course in red ink on his chart, for the encouragement or envy of future navigators.

It has been said that the King of England would consult his dignity by giving audience to foreign ambassadors in the cabin of a man-of-war. And I think the white path of an Atlantic ship the right avenue to the palace front of this seafaring people, who for hundreds of years claimed the strict sovereignty of the sea, and exacted toll and the striking sail from the ships of all other peoples. When their privilege was disputed by the Dutch and other junior marines, on the plea that you could never anchor on the same wave, or hold property in what was always flowing, the English did not stick to claim the channel or bottom of all the main. 'As if', said they, 'we contended for the drops of the sea, and not for its situation, or the bed of those waters. The sea is bounded by His Majesty's empire.'

As we neared the land, its genius was felt. This was inevitably the British side. In every man's thought arises now a new system, English sentiments, English loves and fears, English history and social modes. Yesterday, every passenger had measured the speed of the ship by watching the bubbles over the ship's bulwarks. To-day, instead of bubbles, we measure by Kinsale, Cork, Waterford, and Ardmore. There lay the green shore of Ireland, like some coast of plenty. We could see towns, towers, churches, harvests; but the curse of eight hundred years we could not discern.

1865

# ALGERNON CHARLES SWINBURNE
## 1837–1909

## 'The Return'

I will go back to the great sweet mother,
  Mother and lover of men, the sea.
I will go down to her, I and none other,
  Close with her, kiss her and mix her with me;
Cling to her, strive with her, hold her fast;
O fair white mother, in days long past
Born without sister, born without brother,
  Set free my soul as thy soul is free.

O fair green-girdled mother of mine,
   Sea, that art clothed with the sun and the rain,
Thy sweet hard kisses are strong like wine,
   Thy large embraces are keen like pain.
Save me and hide me with all thy waves,
Find me one grave of thy thousand graves,
Those pure cold populous graves of thine,
   Wrought without hand in a world without stain.

I shall sleep, and move with the moving ships,
   Change as the winds change, veer in the tide;
My lips will feast on the foam of thy lips,
   I shall rise with thy rising, with thee subside;
Sleep, and not know if she be, if she were,
Filled full with life to the eyes and hair,
As a rose is fulfilled to the roseleaf tips
   With splendid summer and perfume and pride.

This woven raiment of nights and days,
   Were it once cast off and unwound from me,
Naked and glad would I walk in thy ways,
   Alive and aware of thy ways and thee;
Clear of the whole world, hidden at home,
Clothed with the green and crowned with the foam,
A pulse of the life of thy straits and bays,
   A vein in the heart of the streams of the sea.

1866

# MATTHEW ARNOLD
## 1822–1888

## 'Dover Beach'

The sea is calm to-night.
The tide is full, the moon lies fair
Upon the straits; on the French coast the light
Gleams and is gone; the cliffs of England stand,
Glimmering and vast, out in the tranquil bay.
Come to the window, sweet is the night-air!
Only, from the long line of spray
Where the sea meets the moon-blanched land,
Listen! you hear the grating roar
Of pebbles which the waves draw back, and fling,
At their return, up the high strand,
Begin, and cease, and then again begin,
With tremulous cadence slow, and bring
The eternal note of sadness in.

Sophocles long ago
Heard it on the Aegaean, and it brought
Into his mind the turbid ebb and flow
Of human misery; we
Find also in the sound a thought,
Hearing it by this distant northern sea.

The Sea of Faith
Was once, too, at the full, and round earth's shore
Lay like the folds of a bright girdle furled.
But now I only hear
Its melancholy, long, withdrawing roar,
Retreating, to the breath
Of the night-wind, down the vast edges drear
And naked shingles of the world.

Ah, love, let us be true
To one another! for the world, which seems
To lie before us like a land of dreams,
So various, so beautiful, so new,
Hath really neither joy, nor love, nor light,
Nor certitude, nor peace, nor help for pain;
And we are here as on a darkling plain
Swept with confused alarms of struggle and flight,
Where ignorant armies clash by night.

1867

## JOHN MACGREGOR
### 1825–1892

# from *The Voyage Alone in the Yawl*
# *'Rob Roy'*

The barometer mounted steadily all Sunday, so we resolved to start next morning at break of day. But though the night was quiet, the vessels near my berth were also getting ready, therefore at last I gave up all hopes of sleep, and for company's sake got ready also after midnight, that we might have all the tide possible for going round Beachy Head, which, once passed, we could find easy ports all the way to London. So about two o'clock, in the dark, we are rowing out again on the ebbing tide, and the water at the pier-head looks placid now compared with the boiling and dashing it made there when the yawl passed in before.

Dawn broke an hour afterwards with a dank and silent mist skirting up far-away hills, and a gentle east wind faintly breathing as our tea-cup smoked fragrant on deck. The young breeze was only playful yet, so we anchored, waiting for it to rise in earnest or the tide to slacken, as both of them were now contrary; and meantime we rested some hours preparing for a long spell of unknown work; but I could not sleep in such a lovely daybreak, not having that most valuable capacity of being able to sleep when it is wanted for coming work, and not for labour past.

The east wind baffled the yawl and a whole fleet of vessels, all of us trying to do the same thing, namely, to arrive at Beachy Head before two o'clock in the day; for, if this could be managed, we should there find the tide ebbing eastwards, and so get twelve hours of current in our favour.

This feature—the division of the tides there—makes Beachy Head a well-marked point in the navigation of the Channel. The stream from the North Sea meets the other from the Atlantic here, and here also they begin to separate. After beating, in downright sailing, one after another of the schooners and brigs and barques in company, I saw at last with real regret that not one of us could reach the point in time, and yet the yawl got there only a few minutes too late; but it was dead calm, and I even rowed her on to gain the last little mile.

One after another the vessels gave it up, and each cast anchor. Coming to a pilot steamer, I hailed: 'Shall I be able to do it?' 'No, sir,' they said; 'no—very sorry for you, sir; you've worked hard, sir, but you're ten minutes too late.' Within that time the tide had turned against us. We had not crossed the line of division, and so the yawl had to be turned towards shore to anchor there, and to wait the tide until nine o'clock at night, unless a breeze came sooner.

After three hours' work she reached the desired six fathoms' patch of sand, just under the noble white cliff that rears its head aloft about 600 feet, standing ever as a giant wall, sheer, upright, out of the sea.

Dinner done and everything set right (for this is best policy always), I slipped into my cabin and tried to sleep as the sun went down, but a little land-breeze now began, and every now and then my head was raised to see how tide or wind progressed. Then I must have fallen once into a mild nap, and perhaps a dream, for sudden and strong a rough hand seemed to shake the boat, and, on my leaping up, there glanced forth a brilliant flash of lightning that soon put everybody on the *qui vive*.

Now was heard the clink of distant cables, as I raised mine also in the dark, with only the bright shine of the lighthouse like a keen and full-opened eye gazing down from the cliff overhead.

Compass lighted, ship-lantern fixed, a reef in each sail, and, with a moment's thought of the very similar events that had passed only a few nights ago, we steered right south, away, away to the open sea.

It was black enough all around; but yet the strong wind expected after thunder had not come, and we edged away eastward, doubly watchful, however, of the dark, for the crowd of vessels here was the real danger, and not the sea.

The ghost of Rob Roy is flitting on the white sail as the lamp shines brightly. Down comes the rain, and with it flash after flash, peal upon peal of roaring thunder, and the grandeur of the scene is unspeakable. The wind changed every few minutes, and vessels and boats and steamers whirled past like visions, often much too near to be welcome.

A white dazzling gleam of forked lightning cleaves the darkness, and, behold! a huge vessel close at hand, but hitherto unseen, lofty and full-sailed, and for a moment black against the instant of light, and then utterly lost again. The plashing of rain hissed in the sea, and a voice would come out of the unseen—'Port, you lubber!' The ship or whatever it is has no lights at all, though on board it they can see mine. Ah, it's no use peering forward to discover on which side is the new danger; for when your eye has gazed for a time at the lighted compass it is powerless for a minute or two to see in the dark space forward, or, again, if you stare into the blackness to scan the faintest glimmer of a sail ahead, then for some time after you cannot see the compass when looking at it dazzled. This difficulty in sailing alone is the only one we felt to be quite insuperable.

Again a steam whistle shrieked amid the thunder, and two eyes glared out of the formless vapour and rain—the red and the green lights—the signals that showed where she was steaming. There was shouting from her deck as she kept rounding and backing, no doubt for a man overboard. As we slewed to starboard to avoid her, another black form loomed close on the right; and what with wind, rain, thunder, and ships, there was everything to confuse just when there was all need of cool decision.

It would be difficult for me to exaggerate the impressive spectacle that passed along on the dark background of this night. To show what others thought, we may quote the following paragraph from the *Pall Mall Gazette* of next day, August 20:[1]

The storm which raged in London through the whole of last night was beyond question by far the most severe and protracted which has occurred for many years. It began at half-past eight o'clock, after a day of intense heat, which increased as the evening advanced, though it never reached the

---

[1] The singular volcanic eruptions in Iceland occurred also this day.

sultriness which was remarked before the storm of last week. The first peal of thunder was heard about nine, and from that time till after five this morning it never ceased for more than a few minutes, while the lightning may be said to have been absolutely continuous. Its vivid character was something quite unusual in the storms of recent summers, and the thunder by which it was often instantaneously followed can only be described as terrific. The storm reached its greatest violence between two and three o'clock, when a smart gale of wind sprang up, and for about ten minutes the tempest was really awful.

We had noticed some rockets sent up from Eastbourne earlier in the evening; probably these were fireworks at a fête there, but the rain must have soon drowned the gala. Certainly it closed up my view of all other lights but the lightning, though sometimes a shining line appeared for a moment in the distance, perhaps from Hastings; and at one time the moon came out red and full, and exactly at the top of a vessel's lofty sails. One steamer had puzzled me much by its keeping nearly still. This drifted close up at last, and they called out,. 'Ahoy, there!—are you a fishing-boat?' They wanted to know their bearings, as the current and shifting wind made the position of Beachy Head quite uncertain in the dark.[2] I replied to their hail—'No, I'm the yacht *Rob Roy*, crew of one man; don't you see my white sails?' and they answered—'See? why, who can see to-night?'

Sometimes a sudden and dead lull came with an ominous meaning, and then the loud hissing of rain could be heard advancing to us in the dark till it poured on the yawl in sheets of water, and the mere dripping from the peak of my sou'wester was enough to obscure vision.

And yet, after a few hours of the turmoil and excitement, this state of things became quite as if it were natural, so soon does one get accustomed to any circumstances, however strange at first. I even cooked hot tea; it was something to do, as well as to drink, and singing and whistling also beguiled the dark hours of eager, strained watching. In a lighter moment, once a great lumbering sloop sailed near, and we hailed her loudly, 'How's the wind going to be?'—for the wind kept ever changing (but the thunder and lightning were going on still). A gruff voice answered, 'Can't say; who *can* say— night this sort—think it'll settle east.' This was bad news for me,

[2] The numerous vessels met now were some of those we had been with in the morning, and they looked even more in number, for we crossed and recrossed each other frequently, and this part of the Channel is a highway for nations.

but it did not come true. The sloop's skipper wished for an east wind, and so he expected it.

A stranger sound than any before now forced attention as it rapidly neared us, and soon the sea was white around with boiling, babbling little waves—what could it be? Instantly I sounded with the lead, but there was no bottom—we were not driving on shore—it was one of the 'overfalls' or 'ripples' we have mentioned before, where a turbid sea is raised in deep water by some far-down precipice under the waves.

The important question at once arose as to which of the 'overfalls' on my chart this could be—the one marked as only a mile from Beachy Head, or the other ten miles further on. Have we been turning and wheeling about all this dreary night in only a few square miles of sea, or have we attained the eastern tide, and so are now running fast on our course?

The incessant and irksome pitching and rolling which the overfalls caused, might be patiently borne, if only we could be assured the yawl progressed. But all was still left in doubt.

So sped the storm for eight long hours, with splendours for the eye, and deep long thrills of the sublime, that stirred deep the whole inner being with feelings vivid and strong and loosed the most secret folds of consciousness with thoughts I had never felt before, and perhaps shall never know again. The mind conjured up the most telling scenes it had known of 'alone' and of 'thunder', to compare with this where both were now combined.

To stand on the top of Mont Blanc, that round white icicle highest in Europe, and all alone to gaze on a hundred peaks around—that was indeed impressive.

More so was it to kneel alone at the edge of Etna, and to fill the mind from the smoking crater with thoughts and fancies teeming out of the hot, black, and wide abyss.

Thunder and lightning, also, in the crater of Vesuvius we had wondered at before; and it had been grander still, when the flashes lighted up Niagara, pouring out its foam that glistened for a moment dazzling white and then vanished, while the thundering heavens sounded louder than the heavy torrent tumbling into the dark. But here, in my yawl on the sea, was more splendid than these. Imagination painted its own free picture on a black and boundless background of mind strung tight by near danger; and from out this spoke the deep loud diapason, while the quick flashing at intervals gave point to all.

Then that glorious anthem came to my memory, where these words of the 18th Psalm are nobly rendered:

He bowed the heavens and came down, and darkness was under His feet.
He rode upon a cherub and did fly; yea, He did fly upon the wings of the wind.
He made darkness His secret place; the pavilion round about Him were dark waters and thick clouds of the skies.
The Lord also thundered in the heavens, and the Highest gave His voice: hail stones and coals of fire.
Then the channels of waters were seen, and the foundations of the world were discovered: at Thy rebuke, O Lord, at the blast of the breath of Thy nostrils.
He sent down from above, He took me, He drew me up out of many waters.

The sensations were prolonged enough to be analysed and reasoned upon, and it was a difficult question which cannot yet be answered— 'Would I willingly have all this over again?' Lying on a sofa in a comfortable room, I would not go out to this scene; but in a boat, if all this began again, I certainly would not go ashore to avoid its discomforts and lose its grandeurs.

The profound uncertainty as to what was to come next moment being one of the most exciting features of the occasion, perhaps the whole scene would be tamed sadly by a mere repetition; but one sentiment was dominant over all at the time, that I had lived a long year in a night.

Soon after four o'clock, there suddenly stretched out what seemed to be a reef of breakers for miles under the sullen rain-clouds, and, with instant attention, the yawl was put about to avoid them.

This extraordinary optical illusion was the dawn opening on the coast, then actually ten miles away, and in a very few minutes, as the cloud lifted, the land seemed to rush off to its proper distance, until at last the curtain split in two, and I found to my intense delight that in the night we had crossed the bay!

1867

# GERARD MANLEY HOPKINS
## 1844–1889

# from *Journal*

## 1872

*Aug. 10.* I was looking at high waves. The breakers always are parallel to the coast and shape themselves to it except where the curve is sharp however the wind blows. They are rolled out by the shallowing shore just as a piece of putty between the palms whatever its shape runs into a long roll. The slant ruck or crease one sees in them shows the way of the wind. The regularity of the barrels surprised and charmed the eye; the edge behind the comb or crest was as smooth and bright as glass. It may be noticed to be green behind and silver white in front: the silver marks where the air begins, the pure white is foam, the green/solid water. Then looked at to the right or left they are scrolled over like mouldboards or feathers or jibsails seen by the edge. It is pretty to see the hollow of the barrel disappearing as the white comb on each side runs along the wave gaining ground till the two meet at a pitch and crush and overlap each other

About all the turns of the scaping from the break and flooding of the wave to its run out again I have not yet satisfied myself. The shores are swimming and the eyes have before them a region of milky surf but it is hard for them to unpack the huddling and gnarls of the water and law out the shapes and the sequence of the running: I catch however the looped or forked wisp made by every big pebble the backwater runs over—if it were clear and smooth there would be a network from their overlapping, such as can in fact be seen on smooth sand after the tide is out; then I saw it run browner, the foam dwindling and twitched into long chains of suds, while the strength of the backdraught shrugged the stones together and clocked them one against another

Looking from the cliff I saw well that work of dimpled foam-laps—strings of short loops or halfmoons—which I had studied at Freshwater years ago

It is pretty to see the dance and swagging of the light green tongues or ripples of waves in a place locked between rocks

1873

*Aug. 1.* To Derby Castle at Douglas [Isle of Man] as last year

*Aug. 16.* We rose at four, when it was stormy and I saw dun-coloured waves leaving trailing hoods of white breaking on the beach. Before going I took a last look at the breakers, wanting to make out how the comb is morselled so fine into string and tassel, as I have lately noticed it to be. I saw big smooth flinty waves, carved and scuppled in shallow grooves, much swelling when the wind freshened, burst on the rocky spurs of the cliff at the little cove and break into bushes of foam. In an enclosure of rocks the peaks of the water romped and wandered and a light crown of tufty scum standing high on the surface kept slowly turning round: chips of it blew off and gadded about without weight in the air. At eight we sailed for Liverpool in wind and rain. I think it is the salt that makes rain at sea sting so much. There was a good-looking young man on board that got drunk and sung 'I want to go home to Mamma'. I did not look much at the sea: the crests I saw ravelled up by the wind into the air in arching whips and straps of glassy spray and higher broken into clouds of white and blown away. Under the curl shone a bright juice of beautiful green. The foam exploding and smouldering under water makes a chrysoprase green.

# ROBERT LOUIS STEVENSON
## 1850–1894

# from 'The English Admirals'

If an Englishman wishes to have such a [patriotic] feeling, it must be about the sea. The lion is nothing to us; he has not been taken to the hearts of the people, and naturalised as an English emblem. We know right well that a lion would fall foul of us as grimly as he would of a Frenchman or a Moldavian Jew, and we do not carry him before us in the smoke of battle. But the sea is our approach and bulwark; it has been the scene of our greatest triumphs and dangers; and we are accustomed in lyrical strains to claim it as our own. The prostrating experiences of foreigners between Calais and Dover have always an agreeable side to English prepossessions. A man from Bedfordshire, who does not know one end of the ship from the other until she begins to move, swaggers among such persons with a sense of hereditary nautical experience. To suppose yourself endowed with natural parts for the sea because you are the countryman of Blake and mighty Nelson is perhaps just as unwarrantable as to imagine Scotch extraction a sufficient guarantee that you will look well in a kilt. But the feeling is there, and seated beyond the reach of argument. We should consider ourselves unworthy of our descent if we did not share the arrogance of our progenitors, and please ourselves with the pretension that the sea is English. Even where it is looked upon by the guns and battlements of another nation we regard it as a kind of English cemetery, where the bones of our seafaring fathers take their rest until the last trumpet; for I suppose no other nation has lost as many ships or sent as many brave fellows to the bottom.

1881

# RUDYARD KIPLING

## 1865–1936

# 'The Sea and the Hills'

Who hath desired the Sea?—the sight of salt water unbounded—
The heave and the halt and the hurl and the crash of the comber wind-
  hounded?
The sleek-barrelled swell before storm, grey, foamless, enormous,
  and growing—
Stark calm on the lap of the Line or the crazy-eyed hurricane
  blowing—
His Sea in no showing the same—his Sea and the same 'neath each
  showing:
       His Sea as she slackens or thrills?
So and no otherwise—so and no otherwise—hillmen desire their
  Hills!

Who hath desired the Sea?—the immense and contemptuous surges?
The shudder, the stumble, the swerve, as the star-stabbing bowsprit
  emerges?
The orderly clouds of the Trades, the ridged, roaring sapphire
  thereunder—
Unheralded cliff-haunting flaws and the headsail's low volleying
  thunder—
His Sea in no wonder the same—his Sea and the same through each
  wonder:
       His Sea as she rages or stills?
So and no otherwise—so and no otherwise—hillmen desire their
  Hills.

Who hath desired the Sea? Her menaces swift as her mercies?
The in-rolling walls of the fog and the silver-winged breeze that
  disperses?
The unstable mined berg going South and the calvings and groans
  that declare it—

White water half-guessed overside and the moon breaking timely to
     bare it—
His Sea as his fathers have dared—his Sea as his children shall dare it:
          His Sea as she serves him or kills?
So and no otherwise—so and no otherwise—hillmen desire their
     Hills.


Who hath desired the Sea? Her excellent loneliness rather
Than forecourts of kings, and her outermost pits than the streets
     where men gather
Inland, among dust, under trees—inland where the slayer may slay
     him—
Inland, out of reach of her arms, and the bosom whereon he must lay
     him—
His Sea from the first that betrayed—at the last that shall never
     betray him:
          His Sea that his being fulfils?
So and no otherwise—so and no otherwise—hillmen desire their
     Hills.

                                                                      1902


# from 'A Matter of Fact'


The *Rathmines* kicked her way northward through the warm water.

   In the morning of one specially warm night we three were sitting
immediately in front of the wheel-house, where an old Swedish
boatswain whom we called 'Frithiof the Dane' was at the wheel,
pretending that he could not hear our stories. Once or twice Frithiof
spun the spokes curiously, and Keller lifted his head from a long chair
to ask, 'What is it? Can't you get any steerage-way on her?'

   'There is a feel in the water,' said Frithiof, 'that I cannot understand. I
think that we run downhills or somethings. She steers bad this
morning.'

   Nobody seems to know the laws that govern the pulse of the big
waters. Sometimes even a landsman can tell that the solid ocean is atilt,
and that the ship is working herself up a long unseen slope; and
sometimes the captain says, when neither full steam nor fair wind
justifies the length of a day's run, that the ship is sagging downhill;

but how these ups and downs come about has not yet been settled authoritatively.

'No, it is a following sea,' said Frithiof, 'and with a following sea you shall not get good steerage-way.'

The sea was as smooth as a duck-pond, except for a regular oily swell. As I looked over the side to see where it might be following us from, the sun rose in a perfectly clear sky and struck the water with its light so sharply that it seemed as though the sea should clang like a burnished gong. The wake of the screw and the little white streak cut by the log-line hanging over the stern were the only marks on the water as far as eye could reach.

Keller rolled out of his chair and went aft to get a pine-apple from the ripening stock that was hung inside the after awning.

'Frithiof, the log-line has got tired of swimming. It's coming home,' he drawled.

'What?' said Frithiof, his voice jumping several octaves.

'Coming home,' Keller repeated, leaning over the stern. I ran to his side and saw the log-line, which till then had been drawn tense over the stern railing, slacken, loop, and come up off the port quarter. Frithiof called up the speaking-tube to the bridge, and the bridge answered, 'Yes, nine knots.' Then Frithiof spoke again, and the answer was, 'What do you want of the skipper?' and Frithiof bellowed, 'Call him up.'

By this time Zuyland, Keller, and myself had caught something of Frithiof's excitement, for any emotion on shipboard is most contagious. The captain ran out of his cabin, spoke to Frithiof, looked at the log-line, jumped on the bridge, and in a minute we felt the steamer swing round as Frithiof turned her.

''Going back to Cape Town?' said Keller.

Frithiof did not answer, but tore away at the wheel. Then he beckoned us three to help, and we held the wheel down till the *Rathmines* answered it, and we found ourselves looking into the white of our own wake, with the still oily sea tearing past our bows, though we were not going more than half steam ahead.

The captain stretched out his arm from the bridge and shouted. A minute later I would have given a great deal to have shouted too, for one-half of the sea seemed to shoulder itself above the other half, and came on in the shape of a hill. There was neither crest, comb, nor curl-over to it; nothing but black water with little waves chasing each other about the flanks. I saw it stream past and on a level with the

*Rathmines'* bow-plates before the steamer hove up her bulk to rise, and I argued that this would be the last of all earthly voyages for me. Then we lifted for ever and ever and ever, till I heard Keller saying in my ear, 'The bowels of the deep, good Lord!' and the *Rathmines* stood poised, her screw racing and drumming on the slope of a hollow that stretched downwards for a good half-mile.

We went down that hollow, nose under for the most part, and the air smelt wet and muddy, like that of an emptied aquarium. There was a second hill to climb; I saw that much: but the water came aboard and carried me aft till it jammed me against the wheel-house door, and before I could catch breath or clear my eyes again we were rolling to and fro in torn water, with the scuppers pouring like eaves in a thunderstorm.

'There were three waves,' said Keller; 'and the stokehold's flooded.'

The firemen were on deck waiting, apparently, to be drowned. The engineer came and dragged them below, and the crew, gasping, began to work the clumsy Board of Trade pump. That showed nothing serious, and when I understood that the *Rathmines* was really on the water, and not beneath it, I asked what had happened.

'The captain says it was a blow-up under the sea—a volcano,' said Keller.

'It hasn't warmed anything,' I said. I was feeling bitterly cold, and cold was almost unknown in those waters. I went below to change my clothes, and when I came up everything was wiped out in clinging white fog.

'Are there going to be any more surprises?' said Keller to the captain.

'I don't know. Be thankful you're alive, gentlemen. That's a tidal wave thrown up by a volcano. Probably the bottom of the sea has been lifted a few feet somewhere or other. I can't quite understand this cold spell. Our sea-thermometer says the surface water is 44°, and it should be 68° at least.'

'It's abominable,' said Keller, shivering. 'But hadn't you better attend to the fog-horn? It seems to me that I heard something.'

'Heard! Good heavens!' said the captain from the bridge, 'I should think you did.' He pulled the string of our fog-horn, which was a weak one. It sputtered and choked, because the stokehold was full of water and the fires were half-drowned, and at last gave out a moan. It was answered from the fog by one of the most appalling steam-sirens I have ever heard. Keller turned as white as I did, for the fog, the cold

fog, was upon us, and any man may be forgiven for fearing a death he
cannot see.

'Give her steam there!' said the captain to the engine-room. 'Steam
for the whistle, if we have to go dead slow.'

We bellowed again, and the damp dripped off the awnings on to
the deck as we listened for the reply. It seemed to be astern this time,
but much nearer than before.

'The *Pembroke Castle* on us!' said Keller; and then, viciously,
'Well, thank God, we shall sink her too.'

'It's a side-wheel steamer,' I whispered. 'Can't you hear the
paddles?'

This time we whistled and roared till the steam gave out, and the
answer nearly deafened us. There was a sound of frantic threshing in
the water, apparently about fifty yards away, and something shot
past in the whiteness that looked as though it were gray and red.

'The *Pembroke Castle* bottom up,' said Keller, who, being a
journalist, always sought for explanations. 'That's the colours of a
Castle liner. We're in for a big thing.'

'The sea is bewitched,' said Frithiof from the wheel-house. 'There
are *two* steamers!'

Another siren sounded on our bow, and the little steamer rolled in
the wash of something that had passed unseen.

'We're evidently in the middle of a fleet,' said Keller quietly. 'If one
doesn't run us down, the other will. Phew! What in creation is that?'

I sniffed, for there was a poisonous rank smell in the cold air—a
smell that I had smelt before.

'If I was on land I should say that it was an alligator. It smells like
musk,' I answered.

'Not ten thousand alligators could make that smell,' said Zuyland;
'I have smelt them.'

'Bewitched! Bewitched!' said Frithiof. 'The sea she is turned
upside down, and we are walking along the bottom.'

Again the *Rathmines* rolled in the wash of some unseen ship, and a
silver-gray wave broke over the bow, leaving on the deck a sheet of
sediment—the gray broth that has its place in the fathomless deeps of
the sea. A sprinkling of the wave fell on my face, and it was so cold
that it stung as boiling water stings. The dead and most untouched
deep water of the sea had been heaved to the top by the submarine
volcano—the chill still water that kills all life and smells of desolation
and emptiness. We did not need either the blinding fog or that

indescribable smell of musk to make us unhappy—we were shivering with cold and wretchedness where we stood.

'The hot air on the cold water makes this fog,' said the captain; 'it ought to clear in a little time.'

'Whistle, oh! whistle, and let's get out of it,' said Keller.

The captain whistled again, and far and far astern the invisible twin steam-sirens answered us. Their blasting shriek grew louder, till at last it seemed to tear out of the fog just above our quarter, and I cowered while the *Rathmines* plunged bows under on a double swell that crossed.

'No more,' said Frithiof, 'it is not good any more. Let us get away, in the name of God.'

'Now if a torpedo-boat with a *City of Paris* siren went mad and broke her moorings and hired a friend to help her, it's just conceivable that we might be carried as we are now. Otherwise this thing is—'

The last words died on Keller's lips, his eyes began to start from his head, and his jaw fell. Some six or seven feet above the port bulwarks, framed in fog, and as utterly unsupported as the full moon, hung a Face. It was not human, and it certainly was not animal, for it did not belong to this earth as known to man. The mouth was open, revealing a ridiculously tiny tongue—as absurd as the tongue of an elephant; there were tense wrinkles of white skin at the angles of the drawn lips, white feelers like those of a barbel sprung from the lower jaw, and there was no sign of teeth within the mouth. But the horror of the face lay in the eyes, for those were sightless—white, in sockets as white as scraped bone, and blind. Yet for all this the face, wrinkled as the mask of a lion is drawn in Assyrian sculpture, was alive with rage and terror. One long white feeler touched our bulwarks. Then the face disappeared with the swiftness of a blindworm popping into its burrow, and the next thing that I remember is my own voice in my own ears, saying gravely to the mainmast, 'But the air-bladder ought to have been forced out of its mouth, you know.'

Keller came up to me, ashy white. He put his hand into his pocket, took a cigar, bit it, dropped it, thrust his shaking thumb into his mouth and mumbled, 'The giant gooseberry and the raining frogs! Gimme a light—gimme a light! Say, gimme a light.' A little bead of blood dropped from his thumb-joint.

I respected the motive, though the manifestation was absurd. 'Stop, you'll bite your thumb off,' I said, and Keller laughed brokenly as he picked up his cigar. Only Zuyland, leaning over the port bulwarks, seemed self-possessed. He declared later that he was very sick.

'We've seen it,' he said turning round, 'That is it.'

'What?' said Keller, chewing the unlighted cigar.

As he spoke the fog was blown into shreds, and we saw the sea, gray with mud, rolling on every side of us and empty of all life. Then in one spot it bubbled and became like the pot of ointment that the Bible speaks of. From that wide-ringed trouble a Thing came up—a gray and red Thing with a neck—a Thing that bellowed and writhed in pain. Frithiof drew in his breath and held it till the red letters of the ship's name, woven across his jersey, straggled and opened out as though they had been type badly set. Then he said with a little cluck in his throat, 'Ah me! It is blind. *Hur illa!* That thing is blind,' and a murmur of pity went through us all, for we could see that the thing on the water was blind and in pain. Something had gashed and cut the great sides cruelly and the blood was spurting out. The gray ooze of the undermost sea lay in the monstrous wrinkles of the back, and poured away in sluices. The blind white head flung back and battered the wounds, and the body in its torment rose clear of the red and gray waves till we saw a pair of quivering shoulders streaked with weed and rough with shells, but as white in the clear spaces as the hairless, maneless, blind, toothless head. Afterwards, came a dot on the horizon and the sound of a shrill scream, and it was as though a shuttle shot all across the sea in one breath, and a second head and neck tore through the levels, driving a whispering wall of water to right and left. The two Things met—the one untouched and the other in its death-throe—male and female, we said, the female coming to the male. She circled round him bellowing, and laid her neck across the curve of his great turtle-back, and he disappeared under water for an instant, but flung up again, grunting in agony while the blood ran. Once the entire head and neck shot clear of the water and stiffened, and I heard Keller saying, as though he was watching a street accident, 'Give him air. For God's sake, give him air.' Then the death-struggle began, with crampings and twistings and jerkings of the white bulk to and fro, till our little steamer rolled again, and each gray wave coated her plates with the gray slime. The sun was clear, there was no wind, and we watched, the whole crew, stokers and all, in wonder and pity, but chiefly pity. The Thing was so helpless, and, save for his mate, so alone. No human eye should have beheld him; it was monstrous and indecent to exhibit him there in trade waters between atlas degrees of latitude. He had been spewed up, mangled and dying, from his rest on the sea-floor, where he might have lived till the Judgment Day, and we saw the tides of his life go from him as an angry tide goes out across rocks in the teeth of a landward gale. His mate lay rocking on the water a little distance off, bellowing continually, and the smell of musk came down upon the ship making us cough.

At last the battle for life ended in a batter of coloured seas. We saw the writhing neck fall like a flail, the carcase turn sideways, showing the glint of a white belly and the inset of a gigantic hind leg or flipper. Then all sank, and sea boiled over it, while the mate swam round and round, darting her head in every direction. Though we might have feared that she would attack the steamer, no power on earth could have drawn any one of us from our places that hour. We watched, holding our breaths. The mate paused in her search; we could hear the wash beating along her sides; reared her neck as high as she could reach, blind and lonely in all that loneliness of the sea, and sent one desperate bellow booming across the swells as an oyster-shell skips across a pond. Then she made off to the westward, the sun shining on the white head and the wake behind it, till nothing was left to see but a little pin point of silver on the horizon. We stood on our course again; and the *Rathmines*, coated with the sea-sediment from bow to stern, looked like a ship made gray with terror.

1893

# JOSEPH CONRAD

## 1857–1924

# from *The Nigger of the 'Narcissus'*

Next morning, at daylight, the *Narcissus* went to sea.

A slight haze blurred the horizon. Outside the harbour the measureless expanse of smooth water lay sparkling like a floor of jewels, and as empty as the sky. The short black tug gave a pluck to windward, in the usual way, then let go the rope, and hovered for a moment on the quarter with her engines stopped; while the slim, long hull of the ship moved ahead slowly under lower topsails. The loose upper canvas blew out in the breeze with soft round contours, resembling small white clouds snared in the maze of ropes. Then the sheets were hauled home, the yards hoisted, and the ship became a high and lonely pyramid, gliding, all shining and white, through the sunlit mist. The tug turned short round and went away towards the land. Twenty-six pairs of eyes watched her low broad stern crawling languidly over the smooth swell between the two paddle-wheels that turned fast, beating the water with fierce hurry. She resembled an enormous and aquatic black beetle, surprised by the light, overwhelmed by the sunshine, trying to escape with ineffectual effort into the distant gloom of the land. She left a lingering smudge of smoke on the sky, and two vanishing trails of foam on the water. On the place where she had stopped a round black patch of soot remained, undulating on the swell—an unclean mark of the creature's rest.

The *Narcissus* left alone, heading south, seemed to stand resplendent and still upon the restless sea, under the moving sun. Flakes of foam swept past her sides; the water struck her with flashing blows; the land glided away slowly fading; a few birds screamed on motionless wings over the swaying mastheads. But soon the land disappeared, the birds went away; and to the west the pointed sail of an Arab dhow running for Bombay, rose triangular and upright above the sharp edge of the horizon, lingered and vanished like an illusion. Then the ship's wake, long and straight, stretched itself out through a day of immense solitude. The setting sun, burning on the level of the water, flamed crimson below the blackness of heavy rain clouds. The sunset squall, coming up from behind, dissolved itself into the short deluge of a hissing shower. It left the ship glistening from trucks to waterline, and with darkened sails. She ran easily before a fair monsoon, with her decks cleared for the night; and, moving along with her, was heard the sustained and monotonous swishing of the waves, mingled with the low whispers of men mustered aft for the setting of watches; the short plaint of some block aloft; or, now and then, a loud sigh of wind.

Mr Baker, coming out of his cabin, called out the first name sharply before closing the door behind him. He was going to take charge of the deck. On the homeward trip, according to an old custom of the sea, the chief officer takes the first night-watch—from eight till midnight. So Mr Baker, after he had heard the last 'Yes, sir!' said moodily, 'Relieve the wheel and look-out'; and climbed with heavy feet the poop ladder to windward. Soon after Mr Creighton came down, whistling softly, and went into the cabin. On the doorstep the steward lounged, in slippers, meditative, and with his shirt-sleeves rolled up to the armpits. On the main deck the cook, locking up the galley doors, had an altercation with young Charley about a pair of socks. He could be heard saying impressively, in the darkness amidships: 'You don't deserve a kindness. I've been drying them for you, and now you complain about the holes—and you swear, too! Right in front of me! If I hadn't been a Christian—which you ain't, you young ruffian—I would give you a clout on the head. . . . Go away!' Men in couples or threes stood pensive or moved silently along the bulwarks in the waist. The first busy day of a homeward passage was sinking into the dull peace of resumed routine. Aft, on the high poop, Mr Baker walked shuffling and grunted to himself in the pauses of his thoughts. Forward, the look-out man, erect between the flukes of the two anchors, hummed an endless tune, keeping his eyes fixed dutifully ahead in a vacant stare. A multitude of stars coming out into the clear night peopled the emptiness of the sky. They glittered, as if alive above the sea; they surrounded the running ship on all sides; more intense than the eyes of a staring crowd, and as inscrutable as the souls of men.

The passage had begun, and the ship, a fragment detached from the earth, went on lonely and swift like a small planet. Round her the abysses of sky and sea met in an unattainable frontier. A great circular solitude moved with her, ever changing and ever the same, always

monotonous and always imposing. Now and then another wandering
white speck, burdened with life, appeared far off—disappeared;
intent on its own destiny. The sun looked upon her all day, and every
morning rose with a burning, round stare of undying curiosity. She
had her own future; she was alive with the lives of those beings who
trod her decks; like that earth which had given her up to the sea, she
had an intolerable load of regrets and hopes. On her lived timid truth
and audacious lies; and, like the earth, she was unconscious, fair to
see—and condemned by men to an ignoble fate. The august loneliness
of her path lent dignity to the sordid inspiration of her pilgrimage.
She drove foaming to the southward, as if guided by the courage of a
high endeavour. The smiling greatness of the sea dwarfed the extent
of time. The days raced after one another, brilliant and quick like the
flashes of a lighthouse, and the nights, eventful and short, resembled
fleeting dreams.

1897

# from *Heart of Darkness*

The *Nellie*, a cruising yawl, swung to her anchor without a flutter of
the sails, and was at rest. The flood had made, the wind was nearly
calm, and being bound down the river, the only thing for it was to
come to and wait for the turn of the tide.

The sea-reach of the Thames stretched before us like the beginning
of an interminable waterway. In the offing the sea and the sky were
welded together without a joint, and in the luminous space the tanned
sails of the barges drifting up with the tide seemed to stand still in red
clusters of canvas sharply peaked, with gleams of varnished sprits. A
haze rested on the low shores that ran out to sea in vanishing flatness.
The air was dark above Gravesend, and farther back still seemed
condensed into a mournful gloom, brooding motionless over the
biggest, and the greatest, town on earth.

The director of Companies was our captain and our host. We four
affectionately watched his back as he stood in the bows looking to
seaward. On the whole river there was nothing that looked half so
nautical. He resembled a pilot, which to a seaman is trustworthiness

personified. It was dificult to realize his work was not out there in the luminous estuary, but behind him, within the brooding gloom.

Between us there was, as I have already said somewhere, the bond of the sea. Besides holding our hearts together through long periods of separation, it had the effect of making us tolerant of each other's yarns—and even convictions. The Lawyer—the best of old fellows—had, because of his many years and many virtues, the only cushion on deck, and was lying on the only rug. The Accountant had brought out already a box of dominoes, and was toying architecturally with the bones. Marlow sat cross-legged right aft, leaning against the mizzen-mast. He had sunken cheeks, a yellow complexion, a straight back, an ascetic aspect, and, with his arms dropped, the palms of hands outwards, resembled an idol. The Director, satisfied the anchor had good hold, made his way aft and sat down amongst us. We exchanged a few words lazily. Afterwards there was silence on board the yacht. For some reason or other we did not begin that game of dominoes. We felt meditative, and fit for nothing but placid staring. The day was ending in a serenity of still and exquisite brilliance. The water shone pacifically; the sky, without a speck, was a benign immensity of unstained light; the very mist on the Essex marshes was like a gauzy and radiant fabric, hung from the wooded rises inland, and draping the low shores in diaphanous folds. Only the gloom to the west, brooding over the upper reaches, became more somber every minute, as if angered by the approach of the sun.

And at last, in its curved and imperceptible fall, the sun sank low, and from glowing white changed to a dull red without rays and without heat, as if about to go out suddenly, stricken to death by the touch of that gloom brooding over a crowd of men.

Forthwith a change came over the waters, and the serenity became less brilliant but more profound. The old river in its broad reach rested unruffled at the decline of day, after ages of good service done to the race that peopled its banks, spread out in the tranquil dignity of a waterway leading to the uttermost ends of the earth. We looked at the venerable stream not in the vivid flush of a short day that comes and departs for ever, but in the august light of abiding memories. And indeed nothing is easier for a man who has, as the phrase goes, 'followed the sea' with reverence and affection, than to evoke the great spirit of the past upon the lower reaches of the Thames. The tidal current runs to and fro in its unceasing service, crowded with memories of men and ships it had borne to the rest of home or to the

battles of the sea. It had known and served all the men of whom the
nation is proud, from Sir Francis Drake to Sir John Franklin, knights
all, titled and untitled—the great knights-errant of the sea. It had
borne all the ships whose names are like jewels flashing in the night of
time, from the *Golden Hind* returning with her round flanks full of
treasure, to be visited by the Queen's Highness and thus pass out of the
gigantic tale, to the *Erebus* and *Terror*, bound on other conquests—and
that never returned. It had known the ships and the men. They had
sailed from Deptford, from Greenwich, from Erith—the adventurers
and the settlers; kings' ships and the ships of men on 'Change;
captains, admirals, the dark 'interlopers' of the Eastern trade, and the
commissioned 'generals' of East India fleets. Hunters for gold or
pursuers of fame, they all had gone out on that stream, bearing the
sword, and often the torch, messengers of the might within the land,
bearers of a spark from the sacred fire. What greatness had not floated
on the ebb of that river into the mystery of an unknown earth!... The
dreams of men, the seed of commonwealths, the germs of empires.

The sun set; the dusk fell on the stream, and lights began to appear
along the shore. The Chapman lighthouse, a three-legged thing erect on
a mud-flat, shone strongly. Lights of ships moved in the fairway—a
great stir of lights going up and going down. And farther west on the
upper reaches the place of the monstrous town was still marked
ominously on the sky, a brooding gloom in sunshine, a lurid glare
under the stars.

'And this also', said Marlow suddenly, 'has been one of the dark
places of the earth.'

1902

# from *Youth*

'The old man warned us in his gentle and inflexible way that it was
part of our duty to save for the underwriters as much as we could of
the ship's gear. According we went to work aft, while she blazed
forward to give us plenty of light. We lugged out a lot of rubbish.
What didn't we save? An old barometer fixed with an absurd
quantity of screws nearly cost me my life: a sudden rush of smoke
came upon me, and I just got away in time. There were various stores,
bolts of canvas, coils of rope; the poop looked like a marine bazaar,

and the boats were lumbered to the gunwales. One would have thought the old man wanted to take as much as he could of his first command with him. He was very, very quiet, but off his balance evidently. Would you believe it? He wanted to take a length of old steam-cable and a kedge-anchor with him in the long-boat. We said, 'Ay, ay, sir,' deferentially, and on the quiet let the thing slip overboard. The heavy medicine-chest went that way, two bags of green coffee, tins of paint—fancy, paint!—a whole lot of things. Then I was ordered with two hands into the boats to make a stowage and get them ready against the time it would be proper for us to leave the ship.

'We put everything straight, stepped the long-boat's mast for our skipper, who was to take charge of her, and I was not sorry to sit down for a moment. My face felt raw, every limb ached as if broken, I was aware of all my ribs, and would have sworn to a twist in the backbone. The boats, fast astern, lay in a deep shadow, and all around I could see the circle of the sea lighted by the fire. A gigantic flame arose forward straight and clear. It flared fierce, with noises like the whir of wings, with rumbles as of thunder. There were cracks, detonations, and from the cone of flame the sparks flew upwards, as man is born to trouble, to leaky ships, and to ships that burn.

'What bothered me was that the ship, lying broadside to the swell and to such wind as there was—a mere breath—the boats would not keep astern where they were safe, but persisted, in a pig-headed way boats have, in getting under the counter and then swinging alongside. They were knocking about dangerously and coming near the flame, while the ship rolled on them, and, of course, there was always the danger of the masts going over the side at any moment. I and my two boat-keepers kept them off as best we could with oars and boat-hooks; but to be constantly at it became exasperating, since there was no reason why we should not leave at once. We could not see those on board, nor could we imagine what caused the delay. The boatkeepers were swearing feebly, and I had not only my share of the work, but also had to keep at it two men who showed a constant inclination to lay themselves down and let things slide.

'At last I hailed "On deck there," and someone looked over. "We're ready here," I said. The head disappeared, and very soon popped up again. "The captain says, All right, sir, and to keep the boats well clear of the ship."

'Half an hour passed. Suddenly there was a frightful racket, rattle, clanking of chain, hiss of water, and millions of sparks flew up into the shivering column of smoke that stood leaning slightly above the ship. The catheads had burned away, and the two red-hot anchors had gone to the bottom, tearing out after them two hundred fathom of red-hot chain. The ship trembled, the mass of flame swayed as if ready to collapse, and the fore top-gallant-mast fell. It darted down like an arrow of fire, shot under, and instantly leaping up within an oar's-length of the boats, floated quietly, very black on the luminous sea. I hailed the deck again. After some time a man in an unexpectedly cheerful but also muffled tone, as though he had been trying to speak with his mouth shut, informed me, "Coming directly, sir," and vanished. For a long time I heard nothing but the whir and roar of the fire. There were also whistling sounds. The boats jumped, tugged at the painters, ran at each other playfully, knocked their sides together, or, do what we would, swung in a bunch against the ship's side. I couldn't stand it any longer, and swarming up a rope, clambered aboard over the stern.

'It was as bright as day. Coming up like this, the sheet of fire facing me, was a terrifying sight, and the heat seemed hardly bearable at first. On a settee cushion dragged out of the cabin, Captain Beard, with his legs drawn up and one arm under his head, slept with the light playing on him. Do you know what the rest were busy about? They were sitting on deck right aft, round an open case, eating bread and cheese and drinking bottled stout.

'On the background of flames twisting in fierce tongues above their heads they seemed at home like salamanders, and looked like a band of desperate pirates. The fire sparkled in the whites of their eyes, gleamed on patches of white skin seen through the torn shirts. Each had the marks as of a battle about him—bandaged heads, tied-up arms, a strip of dirty rag round a knee   and each man had a bottle between his legs and a chunk of cheese in his hand. Mahon got up. With his handsome and disreputable head, his hooked profile, his long white beard, and with an uncorked bottle in his hand, he resembled one of those reckless sea-robbers of old making merry amidst violence and disaster. "The last meal on board," he explained solemnly. "We had nothing to eat all day, and it was no use leaving all this." He flourished the bottle and indicated the sleeping skipper. "He said he couldn't swallow anything, so I got him to lie down," he went on; and as I stared, "I don't know whether you are aware, young fellow, the man had no sleep to speak of for days—and there will be dam' little sleep in the boats." "There will be no boats by-and-by if you fool about much longer," I said, indignantly. I walked up to the skipper and shook him by the shoulder. At last he opened his eyes, but did not move. "Time to leave her, sir," I said, quietly.

'He got up painfully, looked at the flames, at the sea sparkling round the ship, and black, black as ink farther away; he looked at the stars shining dim through a thin veil of smoke in a sky black, black as Erebus.

" 'Youngest first," he said.

'And the ordinary seaman, wiping his mouth with the back of his hand, got up, clambered over the taffrail, and vanished. Others followed. One, on the point of going over, stopped short to drain his bottle, and with a great swing of his arm flung it at the fire. "Take this!" he cried.

'The skipper lingered disconsolately, and we left him to commune alone for a while with his first command. Then I went up again and brought him away at last. It was time. The ironwork on the poop was hot to the touch.

'Then the painter of the long-boat was cut, and the three boats, tied together, drifted clear of the ship. It was just sixteen hours after the explosion when we abandoned her. Mahon had charge of the second boat, and I had the smallest—the 14-foot thing. The long-boat would have taken the lot of us; but the skipper said we must save as much property as we could—for the underwriters—and so I got my first command. I had two men with me, a bag of biscuits, a few tins of meat, and a breaker of water. I was ordered to keep close to the long-boat, that in case of bad weather we might be taken into her.

'And do you know what I thought? I thought I would part company as soon as I could. I wanted to have my first command all to myself. I wasn't going to sail in a squadron if there were a chance for independent cruising. I would make land by myself. I would beat the other boats. Youth! All youth! The silly, charming, beautiful youth.

'But we did not make a start at once. We must see the last of the ship. And so the boats drifted about that night, heaving and setting on the swell. The men dozed, waked, sighed, groaned. I looked at the burning ship.

'Between the darkness of earth and heaven she was burning fiercely upon a disc of purple sea shot by the blood-red play of gleams; upon a disc of water glittering and sinister. A high, clear flame, an immense and lonely flame, ascended from the ocean, and from its summit the black smoke poured continuously at the sky. She burned furiously, mournful and imposing like a funeral pile kindled in the night, surrounded by the sea, watched over by the stars. A magnificent death had come like a grace, like a gift, like a reward to that old ship at the end of her laborious days. The surrender of her weary ghost to the keeping of stars and sea was stirring like the sight of a glorious triumph. The masts fell just before daybreak, and for a moment there was a burst and turmoil of sparks that seemed to fill with flying fire the night patient and watchful, the vast night lying silent upon the sea. At daylight she was only a charred shell, floating still under a cloud of smoke and bearing a glowing mass of coal within.

'Then the oars were got out, and the boats forming in a line moved round her remains as if in procession—the long-boat leading. As we pulled across her stern a slim dart of fire shot out viciously at us, and suddenly she went down, head first, in a great hiss of steam. The unconsumed stern was the last to sink; but the paint had gone, had cracked, had peeled off, and there were no letters, there was no word, no stubborn device that was like her soul, to flash at the rising sun her creed and her name.

'We made our way north. A breeze sprang up, and about noon all the boats came together for the last time. I had no mast or sail in mine, but I made a mast out of a spare oar and hoisted a boat-awning for a sail, with a boat-hook for a yard. She was certainly over-masted, but I had the satisfaction of knowing that with the wind aft I could beat the other two. I had to wait for them. Then we all had a look at the captain's chart, and, after a sociable meal of hard bread and water, got our last instructions. These were simple: steer north, and keep together as much as possible. "Be careful with that jury rig, Marlow," said the captain; and Mahon, as I sailed proudly past his boat, wrinkled his curved noise and hailed, "You will sail that ship of yours under water, if you don't look out, young fellow." He was a malicious old man—and may the deep sea where he sleeps now rock him gently, rock him tenderly to the end of time!

'Before sunset a thick rain-squall passed over the two boats, which were far astern, and that was the last I saw of them for a time. Next day I sat steering my cockle-shell—my first command—with nothing but water and sky around me. I did sight in the afternoon the upper sails of a ship far away, but said nothing, and my men did not notice her. You see I was afraid she might be homeward bound, and I had no mind to turn back from the portals of the East. I was steering for

Java—another blessed name—like Bankok, you know. I steered many days.

'I need not tell you what it is to be knocking about in an open boat. I remember nights and days of calm when we pulled, we pulled, and the boat seemed to stand still, as if bewitched within the circle of the sea horizon. I remember the heat, the deluge of rain-squalls that kept us baling for dear life (but filled our water-cask), and I remember sixteen hours on end with a mouth dry as a cinder and a steering-oar over the stern to keep my first command head on to a breaking sea. I did not know how good a man I was till then. I remember the drawn faces, the dejected figures of my two men, and I remember my youth and the feeling that will never come back any more—the feeling that I could last for ever, outlast the sea, the earth, and all men; the deceitful feeling that lures us on to joys, to perils, to love, to vain effort—to death; the triumphant conviction of strength, the heat of life in the handful of dust, the glow in the heart that with every year grows dim, grows cold, grows small, and expires—and expires, too soon, too soon—before life itself.

'And this is how I see the East. I have seen its secret places and have looked into its very soul; but now I see it always from a small boat, a high outline of mountains, blue and afar in the morning; like faint mist at noon; a jagged wall of purple at sunset. I have the feel of the oar in my hand, the vision of a scorching blue sea in my eyes. And I see a bay, a wide bay, smooth as glass and polished like ice, shimmering in the dark. A red light burns far off upon the gloom of the land, and the night is soft and warm. We drag at the oars with aching arms, and suddenly a puff of wind, a puff faint and tepid and laden with strange odors of blossoms, of aromatic wood, comes out of the still night— the first sigh of the East on my face. That I can never forget. It was impalpable and enslaving, like a charm, like a whispered promise of mysterious delight.

'We had been pulling this finishing spell for eleven hours. Two pulled, and he whose turn it was to rest sat at the tiller. We had made out the red light in that bay and steered for it, guessing it must mark some small coasting port. We passed two vessels, outlandish and high-sterned, sleeping at anchor, and, approaching the light, now very dim, ran the boat's nose against the end of a jutting wharf. We were blind with fatigue. My men dropped the oars and fell off the thwarts as if dead. I made fast to a pile. A current rippled softly. The scented obscurity of the shore was grouped into vast masses, a density of colossal clumps of vegetation, probably—mute and fantastic shapes. And at their foot the semicircle of a beach gleamed faintly, like an illusion. There was not a light, not a stir, not a sound. The mysterious East faced me, perfumed like a flower, silent like death, dark like a grave.

1902

# from *The Mirror of the Sea*

The sea—this truth must be confessed—has no generosity. No display of manly qualities—courage, hardihood, endurance, faithfulness—has ever been known to touch its irresponsible consciousness of power. The ocean has the conscienceless temper of a savage autocrat spoiled by much adulation. He cannot brook the slightest appearance of defiance, and has remained the irreconcilable enemy of ships and men ever since ships and men had the unheard-of audacity to go afloat together in the face of his frown. From that day he has gone on swallowing up fleets and men without his resentment being glutted by the number of victims—by so many wrecked ships and wrecked lives. To-day, as ever, he is ready to beguile and betray, to smash and to drown the incorrigible optimism of men who, backed by the fidelity of ships, are trying to wrest from him the fortune of their house, the dominion of their world, or only a dole of food for their hunger. If not always in the hot mood to smash, he is always stealthily ready for a drowning. The most amazing wonder of the deep is its unfathomable cruelty.

I felt its dread for the first time in mid-Atlantic one day, many years ago, when we took off the crew of a Danish brig homeward bound from the West Indies. A thin, silvery mist softened the calm and majestic splendour of light without shadows—seemed to render the sky less remote and the ocean less immense. It was one of the days, when the might of the sea appears indeed lovable, like the nature of a strong man in moments of quiet intimacy. At sunrise we had made out a black speck to the westward, apparently suspended high up in the void behind a stirring, shimmering veil of silvery blue gauze that seemed at times to stir and float in the breeze which fanned us slowly along. The peace of that enchanting forenoon was so profound, so untroubled, that it seemed that every word pronounced loudly on our deck would penetrate to the very heart of that infinite mystery born from the conjunction of water and sky. We did not raise our voices. 'A water-logged derelict, I think, sir,' said the second officer quietly, coming down from aloft with the binoculars in their case˙slung across his shoulders; and our captain, without a word, signed to the helmsman to steer for the black speck. Presently we made out a low, jagged stump sticking up forward—all that remained of her departed masts.

The captain was expatiating in a low conversational tone to the chief mate upon the danger of these derelicts, and upon his dread of coming upon them at night, when suddenly a man forward screamed out, 'There's people on board of her, sir! I see them!' in a most extra-ordinary voice—a voice never heard before in our ship; the amazing voice of a stranger. It gave the signal for a sudden tumult of shouts. The watch below ran up the forecastle head in a body, the cook dashed out of the galley. Everybody saw the poor fellows now. They were there! And all at once our ship, which had the well-earned name of being without a rival for speed in light winds, seemed to us to have lost the power of motion, as if the sea, becoming viscous, had clung to her sides. And yet she moved. Immensity, the inseparable companion of a ship's life, chose that day to breathe upon her as gently as a sleeping child. The clamour of our excitement had died out, and our living ship, famous for never losing steerage way as long as there was air enough to float a feather, stole, without a ripple, silent and white as a ghost, towards her mutilated and wounded sister, come upon at the point of death in the sunlit haze of a calm day at sea.

With the binoculars glued to his eyes, the captain said in a quavering tone: 'They are waving to us with something aft there.' He put down the glasses on the skylight brusquely, and began to walk about the poop. 'A shirt or a flag,' he ejaculated irritably. 'Can't make it out. . . . Some damn rag or other!' He took a few more turns on the poop, glancing down over the rail now and then to see how fast we were moving. His nervous footsteps rang sharply in the quiet of the ship, where the other men, all looking the same way, had forgotten themselves in a staring immobility. 'This will never do!' he cried out suddenly. 'Lower the boats at once! Down with them!'

Before I jumped into mine he took me aside, as being an inexperi-enced junior, for a word of warning:

'You look out as you come alongside that she doesn't take you down with her. You understand?'

He murmured this confidentially, so that none of the men at the falls should overhear, and I was shocked. 'Heavens! as if in such an emergency one stopped to think of danger!' I exclaimed to myself mentally, in scorn of such cold-blooded caution.

It takes many lessons to make a real seaman, and I got my rebuke at once. My experienced commander seemed in one searching glance to read my thoughts on my ingenuous face.

'What you're going for is to save life, not to drown your boat's crew for nothing,' he growled severely in my ear. But as we shoved off he leaned over and cried out: 'It all rests on the power of your arms, men. Give way for life!'

We made a race of it, and I would never have believed that a common boat's crew of a merchantman could keep up so much determined fierceness in the regular swing of their stroke. What our captain had clearly perceived before we left had become plain to all of us since. The issue of our enterprise hung on a hair above that abyss of waters which will not give up its dead till the Day of Judgment. It was a race of two ship's boats matched against Death for a prize of nine men's lives, and Death had a long start. We saw the crew of the brig from afar working at the pumps—still pumping on that wreck, which already had settled so far down that the gentle, low swell, over which our boats rose and fell easily without a check to their speed, welling up almost level with her head rails, plucked at the ends of broken gear swinging desolately under her naked bowsprit.

We could not, in all conscience, have picked out a better day for our regatta had we had the free choice of all the days that ever dawned upon the lonely struggles and solitary agonies of ships since the Norse rovers first steered to the westward against the run of Atlantic waves. It was a very good race. At the finish there was not an oar's length between the first and second boat, with Death coming in a good third on the top of the very next smooth swell, for all one knew to the contrary. The scuppers of the brig gurgled softly all together when the water rising against her sides subsided sleepily with a low wash, as if playing about an immovable rock. Her bulwarks were gone fore and aft, and one saw her bare deck low-lying like a raft and swept clean of boats, spars, houses—of everything except the ringbolts and the heads of the pumps. I had one dismal glimpse of it as I braced myself up to receive upon my breast the last man to leave her, the captain, who literally let himself fall into my arms.

It had been a weirdly silent rescue—a rescue without a hail, without a single uttered word, without a gesture or a sign, without a conscious exchange of glances. Up to the very last moment those on board stuck to their pumps, which spouted two clear streams of water upon their bare feet. Their brown skin showed through the rents of their shirts; and the two small bunches of half-naked, tattered men went on bowing from the waist to each other in their back-breaking labour, up and down, absorbed, with no time for a glance over the shoulder at the help that was coming to them. As we dashed, unregarded, alongside a voice let out one, only one hoarse howl of command, and then, just as they stood, without caps, with the salt drying grey in the wrinkles and folds of their hairy, haggard faces, blinking stupidly at us their red eyelids, they made a bolt away from the handles, tottering and jostling against each other, and positively flung themselves over upon our very heads. The clatter they made tumbling into the boats had an extraordinarily destructive effect upon the illusion of tragic dignity our self-esteem had thrown over the contests of mankind with the sea. On that exquisite day of gently breathing peace and veiled sunshine perished my romantic love to what men's imagination had proclaimed the most august aspect of Nature. The cynical indifference of the sea to the merits of human suffering and courage, laid bare in this ridiculous, panic-tainted performance extorted from the dire extremity of nine good and honourable seamen, revolted me. I saw the duplicity of the sea's most tender mood. It was so because it could not help itself, but the awed respect of the early days was gone. I felt ready to smile bitterly at its enchanting charm and glare viciously at its furies. In a moment, before we shoved off, I had looked coolly at the life of my choice. Its illusions were gone, but its fascination remained. I had become a seaman at last.

1906

# STEPHEN CRANE

1871–1900

# from 'The Open Boat'

A tale intended to be after the fact: being the experience of
four men from the sunk steamer *Commodore*

None of them knew the color of the sky. Their eyes glanced level, and
were fastened upon the waves that swept toward them. These waves
were of the hue of slate, save for the tops, which were of foaming
white, and all of the men knew the colors of the sea. The horizon
narrowed and widened, and dipped and rose, and at all times its edge
was jagged with waves that seemed thrust up in points like rocks.

Many a man ought to have a bathtub larger than the boat which
here rode upon the sea. These waves were most wrongfully and
barbarously abrupt and tall, and each froth-top was a problem in
small-boat navigation.

The cook squatted in the bottom, and looked with both eyes at the
six inches of gunwale which separated him from the ocean. His
sleeves were rolled over his fat forearms, and the two flaps of his
unbuttoned vest dangled as he bent to bail out the boat. Often he said,
'Gawd! that was a narrow clip.' As he remarked it he invariably gazed
eastward over the broken sea.

The oiler, steering with one of the two oars in the boat, sometimes
raised himself suddenly to keep clear of water that swirled in over the
stern. It was a thin little oar, and it seemed often ready to snap.

The correspondent, pulling at the other oar, watched the waves
and wondered why he was there.

The injured captain, lying in the bow, was at this time buried in
that profound dejection and indifference which comes, temporarily
at least, to even the bravest and most enduring when, willy-nilly, the
firm fails, the army loses, the ship goes down. The mind of a master
of a vessel is rooted deep in the timbers of her, though he command
for a day or a decade; and this captain had on him the stern
impression of a scene in the grays of dawn of seven turned faces, and

later a stump of a topmast with a white ball on it, that slashed to and fro at the waves, went low and lower, and down. Thereafter there was something strange in his voice. Although steady, it was deep with mourning, and of a quality beyond oration or tears.

'Keep 'er a little more south, Billie,' he said.

'A little more south, sir,' said the oiler in the stern.

A seat in his boat was not unlike a seat upon a bucking broncho, and by the same token a broncho is not much smaller. The craft pranced and reared and plunged like an animal. As each wave came, and she rose for it, she seemed like a horse making at a fence outrageously high. The manner of her scramble over these walls of water is a mystic thing, and, moreover, at the top of them were ordinarily these problems in white water, the foam racing down from the summit of each wave requiring a new leap, and a leap from the air. Then, after scornfully bumping a crest, she would slide and race and splash down a long incline, and arrive bobbing and nodding in front of the next menace.

A singular disadvantage of the sea lies in the fact that after successfully surmounting one wave you discover that there is another behind it just as important and just as nervously anxious to do something effective in the way of swamping boats. In a ten-foot dinghy one can get an idea of the resources of the sea in the line of waves that is not probable to the average experience which is never at sea in a dinghy. As each slaty wall of water approached, it shut all else from the view of the men in the boat, and it was not difficult to imagine that this particular wave was the final outburst of the ocean, the last effort of the grim water. There was a terrible grace in the move of the waves, and they came in silence, save for the snarling of the crests.

In the wan light the faces of the men must have been gray. Their eyes must have glinted in strange ways as they gazed steadily astern. Viewed from a balcony, the whole thing would doubtless have been weirdly picturesque. But the men in the boat had no time to see it, and if they had had leisure, there were other things to occupy their minds. The sun swung steadily up the sky, and they knew it was broad day because the color of the sea changed from slate to emerald green streaked with amber lights, and the foam was like tumbling snow. The process of the breaking day was unknown to them. The were aware only of this effect upon the color of the waves that rolled toward them.

In disjointed sentences the cook and the correspondent argued as to the difference between a life-saving station and a house of refuge. The cook had said: 'There's a house of refuge just north of the Mosquito Inlet Light, and as soon as they see us they'll come off in their boat and pick us up.'

'As soon as who see us?' said the correspondent.

'The crew,' said the cook.

'Houses of refuge don't have crews,' said the correspondent. 'As I understand them, they are only places where clothes and grub are stored for the benefit of shipwrecked people. They don't carry crews.'

'Oh, yes, they do,' said the cook.

'No, they don't,' said the correspondent.

'We'll, we're not there yet, anyhow,' said the oiler, in the stern.

'Well,' said the cook, 'perhaps it's not a house of refuge that I'm thinking of as being near Mosquito Inlet Light; perhaps it's a life-saving station.'

'We're not there yet,' said the oiler in the stern.

As the boat bounced from the top of each wave the wind tore through the hair of the hatless men, and as the craft plopped her stern down again the spray slashed past them. The crest of each of these waves was a hill, from the top of which the men surveyed for a moment a broad tumultuous expanse, shining and wind-riven. It was probably splendid, it was probably glorious, this play of the free sea, wild with lights of emerald and white and amber.

'Bully good thing it's an on-shore wind,' said the cook. 'If not, where would we be? Wouldn't have a show.'

'That's right,' said the correspondent.

The busy oiler nodded his assent.

Then the captain, in the bow, chuckled in a way that expressed humor, contempt, tragedy, all in one. 'Do you think we've got much of a show now, boys?' said he.

Whereupon the three were silent, save for a trifle of hemming and hawing. To express any particular optimism at this time they felt to be childish and stupid, but they all doubtless possessed this sense of the situation in their minds. A young man thinks doggedly at such times. On the other hand, the ethics of their condition was decidedly against any open suggestion of hopelessness. So they were silent.

'Oh, well,' said the captain, soothing his children, 'we'll get ashore all right.'

But there was that in his tone which made them think; so the oiler quoth, 'Yes, if this wind holds.'

The cook was bailing. 'Yes! if we don't catch hell in the surf.'

Canton-flannel gulls flew near and far. Sometimes they sat down on the sea, near patches of brown seaweed that rolled over the waves with a movement like carpets on a line in a gale. The birds sat comfortably in groups, and they were envied by some in the dinghy, for the wrath of the sea was no more to them then it was to a covey of prairie chickens a thousand miles inland. Often they came very close and stared at the men with black bead-like eyes. At these times they were uncanny and sinister in their unblinking scrutiny, and the men hooted angrily at them, telling them to be gone. One came, and evidently decided to alight on the top of the captain's head. The bird flew parallel to the boat and did not circle, but made short sidelong jumps in the air in chicken-fashion. His black eyes were wistfully fixed upon the captain's head. 'Ugly brute,' said the oiler to the bird. 'You look as if you were made with a jack-knife.' The cook and the correspondent swore darkly at the creature. The captain naturally wished to knock it away with the end of the heavy painter, but he did not dare do it, because anything resembling an emphatic gesture would have capsized this freighted boat; and so, with his open hand, the captain gently and carefully waved the gull away. After it had been discouraged from the pursuit the captain breathed easier on account of his hair, and others breathed easier because the bird struck their minds at this time as being somehow gruesome and ominous.

In the meantime the oiler and the correspondent rowed. They sat together in the same seat, and each rowed an oar. Then the oiler took both oars; then the correspondent took both oars; then the oiler; then the correspondent. They rowed and they rowed. The very ticklish part of the business was when the time came for the reclining one in the stern to take his turn at the oars. By the very last star of truth, it is easier to steal eggs from under a hen than it was to change seats in the dinghy. First the man in the stern slid his hand along the thwart and moved with care, as if he were of Sèvres. Then the man in the rowing-seat slid his hand along the other thwart. It was all done with the most extraordinary care. As the two sidled past each other, the whole party kept watchful eyes on the coming wave, and the captain cried: 'Look out, now! Steady, there!'

The brown mats of seaweed that appeared from time to time were like islands, bits of earth. They were traveling, apparently, neither one way nor the other. They were, to all intents, stationary. They informed the men in the boat that it was making progress slowly toward the land.

The captain, rearing cautiously in the bow after the dinghy soared on a great swell, said that he had seen the lighthouse at Mosquito Inlet. Presently the cook remarked that he had seen it. The correspondent was at the oars then, and for some reason he too wished to look at the lighthouse; but his back was toward the far shore, and the waves were important, and for some time he could not seize an opportunity to turn his head. But at last there came a wave more gentle than the others, and when at the crest of it he swiftly scoured the western horizon.

'See it?' said the captain.

'No,' said the corespondent, slowly; 'I didn't see anything.'

'Look again,' said the captain. He pointed. 'It's exactly in that direction.'

At the top of another wave the correspondent did as he was bid, and this time his eyes chanced on a small, still thing on the edge of the swaying horizon. It was precisely like the point of a pin. It took an anxious eye to find a lighthouse so tiny.

'Think we'll make it, Captain?'

'If this wind holds and the boat don't swamp, we can't do much else,' said the captain.

The little boat, lifted by each towering sea and splashed viciously by the crests, made progress that in the absence of seaweed was not apparent to those in her. She seemed just a wee thing wallowing, miraculously top up, at the mercy of five oceans. Occasionally a great spread of water, like white flames, swarmed into her.

'Bail her, cook,' said the captain, serenely.

'All right, Captain,' said the cheerful cook.

It would be difficult to describe the subtle brotherhood of men that was here established on the seas. No one said that it was so. No one mentioned it. But it dwelt in the boat, and each man felt it warm him. They were a captain, an oiler, a cook, and a correspondent, and they were friends—friends in a more curiously iron-bound degree than may be common. The hurt captain, lying against the water-jar in the bow, spoke always in a low voice and calmly; but he could never

command a more ready and swiftly obedient crew than the motley
three of the dinghy. It was more than a mere recognition of what was
best for the common safety. There was surely in it a quality that was
personal and heart-felt. And after this devotion to the commander of
the boat, there was this comradeship, that the correspondent, for
instance, who had been taught to be cynical of men, knew even at the
time was the best experience of his life. But no one said that it was so.
No one mentioned it.

'I wish we had a sail,' remarked the captain. 'We might try my
overcoat on the end of an oar, and give you two boys a chance to rest.'
So the cook and correspondent held the mast and spread wide the
overcoat; the oiler steered; and the little boat made good way with
her new rig. Sometimes the oiler had to scull sharply to keep a sea
from breaking into the boat, but otherwise sailing was a success.

Meanwhile the lighthouse had been growing slowly larger. It had
now almost assumed color, and appeared like a little gray shadow on
the sky. The man at the oars could not be prevented from turning his
head rather often to try for a glimpse of this little gray shadow.

At last, from the top of each wave, the men in the tossing boat
could see land. Even as the lighthouse was an upright shadow on the
sky, this land seemed but a long black shadow on the sea. It certainly
was thinner than paper. 'We must be about opposite New Smyrna,'
said the cook, who had coasted this shore often in schooners.
'Captain, by the way, I believe they abandoned that life-saving
station there about a year ago.'

'Did they?' said the captain.

The wind slowly died away. The cook and the correspondent were
not now obliged to slave in order to hold high the oar. But the waves
continued their old impetuous swooping at the dinghy, and the little
craft, no longer under way, struggled woundily over them. The oiler
or the correspondent took the oars again.

Shipwrecks are apropos of nothing. If men could only train for
them and have them occur when the men had reached pink condition,
there would be less drowning at sea. Of the four in the dinghy none
had slept any time worth mentioning for two days and two nights
previous to embarking in the dinghy, and in the excitement of
clambering about the deck of a foundering ship they had also
forgotten to eat heartily.

For these reasons, and for others, neither the oiler nor the correspondent was fond of rowing at this time. The correspondent wondered

ingenuously how in the name of all that was sane could there be people who thought it amusing to row a boat. It was not an amusement; it was a diabolical punishment, and even a genius of mental aberrations could never conclude that it was anything but a horror to the muscles and a crime against the back. He mentioned to the boat in general how the amusement of rowing struck him, and the weary-faced oiler smiled in full sympathy. Previously to the foundering, by the way, the oiler had worked a double watch in the engine-room of the ship.

'Take her easy now, boys,' said the captain. 'Don't spend yourselves. If we have to run a surf you'll need all your strength, because we'll sure have to swim for it. Take your time.'

Slowly the land arose from the sea. From a black line it became a line of black and a line of white—trees and sand. Finally the captain said that he could make out a house on the shore. 'That's the house of refuge, sure,' said the cook. 'They'll see us before long, and come out after us.'

The distant lighthouse reared high. 'The keeper ought to be able to make us out now, if he's looking through a glass,' said the captain. 'He'll notify the life-saving people.'

'None of those other boats could have got ashore to give word of this wreck,' said the oiler, in a low voice, 'else the life-boat would be out hunting us.'

Slowly and beautifully the land loomed out of the sea. The wind came again. It had veered from the north-east to the south-east. Finally a new sound struck the ears of the men in the boat. It was the low thunder of the surf on the shore. 'We'll never be able to make the lighthouse now,' said the captain. 'Swing her head a little more north, Billie.'

'A little more north, sir,' said the oiler.

Whereupon the little boat turned her nose once more down the wind, and all but the oarsman watched the shore grow. Under the influence of this expansion doubt and direful apprehension were leaving the minds of the men. The management of the boat was still most absorbing, but it could not prevent a quiet cheerfulness. In an hour, perhaps, they would be ashore.

Their backbones had become thoroughly used to balancing in the boat, and they now rode this wild colt of a dinghy like circus men. The correspondent thought that he had been drenched to the skin, but happening to feel in the top pocket of his coat, he found therein eight cigars. Four of them were soaked with sea-water; four were perfectly scatheless. After a search, somebody produced three dry matches; and thereupon the four waifs rode impudently in their little boat and, with an assurance of an impending rescue shining in their eyes, puffed at the big cigars, and judged well and ill of all men. Everybody took a drink of water.

1897

# FRANK T. BULLEN

## 1857–1915

## from *Idylls of the Sea*

### A SUBMARINE EARTHQUAKE

There was a delicate tint of green over all the sky instead of its usual deep, steadfast blue. All around the horizon the almost constant concomitants of the Trade winds, fleecy masses of cumuli, were lying peacefully, their shape unaltered from hour to hour. Their usual snowy whiteness, however, was curiously besmirched by a shading of dirty brown which clung around their billowy outlines, giving them a stale appearance greatly at variance with the normal purity of these lovely cloud-forms. The afternoon sun, gliding swiftly down the shining slope of heaven toward the western edge of that placid sea, had an air of mystery about his usually glorious disc, a wondrous glow of unnameable tints that, streaming away from him into the clear firmament, encircled him with a halo of marvellous shades, all lacking the palpitating brightness usually inseparable from solar displays near the Equator. And over the sea-surface also was spread, as upon a vast palette, great splashes of colour, untraceable to any definite source, mysterious in their strange beauty. At irregular intervals, across that silent expanse of peaceful limpidity, came, in stately onset, an undulating throb of ocean's heart—a shining knoll of water one hundred leagues in length, but so mobile, so gentle in its gliding incidence, that it was beautiful as the heaving bosom of a sleeping naiad. The very silence, deep and solemn as that of the stellar spaces, was sweet—a peaceful sweetness that fell upon the soul like the most exquisite music, and soothed as does a dreamless sleep.

And yet, in spite of the indescribable charm of that divine day, there was on board the solitary ship that gave the needed touch of human interest to that ocean Elysium a general air of expectancy, a sense of impending change which as yet could not be called uneasiness, and still was indefinably at variance with the more manifest influences that made for rest of mind and body. The animals on board, pigs and cats and fowls, were evidently ill at ease. Their finer perceptions, unbiassed by reasoning appreciation of Nature's beauties, were palpably disturbed, and they roamed restlessly about, often composing themselves as if to sleep, only to resume their agitated prowling almost immediately. Lower sank the sun, stranger and more varied grew the colour-schemes in sky and sea. Up from the Eastern horizon crept gradually a pale glow as of a premature dawn, the breaking of an interpolated day shed by some visitant sun from another system. The moon was not yet due for six hours, so that none could attribute this unearthly radiance to her rising. Busy each with the eager questionings of his own perturbed mind, none spoke a word as the sun disappeared, but watched in suspense that was almost pain the brightening of this spectral glare. Suddenly, as if reflected from some unimaginable furnace, the zenith was all aflame. That fiery glow above turned the sea into the semblance of a lake of blood, and horror distorted every face. The still persisting silence now lay like the paralysis of a trance upon all, and an almost frantic desire for sound racked them to the core.

At last, when it seemed as if the tension of their nerves had almost reached the snapping point, there was an overwhelming sulphurous stench, followed by a muttering as of thunder beneath the sea. A tremendous concussion below the keel made the stout hull vibrate through every beam, and the tall masts quivered like willow twigs in a squall. The air was full of glancing lights, as if legions of fire-flies disported themselves. Slowly the vessel began to heave and roll, but with an uncertain staggering motion, unlike even the broken sea of a cyclone centre. Gradually that dreadful light faded from the lurid sky, and was replaced by a smoky darkness, alien to the overshadowing gloom of any ordinary tempest. Strange noises arose from the deep, not to be compared with any of the manifold voices of the ocean so well known to those who do business in great waters. And the myriad brightnesses which make oceans' depths so incomparably lovely throughout the tropical nights were all gone. All was dark beneath as above. Not only so, but those anxious mariners could feel, though they could not see, that while the atmospheric ocean was calm almost to stagnation, the hidden deeps under them were being rent and disintegrated by such an unthinkable storm as the air had never witnessed. The fountains of the great deep were broken up, but the floods issuing therefrom were of cosmic flame, able to resolve even that immensity of superincumbent ocean into its original gases and change the unchangeable.

Tossing helplessly upon that tortured sea, face to face with those elemental forces that only to think of makes the flesh shrink on the bones like a withered leaf, the men suffered the passage of the hours. What was happening or was about to happen they could only dimly imagine. They could but endure in helplessness and hope for the day. Yet their thoughts would wander to those they loved, wondering dimly whether the catastrophe apparently impending was to be universal and the whole race of man about to be blotted out—whether the world were dying. What *they* suffered could not be told, but the animals died. Perhaps the scorching heat-waves which continually arose, making mouths and nostrils crack like burnt leather, and cauterising taste and smell as if with the fumes of molten sulphur, had slain the beasts. The discovery of this ghastly detail of the night's terrors did not add much to their fears. It could not; for the mind of man can only contain a limited amount of terror, as the body can only feel a limited amount of pain, which is something to be deeply thankful for.

Shortly after midnight there was a deafening uproar, a hissing as of the Apocalyptic Star being quenched, and immediately the gloom became filled with steam, an almost scalding fog, through which as through a veil came a red sheen. At the same time a mighty swell swept toward them from east to west, striking the ship full in the stem. Gallantly she rose to the advancing wall of water until she seemed upreared upon her stern, but in spite of her wonderful buoyancy a massive sea broke on board, clearing the decks like a besom of destruction. Down the receding slope of this gigantic billow she fled, as if plunging headlong to the sea-bed, and before she had time to recover herself was met by another almost as huge. Clinging for life to such fragments as still held on the clean-swept

decks, the crew felt that at last all was over. But the good ship
survived the third wave, being then granted a brief respite before
another series appeared. This allowed all hands a breathing space, and
an opportunity to notice that there was a healthier smell in the air,
and that the terror-striking noises were fast dying away. When the
next set of rollers came thundering along they were far less dangerous
than before, nor, although they made a clean breach over the much-
enduring ship, were they nearly as trying to the almost worn-out
crew. And now, breaking through the appalling drapery that had
hidden the bright face of the sky, suddenly shone the broad smile of
the silver moon. Like the comforting face of a dear friend, that
pleasant sight brought renewed hope and vigour to all. Again the
cheery voices of the officers were heard, and all wrought manfully to
repair the damage done by the terrible sea. One by one the glittering
stars peeped out as the gloomy canopy melted away, revealing again
the beautiful blue of the sky. A gentle breeze sprang up, but for
awhile it was only possible to lay the ship's head approximately on
her course, because the compasses were useless. The needles had
temporarily lost their polarity in the seismic disturbance that had
taken place beneath them. But that was a small matter. As long as the
celestial guides were available, the navigators could afford to wait
until, with the rest of Nature's forces, magnetism regained its normal
conditions. So, during the energetic labours of the men, the morning
quickly came, hailed by them as a sight they had never again expected
to see. And what a dawn it was. Surely never had the abundant day
been so delightful, the heaven so stainless, the air so pure. All the
more because of the extraordinary contrast between sky and sea; for
old ocean was utterly unlike any sea they had ever before sailed upon.
As far as the eye could reach the surface was covered with floating
pumice, so that the vessel grated through it as if ploughing over a
pebbly beach. Wherever the water could be seen it was actually
muddy, befouled like any ditch. Dead fish, floating and distorted,
added to the ugliness of what overnight was so beautiful. Most
pathetic of all, perhaps, upon that dead sea was the sight of an
occasional spot of white, a tiny patch of ruffled feathers floating, that
had been one of the fearless winged wanderers who add so much to
the beauty of the sea, its joyous life quenched by the poisonous fumes
of the submarine earthquake.

1899

# JOSHUA SLOCUM

## 1844–1909

# from *Sailing Alone Around the World*

[July 1895] The *Spray* was alone, and sailing on, she held her course. July 4, at 6 a.m. I put in double reefs, and at 8.30 a.m. turned out all reefs. At 9.40 p.m. I raised the sheen only of the light on the west end of Sable Island, which may also be called the Island of Tragedies. The fog, which till this moment had held off, now lowered over the sea like a pall. I was in a world of fog, shut off from the universe. I did not see any more of the light. By the lead, which I cast often, I found that a little after midnight I was passing the east point of the island, and should soon be clear of dangers of land and shoals. The wind was holding free, though it was from the foggy point, south-south-west. It is said that within a few years Sable Island has been reduced from forty miles in length to twenty, and that of three lighthouses built on it since 1880, two have been washed away and the third will soon be engulfed.

On the evening of July 5 the *Spray*, after having steered all day over a lumpy sea, took it into her head to go without the helmsman's aid. I had been steering southeast by south, but the wind hauling forward a bit, she dropped into a smooth lane, heading southeast, and making about eight knots her very best work. I crowded on sail to cross the track of the liners without loss of time, and to reach as soon as possible the friendly Gulf Stream. The fog lifting before night, I was afforded a look at the sun just as it was touching the sea. I watched it go down and out of sight. Then I turned my face eastward, and there, apparently at the very end of the bowsprit, was the smiling full moon rising out of the sea. Neptune himself coming over the bows could not have startled me more. 'Good evening, sir,' I cried; 'I'm glad to see you.' Many a long talk since then I have had with the man in the moon; he had my confidence on the voyage.

About midnight the fog shut down again denser than ever before. One could almost 'stand on it'. It continued so for a number of days, the wind increasing to a gale. The waves rose high, but I had a good ship. Still, in the dismal fog I felt myself drifting into loneliness, an insect on a straw in the midst of the elements. I lashed the helm, and my vessel held her course, and while she sailed I slept.

During these days a feeling of awe crept over me. My memory worked with startling power. The ominous, the insignificant, the great, the small, the wonderful, the commonplace—all appeared before my mental vision in magical succession. Pages of my history were recalled which had been so long forgotten that they seemed to belong to a previous existence. I heard all the voices of the past laughing, crying, telling what I had heard them tell in many corners of the earth.

The loneliness of my state wore off when the gale was high and I found much work to do. When fine weather returned, then came the sense of solitude, which I could not shake off. I used my voice often, at first giving some order about the affairs of a ship, for I had been told that from disuse I should lose my speech. At the meridian altitude of the sun I called aloud, 'Eight bells,' after the custom on a ship at sea. Again from my cabin I cried to an imaginary man at the helm, 'How does she head there?' and again, 'Is she on her course?' But getting no reply, I was reminded the more palpably of my condition. My voice sounded hollow on the empty air, and I dropped the practice. However, it was not long before the thought came to me that when I was a lad I used to sing; why not try that now, where it would disturb no one? My musical talent had never bred envy in others, but out on the Atlantic, to realize what it meant, you should have heard me sing. You should have seen the porpoises leap when I pitched my voice for the waves and the sea and all that was in it. Old turtles, with large eyes, poked their heads up out of the sea as I sang 'Johnny Boker', and 'We'll Pay Darby Doyl for his Boots', and the like. But the porpoises were, on the whole, vastly more appreciative than the turtles; they jumped a deal higher. One day when I was humming a favourite chant, I think it was 'Babylon's a-Fallin', a porpoise jumped higher than the bowsprit. Had the *Spray* been going a little faster she would have scooped him in. The sea-birds sailed around rather shy.

[ July 1895] Passing the island of Pico, after the rigging was mended, the *Spray* stretched across to leeward of the island of St Michael's, which she was up with early on the morning of July 26, the wind blowing hard. Later in the day she passed the Prince of Monaco's fine

steam-yacht bound to Fayal, where, on a previous voyage, the prince
had slipped his cables to 'escape a reception' which the padres of the
island wished to give him. Why he so dreaded the 'ovation' I could
not make out. At Horta they did not know. Since reaching the islands
I had lived most luxuriously on fresh bread, butter, vegetables, and
fruits of all kinds. Plums seemed the most plentiful on the *Spray*, and
these I ate without stint. I had also a Pico white cheese that General
Manning, the American consul-general, had given me, which I
supposed was to be eaten, and of this I partook with the plums. Alas!
by night-time I was doubled up with cramps. The wind, which was
already a smart breeze, was increasing somewhat, with a heavy sky to
the sou'west. Reefs had been turned out, and I must turn them in
again somehow. Between cramps I got the mainsail down, hauled out
the earings as best I could, and tied away point by point, in the double
reef. There being sea-room, I should, in strict prudence, have made
all snug and gone down at once to my cabin. I am a careful man at sea,
but this night, in the coming storm, I swayed up my sails, which,
reefed though they were, were still too much in such heavy weather;
and I saw to it that the sheets were securely belayed. In a word, I
should have laid to, but did not. I gave her the double-reefed mainsail
and whole jib instead, and set her on her course. Then I went below,
and threw myself upon the cabin floor in great pain. How long I lay
there I could not tell, for I became delirious. When I came to, as I
thought, from my swoon, I realized that the sloop was plunging into
a heavy sea, and looking out of the companionway, to my amazement
saw a tall man at the helm. His rigid hand, grasping the spokes of the
wheel, held them as in a vice. One may imagine my astonishment. His
rig was that of a foreign sailor, and the large red cap he wore was
cockbilled over his left ear, and all was set off with shaggy black
whiskers. He would have been taken for a pirate in any part of the
world. While I gazed upon his threatening aspect I forgot the storm,
and wondered if he had come to cut my throat. This he seemed to
divine. 'Señor,' said he, doffing his cap, 'I have come to do you no
harm.' And a smile, the faintest in the world, but still a smile, played
on his face, which seemed not unkind when he spoke. 'I have come to
do you no harm. I have sailed free,' he said, 'but was never worse than
a *contrabandista*. I am one of Columbus's crew,' he continued. 'I am
the pilot of the *Pinta* come to aid you. Lie quiet, señor captain,' he
added, 'and I will guide your ship to-night. You have a *calentura*, but
you will be all right to-morrow.' I thought what a very devil he was to

carry sail. Again, as if he read my mind, he exclaimed: 'Yonder is the
*Pinta* ahead; we must overtake her. Give her sail; give her sail! *Vale,
vale, muy vale!*' Biting off a large quid of black twist, he said: 'You
did wrong, captain, to mix cheese with plums. White cheese is never
safe unless you know whence it comes. *Quien sabe*, it may have been
from *leche de Capra* and becoming capricious—'
  'Avast, there!' I cried. 'I have no mind for moralizing.'
  I made shift to spread a mattress and lie on that instead of the hard
floor, my eyes all the while fastened on my strange guest, who,
remarking again that I would have 'only pains and calentura', chuckled
as he chanted a wild song:

> High are the waves, fierce, gleaming,
>   High is the tempest roar!
> High the sea-bird screaming!
>   High the Azore!

I suppose I was now on the mend, for I was peevish, and complained:
'I detest your jingle. Your Azore should be at roost, and would have
been were it a respectable bird!' I begged he would tie a rope-yarn on
the rest of the song, if there was any more of it. I was still in agony.
Great seas were boarding the *Spray*, but in my fevered brain I thought
they were boats falling on deck, that careless draymen were throwing
from wagons on the pier to which I imagined the *Spray* was now
moored, and without fenders to breast her off. 'You'll smash your
boats!' I called out again and again, as the seas crashed on the cabin
over my head. 'You'll smash your boats, but you can't hurt the *Spray*.
She is strong!' I cried.
  I found, when my pains and calentura had gone, that the deck, now
as white as a shark's tooth from seas washing over it, had been swept
of everything movable. To my astonishment, I saw now at broad day
that the *Spray* was still heading as I had left her, and was going like a
race-horse. Columbus himself could not have held her more exactly
on her course. The sloop had made ninety miles in the night through a
rough sea. I felt grateful to the old pilot, but I marvelled some that he
had not taken in the jib. The gale was moderating, and by noon the
sun was shining. A meridian altitude and the distance on the patent
log, which I always kept towing, told me that she had made a true
course throughout the twenty-four hours. I was getting much better
now, but was very weak, and did not turn out reefs that day or the
night following, although the wind fell light; but I just put my wet

clothes out in the sun when it was shining, and, lying down there myself, fell asleep. Then who should visit me again but my old friend of the night before, this time, of course, in a dream. 'You did well last night to take my advice,' said he, 'and if you would, I should like to be with you often on the voyage, for the love of adventure alone.' Finishing what he had to say, he again doffed his cap and disappeared as mysteriously as he came, returning, I suppose, to the phantom *Pinta*. I awoke much refreshed, and with the feeling that I had been in the presence of a friend and a seaman of vast experience. I gathered up my clothes, which by this time were dry, then, by inspiration, I threw overboard all the plums in the vessel.

July 28 was exceptionally fine. The wind from the northwest was light and the air balmy. I overhauled my wardrobe, and bent on a white shirt against nearing some coasting-packet with genteel folk on board. I also did some washing to get the salt out of my clothes. After it all I was hungry, so I made a fire and very cautiously stewed a dish of pears and set them carefully aside till I had made a pot of delicious coffee, for both of which I could afford sugar and cream. But the crowning dish of all was a fish-hash, and there was enough of it for two. I was in good health again, and my appetite was simply ravenous. While I was dining I had a large onion over the double lamp stewing for a luncheon later in the day. High living to-day!

In the afternoon the *Spray* came upon a large turtle asleep on the sea. He awoke with my harpoon through his neck, if he awoke at all. I had much difficulty in landing him on deck, which I finally accomplished by hooking the throat-halyards to one of his flippers, for he was about as heavy as my boat. I saw more turtles, and I rigged a burton ready with which to hoist them in; for I was obliged to lower the mainsail whenever the halyards were used for such purposes, and it was no small matter to hoist the large sail again. But the turtle-steak was good. I found no fault with the cook, and it was the rule of the voyage that the cook found no fault with me. There was never a ship's crew so well agreed. The bill of fare that evening was turtle-steak, tea and toast, fried potatoes, stewed onions; with dessert of stewed pears and cream.

[February 1896] From the time the great wave swept over the *Spray* until she reached Cape Virgins nothing occurred to move a pulse and set blood in motion. On the contrary, the weather became fine and the sea smooth and life tranquil. The phenomenon of mirage frequently occurred. An albatross sitting on the water one day loomed up like a large ship; two fur-seals asleep on the surface of the sea appeared like great whales, and a bank of haze I could have sworn was high land. The kaleidoscope then changed, and on the following day I sailed in a world peopled by dwarfs.

[May 1896] On the morning of May 5, 1896, I sailed from Juan Fernandez, having feasted on many things but on nothing sweeter than the adventure itself of a visit to the home and to the very cave of Robinson Crusoe. From the island the *Spray* bore away to the north, passing the island of St Felix before she gained the trade-winds, which seemed slow in reaching their limits.

If the trades were tardy, however, when they did come they came with a bang, and made up for lost time; and the *Spray*, under reefs, sometimes one, sometimes two, flew before a gale for a great many days, with a bone in her mouth, toward the Marquesas, in the west, which she made on the forty-third day out, and still kept on sailing. My time was all taken up those days—not by standing at the helm; no man, I think, could stand or sit and steer a vessel round the world: I did better than that; for I sat and read my books, mended my clothes, or cooked my meals and ate them in peace. I had already found that it was not good to be alone, and so I made companionship with what there was around me, sometimes with the universe and sometimes with my own insignificant self; but my books were always my friends, let fail all else. Nothing could be easier or more restful than my voyage in the trade-winds.

I sailed with a free wind day after day, marking the position of my ship on the chart with considerable precision; but this was done by intuition, I think, more than by slavish calculations. For one whole month my vessel held her course true; I had not, the while, so much as a light in the binnacle. The Southern Cross I saw every night abeam. The sun every morning came up astern; every evening it went down ahead. I wished for no other compass to guide me, for these were true. If I doubted my reckoning after a long time at sea I verified it by reading the clock aloft made by the Great Architect, and it was right.

There was no denying that the comical side of the strange life appeared. I awoke, sometimes, to find the sun already shining into my cabin. I heard water rushing by, with only a thin plank between me and the depths, and I said, 'How is this?' But it was all right; it was my ship on her course, sailing as no other ship had ever sailed before in the world. The rushing water along her side told me that she was sailing at full speed. I knew that no human hand was at the helm; I knew that all was well with 'the hands' forward, and that there was no mutiny on board.

The phenomena of ocean meteorology were interesting studies even here in the trade-winds. I observed that about every seven days the wind freshened and drew several points farther than usual from the direction of the pole; that is, it went round from east-southeast to south-southeast, while at the same time a heavy swell rolled up from the southwest. All this indicated that gales were going on in the anti-trades. The wind then hauled day after day as it moderated, till it stood again at the normal point, east-southeast. This is more or less the constant state of the winter trades in latitude 12° S., where I 'ran down the longitude' for weeks. The sun, we all know, is the creator of the trade-winds and of the wind system over all the earth. But ocean meteorology is, I think, the most fascinating of all. From Juan Fernandez to the Marquesas I experienced six changes of these great palpitations of sea-winds and of the sea itself, the effect of far-off gales. To know the laws that govern the winds, and to know that you know them, will give you an easy mind on your voyage round the world; otherwise you may tremble at the appearance of every cloud. What is true of this in the trade-winds is much more so in the variables, where changes run more to extremes.

To cross the Pacific Ocean, even under the most favourable circumstances, brings you for many days close to nature, and you realize the vastness of the sea. Slowly but surely the mark of my little ship's course on the track-chart reached out on the ocean and across it, while at her utmost speed she marked with her keel still slowly the sea that carried her. On the forty-third day from land—a long time to be at sea alone—the sky being beautifully clear and the moon being 'in distance' with the sun, I threw up my sextant for sights. I found from the result of three observations, after long wrestling with lunar tables, that her longitude by observation agreed within five miles of that by dead-reckoning.

This was wonderful; both, however, might be in error, but somehow I felt confident that both were nearly true, and that in a few hours more I should see land; and so it happened, for then I made the island of Nukahiva, the southernmost of the Marquesas group, clear-cut and lofty. The verified longitude when abreast was somewhere between the two reckonings; this was extraordinary. All navigators will tell you that from one day to another a ship may lose or gain more than five miles in her sailing-account, and again, in the matter of lunars, even expert lunarians are considered as doing clever work when they average within eight miles of the truth.

I hope I am making it clear that I do not lay claim to cleverness or to slavish calculations in my reckonings. I think I have already stated that I kept my longitude, at least, mostly by intuition. A rotator log always towed astern, but so much has to be allowed for currents and for drift, which the log never shows, that it is only an approximation, after all, to be corrected by one's own judgment from data of a thousand voyages; and even then the master of the ship, if he be wise, cries out for the lead and the lookout.

Unique was my experience in nautical astronomy from the deck of the *Spray*—so much so that I feel justified in briefly telling it here. The first set of sights, just spoken of, put her many hundred miles west of my reckoning by account. I knew that this could not be correct. In about an hour's time I took another set of observations with the utmost care; the mean result of these was about the same as that of the first set. I asked myself why, with my boasted self-dependence, I had not done at least better than this. Then I went in search of a discrepancy in the tables, and I found it. In the tables I found that the column of figures from which I had got an important logarithm was in error. It was a matter I could prove beyond a doubt, and it made the difference as already stated. The tables being corrected, I sailed on with self-reliance unshaken, and with my tin clock fast asleep. The result of these observations naturally tickled my vanity, for I knew that it was something to stand on a great ship's deck and with two assistants take lunar observations approximately near the truth. As one of the poorest of American sailors, I was proud of the little achievement alone on the sloop, even by chance though it may have been.

I was *en rapport* now with my surroundings, and was carried on a vast stream where I felt the buoyancy of His hand who made all the worlds. I realized the mathematical truth of their motions, so well known that astronomers compile tables of their positions through the years and the days, and the minutes of a day, with such precision that one coming along over the sea even five years later may, by their aid, find the standard time of any given meridian on the earth.

To find local time is a simpler matter. The difference between local and standard time is longitude expressed in time—four minutes, we all know, representing one degree. This, briefly, is the principle on which longitude is found independent of chronometers. The work of the lunarian, though seldom practised in these days of chronometers, is beautifully edifying, and there is nothing in the realm of navigation that lifts one's heart up more in adoration.

1900

# JOHN MASEFIELD

## 1878–1967

## 'Sea-Fever'

I must go down to the seas again, to the lonely sea and the sky,
And all I ask is a tall ship and a star to steer her by,
And the wheel's kick and the wind's song and the white sail's
    shaking,
And a grey mist on the sea's face and a grey dawn breaking.

I must go down to the seas again, for the call of the running tide
Is a wild call and a clear call that may not be denied;
And all I ask is a windy day with the white clouds flying,
And the flung spray and the blown spume, and the seagulls crying.

I must go down to the seas again to the vagrant gypsy life,
To the gull's way and the whale's way where the wind's like a
    whetted knife;
And all I ask is a merry yarn from a laughing fellow-rover,
And quiet sleep and a sweet dream when the long trick's over.

1902

# 'Cardigan Bay'

Clean, green, windy billows notching out the sky,
Grey clouds tattered into rags, sea-winds blowing high,
And the ships under topsails, beating, thrashing by,
    And the mewing of the herring gulls.

Dancing, flashing green seas shaking white locks,
Boiling in blind eddies over hidden rocks,
And the wind in the rigging, the creaking of the blocks,
    And the straining of the timber hulls.

Delicate, cool sea-weeds, green and amber-brown,
In beds where shaken sunlight slowly filters down
On many a drowned seventy-four, many a sunken town,
    And the whitening of the dead men's skulls.

                                      1902

# 'Sea Superstition'

One moonlit night in the tropics, as my ship was slipping south under
all sail, I was put to walking the deck on the lee side of the poop, with
orders to watch the ship's clock and strike the bell at each half-hour.
It was a duty I had done nightly for many nights, but this night was
memorable to me. The ship was like a thing carved of pearl. The
sailors, as they lay sleeping in the shadows, were like august things in
bronze. And the skies seemed so near me, I felt as though we were
sailing under a roof of dim branches, as of trees, that bore the moon
and the stars like shining fruits.

    Gradually, however, the peace in my heart gave way to an eating
melancholy, and I felt a sadness, such as has come to me but twice in
my life. With the sadness there came a horror of the water and of the
skies, till my presence in that ship, under the ghastly corpse-light of
the moon, among that sea, was a terror to me past power of words to
tell. I went to the ship's rail, and shut my eyes for a moment, and then
opened them to look down upon the water rushing past. I had shut

my eyes upon the sea, but when I opened them I looked upon the
forms of the sea-spirits. The water was indeed there, hurrying aft as
the ship cut through; but in the bright foam for far about the ship I
saw multitudes of beautiful, inviting faces that had an eagerness and a
swiftness in them unlike the speed or the intensity of human beings. I
remember thinking that I had never seen anything of such passionate
beauty as those faces, and as I looked at them my melancholy fell
away like a rag. I felt a longing to fling myself over the rail, so as to be
with that inhuman beauty. Yet even as I looked that beauty became
terrible, as the night had been terrible but a few seconds before. And
with the changing of my emotions the faces changed. They became
writhelled and hag-like: and in the leaping of the water, as we rushed,
I saw malevolent white hands that plucked and snapped at me. I
remember I was afraid to go near the rail again before the day
dawned.

Not very long after that night, when I was sitting with a Danish
sailor who was all broken on the wheel of his vices and not far from
his death, I talked about the sea-spirits and their beauty and their
wildness, feeling that such a haunted soul as my companion's would
have room in its crannies for such wild birds. He told me much that
was horrible about the ghosts who throng the seas. And it was he who
gave me the old myth of the seagulls, telling me that the souls of old
sailors follow the sea, in birds' bodies, till they have served their
apprenticeship or purged their years of penitence. He told me of two
sailors in a Norway barque, though I believe he lied when he said that
he was aboard her at the time, who illustrated his sermon very aptly.
The barque was going south from San Francisco, bound home round
the Horn, and the two men were in the same watch. Somehow they
fell to quarrelling as to which was the better dancer, and the one killed
the other and flung him overboard during one of the night watches.
The dead body did not sink, said my friend, because no body dares to
sink to the undersea during the night-time; but in the dawn of the
next day, and at the dawn of each day till the barque reached Norway,
a white gull flew at the slayer, crying the cry of the gulls. It was the
dead man's soul, my friend said, getting her revenge. The slayer gave
himself up on his arrival at the home port, and took poison while
awaiting trial.

When he had told me this tale, the Dane called for a tot of the raw
spirits of that land, though he must have known, he being so old a
sailor, that drink was poison to him. When he had swallowed the

liquor, he began a story of one of his voyages to the States. He said
that he was in a little English ship coming from New York to
Hamburg, and that the ship—the winds being westerly—was making
heavy running, under upper topsails, nearly all the voyage. When he
was at the wheel with his mate (for two men steered in the pitch and
hurry of that sailing) he was given to looking astern at the huge
comber known as 'the following sea', which topples up, green and
grisly, astern of every ship with the wind aft. The sight of that water
has a fascination for all men, and it fascinated him, he said, till he
thought he saw in the shaking wave the image of an old halt man who
came limping, bent on a crutch, in the ship's wake. So vivid was the
image of that cripple, he leaned across the wheel-box to his mate,
bidding him to look; and his mate looked, and immediately went
white to the lips, calling to the saints to preserve him. My friend then
told me that the cripple only appears to ships foredoomed to shipwreck,
'And', he said, 'we were run down in the Channel and sunk in ten
minutes' by a clumsy tramp from London.

After a while I left that country in a steamer whose sailors were of
nearly every nation under the sun, and from a Portuguese aboard her
I got another yarn. In the night watches, when I was alone on the
poop, I used to lean on the taffrail to see the water reeling away from
the screws. While loafing in this way one night, a little while before
the dawn, I was joined by the Portuguese, an elderly, wizened fellow,
who wore earrings. He said he had often seen me leaning over the
taffrail, and had come to warn me that there was danger in looking
upon the sea in that way. Men who looked into the water, he told me,
would at first see only the bubbles, and the eddies, and the foam.
Then they would see dim pictures of themselves and of the ship. But
at the last they always saw some unholy thing, and the unholy thing
would lure them away to death. And it was a danger, he said, no
young man should face, for though the other evil spirits, those of the
earth and air, had power only upon the body, the evil sprits of the sea
were deadly to the soul. There was a lad he had known in Lisbon who
had gone along the coast in a brig, and this lad was always looking
into the sea, and had at last seen the unholy things and flung his body
to them across the rail. The brig was too near the coast, and it blew
too freshly inshore, for the sailors to round-to to pick him up. But
they found the lad in Lisbon when they got home. He said he had
sunken down into the sea, till the sea opened about him and showed
him a path among a field of green corn. He had gone up the path and

come at last to a beautiful woman, surrounded by many beautiful women, but the one seemed to him to be the queen. She was so beautiful, he said, the sight of her was like strong wine; but she shook her head when she saw him, as though she could never give him her love, and immediately he was at the surface, under the skies, struggling towards some rocks a little distance from him. He reached the shore and went home to Lisbon in a fisher-boat, but he was never quite sane after seeing that beauty beneath the sea. He became very melancholy, and used to go down the Tagus in a row-boat, singing to himself and looking down into the water.

Before I left that ship I had to help clean her for her decent entry to the Mersey. I spent one afternoon with an old man from the Clyde doing up some ironwork, first with rope yarn and paraffin, then with red lead. The mate left us to ourselves all the watch, because the old man was trusty, and we had a fine yarn together about the things of the sea. He said that there were some who believed in the white whale, though it was all folly their calling him the king of all the fishes. The white whale was nothing but a servant, and lay low, 'somewhere nigh the Poles', till the last day dawned. And then, said the old man 'he's a busy man raising the wrecks'. When I asked him who was the king of all the fishes, he looked about to see that there were no listeners, and said, in a very earnest voice, that the king of the fish was the sea-serpent. He lies coiled, said the old man, in the hot waters of the Gulf, with a gold crown on his head, and a 'great sleep upon him', waiting till the setting of the last sun. 'And then?' I asked. 'Ah, then,' he answered, 'there'll be fine times going for us sailors.'

1905

# ERSKINE CHILDERS
## 1870–1922

# from *The Riddle of the Sands*

So behold us, then, at eight o'clock on 5th October, standing down
the river towards the field of our first labours. It is fifteen miles to the
mouth; drab, dreary miles like the dullest reaches of the lower
Thames; but scenery was of no concern to us, and a south-westerly
breeze blowing out of a grey sky kept us constantly on the verge of
reefing. The tide as it gathered strength swept us down with a force
attested by the speed with which buoys came in sight, nodded above
us and passed, each boiling in its eddy of dirty foam. I scarcely noticed
at first—so calm was the water, and so regular were the buoys, like
milestones along a road—that the northern line of coast was rapidly
receding and that the 'river' was coming to be but a belt of deep water
skirting a vast estuary, three—seven—ten miles broad, till it merged
in open sea.

'Why, we're at sea!' I suddenly exclaimed, 'after an hour's sailing!'

'Just discovered that?' said Davies, laughing.

'You said it was fifteen miles,' I complained.

'So it is, till we reach this coast at Cuxhaven; but I suppose you
may say we're at sea; of course that's all sand over there to starboard.
Look! some of it's showing already.'

He pointed into the north. Looking more attentively I noticed that
outside the line of buoys patches of the surface heaved and worked;
in one or two places streaks and circles of white were forming; in the
midst of one such circle a sleek mauve hump had risen, like the back
of a sleeping whale. I saw that an old spell was enthralling Davies as
his eye travelled away to the blank horizon. He scanned it all with a
critical eagerness, too, as one who looks for a new meaning in an old
friend's face. Something of his zest was communicated to me, and
stilled the shuddering thrill that had seized me. The protecting land
was still a comforting neighbour; but our severance with it came
quickly. The tide whirled us down, and our straining canvas aiding it,
we were soon off Cuxhaven, which crouched so low behind its

mighty dyke, that of some of its houses only the chimneys were
visible. Then, a mile or so on, the shore sharpened to a point like a
claw, where the innocent dyke became a long, low fort, with some
great guns peeping over; then of a sudden it ceased, retreating into the
far south in a dim perspective of groins and dunes.

We spun out into the open and leant heavily over to the now
unobstructed wind. The yacht rose and sank to a little swell, but my
first impression was one of wonder at the calmness of the sea, for the
wind blew fresh and free from horizon to horizon.

'Why, it's all sand *there* now, and we're under the lee of it,' said
Davies, with an enthusiastic sweep of his hand over the sea on our
left, or port, hand. That's our hunting ground.'

'What are we going to do?' I inquired.

'Pick up Sticker's Gat,' was the reply. 'It ought to be near Buoy
K.'

A red buoy with a huge K on it soon came into view. Davies peered
over to port.

'Just pull up the centre-board, will you?' he remarked abstractedly,
adding, 'and hand me up the glasses as you're down there.'

'Never mind the glasses. I've got it now; come to the main-sheet,'
was the next remark.

He put down the helm and headed the yacht straight for the
troubled and discoloured expanse which covered the submerged
sands. A 'sleeping whale', with a light surf splashing on it, was right in
our path.

'Stand by the lead, will you?' said Davies, politely. 'I'll manage the
sheets, it's a dead beat in. Ready about!'

The wind was in our teeth now, and for a crowded half-hour we
wormed ourselves forward by ever-shortening tacks into the sinuous
recesses of a channel which threaded the shallows westward. I knelt
in a tangle of line and, under the hazy impression that something very
critical was going on, plied the lead furiously, bumping and splashing
myself, and shouting out the depths, which lessened steadily, with a
great sense of the importance of my function. Davies never seemed to
listen, but tacked on imperturbably, juggling with the tiller, the
sheets, and the chart, in a way that made one giddy to look at. For all
our zeal we seemed to be making very slow progress.

'It's no use, tide's too strong; we must chance it,' he said at last.

'Chance what?' I wondered to myself. Our tacks suddenly began
to grow longer, and the depths, which I registered, shallower. All

went well for some time though, and we made better progress. Then came a longer reach than usual.

'Two and half—two—one and a half—one—only five feet,' I gasped, reproachfully. The water was growing thick and frothy.

'It doesn't matter if we do,' said Davies, thinking aloud. 'There's an eddy here, and it's a pity to waste it—ready about! Back the jib!'

But it was too late. The yacht answered but faintly to the helm, stopped, and heeled heavily over, wallowing and grinding. Davies had the mainsail down in a twinkling; it half smothered me as I crouched on the lee-side among my tangled skeins of line, scared and helpless. I crawled out from the folds, and saw him standing by the mast in a reverie.

'It's not much use,' he said, 'on a falling tide, but we'll try kedging-off. Pay that warp out while I run out the kedge.'

Like lightning he had cast off the dinghy's painter, tumbled the kedge-anchor and himself into the dinghy, pulled out fifty yards into the deeper water, and heaved out the anchor. 'Now haul,' he shouted.

I hauled, beginning to see what kedging-off meant.

'Steady on! Don't sweat yourself,' said Davies, jumping aboard again.

'It's coming,' I spluttered, triumphantly.

'The warp is, the yacht isn't; you're dragging the anchor home. Never mind, she'll lie well here. Let's have lunch.'

The yacht was motionless, and the water round her visibly lower. Petulant waves slapped against her sides, but, scattered as my senses were, I realized that there was no vestige of danger. Round us the whole face of the waters was changing from moment to moment, whitening in some places, yellowing in others, where breadths of sand began to be exposed. Close on our right the channel we had left began to look like a turbid little river; and I understood why our progress had been so slow when I saw its current racing back to meet the Elbe. Davies was already below, laying out a more than usually elaborate lunch, in high content of mind.

'Lies quiet, doesn't she?' he remarked. 'If you *do* want a sitdown lunch, there's nothing like running aground for it. And, anyhow, we're as handy for work here as anywhere else. You'll see.' . . .

The yacht lay with a very slight heel (thanks to a pair of small bilge-keels on her bottom) in a sort of trough she had dug for herself, so that she was still ringed with a few inches of water, as it were with a moat.

For miles in every direction lay a desert of sand. To the north it touched the horizon, and was only broken by the blue dot of Neuerk Island and its lighthouse. To the east it seemed also to stretch to infinity, but the smoke of a steamer showed where it was pierced by the stream of the Elbe. To the south it ran up to the pencil-line of the Hanover shore. Only to the west was its outline broken by any vestiges of the sea it had risen from. There it was astir with crawling white filaments, knotted confusedly at one spot in the north-west, whence came a sibilant murmur like the hissing of many snakes. Desert as I call it, it was not entirely featureless. Its colour varied from light fawn, where the highest levels had dried in the wind, to brown or deep violet, where it was still wet, and slate-grey where patches of mud soiled its clean bosom. Here and there were pools of water, smitten into ripples by the impotent wind; here and there it was speckled by shells and seaweed. And close to us, beginning to bend away towards that hissing knot in the north-west, wound our poor little channel, mercilessly exposed as a stagnant, muddy ditch with scarcely a foot of water, not deep enough to hide our small kedge-anchor, which perked up one fluke in impudent mockery. The dull, hard sky, the wind moaning in the rigging as though crying in despair for a prey that had escaped it, made the scene inexpressibly forlorn.

Davies scanned it with gusto for a moment, climbed to a point of vantage on the boom, and swept his glasses to and fro along the course of the channel.

'Fairly well boomed,' he said, meditatively, 'but one or two are very much out. By Jove! that's a tricky bend there.' He took a bearing with the compass, made a note or two, and sprang with a vigorous leap down on to the sand.

This, I may say, was the only way of 'going ashore' that he really liked. We raced off as fast as our clumsy sea-boots would let us, and followed up the course of our channel to the west, reconnoitring the road we should have to follow when the tide rose.

'The only way to learn a place like this,' he shouted, 'is to see it at low water. The banks are dry then, and the channels are plain. Look at that boom'—he stopped and pointed contemptuously—'it's all out of place. I suppose the channel's shifted there. It's just at, an important bend too. If you took it as a guide when the water was up you'd run aground.'

'Which would be very useful,' I observed.

'Oh, hang it!' he laughed, 'we're exploring. I want to be able to run through this channel without a mistake. We will, next time.' He stopped, and plied compass and notebook. Then we raced on till the next halt was called.

'Look,' he said, 'the channel's getting deeper, it was nearly dry a moment ago; see the current in it now? That's the flood tide coming up—from the *west*, mind you; that is, from the Weser side. That shows we're past the watershed.'

'Watershed?' I repeated, blankly.

'Yes, that's what I call it. You see, a big sand such as this is like a range of hills dividing two plains, it's never dead flat though it looks it; there's always one point, one ridge, rather, where it's highest. Now a channel cutting right through the sand is, of course, always at its shallowest when it's crossing this ridge; at low water it's generally dry there, and it gradually deepens as it gets nearer to the sea on either side. Now at high tide, when the whole sand is covered, the water can travel where it likes; but directly the ebb sets in the water falls away on either side the ridge and the channel becomes two rivers flowing in opposite directions *from* the centre, or watershed, as I call it. So, also, when the ebb has run out and the flood begins, the channel is fed by two currents flowing *to* the centre and meeting in the middle. Here the Elbe and the Weser are our two feeders. Now this current here is going eastwards; we know by the time of day that the tide's rising, *therefore* the watershed is between us and the yacht.'

'Why is it so important to know that?'

'Because these currents are strong, and you want to know when you'll lose a fair one and strike a foul one. Besides, the ridge is the critical point when you're crossing on a falling tide, and you want to know when you're past it.'

We pushed on till our path was barred by a big lagoon. It looked far more imposing than the channel; but Davies, after a rapid scrutiny, treated it to a grunt of contempt.

'It's a *cul de sac*,' he said. 'See that hump of sand it's making for, beyond?'

'It's boomed,' I remonstrated, pointing to a decrepit stem drooping over the bank, and shaking a palsied finger at the imposture.

'Yes, that's just where one goes wrong, it's an old cut that's silted up. That boom's a fraud; there's no time to go farther, the flood's making fast. I'll just take bearings of what we can see.'

The false lagoon was the first of several that began to be visible in the west, swelling and joining hands over the ribs of sand that divided them. All the time the distant hissing grew nearer and louder, and a deep, thunderous note began to sound beneath it. We turned our backs to the wind and hastened back towards the *Dulcibella*, the stream in our channel hurrying and rising alongside of us.

'There's just time to do the other side,' said Davies, when we reached her, and I was congratulating myself on having regained our base without finding our communications cut. And away we scurried in the direction we had come that morning, splashing through pools and jumping the infant runnels that were stealing out through rifts from the mother-channel as the tide rose. Our observations completed, back we travelled, making a wide circuit over higher ground to avoid the encroaching flood, and wading shin-deep in the final approach to the yacht.

As I scrambled thankfully aboard, I seemed to hear a far-off voice saying, in languid depreciation of yachting, that it did not give one enough exercise. It was mine, centuries ago, in another life. From east and west two sheets of water had overspread the desert, each pushing out tongues of surf that met and fused.

I waited on deck and watched the death-throes of the suffocating sands under the relentless onset of the sea. The last strongholds were battered, stormed, and overwhelmed; the tumult of sounds sank and steadied, and the sea swept victoriously over the whole expanse. The *Dulcibella*, hitherto contemptuously inert, began to wake and tremble under the buffetings she received. Then, with an effort, she jerked herself on to an even keel and bumped and strained fretfully, impatient to vanquish this insolent invader and make him a slave for her own ends. Soon her warp tightened and her nose swung slowly round; only her stern bumped now, and that with decreasing force. Suddenly she was free and drifting broadside to the wind till the anchor checked her and she brought up to leeward of it, rocking easily and triumphantly. Good-humoured little person! At heart she was friends alike with sand and sea. It was only when the old love and the new love were in mortal combat for her favours, and she was mauled in the *fracas*, that her temper rose in revolt.

We swallowed a hasty cup of tea, ran up the sails, and started off west again. Once across the 'watershed' we met a strong current, but the trend of the passage was now more to the north-west, so that we could hold our course without tacking, and consequently could stem the tide. 'Give her just a foot of the centre-plate,' said Davies. 'We know the way here, and she'll make less leeway; but we shall generally have to do without it—always on a falling tide. If you run aground with the plate down you deserve to be drowned.' I now saw how valuable our walk had been. The booms were on our right; but they were broken reeds, giving no hint as to the breadth of the channel. A few had lost their tops, and were being engulfed altogether by the rising water. When we came to the point where they ceased, and the false lagoon had lain, I should have felt utterly lost. We had crossed the high and relatively level sands which form the base of the Fork, and were entering the labyrinth of detached banks which obstruct the funnel-shaped cavity between the upper and middle prongs. This I knew from the chart. My unaided eye saw nothing but the open sea, growing dark green as the depths increased; a dour, threatening sea, showing its white fangs. The waves grew longer and steeper, for the channels, though still tortuous, now begin to be broad and deep.

Davies had his bearings, and struck on his course confidently. 'Now for the lead,' he said; 'the compass'll be little use soon. We must feel the edge of the sands till we pick up more booms.'

'Where are we going to anchor for the night?' I asked.

'Under the Hohenhörn,' said Davies, 'for auld lang syne!'

Partly by sight and mostly by touch we crept round the outermost alley of the hidden maze till a new clump of booms appeared, meaningless to me, but analysed by him into two groups. One we followed for some distance, and then struck finally away and began another beat to windward.

Dusk was falling. The Hanover coast-line, never very distinct, had utterly vanished; an ominous heave of swell was underrunning the short sea. I ceased to attend to Davies imparting instruction on his beloved hobby, and sought to stifle in hard manual labour the dread that had been latent in me all day at the prospect of our first anchorage at sea.

'Sound, like blazes now!' he said at last. I came to a fathom and a half. 'That's the bank,' he said; 'we'll give it a bit of a berth and then let go.'

'Let go now!' was the order after a minute, and the chain ran out

with a long-drawn moan. The *Dulcibella* snubbed up to it and
jauntily faced the North Sea and the growing night.

1903

===

# EDMUND GOSSE
## 1849–1928

# from '*Father and Son*'

It was down on the shore, tramping along the pebbled terraces of the
beach, clambering over the great blocks of fallen conglomerate which
broke the white curve with rufous promontories that jutted into the
sea, or, finally, bending over those shallow tidal pools in the limestone
rocks which were our proper hunting-ground—it was in such circumstances as these that my Father became most easy, most happy,
most human. That hard look across his brows, which it wearied me to
see, the look that came from sleepless anxiety of conscience, faded
away, and left the dark countenance still aways stern indeed, but
serene and unupbraiding. Those pools were our mirrors, in which,
reflected in the dark hyaline and framed by the sleek and shining
fronds of oar-weed, there used to appear the shapes of a middle-aged
man and a funny little boy, equally eager, and, I almost find the
presumption to say, equally well prepared for business.

If any one goes down to those shores now, if man or boy seeks to
follow in our traces, let him realise at once, before he takes the trouble
to roll up his sleeves, that his zeal will end in labour lost. There is
nothing, now, where in our days there was so much. Then the rocks
between tide and tide were submarine gardens of a beauty that
seemed often to be fabulous, and was positively delusive, since, if we
delicately lifted the weed-curtains of a windless pool, though we
might for a moment see its sides and floor paven with living blossoms,
ivory-white, rosy-red, orange and amethyst, yet all that panoply
would melt away, furled into the hollow rock, if we so much as
dropped a pebble in to disturb the magic dream.

Half a century ago, in many parts of the coast of Devonshire
and Cornwall, where the limestone at the water's edge is wrought
into crevices and hollows, the tide-line was, like Keats' Grecian
vase, 'a still unravished bride of quietness'. These cups and basins
were always full, whether the tide was high or low, and the only
way in which they were affected was that twice in the twenty-four
hours they were replenished by cold streams from the great sea,
and then twice were left brimming to be vivified by the temperate
movement of the upper air. They were living flower-beds, so exquisite
in their perfection, that my Father, in spite of his scientific require-
ments, used not seldom to pause before he began to rifle them,
ejaculating that it was indeed a pity to disturb such congregated
beauty. The antiquity of these rock-pools, and the infinite succession
of the soft and radiant forms, sea-anemones, sea-weeds, shells, fishes,
which had inhabited them, undisturbed since the creation of the
world, used to occupy my Father's fancy. We burst in, he used to
say, where no one had ever thought of intruding before; and if the
Garden of Eden had been situate in Devonshire, Adam and Eve,
stepping lightly down to bathe in the rainbow-coloured spray, would
have seen the identical sights that we now saw—the great prawns
gliding like transparent launches, anthea waving in the twilight its
thick white waxen tentacles, and the fronds of the dulse faintly
streaming on the water, like huge red banners in some reverted
atmosphere.

All this is long over, and done with. The ring of living beauty
drawn about our shores was a very thin and fragile one. It had existed
all those centuries solely in consequence of the indifference, the
blissful ignorance of man. These rock-basins, fringed by corallines,
filled with still water almost as pellucid as the upper air itself,
thronged with beautiful sensitive forms of life—they exist no longer,
they are all profaned, and emptied, and vulgarised. An army of
'collectors' has passed over them, and ravaged every corner of them.
The fairy paradise has been violated, the exquisite product of centuries
of natural selection has been crushed under the rough paw of well-
meaning, idle-minded curiosity. That my Father, himself so reverent,
so conservative, had by the popularity of his books acquired the
direct responsibility for a calamity that he had never anticipated,
became clear enough to himself before many years had passed, and
cost him great chagrin. No one will see again on the shore of England
what I saw in my early childhood, the submarine vision of dark

rocks, speckled and starred with an infinite variety of colour, and
streamed over by silken flags of royal crimson and purple.

1907

———

## EZRA POUND

### 1885–1972

## 'The Seafarer'

From the Anglo-Saxon

May I for my own self song's truth reckon,
Journey's jargon, how I in harsh days
Hardship endured oft.
Bitter breast-cares have I abided,
Known on my keel many a care's hold,
And dire sea-surge, and there I oft spent
Narrow nightwatch nigh the ship's head
While she tossed close to cliffs. Coldly afflicted,
My feet were by frost benumbed.
Chill its chains are; chafing sighs
Hew my heart round and hunger begot
Mere-weary mood. Lest man know not
That he on dry land loveliest liveth,
List how I, care-wretched, on ice-cold sea,
Weathered the winter, wretched outcast
Deprived of my kinsmen;
Hung with hard ice-flakes, where hail-scur flew,
There I heard naught save the harsh sea
And ice-cold wave, at whiles the swan cries,
Did for my games the gannet's clamour,
Sea-fowls' loudness was for me laughter,
The mews' singing all my mead-drink.

Storms, on the stone-cliffs beaten, fell on the stern
In icy feathers; full oft the eagle screamed
With spray on his pinion.
                              Not any protector
May make merry man faring needy.
This he little believes, who aye in winsome life
Abides 'mid burghers some heavy business,
Wealthy and wine-flushed, how I weary oft
Must bide above brine.
Neareth nightshade, snoweth from north,
Frost froze the land, hail fell on earth then,
Corn of the coldest. Nathless there knocketh now
The heart's thought that I on high streams
The salt-wavy tumult traverse alone.
Moaneth alway my mind's lust
That I fare forth, that I afar hence
Seek out a foreign fastness.
For this there's no mood-lofty man over earth's midst,
Not though he be given his good, but will have in his youth greed;
Nor his deed to the daring, nor his king to the faithful
But shall have his sorrow for sea-fare
Whatever his lord will.
He hath not heart for harping, nor in ring having
Nor winsomeness to wife, nor world's delight
Nor any whit else save the wave's slash,
Yet longing comes upon him to fare forth on the water.
Bosque taketh blossom, cometh beauty of berries,
Fields to fairness, land fares brisker,
All this admonisheth man eager of mood,
The heart turns to travel so that he then thinks
On flood-ways to be far departing.
Cuckoo calleth with gloomy crying,
He singeth summerward, bodeth sorrow,
The bitter heart's blood. Burgher knows not—
He the prosperous man—what some perform
Where wandering them widest draweth.
So that but now my heart burst from my breastlock,
My mood 'mid the mere-flood,
Over the whale's acre, would wander wide.
On earth's shelter cometh oft to me,

Eager and ready, the crying lone-flyer,
Whets for the whale-path the heart irresistibly,
O'er tracks of ocean; seeing that anyhow
My lord deems to me this dead life
On loan and on land, I believe not
That any earth-weal eternal standeth
Save there be somewhat calamitous
That, ere a man's tide go, turn it to twain.
Disease or oldness or sword-hate
Beats out the breath from doom-gripped body.
And for this, every earl whatever, for those speaking after—
Laud of the living, boasteth some last word,
That he will work ere he pass onward,
Frame on the fair earth 'gainst foes his malice,
Daring ado, . . .
So that all men shall honour him after
And his laud beyond them remain 'mid the English,
Aye, for ever, a lasting life's-blast,
Delight 'mid the doughty.
                              Days little durable,
And all arrogance of earthen riches,
There come now no kings nor Caesars
Nor gold-giving lords like those gone.
Howe'er in mirth most magnified,
Whoe'er in life most lordliest,
Drear all this excellence, delights undurable!
Waneth the watch, but the world holdeth.
Tomb hideth trouble. The blade is layed low.
Earthly glory ageth and seareth.
No man at all going the earth's gait,
But age fares against him, his face paleth,
Grey-haired he groaneth, knows gone companions,
Lordly men, are to earth o'ergiven,
Nor may he then the flesh-cover, whose life ceaseth,
Nor eat the sweet nor feel the sorry,
Nor stir hand nor think in mid heart,
And though he strew the grave with gold,
His born brothers, their buried bodies
Be an unlikely treasure hoard.

                                                    1909

# H. M. TOMLINSON

## 1873-1958

## from *The Sea and the Jungle*

The sun died at birth. The wind we had lost we found again as a gale from the south-east. The waters quickly increased again, and by noon the saloon was light and giddy with the racing of the propeller. I moved about like an infant learning to walk. We were 201 miles from the Mumbles, course SW ½W; it was cold, and I was still looking for the pleasures of travel. The Doctor came to introduce himself, like a good man, and tried me with such things as fevers, Shaw, Brazilian entomology, the evolution of sex, the medical profession under socialism, the sea and the poets. But my thoughts were in retreat, with the black dog in full cry. It was too cold and damp to talk even of sex. When my oil lamp began to throw its rays of brown smell, the Doctor, tired of the effort to exalt the sour dough which was my mind, left me. It was night. O, the sea and the poets!

By next morning the gale, now from the south-west, like the seas, was constantly reinforced with squalls of hurricane violence. The Chief put a man at the throttle. In the early afternoon the waves had assumed serious proportions. They soared by us in broad sombre ranges, with hissing white ridges, an inhospitable and subduing sight. They were a quite different tribe of waves from the volatile and malicious natives of the Bristol Channel. Those channel waves had no serried ranks in the attack; they were but a horde of undisciplined savages, appearing to assault without design or plan, but getting at us as they could, depending on their numbers. The waves in the channel were smaller folk, but more athletic, and very noisy; they appeared to detach themselves from the sea, and to leap at us, shouting.

These western ocean waves had a different character. They were the sea. We did not have a multitude of waves in sight, but the sea floor itself might have been undulating. The ocean was profoundly convulsed. Our outlook was confined to a few heights and hollows, and the moving heights were swift, but unhurried and stately. Your alarm, as you saw a greater hill appear ahead, tower, and bear down, had no time to get more than just out of the stage of surprise and wonder when the 'Capella's' bows were pointing skyward on a long up-slope of water, the broken summit of which was too quick for the 'Capella'—the bows disappeared in a white explosion, a volley of spray, as hard as shot, raked the bridge, the foredeck filled with raging water, and the wave swept along our run, dark, severe, and immense; with so little noise too; with but a faint hissing of foam, as in a deliberate silence. The 'Capella' then began to run down a valley.

The engines were reduced to half speed; it would have been dangerous to drive her at such seas. Our wet and slippery decks were bleak, wind-swept, and deserted. The mirror of water on the iron surfaces, constantly renewed, reflected and flashed the wild lights in the sky as she rolled and pitched, and somehow those reflections from her polish made the steamer seem more desolate and forlorn. Not a man showed anywhere on the vessel's length, except merely to hurry from one vantage to another—darting out of the ship's interior, and scurrying to another hole and vanishing abruptly, like a rabbit.

The gale was dumb till it met and was torn in our harsh opposition, shouting and moaning then in anger and torment as we steadily pressed our iron into its ponderable body. You could imagine the flawless flood of air pouring silently express till it met our pillars and pinnacles, and then flying past rift, the thousand punctures instantly spreading into long shrieking lacerations. The wounds and mouths were so many, loud, and poignant, that you wondered you could not see them. Our structure was full of voices, but the weighty body which drove against our shrouds and funnel guys, and kept them strongly vibrating, was curiously invisible. The hard jets of air spurted hissing through the winches. The sound in the shrouds and stays began like that of something tearing, and rose to a high keening. The deeper notes were amidships, in the alleyways and round the engine-room casing; but there the ship itself contributed a note, a metallic murmur so profound that it was felt as a tremor rather than heard. It was almost below human hearing. It was the hollow ship resonant, the steel walls, decks, and bulkheads quivering under the drumming of the seas, and the regular throws of the crank-shaft far below.

It was on this day the 'Capella' ceased to be a marine engine to me. She was not the 'Capella' of the Swansea docks, the sea waggon squatting low in the water, with bows like a box, and a width of beam which made her seem a wharf fixture. To-day in the Atlantic her bluff bows rose to meet the approaching bulk of each wave with such steady honesty, getting up heavily to meet its quick wiles, it is true, but often with such success that we found ourselves perched at a height above the gloom of the hollow seas, getting more light and seeing more world; though sometimes the hill-top was missed; she was not quick enough, and broke the inflowing ridge with her face. She behaved so like a brave patient thing that now her portrait, which I treasure, is to me that of one who has befriended me, a staunch and homely body who never tired in faithful well-doing. She became our little sanctuary, especially near dayfall, with those sombre mounts close round us bringing twilight before its time.

Your glance caught a wave passing amidships as a heaped mass of polished obsidian, having minor hollows and ridges on its slopes, conchoidal fractures in its glass. It rose directly and acutely from your feet to a summit that was awesome because the eye travelled to it over a long and broken up-slope; this hill had intervened suddenly to obscure thirty degrees of light; and the imagination shrank from contemplating water which overshadowed your foothold with such high dark bulk toppling in collapse. The steamer leaning that side, your face was quite close to the beginning of the bare mobile down, where it swirled past in a vitreous flux, tortured lines of green foam buried far but plain in its translucent deeps. It passed; and the light released from the sky streamed over the 'Capella' again as your side of her lifted in the roll, the sea falling down her iron wall as far as the bilge. The steamer spouted violently from her choked valve, as it cleared the sea, like a swimmer who battles, and then gets his mouth free from a smother.

Her task against those head seas and the squalls was so hard and continuous that the murmur of her heart, which I fancied grew louder almost to a moaning when her body sank to the rails, the panic of her cries when the screw raced, when she lost her hold, her noble and rhythmic labourings, the sense of her concentrated and unremitting power given by the smoke driving in violence from her swaying funnel, the cordage quivering in tense curves, the seas that burst in her face as clouds, falling roaring inboard then to founder half her length, she presently to raise her heavy body slowly out of an acre of foam, the cascades streaming from her in veils—all this was like great music. I learned why a ship has a name. It is for the same reason that you and I have names. She has happenings according to her own weird. She shows perversities and virtues her parents never dreamed into the plans they laid for her. Her heredity cannot be explained by the general chemics of iron and steel and the principles of the steam engine; but something counts in her of the moods of her creators, both of the happy men and the sullen men whose bright or dark energies poured into her rivets and plates as they hammered, and now suffuse her body. Something of the 'Capella' was revealed to me, 'our' ship. She was one for pride and trust. She was slow, but that slowness was of her dignity and size; she had valour in her. She was not a light yacht. She was strong and hard, taking heavy punishment, and then lifting her broad face over the seas to look for the next enemy. But was she slow? She seemed but slow. The eye judged by those assailing hills, so vast and whelmingly quick. The hills were so dark, swift, and great, moving barely inferior to the clouds which travelled with them, the collapsing roof which fell over the seas, flying with the same impulse as the waters. There was the uplifted ocean, and pressing down to it, sundered from it only by the gale— the gale forced them apart—the foundered heavens, a low ceiling which would have been night itself but that it was thinned in patches by some solvent day. And our 'Capella', heavy as was her body, and great and swift as were the hills, never failed to carry us up the long slopes, and over the white summits which moved down on us like the marked approach of catastrophe. If one of the greater hills but hit us, I thought—

One did. Late that afternoon the second mate, who was on watch, saw such a wave bearing down on us. It was so dominantly above us that instinctively he put his hand in his pocket for his whistle. It was his first voyage in an ocean steamer; he was not long out of his apprenticeship in 'sails', and so he did not telegraph to stop the engines. The Skipper looked up through the chartroom window, saw the high gloom of this wave over us, and jumped out for the bridge ladder to get at the telegraph himself. He was too late.

We went under. The wave stopped us with the shock of a grounding, came solid over our forelength, and broke on our structure amidships. The concussion itself scattered things about my cabin. When the 'Capella' showed herself again the ventilators had gone, the windlass was damaged, and the iron ends of the drum on the forecastle head, on which a steel hawser was wound, had been doubled on themselves, like tinfoil.

By day these movements of water on a grand scale, the harsh and deep noises of gale and breaking seas, and the labouring of the steamer, no more than awed me. At least, my sight could escape. But courage went with the light. At dusk, the eye, which had the liberty during the hours of light to range up the inclines of the sea to distant summits, and note that these dangers always passed, was imprisoned by a dreadful apparition. When there was more night than day in the dusk you saw no waves. You saw, and close at hand, only vertical shadows, and they swayed noiselessly without progressing on the fading sky high over you. I could but think the ocean level had risen greatly, and was see-sawing much superior to us all round. The 'Capella' remained then in a precarious nadir of the waters. Looking aft from the Chief's cabin I could see of our ship only the top of our mainmast, because that projected out of the shadow of the hollow into the last of the day overhead; and often the sheer apparitions oscillating around us swung above the truck of it, and the whole length vanished. The sense of onward movement ceased because nothing could be seen passing us. At dusk the steamer appeared to be rocking helplessly in a narrow sunken place which never had an outlet for us; the shadows of the seas erect over us did not move away, but their ridges pitched at changing angles.

You know the Sussex chalk hills at evening, just at that time when, from the foot of them, they lose all detail but what is on the skyline, become an abrupt plane before you of unequal height. That was the view from the 'Capella', except that the skyline moved. And when we passed a barque that evening it looked as looks a solitary bush far on the summit of the downs. The barque did not pass us; we saw it fade, and the height it surmounted fade, as shadows do when all light has gone. But where we saw it last a green star was adrift and was ranging up and down in the night.

1912

# ELINOR WYLIE

## 1885–1928

## 'Sea Lullaby'

The sea creeps to pillage,
She leaps on her prey;
A child of the village
Was murdered today.

She came up to meet him
In a smooth golden cloak,
She choked him and beat him
To death, for a joke.

Her bright locks were tangled,
She shouted for joy,
With one hand she strangled
A strong little boy.

Now in silence she lingers
Beside him all night
To wash her long fingers
In silvery light.

1921

# APSLEY CHERRY-GARRARD

## 1886–1959

# from *The Worst Journey in the World*

The voyage itself on the sailing track from Madeira to the Cape was at first uneventful. We soon got into hot weather, and at night every available bit of deck space was used on which to sleep. The more particular slung hammocks, but generally men used such deck space as they could find, such as the top of the icehouse, where they were free from the running tackle, and rolled themselves into their blankets. So long as we had a wind we ran under sail alone, and on those days men would bathe over the side in the morning, but when the engines were going we could get the hose in the morning, which was preferred, especially after a shark was seen making for Bower's red breast as he swam.

The scene on deck in the early morning was always interesting. All hands were roused before six and turned on to the pumps, for the ship was leaking considerably. Normally, the well showed about ten inches of water when the ship was dry. Before pumping, the sinker would show anything over two feet. The ship was generally dry after an hour to an hour and a half's pumping, and by that time we had had quite enough of it. As soon as the officer of the watch had given the order, "Vast pumping,' the first thing to do was to strip, and the deck was dotted with men trying to get the maximum amount of water from the sea in a small bucket let down on a line from the moving ship. First efforts in this direction would have been amusing had it not been for the caustic eye of the 'Mate' on the bridge. If the reader ever gets the chance to try the experiment, especially in a swell, he will soon find himself with neither bucket nor water. The poor Mate was annoyed by the loss of his buckets.

Everybody was working very hard during these days; shifting coal, reefing and furling sail aloft, hauling on the ropes on deck, together with magnetic and meteorological observations, tow-netting, collecting and making skins and so forth. During the first weeks there was more cargo stowing and paintwork than at other times, otherwise the work ran in very much the same lines all the way out—a period of nearly five months. On July 1 we were overhauled by the only ship we ever saw, so far as I can remember, during all that time, the *Inverclyde*, a barque out from Glasgow to Buenos Ayres. It was an oily, calm day with a sea like glass, and she looked, as Wilson quoted, 'like a painted ship upon a painted ocean', as she lay with all sail set.

We picked up the NE Trade two days later, being then north of the Cape Verde Islands (latitude 22° 28′ N., longitude 23° 5′ W. at noon). It was a Sunday, and there was a general 'make and mend' throughout the ship, the first since we sailed. During the day we ran from deep, clear blue water into a darkish and thick green sea. This remarkable change of colour, which was observed by the Discovery Expedition in much the same place, was supposed to be due to a large mass of pelagic fauna called plankton. The plankton, which drifts upon the surface of the sea, is distinct from the nekton, which swims submerged. The *Terra Nova* was fitted with tow nets with very fine meshes for collecting these inhabitants of the open sea, together with the algae, or minute plant organisms, which afford them an abundant food supply.

The plankton nets can be lowered when the ship is running at full speed and a great many such hauls were made during the expedition.

July 5 had an unpleasant surprise in store. At 10.30 a.m. the ship's bell rang and there was a sudden cry of 'Fire quarters'. Two Minimax fire extinguishers finished the fire, which was in the lazarette, and was caused by a lighted lamp which was upset by the roll of the ship. The result was a good deal of smoke, a certain amount of water below, and some singed paper, but we realized that a fire on such an old wooden ship would be a very serious matter, and greater care was taken after this.

Such a voyage shows Nature in her most attractive form, and always there was a man close by whose special knowledge was in the whales, porpoises, dolphins, fish, birds, parasites, plankton, radium and other things which we watched through microscopes or field-glasses. Nelson caught a Portuguese man-of-war (Arethusa) as it sailed past us close under the counter. These animals are common, but few can realise how beautiful they are until they see them, fresh-coloured from the deep sea, floating and sailing in a big glass bowl. It vainly tried to sail out, and vigorously tried to sting all who touched it. Wilson painted it.

From first to last the study of life of all kinds was of absorbing interest to all on board, and when we landed in the Antarctic, as well as on the ship, everybody worked and was genuinely interested in all that lived and had its being on the fringe of that great sterile continent. Not only did officers who had no direct interest in anything but their own particular work or scientific subject spend a large part of their time in helping, making notes and keeping observations, but the seamen also had a large share in the specimens and data of all descriptions which have been brought back. Several of them became good pupils for skinning birds.

Meanwhile, perhaps the constant cries of 'Whale, whale!' or 'New bird!' or 'Dolphins!' sometimes found the biologist concerned less eager to leave his meal than the observers were to call him forth. Good opportunities of studying the life of sea birds, whales, dolphins and other forms of life in the sea, even those comparatively few forms which are visible from the surface, are not too common. A modern liner moves so quickly that it does not attract life to it in the same way as a slow-moving ship like the *Terra Nova*, and when specimens are seen they are gone almost as soon as they are observed. Those who wish to study sea life—and there is much to be done in this field—should travel by tramp steamers, or, better still, sailing vessels.

Telegrams from all parts of the world, special trains, all ships dressed, crowds and waving hands, steamers out to the Heads and a general hullabaloo—these were the incidents of Saturday, November 26, 1910, when we slipped from the wharf at Lyttelton at 3 p.m. We were to call at Dunedin before leaving civilization, and arrived there on Sunday night. Here we took on the remainder of our coal. On Monday night we danced, in fantastic clothing, for we had left our grand clothes behind, and sailed finally for the South the following afternoon amidst the greatest enthusiasm. The wives remained with us until we reached the open sea. Amongst those who only left us at the last minute was Mr Kinsey of Christchurch. He acted for Scott in New Zealand during the *Discovery* days, and for Shackleton in 1907. We all owe him a deep debt of gratitude for his help. 'His interest in the expedition is wonderful, and such interest on the part of a thoroughly shrewd business man is an asset of which I have taken full advantage. Kinsey will act as my agent in Christchurch during my absence; I have given him an ordinary power of attorney, and I think have left him in possession of all the facts. His kindness to us was beyond words.'

'Evening—Loom of land and Cape Saunders Light blinking.'

The ponies and dogs were the first consideration. Even in quite ordinary weather the dogs had a wretched time. 'The seas continually break on the weather bulwarks and scatter clouds of heavy spray over the backs of all who must venture into the waist of the ship. The dogs sit with their tails to this invading water, their coats wet and dripping. It is a pathetic attitude deeply significant of cold and misery; occasionally some poor beast emits a long pathetic whine. The group forms a picture of wretched dejection; such a life is truly hard for these poor creatures.'

The ponies were better off. Four of them were on deck amidships and they were well boarded round. It is significant that these ponies had a much easier time in rough weather than those in the bows of the ship. 'Under the forecastle fifteen ponies close side by side, seven one side, eight the other, heads together, and groom between—swaying, swaying continually to the plunging, irregular motion.'

'One takes a look through a hole in the bulkhead and sees a row of heads with sad, patient eyes come swinging up together from the starboard side, whilst those on the port swing back; then up come the port heads, while the starboard recede. It seems a terrible ordeal for these poor beasts to stand this day after day for weeks together, and indeed though they continue to feed well the strain quickly drags down their weight and condition; but nevertheless the trial cannot be gauged from human standards.'

The seas through which we had to pass to reach the pack-ice must be the most stormy in the world. Dante tells us that those who have committed carnal sin are tossed about ceaselessly by the most furious winds in the second circle of Hell. The corresponding hell on earth is found in the southern oceans which encircle the world without break, tempest-tossed by the gales which follow one another round and round the world from West to East. You will find albatross there—great Wanderers, and Sooties, and Mollymawks—sailing as lightly before those furious winds as ever did Paolo and Francesca. Round the world they go. I doubt whether they land more than once a year, and then they come to the islands of these seas to breed.

There are many other beautiful sea-birds, but most beautiful of all are the Snowy petrels, which approach nearer to the fairies than anything else on earth. They are quite white, and seemingly transparent. They are the familiar spirits of the pack, which, except to nest, they seldom if ever leave, flying 'here and there independently in a mazy fashion, glittering against the blue sky like so many white moths, or shining snowflakes'. And then there are the Giant petrels, whose coloration is a puzzle. Some very nearly white, others brown, and they exhibit every variation between the one and the other. And, on the whole, the white forms become more general the farther south you go. But the usual theory of protective coloration will not fit in, for there are no enemies against which this bird must protect itself. Is it something to do with radiation of heat from the body?

A ship which sets out upon this journey generally has a bad time, and for this reason the overladen state of the *Terra Nova* was a cause of anxiety. The Australasian meteorologists had done their best to forecast the weather we must expect. Everything which was not absolutely necessary had been ruthlessly scrapped. Yet there was not a square inch of the hold and between decks which was not crammed almost to bursting, and there was as much on the deck as could be expected to stay there. Officers and men could hardly move in their living quarters when standing up, and certainly they could not all sit down. To say that we were heavy laden is a very moderate statement of the facts.

Thursday, December 1, we ran into a gale. We shortened sail in the afternoon to lower topsails, jib and stay-sail. Both wind and sea rose with great rapidity, and before the night came our deck cargo had begun to work loose. 'You know how carefully everything had been lashed, but no lashing could have withstood the onslaught of these coal sacks for long. There was nothing for it but to grapple with the evil, and nearly all hands were labouring for hours in the waist of the ship, heaving coal sacks overboard and re-lashing the petrol cases, etc., in the best manner possible under such difficult and dangerous circumstances. The seas were continually breaking over these people and now and again they would be completely submerged. At such times they had to cling for dear life to some fixture to prevent themselves being washed overboard, and with coal bags and loose cases washing about, there was every risk of such hold being torn away.

'No sooner was some semblance of order restored than some exceptionally heavy wave would tear away the lashing, and the work had to be done all over again.'

The conditions became much worse during the night and things were complicated for some of us by sea-sickness. I have lively recollections of being aloft for two hours in the morning watch on

Friday and being sick at intervals all the time. For sheer downright misery give me a hurricane, not too warm, the yard of a sailing ship, a wet sail and a bout of sea-sickness.

It must have ben about this time that orders were given to clew up the jib and then to furl it. Bowers and four others went out on the bowsprit, being buried deep in the enormous seas every time the ship plunged her nose into them with great force. It was an education to see him lead those men out into that roaring inferno. He has left his own vivid impression of this gale in a letter home. His tendency was always to underestimate difficulties, whether the force of wind in a blizzard, or the troubles of a polar traveller. This should be remembered when reading the vivid accounts which his mother had so kindly given me permission to use:

'We got through the forties with splendid speed and were just over the fifties when one of those tremendous gales got us. Our Lat. was about 52° S., a part of the world absolutely unfrequented by shipping of any sort, and as we had already been blown off Campbell Island we had nothing but a clear sweep to Cape Horn to leeward. One realized then how in the *Nimrod*—in spite of the weather—they always had the security of a big steamer to look to if things came to the worst. We were indeed alone, by many hundreds of miles, and never felt anxious about a ship before, the old whaler was to give me a new experience.

'In the afternoon of the beginning of the gale I helped make fast the TG sails, upper topsails and foresail, and was horrified on arrival on deck to find that the the heavy water we continued to ship was starting the coal bags floating in places. These, acting as battering-rams, tore adrift some of my carefully stowed petrol cases and endangered the lot. I had started to make sail fast at 3 p.m. and it was 9.30 p.m. when I had finished putting on additional lashings to everything I could. So rapidly did the sea get up that one was continually afloat and swimming about. I turned in for two hours and lay awake hearing the crash of the seas and thinking how long those cases would stand it, till my watch came at midnight as a relief. We were under two lower topsails and hove to, the engines going dead slow to assist keeping head to wind. At another time I should have been easy in my mind; now the water that came aboard was simply fearful, and the wrenching on the old ship was enough to worry any sailor called upon to fill his decks with garbage fore and aft. Still 'Risk nothing and do nothing', if funds could not supply another ship, we simply had to overload the one we had, or suffer worse things down south. The watch was eventful as the shaking up got the fine coal into the bilges, and this mixing with the oil from the engines formed balls of coal and grease which, ordinarily, went up the pumps easily; now, however, with the great strains and hundreds of tons on deck, as she continually filled, the water started to come in too fast for the half-clogged pumps to cope with. An alternative was offered to me in going faster so as to shake up the big pump on the main engines, and this I did—in spite of myself and in defiance of the first principles of seamanship. Of course, we shipped water more and more, and only to save a clean breach of the decks did I slow down again and let the water gain. My next card was to get the watch on the hand-pumps as well, and these were choked, too, or nearly so.

'Anyhow, with every pump—hand and steam—going, the water continued to rise in the stokehold. At 4 a.m. all hands took in the fore lower topsail, leaving us under a minimum of sail. The gale increased to storm force (force 11 out of 12) and such a sea got up as only the Southern Fifties can produce. All the afterguard turned out and the pumps were vigorously shaken up—sickening work as only a dribble came out. We had to throw some coal overboard to clear the after deck round the pumps, and I set to work to rescue cases of petrol which were smashed adrift. I broke away a plank or two of the lee bulwarks to give the seas some outlet as they were right over the level of the rail, and once was constantly on the verge of floating clean over the side with the cataract force of the backwash. I had all the swimming I wanted that day. Every case I rescued was put on the weather side of the poop to help get us on a more even keel. She sagged horribly and the unfortunate ponies—though under cover—were so jerked about that the weather ones could not keep their feet in their stalls, so great was the slope and strain on their forelegs. Oates and Atkinson worked among them like Trojans, but morning saw the death of one, and the loss of one dog overboard. The dogs, made fast on deck, were washed to and fro, chained by the neck, and often submerged for a considerable time. Though we did everything in our power to get them up as high as possible, the sea went everywhere. The ward-room was a swamp and so were our bunks with all our nice clothing, books, etc. However, of this we cared little, when the water had crept up to the furnaces and put the fires out, and we realized for the first time that the ship had met her match and was slowly filling. Without a pump to suck we started the forlorn hope of buckets and began to bale her out. Had we been able to open a hatch we could have cleared the main pump well at once, but with those appalling seas literally covering her, it would have meant less than 10 minutes to float, had we uncovered a hatch.

'The Chief Engineer (Williams) and carpenter (Davies), after we had all put our heads together, started cutting a hole in the engine-room bulkhead, to enable us to get into the pump-well from the engine-room; it was iron and, therefore, at least a 12-hours' job. Captain Scott was simply splendid, he might have been at Cowes, and to do him and Teddy Evans credit, at our worst strait none of our landsmen who were working so hard knew how serious things were. Captain Scott said to me quietly—'I am afraid it's a bad business for us—What do you think?' I said we were by no means dead yet, though at that moment Oates, at peril to his life, got aft to report another horse dead; and more down. And then an awful sea swept away our lee bulwarks clean, between the fore and main riggings— only our chain lashings saved the lee motor sledge then, and I was soon diving after petrol cases. Captain Scott calmly told me that they 'did not matter'—This was our great project for getting to the Pole— the much-advertised motors that 'did not matter'; our dogs looked finished, and horses were finishing, and I went to bale with a strenuous prayer in my heart, and 'Yip-i-addy' on my lips, and so we pulled through that day. We sang and re-sang every silly song we ever knew, and then everybody in the ship later on was put on 2-hour reliefs to bale, as it was impossible for flesh to keep heart with no food or rest. Even the fresh-water pump had gone wrong so we drank neat lime-juice, or anything that came along, and sat in our saturated state awaiting our next spell. My dressing-gown was my great comfort as it was not very wet, and it is a lovely warm thing.

'To make a long yarn short, we found later in the day that the storm was easing a bit and that though there was a terrible lot of water in the ship, which, try as we could, we could not reduce, it certainly had ceased to rise to any great extent. We had reason to hope that we might keep her afloat till the pump wells could be cleared. Had the storm lasted another day, God knows what our state would have been, if we had been above water at all. You cannot imagine how utterly helpless we felt in such a sea with a tiny ship—the great expedition with all its hopes thrown aside for its life. God had shown us the weakness of man's hand and it was enough for the best of us—the people who had been made such a lot of lately—the whole scene was

one of pathos really. However, at 11 p.m. Evans and I with the
carpenter were able to crawl through a tiny hole in the bulkhead,
burrow over the coal to the pump-well cofferdam, where, another
hole having been easily made in the wood, we got down below with
Davy lamps and set to work. The water was so deep that you had to
continually dive to get your hand on to the suction. After 2 hours or
so it was cleared for the time being and the pumps worked merrily. I
went in again at 4.30 a.m. and had another lap at clearing it. Not till
the afternoon of the following day, though, did we see the last of the
water and the last of the great gale. During the time the pumps were
working, we continued the baling till the water got below the
furnaces. As soon as we could light up, we did, and got the other
pumps under way, and, once the ship was empty, clearing away the
suction was a simple matter. I was pleased to find that after all I had
only lost about 100 gallons of the petrol and bad as things had been
they might have been worse. . . .

'You will ask where all the water came from seeing our forward
leak had been stopped. Thank God we did not have that to cope with
as well. The water came chiefly through the deck where the tremendous
strain—not only of the deck load, but of the smashing sea—was
beyond conception. She was caught at a tremendous disadvantage
and we were dependent for our lives on each plank standing its own
strain. Had one gone we would all have gone, and the great anxiety
was not so much the existing water as what was going to open up if
the storm continued. We might have dumped the deck cargo, a
difficult job at best, but were too busy baling to do anything else. . . .

'That Captain Scott's account will be moderate you may be sure.
Still, take my word for it, he is one of the best, and behaved up to our
best traditions at a time when his own outlook must have been the
blackness of darkness. . . . '

'Characteristically Bowers ends his account:
'Under its worst conditions this earth is a good place to live in.'
Priestley wrote in his diary:
'If Dante had seen our ship as she was at her worst, I fancy he
would have got a good idea for another Circle of Hell, though he
would have been at a loss to account for such a cheerful and ribald lot
of Souls.'

The situation narrowed down to a fight between the incoming
water and the men who were trying to keep it in check by baling her
out. The *Terra Nova* will never be more full of water, nearly up to the

furnaces, than she was that Friday morning, when we were told to go and do our damndest with three iron buckets. The constructors had not allowed for baling, only for the passage of one man at a time up and down the two iron ladders which connected the engine-room floor plates with the deck. If we used more than three buckets the business of passing them rapidly up, emptying them out of the hatchway, and returning them empty, became unprofitable. We were divided into two gangs, and all Friday and Friday night we worked two hours on and two hours off, like fiends.

Wilson's Journal describes the scene:

'It was a weird night's work with the howling gale and the darkness and the immense seas running over the ship every few minutes and no engines and no sail, and we all in the engine-room oil and bilge water, singing chanties as we passed up slopping buckets full of bilge, each man above slopping a little over the heads of all below him; wet through to the skin, so much so that some of the party worked altogether naked like Chinese coolies; and the rush of the wave backwards and forwards at the bottom grew hourly less in the dim light of a couple of engine-room oil-lamps whose light just made the darkness visible, the ship all the time rolling like a sodden lifeless log, her lee gunwale under water every time.'

'There was one thrilling moment in the midst of the worst hour on Friday when we were realizing that the fires must be drawn, and when every pump had failed to act, and when the bulwarks began to go to pieces and the petrol cases were all afloat and going overboard, and the word was suddenly passed in a shout from the hands at work in the waist of the ship trying to save petrol cases that smoke was coming up through the seams in the afterhold. As this was full of coal and patent fuel and was next the engine-room, and as it had not been opened for the airing it required to get rid of gas, on account of the flood of water on deck making it impossible to open the hatchway, the possibility of a fire there was patent to every one, and it could not possibly have been dealt with in any way short of opening the hatches and flooding the ship, when she must have foundered. It was therefore a thrilling moment or two until it was discovered that the smoke was really steam, arising from the bilge at the bottom having risen to the heated coal.'

Meanwhile men were working for all our lives to cut through two bulkheads which cut off all communication with the suction of the hand-pumps. One bulkhead was iron, the other wood.

Scott wrote at this time:

'We are not out of the wood, but hope dawns, as indeed it should for me, when I find myself so wonderfully served. Officers and men are singing shanties over their arduous work. Williams is working in sweltering heat behind the boiler to get the door made in the bulkhead. Not a single one has lost his good spirits. A dog was drowned last night, one pony is dead, and two others in a bad condition—probably they too will go. Occasionally a heavy sea would bear one of them away, and he was only saved by his chain. Meares with some helpers had constantly to be rescuing these wretched creatures from hanging, and trying to find them better shelter, an almost hopeless task. One poor beast was found hanging when dead; one was washed away with such force that his chain broke and he disappeared overboard; the next wave miraculously washed him on board again and he is fit and well. (I believe the dog was Osman.) The gale has exacted heavy toll, but I feel all will be well if we can only cope with the water. Another dog has just been washed overboard—alas! Thank God the gale is abating. The sea is still mountainously high, but the ship is not labouring so heavily as she was.'

The highest waves of which I can find any record were 36 feet high. These were observed by Sir James C. Ross in the North Atlantic.

On December 2 the waves were logged, probably by Pennell, who was extremely careful in his measurements, as being 'thirty-five feet high (estimated)'. At one time I saw Scott, standing on the weather rail of the poop, buried to his waist in green sea. The reader can then imagine the condition of things in the waist of the ship, 'over and over again the rail, from the fore-rigging to the main, was covered by a solid sheet of curling water which swept aft and high on the poop'. At another time Bowers and Campbell were standing upon the bridge, and the ship rolled sluggishly over until the lee combings of the main hatch were under the sea. They watched anxiously and slowly she righted herself, but 'she won't do that often,' said Bowers. As a rule if a ship gets that far over she goes down.

1922

# VIRGINIA WOOLF

## 1882–1941

# from *Jacob's Room*

What's the use of trying to read Shakespeare, especially in one of those little thin paper editions whose pages get ruffled, or stuck together with sea-water? Although the plays of Shakespeare had frequently been praised, even quoted, and placed higher than the Greek, never since they started had Jacob managed to read one through. Yet what an opportunity!

For the Scilly Isles had been sighted by Timmy Durrant lying like mountain-tops almost a-wash in precisely the right place. His calculations had worked perfectly, and really the sight of him sitting there, with his hand on the tiller, rosy gilled, with a sprout of beard, looking sternly at the stars, then at a compass, spelling out quite correctly his page of the eternal lesson-book, would have moved a woman. Jacob, of course, was not a woman. The sight of Timmy Durrant was no sight for him, nothing to set against the sky and worship; far from it. They had quarrelled. Why the right way to open a tin of beef, with Shakespeare on board, under conditions of such splendour, should have turned them to sulky schoolboys, none can tell. Tinned beef is cold eating, though; and salt water spoils biscuits; and the waves tumble and lollop much the same hour after hour— tumble and lollop all across the horizon. Now a spray of seaweed floats past—now a log of wood. Ships have been wrecked here. One or two go past, keeping their own side of the road. Timmy knew where they were bound, what their cargoes were, and, by looking through his glass, could tell the name of the line, and even guess what dividends it paid its shareholders. Yet that was no reason for Jacob to turn sulky.

The Scilly Isles had the look of mountain-tops almost a-wash. . . . Unfortunately, Jacob broke the pin of the Primus stove.

The Scilly Isles might well be obliterated by a roller sweeping straight across.

But one must give young men the credit of admitting that, though breakfast eaten under these circumstances is grim, it is sincere enough. No need to make conversation. They got out their pipes.

Timmy wrote up some scientific observations; and—what was the question that broke the silence—the exact time or the day of the month? anyhow, it was spoken without the least awkwardness; in the most matter-of-fact way in the world; and then Jacob began to unbutton his clothes and sat naked, save for his shirt, intending, apparently, to bathe.

The Scilly Isles were turning bluish; and suddenly blue, purple, and green flushed the sea; left it grey; struck a stripe which vanished; but when Jacob had got his shirt over his head the whole floor of the waves was blue and white, rippling and crisp, though now and again a broad purple mark appeared, like a bruise; or there floated an entire emerald tinged with yellow. He plunged. He gulped in water, spat it out, struck with his right arm, struck with his left, was towed by a rope, gasped, splashed, and was hauled on board.

The seat in the boat was positively hot, and the sun warmed his back as he sat naked with a towel in his hand, looking at the Scilly Isles which—confound it! the sail flapped. Shakespeare was knocked overboard. There you could see him floating merrily away, with all his pages ruffling innumerably; and then he went under.

Strangely enough, you could smell violets, or if violets were impossible in July, they must grow something very pungent on the mainland then. The mainland, not so very far off—you could see clefts in the cliffs, white cottages, smoke going up—wore an extra-ordinary look of calm, of sunny peace, as if wisdom and piety had descended upon the dwellers there. Now a cry sounded, as of a man calling pilchards in a main street. It wore an extraordinary look of piety and peace, as if old men smoked by the door, and girls stood, hands on hips, at the well, and horses stood; as if the end of the world had come, and cabbage fields and stone walls, and coast-guard stations, and, above all, the white sand bays with the waves breaking unseen by any one, rose to heaven in a kind of ecstasy.

But imperceptibly the cottage smoke droops, has the look of a mourning emblem, a flag floating its caress over a grave. The gulls making their broad flight and then riding at peace, seem to mark the grave.

No doubt if this were Italy, Greece, or even the shores of Spain, sadness would be routed by strangeness and excitement and the nudge of a classical education. But the Cornish hills have stark chimneys standing on them; and, somehow or other, loveliness is infernally sad. Yes, the chimneys and the coast-guard stations and the little bays with the waves breaking unseen by anyone make one remember the overpowering sorrow. And what can this sorrow be?

It is brewed by the earth itself. It comes from the houses on the coast. We start transparent, and then the cloud thickens. All history backs our pane of glass. To escape is vain.

But whether this is the right interpretation of Jacob's gloom as he sat naked, in the sun, looking at the Land's End, it is impossible to say; for he never spoke a word. Timmy sometimes wondered (only for a second) whether his people bothered him . . . No matter. There are things that can't be said. Let's shake it off. Let's dry ourselves, and take up the first thing that comes handy. . . . Timmy Durrant's notebook of scientific observations.

'Now . . . ' said Jacob.

It is a tremendous argument.

Some people can follow every step of the way, and even take a little one, six inches long, by themselves at the end; others remain observant of the external signs.

The eyes fix themselves upon the poker; the right hand takes the poker and lifts it; turns it slowly round, and then, very accurately, replaces it. The left hand, which lies on the knee, plays some stately but intermittent piece of march music. A deep breath is taken; but allowed to evaporate unused. The cat marches across the hearth-rug. No one observes her.

'That's about as near as I can get to it,' Durrant wound up.

The next minute is quiet as the grave.

'It follows . . .' said Jacob.

Only half a sentence followed; but these half-sentences are like flags set on tops of buildings to the observer of external sights down below. What was the coast of Cornwall, with its violet scents, and mourning emblems, and tranquil piety, but a screen happening to hang straight behind as his mind marched up?

'It follows . . .' said Jacob.

'Yes,' said Timmy, after reflection. 'That is so.'

Now Jacob began plunging about, half to stretch himself, half in a kind of jollity, no doubt, for the strangest sound issued from his lips as he furled the sail, rubbed the plates—gruff, tuneless—a sort of paean, for having grasped the argument, for being master of the situation, sunburnt, unshaven, capable into the bargain of sailing round the world in a ten-ton yacht which, very likely, he would do one of these days instead of settling down in a lawyer's office, and wearing spats.

'Our friend Masham', said Timmy Durrant, 'would rather not be seen in our company as we are now.' His buttons had come off.

'D'you know Masham's aunt?' said Jacob.

'Never knew he had one,' said Timmy.

'Masham has millions of aunts,' said Jacob.

'Masham is mentioned in Domesday Book,' said Timmy.

'So are his aunts,' said Jacob.

'His sister,' said Timmy, 'is a very pretty girl.'

'That's what'll happen to you, Timmy,' said Jacob.

'It'll happen to you first,' said Timmy.

'But this woman I was telling you about—Masham's aunt—'

'Oh, do get on,' said Timmy, for Jacob was laughing so much that he could not speak.

'Masham's aunt . . . '

Timmy laughed so much that he could not speak.

'Masham's aunt . . . '

'What is there about Masham that makes one laugh?' said Timmy.

'Hang it all—a man who swallows his tie-pin,' said Jacob.

'Lord Chancellor before he's fifty,' said Timmy.

'He's a gentleman,' said Jacob.

'The Duke of Wellington was a gentleman,' said Timmy.

'Keats wasn't.'

'Lord Salisbury was.'

'And what about God?' said Jacob.

The Scilly Isles now appeared as if directly pointed at by a golden finger issuing from a cloud; and everybody knows how portentous that sight is, and how these broad rays, whether they light upon the Scilly Isles or upon the tombs of crusaders in cathedrals, always shake the very foundations of scepticism and lead to jokes about God.

> Abide with me:
> Fast falls the eventide;
> The shadows deepen;
> Lord, with me abide,

sang Timmy Durrant.

'At my place we used to have a hymn which began

Great God, what do I see and hear?

said Jacob.

Gulls rode gently swaying in little companies of two or three quite near the boat; the cormorant, as if following his long strained neck in eternal pursuit, skimmed an inch above the water to the next rock; and the drone of the tide in the caves came across the water, low, monotonous, like the voice of someone talking to himself.

Rock of Ages, cleft for me,<br>Let me hide myself in thee,

sang Jacob.

Like the blunt tooth of some monster, a rock broke the surface; brown; overflown with perpetual waterfalls.

Rock of Ages,

Jacob sang, lying on his back, looking up into the sky at mid-day, from which every shred of cloud had been withdrawn, so that it was like something permanently displayed with the cover off.

By six o'clock a breeze blew in off an icefield; and by seven the water was more purple than blue; and by half-past seven there was a patch of rough gold-beater's skin round the Scilly Isles, and Durrant's face, as he sat steering, was of the colour of a red laquer box polished for generations. By nine all the fire and confusion had gone out of the sky, leaving wedges of apple-green and plates of pale yellow; and by ten the lanterns on the boat were making twisted colours upon the waves, elongated or squab, as the waves stretched or humped themselves. The beam from the lighthouse strode rapidly across the water. Infinite millions of miles away powdered stars twinkled; but the waves slapped the boat, and crashed, with regular and appalling solemnity, against the rocks.

1922

# JAMES JOYCE
1882–1941

## from *Ulysses*

In long lassoes from the Cock lake the water flowed full, covering
greengoldenly lagoons of sand, rising, flowing. My ashplant will float
away. I shall wait. No, they will pass on, passing chafing against the
low rocks, swirling, passing. Better get this job over quick. Listen: a
fourworded wavespeech: seesoo, hrss, rsseeiss, ooos. Vehement
breath of waters amid seasnakes, rearing horses, rocks. In cups of
rocks it slops: flop, slop, slap: bounded in barrels. And, spent, its
speech ceases. It flows purling, widely flowing, floating foampool,
flower unfurling.

Under the upswelling tide he saw the writhing weeds lift languidly
and sway reluctant arms, hising up their petticoats, in whispering
water swaying and upturning coy silver fronds. Day by day: night by
night: lifted, flooded and let fall. Lord, they are weary: and, whispered
to, they sigh. Saint Ambrose heard it, sigh of leaves and waves,
waiting, awaiting the fullness of their times, *diebus ac noctibus
iniurias patiens ingemiscit*. To no end gathered: vainly then released,
forth flowing, wending back: loom of the moon. Weary too in sight
of lovers, lascivious men, a naked woman shining in her courts, she
draws a toil of waters.

Five fathoms out there. Full fathom five thy father lies. At one he
said. Found drowned. High water at Dublin bar. Driving before it a
loose drift of rubble, fanshoals of fishes, silly shells. A corpse rising
saltwhite from the undertow, bobbing landward, a pace a pace a
porpoise. There he is. Hook it quick. Sunk though he be beneath the
water floor. We have him. Easy now.

Bag of corpsegas sopping in foul brine. A quiver of minnows, fat of
a spongy titbit, flash through the slits of his buttoned trouserfly. God
becomes man becomes fish becomes barnacle goose becomes feather-
bed mountain. Dead breaths I living breathe, tread dead dust, devour
a urinous offal from all dead. Hauled stark over the gunwale he
breathes upward the stench of his green grave, his leprous nosehole
snoring to the sun.

A seachange this, brown eyes saltblue. Seadeath, mildest of all deaths known to man. Old Father Ocean. *Prix de Paris*: beware of imitations. Just you give it a fair trial. We enjoyed ourselves immensely.

1922

# HILAIRE BELLOC

## 1870–1953

# from *The Cruise of the 'Nona'*

Portland Race should, by rights, be the most famous thing in all the seas of the world. I will tell you why. It is a dreadful, unexpected, enormous, unique business, set right upon the highway of all our travel: it is the marvel of our seas. And yet it has no fame. There is not a tired man writing with a pencil at top speed in the middle of the night to the shaking of machinery in Fleet Street, who will not use the word 'Maelstrom' or 'Charybdis'. I have seen Charybdis—piffling little thing; I have not seen the Maelstrom, but I have talked to men who told me they had seen it. But Portland Race could eat either of them and not know it had had breakfast.

I have nearly always been successful in catching the smooth, narrow belt near the point: but I also once found that smooth belt fail me, and so have gone through the tail-end of Portland Race; only the very tail-end. I had seen it from close by half a dozen times before in my life. I had very nearly got into it twice. But this time I did actually make knowledge of the 'thing in itself'—and there is no mistaking it. It is one of the wonderful works of God.

Portland Bill stands right out into the Channel and challenges the Atlantic tide. It is a gatepost, with Alderney and the Hogue for gate-posts on the other side. They make the gate of the narrow sea; outside them you are really (in spite of names) in the air of the ocean, and look toward the Americas. Inside them is the domestic pond. Portland Bill thrusts out into the Channel and challenges the Atlantic sea. In my folly, for many years I used to call it 'William', but I will do so no longer. For there is something awful about the snake-like descending point, and dreadful menace in the waters beyond. And here Portland Bill differs from his namesake of the land. It would be familiar to call a William of the land 'Bill'. But in the matter of Portland it is familiar to call the Bill 'William'. I will never call him William again.

I thought I had well known what the Race was before I first heard it bellowing years ago. I knew after the fashion of our shadowy nominal knowledge. I knew it in printed letters. I knew it on the chart. I knew it in the Channel Pilot. Then I came to it in the flesh, and I knew it by the senses, I saw it with my eyes, and I had heard it with my ears. I had heard it roaring like a herd, or park, or pride, of lions miles away. I had seen its abominable waste of white water on a calm day: shaving it by a couple of hundred yards. But there is all the difference in the world between that kind of knowledge and knowledge from within!

He that shall go through even the tail-end of Portland Race in a small boat and in calm weather will know what he is taking about, and for so vast an accession of real knowledge, even that pain is worth while.

Portland Race lies in a great oval, sometimes three, sometimes four or five miles out from Portland Bill, like a huge pendant hanging from the tip of a demon's ear. It is greater or smaller, according to whether the wind be off-shore or on, but it is immense always, for it is two miles or more across. It lumps, hops, seethes and bubbles, just like water boiling over the fire, but the jumps are here in feet, and the drops are tons.

There is no set of the sea in Portland Race: no run and sway: no regular assault. It is a chaos of pyramidical waters leaping up suddenly without calculation, or rule of advance. It is not a charge, but a scrimmage; a wrestling bout; but a wrestling bout of a thousand against one. It purposely raises a clamour to shake its adversary's soul, wherein it most resembles a gigantic pack of fighting dogs, for it snarls, howls, yells, and all this most terrifically. Its purpose is to kill, and to kill with a savage pride.

And all these things you find out if you get mixed up in it on a very small boat.

Perhaps the reason why Portland Race does not take the beetling place it should in the literature of England is that those who turn out the literature of England by the acre to-day never go through it, save in craft as big as towns—liners and the rest. Even these have been taught respect. During the War Portland Race sank a ship of 14,000 tons, loaded with machinery, and if you were to make a list of all the things which Portland Race has swallowed up it would rival Orcus. Portland Race is the master terror of our world.

And here I can imagine any man who had sailed saying to me that there are many other races abominable in their various degrees. I have not been through Alderney Race since the 'nineties, but I suppose it is still going strong. The Wild Goose Race you have already heard of—a very considerable thing. The Skerries also—I mean the one off Anglesey—is worthy to be saluted. And even little St Albans, though it is a toy compared with Portland, is a nuisance in any wind.

But the reason Portland deserves the master name, which it has never achieved, the reason I write so strongly of the ignorance of England toward this chief English thing, the reason that Portland Race makes me seriously consider whether literary gents be not, after all, the guardians of greatness, and whether their neglect be not, after all, the doom of the neglected, is that this incredible thing lies to everybody's hand, and yet has no place in the English mind. The Saxon and Danish pirates of the Dark Ages must have gone through it (and—please God—foundered). Every one making Dorset from France for 2,000 years must have risked it. To-day the straight course of innumerable ships out of Southampton, making for the Start and the Lizard to the ocean, leads them right past it—yet I know nothing of it in our Letters, unless it be one allusion of Mr Hardy's to the ghosts which wander above it. But there is no ghost so full of beef as to wander above Portland Race!

It is, perhaps, in that word 'Southampton' that I have struck the cause. Until Southampton became the port for the Americas the Race lay off the track. No man running down Channel from the Thames need touch the Race: no man running up. Even beating down or up Channel you are free to go about before you touch the broken water; running, you need not go near it. And steam need have nothing to do with it—except all that steam, which, during the last thirty years, has begun to use again more and more of our one inland water of the south inside the Isle of Wight.

There is a great deal more I had intended to write about Portland Race. I had intended to talk about the folly of the Bill challenging the sea, and how it ought to be an island, as it was for centuries. I had intended to say something of that canal between Portland Roads and the West Bay, which ought to have been dug long ago, and which some day people will wish they had dug, when it is too late. I had intended to give rules for getting round by the narrow smooth. I had intended to curse the absurd arrangement whereby the tide, instead of behaving like a reasonable human tide, and running six hours either way, runs southerly nine hours out of the twelve from both sides of the Bay, leaving only three for the dodge round. I had intended to add much more.

But I cannot. Let me end with this piece of advice.

Never trust any man unless he has gone round Portland Bill in something under ten tons. Never allow any man to occupy any position of import to the State until he has gone round Portland Bill under his own sail in something under ten tons. But most of all, never believe any man—no, not even if you see it printed on this page—who says that he himself has done the thing.

1925

---

# WILLIAM BEEBE

## 1877–1962

# from *The Arcturus Adventure*

For countless voyages I have hung over the bow of passenger steamers in mid-ocean, making of myself a figurehead of sorts, straining my eyes downward to watch the living creatures which whirled into sight and swept past. Dolphins, flyingfish, tunny, an occasional shark—these are familiar to all who have ever glanced over the bow. But the rays of the slanting sun striking obliquely into the smooth surface often revealed a myriad, myriad motes—more like aquatic dust than individual organisms, which filled the water from the very surface to as deep as the eye could penetrate.

Toward sunset these would vanish in the increasing dimness, and finally the bow would cut its way through an opaque, oxidized liquid, as unlike water as tar to glass. The moon overhead which showed in the waning day as a crescent of cloud, now cuts through the darkness like a sliver of gold. So the minute sea life becomes, in the dark, redoubly visible, and the ship ploughs a deep furrow through miles of star dust—phosphorescence which will fill the last imaginative human being as full of wonder and awe as it did the first who ever ventured out to sea.

As I have elsewhere explained, the floating oceanic life is known as plankton—indicating the helplessness of these wanderers, drifting about at the direction of the winds and currents. Even vaguely to estimate the abundance or numbers of these powdery clouds of animals of the ocean is to attempt a Herculean task, second only to numbering the sands of the shore or the proverbial hairs of our head. One dark, moonless evening I put out a silk surface net the mouth of which was round, and about a metre or a yard in diameter. At the farther end of the net a quart preserve jar was tied to receive and hold any small creatures which might be caught as the net was drawn slowly along the surface of the water. This was done at the speed of two knots and kept up for the duration of one hour. When drawn in, the net sagged heavily and we poured out an overflowing mass of rich pink jelly into a white flat tray. This I weighed carefully and then took, as exactly as possible, a one-hundred-and-fiftieth portion. I began to go over this but soon became discouraged, and again divided it and set to work on one sixth of the fraction on which I had first started. After many hours of eye-straining and counting under the microscope, I conservatively estimated my 1/150 part of the hour's plankton haul as follows:

| | |
|---|---:|
| Feathery copepods—Candace-like | 7,920 |
| Bright blue copepods—Pontella-like | 71,400 |
| Other copepods—Calanus-like, pink | 139,320 |
| Bivalve crustacea—Ostracod-like | 4,920 |
| Short-eyed shrimps | 720 |
| Siphonophores | 14,400 |
| Helix snails | 8,880 |
| Purple Ianthina snails | 13,440 |
| Egg masses of snails | 1,080 |
| Free eggs, various | 5,280 |
| Arrow-like flying snails | 2,520 |
| Nautilus-like flying snails | 240 |
| Oyster-like flying snails | 960 |
| | 271,080 |

If we multiply this by one hundred and fifty we get forty million, six hundred and sixty-two thousand individuals. Please remember that this is a very conservative estimate of only a few of the more easily counted groups in one small haul of an hour's duration, and the magnitude of the life of the sea will begin to dawn upon our minds. Twelve hours later—in full daylight—I repeated the haul as closely as possible and, instead of forty million, I captured about one thousand individuals of the corresponding groups. So although plankton is an involuntary horizontal wanderer, yet vertically it has more perfect control, and having developed its own system of lighting it will have nothing of the sun or even of moonlight, and remains well below reach of the stronger rays.

My own interest in plankton is wholly that of trying to disentangle the lives of some of the small people—to put myself in their places by day and night, but I feel that I must establish their importance in the minds of more practical and farseeing readers. Realize then, that even for our human race, the universe of plankton is of vital importance. The surface-loving copepods are commonly and correctly known as 'whale food', and they are also the most important food of many fishes. Only at the surface can vegetable life exist and develop, changing sunlight into edible materials, and in plankton diatoms and other plants affording satisfactory aquatic fodder to the small grazing animals about them. They thus start the ball of life rolling, which does not cease until it includes the possibility of continued existence for whales and food fishes, while, in the future, the whole human race may come to depend upon this larder of ocean.

Indeed it is a remarkable fact that ship-wrecked men in an open boat, if their lot is cast on waters rich in plankton, need never starve to death if they can manage to drag an old shirt, net fashion, through the water at night. The great percentage of crustaceans makes plankton a rich, nourishing food, even raw.

I can imagine no swifter way of killing anyone's interest in plankton than to put him in front of a pan of forty million swarming small folk. We have only a sort of hypnotic or at most superficial interest in a regiment or mob; and so I gave but the merest mechanical attention to the thirteen thousand odd *Ianthina* snails in my counting tray. But when I lay flat on my pulpit platform and began scooping up, one by one, the creatures which for years I had watched go past out of reach, then my distant longings began to change into intimate acquaintanceships, and I learned to admire and to have a real affection for these little fellow beings who lived their lives with me on this whirling planet.

Hummingbirds vibrate before flowers, albatrosses skim for hour after hour over the waves, but sooner or later every bird must come to rest—its muscles exhausted, its wings aweary. But for the mid-ocean folk there is no rest as we know it. Somehow or other they must keep themselves suspended. A list of possible ways, thinking as always from our own experience, would include swimming or flying, treading water, balloons of air or gas, or clinging to some bit of floating wreckage, whether from a storm-broken ship, a bit of porous lava, or a pinion dropped by a passing seabird. All these and many others are actually in use, and had been so for millions of years before man had brain enough to make a list.

Oblong pieces of whitish scum had tantalized me for many voyages, and even when I had emptied one of these bits from my net into a small aquarium I could make nothing of the mass of bubbles, until I looked beneath the surface and there saw that exquisite violet sea-shell with the euphonious name of *Ianthina*. Although this snail lives in a home of tissue-thin lime, it yet spends its entire life at the surface of the ocean. Its relations which we know on land leave a trail of glairy slime wherever they walk, and *Ianthina* still has the gland which secretes this, but has etherealized its use. The thin secretion is poured forth, and then, by successive upreachings of a part of the foot, bubbles of air are caught and entangled in the slime, which soon extends out as a narrow buoyant raft, the shell hanging down at one end. The bubble slime is not only balloon but nursery, and egg after egg is suspended from the lower surface. So abundant were these snails that I observed them with only general interest, thinking of course that their whole life history was well known, but on my return I found that this was far from the case, and that few facts are known about them.

There are two kinds of thrills in science; one is the result of long, patient, intellectual study. An example of this is the years of astronomical calculation whereby movements of certain heavenly bodies can be explained only by the existence of some unknown factor, and then one day this unknown but expected star is found at the very spot indicated by mathematical necessity.

Another thrill lies in an absolutely unexpected discovery. Night after night small white spots floated about on the water just beyond the glare of the gangway electric lights. In vain we tried to net them.

Now and then several would join together in a sinuous row and swim slowly along. At last, with an effort which almost precipitated him into the sea, Serge Chetyrkin scooped one up and dropped it into a small jar. To my astonishment I saw it was an argonaut or nautilus—a paper nautilus—which, in other words, is a diminutive octopus with the most exquisite shell in the world. Never have I seen a creature with a more explosive temper—we named her Mrs Bang on the spot. Hardly had I changed her to a small aquarium when she angrily shot forth a cloud of sepia, and had to be transferred twice before her inkbag was emptied and I could observe her clearly.

She rested quietly on the bottom with her many arms wrapped about her beautiful brown and white shell. But as soon as my face approached the glass, she rushed back and forth, shooting directly at me or bumping against the opposite glass, and finally backing into a corner. Here she spitefully squirted spouts of water through her siphon, until I gave her a small fish. She snatched it ungraciously, bit its head off and ate the body, feeling suspiciously about with three or four arms in my direction the while.

Two days later she went into such a paroxysm of rage that she flung herself clear out of her shell. I carefully picked this up and found her eggs still remaining inside. There were thirteen hundred of them, even-ended ovals, about ten by fifteen millimetres, with a tiny thread at one end which attached them loosely together, exactly like a miniature bunch of grapes—the smaller stems growing out from larger and these in turn from a twisted, central rope. The embryos were in various, well-advanced stages, with the future eyes of the infant argonauts marked by two large, red spots.

The shell of the argonaut is secreted by two great flat plates on the arms, and it was formerly thought that when, in calm weather, the owner rose to the surface, it sat back comfortably in its shell, raised the two broad arms aloft and used them as sails. Such a performance should properly take place only within sight of the fleets of entangled ships in the Sargasso Sea!

I never tired of watching the squids and octopuses which we captured. Soon after we landed the nautilus, Serge, with his usual skill, caught a two-foot squid which I studied for many minutes. It squirted sepia all over us and bit our hands before we could drop it in an aquarium. When it quieted down it pulsated slowly, while the colors came and went over the body in such a way that new adjectives will have to be coined adequately to describe it—reds, blacks,

browns, yellows, rolling, surging, springing into vision as the pigment
spots contracted or expanded, a living, liquid palette.

The staring eyes were oval, and of an astonishing turquoise blue,
and even on this surface, scarlet spots grew and passed—vanishing
completely, only to reappear and coalesce so that the turquoise
became carnelian. I looked into the sinister, narrow, cat-like pupils,
and they seemed to express all the horrible mystery of things which
should not be—such as these monstrous, flabby creatures calling the
snail, the slug, the nautilus and the oyster brothers—possessing not
even the prestige of having fallen, like the humble sea-squirts, from
higher aspirations—shellfish they are and nothing else. And yet
unreasonably possessing an eye, as well as or better developed than
our own. When to a low evolved mollusk thing, there has been given
a 'window of the soul' such as this, one wonders what secret, what
thing of enormous value must have been bartered for it, what sinister
transaction at some nefarious 'Bureau d'Échange de Maux'. A hand
even, would not have been so unexpected, nor a foot patterned after
those of infinitely higher beings, but such an eye should not be in
such a body.

Before we lose ourselves among the small folk of mid-ocean let us
strike a contrast. Day after day, from the crow's nest or the bridge we
caught sight of the monsters of the ocean's surface—occasional
sunfish so gigantic that, so long as they remained out of reach of a
yard-stick, it were better for a scientist to call them merely exceedingly
large. A layman might use the simile of a vertical barn-door and not
exceed the truth. Indeed the same time-worn phrase if considered
horizontally would be less than the actual fact if applied to some of
the devilfish or giant rays which we saw. Now and then a playful one
would leap almost out of the water, or pass close to the bow on its
graceful, leisurely aquatic flight.

North of Narborough they were so numerous that three of the
staff, Dickerman, Franklin and Cady, made up their minds to capture
one. Assembling every weapon, legitimate and otherwise, which the
Arcturus afforded, they set out in a tiny rowboat and made good.
When, later on, we analyzed the fight from the motion pictures, we
realized that luck had surely been with us, for if the great fish had
slapped its wing tips a little nearer and higher, the rowboat and
devilfishers would have been flattened. When once a harpoon was
deeply fastened to the fish, the battle became merely a question of
trying to tire it out, and to hope that the injury inflicted by the hail of
deeply fastened to the fish, the battle became merely a question
of trying to tire it out, and to hope that the injury inflicted by

the hail of bullets would antedate the effect of their accumulating weight!

Something at last was effective and after two hours the devilfish surrendered and was towed to the *Arcturus*. Several lashings were broken before it was at last drawn out of the water and lowered on the deck. Here was a specimen indeed, not to be placed on the stage of the microscope, but studied by walking around, over and almost into, for its gaping mouth was quite four feet wide. From fin tip to fin tip it measured exactly eighteen feet, and little by little as we cut it up we weighed the pieces and found it to total two thousand, three hundred and ten pounds. The liver alone weighed as much as a man, and we found a young devilfish about to be born—a lusty infant weighing twenty eight pounds and with a fin spread of over three and a half feet. As usual the fish had many interesting parasites. I took eight sucking fish from its gills and at least thirty more fell off when it left the water. On the skin were many weird-looking parasitic crustaceans.

These great fish are not especially wary and a few days before when returning from a diving excursion near shore we played with one for an hour, bumping into it continually with our bow and being splashed by the threshing fin-tips as it half turned over. There were two close together, each with a ten foot expanse of wings. They refused to leave or to go down although we pummeled them with the oars, and they were still swimming and rolling about when we left.

Merely to enumerate the species of floating, living beings which we took in our surface nets would fill this chapter, so all we can do is to think for a moment of the most characteristic ones. If a cupful of pond water is examined, tiny creatures will be seen shooting about, and under the lens one of these resolves into a crustacean thing, with two enormously long horns or antennae, and a single, median eye. This is aptly named *Cyclops*, and is a member of the group of copepods. We may recall that these little beasts comprised thirty million of our enumerated plankton haul, and so abundant are they that they usually give the characteristic color to the hauls or even to the ocean for miles around, varying from carnelian red to deep madder blue.

Oceanic crustaceans in general and copepods in particular correspond in numbers and variety to the insects among terrestrial creatures. Indeed as regards beauty and variety I can compare copepods only with snow crystals. Very small species often contained good-sized oil globules which seemed to serve the purpose of buoyancy, but these were lacking in larger, bizarre forms who relied on the most amazing development of appendages, some having widespread, feathery tails affording a great expanse of surface for support in this thin medium.

In the dark a small dish of this plankton would glow like a trayful of diamonds, but in the light no trace of luminescence could be detected. And yet, now and then, even under the binoculars there would come a flash as of fire opal. Little by little I narrowed this down until I had in the field of vision a single oval copepod, about an eighth of an inch long. When viewed from the side it showed as a mere tissuey line, but when it turned on its back every color of the spectrum was kindled. *Sapphirina* is its name, but Opalina would be more appropriate.

Traces of Aquarius or Pisces might reasonably be expected in these submarine regions, but hardly of Sagittarius, and yet hardly any pipette of plankton would fail to show numerous little arrows shooting across the field of vision. These are worms in structure if not in conventional outline, but their name *Sagitta* makes up in aptness what they lack in vermiformity. They are transparent, slender and quite stiff, with well-marked fins. The entire anterior end is composed of a mouth armed with great teeth-like bristles, indicating a type of life and diet far different from that of the quiet, plant-eating copepods.

Many of the day-time animals which called the surface of the ocean home, were ultramarine above and silvery white beneath, stained thus with the very essence of their surroundings—a vital factor in helping to hide them from the eye of enemies which looked down upon them from the air, or upward from the depths. But at night a host of small creatures found safety in being divested of all pigment. In the course of evolution they had scraped off all the mercury from the back of their beings, becoming so transparent that the food which they swallowed was the most conspicuous and opaque part of their anatomy.

I could never quite escape from a decided Alice in Wonderland feeling when I looked into a dish of night plankton scooped from the surface. By keenest scrutiny I could perceive only the usual hosts of small fry, when, reaching down and lifting out what seemed only an area of clear water, there would materialize before my eyes a *Phyllosoma*. This was a creature who cast no more shadow than the thinnest skim of clear ice. Yet it was a living animal, more than three inches long, with all the general organs which we ourselves possess—eyes, mouth, feet, stomach, nerves, muscles and a strong will to live. *Phyllosoma*, or leaf person, was the only name I could give them, although glass crab would be more appropriate, for they were the young of some lobster-like crustacean and nothing is known of the intermediate stages.

On land the barriers which confront animals are very apparent and tangible—mountains, deep valleys, rivers, lakes, the presence or absence of treeless plains, etc. At sea, living creatures are confined with almost equal rigidity by invisible walls. Temperature, salinity, pressure and light are some of the intangible and impassable frontiers. But the study of these requires a maximum of diagrams and schedules which would be out of place in this volume. Nevertheless, there is drama and tragedy, plot and adventure, so let us consider sunlight and darkness, or even light and shadow. I have already told how the beings who love the surface of the sea at night are all but absent from it in the daylight, but many others are willing to come up if they can find the merest excuse or parody of a sheltering shadow.

I will work up to concrete examples by a few minutes' observation from the pulpit, which always revealed the life and death need for even the slightest protection. The most faithful attendants of the *Arcturus* were the tunny fish, who kept close to the bow hour after hour, yielding to the occasional dolphins but returning at once when they had gone. Looking down through the ultramarine film I saw a score of these fish metamorphosed to rainbow colors—rich violet bodies with yellow finlets and black tails. Now and then an unfortunate flyingfish rose, then a tunny turned aside, there was a flash in the air of molten silver and the tunny was back. A few minutes later a dense mob of several thousand half-beaks rose like hail. These fish are on their way to becoming flyingfish, and sculling frantically with tail fins, skim through the air, like planes near the end of their taxiing run. Every tunny within sight flung itself headlong into the boiling mass, took toll, and returned to the pace-making bow race.

Ten minutes more passed and a *Pyrosoma* drifted by—a great, pink, hollow, cylindrical colony of unfortunates who had just missed being vertebrates like the tunny and ourselves. Beneath this cylinder of jelly was a half-dozen pilot fish. For some reason—and this is the crux of the whole matter—so long as they crowded beneath it, no tunny paid any attention to them, although so far as actual concealment went, they might just as well have been hiding beneath mosquito netting or a Greek peristyle. As our bow approached their living roof they became panic stricken. All six little fish dashed out, and as if moved by the same mechanism, six tunnies gave six snaps in the very foam of the bow wave, and six little pilot fish were relieved from further worry about their destiny. It cannot be that the tunny fish do not see their ambushed prey, but as a cat will often wait until a mouse makes some movement before it springs, so there may be some instinctive, hair-trigger, piscine law, of vital moment to them, but which in our own case we would similize with the sporting chance of a wing shot.

I came to have the feeling that far down beyond where my eyes could penetrate were uncounted hosts of little eyes peering upward, waiting for the revealing sunlight to lessen, as animals and flowers appear along the edge of retreating snow, following it, occupying every bare piece of ground. The cook would throw over an empty tin can, and if it failed to sink there would soon be a small fish swimming close beneath it. I could imagine the widening cone of shadow which the can cast downward and the fish, feeling its comfortable darkness, followed it up until it focussed on the bobbing bit of floating tin.

1926

# CONOR O'BRIEN
## 1880–1952

# from *Across Three Oceans*

Before embarking on the next paragraph, in which I shall have to use some words of strange meaning, I must explain that there is no term in the English language that denotes unequivocally a system of winds rotating round an area of low pressure. The depression beloved of the weather forecaster does not quite fill the bill; besides, it is ambiguous to say 'The depression has passed away from us.' So I fall back, as the meteorologist does, on 'cyclone' for the whole system, and, for brevity, 'storm centre' for the middle of it, without implying any particular strength of wind. For this purpose I use the word 'gale' suitably qualified. Thus 'half a gale' means a wind blowing up to 30 miles an hour; a 'gale' to 40; a 'fresh gale', 'whole gale', 'strong gale' may approach 50, but is generally a simple 'gale' complicated by cold rain or a catastrophe in the galley.

It was obvious that the storm centre was somewhere to the northward; it was probable that it was moving to the eastward; but I had no indication of how far away it lay, and the barometer was very sluggish and unhelpful. But if I kept the ship running before the wind I should eventually get a westerly breeze, and I supposed the barometer would tell me if I were getting imprudently near the centre. It did not; this depression was, like most extra-tropical cyclones, a saucer-shaped affair; and as we proceeded to the northward the wind actually took off a little. In the evening the dull and rather thick weather cleared, and I saw a great commotion in the upper clouds and deduced that we were pretty near the centre. The whole affair must have been quite stationary, or even moving in the wrong direction. While the wind was still tolerably steady we hove-to and had dinner, and then waited to see what would happen.

It fell calm, then the waves, no longer controlled by any order, ran in every direction, climbed upon each other's backs, and hurled misshapen lumps of black water into the air; at times it felt as if they were hurling the ship into the air as well. We had a good view of all this, for right above our heads the moon hung in a small clear space of sky. Round her black clouds, throwing out here and there streamers of brilliant white, whirled in a mad dance, at one moment retreating almost to the horizon which was lurid with lightning, at another rushing towards the charmed centre. At last one invaded it, and there burst into rain. It was overwhelming, stunning. I at the wheel could not see the compass a foot away. The mate, from the shelter of the chart-room, bawled out instructions to me, for I wanted to get steerage way on the ship as soon as possible. Though the wind had eased off gradually, it might come on again with a bang and knock the mast out of us. I do not know just when the wind did come; very little of it was enough to give me command of the ship, for that deluge had knocked the sea flat; and it came gradually, with intervals of calm and comparatively light showers. It was not the conventional behaviour of a cyclone, but since the dirt started the barometer had only dropped fifteen-hundredths of an inch.

Daybreak saw us running before a fresh westerly breeze, and I set the jib and turned one reef out of the mainsail. I should have turned out the crew and sent up the foreyard, but I felt we all needed a bit of rest, and sending up that foreyard was likely to be an all-hands and all-the-morning job. We had not shipped any heavy seas, so it must have been the rain that washed all the gear into an inextricable tangle. By the time that things had dried out and been to some extent cleared up, there was far too much wind and sea to set the sail; for we had now got on the right side of the weather and into a smart westerly gale.

This was my first experience of easting weather. I had sworn, in these circumstances, to take in my mainsail and run under square canvas only. For to a small vessel sea is usually a more serious matter than wind, and if it is really big she has to steer dead before it, and chance a gybe. Being without a main boom we could take that chance, but naturally preferred a rig which eliminated all risk. To-day, however, since I could not set any square canvas, I wanted to avoid reducing the fore-and-afters, nuisance as they were in a heavy sea; for I was not wasting a fair wind. I let the ship run on under two headsails and single-reefed mainsail. I wanted to bring the wind as far out on the starboard quarter as I dared, to make up some of that southing I had lost the day before, and that kept all the sails full, so they were not so much of a nuisance as I had expected. But looking back on it, the sea was not so bad as I thought it was; the ship, however, took a lot of steering, and I took P.'s watch for him. Part of the difficulty of steering was due to the cramped position of the helmsman, but part was due to the benefactions of a friend in Dublin, who had insisted that the wheel chains were not strong enough, and had rove off a stouter chain. Meanwhile the unlucky P. had kicked the original chain overboard. The new chain, naturally enough, jammed in the sheaves when a strain came on it, and, such is the perversity of inanimate things, jammed worst at such moments as I, fearing the ship would broach to, wanted to put the helm hard up. With my heart in my mouth I had to let the wheel run back a spoke or two and have another try at it. I dared not force it for fear of breaking something. But all that evening we ran unscathed.

Dark mountain ranges, their lower slopes netted with the tracery of spindrift, reared snowy crests against the sky; from them jutted sharp-cut spurs, which, growing with incredible rapidity, exploded against the bulwarks and discharged a salvo of spray into the belly of the sails. The ship, her jib-boom sweeping the water already mottled by the fountain thrown from her cut-water, rose on the steep face of the advancing swell and drowned the lighter patter of the drops torn from its summits with the shrieking in the rigging of the now unimpeded wind; then with a great crash the sea spread out under her in a boiling sheet of white. On this, or, as it seemed, suspended over this, and uncontrolled by contact with the firm support of the waters, she flew for a long space, then gradually settled down on the streaked back of the roller; the singing of the wind in the stays dropped to a low murmur, and in an uncanny quiet she shook herself and prepared for the next onset. So hour after hour the rhythm goes on, a hissing, rattling, shrieking crash; and then the bubbling of foam; a hypnotic influence. H. said that I was asleep when he relieved me at the wheel, but I do not believe that was literally true.

I have very frequently been asked whether my sails, which on a day like this would be little more than twenty feet above the water level, were not becalmed between the seas. What I have described in the last paragraph certainly gave the illusion of being becalmed; but it was, I imagine, only an illusion, due to the facts that on the back of a wave one is undoubtedly moving slowly because one is sailing uphill, and that one is in smooth water after a very noisy and agitated few moments. It is physically impossible that the wind should be lighter on this, the windward, slope of the sea, where one might expect a calm would be close under the crest; but here, it seemed to me, probably because it was puffy, that it blew the hardest. In connexion with this I noticed one fact that surprised me very much, that there was always a smooth depression in the crest immediately astern of us (I was not using oil, it was just Providence) and one might expect a strong wind to blow over that as it would over a mountain pass. But the fact that I lost no sails running in heavy weather proves that the puffs cannot have been very heavy or the soft spots very light.

1927

# HENRY BESTON
## 1888–1968

# from *The Outermost House*

This morning I am going to try my hand at something that I do not recall ever having encountered either in a periodical or in a book, namely, a chapter on the ways, the forms, and the sounds of ocean near a beach. Friends are forever asking me about the surf on the great beach and if I am not sometimes troubled or haunted by its sound. To this I reply that I have grown unconscious of the roar, and though it sounds all day long in my waking ears, and all night long in my sleeping ones, my ears seldom send on the long tumult to the mind. I hear the roar the instant I wake in the morning and return to consciousness, I listen to it a while consciously, and then accept and forget it; I hear it during the day only when I stop again to listen, or when some change in the nature of the sound breaks through my acceptance of it to my curiosity.

They say here that great waves reach the coast in threes. Three great waves, then an indeterminate run of lesser rhythms, then three great waves again. On Celtic coasts it is the seventh wave that is seen coming like a king out of the grey, cold sea. The Cape tradition, however, is no half-real, half-mystical fancy, but the truth itself. Great waves do indeed approach this beach by threes. Again and again have I watched three giants roll in one after the other out of the Atlantic, cross the outer bar, break, form again, and follow each other in to fulfilment and destruction on this solitary beach. Coast guard crews are all well aware of this triple rhythm and take advantage of the lull that follows the last wave to launch their boats.

It is true that there are single giants as well. I have been roused by them in the night. Waked by their tremendous and unexpected crash, I have sometimes heard the last of the heavy overspill, sometimes only the loud, withdrawing roar. After the roar came a briefest pause, and after the pause the return of ocean to the night's long cadences. Such solitary titans, flinging their green tons down upon a quiet world, shake beach and dune. Late one September night, as I sat reading, the very father of all waves must have flung himself down before the house, for the quiet of the night was suddenly overturned by a gigantic, tumbling crash and an earthquake rumbling; the beach trembled beneath the avalanche, the dune shook, and my house so shook in its dune that the flame of a lamp quivered and pictures jarred on the wall.

The three great elemental sounds in nature are the sound of rain, the sound of wind in a primeval wood, and the sound of outer ocean on a beach. I have heard them all, and of the three elemental voices, that of ocean is the most awesome, beautiful, and varied. For it is a mistake to talk of the monotone of ocean or of the monotonous nature of its sound. The sea has many voices. Listen to the surf, really lend it your ears, and you will hear in it a world of sounds: hollow boomings and heavy roarings, great watery tumblings and tramplings, long hissing seethes, sharp, rifle-shot reports, splashes, whispers, the grinding undertone of stones, and sometimes vocal sounds that might be the half-heard talk of people in the sea. And not only is the great sound varied in the manner of its making, it is also constantly changing its tempo, its pitch, its accent, and its rhythm, being now loud and thundering, now almost placid, now furious, now grave and solemn-slow, now a simple measure, now a rhythm monstrous with a sense of purpose and elemental will.

Every mood of the wind, every change in the day's weather, every phase of the tide—all these have subtle sea musics all their own. Surf of the ebb, for instance, is one music, surf of the flood another, the change in the two musics being most clearly marked during the first hour of a rising tide. With the renewal of the tidal energy, the sound of the surf grows louder, the fury of battle returns to it as it turns again on the land, and beat and sound change with the renewal of the war.

Sound of surf in these autumnal dunes—the continuousness of it, sound of endless charging, endless incoming and gathering, endless fulfilment and dissolution, endless fecundity, and endless death. I have been trying to study out the mechanics of that mighty resonance. The dominant note is the great spilling crash made by each arriving wave. It may be hollow and booming, it may be heavy and churning, it may be a tumbling roar. The second fundamental sound is the wild seething cataract roar of the wave's dissolution and the rush of its foaming waters up the beach—this second sound *diminuendo*. The third fundamental sound is the endless dissolving hiss of the inmost

slides of foam. The first two sounds reach the ear as a unisonance—
the booming impact of the tons of water and the wild roar of the uprush blending—and this mingled sound dissolves into the foam-
bubble hissing of the third. Above the tumult, like birds, fly wisps of
watery noise, splashes and counter splashes, whispers, seethings,
slaps, and chucklings. An overtone sound of other breakers, mingled
with a general rumbling, fells earth and sea and air.

Here do I pause to warn my reader that although I have recounted
the history of a breaker—an ideal breaker—the surf process must be
understood as mingled and continuous, waves hurrying after waves,
interrupting waves, washing back on waves, overwhelming waves.
Moreover, I have described the sound of a high surf in fair weather. A
storm surf is mechanically the same thing, but it *grinds*, and this same
long, sepulchral grinding—sound of utter terror to all mariners—is a
development of the second fundamental sound; it is the cry of the
breaker water roaring its way ashore and dragging at the sand. A
strange underbody of sound when heard through the high, wild
screaming of a gale.

Breaking waves that have to run up a steep tilt of the beach are
often followed by a dragging, grinding sound—the note of the
baffled water running downhill again to the sea. It is loudest when the
tide is low and breakers are rolling beach stones up and down a slope
of the lower beach.

I am, perhaps, most conscious of the sound of surf just after I have
gone to bed. Even here I read myself to drowsiness, and, reading, I
hear the cadenced trampling roar filling all the dark. So close is the
Fo'castle to the ocean's edge that the rhythm of sound I hear oftenest
in fair weather is not so much a general tumult as an endless arrival,
overspill, and dissolution of separate great seas. Through the dark,
mathematic square of the screened half window, I listen to the rushes
and the bursts, the tramplings, and the long, intermingled thunderings,
never wearying of the sonorous and universal sound.

Away from the beach, the various sounds of the surf melt into one
great thundering symphonic roar. Autumnal nights in Eastham
village are full of this ocean sound. The 'summer people' have gone,
the village rests and prepares for winter, lamps shine from kitchen
windows, and from across the moors, the great levels of the marsh,
and the bulwark of the dunes resounds the long wintry roaring of the
sea. Listen to it a while, and it will seem but one remote and
formidable sound; listen still longer and you will discern in it a

symphony of breaker thunderings, an endless, distant, elemental cannonade. There is beauty in it, and ancient terror. I heard it last as I walked through the village on a starry October night; there was no wind, the leafless trees were still, all the village was abed, and the whole sombre world was awesome with the sound.

The seas are the heart's blood of the earth. Plucked up and kneaded by the sun and the moon, the tides are systole and diastole of earth's veins.

The rhythm of waves beats in the sea like a pulse in living flesh. It is pure force, forever embodying itself in a succession of watery shapes which vanish on its passing.

I stand on my dune top watching a great wave coursing in from sea, and know that I am watching an illusion, that the distant water has not left its place in ocean to advance upon me, but only a force shaped in water, a bodiless pulse beat, a vibration.

Consider the marvel of what we see. Somewhere in ocean, perhaps a thousand miles and more from this beach, the pulse beat of earth liberates a vibration, an ocean wave. Is the original force circular, I wonder? and do ocean waves ring out from the creative beat as they do on a quiet surface broken by a stone? Are there, perhaps, ocean circles so great and so intricate that they are unperceived? Once created, the wave or the arc of a wave begins its journey through the sea. Countless vibrations precede it, countless vibrations follow after. It approaches the continent, swings into the coast line, courses ashore, breaks, dissolves, is gone. The innermost waters it last inhabited flow back in marbly foam to become a body to another beat, and to be again flung down. So it goes night and day, and will go till the secret heart of earth strikes out its last slow beat and the last wave dissolves upon the last forsaken shore.

As I stand on my dune top, however, I do not think of the illusion and the beat of earth, for I watch the waves with my outer rather than my inner eye. After all, the illusion is set off by an extraordinary, an almost miraculous thing—the embodiment of the wave beat in an almost constant shape. We see a wave a quarter of a mile off, then a few hundred yards nearer in, then just offshore; we seem to have been watching the same travelling mass of water—there has been no appreciable change in mass or in shape—yet all the while the original beat has taken on a flowing series of liquid bodies, bodies so alike, so much the same, that our eye will individualize them and follow them

in—the third wave, we say, or the second wave behind the great
wave. How strange it is that this beat of earth, this mysterious
undulation of the seas, moving through and among the other forces
stirring the waters close off the continent, should thus keep its
constancy of form and mass, and how odd a blend of illusion and
reality it all is! On the whole, the outer eye has the best of it.

Blowing all day long, a northwest wind yesterday swept the sky
clear of every tatter and wisp of cloud. Clear it still is, though the
wind has shifted to the east. The sky this afternoon is a harmony of
universal blue, bordered with a surf rim of snowiest blue-white. Far
out at sea, in the northeast and near the horizon, is a pool of the
loveliest blue I have ever seen here—a light blue, a petal blue, blue of
the emperor's gown in a Chinese fairy tale. If you would see waves at
their best, come on such a day, when the ocean reflects a lovely sky,
and the wind is light and onshore; plan to arrive in the afternoon so
that you will have the sun facing the breakers. Come early, for the
glints on the waves are most beautiful and interesting when the light
is oblique and high. And come with a rising tide.

The surf is high, and on the far side of it, a wave greater than its
fellows is shouldering out of the blue, glinting immensity of sea.

Friends tell me that there are certain tropic beaches where waves
miles long break all at once in one cannonading crash: a little of this, I
imagine, would be magnificent; a constancy of it, unbearable. The
surf here is broken; it approaches the beach in long intercurrent
parallels, some a few hundred feet long, some an eighth of a mile long,
some, and the longest, attaining the quarter-mile length and perhaps
just over. Thus, at all times and instants of the day, along the five
miles of beach visible from the Fo'castle deck, waves are to be seen
breaking, coursing in to break, seething up and sliding back.

But to return to the blue wave rolling in out of the blue spaciousness
of sea. On the other side of the world, just opposite the Cape, lies the
ancient Spanish province of Galicia, and the town of Pontevedra and
St James Compostella, renowned of pilgrims. (When I was there they
offered me a silver cockle shell, but I would have none of it, and got
myself a sea shell from some Galician fisherfolk.) Somewhere between
this Spanish land and Cape Cod the pulse of earth has engendered this
wave and sent it coursing westward through the seas. Far off the
coast, the spray of its passing has, perhaps, risen on the windward
bow of some rusty freighter and fallen in rainbow drops upon her
plates; the great liners have felt it course beneath their keels.

A continent rises in the west, and the pulse beat approaches this bulwark of Cape Cod. Two thirds of a mile out, the wave is still a sea vibration, a billow. Slice it across, and its outline will be that of a slightly flattened semicircle; the pulse is shaped in a long, advancing mound. I watch it approach the beach. Closer and closer in, it is rising with the rise of the beach and the shoaling of the water; closer still, it is changing from a mound to a pyramid, a pyramid which swiftly distorts, the seaward side lengthening, the landward side incurving— the wave is now a breaker. Along the ridge of blue forms a rippling crest of clear, bright water; a little spray flies off. Under the racing foam churned up by the dissolution of other breakers the beach now catches at the last shape of sea inhabited by the pulse—the wave is *tripped* by the shoaling sand—the giant stumbles, crashes, and is pushed over and ahead by the sloping line of force behind. The fall of a breaker is never the work of gravity alone.

It is the last line of the wave that has captured the decorative imagination of the world—the long seaward slope, the curling crest, the incurved volute ahead.

Toppling over and hurled ahead, the wave crashes, its mass of glinting blue falling down in a confusion of seething, splendid white, the tumbling water rebounding from the sand to a height almost always a little above that of the original crest. Out of the wild, crumbling confusion born of the dissolution of the force and the last great shape, foamy fountains spurt, and ringlets of spray. The mass of water, still all furiously a-churn and seething white, now rushes for the rim of the beach as it might for an inconceiveable cataract. Within thirty-five feet the water shoals from two feet to dry land. The edge of the rush thins, and the last impulse disappears in inch-deep slides of foam which reflect the sky in one last moment of energy and beauty and then vanish all at once into the sands.

Another thundering, and the water that has escaped and withdrawn is gathered up and swept forward again by another breaking wave. Night and day, age after age, so works the sea, with infinite variation obeying an unalterable rhythm moving through an intricacy of chance and law.

I can watch a fine surf for hours, taking pleasure in all its wild plays and variations. I like to stand on my beach, watching a long wave start breaking in many places, and see the curling water run north and south from the several beginnings, and collide in furious white pyramids built of the opposing energies. Splendid fountains often delight the eye. A towering and deep-bellied wave, toppling, encloses in its volute a quantity of air, and a few seconds after the spill this prisoned and compressed vapour bursts up through the boiling rush in feathery, foamy jets and geyser plumes. I have seen fountains here, on a September day, twenty and twenty-five and even thirty feet high. Sometimes a curious thing happens. Instead of escaping vertically, the rolled-up air escapes horizontally, and the breaker suddenly blows, as from a dragon's mouth, a great lateral puff of steamy spray. On sunny days, the toppling crest is often mirrored in the glassy volute as the wave is breaking. One lovely autumn afternoon, I saw a beautiful white gull sailing along the volute of a breaker accompanied by his reflection in the wave.

I add one curious effect of the wind. When the wind is directly offshore or well offshore, the waves approach fighting it; when the wind is offshore but so little off that its angle with the coast line is oblique—say an angle never greater than twenty-two degrees and never less than about twelve—the waves that approach the coast do not give battle, but run in with their long axis parallel to the wind. Sitting in the Fo'castle, I can often tell the exact quarter of an offshore wind simply by looking at this oblique alignment of the waves.

The long miles of beach are never more beautiful than when waves are rolling in fighting a strong breeze. Then do the breakers actually seem to charge the coast. As they approach, the wind meets them in a shock of war, the chargers rear but go on, and the wind blows back their manes. North and south, I watch them coursing in, the manes of white, sun brilliant spray streaming behind them for thirty and even forty feet. Sea horses do men call such waves on every coast of the world. If you would see them at their best, come to this beach on a bright October day when a northwest wind is billowing off to sea across the moors.

1928

# ROCKWELL KENT

## 1882–1971

# from *N by E*

It seemed, perhaps, too good to be quite true. Certainly the prompt abandon with which all responsibility for our course was forthwith thrust upon me smacked somewhat of a taunt to do or die; while the name Godthaab Kent with which I was threatened was somehow to be the symbol of that everlasting disgrace which must attend my life if now in stating our position I was wrong.

Our narrative approaches so near to its catastrophe that every happening and almost every thought assumes distinction as contributing somehow to our being finally where drama needed us. Bearing in mind accordingly that interest in detail which the High Court in Admiralty for Southern Greenland might in its later investigation have shown—and, graciously, did not—we enter upon such solemn detailing of little events as only those impressed by knowledge of their aftermath may value.

We had been at least two hours on our course for Godthaab when we sighted the first evidence that we were approaching the region of a settlement: there on the summit of a little island stood a cross-shaped beacon.

Two courses, by the chart, now lay before us: the open sea to Godthaab, and an inside passage between successive islands and the mainland. The outside course was longer, and dirty weather was in prospect. That way, however, was my choice; and being then at the tiller I headed seawards.

The skipper and mate were at the charts.

'If we're approaching Godthaab, as you say,' spoke the skipper, 'can't we take this inside passage?'

'We can—but—'

'Then that's what we'll do,' he said.

We headed in.

Putting a cluster of islands with beacons on them to port we entered sheltered waters. Here was less wind; and the surface of the bay, save for the little ripples of the breeze, was as smooth as a fresh-water pond. How sweet it was to sail so evenly, so quietly, and hear again those liquid gurglings on our sides! And see the land again so near! To feel the friendliness of that majestic wilderness, its peacefulness—immense, secure! But a few hours more and we'd go sailing into Godthaab, and drop anchor! And the people would crowd the shores to greet us! How wonderful you are, they'd say! They'd come aboard to see the ship and marvel at it. How small, how strong, how clean and neat and beautiful! How brave you are! And the men—even the hardy Danes—would amire and envy us; and the girls—sweet, gentle, blue-eyed Danish girls—they'd *love* us!

'Clean up!' think I.

'More speed!' says the skipper. And he gets out the spinnaker.

'For God's sake, don't put that on,' I protest.

Green headlands frown upon us. Inlets with canyon walls point like the outspread fingers of a hand toward that arctic rookery of storm, the inland ice. Alaska, Cape Horn; brothers to here: I've felt the violence of their sudden squalls, those dreaded 'wullys'; how with malignant fury they strike down from mountain heights, lashing the sea to foam; so swift, and terrible!

We set the spinnaker. The wind, as if to shame my fear dropped to a gentle breeze.

'Keep on this course,' say I, 'until you have that hive shaped island fair abeam; then bear off sharp to port.' And I go below to cook supper and put everything in order.

It was a splendid supper I prepared that night: corn bread and corned-beef hash and pancakes. And it was with some thought of the scrutiny of Danish housewives that I meanwhile set about that scouring and scrubbing which our long days and nights at sea had put us in such need of. So time passed.

Meanwhile the wind had headed us a bit. This had entailed a change of course and a departure from those simple and, as I now know, correct sailing directions which had been my last word. I was called on deck—only to look upon strange land forms and to share in the general confusion as to where, exactly, we had got to.

But if our course appeared now far from clear it was of no immediate concern; the breeze was failing us. It was nighttime and the sky was so heavily overcast that twilight darkness was around us. A most gentle rain began to fall.

The skipper headed for a small fiord that lay before us. On a faint breeze that scarcely gave us headway, in silence so profound that it became the murmur of the rain, we turned the headland flanking its approach and entered. And all at once, as one—there between mountain walls, sheltered and peaceful, awed by the scale and stillness of that solitude—we knew that rarest and most simple wish: here, for a time so long that it has only a beginning, merely to live!

Just where we anchored I shall never know; we were a long time about it. The sandy bottom of the fiord shoaled rapidly toward the head; and once we gently ran aground. But we poled off to some sufficient depth near to the southern shore. Down in the cabin I took the anchor's splash as signal to serve supper.

How warm and neat and clean they found the cabin! Dressed for port. Port! And tonight we sleep!

'And as late as we want to in the morning,' added the skipper.

But, for an hour after the others had gone to bed, I sat in my trim little fo'castle writing those pages of my diary which should have been these; writing through that grateful, midnight calm and stillness while the rain fell gently on the deck.

And of much that being there at last, in port in Greenland, meant to me, the last line that I wrote may speak: 'Tomorrow,' it read, 'I paint!'

The motion woke me. Where was I? I remembered. Daylight came but faintly through the fo'castle ports, shadowed as they were by the dinghy. My clock showed ten-thirty. How I had slept!

We were rolling violently; a sudden roll, a lurch to starboard. I heard steps on deck, voices, the sound of hawser paying out. Oh, well, we're at anchor; and so no one has called. I braced my knees against the side board of the bunk; I had need to.

Suddenly we were careened so far that I was almost catapulted onto the floor. I got out, dressed hastily and opened the door into the cabin. It was broad daylight there. The skipper was in bed.

'She's drifting with both anchors,' called the mate from deck.

'Give 'em more rope,' answered the skipper.

I reached the ladder. At that moment something rolled us over, far, far down, and held us there; and the green sea came pouring in as if to fill the ship.

'Damn it!' I cried, 'and I'd made everything so neat!'

On deck a hurricane; I'd never felt such wind before. The sea was beaten flat, with every wave crest shorn and whipped to smoke; cold spray and stinging rain drove over us.

I helped the mate. 'We'll need the third anchor,' I said, and started aft.

The skipper appeared. 'Good, get it out,' he said as I passed him. I went below for the last time.

The spare anchor was knocked down and stowed under the coal sacks and provisions in the after hold; it was not easy to come at. Removing the companion ladder I set to work. Hard work it was, cramped in that narrow space on hands and knees. As I dragged the hundred pound sacks out onto the cabin floor—always, strangely, careful not to damage anything—I'd look up and see the gray sky through the opening above my head. Then one time glancing up I saw the brow of the mountain; and always after that more mountain showed and less sky. And at last the mountainside itself seemed to have moved against the ship and to be towering over it.

I had laid a lighted cigarette carefully upon the chart table; this, as I worked, was always in my mind—that it should not be left to burn the wood. And so, from time to time, I'd move it just a bit. We were so careful of our boat, to mar it in no way!

But all the while I had been shifting goods and moving sacks of coal; so that at last I came to the anchor. It was a large anchor and very heavy. I dragged it out into the cabin.

'Come,' I called to the mate, 'and help me get this thing on deck.' And as I looked up I saw the mate in his yellow oilskins, bright against the near dark mountain side.

'Not much use now,' said the mate; but he came down.

It was hard work to lift that anchor up, and we seemed not to be very strong. 'I lose my strength from excitement,' said the mate. I thought that I did too—but I didn't say so.

We lifted the cumbersome affair head high and tumbled it out into the cockpit. As I started to follow, a great sea lifted us and rolled us over; I hung on, half out of the cabin. And I stared straight at an oncoming wall of rock so near astern it seemed about to crush us. The sea rose high against it, and broke and became churned water that seethed around us. It cradled us and lowered us gently; and the dark land drew quietly away.

Then came another sea that hurled us and the land together. 'Now for the crash!' I thought—and I gripped hard and braced myself against it, and watched the moment—thrilled by its impending horror.

There was no crash—that time. Ever so gently, just as we seemed to draw away again, our stern post touched the ledge; so lightly touched it that it made no sound, only a little tremor. And the tremor ran through the iron keel and the oak, and through the ribs and planking, and through every bolt and nail, through every fibre of the boat and us. Maybe we had not known that the end had come; now, as if God whispered it, we knew.

So for a third time we were floated back.

Then, as if the furies of the sea and wind were freed at last to end their coquetry, they lifted us—high, high above the ledge—and dropped us there. And the impact of that shock was only less than those that followed for that half an hour until *Direction* sank.

That half an hour! We lay, caught in the angle of a giant step of rock, keel on the tread and starboard side against the riser; held there by wind and sea; held there to lift and pound; to lift so buoyantly on every wave; to drop—crashing our thirteen iron-shod tons on granite. Lift and pound! There the perfection of our ship revealed itself; only, that having struck just once, she ever lived, a ship, to lift and strike again.

A giant sledge hammer striking a granite mountain; a hollow hammer; and within it a man. Picture yourself the man. I stayed below, and was.

See me as Adam; set full blown into that pandemonium of force, his world—of wind, storm, snow, rain, hail, lightning and thunder, earthquake and flood, hunger and cold, and the huge terrifying presence of the unknown—using his little wit toward self contained-ness against the too-much of immensity; and quietly—for Adam lived—doing the little first-at-hands one on another in their natural course, thinking but little and reflecting less. Adam and Man; and me in that compacted miniature of man's universe, the cabin of the yacht *Direction* on the rocks of Greenland.

We live less by imagination than despite it.

Matches: they're in the fo'castle cupboard. I get out a lot. Next: Keep 'em dry. A big tin on the shelf. Lentils! I pour them out on the floor—no, not all; we don't need all that room for matches. Pack in matches, put on the cover. Good. Now something to put the tin into. Sam's little bag lying there; the very thing! Good neckties and white collars! Out with them!

Put in the tin of matches; add odds and ends of food; close it; that's done.

Kerosene: Five-gallon tin too big to get ashore. The one-gallon. Buried under stores.

Over the coal sacks into the after storage space. God what a mess! Dig in the stores; dig—and find it. Good!

Alcohol for priming: Find it—a small bottle.

And the Primus stove? Crushed on the floor.

There's another in my pack-sack with pup tent, nest of pots, etc. Under the starboard fo'castle bunk. Smothered under spare sails, spare rope, spare clothes, painting supplies. Out with everything. Ha! the sack!

Flour, rice, butter, beans, dried soups, coffee, bacon, chocolate, cigarettes: fill up the sack with them. Done.

Chronometers, the beauties! I take them from their boxes and wrap them carefully in layer on layer of clothes. I partly fill a duffle bag with blankets; put in watches; add the sextant, my silver flute, my movie camera, more blankets.

And this and all the rest, plus now and then a garment or a blanket, I pass on deck to the mate.

'Enough!' I think, with pride.

'Come out of there,' calls the mate for the fourth time, peering down into the havoc of that hold.

Havoc! It's no-man's land; a mass of wreckage: doors, drawers, shelves, sheathing, stove lids, pots and pans and crockery, springs, mattresses, tools, beans and butter and books—torn, splintered, crashed and mashed, lifted and churned and hurled again with every shivering impact of the ship.

Over my writing table in the fo'castle, nailed to a timber, was my sweetheart's picture. I had not forgotten it. I will take that picture, I had thought, tuck it for safety next my skin; and carry it, last thing, ashore with me. Then on my return I'll say, 'Look, darling, what I have brought home!' And I'll take the picture from over my heart to show it to her. And with not so much modesty as to hide my valor I'll tell how in that hour of confusion and terror I had thought of her. And what a fine fellow I shall be!

So I now clambered, somehow, back to the fo'castle; found her image looking out serenely over the carnage; took her down and tucked her next to me; put an envelope containing my money, my passport and my permit to land in Greenland next to me too; and—

wading, climbing, dodging, holding on for dear life—made my way
out and to the deck.

The mate, working like ten stevedores, was getting things to shore. It
was not far: a jump from deck to rocks, jump on a rising sea and
scramble out of it and up before that step of rock was flooded.
Hurling a sack, he'd follow it; clutch it and drag it to the safety of a
higher ledge.

The sack containing the chronometers rolled back into the water.
It was retrieved intact. Some things, washed from the rocks, were
lost. The tide was littered with our gear and goods.

The thrashing of the main boom added confusion to the deck.
Only the too stout standing rigging saved the mast.

The skipper was on shore desperately struggling to secure a mast-
head line to a great boulder. Finished on board I leaped to help him.
The yawing mast-head tore the line away from us each time we'd
nearly made it fast. But once as the mast leant far down toward us we
got two turns of line around the rock; we braced ourselves and held.
The three-inch cable snapped like grocer's twine!

*Direction's* end was near. Quickly undoing the sack I got out the
movie camera. Listen! Even above the noise of sea and wind and rain I
hear for a short minute its small whirring like the beating of a heart.
And by that sound, what happened there, in Karajak Fiord in
Greenland, at eleven in the morning of July 15th, 1929, achieved
soundless immortality.

1930

# ALBERT RICHARD WETJEN

1900–1940

## from *Way for a Sailor!*

When I was wakened to eat at six o'clock the weather was clearing fast and the ship was no longer taking water. The sun was a great red disc behind thin masses of rolling vapor in which cracks were widening to show a blue sky behind. The *Blue Sea Lady* looked badly battered, with lengths of her rail gone, two of her boats smashed, her steam-pipe casing twisted, the woodwork that covered the lower bridge rails all splintered and the port bridge companion all askew. The men had cleared up a lot of other raffle but taking things all round it looked as if we'd come through the blow standing pretty well.

I took over at eight from the mate and there was a gorgeous sunset, the colors flooding the cloud-streaked sky like a paint box gone mad. The sea was running in long high swells, still white-capped before the strong wind, but deep green and sunny and no longer harmful. The ship lifted and sank, rolled heavily on occasion but kept her decks dry. The night dropped down, sudden as always in the tropics, and the stars came out between the clouds, powdery and big, lighting the satiny water. The sea fires ran along the hull, spangling the snowy wake with yellow dust and with the darkness the wind dropped to a cool rushing of soft air . . . It was a mystery and altogether a wonder, to stand on the bridge in that heaving, whispering universe and remember that scarce twelve hours before all the winds of the world had battered you and flung the sea in tepid furious mountains upon your laboring ship.

But there it is! Only in its endless variety is the sea unchanging. It is always the same, and it is never the same. You can say it is blue, and even as you define the color it has turned to purple, or green, or gray, or black, or violet, and back to blue again. You can say it is restless, and while you speak the wind drops, the swells subside and from horizon to horizon there is no ripple, no flaw, no movement, only a vast sheet of pallid satin color. You can say it is calm and it rises and sweeps your coast cities away, throws your ships ashore, washes the keels of the flying clouds above. At the last, when you have sailed long enough and far enough, you come to understand that the sea is everything. It is calm and restless, stormy and laughing, many-hued and one-colored, salty and fresh, warm and cold, an enemy and a friend, a help and a hindrance, a tragedy and a jest. Everything! Sufficient for every mood, for every dream, for every hope, for every sorrow. It will give you health and it will break you. It will teach you strength and turn your courage to water. It is like a woman, a beautiful warm-eyed woman, with magic hands and a whispered voice, with a warm heart and a sad smile; a woman you love; a woman who may turn and blast you under the acid of her anger, under the fire of her gaze, the lash of her voice, the iciness of her hands. She takes your soul away from you and fastens invisible and unbreakable chains round your heart. And you take what she gives, anger or laughter, passion or indifference, smiling and proud because she is your mistress and very, very dear to you.

And this sea, this beautiful warm woman that is the sea, with the winds in her hair and the reefs at her feet, you learn first from the foredeck, by the spume sting on your face, the salt blisters on your hands, the little whispers behind the swells and the low singing surge of the breakers on the shoal. Through pain and work, hunger and cold, night-watch and day watch, sun, moon, and wind you come to know her. She is home to you, some one friendly and comfortable. You can tell her your jests in the night and she will laugh with you; you can whisper your secret dreams and she will sigh for you; you can pour out your angers and she will lash herself to fury that her heart may feel with yours. And so you come to communion with her under the roof of the world, and you lay on her altar your boyhood, your youth, your manhood, your life, your head, heart, and hand.

And then, when you turn from the foredeck and rise to the bridge, it seems all this pre-knowledge is gone. You must start again, from the beginning, and learn of a new sea, of a new woman, beautiful and warm and cruel. From foredeck to bridge is a distance of feet alone, a small space nearer the stars, nearer the suns, and you wonder how such a small space can change things so. But it does. The sea is different. The face you knew mists over, and fades, and a new face comes to enchant you. All your reactions to the sea are turned about. From the foredeck it concerns you, but you alone, you intimately. From the bridge it concerns your ship, your cargo, your men. You lose one intimate touch and gain another. The ship comes between you. The ship takes half of that heart which before belonged only to the gray water. And the sea, that beautiful warm woman who sings from behind the swells and along the ridges of the surf, you regard her now as a foe, as a worthy foe, as a woman you may not escape from, as a woman you must always love, but as a woman you must also watch lest she take your other loves from you.

On the bridge the sea becomes abruptly an immense force, sometimes a definitely malevolent force. Before it was only one vast expanse with moods and colors and whisperings and laughter. Now in the vast expanse appear tides, currents, rips, shoals, rocks, whirlpools, hurricanes, waterspouts, tidal waves, and danger added to danger. Through all these you must steer your ship, that floating shell of wood and steel that has strangely, from the inanimate craft it was before, just a home and a place to work, changed to a personal being, as near to you, as dear to you as your right arm, or as a child. The sense of responsibility grips you. You are not always conscious of this fact but a fact it is just the same. And so in your youth, when the bridge-watch comes, you regard that sea which took your boyhood and gave you a certain wisdom and joy, warily as a fencer regards his foe. And something of the mystery, something of the wonder, something of the clean, innocent, and sincere love you gave to deep-water goes slowly away, never to return.

Isn't that right? If you've sailed you've felt that. That queer change in the sea when you took over your bridge. Didn't all the old gay feeling for it pass, vanish utterly away, and didn't all those menaces you'd never thought about before suddenly loom important, so the old friendly whisperings from behind the sky-line become the sullen mutterings of a threatened storm; the lovely whiteness of the surf a warning of iron rocks below; the smooth black currents turn from fascinating water-snakes to strong fingers plucking you to destruction, you and your ship, your ship and you?

And you've felt the ship change, change from what it was before to a living creature, so that you shivered when a log struck the hull; found an ache inside you when she swung in the rips, perilously close to the shoals; perhaps broke down and cried when she went under. Yes, that's it! That's the sort of thing! And because of it you do things for your vessel you wouldn't do for love, nor for gold, nor for fame. You know what I mean!

1931

# MARIANNE MOORE

## 1887–1972

## 'A Grave'

Man looking into the sea,
taking the view from those who have as much right to it as you have
    to it yourself,
it is human nature to stand in the middle of a thing,
but you cannot stand in the middle of this;
the sea has nothing to give but a well excavated grave.
The firs stand in a procession, each with an emerald turkey foot at the
    top,
reserved as their contours, saying nothing;
repression, however, is not the most obvious characteristic of the
    sea;
the sea is a collector, quick to return a rapacious look.
There are others besides you who have worn that look—
whose expression is no longer a protest; the fish no longer investigate
    them
for their bones have not lasted:
men lower nets, unconscious of the fact that they are desecrating a
    grave,
and row quickly away—the blades of the oars
moving together like the feet of water spiders as if there were no such
    thing as death.
The wrinkles progress among themselves in a phalanx—beautiful
    under networks of foam,
and fade breathlessly while the sea rustles in and out of the sea-
    weed;
the birds swim through the air at top speed, emitting catcalls as
    heretofore—
the tortoise shell scourges about the feet of the cliffs, in motion
    beneath them;
and the ocean, under the pulsation of lighthouses and noise of bell
    buoys,

advances as usual, looking as if it were not that ocean in which
    dropped things are bound to sink—
in which if they turn and twist, it is neither with volition nor
    consciousness.

1935

———

# DORA BIRTLES

## 1903–

# from *North-West by North*

Dog watch on the Arafura sea. It is strange how night, the moon and
silence turn one's thoughts out. I had been thinking of childhood
fantasies and of the mystery of birth. Watching it, as we rocked over
its heaving waters, the sea became for me the All-Mother, the watery
womb that produced the first life, the moon, the eternal female.
'Green-eyed women of the moon.' A Mother Carey's chicken or a
petrel kept flying round and round in circles over my head and over
the wake stretched like a galloping mare's tail behind the boat. The
bird was so black against the moon. I thought that had my dream
desires been fulfilled, I had read them as motherhood longings, it
might be a disembodied spirit trying to get a lodgment within me.
That conviction grew as the bird kept on weaving the rings of its
flight about me. Finally it perched near the end of the boom not a
yard from me. Its tail folded looked like a pair of scissors half-open.
It made no sound, its beak pointing as if it would pierce my breast.
Fascinated I let the ship get off the course a little and was aware of a
wave bigger than any that night, immediately astern, coming sideways
with a hissing indrawn breath and a curl of white on its forehead. So I
had to nurse the boat over that and over two more big ones and when
I looked again the bird had gone.

　　To beware of being moon-fey a second time I sat on the other side
and steered by the compass and by Capella that shone bright in the
sky. We were far from any boat track and it was easy to imagine

anything at night and alone on the sea. Our boat was so tiny, such a duckling of a craft, shaped childishly like the moon above or like a pre-historic drawing of the boat in which the sun-myth hero makes his sea journey, that it became impossible not to think anthropomorphically. I had convinced myself that our journey to the west, like the sun's, was symbolical, that the moon had evil desires on me and that if I stared at her boat much longer mooncraft would prevail and I would be infecundated according to some magical ritual which unconsciously I was following and into whose circle I had stepped when we sailed into that name of magic, the Arafura Sea.

. . . The sea had not changed; it remained mirror smooth. Banks of white clouds were like mountains of snow on the horizon, their reflections combed wool below them. Everything was incredibly still; the clarity of the air, the shine and the reflection of shining, from sea to sky and from sky to sea found no word in my vocabulary to fit it; glitter, glimmer, sheen, luminous, radiance, incandescent, white-hot, were not true, they suggested a movement of light within itself and there was none of that, there was rather a transparency of light and air bound in a permanent state of being stiffly brilliant, starched with heat. The shadow of the ship smouldered blue in the glassiness. Little striped fish that had been with us for a long time darted about, doubtless they imagined we were a convenient rock for the barnacles were thick again and quite large. A crab that belonged to us Sven said he recognized from Pulo Moreaux and swore that since it had been with us it had grown bigger. He cut a barnacle off and tried some surface fishing with it for bait. No luck. Ruth suggested a barnacle stew. We had all been dreaming of food, Henery dreamt of meat, veal cutlets, Joan of lettuce and mashed potato with butter on it, Ruth dreamt she saw me eating apricots under a tree in a garden. I had a long circumstantial shopping dream that ended in oranges and Sven said he dreamed of hot cross buns with currants in them and sugar on the top; he had a bearish taste for buns, filling things, he so often felt empty.

The noon position put us another five miles south.

In the afternoon a dark cloud came about a mile from the starboard beam and from it hung a long gossamer thread waving about like a thick black clotted cobweb. It dangled to and fro as if grappling for something. Out of the sea rose a shorter dark whorl of water to meet it. A waterspout. The two whorls did not join. There was evidently a series of local low-pressure areas around us for a long sheet of black cloud reached out of the southern sky and plainly touched the sea. It slowly approached, travelling on the surface of the water. The incipient waterspout was travelling faster than the cloud and away from us. The upper part of it lifted a little. As the waterspout moved in front of the black sheet of cloud its lower half was visible as a white cylinder of vapour while the upper half moved on without it, still black. Farther away to port, where we had not been watching, a second waterspout had completed itself and hung, a thin black ribbon, from sky to sea. We marvelled but were not apprehensive. They seemed a spectacle not a danger. To go up in a waterspout would be an interesting finish, something to break the monotony of being becalmed.

1935

ROBERT FROST

1874–1963

## 'Neither Out Far Nor In Deep'

The people along the sand
All turn and look one way.
They turn their back on the land.
They look at the sea all day.

As long as it takes to pass
A ship keeps raising its hull;
The wetter ground like glass
Reflects a standing gull.

The land may vary more;
But wherever the truth may be—
The water comes ashore,
And the people look at the sea.

They cannot look out far.
They cannot look in deep.
But when was that ever a bar
To any watch they keep?

1936

# RICHARD HUGHES

## 1900–1976

# from *In Hazard*

Dick Watchett was busy, and excited. This was his first hurricane;
and he looked forward to it. Moreover the Captain—since captains
are schoolmasters as well as everything else—made him in imagination
commander of the ship; required him to repeat, from barometer and
wind-direction, the same calculations that he had made himself, and
say what should be done. It was interesting, but an ordeal (because
the Captain's report on him at the end of the voyage would depend
on the answers he made).

Once that was over, he was like a schoolboy out of school. He hoped
that the hurricane would do something spectacular; that the wind
would bend solid iron rails with its weight, something tangibly to
express its force: something vivid, for letters home. But one could
hardly hope for anything really spectacular on so large and well-found
a ship as the 'Archimedes'. No dismasting. No frozen helmsman
lashed to the wheel, with salt spray glittering in his beard. No: for the
strong wheel-house was up in the centre of the bridge, far above any
waves, and thick panes of glass protected you completely from the
weather. Nor was it a viking figure that stood at the wheel: it was a
little old Chinese quartermaster, with a face like a wrinkled yellow
apple, standing on a little old mat.

At eight, when Mr Buxton had gone his rounds, he had taken Dick
with him. Going about the deck, against this wind, was exactly like
going up hill: the same effort, and the same slant of one's body

towards the ground. The ship might just as well have been standing up on its stern, facing the wind, when you tried to go forward: and coming aft was like falling downstairs.

The loud rustling shriek of the gale was giving place to a deafening roaring. The water sloshing about on the fo'c'sle head was atomised by the wind, and blew aft as mist. The water on the rails was blown off in little glittering fans. Even oil from the winches was carried by the spray to the upper deck.

And over the side one saw, not the familiar sea, but rather whole countrysides of water. The wind picked the skin off the waves, leaving little white pock-marks. Waves broke, and then swallowed their own foam: you could see it far below the surface, engulfed. Suddenly a squall of rain dashed across. The rain-drops bounced on the water, making a surface like the dewy gossamer on a lawn: like wool. It was as if the naked sea were growing hair.

Instantly it was a great pleasure to Dick that Sukie was not there. Wind was better than women. A ship-load of men, none of them—at any rate for the respite of the storm—in love with anyone: all purely bent on the impending battle with the air. That was best.

The thought of Sukie brought the taste of corn-whiskey into his mind; and his mind repelled it with vigour. He felt a sudden conviction that he would never again touch alcohol: it was revolting stuff. Not so much as a glass of beer. Nor smoke. It surprised him a little; for he had always taken a normal pleasure in these things. It was like conversion—a physical conversion, not a spiritual one, for there was no morality nor resolution in it. It was just a sudden reversal of his physical appetites, so strong that he could not believe they would ever change again. A loathing of girls, drink, tobacco; and all wrought by the wind.

Then the exultation which the storm had raised in him whirled up in his head giddily, and he was sea-sick.

At nine o'clock, when the ship was hove-to, the wind-force had been only seven (on the Beaufort scale): and the barometer stood at 29.58. By noon the barometer had dropped to 29.38; and the wind-force was ten. That is a great wind: we don't often get it as strong as that in England, even when the weather seems to be blowing itself inside out: but it still continued to increase.

Plainly the storm was neither of the mildness, nor in the position, predicted. It was lucky that they had had all loose gear and so on secured in plenty of time. It would have been difficult now. It was difficult even to get about.

The seas, huge lumps of water with a point on top, ran about in all directions in a purposeful way at immense speeds. They were as big as houses, and moved as fast as trains. Sometimes they ran into each other, hard, and threw themselves jointly into the air. At others they banged suddenly against the ship, and burst out into a rapid plumage of spray that for a moment hid everything. The windows of the bridge, high up as they were, were completely obscured by spray: it was only through the little 'clear-vision screen' (a fast-spinning wheel of glass which water cannot stick to) that it was possible to see at all. For if you stepped out on to the ends of the bridge, where there was no glass, the wind blew your eyes shut immediately.

Directly beneath the bridge were the deck-officers' quarters, a little room for each: and directly beneath that again, grouped just aft of the common dining-saloon, were the engineers' quarters. On each side there was a short corridor; and the steering-rods, from the bridge above, ran along it. On to the starboard corridor Mr MacDonald's room opened: on the port corridor the doctor lived.

This Dr Frangcon was an elderly man, who never talked about his past. But a ship's doctor's is hardly a life for the professionally ambitious, and few elderly men are to be found in it. The only clue to his past (if it can be called a clue) was a package of medals which he kept hidden in a drawer among his underclothing. No one ever had got a good view of them: and while some said they were Boer War medals, others held that they were foreign decorations: but the steward maintained that they had been had for swimming. And Dr Frangcon collected antique musical instruments—lutes, serpents, recorders and so on. These he brought to sea with him, sealed in glass cases to protect them against the changes of climate. He spent the morning anxiously wadding these glass cases apart with lint and surgical dressings, as the motion of the ship threatened to clap them together.

At two o'clock Mr MacDonald, being rather old, went to his room for a rest: and Dick Watchett also went to his room, to see he had left nothing breakable in a place where it could break. The fourth engineer was left in charge of the hissing engine-room. Captain Edwardes and Mr Buxton were both on the bridge, and intended to remain there. The wind was still increasing. The roaring so hammered on the ears as to tend to frighten the brain within. The atmosphere was almost all spray now: you could not see through it. Except for occasional momentary lulls, you could not see the sea, or the deck even. It was only by the wincing of the ship you knew what huge waves were hitting her: by that, and the thunderous banging. You could not *see* anything. Standing in the damp chartroom, you could descry, through the glass between, the little Chinaman, on his mat, at the wheel; but nothing outside: and it was only by shouting close into each other's ears that they could hear, either.

However, the fiercer a hurricane is, the smaller the area (as a rule) which it covers: and so the sooner it should be over. By that evening, with luck. That was, if nothing untoward happened.

But at two o'clock, there happened something very untoward indeed. For at two o'clock the engines, at half-speed, began to appear to be inadequate to keep her nose into the wind. So Captain Edwardes telegraphed for full speed ahead. Yet that seemed to make no difference: the propeller, unable any more to hold her, only roared in the helpless milk under her stern.

She was turning. The seas were battering more on the starboard side. The wind was on the starboard bow.

The quartermaster was making frantic signs, through the window, that something had gone wrong with the steering. So that was it! However, there was nothing to be done, but watch the compass-needle creep round in the compass. For by the time anyone could get the emergency wheel on the poop in action, she would be broadside; and then no power on earth could straighten her again till the wind eased. It took about five minutes, altogether; and then she was lying broadside on to the wind, heeled over steeply, vulnerable; and Mr Buxton, noting the time, entered it in the log.

He also noted, with satisfaction, that her motion was a short, sharp rolling. This might be uncomfortable, but from the point of view of stability it was satisfactory. But she was heeled over so far that walls and floor seemed to have almost equal claims to represent the horizontal.

In the wheelhouse the little Chinese quartermaster clung to the useless wheel, like a cold monkey to the neck of its master. A sudden lurch tore him off. The mat on which he stood skiddered down the steep slope of the bridge: a snapshot (from the chartroom) of the Chinaman shooting by, with a concentrated expression, on his inadequate toboggan: then he fetched up against the rails at the far end with such a terrific impact as to bend them, and send the shield of the navigating light spinning into the sea. There he stopped, inert, on the brink: till Buxton and the Captain together managed to drag him back. Was he dead or alive? One does not bend iron rails with one's body for nothing. Yet, oddly enough, he was alive.

Gaston, the fourth engineer, a young dark Channel-islander, in temporary charge of the engine-room, telephoned for help. The engine-room skylight had blown off, deluging the engine-room with spray, and fusing the lights; and with the ship heeled right over like that the engines would anyhow have been difficult to work. The second and third engineers came, but not Mr MacDonald. For, leaving his room, he saw that the coir matting in the corridor had got jammed in the steering rods; and he was down on hands and knees, tearing at it with his finger-nails.

These steering-rods were his: and though the matting was Mr Buxton's he knew he ought to have vetoed its presence in that passage, near his rods. But he had not noticed it: and now it had jammed the steering.

As soon as he felt the ship turn, Dick Watchett tried to leave his room. But he could not. The wind had fixed the door shut. It would have held it against an elephant. He was a prisoner there. He would have to stay there till a lull came and let him out.

Captain Edwardes telegraphed to the engine-room to reduce speed to dead slow: if full speed ahead could not hold her, it was better to save the engines.

The force of the wind continued to increase. Through its solid roar nothing—not even the impact of the seas—could now be heard. Captain Edwardes had been through several hurricanes; but never anything like this. He tried to assess its velocity: but he had nothing to go by. There is no figure on the Beaufort Scale to express such a wind-force as this was. No anemometer is made that would register so great a ferocity of air. Any anemometer yet made would be smashed by it. He thrust his hand out, for a moment, into the force of the spray, then drew it back bleeding at the finger-tips, and numbed as if by an electric shock. For the wind was blowing now with a velocity of about two hundred miles an hour. It begins to be called a hurricane when it reaches seventy-five; and the pressure at two hundred would be seven times greater. To be exposed to a wind like this was of the order of having to cling to the bare wings of an aeroplane racing.

1938

# T. S. ELIOT
## 1888–1965

# from 'The Dry Salvages'

The river is within us, the sea is all about us;
The sea is the land's edge also, the granite
Into which it reaches, the beaches where it tosses
Its hints of earlier and other creation:
The starfish, the horseshoe crab, the whale's backbone;
The pools where it offers to our curiosity
The more delicate algae and the sea anemone.
It tosses up our losses, the torn seine,
The shattered lobsterpot, the broken oar
And the gear of foreign dead men. The sea has many voices,
Many gods and many voices.
                              The salt is on the briar rose,
The fog is in the fir trees.
                        The sea howl
And the sea yelp, are different voices
Often together heard: the whine in the rigging,
The menace and caress of wave that breaks on water,
The distant rote in the granite teeth,
And the wailing warning from the approaching headland
Are all sea voices, and the heaving groaner
Rounded homewards, and the seagull:
And under the oppression of the silent fog
The tolling bell
Measures time not our time, rung by the unhurried
Ground swell, a time
Older than the time of chronometers, older
Than time counted by anxious worried women
Lying awake, calculating the future,
Trying to unweave, unwind, unravel
And piece together the past and the future,
Between midnight and dawn, when the past is all deception,

The future futureless, before the morning watch
When time stops and time is never ending;
And the ground swell, that is and was from the beginning,
Clangs
The bell.

1940

F. A. WORSLEY

1872–1943

# from *Shackleton's Boat Journey*

Our eleventh day was splendid—a day's grace. Moderate southeast breezes. Blue sky and passing clouds. The sea was moderate, and the great long westerly swell went shouldering lazily across us. We only shipped an occasional small sea, and, again hanging out our gear, got it into a pleasantly moderate state of dampness. We felt very uppish indeed that night, when we crawled into our sleeping bags and thought with pity of our unfortunate pals on Elephant Island, though they were probably pitying us at that moment.

The day before I had taken observations of the sun, cuddling the mast with one arm and swinging fore and aft round the mast, sextant and all. This day I found the best way was, sitting on the deck, to jam one foot between the mast and halyards, the other against the shroud, and catch the sun when the boat leaped her highest on the crest of a sea, allowing the 'height of eye' accordingly. Position 55°31′S, 44°43′W, run N36°E fifty-two miles; total 496.

From my navigation book: 'In assisting with the Primus' I burn my fingers on the aluminium rest for the cooker. My subsequent antics with the crumpled-up thing that now bears a faint resemblance to a lady's hat that I am endeavouring to trim, sends everyone into yells of laughter, in which, after a while, I cannot help joining too.' This was quite the heartiest laugh we had on the passage, helped, no doubt, by the two good days we had enjoyed. We had one other good laugh, but I cannot now remember what it was about.

The twelfth day a southeast breeze blew strong on the starboard beam. It was clear weather, but overcast and squally, with a lumpy sea and southwest swell. We shipped seas. Everything was wet through again.

Our plug tobacco had gradually disintegrated and washed apart into its original leaves, which were carried by the water under and to and fro through the ballast. Sometimes, with the aid of reindeer hair, they choked the pump. Sea-sodden pieces were salvaged by the seamen, and, while Crean and I were operating the 'Primus', laid on the crumpled rest previously mentioned to be dried or scorched.

After meals the leaves that had not found their way into the hoosh were torn up, shredded laboriously and rolled with toilet paper into a cigarette. Macarty or Vincent then performed prodigies of drawing at it, and when at a dull glow handed it, as a special treat, to Sir Ernest, who, not liking to hurt anyone's feelings, took it gingerly, puffed away for a minute and, when the donor's back was turned, slyly handed it to Crean, who puffed valiantly for a while. It was often too strong even for him, and so by degrees found its way back to the maker, who finished it with gusto.

From the ceaseless cold and soaking we suffered much bodily inconvenience. The constant chafing of wet clothes had also made our thighs sore and inflamed. One thing we were spared, that was small lodgers—too wet and cold for them.

That day was the *James Caird's* biggest twenty-four hours' run, N50°E ninety-six miles; but being by dead reckoning it may have been a little less or a little more. Wallis Island, at the west end of South Georgia, bore N80°E 155 miles. It sounded quite close to us. Our position was 54°30'S, 42°36'W.

The thirteenth day was also clear but overcast, with a north by west gale and a heavy, lumpy sea that increased so much after noon that we were forced to heave to with the reefed jib on the mainmast. Since leaving Elephant Island I had only been able to get the sun four times, two of these being mere snaps or guesses through slight rifts in the clouds.

Our hands had become awful objects to look upon. Crean's and mine, in addition to being almost black with grime, blubber, and soot, were ornamented with recent frostbites, also burns from the 'Primus'. Each successive frostbite on a finger was marked by a ring

where the skin had peeled up to, so that we could count our frostbites by the rings, after the method of a woodman telling the age of
a tree.

From the day after leaving Elephant Island we had been accompanied
at intervals by albatross, the stateliest bird in flight in the world, and
mollyhawks, a smaller species of albatross. These birds, peculiar to
the Southern Ocean, are only seen as far south as the edge of the pack
ice. Their northern limit is 30°S, though I once saw both a few miles
within the tropics to the south of St Helena, following the cool
current. The albatross is sometimes divided into two species, the
Wandering and the Royal, the latter slightly larger, though it is
possibly only an older bird of the same species. Their usual spread of
wings from tip to tip is about eleven feet. I have measured a Royal
fourteen feet across, and there is one in the Adelaide Museum that is
given as sixteen feet! This gives them the largest span of wing of any
bird in the world.

Awkward on the land, ludicrous when struggling to rise from a
smooth sea, the albatross is most graceful and stately on the wing. He
sweeps before the gale with a mighty rush, then, turning sharply, lets
the wind strike his underside, soars almost perpendicularly, and
again turns with the wind, coming down in a long, symmetrical
swoop, carelessly lifting a few inches to clear the top of a breaking
sea, while conforming his flight to the surface of the ridges and
hollows. He is a noble sight when the white cross of his back,
shoulders, neck, and rump shows startlingly against the heavy black
of an advancing squall.

Never seeming to rest, week after week, he follows the sailing ship;
day after day he followed our boat. His poetic motion fascinated us;
the ease with which he swept the miles aside filled us with envy. He
could, with a southwest gale, have made our whole journey in ten
hours.

In some of the few fine watches we had, Crean made noises at the
helm that, we surmised, represented 'The Wearin' o' the Green.'
Another series of sounds, however, completely baffled us.

I sang—Macarty thought it was a recitation—that classic:

> She licked him, she kicked him,
>   She wouldn't let him be;
> She welted him, and belted him,
>   Until he couldn't see.

> But Macarty wasn't hearty;
> Now she's got a different party.
> She might have licked Macarty,
> But she *can't lick me*.

The last part triumphantly to Macarty, but I doubt if he believed it. Then I sang 'We're Bound for the Rio Grande'. No one complained. It's astonishing how long-suffering people become on a trip like this.

The fourteenth day. After being hove to for twelve hours, we again carried on for the land. It was blowing a moderate north-northwest gale with a high northerly sea. Clear till dawn, it then clouded over with fog banks.

Making the land, it was most important to get 'sights' for position, but the conditions for observing the sun were most unfavourable. It was misty, the boat was jumping like a flea, shipping seas fore and aft, and there was no 'limb' to the sun, so I had to observe the centre by guesswork. Astronomically, the limb is the edge of sun or moon. If blurred by cloud or fog, it cannot be accurately 'brought down' to the horizon. The centre is the spot required, so when the limb is too blurred you bring the centre of the bright spot behind the clouds down to the horizon. By practice, and taking a series of 'sights', you can obtain an average that has no bigger error than one minute of arc.

At 9.45 a.m. the sun's limb was clear, but it was so misty that I kept low in the boat to bring the horizon closer, and so a little clearer. The lateness of the hour, and the misty horizon, made a poor observation for longitude. At noon the sun's limb was blurred by a thick haze, so I observed the centre for latitude. Error in latitude throws the longitude out, more so when the latter is observed, as now, too near noon. I told Sir Ernest that I could not be sure of our position to ten miles, so he would not agree to my trying to weather the northwest end of South Georgia, for fear of missing it. We then steered a little more easterly, to make a landfall on the west coast.

In some respects our condition had become worse. The last two days we had only brackish water from the stove-in 'breaker' to drink. This seemed to add to our thirst. We dipped it through the bunghole, with the six-inch by one-inch tube provided for the purpose, and strained it with a piece of medicated gauze, to free it of sediment, dirt, and reindeer hair. One gill a man a day was all that could be spared. The hot milk at night was stopped and hoosh was only made twice daily.

I think the others all suffered badly from thirst; for some reason it did not trouble me so much, though I would have liked a few hot toddies or a jug of cocoa. The situation had grown critical. If we had been driven off the land, or had not seen any ice, we should have been done for, unless we could have killed sea birds for their blood.

When short of water, keeping men wet with sea water compensates to a large extent. This, I think, applies to a normal or hot climate, where, the pores being open, the skin can 'drink'. We were wet all the time, but it did not appear to reduce our thirst, probably because the cold closed our pores.

Just before dark, eighty miles offshore, we saw a piece of kelp. We joyfully hailed it as a sign of nearness to the land, though it may have been borne by the current from the Shag Rocks—the mythical Aurora Islands to the westward.

All night we steered east-northeast, with a strong north-northwest breeze, recklessly burning inches of our precious candle. The seas came fast and merrily over us as usual, but we had a happy feeling that our worst troubles were over; we were nearly there.

At dawn on the fifteenth day, May 8, we saw some pieces of seaweed. Cape pigeons, albatross, mollyhawks, and the bobtailed birds grew numerous.

I looked anxiously for the sun. My navigation had been, perforce, so extraordinarily crude that a good landfall could hardly be looked for. The sky was overcast, and the weather misty and foggy, with a few clear intervals. Cross swells, and a heavy, confused, lumpy sea, made us wetter than usual, but a subdued joy and a species of quiet excitement held us, for we were making the land, and even hoped by dark to be on good solid earth once more, with beautiful clean water gurgling down our parched throats. We talked of how soon we should be at the whaling stations, with clean, dry clothes, and clean, dry beds to sleep in. Poor fools! We didn't know.

Fifteen miles offshore we saw the first shag. The sight of these birds is a guarantee that you are within fifteen miles of the land, as they hardly ever venture farther out.

By noon the fog had cleared, but heavy, ragged, low clouds were driving hard across from west-northwest, and still we had not sighted land.

Misty squalls at times obscured the view. Several patches of kelp were seen; and then, half an hour past noon, Macarty raised the cheerful cry, 'Land ho!' There, right ahead, through a rift in the flying

scud, our glad but salt-blurred eyes saw a towering black crag, with a
lacework of snow around its flanks. One glimpse, and it was hidden
again. We looked at each other with cheerful, foolish grins. The
thoughts uppermost were: 'We've done it. We'll get a drink tonight.
In a week we'll get them off Elephant Island.'

The land, Cape Demidov, the northern headland of King Haakon
Sound, was ten miles distant when sighted. Wonderful to say, the
landfall was quite correct, though we were a little astern through
imperfect rating of my chronometer at Elephant Island.

We had been exactly fourteen days on the passage from land to
land.

An hour later the coast was visible to port and starboard. A
desolate, forbidding coast, but that did not trouble us much.

As we drew inshore we passed close north of an area of huge 'blind'
rollers on an uncharted shoal. Norsemen call them 'blinders'. Ahead
of us, and to the south, sudden great spouts of white and terrific
roaring combers showed where the battle raged between the wild
westerly swell and uncharted reefs off the coast.

By 3 p.m. we could see small patches of green and areas of yellow-
brown tussock showing through the snow on Cape Demidov.

Sir Ernest considered it too dangerous to stand on when I told him
King Haakon Sound was right ahead and Wilson Harbour to the
north. The former lies open to the west, and it would have been
madness to land, in the dark, with a heavy sea, on a beach we had
never seen and which had never been properly charted.

Wilson Harbour would have been good, but it was to wind'ard,
and against the heavy sea we could not make it.

After a fierce, stormy-looking sunset the wind hauled to west-
southwest and blew a hard gale with rain, snow, sleet, and hail to give
a bitter edge to our disappointment.

We stood off on the starboard tack till midnight, then hove to,
eighteen miles offshore.

The heavy westerly swell increased. All night the *Caird* fell about
in a very dangerous, lumpy, and confused sea, that seemed to run in
on us from all directions, so that we sometimes shipped two seas over
from opposite sides at the same time.

All night, even when hove to, with the reefed jib on the main, we
had to bale and pump at very frequent intervals. It seemed to me that
she was leaking badly besides shipping seas overall.

At daybreak on May 9 we were wallowing in a terribly heavy cross sea, with a mountainous westerly swell setting us in on the coast before the furious westerly gale then raging. We felt none too easy in our minds, for we knew the current was aiding the wind and sea in forcing us towards destruction.

All day we were stormed at in turns by rain, hail, sleet, and snow, and half the time our view was obscured by thick, driving, misty squalls that whipped the sea into lines of yeasty foam.

By noon the gale had risen to hurricane force, hauled to southwest, and was driving us, harder than ever, straight for that ironbound coast. We thought but did not say those words, so fateful to the seaman, 'a lee shore'.

Each time we were lifted high on a towering swell we anxiously searched the horizon to leeward for the break of an unknown reef or the dreaded coast. 'Sea room, sea room, or a change of wind', was our mental prayer.

Dead reckoning was of slight use to give us our position in this hurricane, for the currents and tides on this coast, though fast and dangerous, are still unrecorded. All we knew was we were setting onshore.

We remained hove to till 2 p.m., when through a sudden rift in the storm-driven clouds we saw two high, jagged crags and a line of precipitous cliffs and glacier fronts on our lee quarter. We were being literally blown onshore—in the most dangerous and unknown part of the coast—the stretch between King Haakon Sound and Annenkov Island.

As we drove inshore it seemed that only three or four of the giant deep-sea swells separated us from the cliffs of destruction—the coast of death.

If we could have appreciated it, a magnificent, awe-inspiring scene lay before us.

The sky all torn, flying scud—the sea to wind'ard like surf on a shallow coast—one great roaring line of breaking seas behind another, till lost in spume, spindrift, and the fierce squalls that were feeding the seas. Mist from their flying tops cut off by the wind filled the great hollows between the swells. The ocean was everywhere covered by a gauzy tracery of foam with lines of yeasty froth, save where boiling white masses of breaking seas had left their mark on an acre of the surface.

On each sea the boat swept upward till she heeled before the droning fury of the hurricane, then fell staggering into the hollow, almost becalmed. Each sea, as it swept us closer in, galloped madly, with increasing fury, for the opposing cliffs, glaciers, and rocky points. It seemed but a few moments till it was thundering on the coast beneath icy uplands, great snow-clad peaks, and cloud-piercing crags.

It was the most awe-inspiring and dangerous position any of us had ever been in. It looked as though we were doomed—past the skill of man to save.

With infinite difficulty and danger of being washed overboard we got the reefed jib off the main, set it for'ard, set reefed lug and mizen, and with these large handkerchiefs endeavoured to claw offshore, praying to Heaven that the mast would stand it.

She gathered way, then crash! she struck an onrushing sea that swept her fore and aft even to the mastheads. While all baled and pumped for dear life, she seemed to stop, then again charged a galloping wall, of water, slam! like striking a stone wall with such force that the bow planks opened and lines of water spurted in from every seam, as she halted, trembling, and then leaped forward again. The strains, shocks, and blows were tremendous, threatening every minute to start her planking, while the bow seams opened and closed on every sea. Good boat! but how she stood it was a miracle of God's mercy.

While one steered, three worked the pump, one baled with the two-gallon hoosh pot, and the sixth stood by to relieve one of the others. Half the time he assisted with the small baler, and when opportunity offered, passed out a small lump of hoosh or some sea-damped lumps of sugar. Every hour we changed round to reduce fatigue.

As we looked at that hellish rock-bound coast, with its roaring breakers, we wondered, impersonally, at which spot our end was to come.

The thoughts of the others I did not know—mine were regret for having brought my diary and annoyance that no one would ever know we had got so far. At intervals we lied, saying, 'I think she'll clear it.'

For three hours, our thirst almost forgotten, we looked Death square in the eye. It was not so much terrifying as chilling, especially in conjunction with the ceaseless rush of breaking seas over us.

Just then the land parallel to our course, and onto which we were being driven, receded slightly to the eastward, giving us a little more sea room.

Then just as it seemed we might draw clear, a new danger threatened. The mountain peak of Annenkov Island loomed menacingly close on the lee bow. We headed to wind'ard of it, but leeway and the heavy sea appeared to be carrying us on to its western point. We could have kept away and gone to leeward of it, but we dared not, with darkness coming on; besides the danger of the coast we were clearing, an eight-mile-long reef was marked on the chart, between Annenkov and South Georgia. We caught glimpses of it and others not charted and held on to wind'ard. Our chart, imperfect at best, was almost illegible from sea stains, and so was but a doubtful guide.

Darkness settled on six men driving a boat slamming at the seas and steadily baling death overboard. The pale snow-capped peak gleamed spectrally aloft, resting on black shades of cliffs and rocks, fringed by a roaring line of foaming breakers—white horses of the hurricane, whose pounding hooves we felt, in imagination, smashing our frail craft.

We peered under the clew of the sail and said encouragingly to each other, 'She'll do it,' even when we felt it most impossible. The island came so close that we had to crane our necks to look up at the peak. At one time we were almost in the yeasty backwash of the surf; I believe that some eddy of the tide or current drove us clear.

Foot by foot we staggered and lurched drunkenly past the ravening black fangs of the rocky point. The moments became so tense that we feared even to speak—just held our breath or baled harder.

By 9 p.m. we knew we were safe. High, almost overhead it seemed, the great peak loomed mysteriously through the darkness. Right abeam, long pale fingers from the surf reached back—threatening but impotent—no longer did we fear them; every minute the clamorous roar on the rocky point became more faint with distance on the lee quarter.

Strangely, as soon as the worst danger was passed, the hurricane decreased rapidly. Half an hour later the wind came ahead from south-southwest.

We wore her round before the wind and stood back northwest, taking care to pass well to wind'ard of our enemy.

For nine hours we had fought at its height a hurricane so fierce that, as we heard later, a 500-ton steamer from Buenos Ayres to South Georgia had foundered in it with all hands, while we, by the grace of

God, had pulled through in a twenty-two-foot boat. I doubt if any of
us had ever experienced a fiercer blow than that from noon to 9 p.m.

1940

ROBERT LOWELL

1917–1977

## 'The Quaker Graveyard in Nantucket'

(FOR WARREN WINSLOW, DEAD AT SEA)

Let man have dominion over the fishes of the sea and the fowls
of the air and the beasts and the whole earth, and every creeping
creature that moveth upon the earth.

I

A brackish reach of shoal off Madaket—
The sea was still breaking violently and night
Had steamed into our North Atlantic Fleet,
When the drowned sailor clutched the drag-net. Light
Flashed from his matted head and marble feet,
He grappled at the net
With the coiled, hurdling muscles of his thighs:
The corpse was bloodless, a botch of reds and whites,
Its open, staring eyes
Were lustreless dead-lights
Or cabin-windows on a stranded hulk
Heavy with sand. We weight the body, close
Its eyes and heave it seaward whence it came,
Where the heel-headed dogfish barks its nose
On Ahab's void and forehead; and the name
Is blocked in yellow chalk.

Sailors, who pitch this portent at the sea
Where dreadnoughts shall confess
Its heel-bent deity,
When you are powerless
To sand-bag this Atlantic bulwark, faced
By the earth-shaker, green, unwearied, chaste
In his steel scales: ask for no Orphean lute
To pluck life back. The guns of the steeled fleet
Recoil and then repeat
The hoarse salute.

## II

Whenever winds are moving and their breath
Heaves at the roped-in bulwarks of this pier,
The terns and sea-gulls tremble at your death
In these home waters. Sailor, can you hear
The Pequod's sea wings, beating landward, fall
Headlong and break on our Atlantic wall
Off 'Sconset, where the yawing S-boats splash
The bellbuoy, with ballooning spinnakers,
As the entangled, screeching mainsheet clears
The blocks: off Madaket, where lubbers lash
The heavy surf and throw their long lead squids
For blue fish? Sea gulls blink their heavy lids
Seaward. The winds' wings beat upon the stones,
Cousin, and scream for you and the claws rush
At the sea's throat and wring it in the slush
Of this old Quaker graveyard where the bones
Cry out in the long night for the hurt beast
Bobbing by Ahab's whaleboats in the East.

## III

All you recovered from Poseidon died
With you, my cousin, and the harrowed brine
Is fruitless on the blue beard of the god,
Stretching beyond us to the castles in Spain,
Nantucket's westward haven. To Cape Cod
Guns, cradled on the tide,
Blast the eelgrass about a waterclock

Of bilge and backwash, roil the salt and sand
Lashing earth's scaffold, rock
Our warships in the hand
Of the great God, where time's contrition blues
Whatever it was these Quaker sailors lost
In the mad scramble of their lives. They died
When time was open-eyed,
Wooden and childish; only bones abide
There, in the nowhere, where their boats were tossed
Sky-high, where mariners had fabled news
Of IS, the whited monster. What it cost
Them is their secret. In the sperm-whale's slick
I see the Quakers drown and hear their cry:
'If God himself had not been on our side,
If God himself had not been on our side,
When the Atlantic rose against us, why,
Then it had swallowed us up quick.'

IV

This is the end of the whaleroad and the whale
Who spewed Nantucket bones on the thrashed swell
And stirred the troubled waters to whirlpools
To send the Pequod packing off to hell:
This is the end of them, three-quarters fools,
Snatching at straws to sail
Seaward and seaward on the turntail whale,
Spouting out blood and water as it rolls,
Sick as a dog to these Atlantic shoals:
Clamavimus, O depths. Let the sea-gulls wail

For water, for the deep where the high tide
Mutters to its hurt self, mutters and ebbs.
Waves wallow in their wash, go out and out,
Leave only the death-rattle of the crabs,
The beach increasing, its enormous snout
Sucking the ocean's side.
This is the end of running on the waves;
We are poured out like water. Who will dance
The mast-lashed master of Leviathans
Up from this field of Quakers in their unstoned graves?

## V

When the whale's viscera go and the roll
Of its corruption overruns this world
Beyond tree-swept Nantucket and Wood's Hole
And Martha's Vineyard, Sailor, will your sword
Whistle and fall and sink into the fat?
In the great ash-pit of Jehoshaphat
The bones cry for the blood of the white whale,
The fat flukes arch and whack about its ears,
The death-lance churns into the sanctuary, tears
The gun-blue swingle, heaving like a flail,
And hacks the coiling life out: it works and drags
And rips the sperm-whale's midriff into rags,
Gobbets of blubber spill to wind and weather,
Sailor, and gulls go round the stoven timbers
Where the morning stars sing out together
And thunder shakes the white surf and dismembers
The red flag hammered in the mast-head. Hide,
Our steel, Jonas Messias, in Thy side.

## VII

The empty winds are cracking and the oak
Splatters and splatters on the cenotaph,
The boughs are trembling and a gaff
Bobs on the untimely stroke
Of the greased wash exploding on a shoal bell
In the old mouth of the Atlantic. It's well;
Atlantic, you are fouled with the blue sailors,
Sea-monsters, upward angel, downward fish:
Unmarried and corroding, spare of flesh,
Mart once of supercilious, wing'd clippers,
Atlantic, where your bell-trap guts its spoil
You could cut the brackish winds with a knife
Here in Nantucket, and cast up the time
When the Lord God formed man from the sea's slime
And breathed into his face the breath of life,
And blue-lung'd combers lumbered to the kill.
The Lord survives the rainbow of His will.

1946

# ELIZABETH BISHOP

1911–1979

## 'Seascape'

This celestial seascape, with white herons got up as angels,
flying as high as they want and as far as they want sidewise
in tiers and tiers of immaculate reflections;
the whole region, from the highest heron
down to the weightless mangrove island
with bright green leaves edged neatly with bird-droppings
like illumination in silver,
and down to the suggestively Gothic arches of the mangrove roots
and the beautiful pea-green back-pasture
where occasionally a fish jumps, like a wild-flower
in an ornamental spray of spray;
this cartoon by Raphael for a tapestry for a Pope:
it does look like heaven.
But a skeletal lighthouse standing there
in black and white clerical dress,
who lives on his nerves, thinks he knows better.
He thinks that hell rages below his iron feet,
that that is why the shallow water is so warm,
and he knows that heaven is not like this.
Heaven is not like flying or swimming,
but has something to do with blackness and a strong glare
and when it gets dark he will remember something
strongly worded to say on the subject.

1946

# ROBERT CUSHMAN MURPHY

## 1887–1973

## from *Logbook for Grace*

SEPTEMBER 4. A slight breeze, but from the wrong direction. If I could send a letter by the proud ship still in sight, I would not dare say what follows. But something begins to whisper to me that we are going to touch at the Cape Verde Islands, and that the log for all of August and part of September may be in your hands this autumn.

Today we have cut and passed endless bands of sargasso weed, lying parallel and up-and-down wind in the dark blue ocean, just as billow clouds are streaking to the horizon across the mazarine blue of the sky. This is Sargasso weather, such as Columbus described in September, 1492, when he wrote that the mornings were like April in Andalusia—lacking only the songs of the nightingales! Columbus did a good job, too, of fishing up and recording the appearance of the strange little denizens of the weed clumps, which are almost the only surface creatures in this remote hub of the ocean.

There is little or nothing from the land in the vast, deep Sargasso Sea, which forms an area as big as the United States, all enclosed within the currents of the North Atlantic. I don't mean only that there are no mouldering fleets of galleons caught in the tangles; neither are there twigs or straws afloat, nor silt suspended in the water, which is clearer than any pool or spring on earth.

After dinner, when the breeze died away, I had the dory lowered and I rowed off alone for an hour. The appearance of everything was different than the view from shipboard. Channels of bottomless blue, banks of orange vegetation—or so it seemed. But whenever I attempted to pull 'ashore', the masses practically dissolved ahead of me. I could feel no resistance, hear no swish of weed along the flanks and bottom of the *Grace Emeline*, nor could I catch a single elusive strand upon an oar. Solid rafts seemed always yonder; close by, all was fluidity.

I noticed also, when I reached what appeared to be the heart of a great band, that all the weed floated at the very surface of the calm ocean. Six inches below, there was none. And yet not a strand, or a leaf or a 'berry' projected anywhere above the surface. In this respect it differed remarkably from the clusters of ordinary rockweed that float with the tide at home.

Sargasso weed, as was pointed out generations ago, has no reproductive organs. It grows from its tips, like cuttings of land plants. Forever and ever it replenishes itself in this way, while the old strands die and sink. So what I have seen today is merely another pattern of the changeless seascape through which the *Pinta*, *Niña* and *Santa Maria* once skimmed.

SEPTEMBER 5. Lat. 32° 12′ N., long. 35° 15′ W. The day has been squally, with frequent showers.

I have read the Revelation of John the Divine and Shakespeare's *Measure for Measure*. The latter was a new play to me and I found it thrilling and wholly engrossing, and tricked up with magnificent passages. It was not designed for Sunday school reading, however.

As for the Revelation, it has colored the literature of two millennia, but what has it to do with Christianity? Tinsel and might, rather than love, are made the supreme attributes of deity. If the members of a recent Chicago audience had been more thoroughly versed in the Revelation, the joke would not have been on them when T. R. cried, 'We stand at Armageddon and we battle for the Lord!'

SEPTEMBER 6. At evening the heavens opened wide, and the deluge found a way through deck and walls and trickled below. The aftercabin is a forlorn spot during heavy rain. The swinging lamp makes so timid a glimmer that one cannot write there, and the only thing to do is lie down. Fortunately, my special section, both bed and bookshelves, has always remained completely dry.

Today I read *Love's Labour Lost*, of which the lyrics are the only part up to scratch.

SEPTEMBER 7. Lat. 30° N., long. 33° W., by deduced reckoning, more familiarly called dead reckoning. No sunsights were possible.

This morning was ushered in by a brilliant double rainbow in the west, out of which came a 2,000-ton ship under short sail. I hastily closed a letter, but the weather proved too squally for a gam. The three-master passed half a mile astern of us—a beautiful sight, with her wings spread to the strong, driving gusts, and a large bone-in-her-teeth. I could make out neither name nor any other mark of identification, but the Old Man said quite confidently that she was a Spaniard bound for the Canary Islands. (Perhaps his inference was as

subtle as that of the skipper who identified a Scotch ship out of
Glasgow by noting that 'there weren't no gulls follering her.')

Today has been my first truly rainy day at sea. The spattering
winds came in tremendous puffs. Rack scudded across the white-
gray sky, and spume filled the air just above a jumbled, unreal
horizon that looked as though it was studded with half-visible trees
and shrubs. All day there were gleaming cloud lifts and sky windows
here and there in the pall. After dinner I put on my leather hip boots,
sou'wester, and oilskin coat, and paced the deck in the downpour.
How unfortunate are they that don't know the joy implied by the
name of the old Sioux Indian, 'Rain-in-the-face'! Toward evening
there was a rainbow again, which lasted twelve minutes after sundown,
and extended much higher in the air than any I had seen before. A
golden sunset followed a final hard squall, betokening a fair morrow.

SEPTEMBER 8. Sunday, by the clam chowder and baked beans!

A bright day, glassy calm, succeeded by a motionless evening. We
haven't made a really good day's run since we left the Antilles. I have
been three months on my journey, yet I am now within three weeks'
sail of New Bedford. We are not yet back in the tropics, and there are
at least 6,000 miles to go before we shall begin to turn toward you and
home.

The big ship lies becalmed, a few miles ahead of us. The nearest
land is 'the blue Canary Isles'. Do you think that they were named for
the birds? Tut, tut, not at all, not at all! The Roman voyagers found
them full of dogs, so they called the islands Canaria, meaning
'kennels'. And the dicky birds were named after the islands. (I have
just sprung this erudition on the Old Man and his officers.)

SEPTEMBER 9. Lat. 28° 36′ N., long. 31° 45′ W.

The calmest day I have ever seen on the ocean, and excessively hot.
I had not known that the face of the deep could lie so flat and still, like
a polished silver plate. The glare was blinding. The Daisy rested all
day with furled canvas, while our fellow ship did likewise, nearly hull
down on the far horizon.

Here and there, patches of small organisms that the skipper called
'whale feed' or 'tallow drops' discolored the water, and the oceanic
bugs or water striders, which are rarely visible, left long wakes on the
impressionable mirror of the sea.

About the middle of the forenoon a moving speck half a mile off
the starboard beam was pointed out to me by the mastheads. My
trusty field glass, a daily reminder of your thoughtful generosity,

revealed it as a bird, probably a shearwater. Within a few moments I saw also several Mother Carey's chickens, so we lowered the *Grace Emeline* and Conrad rowed me out toward the potential specimens. One of them made the error of flying within gunshot and, when I picked it up, it proved to be Leach's petrel, a breeding species of the northern North Atlantic, now doubtless bound toward its tropical winter range. I chummed for a while with grease from the galley, in the hope of luring other birds, but none approached.

It was very pleasant to be free on the placid water, a mile from the *Daisy* and eight hundred miles from the coast of Africa. When the petrels had flown off, so that they were no longer a distraction, I saw that the ocean around the dory was dotted with the tiny, translucent sails of a siphonophore called the salleeman or 'by-the-wind-sailer'. Its scientific name—which the Old Man demanded of me as soon as I had come on board with specimens—is *Velella*, and it is a small cousin of the Portuguese man-o'-war. Never before had I seen the creature outside a bottle, but now it was an effortless task, because of the perfect calm, to pick up examples by their sails.

Each one rested buoyantly on an oval, gas-filled float about two inches long and of a delicate bubble-blue color. Running at an angle across the float was the stiff, upright sail, tinted with lavender, pink and yellow, but nearly transparent. The sail enables the silent, expressionless salleeman to run before the wind or, more likely, to point into the wind and tack, because otherwise a lee shore would be its ultimate bourne.

Seeing hundreds or thousands of these exquisite little surface dwellers all about me, and realizing that they are always there, though usually hidden from human eyes by the light and movement of a rippling sea, caused a strong and strange upwelling of sentiment, which I can best suggest by lines from *The Rime of the Ancient Mariner*:

> O happy living things! no tongue
> Their beauty might declare:
> A spring of love gushed from my heart,
> And I blessed them unaware.

Later in the day I read *Much Ado about Nothing* and *As You Like It*, and in the latter play I found the perfect description of this, my journal, the sole object of which is to keep you with me while we are absent one from the other:

It is a melancholy of mine own, compounded of many simples, extracted from many objects, and indeed the sundry contemplation of my travels, in which my often rumination wraps me in a most humorous sadness.

1947

────

# W. H. AUDEN

## 1907–1973

# from *The Enchaféd Flood*

### THE SEA

The second verse of the first chapter of the Book of Genesis runs as follows:

And the earth was without form, and void; and darkness was upon the face of the deep. And the Spirit of God moved upon the face of the waters.

On the first day God said, Let there be light, on the second He

made the firmament, and divided the waters which were under the firmament from the waters which were above the firmament.

And on the third He gathered the waters under the heaven

unto one place, and let the dry land appear; and the gathering together of the waters called he Seas.

Similarly in one of the Greek cosmologies, the beginning of everything was when Eros issued from the egg of Night which floated upon Chaos.

The sea or the great waters, that is, are the symbol for the primordial undifferentiated flux, the substance which became created nature only by having form imposed upon or wedded to it.

The sea, in fact, is that state of barbaric vagueness and disorder out of which civilisation has emerged and into which, unless saved by the effort of gods and men, it is always liable to relapse. It is so little of a friendly symbol that the first thing which the author of the Book of Revelation notices in his vision of the new heaven and earth at the end of time is that *there was no more sea.*

1950

———

RACHEL CARSON

1907–1964

## from *The Sea Around Us*

To the human senses, the most obvious patterning of the surface waters is indicated by color. The deep blue water of the open sea far from land is the color of emptiness and barrenness; the green water of the coastal areas, with all its varying hues, is the color of life. The sea is blue because the sunlight is reflected back to our eyes from the water molecules or from very minute particles suspended in the sea. In the journey of the light rays downward into the water and back to our eyes, all the red rays of the spectrum and most of the yellow have been absorbed, so it is chiefly the cool, blue light that we see. Where the water is rich in plankton, it loses the glassy transparency that permits this deep penetration of the light rays. The yellow and brown and green hues of the coastal waters are derived from the minute algae and other micro-organisms so abundant there. Seasonal abundance of certain forms containing reddish or brown pigments may cause the 'red water' known from ancient time in many parts of the world, and so common is this condition in some enclosed seas that they owe their names to it—the Red Sea and the Vermillion Sea are examples.

. . . An observer sitting on a beach can make at least an intelligent guess whether the surf spilling out onto the sand before him has been produced by a gale close offshore or by a distant storm. Young waves, only recently shaped by the wind, have a steep, peaked shape even well out at sea. From far out on the horizon you can see them forming whitecaps as they come in; bits of foam are spilling down their fronts and boiling and bubbling over the advancing face, and the final breaking of the wave is a prolonged and deliberate process. But if a wave, on coming into the surf zone, rears high as though gathering all its strength for the final act of its life, if the crest forms all along its advancing front and then begins to curl forward, if the whole mass of water plunges suddenly with a booming roar into its trough—then you may take it that these waves are visitors from some very distant part of the ocean, that they have traveled long and far before their final dissolution at your feet.

What is true of the Atlantic wave we have followed is true, in general, of wind waves the world over. The incidents in the life of a wave are many. How long it will live, how far it will travel, to what manner of end it will come are all determined, in large measure, by the conditions it meets in its progression across the face of the sea. For the one essential quality of a wave is that it moves; anything that retards or stops its motion dooms it to dissolution and death.

Forces within the sea itself may affect a wave most profoundly. Some of the most terrible furies of the ocean are unleashed when tidal currents cross the path of the waves or move in direct opposition to them. This is the cause of the famous 'roosts' of Scotland, like the one off Sumburgh Head, at the southernmost tip of the Shetland Islands. During northeasterly winds the roost is quiescent, but when the wind-born waves roll in from any other quarter they encounter the tidal currents, either streaming shoreward in flood or seaward on the ebb. It is like the meeting of two wild beasts. The battle of the waves and tides is fought over an area of sea that may be three miles wide when the tides are running at full strength, first off Sumburgh Head, then gradually shifting seaward, subsiding only with the temporary slackening of the tide. 'In this confused, tumbling, and bursting sea, vessels often become entirely unmanageable and sometimes founder,' says the *British Islands Pilot*, 'while others have been tossed about for days together.' Such dangerous waters have been personified in many parts of the world by names that are handed down through generations of seafaring men. As in the time of our grandfathers and of their grandfathers, the Bore of Duncansby and the Merry Men of Mey rage at opposite ends of the Pentland Firth, which separates the Orkney Islands from the northern tip of Scotland. The sailing directions for the Firth in the *North Sea Pilot* for 1875 contained a warning to mariners, which is repeated verbatim in the modern *Pilot*:

Before entering the Pentland Firth all vessels should be prepared to batten down, and the hatches of small vessels ought to be secured even in the finest weather, as it is difficult to see what may be going on in the distance, and the transition from smooth water to a broken sea is so sudden that no time is given for making arrangements.

Both roosts are caused by the meeting of swells from the open ocean and opposing tidal currents, so that at the east end of the Firth the Bore of Duncansby is to be feared with easterly swells and a flood tide, and at the west end the Merry Men of Mey stage their revelries with the ebb tides and a westerly swell. Then, according to the *Pilot*, 'a sea is raised which cannot be imagined by those who have never experienced it.'

Such a rip may offer protection to the near-by coast by the very fury and uncompromisingness of the struggle between waves and tide. Thomas Stevenson long ago observed that as long as the Sumburgh roost was breaking and cresting heavily off the Head there was little surf on shore; once the strength of the tide was spent and it could no longer run down the seas a heavy surf rolled in against the coast and rose to great heights on the cliffs. And in the western Atlantic, the confused and swiftly running tidal currents at the mouth of the Bay of Fundy offer such strong opposition to waves approaching from any quarter from southwest to southeast that such surf as develops within the Bay is almost entirely local in its origin.

Out in the open sea, a train of waves encountering a hostile wind may be rapidly destroyed, for the power that created a wave may also destroy it. So a fresh trade wind in the Atlantic has often flattened out the swells as they rolled down from Iceland toward Africa. Or a friendly wind, suddenly springing up to blow in the direction the waves are moving, may cause their height to increase at the rate of a foot or two per minute. Once a group of moving ridges has been created, the wind has only to fall into the troughs between them to push up their crests rapidly.

Rocky ledges, shoals of sand or clay or rock, and coastal islands in the mouths of bays all play their part in the fate of the waves that advance toward shore. The long swells that roll from the open ocean toward the shores of northern New England seldom reach it in full strength. Their energy is spent in passing over that great submerged highland known as Georges Bank, the crests of whose highest hills approach the surface over the Cultivator Shoals. The hindrance of these submarine hills, and of the tidal currents that swirl around and across them, robs the long ocean swells of their power. Or islands scattered within a bay or about its mouth may so absorb the strength of the waves that the head of the bay is free from surf. Even scattered reefs off a coast may offer it great protection, by causing the highest waves to break there, so that they never reach the shore.

Ice, snow, rain—all are enemies of the waves and under proper conditions may knock down a sea or cushion the force of surf on a beach. Within loose pack ice a vessel may count on smooth seas even if a gale is raging and surf is breaking heavily about the edges of the pack. Ice crystals forming in the sea will smooth the waves by increasing the friction between water particles; even the delicate, crystalline form of a snowflake has such an effect on a smaller scale. A hail storm will knock down a rough sea, and even a sudden downpour of rain may often turn the surface of the ocean to oiled-silk smoothness, rippling to the passage of the swells.

The divers of ancient times who carried oil in their mouths to release beneath the surface when rough water made their work difficult were applying what every seaman today knows—that oil appears to have a calming effect on the free waves of the open ocean. Instructions for the use of oil in emergencies at sea are carried by most official sailing directions of maritime nations. Oil has little effect on surf, however, once the dissolution of the wave form has begun.

In the Southern Ocean where the waves are not destroyed by breaking on any beach, the great swells produced by the westerly winds roll around and around the world. Here the longest waves, and those with the greatest sidewise expanse of crest, are formed. Here, it might be supposed, the highest waves would also be found. Yet there is no evidence that the waves of the Southern Ocean surpass the giants of any other ocean. A long series of reports culled from the publications of engineers and ships' officers show that waves higher than 25 feet from trough to crest are rare in all oceans. Storm waves may grow twice as high, and if a full gale blows long enough in one direction to have a fetch of 600 to 800 miles, the resulting waves may be even higher. The greatest possible height of storm waves at sea is a much debated question, with most textbooks citing a conservative 60 feet, and mariners stubbornly describing much higher waves. Throughout the century that has followed the report of Dumont d'Urville that he encountered a wave 100 feet high off the Cape of Good Hope, science generally has viewed such figures with skepticism. Yet there is one record of a giant wave which, because of the method of measurement, seems to be accepted as reliable.

In February 1933 the USS *Ramapo*, while proceeding from Manila to San Diego, encountered seven days of stormy weather. The storm was part of a weather disturbance that extended all the way from Kamchatka to New York and permitted the winds an unbroken fetch of thousands of miles. During the height of the storm the *Ramapo* maintained a course running down the wind and with the sea. On 6 February the gale reached its fiercest intensity. Winds of 68 knots came in gusts and squalls, and the seas reached mountainous height. While standing watch on the bridge during the early hours of that day, one of the officers of the *Ramapo* saw, in the moonlight, a great sea rising astern to a level above an iron strap on the crow's nest of the mainmast. The *Ramapo* was on even keel and her stern was in the trough of the sea. These circumstances made possible an exact line of sight from the bridge to the crest of the wave, and simple mathematical calculations based on the dimensions of the ship gave the height of the wave. It was 112 feet.

Waves have taken their toll of shipping and of human life on the open sea, but it is around the shorelines of the world that they are most destructive. Whatever the height of storm waves at sea, there is abundant evidence, as some of the case histories that follow will show, that breaking surf and the upward-leaping water masses from thundering breakers may engulf lighthouses, shatter buildings, and hurl stones through lighthouse windows anywhere from 100 to 300 feet above the sea. Before the power of such surf, piers and breakwaters and other shore installations are fragile as a child's toys.

Almost every coast of the world is visited periodically by violent storm surf, but there are some that have never known the sea in its milder moods. 'There is not in the world a coast more terrible than this!' exclaimed Lord Bryce of Tierra del Fuego, where the breakers roar in upon the coast with a voice that, according to report, can be heard 20 miles inland on a still night. 'The sight of such a coast', Darwin had written in his diary, 'is enough to make a landsman dream for a week about death, peril, and shipwreck.'

Others claim that the Pacific coast of the United States from northern California to the Straits of Juan de Fuca has a surf as heavy as any in the world. But it seems unlikely that any coast is visited more wrathfully by the sea's waves than the Shetlands and the Orkneys, in the path of the cyclonic storms that pass eastward between Iceland and the British Isles. All the feeling and the fury of such a storm, couched almost in Conradian prose, are contained in the usually prosaic *British Islands Pilot*:

In the terrific gales which usually occur four or five times in every year all distinction between air and water is lost, the nearest objects are obscured by spray, and everything seems enveloped in a thick smoke; upon the open coast the sea rises at once, and striking upon the rocky shores rises in foam for several hundred feet and spreads over the whole country.

The sea, however, is not so heavy in the violent gales of short continuance as when an ordinary gale has been blowing for many days; the whole force of the Atlantic is then beating against the shores of the Orkneys, rocks of many tons in weight are lifted from their beds, and the roar of the surge may be heard for twenty miles; the breakers rise to the height of 60 feet, and the broken sea on the North Shoal, which lies 12 miles northwestward of Costa Head, is visible at Skail and Birsay.

The first man who ever measured the force of an ocean wave was Thomas Stevenson, father of Robert Louis. Stevenson developed the instrument known as a wave dynamometer and with it studied the waves that battered the coast of his native Scotland. He found that in winter gales the force of a wave might be as great as 6000 pounds to the square foot. Perhaps it was waves of this strength that destroyed the breakwater at Wick on the coast of Scotland in a December storm in 1872. The seaward end of the Wick breakwater consisted of a block of concrete weighing more than 800 tons, bound solidly with iron rods to underlying blocks of stone. During the height of this winter gale the resident engineer watched the onslaught of the waves from a point on the cliff above the breakwater. Before his incredulous eyes, the block of concrete was lifted up and swept shoreward. After the storm had subsided divers investigated the wreckage. They found that not only the concrete monolith but the stones it was attached to had been carried away. The waves had torn loose, lifted, and bodily moved a mass weighing not less than 1350 tons, or 2,700,000 pounds. Five years later it became clear that this feat had been a mere dress rehearsal, for the new pier, weighing about 2600 tons, was then carried away in another storm.

A list of the perverse and freakish doings of the sea can easily be compiled from the records of the keepers of lights on lonely ledges at sea, or on rocky headlands exposed to the full strength of storm surf. At Unst, the most northern of the Shetland Islands, a door in the lighthouse was broken open 195 feet above the sea. At the Bishop

Rock Light, on the English Channel, a bell was torn away from its attachment 100 feet above high water during a winter gale. About the Bell Rock Light on the coast of Scotland one November day a heavy ground swell was running, although there was no wind. Suddenly one of the swells rose about the tower, mounted to the gilded ball atop the lantern, 117 feet above the rock, and tore away a ladder that was attached to the tower 86 feet above the water. There have been happenings that, to some minds, are tinged with the supernatural, like that at the Eddystone Light in 1840. The entrance door of the tower had been made fast by strong bolts, as usual. During a night of heavy seas the door was broken open *from within*, and all its iron bolts and hinges were torn loose. Engineers say that such a thing happens as a result of pneumatic action—the sudden back draught created by the recession of a heavy wave combined with an abrupt release of pressure on the outside of the door.

On the Atlantic coast of the United States, the 97-foot tower on Minot's Ledge in Massachusetts is often completely enveloped by masses of water from breaking surf, and an earlier light on this ledge was swept away in 1851. Then there is the often quoted story of the December storm at Trinidad Head Light on the coast of northern California. As the keeper watched the storm from his lantern 196 feet above high water, he could see the near-by Pilot Rock engulfed again and again by waves that swept over its hundred-foot crest. Then a wave, larger than the rest, struck the cliffs at the base of the light. It seemed to rise in a solid wall of water to the level of the lantern, and it hurled its spray completely over the tower. The shock of the blow stopped the revolving of the light.

Along a rocky coast, the waves of a severe storm are likely to be armed with stones and rock fragments, which greatly increase their destructive power. Once a rock weighing 135 pounds was hurled high above the lightkeeper's house on Tillamook Rock on the coast of Oregon, 100 feet above sea level. In falling, it tore a 20-foot hole through the roof. The same day showers of smaller rocks broke many panes of glass in the lantern, 132 feet above the sea. The most amazing of such stories concerns the lighthouse at Dunnet Head, which stands on the summit of a 300-foot cliff at the southwestern entrance to Pentland Firth. The windows of this light have been broken repeatedly by stones swept from the cliff and tossed aloft by waves.

1951

# ERNEST HEMINGWAY

1899–1961

## from *The Old Man and the Sea*†

'Good luck old man.'

'Good luck,' the old man said. He fitted the rope lashings of the oars onto the thole pins and, leaning forward against the thrust of the blades in the water, he began to row out of the harbour in the dark. There were other boats from the other beaches going out to sea and the old man heard the dip and push of their oars even though he could not see them now the moon was below the hills.

Sometimes someone would speak in a boat. But most of the boats were silent except for the dip of the oars. They spread apart after they were out of the mouth of the harbour and each one headed for the part of the ocean where he hoped to find fish. The old man knew he was going far out and he left the smell of the land behind and rowed out into the clean early morning smell of the ocean. He saw the phosphorescence of the Gulf weed in the water as he rowed over the part of the ocean that the fishermen called the great well because there was a sudden deep of seven hundred fathoms where all sorts of fish congregated because of the swirl the current made against the steep walls of the floor of the ocean. Here there were concentrations of shrimp and bait fish and sometimes schools of squid in the deepest holes and these rose close to the surface at night where all the wandering fish fed on them.

In the dark the old man could feel the morning coming and as he rowed he heard the trembling sound as flying fish left the water and the hissing that their stiff set wings made as they soared away in the

† Long before he began to write *The Old Man and the Sea* in the spring of 1952, Hemingway had the story clearly in his mind. In February 1939, he wrote to Maxwell Perkins (his editor at Scribners'): 'three very long stories I want to write now . . . One about the old commercial fisherman who fought the swordfish all alone in his skiff for 4 days and four nights and the sharks finally eating it after he had it alongside and could not get it into the boat. That's a wonderful story of the Cuban coast. I'm going out with old Carlos in his skiff so as to get it all right. Everything he does and everything he thinks in all that long fight with the boat out of sight of all the other boats all alone on the sea. It's a great story if I can get it right. One that would make the book.'

darkness. He was very fond of flying fish as they were his principal friends on the ocean. He was sorry for the birds, especially the small delicate dark terns that were always flying and looking and almost never finding, and he thought, 'The birds have a harder life than we do except for the robber birds and the heavy strong ones. Why did they make birds so delicate and fine as those sea swallows when the ocean can be so cruel? She is kind and very beautiful. But she can be so cruel and it comes so suddenly and such birds that fly, dipping and hunting, with their small sad voices are made too delicately for the sea.'

He always thought of the sea as *la mar* which is what people call her in Spanish when they love her. Sometimes those who love her say bad things of her but they are always said as though she were a woman. Some of the younger fishermen, those who used buoys as floats for their lines and had motor-boats, bought when the shark livers had brought much money, spoke of her as *el mar* which is masculine. They spoke of her as a contestant or a place or even an enemy. But the old man always thought of her as feminine and as something that gave or withheld great favours and if she did wild or wicked things it was because she could not help them. The moon affects her as it does a woman, he thought.

He was rowing steadily and it was no effort for him since he kept well within his speed and the surface of the ocean was flat except for the occasional swirls of the current. He was letting the current do a third of the work and as it started to be light he saw he was already further out than he had hoped to be at this hour.

I worked the deep wells for a week and did nothing, he thought. Today I'll work out where the schools of bonita and albacore are and maybe there will be a big one with them.

Before it was really light he had his baits out and was drifting with the current. One bait was down forty fathoms. The second was at seventy-five and the third and fourth were down in the blue water at one hundred and one hundred and twenty-five fathoms. Each bait hung head down with the shank of the hook inside the bait fish, tied and sewed solid, and all the projecting part of the hook, the curve and the point, was covered with fresh sardines. Each sardine was hooked through both eyes so that they made a half-garland on the projecting steel. There was no part of the hook that a great fish could feel which was not sweet-smelling and good-tasting.

The boy had given him two fresh small tunas, or albacores, which hung on the two deepest lines like plummets and, on the others, he had a big blue runner and a yellow jack that had been used before; but they were in good condition still and had the excellent sardines to give them scent and attractiveness. Each line, as thick around as a big pencil, was looped onto a green-sapped stick so that any pull or touch on the bait would make the stick dip and each line had two forty-fathom coils which could be made fast to the other spare coils so that, if it were necessary, a fish could take out over three hundred fathoms of line.

Now the man watched the dip of the three sticks over the side of the skiff and rowed gently to keep the lines straight up and down and at their proper depths. It was quite light and any moment now the sun would rise.

The sun rose thinly from the sea and the old man could see the other boats, low on the water and well in toward the shore, spread out across the current. Then the sun was brighter and the glare came on the water and then, as it rose clear, the flat sea sent it back at his eyes so that it hurt sharply and he rowed without looking into it. He looked down into the water and watched the lines that went straight down into the dark of the water. He kept them straighter than anyone did, so that at each level in the darkness of the stream there would be a bait waiting exactly where he wished it to be for any fish that swam there. Others let them drift with the current and sometimes they were at sixty fathoms when the fishermen thought they were at a hundred.

But, he thought, I keep them with precision. Only I have no luck any more. But who knows? Maybe today. Every day is a new day. It is better to be lucky. But I would rather be exact. Then when luck comes you are ready.

The sun was two hours higher now and it did not hurt his eyes so much to look into the east. There were only three boats in sight now and they showed very low and far inshore.

All my life the early sun has hurt my eyes, he thought. Yet they are still good. In the evening I can look straight into it without getting the blackness. It has more force in the evening too. But in the morning it is painful.

Just then he saw a man-of-war bird with his long black wings circling in the sky ahead of him. He made a quick drop, slanting down on his back-swept wings, and then circled again.

'He's got something,' the old man said aloud. 'He's not just looking.'

He rowed slowly and steadily toward where the bird was circling. He did not hurry and he kept his lines straight up and down. But he crowded the current a little so that he was still fishing correctly though faster than he would have fished if he was not trying to use the bird.

The bird went higher in the air and circled again, his wings motionless. Then he dove suddenly and the old man saw flying fish spurt out of the water and sail desperately over the surface.

'Dolphin,' said the old man aloud. 'Big dolphin.'

He shipped his oars and brought a small line from under the bow. It had a wire leader and a medium-sized hook and he baited it with one of the sardines. He let it go over the side and then made it fast to a ring bolt in the stern. Then he baited another line and left it coiled in the shade of the bow. He went back to rowing and to watching the long-winged black bird who was working, now, low over the water.

As he watched the bird dipped again slanting his wings for the dive and then swinging them wildly and ineffectually as he followed the flying fish. The old man could see the slight bulge in the water that the big dolphin raised as they followed the escaping fish. The dolphin were cutting through the water below the flight of the fish and would be in the water, driving at speed, when the fish dropped. It is a big school of dolphin, he thought. They are wide spread and the flying fish have little chance. The bird has no chance. The flying fish are too big for him and they go too fast.

He watched the flying fish burst out again and again and the ineffectual movements of the bird. That school has gotten away from me, he thought. They are moving out too fast and too far. But perhaps I will pick up a stray and perhaps my big fish is around them. My big fish must be somewhere.

The clouds over the land now rose like mountains and the coast was only a long green line with the grey-blue hills behind it. The water was a dark blue now, so dark that it was almost purple. As he looked down into it he saw the red sifting of the plankton in the dark water and the strange light the sun made now. He watched his lines to see them go straight down out of sight into the water and he was happy to see so much plankton because it meant fish. The strange light the sun made in the water, now that the sun was higher, meant good weather and so did the shape of the clouds over the land. But the bird was almost out of sight now and nothing showed on the surface of the water but some patches of yellow, sun-bleached Sargasso weed and the purple, formalized, iridescent, gelatinous bladder of a Portuguese man-of-war floating close beside the boat. It turned on its side and then righted itself. It floated cheerfully as a bubble with its long deadly purple filaments trailing a yard behind it in the water.

'*Agua mala*,' the man said. 'You whore.'

From where he swung lightly against his oars he looked down into the water and saw the tiny fish that were coloured like the trailing filaments and swam between them and under the small shade the bubble made as it drifted. They were immune to its poison. But men were not and when some of the filaments would catch on a line and rest there slimy and purple while the old man was working a fish, he would have welts and sores on his arms and hands of the sort that poison ivy or poison oak can give. But these poisonings from the *agua mala* came quickly and struck like a whiplash.

The iridescent bubbles were beautiful. But they were the falsest thing in the sea and the old man loved to see the big sea turtles eating them. The turtles saw them, approached them from the front, then shut their eyes so they were completely carapaced and ate them filaments and all. The old man loved to see the turtles eat them and he loved to walk on them on the beach after a storm and hear them pop when he stepped on them with the horny soles of his feet.

He loved green turtles and hawks-bills with their elegance and speed and their great value and he had a friendly contempt for the huge, stupid logger-heads, yellow in their armour plating, strange in their love-making, and happily eating the Portuguese men-of-war with their eyes shut.

He had no mysticism about turtles although he had gone in turtle boats for many years. He was sorry for them all, even the great trunk-backs that were as long as the skiff and weighed a ton. Most people are heartless about turtles because a turtle's heart will beat for hours after he has been cut up and butchered. But the old man thought, I have such a heart too and my feet and hands are like theirs. He ate the white eggs to give himself strength. He ate them all through May to be strong in September and October for the truly big fish.

He also drank a cup of shark liver oil each day from the big drum in the shack where many of the fishermen kept their gear. It was there for all fishermen who wanted it. Most fishermen hated the taste. But it was no worse than getting up at the hours that they rose and it was very good against all colds and grippes and it was good for the eyes.

Now the old man looked up and saw that the bird was circling again.

'He's found fish,' he said aloud. No flying fish broke the surface and there was no scattering of bait fish. But as the old man watched, a small tuna rose in the air, turned and dropped head first into the water. The tuna shone silver in the sun and after he had dropped back into the water another and another rose and they were jumping in all directions, churning the water and leaping in long jumps after the bait. They were circling it and driving it.

If they don't travel too fast I will get into them, the old man thought, and he watched the school working the water white and the bird now dropping and dipping into the bait fish that were forced to the surface in their panic.

'The bird is a great help,' the old man said. Just then the stern line came taut under his foot, where he had kept a loop of the line, and he dropped his oars and felt the weight of the small tuna's shivering pull as he held the line firm and commenced to haul it in. The shivering increased as he pulled in and he could see the blue back of the fish in the water and the gold of his sides before he swung him over the side and into the boat. He lay in the stern in the sun, compact and bullet-shaped, his big, unintelligent eyes staring as he thumped his life out against the planking of the boat with the quick shivering strokes of his neat, fast-moving tail. The old man hit him on the head for kindness and kicked him, his body still shuddering, under the shade of the stern.

'Albacore,' he said aloud. 'He'll make a beautiful bait. He'll weigh ten pounds.'

He did not remember when he had first started to talk aloud when he was by himself. He had sung when he was by himself in the old days and he had sung at night sometimes when he was alone steering on his watch in the smacks or in the turtle boats. He had probably started to talk aloud, when alone, when the boy had left. But he did not remember. When he and the boy fished together they usually spoke only when it was necessary. They talked at night or when they were storm-bound by bad weather. It was considered a virtue not to talk unnecessarily at sea and the old man had always considered it so and respected it. But now he said his thoughts aloud many times since there was no one that they could annoy.

'If the others heard me talking out loud they would think that I am crazy,' he said aloud. 'But since I am not crazy, I do not care. And the rich have radios to talk to them in their boats and to bring them the baseball.'

Now is no time to think of baseball, he thought. Now is the time to think of only one thing. That which I was born for. There might be a big one around that school, he thought. I picked up only a straggler from the albacore that were feeding. But they are working far out and fast. Everything that shows on the surface today travels very fast and to the north-east. Can that be the time of day? Or is it some sign of weather that I do not know?

He could not see the green of the shore now but only the tops of the blue hills that showed white as though they were snow-capped and the clouds that looked like high snow mountains above them. The sea was very dark and the light made prisms in the water. The myriad flecks of the plankton were annulled now by the high sun and it was only the great deep prisms in the blue water that the old man saw now with his lines going straight down into the water that was a mile deep.

1952

ALAN ROSS

1922–

## 'Night Patrol'

We sail at dusk, the red moon
Like a paper lantern setting fire
To our wake. Headlands disappear,
Muffled in their own velvet.

Docks dwindle, rubbed out by mists,
Their cranes, like drunks, askew
Over jetties. Coal is unloaded
Under blue arc-lights.

Turning south, the mapped moon
Swings between masts, our aerials
Swollen and lurching. The bag
Of sea squirts black and sooty.

Flashes of gunfire, perhaps lightning,
Straddle our progress, a convoy
Of hearses. The bow-waves of gunboats
Sew us together, helplessly idling.

The watch changes, and changes
Again. We edge through a minefield,
Real or imaginary. The speed of a convoy
Is the speed of the slowest ship.

No one speaks, it might be a funeral.
Altering course, the moon congeals
On a new bearing. The telegraph rings,
And, at speed now, clouds grow visible.

We're on our own, making for harbour.
In tangerine light we sniff greenness,
Tremble like racehorses. Soon minesweepers
Pass us, continuing our business.

1954

# WALTER MUNK

## 1917–

# from 'The Circulation of the Oceans'

The precise mechanism whereby the winds produce the circulation gyres is complex and not clear. First of all, the action of wind upon water is itself a complicated matter. Wind can move water simply by frictional force as it slides over the surface, even when the surface is smooth. It must also accelerate the motion of water when it picks up spray and throws it down again, particularly during hurricanes, when so much water is pulled up into the air that the 'boundary' between the sea and the air is lost. Another important means by which wind drives ocean water is its pressure on the waves as it sweeps over rough water—just as wind blowing over a field bends the blades of grass because pressure is higher on the windward sides than on the lee sides. It turns out that the important elements in the response of water to wind are not the large waves that rock boats and make people seasick, but the tiny bumps, the ripples. If we could cover the North Atlantic with oil and smooth these ripples, the Gulf Stream would lose an appreciable part of its strength. The importance of these tiny waves is surprising. Would any honest seafaring man care to admit that the tiny ripples, to which he paid so little attention, may have been partly responsible for setting him off his course?

How do the driving winds produce the great circulations (gyres) that we see in the oceans? During the last 10 years a theory has been developed. We start with a situation where no land barrier stands in the way of the wind-driven water. The currents will then flow in a great circle around the earth, as they do around the Antarctic Continent. Things get more complicated when we introduce land masses. Suppose we erect barriers and make an enclosed sea. Now if winds blow only from the west and have equal force at all latitudes in this sea, there can be no rotary circulation or currents; just as a paddle wheel subject to equal force from the same direction on its opposite blades will not turn. The wind will simply pile up water on the eastern side of the sea. But if the wind is stronger at some latitudes than at others, the stronger will overpower the weaker and the water will begin to circulate. The circulation will be even stronger, of course, if the winds at different latitudes blow in opposite directions. To this effect we must now add the effect of the earth's rotation. The turning of the earth toward the east exerts a torque on the ocean circulation, with the result that the center is displaced toward the west and the currents are intensified on the western side.

In general the great wind-driven currents in the world's oceans do fit this model and the theory derived from it. The boundaries of the major currents are where they should be in relation to wind systems, and the strong western currents also appear where they should. Moreover, the theory has received some support from a laboratory model simulating ocean circulations. William von Arx, of the Woods Hole Oceanographic Institution, performed these experiments with a rotating basin shaped like a roulette wheel—essentially a hemisphere turned inside out. His 'oceans' consist of a thin film of water clinging in an equilibrium distribution over the surface of the whirling basin, and winds are blown on the water from nozzles on vacuum cleaners. Von Arx projects the Northern Hemisphere into this basin, with the North Pole at the low point in the center. Potassium permanganate crystals are placed in the center, and when ink is introduced into the water, it reacts with the chemical to show the flow patterns in different colors. Von Arx's model faithfully reproduces the gyres of the North Atlantic and the North Pacific, including the intense western currents. The model is especially interesting because the topography and winds can be varied to show possible circulations of the oceans in the past, when conditions were different; for instance, one can investigate how the Gulf Stream might have behaved at a time when there was a separation between North and South America in the place of the present Isthmus of Panama.

It must not be supposed that the theory about how the ocean circulations are produced is fully confirmed by these observations and experiments. There are many inconsistencies; in particular, some of the circulation in the oceans of the Southern Hemisphere refuses to fit into the pattern pictured by the theory.

This is where we stand, then, on the climatic circulation. The era of measurement of the synoptic circulation, or day-to-day ocean weather, began with the recent invention of certain new techniques and instruments, notably (1) the radio location method called 'loran', (2) the instrument for rapidly measuring temperatures at various depths which is called the 'bathythermograph', and (3) an instrument, invented by von Arx and named the 'geomagnetic electrokinetograph', which determines the motion of ocean water by measuring the electric potentials induced in it because of its movement through the earth's magnetic field.

Resurveying the Gulf Stream with these techniques, Columbus O'Donnell Iselin and his collaborators at Woods Hole discovered that the Stream was narrower and much faster than had been thought. As their instruments and techniques improved, the current became even narrower and faster. They also found that the position and direction of the current varied from one cruise to the next. A five-ship expedition called Operation Cabot was organized by the US Navy Hydrographic Office in 1950 to study the Gulf Stream more closely. This cruise detected a most important and dramatic phenomenon: the Gulf Stream meandered off the usual course to form a loop 250 miles long! Within two days the loop broke off and separated as an independent eddy. The eddy then gradually weakened.

It is estimated that this single eddy injected some 10 million million tons of subarctic water from the North Atlantic into the subtropical Atlantic. Obviously such an immense transport of water, with its content of living organisms, must be of considerable importance to the biology of the sea. Possibly similar eddies of water from the south break off toward the north, injecting subtropical water into the colder part of the ocean.

Frederick Fuglister of Woods Hole, an artist who has been in oceanographic work since the war, later discovered some other unsuspected characteristics of the Gulf Stream. Plotting currents by means of temperature gradients measured with the bathythermograph, he found a pattern which suggested that the Gulf Stream consists of a number of long, narrow, separate ribbons, or filaments. They are not continuous over thousands of miles; as a rule one will peter out and another will start somewhere else. In other words, it appears that the concept of a single, continuous Gulf Stream all the way from Florida to Europe must be abandoned. Rather one must visualize the Stream as composed of high-speed filaments of current separated by counter-currents. L. V. Worthington of Woods Hole, using all the modern tools, has substantially confirmed this picture with detailed cross-section studies. In one 30-mile cross section he found three separate major filaments, each flowing at better than three miles per hour. Gunther Wertheim, also of Woods Hole, further demonstrated the

complexity and variability of the Gulf Stream by discovering that the
transport of water by the Florida current section of the Stream
doubled from one month to the next! He computed the movement of
water from measurements of electric potential between Havana and
Key West, made by attaching electrodes to the Western Union
telegraph cable between those points.

Fuglister has satisfied himself that the Japanese current also can be
interpreted as consisting of filaments; in fact almost everywhere we
look the ocean weather seems extremely fickle. Henry Stommel,
monitoring radio drift buoys near Bermuda, found the currents
highly changeable; every sudden waxing or waning of the winds set
up rotary currents.

My interpretation of the new look with regard to the ocean
weather is something like this. The motion of water in the open sea is
highly irregular and variable. If we release a drift buoy, we can expect
the current to carry it something like half a mile in an hour, but the
velocity and the direction will be quite different from one day to the
next. This unsteady motion—the 'noise' of the ocean circulation—
represents in some way the response of the sea to the multiplicity of
shocks it receives from the wind blowing on its surface. The response
is not simple, and the underlying laws have not yet been recognized.
The transient ocean weather, unlike the slow climatic circulation,
apparently has no blow-by-blow counterpart in the circulation of the
atmosphere.

The fine structure of the ocean currents can be tied in with the
climatic circulation only in a general way. It evidently results from
the fact that the broad circulation cannot dissipate all the energy
received by the ocean from the wind, but just why the fine structure
takes the forms it does is a problem awaiting further exploration.

1955

# WILLIAM GOLDING

## 1911–

# from *Pincher Martin*

'Help! Nathaniel! Help—!'

And I gave the right orders too. If I'd done it ten seconds earlier I'd be a bloody hero—Hard a-starboard for Christ's sake!

Must have hit us bang under the bridge. And I gave the right order. And I get blown to buggery.

The snarl fixed itself, worked on the wooden face till the upper lip was lifted and the chattering teeth bared. The little warmth of anger flushed blood back into the tops of the cheeks and behind the eyes. They opened.

Then he was jerking and splashing and looking up. There was a difference in the texture of the darkness; there were smears and patches that were not in the eye itself. For a moment and before he remembered how to use his sight the patches lay on the eyeballs as close as the darkness had been. Then he firmed the use of his eyes and he was inside his head, looking out through the arches of his skull at random formations of dim light and mist. However he blinked and squinted they remained there outside him. He bent his head forward and saw, fainter than an after-image, the scalloped and changing shape of a swell as his body was lifted in it. For a moment he caught the inconstant outline against the sky, then he was floating up and seeing dimly the back top of the next swell as it swept towards him. He began to make swimming motions. His hands were glimmering patches in the water and his movements broke up the stony weight of his legs. The thoughts continued to flicker.

We were travelling north-east. I gave the order. If he began the turn she might be anywhere over there to the east. The wind was westerly. That's the east over there where the swells are running away down hill.

His movements and his breathing became fierce. He swam a sort of clumsy breast-stroke, buoyed up on the inflated belt. He stopped and lay wallowing. He set his teeth, took the tit of the lifebelt and let out air till he was lying lower in the water. He began to swim again. His breathing laboured. He stared out of his arches intently and painfully at the back of each swell as it slunk away from him. His legs slowed and stopped; his arms fell. His mind inside the dark skull made swimming movements long after the body lay motionless in the water.

The grain of the sky was more distinct. There were vaporous changes of tone from dark to gloom, to grey. Near at hand the individual hillocks of the surface were visible. His mind made swimming movements.

Pictures invaded his mind and tried to get between him and the urgency of his motion towards the east. The jam jar came back but robbed of significance. There was a man, a brief interview, a desk-top so polished that the smile of teeth was being reflected in it. There was a row of huge masks hung up to dry and a voice from behind the teeth that had been reflected in the desk spoke softly.

'Which one do you think would suit Christopher?'

There was a binnacle-top with the compass light just visible, there was an order shouted, hung up there for all heaven and earth to see in neon lighting.

'Hard a-starboard, for Christ's sake!'

Water washed into his mouth and he jerked into consciousness with a sound that was half a snore and half a choke. The day was inexorably present in green and grey. The seas were intimate and enormous. They smoked. When he swung up a broad, hilly crest he could see two other smoking crests then nothing but a vague circle that might be mist or fine spray or rain. He peered into the circle, turning himself, judging direction by the run of the water until he had inspected every part. The slow fire of his belly, banked up to endure, was invaded. It lay defenceless in the middle of the clothing and sodden body.

'I won't die! I wont!'

The circle of mist was everywhere alike. Crests swung into view on that side, loomed, seized him, elevated him for a moment, let him down, and slunk off, but there was another crest to take him, lift him so that he could see the last one just dimming out of the circle. Then he would go down again and another crest would loom weltering towards him.

He began to curse and beat the water with the flat of his white hands. He struggled up the swells. But even the sounds of his

working mouth and body were merged unnoticed in the innumerable
sounds of travelling water. He hung still in his belt, feeling the cold
search his belly with its fingers. His head fell on his chest and the stuff
slopped weakly, persistently over his face. Think. My last chance.
Think what can be done.

She sank out in the Atlantic. Hundreds of miles from land. She was
alone, sent north-east from the convoy to break WT silence. The
U-boat may be hanging round to pick up a survivor or two for
questioning. Or to pick off any ship that comes to rescue survivors.
She may surface at any moment, breaking the swell with her heavy
body like a half-tide rock. Her periscope may sear the water close by,
eye of a land-creature that has defeated the rhythm and necessity of
the sea. She may be passing under me now, shadowy and shark-like,
she may be lying down there below my wooden feet on a bed of salty
water as on a cushion while her crew sleeps. Survivors, a raft, the
whaler, the dinghy, wreckage may be jilling about only a swell or two
away hidden in the mist and waiting for rescue with at least bully and
perhaps a tot.

He began to rotate in the water again, peering blearily at the mist,
he squinted at the sky that was not much higher than a roof; he
searched the circle for wreckage or a head. But there was nothing. She
had gone as if a hand had reached up that vertical mile and snatched
her down in one motion. When he thought of the mile he arched in
the water, face twisted, and began to cry out.

'Help, curse you, sod you, bugger you—Help!'

Then he was blubbering and shuddering and the cold was squeezing
him like the hand that had snatched down the ship. He hiccuped
slowly into silence and started to rotate once more in the smoke and
green welter.

One side of the circle was lighter than the other. The swell was
shouldering itself on towards the left of this vague brightness; and
where the brightness spread the mist was even more impenetrable
than behind him. He remained facing the brightness not because it
was of any use to him but because it was a difference that broke the
uniformity of the circle and because it looked a little warmer than
anywhere else. He made swimming movements again without thought
and as if to follow in the wake of that brightness was an inevitable
thing to do. The light made the sea-smoke seem solid. It penetrated
the water so that between him and the very toss of the restless hillocks
it was bottle green. For a moment or two after a wave had passed he

could see right into it but the waves were nothing but water—there was no weed in them, no speck of solid, nothing drifting, nothing moving but green water, cold persistent idiot water. There were hands to be sure and two forearms of black oilskin and there was the noise of breathing, gasping. There was also the noise of the idiot stuff, whispering, folding on itself, tripped ripples running tinkling by the ear like miniatures of surf on a flat beach; there were sudden hisses and spats, roars and incompleted syllables and the soft friction of wind. The hands were important under the bright side of the circle but they had nothing to seize on. There was an infinite drop of the soft, cold stuff below them and under the labouring, dying, body.

The sense of depth caught him and he drew his dead feet up to his belly as if to detach them from the whole ocean. He arched and gaped, he rose over the chasm of deep sea on a swell and his mouth opened to scream against the brightness.

It stayed open. Then it shut with a snap of teeth and his arms began to heave water out of the way. He fought his way forward.

'Ahoy—for Christ's sake! Survivor! Survivor! Fine on your starboard bow!'

He threshed with his arms and legs into a clumsy crawl. A crest overtook him and he jerked himself to the chest out of water.

'Help! Help! Survivor! For God's sake!'

The force of his return sent him under but he struggled up and shook the wave from his head. The fire of his belly had spread and his heart was thrusting the sluggish blood painfully round his body. There was a ship in the mist to port of the bright patch. He was on her starboard bow—or—and the thought drove him to foam in the water—he was on her port quarter and she was moving away. But even in his fury of movement he saw how impossible this was since then she would have passed by him only a few minutes ago. So she was coming towards, to cut across the circle of visibility only a few yards from him.

Or stopped.

At that, he stopped too, and lay in the water. She was so dull a shape, little more than a looming darkness that he could not tell both her distance and her size. She was more nearly bows on than when he had first seen her and now she was visible even when he was in a trough. He began to swim again but every time he rose on a crest he screamed.

'Help! Survivor!'

But what ship was ever so lop-sided? A carrier? A derelict carrier, deserted and waiting to sink? But she would have been knocked down by a salvo of torpedoes. A derelict liner? Then she must be one of the Queens by her bulk—and why lop-sided? The sun and the mist were balanced against each other. The sun could illumine the mist but not pierce it. And darkly in the sun-mist loomed the shape of a not-ship where nothing but a ship could be.

He began to swim again, feeling suddenly the desperate exhaustion of his body. The first, fierce excitement of sighting had burned up the fuel and the fire was low again. He swam grimly, forcing his arms through the water, reaching forward under his arches with sight as though he could pull himself into safety with it. The shape moved. It grew larger and not clearer. Every now and then there was something like a bow-wave at the forefoot. He ceased to look at her but swam and screamed alternately with the last strength of his body. There was green force round him, growing in strength to rob, there was mist and glitter over him; there was a redness pulsing in front of his eyes—his body gave up and he lay slack in the waves and the shape rose over him. He heard through the rasp and thump of his works the sound of waves breaking. He lifted his head and there was rock stuck up in the sky with a sea-gull poised before it. He heaved over in the sea and saw how each swell dipped for a moment, flung up a white hand of foam then disappeared as if the rock had swallowed it. He began to think swimming motions but knew now that his body was no longer obedient. The top of the next swell between him and the rock was blunted, smoothed curiously, then jerked up spray. He sank down, saw without comprehension that the green water was no longer empty. There was yellow and brown. He heard not the formless mad talking of uncontrolled water but a sudden roar. Then he went under into a singing world and there were hairy shapes that flitted and twisted past his face, there were sudden notable details close to of intricate rock and weed. Brown tendrils slashed across his face, then with a destroying shock he hit solidity. It was utter difference, it was under his body, against his knees and face, he could close fingers on it, for an instance he could even hold on. His mouth was needlessly open and his eyes so that he had a moment of close and intent communion with three limpets, two small and one large, that were only an inch or two from his face. Yet this solidity was terrible and apocalyptic after the world of inconstant wetness. It was not vibrant as a ship's hull might be but merciless and mother of panic. It had no business to interrupt the thousands of miles of water going about their purposeless affairs and therefore the world sprang here into sudden war. He felt himself picked up and away from the limpets, reversed, tugged, thrust down into weed and darkness. Ropes held him, slipped, and let him go. He saw light, got a mouthful of air and foam. He glimpsed a riven rock face with trees of spray growing up it and the sight of this rock floating in mid Atlantic was so dreadful that he wasted his air by screaming as if it had been a wild beast. He went under into a green calm, then up and was thrust sideways. The sea no longer played with him. It stayed its wild movement and held him gently, carried him with delicate and careful motion like a retriever with a bird. Hard things touched him about the feet and knees. The sea laid him down gently and retreated. There were hard things touching his face and chest, the side of his forehead. The sea came back and fawned round his face, licked him. He thought movements that did not happen. The sea came back and he thought the movements again and this time they happened because the sea took most of his weight. They moved him forward over the hard things. Each wave and each movement moved him forward. He felt the sea run down to smell at his feet then come back and nuzzle under his arm. It no longer licked his face. There was a pattern in front of him that occupied all the space under the arches. It meant nothing. The sea nuzzled under his arm again.

He lay still.

1956

# CHARLES TOMLINSON

1927–

## 'The Atlantic'

Launched into an opposing wind, hangs
Grappled beneath the onrush,
And there, lifts, curling in spume,
Unlocks, drops from that hold
Over and shoreward. The beach receives it,
A whitening line, collapsing
Powdering-off down its broken length;
Then, curded, shallow, heavy
With clustering bubbles, it nears
In a slow sheet that must climb
Relinquishing its power, upward
Across tilted sand. Unravelled now
And the shore, under its lucid pane,
Clear to the sight, it is spent:
The sun rocks there, as the netted ripple
Into whose skeins the motion threads it
Glances athwart a bed, honey-combed
By heaving stones. Neither survives the instant
But is caught back, and leaves, like the after-image
Released from the floor of a now different mind,
A quick gold, dyeing the uncovering beach
With sunglaze. That which we were,
Confronted by all that we are not,
Grasps in subservience its replenishment.

1958

## 'On Water'

'Furrow' is inexact:
no ship could be
converted to a plough
travelling this vitreous ebony:

seal it in sea-caves and
you cannot still it:
image on image bends
where half-lights fill it

with illegible depths
and lucid passages,
bestiary of stones,
book without pages:

and yet it confers
as much as it denies:
we are orphaned and fathered
by such solid vacancies:

                              1972

# LANGSTON HUGHES
## 1902–1967

## 'Sea Calm'

How still,
How strangely still
The water is today.
It is not good
For water
To be so still that way.

1959

―――――

# MILES SMEETON
## 1906–1988

## from *Once is Enough*

On February 1 we had been thirty-six days at sea and we had only
done 3,523 miles on the chart, but we knew that we would soon catch
up on our estimate of 100 miles a day, if only the winds stayed
favourable. We were soon down to 48° south again, with glorious
westerly weather, cold and sunny, and John was busy about the ship
with his camera. He did a lot of filming from the cross-trees. Beryl
and John said that they preferred the dull grey days that we had had
further south, with the low driven cloud and the big swinging grey
seas. A monotone, cold, powerful and impersonal. That was what
they had expected down here.

'Not the cruel sea,' Beryl said. 'The sea is impersonal. I don't see
how you can call it cruel. It's the people on it who are apt to be cruel. I

don't think that you would call mountains or the sea cruel. It's only that we are so small and ineffective against them, and when things go wrong we start blaming them and calling them cruel.'

'Got to blame something,' said John. 'You never get anywhere blaming yourself.'

'No, I think that it's jolly hard luck on them. I think that they are kind, both the mountains and the sea, and it's only that they are so big that they don't notice us, or seem to forget about us.'

'I thought that you said they were impersonal.'

'Well, impersonal in that they don't feel spite against us. We are just so small that they don't notice us.'

'Didn't Hilary say, after he had climbed Everest, that he felt as if the mountain had sort of noticed them, and given them permission? Same sort of thing in reverse.'

'Yes, I don't think that anyone should ever mention victory or conquest with regard to the sea or the mountains. I think that you can talk about a fight or a struggle, in the same way as an ant could talk about struggling up your trousers, but I don't think that it could talk of victory, when it got to the top.'

'You wouldn't like the sea if there wasn't an almost continual struggle,' I said, and then to John: 'Life with Beryl has been one long struggle for survival. The army ought to hire her to run a battle course for the next war.'

'No wonder you look your age.'

'I once had a confidential report which said, "This Officer shows great skill in getting out of situations he should never have got into". It should have been "getting out of situations his wife has got him into".'

Beryl and John might prefer the grey smoking seas, but I liked this sun and movement, this sparkle on the water, the blues and the greens, the dazzle and flash of the spray at the bow, and the small white clouds.

For three days the wind stayed fresh in the west, and never had we had such sailing. The stove was kept on all day and it was warm and snug in the cabin, and on deck *Tzu Hang* seemed to be singing a wild saga of high adventure. The big swells built up, showing a greenish blue at their tops against the sky and as they rolled up from behind, *Tzu Hang* leaped forward in a flurry of foam, weaving, swaying and surging, in an ecstasy of movement and sun and spray.

✻

. . . The sea was a wonderful sight. It was as different from an ordinary rough sea, as a winter's landscape is from a summer one, and the thing that impressed me most was that its general aspect was white. This was due to two reasons: firstly because the wide breaking crests left swathes of white all over the sea, and secondly because all over the surface of the great waves themselves, the wind was whipping up lesser waves, and blowing their tops away, so that the whole sea was lined and streaked with this blown spume, and it looked as if all the surface was moving. Here and there, as a wave broke, I could see the flung spray caught and whirled upwards by the wind, which raced up the back of the wave, just like a whirl of wind-driven sand in the desert. I had seen it before, but this moving surface, driving low across a sea all lined and furrowed with white, this was something new to me, and something frightening, and I felt exhilarated with the atmosphere of strife. I have felt this feeling before on a mountain, or in battle, and I should have been warned. It is apt to mean trouble.

For the first time since we entered the Tasman there were no albatrosses to be seen. I wondered where they had gone to, and supposed that however hard the wind blew it could make no difference to them. Perhaps they side-slipped out of a storm area, or perhaps they held their position as best they could until the storm passed, gliding into the wind and yet riding with the storm until it left them.

I kept looking aft to make sure that *Tzu Hang* was dead stern on to the waves. First her stern lifted, and it looked as if we were sliding down a long slope into the deep valley between this wave and the one that had passed, perhaps twenty seconds before; then for a moment we were perched on the top of a sea, the wind force rose, and I could see the white desolation around me. Then her bowsprit drove into the sky, and with a lurch and a shrug, she sent another sea on its way. It was difficult to estimate her speed, because we had brought the log in, and the state of the water was very disturbed, but these waves were travelling a great deal faster than she was, and her speed seemed to be just sufficient to give her adequate steerage way, so that I could correct her in time to meet the following wave.

Suddenly there was a roar behind me and a mass of white water foamed over the stern. I was knocked forward out of the cockpit on to the bridge deck, and for a moment I seemed to be sitting in the sea with the mizzen mast sticking out of it upright beside me. I was surprised by the weight of the water, which had burst the canvas windscreen behind me wide open, but I was safely secured by my body-line to the after shroud. I scrambled back into the cockpit and grabbed the tiller again, and pushed it hard over, for *Tzu Hang* had swung so that her quarter was to the sea. She answered slowly but in time, and as the next sea came up, we were stern on to it again. The canvas of the broken windbreak lashed and fluttered in the wind until its torn ends were blown away.

Now the cloud began to break up and the sun to show. I couldn't look at the glass, but I thought that I felt the beginning of a change. It was only the change of some sunlight, but the sunlight seemed to show that we were reaching the bottom of this depression. Perhaps we would never get a chance again to film such a sea, in these fleeting patches of brilliance. I beat on the deck above John's bunk and called him up. I think that he had just got to sleep, now that the sails were off her, and there was someone at the helm. I know that I couldn't sleep before. He looked sleepy and disgruntled when he put his head out of the hatch.

'What about some filming, John?'

'No, man, the sea never comes out.'

'We may never get a sea like this again.'

'I don't want to get the camera wet, and there's not enough light.'

'No, look, there's a bit of sun about.'

As he was grumbling, like an old bear roused out of its winter quarters, he looked aft and I saw his expression change to one of interest.

'Look at this one coming up,' he said, peering over the top of the washboards, just the top of his head and his eyes showing. 'Up she goes,' he ducked down as if he expected some spray to come over, and then popped his head up again. 'Wait a minute,' he said. 'I'll fix something up,' and he slammed the hatch shut and disappeared below again.

He came up in a few minutes, fully equipped. He had the camera in a plastic bag with the lens protruding through a small hole. He took some shots. The lens had to be dried repeatedly, but the camera was safe in its bag, and we had no more wave tops on board. Presently he went down again.

John relieved me for breakfast, and when I came up it seemed to be blowing harder than ever.

'How's she steering?' I asked him.

'Not bad,' he said. 'I think she's a bit sluggish, but she ought to do.'

I took over again, and he went below; no one wanted to hang about in this wind. I watched the sixty fathoms of 3-inch hawser streaming behind. It didn't seem to be making a damn of difference, although I suppose that it was helping to keep her stern on to the seas. Sometimes I could see the end being carried forward in a big bight on the top of a wave. We had another sixty fathoms, and I considered fastening it to the other and streaming the two in a loop, but I had done this before, and the loop made no difference, although the extra length did help to slow her down. We had oil on board, but I didn't consider the emergency warranted the use of oil. For four hours now we had been running before this gale, running in the right direction, and we had only had one breaking top on board, and although I had been washed away from the tiller, *Tzu Hang* had shown little tendency to broach to. To stop her and to lie a-hull in this big sea seemed more dangerous than to let her run, as we were doing now. It was a dangerous sea I knew, but I had no doubt that she would carry us safely through, and as one great wave after another rushed past us, I grew more and more confident.

Beryl relieved me at nine o'clock. She looked so gay when she came on deck, for this is the sort of thing that she loves. She was wearing her yellow oilskin trousers and a yellow jumper with a hood, and over all a green oilskin coat. So that she could put on enough pairs of socks, she was wearing a spare pair of John's sea-boots. She was wearing woollen gloves, and she had put a plastic bag over her left hand, which she wouldn't be using for the tiller. She snapped the shackle of her body-line on to the shroud, and sat down beside me, and after a minute or two she took over. I went below to look at the glass and saw that it had moved up a fraction. My camera was in the locker in the doghouse, and I brought it out and took some snaps of the sea. Beryl was concentrating very hard on the steering. She was looking at the compass, and then aft to the following sea, to make sure that she was stern on to it, and then back to the compass again, but until she had the feel of the ship she would trust more to the compass for her course than to the wind and the waves. I took one or two snaps of Beryl, telling her not to look so serious, and to give me a smile. She laughed at me.

'How do you think she's steering?'

'Very well, I think.'

'We could put the other line out. Do you think she needs it? The glass is up a bit.'

'No, I think she's all right.'

'Sure you're all right?'

'Yes, fine, thanks.'

I didn't want to leave her and to shut the hatch on her, and cut her off from us below, but we couldn't leave the hatch open, and there was no point in two of us staying on deck. I took off my oilskins, put the camera back in its plastic bag in the locker, and climbed up into my bunk. The cat joined me and sat on my stomach. She swayed to the roll and purred. I pulled my book out of the shelf and began to read. After a time, I heard John open the hatch again and start talking to Beryl. A little later he went up to do some more filming. As the hatch opened there was a roar from outside, but *Tzu Hang* ran on straight and true, and I felt a surge of affection and pride for the way she was doing. 'She's a good little ship, a good little ship,' I said to her aloud, and patted her planking.

I heard the hatch slam shut again, and John came down. He went aft, still dressed in his oilskins, and sat on the locker by his bunk, changing the film of his camera. Beneath him, and lashed securely to ring-bolts on the locker, was his tool-box, a large wooden chest, about 30 inches by 18 inches by 8 inches, crammed full with heavy tools.

My book was called *Harry Black*, and Harry Black was following up a wounded tiger, but I never found out what happened to Harry Black and the tiger.


When John went below, Beryl continued to steer as before, continually checking her course by the compass, but steering more by the wind and the waves. She was getting used to them now, but the wind still blew as hard as ever. In places the sun broke through the cloud, and from time to time she was in sunshine. A wave passed under *Tzu Hang*, and she slewed slightly. Beryl corrected her easily, and when she was down in the hollow she looked aft to check her alignment. Close behind her a great wall of water was towering above her, so wide that she couldn't see its flanks, so high and so steep that she knew *Tzu Hang* could not ride over it. It didn't seem to be breaking as the other waves had broken, but water was cascading down its front, like a waterfall. She thought, 'I can't do anything, I'm absolutely straight.' This was her last visual picture, so nearly truly her last, and it has remained with her. The next moment she seemed to be falling out of the cockpit, but she remembers nothing but this sensation.

Then she found herself floating in the sea, unaware whether she had been under or not.

   She could see no sign of *Tzu Hang*, and she grabbed at her waist for her life-line, but felt only a broken end. She kicked to tread water, thinking, 'Oh, God, they've left me!' and her boots, those good roomy boots of John's, came off as she kicked. Then a wave lifted her, and she turned in the water, and there was *Tzu Hang*, faithful *Tzu Hang*, lying stopped and thirty yards away. She saw that the masts were gone and that *Tzu Hang* was strangely low in the water, but she was still afloat and Beryl started to swim towards the wreckage of the mizzenmast.

1959

# NORMAN MACCAIG
## 1910–

## 'Midnight, Lochinver'

Wine-coloured, Homer said, wine-dark . . .
The seaweed on the stony beach,
Flushed darker with that wine, was kilts
And beasts and carpets . . . A startled heron
Tucked in its cloud two yellow stilts.

And eiderducks were five, no, two—
No, six. A lounging fishbox raised
Its broad nose to the moon. With groans
And shouts the steep burn drowned itself;
And sighs were soft among the stones.

All quiet, all dark: excepting where
A cone of light stood on the pier
And in the circle of its scope
A hot winch huffed and puffed and gnashed
Its iron fangs and swallowed rope.

The nursing tide moved gently in.
Familiar archipelagoes
Heard her advancing, heard her speak
Things clear, though hard to understand
Whether in Gaelic or in Greek.

1962

———

# WILLARD BASCOM

## 1916–

# from *The Crest of the Wave: Adventures in Oceanography*

### THE SURF AT TABLE BLUFF

Humboldt Bay, 300 miles north of San Francisco, is shallow and muddy, about a quarter mile wide and three or four miles long. A ridge of sand perhaps 200 yards wide separates the calm bay from the ocean. Near the middle of the bay this sandy barrier is dissected by a pair of rock jetties that contain the entrance channel through which tidal currents rush in and out twice a day. At the south end of the bay, a green meadow slopes upward toward the ocean and terminates against the beach in a cliff more than 100 feet high, known as Table Bluff. Atop the bluff there was a light and two tall radio towers operated by the Coast Guard. The surf below the lighthouse was the place selected for our party to make definitive measurements of the encounter between the great North Pacific swell and one of the roughest beaches known.

The beach party left for the northern coast encouraged by a pronouncement from the big boss, Mike O'Brien, dean of engineering at Berkeley: 'If you can work in the winter surf north of Cape Mendocino, you can work anywhere.' We accepted that statement as a fact without thinking through its implications. He did not mention that we might drown while finding out.

Late on a rainy November afternoon, our expedition arrived at a motel on the inner side of the bay. John stood atop the dukws and pointed across the bay and the sand spit to exploding masses of white water. 'Out there', he said, 'is where we will work. Those are *big* breakers maybe thirty feet high.' It was the first time I had seen the Pacific Ocean and, like the others, was not sufficiently experienced to make a suitable comment. What did we know? Thirty feet didn't sound big for an ocean the size of the Pacific, but that depends on where you are, relative to the wave.

The following day Isaacs, Lieutenant Dickey, our Marine Corps liaison officer, and I visited the beach for a closer look.

... The sky was dark, and it was raining and blowing as we picked our way over the crest of a driftwood-strewn sand ridge to confront the Pacific. To both north and south, a rough spume-crossed beach stretched away to foggy vanishing points; we could see about one quarter of the fifteen miles of desolate, unbroken beach between the Eel River and the Humboldt Bay jetties. In that entire length there was not a person or a house to interrupt the desolation. The top of the sand spit behind us was crowned with a jumbled mass of driftwood. Large logs, some escapees from log rafts or lumber mills, were represented; so were whole trees with stubs of branches still attached that had floated down rivers in flood and had been heaved by the largest waves above the highest tide. This bristling rampart was tangible evidence of how waves shaped beaches.

We squinted into the gusting wind to avoid the flying sand grains, and the water trickling down our cheeks tasted salty. The surf roared at us, which is to say that the wide spectrum of frequencies created by all the waves crashing, colliding, swashing, and releasing bubbles produced a high volume of white noise—a hiss of astonishing proportions broken only by the occasional crack of a single breaker slapping the water extra hard. We could feel the beach shake under our feet when a long plunging breaker collapsed.

Then we became aware of a distinctive smell. The flavor of the open sea on the Pacific Northwest is not to be confused with that of Southern California or of East Coast harbors or of tidal flats. It is a not unpleasant odor but a natural perfume, probably flavored by plankton that are churned into a froth to create an aerosol that is carried shoreward by the wind.

When the violent gusts subsided, we opened our eyes and tried to make some sense out of the mass of breaking waves churning the half-

mile-wide band of water nearest the shoreline. As we huddled
watching the white confusion, Isaacs decided that we inlanders were
entitled to a short background lecture on what was going on.

'Most waves are caused by wind blowing across the water surface.
The stronger the wind and the longer distance it blows, the bigger the
waves. In the area where they are generated, waves can be large and
rough, but as they move out from under the wind that created them
they become long low undulations called swell.

'Swell can travel long distances with little loss of energy. Only the
wave form moves forward; after it passes, the water particles end up
about where they were before. Individual waves are primarily described
by their period, which is the time in seconds for successive crests to
pass a fixed point such as a rock.

'As swell approaches a shore, it feels bottom, and as the depth
continues to shoal, the crests of the waves become more peaked.
Finally, when the water depth is only about 1.2 times the wave
height, the wave becomes unstable. As the water at the bottom slows,
the crest rushes forward, and the wave breaks. If the top curls over an
air-filled tunnel and falls into the trough ahead, the breaker is said to
"plunge"; if the top merely turns white and tumbles down the wave
front, it is a "spilling" breaker.'

Our inexperienced eyes still saw only confusion, so we climbed
Table Bluff to get a better perspective. Before us there was spread a
grand panorama of Pacific violence, a texture of white turbulence
atop the green-gray fabric of sea and sky. We could make out three
broad strips of broken white water, each with green water between.
Beyond, as far as the eye could see, a procession of long-crested
waves advanced and furiously harled themselves onto the submerged
outer bar. Then they would re-form in the deeper green water inside
that bar and break a second time on the inner bar. Finally, on reaching
the beach face, they would break one last time, and the last dregs of
energy would be expended in a thin white swash; when this slid back
down and ended in a muddy swirl called the backrush, the wave was
finished.

Although John patiently explained the inner workings of the
waves, we did not then appreciate such details. 'A man wouldn't live
long in that surf,' he added. That certainly seemed to be true but who
would be foolish enough to go there anyway? Who indeed?

The beach party established a wave observation post atop Table
Bluff, where we could observe sea and surf conditions, time wave

periods, and measure the height of breakers on the outer bar. In order
to capture details of the outer breakers a half mile offshore, we used
long-focal-length aerial cameras borrowed from the Navy. These
were bulky and heavy, but they had excellent lenses, used negatives
8 inches square, with 200 exposures per roll. An internal clock
showed in the corner of every picture, so we knew exactly when it
was taken. This was very advantageous in following a sequence of
events or for calculating the height of the tide. Twice a day we
photographed the surf zone and recorded its vital statistics from that
observation post at the edge of the bluff. Later the height of the waves
could be measured on these pictures.

Sometimes, on days when the waves were large and the sky was
clear, the Navy would send reconaissance planes to take a sequence of
vertical photos of the surf zone. From these we could obtain water
depths on and between the submerged sand bars by measuring the
speed of advance of the wave front on a series of pictures taken at
3-second intervals.

Having estimated wave height and water depth from the safety of
shore, we felt honor bound to check up on ourselves by making
direct measurements of the profile of the sand under the surf to find
out if those figures were correct. This was more than a point of pride;
one of our jobs was to determine the exact configuration of the sand
bars that caused the waves to break when and where they did. Did
large waves in the real ocean do the same things as those in a model
tank? That meant surveying the surf zone during or immediately
after large waves were breaking, because when the waves changed,
the shapes of the sand bars changed.

We learned a simple way for a person on the beach to measure the
height of the big breakers, even though they are far offshore. Just
stand at a level on the beach where your eyes are exactly aligned with
both the high point of the breaker and the distant horizon; then the
height of the wave is the vertical distance between your eyes and
the backrush. We would often do that before risking a run through
the surf, but rarely did we do it long enough to get the highest
breakers, because wave heights vary so much. We found that about
every 3 minutes there would be a series of three higher-than-average
waves. But sometimes, because the three highest in one group were
not the same height as those in the next group, we got into trouble.

The line along which we would take soundings was established by
pairs of red and white banded range boards 10 feet high that were

visible a mile at sea. In the system that Isaacs had developed, a dukw moved shoreward along that line while a surveyor, a thousand feet down the beach, would follow it with the telescope of a surveyor's transit. The leadsman in the dukw would heave a sounding lead out ahead and call, 'Mark' into a walkie-talkie radio. The surveyor would see the splash of the lead and read the angle between it and the base line. Then, as the dukw came even with the lead and the line became vertical, the leadsman would tap the lead on the bottom, read the water level on the line, and call the depth into the radio. The recorder on shore would write the angle and depth in a notebook, and these would later be converted to profiles and contour maps.

Such surveying is easy in low waves. But in the winter breakers at Table Bluff, it was a stimulating experience, because a dukw has about 2 feet of freeboard, and the breakers were often 10 to 15 feet high occasionally more. There was an excellent chance that the leadsman (me) would get cold seawater down the back of his neck, not to mention the possibility of drowning.

First it was necessary to get out through the lines of breakers to the relative calm beyond, where a survey run could be started. On the way out, the driver and I were forcibly reminded that the energy in a breaking wave is proportional to the square of its height. That is, a 14-foot breaker on the outer bar has four times as much energy as a 7-foot breaker on the inner bar. The driver and I often made that kind of calculation in our heads when the breakers ahead were unexpectedly large. That was because it was our considered opinion that the chances of *not* returning to the beach alive increased along with the energy of the breaker. If the dukw foundered or rolled over on the outer bar when the breakers were large, there was a very small chance that either of us could have made it ashore.

On days when the outer breakers were relatively low, which meant 10 to 12 feet, the dukw would buck its way out, usually taking two or three breaking waves head-on at each of the two bars. Since the top of a dukw cab is only 4 feet above the still-water line, driving deliberately into an onrushing wall of water two or three times higher than your head takes either nerve or poor judgment. We had a lot of both.

It was much better to take a breaker head-on than to turn at the last minute and take the chance of being hit broadside and perhaps being rolled over. As dukw and wave collided at about 20 miles per hour, there would be a resounding metallic thud. The hull would shudder, forward motion would be momentarily reversed, and the impact would fling a hugh white splash in all directions. There were small holes where the canvas roof joined the coners of the windows through which water would squirt like a high pressure hose on the men inside. Green water crashing on top would pour onto the grating between the cab and the cargo compartment and the automatic bilge pumps would start throwing 3-inch jets of water into the air on both sides. It was not unusual for the canvas seams in the roof to split or for the windshield wipers and rear-view mirrors to be torn away by these impacts. The original light-steel frames that supported the canvas over the cargo compartment soon buckled under plunging breakers and were replaced with heavy pipe.

Once the dukw was outside the breaker zone and aligned with red-striped range markers, we would check to see if the radio was working and make sure the transit man was ready before heading landward. Then we would select what we hoped would be the lowest of the oncoming waves for a ride across the outer bar. Once committed, there was no possibility of turning back.

When that wave overtook us, the dukw would begin to surfboard. I would heave the sounding lead ahead and to one side into the trough; as we passed it, and the line became vertical, I could read the water depth in the trough. Then the dukw's stern would begin to rise as the crest overtook us, and the bow tilted downward. As its slope increased, our seagoing truck would begin to slide down the front of the breaker that was peaking behind us, and the driver would fight desperately with throttle and rudder to maintain its position at right angles to the wave front. While running before the wave, we were traveling at twice normal speed, often with the bow plowing the slick green water of the trough ahead, sometimes up to the windshield.

While balancing under this incipient waterfall, I would estimate the height of the wave that was about to come crashing down, add one third of that (5 feet for a 15-foot wave) to the trough depth, call the answer into the microphone, and duck. Then the reaching crest of the plunging wave would collapse on us, not quite capsizing the dukw.

Now the bow would rise, and the wave would pass underneath, lifting us on its shoulders. The dukw would become level again, its deck 8 feet or so above the surface of the trough just ahead. We found it exhilarating to ride the crest of a wave, driven forward by the pressure of the moving water against the wheels and axles that hung below. After a few seconds atop this rolling pinnacle of water, the

wave would pass on, and the dukw would slide down the spent
breaker's back side.

Now the idling engine would begin to roar as the driver redlined
the tachometer to get clear of the bar before the next wave broke. The
total time elapsed for a ride on an outer breaker was not much more
than 15 seconds, but those were long seconds. By comparison the
breakers on the inner bar were pretty tame.

At the end of the run as the dukw neared the beach, the wheels
would touch bottom gently as the springs resumed their load. The
driver would shift power from the propeller to the wheels, and with
gears grinding and canvas dripping, our dukw would slosh out of the
water. Once safely up on the beach the driver would threaten to quit,
logically arguing that his life was worth more than a beach profile. I
would agree sympathetically, check with the transit party by radio to
see if they had gotten the data, and after a short breather, we'd agree
that this was really fun and head back out to sea to run another line of
soundings farther down the beach.

1958

# from *Waves and Beaches:*<br>*The Dynamics of the Ocean Surface*

Waves have many stages in their lives. They are born as ripples, grow
into whitecaps, chop, wind waves, and finally into fully developed
storm seas. As these seas pass out from under the winds that formed
them, they diminish in height and steepness into low sine-shaped
swell. As swell, waves may traverse great stretches of open ocean
without much loss of energy. Eventually they reach the shoaling
waters of a continental shelf. Once on the shelf the wave fronts are
bent until they almost parallel the shoreline.

All this seems to be merely preparation for the final and most
exciting step. The irregular waves of deep water are organized by the
effect of the bottom into long regular lines of crests moving in the
same direction at similar velocities. The romanticist thinks of the
forces of the sea being marshaled for an exuberant death against
an ancient enemy. The depth continues to decrease until finally in
very shallow water it becomes impossible for the oscillating water
particles to complete their orbits. When the orbits break the wave

breaks. The crest tumbles forward, falling into the trough ahead as a mass of foaming white water. The momentum carries the broken water onward until the wave's last remaining energy is expended in a gentle swash that rushes up the sandy beach face and sinks from sight. The wave is gone!

This zone where waves give up their energy and where systematic water motions give way to violent turbulence is the surf. It is the most exciting part of the ocean.

## BREAKING WAVES

As the swell from the deep sea moves into very shallow water, it is traveling at a speed of fifteen to twenty miles an hour, and the changes in its character over the final few dozen yards to shore come very rapidly.

In the approach to shore the drag of the bottom causes the wave velocity to decrease. The decrease causes the phenomenon of refraction, which was described earlier, and one of its effects is to shorten the wave length. As length decreases, wave steepness increases, tending to make the waves less stable. Moreover, as a wave crest moves into water whose depth is about twice the wave height, another effect is observed which further increases wave steepness. The crest 'peaks up'. That is, the rounded crest that is identified with swell is transformed into a higher, more pointed mass of water with steeper flanks. As the depth of water continues to decrease, the circular orbits are squeezed into a tilted ellipse and the orbital velocity at the crest increases with the increasing wave height.

This sequence of changes in wave length and steepness is the prelude to breaking. Finally, at a depth of water roughly equal to 1.3 times the wave height, the wave becomes unstable. This happens when not enough water is available in the shallow water ahead to fill in the crest and complete a symmetrical wave form. The top of the onrushing crest becomes unsupported and it collapses, falling in uncompleted orbits. The wave has broken; the result is surf.

Having broken into a mass of turbulent tumbling foam, carried landward by its own momentum, the ex-wave will, if the water deepens again as it does after passing over a bar, reorganize itself into a new wave with systematic orbital motion. This reorganization is probably the result of dumping the mass of water from the wave crest into the relatively quiet water inside the breaker zone; the impulse generates a new wave. The new wave is smaller than the original one, the difference in heights representing the energy lost in breaking. The new wave, being smaller, proceeds into water equal to 1.3 times its height; then it, too, breaks.

Again a mass of water, white with bubbles of entrained air, is produced, but the water is likely to be too shallow for a new oscillatory wave to form. Now the front of the water becomes a step-shaped wave of translation—a different sort of wave in which the water actually moves forward with the wave form rather than merely oscillating as the wave form passes. Finally, at the beach face, the momentum of the water carries it into an uprush; the water slides and sprawls in a thin swash up and across the face of the beach. As it reaches its uppermost limit the wave dies; all the energy so carefully gleaned from the winds of the distant storm and hoarded for a thousand miles of ocean crossing is gone, expended in a few wild moments. Because the energy is released so rapidly, the energy density in the surf is actually much higher than in the storm which originally created the waves.

The surf changes from moment to moment, day to day, and beach to beach. The waves are influenced by the bottom and the bottom is changed by the waves. And since the waves arriving at a beach are highly variable in height, period, and direction, each wave creates a slightly different bottom configuration for the ones that come after it. The water level changes with the tide and the waves change as the storms at sea develop, shift position, and die out again. The result is that the sand bottom is forever being rearranged. Even in glass-sided wave channels where an endless number of waves, each exactly the same, can be produced, equilibrium is never reached; the sand continues to change as long as the wave machine is running.

Thus the waves change the sand at the same time the sand is changing the waves. First, consider the effect of the bottom on the waves as they break. It may make them plunge or spill.

Plunging breakers are the most impressive. Their principal characteristic is very rapid release of energy from a wave moving at high velocity. There is a sudden deficiency in water ahead of the wave which causes high-velocity currents in the trough as the water rushes seaward to fill the cavity beneath the oncoming crest. When there is not enough water to complete the wave form, the water in the crest, attempting to complete its orbit, is hurled ahead of its steep forward side and lands in the trough. This curling mass of falling water will often entrap air and then, as the upper part of the wave collapses, the air is compressed. When the compressed air finally bursts through the watery cap, a geyser of water is hurled into the air—sometimes over fifty feet.

If there is a strong offshore breeze, the thin crest of the wave will be blown off as it plunges forward, leaving a veil of rising spray behind to mark the path it has followed. This delicate tracery of spray has been likened by poets to the 'white manes of plunging horses'. Anyone who has observed such breakers, backlighted by a low sun, will understand the comparison and agree that this circumstance is worthy of poetic description.

To understand the reasons why breakers plunge calls for a somewhat more scientific approach. The wave must retain most of its energy right up to the moment of breaking. That is, there should be nothing, such as a rough bottom, a strong wind, or substantial currents, to make the wave prematurely unstable. Any of these conditions will degrade a wave's energy by slowing it down and warping its orbits so that it breaks gradually rather than abruptly. Thus, when a large clearly defined swell passes over a steep smooth underwater slope of the proper depth on a calm day, a perfect plunging breaker will result. If, however, the bottom is gently sloping and studded with rocky irregularities, or if the approaching waves appear confused, a spilling breaker is more likely to be produced.

A spilling wave breaks slowly and without the violent release of energy needed to fling the crest forward into the trough ahead. Its crest merely tumbles down a more gently sloping forward side, sometimes over a considerable distance and lasting for several minutes. Therefore, spilling waves are much favored by surfers, who ride on the face of the wave, their boards doing much the same thing the tumbling white water is doing.

1964

# SAMUEL ELIOT MORISON

## 1887–1976

# from *Spring Tides*

Since high water of a spring tide comes at noon or midnight, low water occurs shortly before sunrise and sunset, depending on the season. The October spring low is something I would not miss. After a day of brisk northwest wind the harbor is glassy calm, reflecting sunset clouds, the brilliant maples on the shore, and the white hulls of yachts waiting to be hauled out. Around the edge of the sand flats, well below the blue mussel beds, is a rod-wide belt of eel grass catching its fortnightly chance to breathe plenty of oxygen. Big black-backed gulls walk through the grass with a dignified gait, stalking the tiny crabs and little fishes which normally obtain protection among the grass but are now laid bare to the piercing eye and hungry beak.

My favorite spring high on the rocky Maine coast comes in May. It is an esthetic delight to sail in a gentle breeze close to shore when the shadbush is flinging out its white banners among the dark green spruce, the birches are putting forth leaves of the tenderest green, and the birds are 'singing like crazy'. Equally beautiful, however, are the spring highs on one of those halcyon days in October, when the blueberry bushes on top of the granite cliffs turn a brilliant crimson and the maple near shore sends up torches of gold and scarlet among the evergreen, all reflected in the quiet waters. No birds sing, but the crickets are lively, and if you sail close to where a meadow touches the shore you can hear a violin concerto of their little *cri-cri*. Lovers of Vermont and other inland states assert that their regions display the world's most brilliant colors in the fall of the year. Perhaps so; for who could test them with a color card? But the maples of Maine and the Maritime Provinces at least seem more brilliant, because of their background of dark green spruce and bright blue sea.

The 'salacious, supple sea' nibbles at the land in every spring high. One can observe the change in the shoreline over a series of years. Here a boulder is unbalanced and rolls onto the beach; there a spruce which has hopefully stretched out over the water to gather sunlight, loses its balance when a spring high sucks at its roots, and falls overboard; a clump of birches, undermined by the sea viciously undercutting the sandbank where it has been growing, topples and lies forlornly, roots in air, unless someone cuts it up for firewood. This is why people who love their shoreline build stone sea walls to restrain the robber tide; but if the present trend continues the sea will have its way in the end. Highland Light has had to be moved twice in our time, as the sea bites further and further into the skinny arm of Cape Cod.

Shakespeare has Brutus remark:

> There is a tide in the affairs of men,
> Which, taken at the flood, leads on to fortune.

True enough, as Shakespeare had ample opportunity to observe in London River. There, if a sailing barge 'missed its tide' it had to wait twelve hours, half of them sitting miserably on the bottom alongside an odorous dock, to catch another ebb to take her down the Thames. You may still see what the tide can do every day in the Tagus off Lisbon. A fleet of *fragatas*, the sailing lighters, part drifts, part sails up that noble river with the flood. The wind drops, the tide turns, and of a sudden you hear the rattle of forty chain cables off Black Horse Square as every vessel bound upriver anchors to await the next unpredictable fair wind or predictable fair tide.

Their predictability explains why tides are the sailor's friend. With a tide and current table he can figure them out to a minute; and even without modern aids he knows the full-and-change factor for his neighborhood, and has been shown by his grandfather how the currents work. Years ago, struggling with engine against a flood tide current between East Quoddy Head and Cutler, I barely overtook a fisherman who, with no other means of propulsion than sweep and sail, worked the eddies so close to that ironbound coast that he made good progress against the strong tidal current. Shipbuilders loved the spring tide, enabling them to build large vessels on convenient spots, at the very head of tidewater, in their very backyards; yet launch and float them at the top of a spring ebb. At low water, take a look from the head of tide in Kennebunkport, or over Duxbury Bay, now a green meadow of eelgrass, and you can hardly believe that hundreds of tall ships were there built, launched, and sailed or poled down to deep water. At the North River in Massachusetts, ships were built as

high upstream as Hanover bridge, launched on a spring high and
towed downstream on the ebb; a gang of men with a hawser on each
bank, and the pilot, at the knightheads, ordering, 'A leetle more over
toward Scituate!' or, 'Marshfield side, and put more back into it!'

Since tides, like the movements of sun, moon and stars, were
phenomena that man could not influence, it was man's natural
conclusion that they affected his life. Just as farmers regulated
plowing and sowing by the phases of the moon, so sailors and
fishermen believed that flood tide meant strength, and ebb tide,
weakness. If an old salt lay at death's door, his family and friends
watched the tide. If he survived an ebb he would improve with the
flood, but he would always die on the ebb. It was a pretty conception
that the sailor's spirit would wish to float out of harbor with the ebb
and once more survey familiar scenes—kelp-marked ledges, foaming
tide rips, circling sea birds, friendly lighthouses—before it left for
another world. That this belief was not confined to the coast is
attested by Walt Whitman on the Civil War:

'He went out with the tide and the sunset,' was a phrase I heard from a
surgeon describing an old sailor's death under peculiarly gentle conditions.

During the Secession War, 1863 and '64, visiting the army hospitals around
Washington, I formed the habit and continued it to the end, whenever the
ebb or flood tide began the latter part of day, of punctually visiting those at
that time populous wards of suffering men. Somehow (or I thought so) the
effect of the hour was palpable. The badly wounded would get some ease and
would like to talk a little or be talked to. Intellectual and emotional natures
would be at their best; deaths were always easier; medicines seemed to have
better effect when given then; and a lulling atmosphere would pervade the
wards.

Similar influences, similar circumstances and hours, day-close, after great
battles, even with all their horrors. I had more than once the same experiences
on the fields covered with the fallen or dead.

Something of the same feeling comes over every lover of the sea at
the turn of a spring tide, especially if the wind is offshore. His soul
seems to be pulling his body seaward. He feels an almost irresistible
impulse to knock off whatever he may be doing, launch the punt, row
out to his sail or motor boat, make sail or start the engine, and speed
out into blue water with the ebb, which on a spring tide will carry him
through the narrow channel with unusual speed. Around sunset,
when the tide turns, he can point his prow home once more, and feel
the ineffable delight of half sailing, half drifting to his mooring with

the lightest of sea breezes, under a full moon; or in the new-moon
spring, under stars that have guided mariners for thousands of years.

1964

H. W. TILMAN

1898–?1977–8

# from *Mostly Mischief*

The extensive repairs to *Mischief*'s ribs having been completed the
crew began to assemble from May 20th onwards. One or two of them
I had met only once before for a few brief moments, so that when
they stepped on board, instead of a welcoming smile, my face must
have worn a look of shocked surprise. Had I or had I not met this
chap before somewhere? Surely I had not asked him to come? The
lean, wiry Charles Sewell bore a horrible resemblance to someone I
had sailed with many years before and when he upset the varnish tin
twice the first day this fear was almost confirmed. Charles Marriott
ran true to form by deferring his arrival from day to day and
consequently our departure. It did not matter. Rain delayed the
fitting out and for two days I myself felt more like going to bed than
going to sea.

   Our wireless set, a type that is fitted in motor cars, had at last
succumbed to sea-air and damp. I invested in a Decca transistor set,
supposed to give world-wide coverage, so that we need no longer
depend upon the battery and the charging engine. With a good
chronometer watch a wireless receiving set is not essential. Watches,
however, have been known to stop, especially if one forgets to wind
them, and if Test Matches are being played a reliable receiving set is
important. Weather forecasts can be obtained only for home waters
and need not necessarily be taken too much to heart. West of the areas
Shannon and Rockall forecasts for the Atlantic are transmitted in
Morse too fast for the average yachtsman, while those for Iceland or
Greenland waters will be in some unknown tongue.

Charles Marriott arrived on May 30th at 11.30 and we cast off at 12.30 after a hurried lunch. As we motored down the river the Royal Lymington Yacht Club honoured us with a salute from their starting gun. With the ebb tide and a light wind we soon cleared the Needles, but in the evening a violent squall ushered in a night of torrential rain, thunder, lightning, and squalls from all points of the compass. Not at all the sort of night to be at sea with a green crew. We had several Chinese gybes, were scared by steamers, and enjoyed five minutes pandemonium when the staysail sheet got out of control. The next night was a repetition of the first, worse in fact, for Charles Marriott lost overboard his yachting cap, a veteran of many voyages, at least ten years old to my knowledge, much prized by him and greatly admired by the crew. No longer would a slimmer edition of King Edward VII be seen disembarking from *Mischief* as though from the royal yacht *Britannia*.

By June 1st the weather had faired up and the wind died down to leave us rolling heavily. A corvette steamed slowly past and hailed us by name to know if we were all right. The crew discomfited by the heavy rolling, might not have agreed with my affirmative reply. We discovered now that the metal collar for the twin staysail booms had been left behind, like the proverbial Dutchman's anchor. It was infuriating to have the sails on board and no means of setting them. Our course down Channel had no doubt been tortuous. On June 2nd the visibility being poor, I reckoned we must be somewhere near the Manacles. But life is full of surprises. When the wind fell light we handed the mainsail in order to stitch a slender seam and while I was busy with this Noddy sighted through the haze a slender tower to the north-east—no doubt, the Eddystone. But when the sun went down and the lights came on it proved to be the Wolf Rock light. We were at least twenty miles and two points out in our reckoning. I concluded that *Mischief* knew the way down Channel better than her skipper.

Astonishment is an emotion salutary for the young—and the old, too, for that matter. Presently we were to have even greater cause than this for astonishment, and these two strange occurrences went far to confirm my belief that navigation is far from being an exact science. Bound for east Greenland via the Faeroes and Iceland our best course lay up the Irish Sea and through the Minches. Upon rounding Land's End, therefore, we set a course for the Smalls. Thick weather obliged us to go about before sighting them but on the evening of June 4th we had the Tuskar rock abeam five miles off.

Taking our departure from this unmistakable mark we set a course for Holyhead eighty miles away, a course that enabled us to make the most of a fine quartering wind. The wind held steady all night and next day, which was hazy, we were puzzled but not dismayed when we found we had run 100 miles without either hitting or even sighting Holyhead Island. At last about tea-time, when land began to loom vaguely to port, to starboard, and also ahead, we realized that we were near the head of Cardigan Bay, two points off course and some forty miles from Holyhead. Currents, the compass, the helmsmen, even the navigator, may be responsible for these anomalies. It is not, however, for the navigator to accept responsibility for them or to show surprise, or he may sap what confidence the crew have in him. Attack is the best form of defence. A few remarks about the impossibility of navigating the ship if it is not steered straight will restore his own confidence and subdue and mystify the crew.

> Where lies the land to which the ship will go?
> Far, far ahead is all her seamen know.
> And where the land she travels from? Away
> Far, far behind is all that they can say.

The tide being foul we went outside Bardsey Island and headed across to Ireland, the wind by now round at north. In poor visibility we were lucky to sight St Johns lighthouse whence we set a course to clear South Rock, the most easterly point of Ireland. The night closed down dark and foggy and we were sailing fast, so mindful of recent events I prudently decided to heave to. Several ships were about with their foghorns blaring and before dawn we received aid and comfort by hearing away on our beam the bleating of Mew Island lighthouse south of Belfast Lough. Approaching the North Channel on a clear, sunny evening, the wind light, we had the doubtful pleasure of watching the Stranraer-Larne ferry cross and recross no less than four times. Here the tides run strongly and, perhaps, I had not been explicit enough about the course to steer if the wind freshened. Coming on deck early next morning I found we were up behind the Mull of Kintyre, none of the helmsmen in the night having realized that he was steering blithely into a cul-de-sac. By the time we had regained the North Channel, and once more sighted the ferryboat, the tide had turned against us, leaving us no choice but to steer west for Red Bay and anchor there.

Leaving on the north-going tide, by 1 p.m. of June 9th we had

Inishtrahull abeam, whence we set a course for Skerryvore. Inishtrahull and Skerryvore! What stirring, romantic names for the two
lonely, Atlantic-facing outposts of Ireland and Scotland! Skerryvore
is one of a shoal of above-water and sunken rocks extending for
twelve miles to the south of the Isle of Tiree. It must be a fearsome
sight in a gale when the whole of this twelve miles is a mass of
breakers. The lighthouse, designed by Alan Stevenson and finished in
1844, must be one of the most exposed of any, wide open as it is to the
unbroken sweep of the Atlantic.

After passing Skerryvore we had a grand sail through the Passage
of Tiree, the five-miles-wide strait between Mull and the two bleak,
barren islands of Tiree and Coll. Johnson and Boswell in their tour of
the Hebrides were driven by a storm to take refuge in Coll where
they remained weatherbound for nearly a fortnight:

We were doomed to experience, like others, the dangers of trusting to the
wind, which blew against us in a short time with such violence that we, being
so seasoned sailors, were willing to call it a tempest. I was sea-sick and lay
down. Mr Boswell kept the deck. The master knew not well whither to go;
and our difficulties might well have filled a very pathetic page, had not
Maclean of Coll, who with every other qualification that insular life requires
is a very active and skilful mariner, piloted us safe into his own harbour.

Boswell devotes several pages to this adventure of which the following is
a brief sample:

. . . a prodigious sea with immense billows coming upon the vessel so that it
seemed hardly possible to escape. There was something grandly horrible in
the sight . . . As I saw them all busy doing something, I asked Coll what I
could do. He, with a happy readiness, put into my hand a rope, which was
fixed to the top of one of the masts, and told me to hold it till he bade me pull.
If I had considered the matter I might have seen that this could not be of the
least service but his object was to keep me out of the way of those who were
busy working the vessel, and at the same time divert my fear by employing
me, and making me think I was of use. Thus did I stand firm to my post while
the wind and rain beat upon me, always expecting a call to pull my rope.

From what we saw of Coll and its small harbour as we sailed by I
think Boswell had good reason to be afraid, running as they were for
a small, unlit harbour, in a gale, on a black night. Among the
Hebrides with their strong tides, strong winds, and much rain, the
perils of navigation when there were no harbour lights or lighthouses are hardly imaginable. Nowadays, in summer at least, there

are no difficulties thanks to the numerous lights. Rounding the north
end of Coll we stood across to Ushinish lighthouse on South Uist
passing on the way the rocks of Oigh Sgeir where there is also a light.
From Ushinish we made for the Little Minch at the north end of Skye,
faithfully following the pecked line on the chart, the recommended
route for north-bound vessels, like a hen following a chalk-line.
Once through the pass of the Little Minch we were in the clear, for
the North Minch is over thirty miles wide.

It seemed a shame to pass non-stop through this perfect cruising
ground with only the vaguest glimpse of the mountains of Skye.
These western isles were no more familiar to the crew than Greenland
but at this stage of the voyage they were more interested in sleep than
in scenery. On the evening of June 11th we passed the Butt of Lewis
and sailed out into the Atlantic. The Faeroes lie due north, only 180
miles away, with nothing in between but the small uninhabited
islands of Sula Sgeir and Rona. We sighted the former on the 12th; it
is visited in summer by people from Lewis to collect the eggs of the
gannet or solan goose. A mixture of rain and fog, flat calms and high
winds, made this short passage slow and uncertain. I got no sun
sights, only a sight of Vega, and one star by itself is not of great value.
Sailing north in summer the nights soon become so light that only
planets or the very brightest stars are visible—visible, that is to say, to
the navigator with a sextant that is a little antique like mine, with a
telescope that hinders rather than helps the picking up of stars. Even
when the nights are dark the North Atlantic sky, after remaining
clear all night, has a mean trick of clouding over before dawn when
one is hoping to take star sights. The exasperated navigator then feels
like echoing the impious outburst ascribed to Lord Jeffrey, a contemporary of Sydney Smith, though what circumstances occasioned the
outburst I have not discovered: 'Damn the solar system; bad light;
planets too distant; pestered with comets; feble contrivance; could
make a better with ease.'

After remaining hove to most of the night in a near gale and heavy
rain, still uncertain of our position, we let draw on the morning of the
14th, steering east. Two trawlers were in sight and at noon a high
island showed up on the starboard bow some twenty miles away. It
could be only Syderö the southernmost of the Faeroes. There are
altogether eighteen islands, all but one inhabited, spread over about
sixty miles of sea. There are many good harbours, a few of them
classed as 'winter harbours' safe in all weather conditions, and the

rest are 'summer harbours'. My only knowledge of the Faeroes, strictly practical, came from the *Pilot*; we did not know where to find the choicest beauty spots or the cheapest beer; even Charles Marriott, a rich store of general knowledge, was at a loss. I inclined to the capital, Thorshaven, or Vaag Fjord on Syderö, both on the east side of the group and therefore sheltered.

Three miles off the south end of Syderö is a thirty-seven-foot-high rock called Munken and in the vicinity of the rock there are heavy tide rips even in fine weather. That evening we were sailing eastwards about two miles south of Munken, thinking that was enough. Apparently it was not. The wind dropped and almost at once the sea, as if glad to be free of its control, began to boil like a pot. All around us waves shot up and collapsed in confusion. As we had no steerage way the sails and spars slammed and banged, the mast quivered. Broken water extended as far as the eye could reach. We were being set westwards anyway, so we forgot about Thorshaven and Vaag Fjord, started the engine, and steered north-west, intent only on getting out of this miniature maelstrom.

When we were well west of Syderö conditions improved except for a heavy swell running and an absence of wind. We handed all sails except the genoa which we stupidly left up with the result that it split right across. But we had by no means finished with our Faeroe Island troubles. Our best bet now seemed to be Vestmanhavn in Vestmanha Sund, the narrow channel between the main island Strömö and the westernmost island Vaagö. From there, to continue our voyage to Iceland, we should merely have to complete the passage of the Sund to fetch clear of the islands and be out in the Atlantic. Entering Vestmanhavn we should have to fly a 'Q' flag which we now discovered we had also left behind. So while waiting for a wind I made up a flag with canvas and curry powder.

Towards noon a breeze came in from west enabling us just to lay the desired course. All seemed set fair for a quick passage to Vaagö Fjord followed by a quiet night at anchor in Vestmanhavn. In the afternoon, however, the weather deteriorated, squalls of wind and rain became gradually heavier and more frequent, blotting out all the land except for two 1,500-foot-high islands close on our starboard hand. Prudence suggested reefing or even standing out to sea for the night, for the wind had in it a note of malice and we were on a lee shore in thick weather. But without the driving power of the full mainsail we should never clear Kolter, the northernmost of the two islands now fine on the lee bow. With Vaagö Fjord and its promise of shelter only five miles away we drove on under all plain sail, the lee scuppers awash, praying that the gear would stand and that we could weather Kolter. As if to enhance the wild, adventurous aspect of the scene—the hard-driven ship, the angry sea, the dim, menacing outline of the island—a blue whale, close aboard, jumped half clear of the water, fell back with a splash that could be heard above the roar of the wind, and then towered, head and shoulders clear of the water, before sounding.

With Kolter gradually drawing safely aft we could turn our attention to what lay ahead, peering through the gathering gloom of rain and nightfall in search of the fjord entrance. Between the heavier curtains of rain that swept across we made out the black outline of an immense vertical wall of rock fine on the weather bow. For this we steered, certain that it would provide us with a lee and trusting that it marked the entrance to the fjord. In the smooth water in the lee of this precipice we got the sails off, for the wind now whistled straight down the fjord which lay directly ahead. Vestmanhavn is some eight miles up the fjord and we had not gone more than a couple of miles, motoring into the teeth of the blast, when we began to have doubts about reaching it. Either the wind had increased or the tide turned against us, for we almost stood still. There was no anchoring anywhere in this wall-sided fjord so once more we abandoned our immediate objective, turned tail, and shot back down the fjord.

About three miles west of the fjord entrance and the great cliff which we now knew was Stakken there is a small harbour called Midvaag. Although it was on the weather side of Stakken we hoped that by creeping close along the shore we could cheat the wind and find moderately smooth water. As we rounded close under Stakken we regarded with awe its lesser but more extraordinary neighbour, a detached pinnacle like a gigantic Napes Needle, over 1,000 feet high, called Troldkonefinger. Bucking the wind and sea, our speed reduced to a crawl, we watched the rocks close inshore anxiously as we crept slowly by. Soon we were in more sheltered water and at last at midnight we let go in three fathoms between some fishing craft and a small breakwater. There had been no time for supper in the stress and strain of the last few hours. Before turning in Charles dished up soup, bully, and spuds, alleviating this austerity with cocoa and rum.

1966

# LAURENCE DRAPER

# Appendix to J. Adlard Coles, *Heavy Weather Sailing*

## FREAK WAVES

Whenever there are waves on the surface of the sea there is a small but finite possibility of the occurrence of one or more waves which are noticeably higher than the others, and when they occur they are often labelled 'freak waves'. Amongst sailors there are many stories of freak waves, usually concerning great waves maybe 100 ft. high (which may or may not have grown with the telling) and which overwhelmed or badly damaged many a vessel, but to a yachtsman a wave 15 ft. high occurring on a day when the highest he's seen had been perhaps 8 or 10 ft. high is in every sense a freak.

There is no need to invoke the supernatural to account for such oddities, because the occurrence of unusually high waves does seem to fit into established patterns. The explanation as to why, on a day when there is only a comfortable breeze and no storm within perhaps hundreds of miles, a nasty-looking wave arises out of an otherwise friendly sea is that no wave system consists of just one wave train; there are many wave components present, each with its own period and height, travelling along together at slightly different, but constant, speeds. As the components continually get into and out of step with each other they produce the groups of high waves followed by brief intervals of relatively quiet water which are characteristic of all sea waves. Every now and then, just by chance, it so happens that a large number of these components get into step at the same place and an exceptionally high wave ensues. The life of such a wave is only a transient one, being not much more than a minute or two in the deep ocean and even less in sheltered waters where the wave period is smaller. Because each wave component is travelling at its own characteristic speed, the faster ones will escape from the others and the monster wave will die just as surely as it was born. The energy it contains belongs to its component wave trains, which still exist and travel on, taking their energy with them. Somewhere else on the water surface at some other time some other wave trains will, again just by chance, coincide and produce another large wave which will have its brief moment of glory before disappearing for ever into the random jumble of the sea. Although we are never likely to be able to predict just where and when an exceptionally high wave will appear, because the instrumentation problems are immense, the probability of occurrence of any such wave is finite and can be predicted; its calculation has the apparently contradictory title of Statistics of a Stationary Random Process. Using this theory, it has been shown that whilst one wave in twenty-three is over twice the height of the average wave, and one in 1,175 is over three times the average height, only one wave in over 300,000 exceeds four times the average height. The wave which *Puffin* experienced in the Mediterranean is an authenticated example of the effect of this phenomenon, and graphically illustrates the rule that a seaman must never relax his watch even though the worst of the storm appears to be over.

Reports of freak waves usually concern waves with unexpectedly high crests, as in most of the instances described in previous chapters, but there is just as much chance of an unusually low trough occurring. The reason why they are not often reported must be that a high crest can be seen from a large distance, but a vessel would have to be on the very edge of a deep trough to notice it. Two reports of deep troughs (at least, that is what we believe them to have been) were described in the *Marine Observer* under the heading 'The one from nowhere'. The following is an extract from the report of Commodore W. S. Byles RD, master of the *Edinburgh Castle*, and a similar report of a wartime experience by Commander I. R. Johnston, RN (Retired), appearing in that article:

Ever since the *Waratah* was lost without trace, having sailed from Durban to Cape Town on 26th July 1909, Cape coastal waters have been suspect and especially in the vicinity of Port St. Johns. There was a report that she had been 'spoken' and reported 'all well' off Port Shepstone; she had a morse lamp but no wireless.

On 21st August 1964 in 31° 39' S, 29° 46' E the *Edinburgh Castle* was experiencing a strong south-west wind and a heavy south-west swell, but, being 750 ft. long and of 28,600 gross tonnage, these conditions presented no serious problem to her. As she dipped into the swell she was spraying forward a little, and (on the big ones) shovelling up a little water through the hawse pipes. The reputation of the coast, my previous experience and my desire to avoid damage of any sort, decided me to abandon the benefit of the

LAURENCE DRAPER

Agulhas current, put up with a later arrival and close the coast. To further ensure that no untoward incident should occur, I took a knot off her speed and, to close the coast I had, of course, put the swell cosily on the bow instead of driving into it head-on. Under these conditions she was very comfortable for three-quarters of an hour or so. The distance from one wave top to the next was about 150 ft. and the ship was pitching and scending about 10–15 degrees to the horizontal. And then it happened. Suddenly, having scended normally, the wave length appeared to be double the normal, about 300 ft., so that when she pitched she charged, as it were, into a hole in the ocean at an angle of 30 degrees or more, shovelling the next wave on board to a height of 15 or 20 ft. before she could recover, as she was 'out of step'.

It was a hot night and so that the passenger accommodation might get some air, the steel doors at the after end of the foredeck had been left open, but, due to an oversight, this information was not passed to the bridge, so that not only was the foredeck swept with a wall of water which unseated the insurance wire reel which damaged a winch in its travel, and swept away the athwartship rails and the ladder to the well-deck, but a great quantity of water flooded into the passenger accommodation.

The lessons to be learned are twofold. Firstly, that whatever the weather prevailing the forward steel doors must always be shut and remain shut on passage from Durban to East London, because when this happens there will be no warning. The waves are no higher than their fellows, and in perspective the 'hole' is not visible until the ship is about to fall into it! Secondly, that as this is out of keeping with the weather prevailing at the time, such a thing could happen in conditions of little or no wind at all.

Another question which poses itself is: why, after hundreds of voyages between Durban and East London, have I never experienced this before? I think the answer to that is that, in any event, it is very locally confined, and if it be a line as opposed to a spot, it is still easily possible to pass outside it, inside it, or to close or open the coast north or south of it. I have closed the coast before to get out of an awkward swell, but the decision to do this was taken at the time and my ship may well have been north or south of her position on this occasion, though, as far as I can recall, the action was always taken somewhere 'off St. Johns'. In this case the ship was just closing the hundred-fathom line on a true course of 260 degrees.

Commander Byles's article was reported in the national Press and brought the following comments from Commander I. R. Johnston, RN (Retired):

When I was serving in the cruiser *Birmingham* during the Second World War we had a similar experience in those waters one night which I recall the more vividly for being on watch at the time. We were about 100 miles south-south-west of Durban on our way to Cape Town, steaming fast but quite comfortably into a moderate sea and swell when suddenly we hit the 'hole' and went down like a plummet into the next sea which came green over A and B turrets and broke over our open bridge. I was knocked violently off my feet, only to recover and find myself wading around in 2 ft. of water at a height of 60 ft. above normal sea-level.

The ship was so jarred by the impact that many of the watch below thought we had been torpedoed and went to emergency stations. The Captain immediately reduced speed, but the precaution proved unnecessary, as the moderate conditions returned as before and no further 'holes' appeared.

This experience, occurring as it did in pitch darkness in a blacked-out ship, was quite one of my most alarming at sea and I can well believe that a deeply laden ship might founder under similar circumstances.

In subsequent discussions we put the phenomenon down to the shelving of the Agulhas bank; this would account for the steepness of the swell, but not entirely for the sudden increase in swell length.

The conditions in which the 'holes' appeared were those of a fairly heavy swell, the familiar characteristics of which are groups of large waves followed by an interval of relatively low waves. It seems possible that the holes were caused by the chance coincidence, already explained, of a large number of wave components in exactly the same way as high crests are formed. If the depth of the 'hole' were, say, more than five times the average trough depth, the chance of it occurring to one vessel would require the time equivalent of scores of lifetimes at sea, so perhaps there is no wonder that such things are rarely seen.

On many occasions a freak wave is not just alone—sometimes two or three waves, all much bigger than the general run of large waves, are seen to occur together, and, of course, in such cases they have deep troughs between them. Many a vessel must have been lost when the first wave laid her over on her side and she did not have time to right herself before another and possibly larger wave crashed down on her exposed side. In those conditions no one survives to tell what happened.

One of the most damaging features to a small yacht must be the breaking of waves, when the actual slope of the surface can reach the vertical. There is a theoretical limit to the height which a progressive wave can sustain for a given wave length; when the wave height reaches one-seventh of its length the accelerations required of the particles become too large for gravity to restrain, and the wave crest disintegrates. If the combined wave components reach this height, it needs little imagination to decide what will happen to any luckless vessel which finds itself at the crest. Of course, in a strong wind the higher waves can appear to break purely by having their tops blown off, giving the familiar 'white horses', and the mass of water blown off on to a vessel temporarily in the lee can make life uncomfortable to say the least.

It is not only on the deep sea where frightening wave heights can occur in generally moderate conditions. If a wave runs over a shallow bank its speed is reduced and therefore the distance between one crest and the following one [the wavelength] is reduced, the energy is compressed into a smaller area and therefore the wave height has to increase. The result is that over shallow banks, and on a beach as well, the wave activity can be more dangerous than over deeper water. A similar result occurs when waves run into an opposing current, in fact a wave will be stopped completely when it meets an opposing current travelling at a quarter of the speed of the wave, which will build up into a frightening wall of water. In both of these cases there will be an area of turbulent water which is continually being disturbed and which can be seen from a distance. Of course, waves in such places cannot truly be called freaks, but nevertheless it is always wise to give them a wide berth.

Although freak waves have been illustrated by reference to observations from ocean-going vessels, the same mechanisms must apply to sea waves of all heights and periods, so that the skipper of a small yacht cruising for pleasure in coastal waters should keep as alert an eye for the unusual as the skipper of a racer in mid-ocean and the master of a liner in a storm. Although freak waves over deep water come in a vast assortment of shapes and sizes, they have the common characteristics that they appear with little or no warning, any one wave has a very short life, and they can all be fatal to the unwary.

1967

# THOM GUNN

1929–

## 'From the Wave'

It mounts at sea, a concave wall
   Down-ribbed with shine,
And pushes forward, building tall
   Its steep incline.
Then from their hiding rise to sight
   Black shapes on boards
Bearing before the fringe of white
   It mottles towards.

Their pale feet curl, they poise their weight
   With a learned skill.
It is the wave they imitate
   Keeps them so still.

The marbling bodies have become
   Half wave, half men,
Grafted it seems by feet of foam
   Some seconds, then,

Late as they can, they slice the face
   In timed procession:
Balance is triumph in this place,
   Triumph possession.

The mindless heave of which they rode
   A fluid shelf
Breaks as they leave it, falls and, slowed,
Loses itself.

Clear, the sheathed bodies slick as seals
  Loosen and tingle;
And by the board the bare foot feels
  The suck of shingle.

They paddle in the shallows still;
  Two splash each other;
Then all swim out to wait until
  The right waves gather.

1968

# DAVID LEWIS

## 1917–

# from *We, the Navigators*

The procedure of steering by swells in the open sea should be distinguished from land-finding techniques based on the distortion of swells by islands.

A few non-technical remarks about the nature of ocean swells may help explain their role in orientation. In the first place the word 'swells' denotes waves that have travelled beyond the wind systems that generated them, or that remain after the wind has died away. 'Waves', strictly speaking, are produced by contemporary winds. The two terms are frequently used as synonyms and indeed it is often impossible to distinguish one from the other at sea.

For swells to remain perceptible after travelling hundreds of miles, they must have their origin in regions of strong and persistent winds, the more important swells originating in 'permanent' weather systems such as the Trades. Trade wind generated swells tend to be from east, north-east, or south-east, depending on latitude and season. The other main source is the Southern Ocean belt of strong westerlies, whence long southerly swells sweep even beyond the equator. Largely seasonal swells originate in the monsoons of the western Pacific and others, more temporary still, are caused by tropical revolving storms.

Waves thrown up by the immediate wind tend to be temporary as well as having breaking crests and other recognisable characteristics. This distinction is well recognised by Pacific Island navigators and its importance was repeatedly stressed to me by Tevake and Teeta among others. The Papuans Lohia Loa and Frank Rei carefully explained that the swells they used were 'not wind waves', but were more permanent.

Swells from relatively distant origins are long in wavelength from crest to crest and move past with a slow swelling undulation, while wind waves and swells from nearby sources are shorter and steeper. The former are not readily abolished even by prolonged gales.

The ocean wave and swell pattern is almost always a complex one, with several systems that differ in height, length, shape, and speed moving across each other from different directions at the same time. It follows that every Island navigator must select those swells that he considers most significant and reliable, and though there are patterns that are generally recognised throughout each navigational area, there can also be a personal element in this selectivity. In the Gilberts, for instance, it was certainly not due to confusion and ignorance that Iotiebata described the most important swell as coming from the east, while the equally accomplished Abera drew a diagram that showed it to come from the south, and Rewi asserted that the main swell was easterly but with a less prominent southerly component. The fact that these three navigators came from different islands either might or might not explain how their particular schools came to place emphasis on different swell components. However, wave patterns should not vary markedly in the archipelago. In any case there would be no confusion for a navigator sailing from one area to another because 'his' familiar 'main swell' would probably still be identifiable to a trained eye. Even should it disappear altogether, the prevailing pattern could readily be sorted out at sea from the sun or stars.

Holding course by swells seems always to be a matter more of feel than sight—which emphasises the value of the art on overcast nights. Tevake told me he would sometimes retire to the hut on his canoe's outrigger platform, where he could lie down and without distraction more readily direct the helmsman onto the proper course by analysing the roll and pitch of the vessel as it corkscrewed over the waves. In distinguishing swells, he stressed, you have to wait patiently until the

one you want has a spell of being prominent and discernible. Rafe of
Tikopia also spoke about 'feeling' the swell, and Gladwin points out
that Puluwatans too 'steer by the feel of the waves under the canoe,
not visually'. One might perhaps be tempted to refer to keeping
course by the swells as 'steering by the seat of one's pants', were it not
for the more anatomically specific detail supplied by the veteran
island skipper Captain Ward, who writes, 'I have heard from several
sources, that the most sensitive balance was a man's testicles, and that
when at night or when the horizon was obscured, or inside the cabin
this was the method used to find the focus of the swells off an island.'

Examples of the practice of orientation by swells can be collected
from virtually any part of the Pacific. Andia y Varela, for instance,
gives one from Tahiti. Vili Mailau spoke of the swell from the south
as being the most valuable for orientation in Tongan waters. Ton-
naku of Bougainville described a canoe voyage down the 60-mile-
long 'corridor', traditionally flanked by waves from the north and
from the south, that extends between Vella Lavella and the Shortland
Islands. Ninigo informants also referred to using swells for direction.
We cannot consider all these in detail, so will concentrate on the Santa
Cruz and Caroline areas.


*Santa Cruz Group.*    Three swells are considered to be present all the
year round, varying in relative prominence with the wind, and one or
other being sometimes difficult to detect, especially when overlaid by
wind waves. Tevake insisted that they could be discerned even after
long stretches of calm and that all three are generally present during
both the north-west monsoon and south-east Trade seasons. Rarely
the storm waves of a cyclone would temporarily abolish them all.
They were:

*Hoahualoa*, the 'Long Swell', from the south-east.
*Hoahuadelatai*, the 'Sea Swell', from east-north-east.
*Hoahuadelahu*, from the north-west.

I would suspect these to originate from the south-east trades, the
north-east trades (whose more common direction towards their
southern limit is east-north-east) and the north-west monsoon,
respectively. As to the likely geographical extent of this swell pattern,
it would seem probable that it would be fairly general in the south-
west segment of the Pacific, subject to the degree of interference by
land. Further eastward but still south of the equator we might expect

the effects of the monsoon to be lost and, once clear of the big
Melanesian islands, for the Southern Ocean swell to sweep unhindered
up from the southward. This indeed is the pattern in the Gilberts and
Tonga, with their 'great swells' from the east and south.

Tevake demonstrated the three Santa Cruz swells on the passages
between the Reef Islands and Taumako during December, the monsoon
season of variable winds and calms. On this occasion the 'Long Swell'
from the south-east was very low and hard to detect, the 'Sea Swell'
from east-north-east was low and long and the north-west swell was
very noticeable, having been reinforced by a recent cyclone. The
north-west and south-east swells pass 'through' each other like the
interlocked fingers of two hands, said Tevake, demonstrating. Some
time in the late afternoon a northerly swell from a recent or nearby
wind began to roll by, and for some hours remained the most
prominent.

Much more stress was laid by Tevake on the swells than the sun for
daytime orientation. It would be wrong, I think, to conclude from
this that Santa Cruz navigation must needs incorporate the same
preference as was shown by this one particular Santa Cruz navigator.
More especially, since Tevake is virtually the sole surviving exponent,
must we be on guard against accepting his personal practice as
necessarily representative of the whole area. A teacher's bias or his
pupil's special aptitudes might be expected to give rise to differences
between the arts of different Island navigators, as we have already
seen in the three swell interpretations of as many learned Gilbertese
*tani borau*. Such individualism is a characteristic of orally taught
lore that we, who are accustomed to all the data of a particular field
being systematically set out in a textbook, are only too apt to
forget.

The course towards Taumako was east-north-east, directly into
the 'Sea Swell' that came from the same direction, though it was only
present, or at any rate detectable, occasionally. At such times it could
be picked out by eye and the ship rode up and over it (pitched)
without any roll at all, except when the steep northerly wind-wave
happened to coincide, when *Isbjorn* was rolled to starboard at the
same moment as she was pitching over the head-on 'Sea Swell'. In
those long intervals when the 'Sea Swell' was absent, the wind-wave
rolled us to starboard about once every five seconds without there
being any pitching component. I could feel little effect from the
south-east or north-west swells. After nightfall we steered by the

stars, the swells remaining unchanged except that the wind-wave declined.

The return from Taumako to the Reef Islands was commenced an hour before daybreak. The course was west-south-west and the distance 60 miles. The wind being south-east, the 'Long Swell' from that quarter was much the most obtrusive and only occasionally could we feel the stern being lifted up by the following east-north-east 'Sea Swell'. Nevertheless, Tevake bade me disregard the roll imparted by the former.

From approximately 06.00, when clouds shut down, we had to steer exclusively by the swell. A violent squall came in from the north around 08.30 and over the next five hours the wind veered suddenly in turn to north-east, east-north-east, and finally south-east. Heavy overcast persisted with visibility remaining poor even between rain showers.

Tevake was piloting us by the east-north-east 'Sea Swell' from astern, he told me, but the steep northerly waves kicked up by the squall effectively prevented me from sorting out the pattern, and I only succeeded in doing so thanks to his repeated demonstrations. At each fresh wind change (which I by myself could not have detected at all) I became disorientated anew so that the laborious process of instruction had to be gone over again.

It was for eight solid hours that Tevake stood on the fore-deck with a plastic tablecloth decorated with roses or an umbrella palm leaf held over his head and a sopping *lava lava* flapping round his legs, gazing intently at the sea and only moving to gesture from time to time to guide the helmsman. Then around 14.00 something more substantial than mist loomed up through the murk fine on the port bow perhaps two miles off. 'Lomlom', said Tevake, with satisfaction. Very soon afterwards Fenualoa also became visible to starboard and it was apparent that Tevake had made a perfect landfall on the middle of the half-mile-wide Forrest Passage between the two, after covering an estimated 45 to 48 miles since his last glimpse of the sky.

1972

# PHILIP LARKIN

## 1922–1985

## 'To the Sea'

To step over the low wall that divides
Road from concrete walk above the shore
Brings sharply back something known long before—
The miniature gaiety of seasides.
Everything crowds under the low horizon:
Steep beach, blue water, towels, red bathing caps,
The small hushed waves' repeated fresh collapse
Up the warm yellow sand, and further off
A white steamer stuck in the afternoon—

Still going on, all of it, still going on!
To lie, eat, sleep in hearing of the surf
(Ears to transistors, that sound tame enough
Under the sky), or gently up and down
Lead the uncertain children, frilled in white
And grasping at enormous air, or wheel
The rigid old along for them to feel
A final summer, plainly still occurs
As half an annual pleasure, half a rite,

As when, happy at being on my own,
I searched the sand for Famous Cricketers,
Or, farther back, my parents, listeners
To the same seaside quack, first became known.
Strange to it now, I watch the cloudless scene:
The same clear water over smoothed pebbles,
The distant bathers' weak protesting trebles
Down at its edge, and then the cheap cigars,
The chocolate-papers, tea-leaves, and, between

The rocks, the rusting soup-tins, till the first
Few families start the trek back to the cars.
The white steamer has gone. Like breathed-on glass
The sunlight has turned milky. If the worst
Of flawless weather is our falling short,
It may be that through habit these do best,
Coming to water clumsily undressed
Yearly; teaching their children by a sort
Of clowning; helping the old, too, as they ought.

1974

---

## JOHN FOWLES

### 1926–

# from *Shipwreck*

No other element has such accreted layers of significance for us, such complex archetypal meaning. The sea's moods and uses sex it. It is the great creatrix, feeder, womb and vagina, place of pleasure; the gentlest thing on earth, the most maternal; the most seductive whore, and handsomely the most faithless. It has the attributes of all women, and men too. It can be subtle and noble, brave and energetic; and far crueller than the meanest, most sadistic human king who ever ruled. ('I believe in the Bible,' an old sailor once told Lord Fisher, 'because it don't mention no sea in Paradise.') I happen to live over the sea myself, I watch it every day, I hear it every night. I do not like it angry, but I've noticed that most urban and inland people adore it so. Storms and gales seem to awaken something joyous and excited in them: the thunder on the shingle, the spray and spume, the rut and rage.

No doubt this is partly a product of a life where the elements have largely receded out of daily notice; but I think it goes deeper, into a kind of Freudian double identification, in which the wrath of the sea is interpreted both as *super-ego* and as *id*. It is on the one hand a thing

without restraint, a giant bull in a salt ring; on the other it is the great
punisher of presumption, the patriarch who cuts that green stripling,
man, down to size. It is strangely—or perhaps not so strangely, in
these days of the universal oil-slick—as if we had committed a crime
against the sea by ever leaving it in the first place; and as if we liked to
be told (through convenient scapegoats, of course) that we merit
retribution for our ambitious folly. In its rages we admire the total
lack of reason and justice, the blindness to all but the laws of its own
nature; and quite naturally, since similar feelings and desires lurk
deep inside our own minds. A wrecking sea is part of what we all
dream ourselves to be every night; and the ship becomes our own
puny calculations, our repressions, our compromises, our kowtowings
to convention, duty and a dozen other idols of the top-hamper we
call civilization. A psychiatrist tells me that a morbid obsession with
disaster is a common defence against depression; its enjoyment
brings a vicarious sense of manic triumph over normal reality. So the
shipwreck is not only what we are thankful will never happen to us; it
is also what we secretly want to happen, and finally to ourselves.

The other great nexus of metaphors and feeling is the ship itself.
No human invention, with all its associated crafts in building and
handling, has an older history—or received more love. That is why
we have sexed it without ambiguity, at least in the West; which in this
context casts the sea, the domaine of Neptune, as raper, berserker,
Bluebeard. Even our judgment of a ship's beauty has tended to be
that of the male upon the female—that is, we put a greater value on
outward line than on soul or utility, and nowhere more than with the
last of the sailing-ships, that splendid and sharply individualized
zenith of five thousand years of hard-earned knowledge and aesthetic
instinct. The vocabulary of the aeroplane seduced us for a while; but I
think it is interesting that we have come back to star- and space-*ships*.
*Jet* will do for a transport shorthand; yet when man really reaches,
across the vast seas of space, he still reaches in ships. Other words
may function as well; no other has the poetrics.

1974

# E. B. WHITE

### 1899–1985

## 'The Sea and the Wind that Blows'

Waking or sleeping, I dream of boats—usually of rather small boats under a slight press of sail. When I think how great a part of my life has been spent dreaming the hours away and how much of this total dream life has concerned small craft, I wonder about the state of my health, for I am told that it is not a good sign to be always voyaging into unreality, driven by imaginary breezes.

I have noticed that most men, when they enter a barber shop and must wait their turn, drop into a chair and pick up a magazine. I simply sit down and pick up the thread of my sea wandering, which began more than fifty years ago and is not quite ended. There is hardly a waiting room in the East that has not served as my cockpit, whether I was waiting to board a train or to see a dentist. And I am usually still trimming sheets when the train starts or the drill begins to whine.

If a man must be obsessed by something, I suppose a boat is as good as anything, perhaps a bit better than most. A small sailing craft is not only beautiful, it is seductive and full of strange promise and the hint of trouble. If it happens to be an auxiliary cruising boat, it is without question the most compact and ingenious arrangement for living ever devised by the restless mind of man—a home that is stable without being stationary, shaped less like a box than like a fish or a bird or a girl, and in which the homeowner can remove his daily affairs as far from shore as he has the nerve to take them, close-hauled or running free—parlor, bedroom, and bath, suspended and alive.

Men who ache all over for tidiness and compactness in their lives often find relief for their pain in the cabin of a thirty-foot sailboat at anchor in a sheltered cove. Here the sprawling panoply of The Home is compressed in orderly miniature and liquid delirium, suspended between the bottom of the sea and the top of the sky, ready to move on in the morning by the miracle of canvas and the witchcraft of rope. It is small wonder that men hold boats in the secret place of their mind, almost from the cradle to the grave.

Along with my dream of boats has gone the ownership of boats, a long succession of them upon the surface of the sea, many of them makeshift and crank. Since childhood I have managed to have some sort of sailing craft and to raise a sail in fear. Now, in my seventies, I still own a boat, still raise my sail in fear in answer to the summons of the unforgiving sea. Why does the sea attract me in the way it does? Whence comes this compulsion to hoist a sail, actually or in dream? My first encounter with the sea was a case of hate at first sight. I was taken, at the age of four, to a bathing beach in New Rochelle. Everything about the experience frightened and repelled me: the taste of salt in my mouth, the foul chill of the wooden bathhouse, the littered sand, the stench of the tide flats. I came away hating and fearing the sea. Later, I found that what I had feared and hated, I now feared and loved.

I returned to the sea of necessity, because it would support a boat; and although I knew little of boats, I could not get them out of my thoughts. I became a pelagic boy. The sea became my unspoken challenge: the wind, the tide, the fog, the ledge, the bell, the gull that cried help, the never-ending threat and bluff of weather. Once having permitted the wind to enter the belly of my sail, I was not able to quit the helm; it was as though I had seized hold of a high-tension wire and could not let go.

I liked to sail alone. The sea was the same as a girl to me—I did not want anyone else along. Lacking instruction, I invented ways of getting things done, and usually ended by doing them in a rather queer fashion, and so did not learn to sail properly, and still cannot sail well, although I have been at it all my life. I was twenty before I discovered that charts existed; all my navigating up to that time was done with the wariness and the ignorance of the early explorers. I was thirty before I learned to hang a coiled halyard on its cleat as it should be done. Until then I simply coiled it down on deck and dumped the coil. I was always in trouble and always returned, seeking more trouble. Sailing became a compulsion: there lay the boat, swinging to her mooring, there blew the wind; I had no choice but to go. My earliest boats were so small that when the wind failed, or when I failed, I could switch to manual control—I could paddle or row home. But then I graduated to boats that only the wind was strong enough to move. When I first dropped off my mooring in such a boat, I was an hour getting up the nerve to cast off the pennant. Even now, with a thousand little voyages notched in my belt, I still feel a memorial chill on casting off, as the gulls jeer and the empty mainsail claps.

Of late years, I have noticed that my sailing has increasingly become a compulsive activity rather than a simple source of pleasure. There lies the boat, there blows the morning breeze—it is a point of honor, now, to go. I am like an alcoholic who cannot put his bottle out of his life. With me, I cannot not sail. Yet I know well enough that I have lost touch with the wind and, in fact, do not like the wind anymore. It jiggles me up, the wind does, and what I really love are windless days, when all is peace. There is a great question in my mind whether a man who is against wind should longer try to sail a boat. But this is an intellectual response—the old yearning is still in me, belonging to the past, to youth, and so I am torn between past and present, a common disease of later life.

When does a man quit the sea? How dizzy, how bumbling must he be? Does he quit while he's ahead, or wait till he makes some major mistake, like falling overboard or being flattened by an accidental jibe? This past winter I spent hours arguing the question with myself. Finally, deciding that I had come to the end of the road, I wrote a note to the boatyard, putting my boat up for sale. I said I was 'coming off the water'. But as I typed the sentence, I doubted that I meant a word of it.

If no buyer turns up, I know what will happen: I will instruct the yard to put her in again—'just till somebody comes along'. And then there will be the old uneasiness, the old uncertainty, as the mild south-east breeze ruffles the cove, a gentle, steady, morning breeze, bringing the taint of the distant wet world, the smell that takes a man back to the very beginning of time, linking him to all that has gone before. There will lie the sloop, there will blow the wind, once more I will get under way. And as I reach across to the red nun off the Torry Islands, dodging the trap buoys and toggles, the shags gathered on the ledge will note my passage. 'There goes the old boy again,' they will say. 'One more rounding of his little Horn, one more conquest of his Roaring Forties.' And with the tiller in my hand, I'll feel again the wind imparting life to a boat, will smell again the old menace, the one that imparts life to me: the cruel beauty of the salt world, the barnacle's tiny knives, the sharp spine of the urchin, the stinger of the sun jelly, the claw of the crab.

1977

# ANNE STEVENSON

1933–

## 'North Sea off Carnoustie'

### for Jean Rubens

You know it by the northern look of the shore,
by the salt-worried faces,
by an absence of trees, and an abundance of lighthouses.
It's a serious ocean.


Along marram-scarred, sandbitten margins
wired roofs straggle out to where
a cold little holiday fair
has floated in and pitched itself
safely near the prairie of the golf course.
Coloured lights are sunk deep into the solid wind,
but all they've caught is a pair of lovers
and three silly boys.
Everyone else has a dog.
Or a room to get to.


The smells are of fish and of sewage and cut grass.
Oystercatchers, doubtful of habitation,
clamour 'weep, weep, weep' as they fuss over
scummy black rocks the tide leaves for them.


The sea is as near as we come to another world.


But there in your stony and windswept garden
a blackbird is confirming the grip of the land.
'You, you,' he murmurs, dark purple in his voice.

And now in far quarters of the horizon
lighthouses are awake, sending messages—
invitations to the landlocked,
warnings to the experienced,
but to anyone returning from the planet ocean,
candles in the windows of a safe earth.

1977

—————

# DEREK WALCOTT

1930–

## 'The Sea is History'

Where are your monuments, your battles, martyrs?
Where is your tribal memory? Sirs,
in that grey vault. The sea. The sea
has locked them up. The sea is History.

First, there was the heaving oil,
heavy as chaos;
then, like a light at the end of a tunnel,

the lantern of a caravel,
and that was Genesis.
Then there were the packed cries,
the shit, the moaning:

Exodus.
Bone soldered by coral to bone,
mosaics
mantled by the benediction of the shark's shadow,

that was the Ark of the Covenant.
Then came from the plucked wires
of sunlight on the sea floor

the plangent harps of the Babylonian bondage,
as the white cowries clustered like manacles
on the drowned women,

and those were the ivory bracelets
of the Song of Solomon,
but the ocean kept turning blank pages

looking for History.
Then came the men with eyes heavy as anchors
who sank without tombs,

brigands who barbecued cattle,
leaving their charred ribs like palm leaves on the shore,
then the foaming, rabid maw

of the tidal wave swallowing Port Royal,
and that was Jonah,
but where is your Renaissance?

Sir, it is locked in them sea-sands
out there past the reef's moiling shelf,
where the men-o'-war floated down;

strop on these goggles, I'll guide you there myself.
It's all subtle and submarine,
through colonnades of coral,

past the gothic windows of sea-fans
to where the crusty grouper, onyx-eyed,
blinks, weighted by its jewels, like a bald queen;

and these groined caves with barnacles
pitted like stone
are our cathedrals,

and the furnace before the hurricanes:
Gomorrah. Bones ground by windmills
into marl and cornmeal,

and that was Lamentations—
that was just Lamentations,
it was not History;


then came, like scum on the river's drying lip,
the brown reeds of villages
mantling and congealing into towns,


and at evening, the midges' choirs,
and above them, the spires
lancing the side of God


as His son set, and that was the New Testament.


Then came the white sisters clapping
to the waves' progress,
and that was Emancipation—


jubilation, O jubilation—
vanishing swiftly
as the sea's lace dries in the sun,


but that was not History,
that was only faith,
and then each rock broke into its own nation;


then came the synod of flies,
then came the secretarial heron,
then came the bullfrog bellowing for a vote,


fireflies with bright ideas
and bats like jetting ambassadors
and the mantis, like khaki police,


and the furred caterpillars of judges
examining each case closely,
and then in the dark ears of ferns

and in the salt chuckle of rocks
with their sea pools, there was the sound
like a rumour without any echo

of History, really beginning.

                                    1979

─────

# JOHN BARTH
## 1931–

# from *Sabbatical*

*Blam! Blooey!* From calm to half-gale in so sudden a wallop that Fenn
is pitched down the companionway, mightily bruising arms, ribs,
and legs, but luckily breaking none, only lacerating his scalp a bit. For
a stunned second he wonders what exploded: our engine fuel is
diesel, but we cook with propane, whose vapors have been known to
sink like gasoline's into bilges and turn pleasure boats into bombs.
Then he feels *Pokey* roll almost to his[1] beam-ends, sees Susan
clutching a stanchion for dear life, hears her shriek his[2] name, and
realizes as he yells back that what has blown up is the weather. He
struggles up into the cockpit and roller-furls the genoa while Susan at
the helm sheets in the main just enough to bring the bow a bit to
windward. We are five minutes into the storm, and already steep seas
are building. Fenwick scrambles below, where all is chaos, to don
life-vest and safety harness, never mind foul-weather gear yet; then

---

[1] Our vessel is 33′4″ long, cutter rigged, tiller steered, diesel auxiliary powered, and
male.

[2] Fenwick Scott Key Turner, age 50, son of 'Chief' Herman Turner and Virginia
Scott Key of Wye Island, Md.: former United States Central Intelligence Agency
officer, more recently (until 1978) a consultant to that agency; even more recently
(1979) author of *KUDOVE*, an exposé of the CIA's Clandestine Services division
(CS); currently on unpaid 'sabbatical leave' between careers. But his wife of seven
years, Susan Rachel Allan Seckler, BA, PhD, age 35, associate professor of American
literature and creative writing at Washington College, Chestertown, Md., on sabbatical
leave at half salary for the academic year 1979/80, shrieks only 'Fenn!'

scrambles back to the dangerous work of going forward to reef the main. Though he is clipped to a lifeline, Sue's relieved when the job is done; she angles *Pokey's* bow into the seas with the club jib staysail while the main luffs. So rapidly does the wind increase, by the time Fenn returns to the cockpit and trims the mainsheet, we are over-powered and must shorten sail again. He delays by luffing until Susan is slickered, jacketed, and safety-harnessed; then he goes forward a second time on the pitching deck, in the howling spray, soaked and chilled, to reef the club jib and double-reef the main. Now we have a measure of control: with Susan safely harnessed at the helm and *Pokey* temporarily holding his own, Fenn goes below to towel himself quickly, suit up in foul-weather gear, and secure loose items in the cabin before rejoining his frightened friend.

We have precarious leisure now to exclaim together at the sudden violence of the gale: *Blam! Blooey!* The anemometer hangs at thirty to forty knots and gusts higher, but stars can still be seen between the scudding clouds. We survey our damage: Fenn's head-cut is bloody but superficial; our self-steering vane seems kaput; we have shipped a bit of water, and discover that our automatic bilge-pump switch has died, though the pump still operates. Everything on deck and aloft appears secure. We begin, if not to relax, at least to breathe more normally.

But the seas are rough and growing; the wind shows no sign of abating; minding the helm is white-knuckled work. We are both too shaken for either of us to go below and leave everything to the other. For the next thirty-six hours we remain in the cockpit except for short excursions to the head, to the radio direction finder, or to the galley for a quick fix of chocolate, cheese, raisins, water, rum— whatever can be swigged and swallowed in a hurry. We spell each other hourly at the tiller and catnap against the cabin bulkhead, under the spray dodger.

By dawn the bilge-pump motor has gone the way of its automatic switch; fortunately we have a manual backup system. The self-steering linkage is stripped and unusable; the radio direction finder operates only intermittently; the VHF masthead antenna has worked itself loose. Minor nuisances all, since we're near the end of our ocean passage. Of more concern is a certain fitting at the mast spreader, to which a starboard lower shroud is attached: surveying the rig by daylight, sharp-eyed Fenn observes that this fitting has developed a tiny, alarming wobble. On our present tack, no immediate peril;

the tension is on the portside shrouds. But the slack that permits the
wobble may also work the fitting loose: should it let go, so might the
mast on any other point of sail, and this is no weather for going aloft
to attempt repairs.

Our other concern is our position. The wind is too northerly, and
our last estimated position too close to land, for us to run before the
gale without fear of piling up on the Outer Banks. On the other hand,
we are too near the big shipping lanes to risk heaving to and going
below to ride out the storm. Hence our toiling north-northeast on
the port tack under triple-reefed main and double-reefed jib, to
preserve our sea-room without being carried too far offshore, while
keeping an eye out for freighters. But during the day, though the sun
perversely breaks through from time to time, the wind slightly
increases: while the Norfolk weather station reports thirty knots
with gusts to forty, our indicator indicates ten and twelve above that.
We run the engine slowly to keep our bow from falling off the wind.
We are weary, wet, and duly (but not unduly) scared, especially as the
long day ends and our second stormy night approaches. We have seen
no freighters since mid-afternoon. We daresay we have a proper
offing; we wish we knew how far south of the 37th parallel our
leeway has carried us.

At dark, Susan straps herself into the pitching galley to make hot
thermoses of coffee and bouillon and a supply of peanut-butter
sandwiches. Fenwick, at the helm, decides we'd better have Chart
12221, Chesapeake Bay Entrance, at hand in its clear plastic case as
well as its southern neighbor and the smaller-scale ocean chart. Since
Susan is busy with both the galley stove and the RDF beside it, Fenn
breaks a rule[3] and extracts the chart from between two others in order
to replace it on top. He steers with one foot, keeps an eye on the steep
black growlers, and holds a penlight between his teeth.

Brava! Sue charms the RDF into confessing a positive, unequivocal
bearing on Chesapeake Radio Beacon 290, dot dash dash dot at 300°;
she calls it out, then twists the antenna to find a second bearing for
plotting a fix. But the gadget dies just as Fenwick, bending to look for
that beacon with his purse-mouthed light on the half-secured chart,
inadvertently lets *Pokey's* bow fall ten degrees off: the next sea strikes
us more abeam than its forerunners, flings Susan against the galley
sink (another green-and-purple hip), obliges Fenn to grab a stanchion

[3] The rule: do not remove nautical charts from their cases while on deck in rain or
breeze, except in greater emergencies than this.

with his chart-case hand and the tiller with his right. Chart 12221 flaps off toward Kitty Hawk. Groaning Fenn slaps the chart-case under his left buttock to secure it, returns the bow quickly into position to meet the next wave, removes the penlight from his mouth to shout Shit, there went Twelve Two Twenty-one; you okay, Suse? and hearing she is, to announce loudly over his left shoulder to the black Atlantic, the eye of the wind, the teeth of the gale: You win, Poseidon! We're going to heave our ass to and get some rest!

Susan wonders Is it safe? Fenn hopes so. It is *not* safe, anyhow, to wear the both of us into exhaustion: look what happened to Odysseus, in very sight of home. What shall we do for a chart? Fenn hopes he knows the approach well enough to manage without it; we can always follow the freighters in; then we've got the Cruising Guide. We switch on the masthead strobe, upon which, with the radar reflector, we depend to avoid being run down in the shipping lanes: it flashes thrice and dies, perhaps short-circuited somehow by that loose antenna. Fenn complains to Poseidon: Overkill!

Very well, then, we must return to two-hour watches: Fenwick will take the first, to adjust and monitor the heaving-to and look out for ships while Susan sleeps, at least rests, below. No stars tonight; the wild air is filled with spray. We kiss seriously through the companionway, and Sue retires to the leeward settee berth wishing she were religious. Fenn sheets the reefed main in hard, backs the jib, lashes the tiller hard over, and adjusts the engine RPMs for just enough thrust to keep the bow at a safe angle to the seas. Once he gets it right, he sits with his back to the wind, in the lee of the cabin, and judges by the compass whether we're holding our position.

The view astern is terrifying; the view ahead more so. But with occasional fine tuning *Pokey* holds position, and at last the wind begins slowly to abate. By midnight, when Fenwick relieves Susan for his second watch, the anemometer is averaging thirty. We shake out one reef from each sail and cut the engine. The silence is welcome, and the boat tracks better under sail alone. Off-watch at 3 a.m., groggy Fenn is drowsing in his berth and trying to recall the main features of Chart 12221 when Susan shrieks his name again. He piles up the companionway ladder and finds her wrestling to unlash the tiller and free the jibsheet: before she can do either, a fair-size ship thunders across our bows, so close that its wake broaches us. Fenn has just time, before the next wave rolls *Pokey* on his beam-ends like that first blam-blooey blow, to catch sight of the diagonal red-orange slash of a Coast Guard cutter; by the time we're righted and back on course, the ship has disappeared.

Sue's in tears. Fenn's heart slams; he is too shocked to curse. Unharnessed, he very nearly went over the side in that knockdown. Why did the cutter not veer to starboard and cross our stern? Why did it not now return to determine our safety? For that matter, how did it manage not to remark us on its fancy radar and avoid the near-collision? Hands shaking, Fenwick calls angrily on Channel 16. No reply: perhaps our VHF has joined the list of casualties? The best excuse we can imagine is a poor one: that the cutter was rushing full speed to some rescue so dire that even a near-ramming had to be ignored. More likely, a green watch officer simply missed our blip on his/her radar screen and charged on without ever seeing us.

By dawn our gale has blown itself out and is replaced by a mild breeze from the south-southwest. In time the seas subside. With our last strength we unreef the main and the jib staysail, unfurl the genoa, and settle down for an easy reach across the swells. However spent and shaken, we have much to be thankful for: we are alive and physically intact, as certain people dear to us are not; the rigging-strain is still safely on the port shrouds, and upon climbing the mast-steps to inspect that wobbly tang, Fenn finds he can simply tighten its bolt; the RDF, with much coaxing, yields another reasonable bearing on that Chesapeake beacon, which we find in the binoculars soon after sunrise and salute it with a weary kiss. From there it is a mere fifteen or twenty nautical miles west-northwestward to the threshold of the Bay: the combination bridge and tunnel between Hank and Chuck. At 1000 hours we raise the Capes themselves: Sue's fast asleep. Ninety minutes later we're at the bridge, in a thicket of freighters, tankers, and naval craft from Hampton Roads. Fenn wakes his wife to say hello to the USA and relieve him at the helm.

Hello America.

1982

# MARY OLIVER

1935–

## 'The Waves'

The sea
   isn't a place
     but a fact, and
     a mystery

under its green and black
   cobbled coat that never
     stops moving.
     When death

happens on land, on some
   hairpin piece of road,
     we crawl past,
     imagining

over and over that moment
   of disaster. After the storm
     the other boats didn't
       hesitate—they spun out

from the rickety pier, the men
   bent to the nets or turning
     the weedy winches.
     Surely the sea

is the most beautiful face
   in our universe, but
     you won't find a fisherman
     who will say so;

what they say is,
   *See you later.*
      Gulls white as angels scream
     as they float in the sun


just off the sterns;
   everything is here
      that you could ever imagine.
     And the bones


of the drowned fisherman
   are returned, half a year later,
     in the glittering,
      laden nets.

              1986


---

# JOHN UPDIKE

## 1932–


## 'Sea Knell'

Pulsating Tones in Ocean
Laid to Whale Heartbeats
      —*The Times*


There is a rapture on the lonely shore,
There is society, where none intrudes,
By the deep sea, and music in its roar . . .
       —*Byron*


I wandered to the surfy marge
  To eavesdrop on the surge;

The ocean's pulse was slow and large
And solemn as a dirge.

'Aha,' mused I, 'the beat of Time,
Eternally sonorous,
Entombed forever in the brine,
A fatal warning for us.'

'Not so!' bespoke a jolly whale
Who spouted into view,
'That pulsing merely proves I'm hale
And hearty, matey, too!

'Rejoice, my lad—my health is sound,
The very deeps attest!
It permeates the blue profound
And makes the wavelets crest!'

With that, he plunged in sheer excess
Of spirits. On the shore,
I harkened with an ear much less
Byronic than before.

1969


## 'Bath after Sailing'

From ten to five we whacked the waves,
the hostile, mobile black
that lurched beneath the leeward winch
as helplessly we heeled.

Now after six I lie at ease,
at ease in a saltless sea my size,
my fingertips shrivelled as if dead,
the sway of the sloop still haunting the tub.

I can't stop seeing the heartless waves
the mirthless color of green tar
sliding on themselves like ball-bearings,
deep and opaque and not me,

not me: I was afraid,
afraid of heeling over in the wind
and inhaling bubbling lead
and sinking, opaque as stone.

Lord, how light my feet,
wed to their salt-soaked sneakers,
felt on the dock, amid the mysterious
steadiness of trees and air.

I did not want, I had not wanted
to die. I saw death's face
in that mass absorbed
in shrugging off its timeless weight,

the same dull mass blond Vikings scanned,
impervious to all the sailor love
thrust onto it. My shredded hand
ached on the jib sheet line.

The boat would clumsily, broken
wings flapping, come about,
and the slickered skipper search
the sea-face and finds me gone,

his surprise not total,
and one wave much like the rest,
a toppling ton, a rib of time,
an urgent message from nothing to nothing.

I thank you, God of trees and air,
whose steeples testify
to something steady slipped by chance
upon Your tar-green sliding face,

for this my mock survival.
My children's voices plumb my death.
My rippling legs are hydra limbs.
My penis, my representative,

my emissary to darkness, survivor
of many a plunge, flipflops
sideways, alive and small
and pallid in reprieve.

Black sea, deep sea, you dangle
beneath my bliss like a dreadful gamble.
Mute, white as a swimming pool cork,
I float on the skin

of sleepiness, of my sleep,
of all sleep . . . how much I prefer
this microcosmic version
of flirting with immersion.

1977

## from *Rabbit at Rest*

Judy is stationed on this side of the mast, poised to push the centerboard down its slot; Harry sits awkwardly on the wet Fiberglas with his legs bent and one hand behind him on the tiller and the other clutching the sheet. His mind begins to assemble a picture of directional arrows, the shining wind pressing on the sail's straining striped height. Certain tense slants begin in his hands and fan out to the horizon and zenith. *Like a scissors*, Cindy had said, and a sensation of funnelled invisible power grows upon him. 'Centerboard down,' he commands, a captain at last, at the mere age of fifty-five. His scraped shin stings and his buttocks in his thin wet bathing suit resent the pressure of bald Fiberglas. His weight is so much greater than Judy's the hollow hull tips upward in front. The waves are choppier, the tugs on the sail ruder, and the water a dirtier green than in his enhanced memory of that Caribbean adventure at the beginning of this decade.

Still, his companion is happy, her bright face beaded with spray. Her thin little arms stick goosebumped out of her dull-black rubber vest, and her whole body shivers with the immersion in motion, the newness, the elemental difference. Rabbit looks back toward land:

Pru, the sun behind her, is a forked silhouette against the blaze of the
beach. Her figure in another minute will be impossible to distinguish
from all the others tangled along the sand, the overprinted alphabet of
silhouettes. Even the hotel has shrunk in the growing distance, a tall
slab among many, hotels and condos for as far as he can see in either
direction along this stretch of the Florida coast. The power he finds in
his hands to change perspectives weighs on his chest and stomach.
Seeing the little triangular sails out here when he and Janice drove the
shore route or visited their bank in downtown Deleon had not
prepared him for the immensity of his perspectives, any more than
the sight of men on a roof or scaffold conveys the knee-grabbing
terror of treading a plank at that height. 'Now, Judy,' he says, trying
to keep any stiffness of fear from his voice, yet speaking loudly lest
the dazzling amplitudes of space suck all sense from his words, 'we
can't keep going forever in this direction or we'll wind up in Mexico.
What I'm going to do is called coming about. I say—I know it seems
silly—"Coming about, hard alee," and you duck your head and
don't slide off when the boat changes direction. Ready? Coming
about, hard alee.'

He is not quite decisive enough in pushing the tiller away from
him, and for too many seconds, with Judy crouched in a little
acrobatic ball though the boom has already passed over her head,
they head lamely into the wind, in a stillness wherein the slapping of
water sounds idle and he feels they are being carried backward. But
then an inertia not quite squandered by his timidity swings the bow
past the line of the wind and the sail stops impatiently rippling and
bellies with a sulky ripple in the direction of the horizon and goes
tight, and Judy stops looking worried and laughs as she feels the boat
tug forward again, over the choppy, opaque waves. He pulls in sail
and they move at right angles to the wind, parallel to the color-
flecked shore. In their moment of arrested motion the vastness all
around had transfixed them as if with arrows from every empty
shining corner of air and sea, but by moving they escape and turn
space to their use; the Gulf, the boat, the wind, the sun burning the
exposed tips of their ears and drying the spray from the erect pale
body hairs on their goosebumped arms all make together a little
enclosed climate, a burrow of precise circumstance that Harry gradually
adjusts to. He begins to know where the wind is coming from
without squinting up at the faded telltale at the top of the mast, and to
feel instinctively the planes of force his hands control, just as on a fast

break after a steal or rebound of the basketball in the old days he
would picture without thinking the passing pattern, this teammate to
that, and the ball skidding off the backboard into the hoop on the
layup. Growing more confident, he comes about again and heads
toward a distant green island tipped with a pink house, a mansion
probably but a squat hut from this distance, and pulls in the sail, and
does not flinch when the boat heels on this new tack.

Like a good grandfather, he explains his actions to Judy as they go
along, the theory and the practice, and both of them become infected
by confidence, by the ease with which this toy supporting them can
be made to trace an angled path back and forth, teasing the wind and
the water by stealing a fraction of their glinting great magnitudes.

Judy announces, 'I want to steer.'

'You don't *steer* it, sweetie, like you steer a bicycle. You can't just
point it where you want to go. You have to keep the wind in mind,
what direction it's coming from. But yeah, OK, scrootch your like
backside back toward me and take hold of the tiller. Keep the boat
pointed at that little island with the pink house out there. That's right.
That's good. Now you're slipping off a little. Pull it a bit toward you
to make it come left. That's called port. Left is port, starboard is right.
Now I'm letting out the sail a little, and when I say "Ready about,"
you push the tiller toward me as hard as you can and hold it. Don't
panic, it takes a second to react. Ready? Ready, Judy? OK. Ready
about, hard alee.'

He helps her through the last part of the arc, her little arm doesn't
quite reach. The sail slackens and flaps. The boom swings nervously
back and forth. The aluminium mast squeaks in its Fiberglas socket.
A far gray freighter sits on the horizon like a nickel on a high
tabletop. A bent-winged tern hangs motionless against the wind and
cocks its head to eye them as if to ask what they are doing so far out of
their element. And then the sail fills; Harry tugs it in, his hand on top
of Judy's little one sets the angle of the tiller for this tack. Their two
weights toward the stern lift the bow and make the Sunfish slightly
wallow. The patter of waves on the hull has settled into his ears as a
kind of deafness. She tacks a few more times and, seeing that's all
there is to it, grows bored. Her girlish yawn is a flower of flawless
teeth (the chemicals they put in toothpaste now, these kids will never
know the agony he did in dental chairs) and plush arched tongue.
Some man some day will use that tongue.

'You kind of lose track of time out here,' Harry tells her. 'But from the way the sun is it must be near noon. We should head back in. That's going to take some time, since the wind's coming out against us. We don't want your mother to get worried.'

'That man said he'd sent a launch out.'

Harry laughs, to release the tension of the tenderness he feels toward this perfect child, all coppery and bright and as yet unmarred. 'That was just for an emergency. The only emergency we have is our noses are getting sunburned. We can sail in, it's called beating against the wind. You work as close to the wind as you can. Here, I'll pull in the sail and you try to keep us pointed toward that hotel. Not the hotel at the very far right. The one next to it, the one like a pyramid.'

The merged bodies on the beach have lost their flecks of color, the twinkle of their bathing suits, and seem a long gray string vibrating along the Bay for miles. The water out here is an uglier color, a pale green on top of a sunken bile green, than it seems from the shore.

'Grandpa, are you cold?'

'Getting there,' he admits, 'now that you ask. It's chilly, this far out.'

'I'll say.'

'Isn't your life jacket keeping you warm?'

'It's slimy and awful. I want to take it off.'

'Don't.'

Time slips by, the waves idly slap, the curious tern keeps watch, but the shore doesn't seem to be drawing closer, and the spot where Roy and Pru wait seems far behind them. 'Let's come about,' he says, and this time, what with the child's growing boredom and his own desire to get in and conclude this adventure, he tries to trim the wind too closely. A puff comes from an unexpected direction, from the low pirate islands instead of directly offshore, and instead of the Sunfish settling at a fixed heel in a straight line at a narrow angle to the direction they have been moving in, it heels and won't stop heeling, it loses its grip on the water, on the blue air. The mast passes a certain point up under the sun and as unstoppably as if pushed by a giant malevolent hand topples sideways into the Gulf. Rabbit feels his big body together with Judy's little lithe one pitch downward feet-first into the abyss of water, his fist still gripping the line in a panic and his shin scraped again, by an edge of Fiberglas. A murderous dense cold element encloses his head in an unbreathable dark green that clamps his mouth and eyes and then pales and releases him to air, to sun, and to the eerie silence of halted motion.

His brain catches up to what has happened. He remembers how Cindy that time stood on the centerboard and the Sunfish came upright again, its mast hurling arcs of droplets against the sky. So there is no great problem. But something feels odd, heart-suckingly wrong. Judy. Where is she? 'Judy?' he calls, his voice not his out here between horizons, nothing solid under him and waves slapping his face with a teasing malice and the hull of the Sunfish resting towering on its edge casting a narrow shade and the striped sail spread flat on the water like a many-colored scum. *'Judy!'* Now his voice belongs entirely to the hollow air, to the heights of terror; he shouts so loud he swallows water, his immersed body offering no platform for him to shout from; a bitter molten lead pours instead of breath into his throat and his heart's pumping merges with the tugs and swellings of the sea. He coughs and coughs and his eyes take on tears. She is not here. There are only the dirty-green waves, kicking water, jade where the sun shines through, layered over bile. And clouds thin and slanting in the west, forecasting a change in the weather. And the hollow mute hull of the Sunfish hulking beside him. His bladder begs him to pee and perhaps he does.

The other side. She must be there. He and the boat and sail exist in a few square yards yet enormous distances feel ranged against him. He must dive under the hull, quickly. Every second is sinking everything. The life jacket buoys him but impedes. Currents in the water push against him. He has never been a natural swimmer. Air, light, water, silence all clash inside his head in a thunderous demonstration of mercilessness. Even in this instant of perfectly dense illumination there is space for his lifelong animal distaste for putting his head underwater, and for the thought that another second of doing nothing might miraculously bring it all right; the child's smiling face will surface with saltwater sparkling in her eyelashes. But the noon sun says now or never and something holy in him screams that all can be retrieved and he opens his mouth and sucks down panicked breath through a sieve of pain in his chest and tries to burrow through a resistant opacity where he cannot see or breathe. His head is pressed upward against something hard while his hands sluggishly grope for a snagged body and find not even a protuberance where a body could snag. He tries to surface. Fiberglas presses on his back like sharkskin and then the tiller's hinged wood, dangling down dripping, scrapes his face.

'Judy!' This third time he calls her name he is burbling; gobbets of water make rainbow circles in his vision as he faces straight up into the sun; in these seconds the boat is slowly twirling and its relation to the sun, the shadow it casts on the water, is changing.

Under the sail. She must be under the sail. It seems vast in the water, a long nylon pall with its diagonal seams, its stitched numbers and sunfish silhouette. He must. His bowels burn with all the acid guilt that has accumulated since creation; he again forces himself under into a kind of dirty-green clay where his bubbles are jewels. Against the slither of cloth on his back he tries to tunnel forward. In this tunnel he encounters a snake, a flexible limp limb that his touch panics so it tries to strangle him and drag him down deeper. It claws his ear; his head rises into the sail and a strained white light breaks upon his eyes and there is a secret damp nylon odor but no air to breathe. His body convulsively tries to free itself from this grave; he flounders with his eyes shut; the sail's edge eventually nuzzles past his drowning face and he has dragged along Judy into the light.

# Acknowledgements

The editor and publisher are grateful for permission to include the following copyright material in this collection.

All rights in respect of the Authorized King James Version of the Holy Bible and the Book of Common Prayer 1662 are vested in the Crown in the United Kingdom and controlled by royal Letters Patent.

W.H. Auden, from *The Enchafèd Flood*. Copyright the Rector and Visitors of the University of Virginia. Published in the UK by Faber and Faber (1950) and in the US by The University Press of Virginia (1979) and reprinted by their permission.

John Barth, from *Sabbatical* (1982). © 1982 John Barth. Reprinted by permission of Martin Secker & Warburg Limited.

Willard Bascom, from *Waves and Beaches: The Dynamics of the Ocean Surface*. © 1980 by Willard Bascom. Used by permission of Doubleday, a division of Bantam Doubleday Dell Publishing Group, Inc. From *The Crest of the Waves: Adventures in Oceanography*. © 1988 by Willard Bascom. Reprinted by permission of Harper-Collins Publishers, New York.

William Beebe, from *The Arcturus Adventure* (G.P. Putnam's Sons, 1926).

Hilaire Belloc, from *The Cruise of the Nona*. Reprinted by permission of the Peters Fraser & Dunlop Group Ltd.

Henry Beston, from *The Outermost House* (1928). Published by Henry Holt & Co. Inc.

Dora Birtles, from *North-West by North*. Reprinted by permission of Virago Press.

Elizabeth Bishop, "Seascape" from *The Complete Poems, 1927–1979*. © 1979, 1983 by Alice Helen Methfessel. Reprinted by permission of Farrar, Straus and Giroux Inc.

Rachel Carson, from *The Sea Around Us*. Reprinted by permission of Laurence Pollinger Ltd. Published in the US by Oxford University Press, New York.

Apsley Cherry-Garrard, from *The Worst Journey in the World* (1922). Reprinted by permission of Angela Mathias.

Kevin Crossley-Holland, "I can sing a true song . . ." from *The Seafarer*, translated by Kevin Crossley-Holland, © 1982. Reprinted by permission of Rogers Coleridge & White Ltd.

Laurence Draper, "Freak Waves", Appendix 2 to J. Adlard Coles, *Heavy Weather Sailing* (Adlard Coles Ltd., 1967). © 1967, Laurence Draper.

T.S. Eliot, from "The Dry Salvages" from *Collected Poems 1909–1962*. Copyright 1936 by Harcourt Brace Jovanovich, Inc. Copyright © 1963, 1964 by T.S. Eliot. Reprinted by permission of Faber & Faber.

John Fowles, from *Shipwreck* (Cape, 1974). Reprinted by permission of the Random Century Group Ltd on behalf of the author and publisher.

Robert Frost, "Neither Out Far Nor In Deep" from *The Poetry of Robert Frost*, edited by Edward Connery Lathem. Copyright 1930, 1939, © 1969 by Holt, Rinehart & Winston, © 1958 by Robert Frost, © 1967 by Lesley Frost Ballantine. Published in the UK by Jonathan Cape Ltd. Reprinted by permission of Jonathan Cape Ltd. on behalf of the estate of Robert Frost. Published in the US by Henry Holt & Co.

William Golding, from *Pincher Martin*. Reprinted by permission of Faber & Faber Ltd.

Thom Gunn, "From the Wave" from *Selected Poems 1950–1975*. © 1979 by Thom Gunn. Reprinted by permission of Faber & Faber Ltd. and Farrar, Straus and Giroux Inc.

Ernest Hemingway, from *The Old Man and the Sea*. Copyright 1952 by Ernest Hemingway, renewal copyright © 1980 by Mary Hemingway. Copyright 1952 all rights outside US, Hemingway Foreign Rights Trust. Passage from letter of February 7, 1939 to Maxwell Perkins from *Ernest Hemingway: Selected Letters 1917–1961*, edited by Carlos Baker. © 1981 The Ernest Hemingway Foundation, Inc. Reprinted by permission of Mayer Brown & Platt and Charles Scribner's Sons, an imprint of Macmillan Publishing Company.

Gerard Manley Hopkins, from *The Journals and Papers of Gerard Manley Hopkins*, edited by Humphrey House and Graham Storey (1959), © The Society of Jesus 1959. Reprinted by permission of Oxford University Press on behalf of the Society of Jesus.

Langston Hughes, "Sea Calm". First published Alfred A. Knopf 1959. © Langston Hughes 1959.

Richard Hughes, from *In Hazard* (Harper, 1938). Reprinted by permission of David Higham Associates Ltd.

Rockwell Kent, from *N by E*. Courtesy of the Rockwell Kent Legacies.

Philip Larkin, from "To the Sea" from *High Windows*. © 1974 by Philip Larkin. Reprinted by permission of Faber & Faber Ltd. and Farrar, Straus & Giroux, Inc.

David Lewis, from *We, the Navigators*, © 1972 David Lewis. Reprinted by permission of the University of Hawaii Press.

Robert Lowell, from "The Quaker Graveyard in Nantucket" published in the UK in *Poems 1938–1949*, and in the US in *Lord Weary's Castle*, copyright 1946 and renewed 1974 by Robert Lowell. Reprinted by permission of Faber & Faber Ltd. and Harcourt Brace Jovanovich, Inc.

Norman MacCaig, "Midnight, Lochinvar" from *Selected Poems* (Hogarth Press, 1962). Reprinted by permission of the Random Century Group Ltd on behalf of the author and publisher.

John Masefield, "Sea Fever", "Cardigan Bay" and "Sea Superstition". Reprinted by permission of The Society of Authors as the literary representative of the Estate of John Masefield.

Marianne Moore, "A Grave" from *Collected Poems*. Reprinted by permission of Faber & Faber Ltd.

Samuel Eliot Morison, from *Spring Tides* (Houghton Mifflin, 1965). © Samuel Eliot Morison 1965.

Walter Munk, extract from "The Circulation of the Oceans" from *Scientific American* September 1955, pp. 99–104, © 1955 Scientific American Inc. All rights reserved. Used with permission.

Robert Cushman Murphy, from *Logbook for Grace*. Copyright 1947 by Robert Cushman Murphy, renewed © 1974 by Grace E. Barston Murphy. Reprinted by permission of Robert Hale Limited, and Macmillan Publishing Company.

Conor O'Brien, from *Across Three Oceans*. Reprinted by permission of Rupert Hart Davis, a division of Harper-Collins Publishers Limited.

Alan Ross, "Night Patrol". Reprinted by permission of the author.

Miles Smeeton, from *Once Is Enough*. © 1959 by Miles Smeeton. Copyright renewed 1987 by Miles Smeeton. Reprinted by permission of W.W. Norton & Company, Inc and Harper-Collins Publishers Limited.

H.W. Tilman, from *Mostly Mischief* (Hollis & Carter, 1966). © 1966 H.W. Tilman.

H.M. Tomlinson, from *The Sea and the Jungle*. © The Estate of H.M. Tomlinson.

John Updike, "Bath After Sailing" from *Tossing and Turning*, © John Updike 1977; extract from *Rabbit at Rest*, © John Updike 1990. Reprinted by permission of André Deutsch Ltd., published in the US by Random House Inc. "Sea Knell", from *Midpoint*, © 1969 John Updike. Reprinted by permission of Andre Deutsch Ltd. Published in the US by Alfred A. Knopf, Inc.

Derek Walcott, "The Sea is History" from *The Star-Apple Kingdom*. © 1979 by Derek Walcott. Reprinted by permission of Farrar, Straus and Giroux Inc. and Jonathan Cape Ltd.

Albert Richard Wetjen, from *Way for a Sailor!* (1931). Reprinted by permission of A.M. Heath & Co Ltd., Authors' Agents.

E.B. White, "The Sea and the Wind That Blows" from *Essays of E.B. White*. © 1963 by E.B. White. Reprinted by permission of Harper-Collins Publishers, New York.

Virginia Woolf, from *Jacob's Room*. Copyright 1923 by Harcourt Brace Jovanovich, Inc. and renewed 1951 by Leonard Woolf. Reprinted by permission of the publisher.

Frank Arthur Worsley, from *Shackleton's Boat Journey*. Copyright Frank Arthur Worsley 1940. Reprinted by permission of Sheil Land Associates Ltd on behalf of the Estate of Frank Arthur Worsley.

Although every effort has been made to secure permissions prior to printing this has not always been possible. The publisher apologises for any errors or omissions but if contacted will rectify these at the earliest opportunity.

# Index of Authors